RARE BOOKS
and SPECIAL COLLECTIONS

SIDNEY E. BERGER

RARE BOOKS

and SPECIAL COLLECTIONS

An imprint of the American Library Association

CHICAGO 2014

SIDNEY E. BERGER is currently the Ann C. Pingree Director of the Phillips Library at the Peabody Essex Museum in Salem, Massachusetts. It is the third-largest library in an art museum in the United States. Sid and his wife, Michèle Cloonan, are proprietors of the Doe Press, for which they hand print books of poetry and other works, some by Pulitzer Prize winners. He makes paper and casts type by hand. Since 2002, he has been an English, Communications, and GSLIS (Graduate School of Library and Information Science) professor at Simmons College in Boston, where he teaches Editing Copy and Proof, History of the Book, and Rare Books and Special Collections Librarianship. Sid is also an adjunct professor in the Graduate School of Library and Information Science at the University of Illinois, Urbana-Champaign. He has published and lectured widely on literary, bibliographical, and library subjects.

Printed in the United States of America
18 17 16 15 14   5 4 3 2 1

ISBN: 978-1-55570-964-8 (paper)

Library of Congress Cataloging-in-Publication Data

Berger, Sidney E.
    Rare books and special collections / Sidney E. Berger.
        pages   cm
    Includes bibliographical references and index.
    ISBN 978-1-55570-964-8 (alk. paper)
    1. Libraries—Special collections—Rare books. 2. Libraries—Special collections—Administration. 3. Libraries—Special collections—Nonbook materials. 4. Libraries—Special collections. 5. Nonbook materials—Collectors and collecting. I. Title.
Z688.R3B47 2014
025.2'816—dc23   2014006055

Book design by Kim Thornton in the Charis SIL and Proxima Nova typefaces.
Cover image from Harley MS 4986; courtesy of the British Library;
www.bl.uk/manuscripts.

∞ This paper meets the requirements of ANSI/NISO Z39.48-1992
(Permanence of Paper).

*To Joe and Frances, without whom none of this could have
been written, to Rafe and Aaron for their enduring love, and to
Michèle, for her encouragement and inspiration*

CONTENTS

ILLUSTRATIONS

Illustrations are listed by chapter,
"4.1" being the first illustration in chapter 4.

FOREWORD

HAT ARE LIBRARIANS SUPPOSED TO DO NOW? FOR A LONG time, what librarians did was provide people with the books that they wanted to read, and help people find information about what they wanted to know. This information was usually available somewhere in print, in places not obvious to casual readers or even to many scholars, and it was the librarian's job to locate it and pass it on. With the development in recent years of widely available online resources, including searchable access to millions of books and journals, the work of librarians has changed, and where it goes from here isn't at all clear. A librarian doesn't have to attend many professional meetings before encountering a new and popular philosophy of librarianship, which holds that "Services Are the New Collections."

For many librarians, this slogan makes a lot of sense. Librarians have spent decades competing with each other to build large collections of printed materials, and now, with the availability of free and subscription-based online resources, much of the information that library users want is available without the need to consult these collections. Readers and researchers may not even need to go to the library, since what they're looking for is available to them electronically wherever they are. For some of today's research libraries, large collections of books and journals have been quickly transformed from assets into liabilities, and printed materials are increasingly being relocated from central library spaces to offsite storage-and-retrieval facilities. Since a large number of libraries can now have access to the same resources, focusing acquisitions resources on electronic information, and concentrating staff time on making this information available at all times and in the forms most convenient to users, sounds sensible. Libraries have long been understaffed and underfunded, and being able to provide needed information to the widest possible audience is a desirable goal.

But that doesn't mean that all libraries are the same. As Sidney Berger makes very clear, there is much more "information" in physical objects such as books and manuscripts than can be reproduced by any surrogates, including online reproductions. Library administrators have now taken notice that what distinguishes a library or library system, other than 24/7 reference chat or apps for using library resources on mobile devices, are the irreplaceable holdings of their special collections departments. Whether for research by scholars, or viewing by students and the general public, the physical objects in special collections libraries have a significance and evocative presence that is tangible, but sometimes difficult to define. It's the duty of special collections librarians to acquire, preserve, make available, and interpret these objects, and how this may be done, intelligently and effectively, forms a large part of the subject matter of this book.

More important than this, however, is the foundation on which special collections librarianship rests—a knowledge of the objects themselves, including what they are, what they're made of, how they were created, and what's happened to them since then. This kind of knowledge is becoming rarer among librarians these days, as older librarians retire, and as younger students work increasingly, even in library schools, with online rather than with print resources. This relative lack of familiarity with original resources is by no means limited to librarians, as anyone who has worked in reference or public services in a special collections library can attest. Fifty years ago, much of the traffic in any large rare book reading room came from faculty members in the departments of English and history. Research has changed a great deal in these fields since then, and practically all of today's hires in history and English have never really worked with original books and manuscripts, even in graduate school.

A few years ago, I gave a tour of the Lilly Library to a lecturer visiting Bloomington, who was interested in seventeenth-century England in general, and John Milton in particular. When he told me that his recent research related to early opinions of *Paradise Lost*, I showed him our copy of the first edition of 1667, which is one of just a few copies to survive in its original binding. When he said that he had never seen a copy, I misunderstood him, because I thought he meant that he had never seen a copy in an early binding. As it turned out, he had never seen a copy

of the first edition at all, and, in fact, he'd never seen any edition of the book that predated the twentieth century. He was quite surprised that the first edition, which is a smallish quarto, wasn't larger, since he was imagining it to be a big folio volume, as befitted its historical importance.

It's easy to lament the lack of coverage of books and their histories in current education in the humanities and social sciences, but it's more productive to realize that this creates a wonderful opportunity for special collections libraries. It's up to us as librarians to make our collections better known, and to demonstrate how transformative they can be. To do this well, we need to learn as much as we can about what we have, and we should be willing to spend the rest of our careers learning more.

In his masterly survey *The Portuguese Seaborne Empire: 1415–1825* (London: Hutchinson, 1969), eminent historian and book collector Charles R. Boxer noted that his book was based on the resources of his own private library, along with those of other major libraries around the world. He also told readers that he had "been able to visit at one time or another most of the places concerned, from the Spice Islands of the Moluccas to the Backlands of the Mato Grosso." Just as Professor Boxer's book was the product of more than forty years of immersion in all aspects of his subject, so is this present volume the result of many decades of Sidney Berger's complete involvement in all aspects of books, from their creation to their institutional care. His experiences as a papermaker, typefounder, compositor, printer, collector, antiquarian bookseller, author, bibliographer, librarian, and teacher enable him to consider and describe the world of rare books and manuscripts with a perspective that few others can match. This is a challenging time for librarians, and while we can't foresee exactly what libraries of the future will look like, for those of us who work with special collections today, this book provides needed and thoughtful answers to the question of "what are librarians supposed to do now?"

Joel Silver
Bloomington, Indiana
February 2014

ACKNOWLEDGMENTS

IN WRITING THIS BOOK, I HAVE DRAWN ON THE ASSISTANCE OF many people who must be acknowledged.

Charles Harmon of Neal-Schuman got this started, with his insight and encouragement, and his colleague Sandy Wood did a superb job editing the first half of this book. Eventually that task was ceded to Rachel Chance of ALA, whose reinforcement kept it going. More recently, Russell Harper and Carolyn Crabtree, also of ALA, stepped in and wonderfully ushered this volume through the press.

Tamara Gaydos, Tom Horrocks, and Maureen Whalen also read various chapters and made many valuable suggestions. And my deep appreciation to Jeff Dykes, whose brilliant photography brings much to light here.

Matt T. Roberts and Don Etherington's book *Bookbinding and the Conservation of Books*, cited many times in the present volume, has been invaluable in its breadth and clarity. Equally amazing are this volume's excellent drawings by Margaret R. Brown, who graciously allowed their use. The "pictures-worth-thousands-of-words" cliché works here: Brown has saved me thousands upon thousands of words with her outstanding artistry.

Thanks also to Stanley Nelson, whose illustrations of typecasting are superb, to Bill Stoneman for permission to use the Houghton Library digital camera policy, and to Valerie Hotchkiss of the University of Illinois, Urbana-Champaign, Rare Book and Manuscript Library for allowing me to have access to that magnificent collection.

And of course, as the notes and bibliographical entries indicate, this volume owes a great deal to the many scholars who have worked in this endlessly broad field.

INTRODUCTION

HE LIBRARY AND THE CLASSROOM ARE THE CENTERS OF INTEL-
lectual ferment at many institutions, and in many of these orga-
nizations, the rare book and special collections department is the
jewel in their crown. Here are held the works of the world's great
thinkers and artists, scholars and printers and bookmakers, the
most important scientists and writers—all available locally and, in
many instances, remotely for patrons' use. This department is the locus of the central educational mission of the institution. And it is also the venue of the most intellectually and fiscally valuable materials in the library.

A good deal of literature exists on special collections and rare books, including
scholarship on just about every aspect of the field. After all, rare books have been
with us for millennia, rare book collections have been around for centuries, and rare
book and special collections departments have existed for a long time as well. The
field is extremely broad, and no single volume—nor, perhaps, a hundred volumes—
can cover it comprehensively. Nonetheless, those working in these areas—including
librarians, archivists, booksellers, collectors, historians, other scholars, and anyone
else interested in them—could profit from an overview of the realm. The present
volume aims to be that overview.

■ ■ ■

For decades I have been teaching courses relating to books: Rare Book Librarianship; History of the Book; Medieval Codicology: The Medieval Book from Sheep
to Shelf; Enumerative, Descriptive, Historical, and Textual Bibliography; The History, Materials, Manufacture, and Bibliographical Description of Paper; Preservation Management; Preservation and Conservation of Library Materials; The Book as
Physical Object; and others. And through the years I have had to assemble readings
for my students from myriad sources because no one volume on the market offered
the information I wished to convey.

Naturally, no single text could ever be sufficient, because the topics for each individual class are wide-ranging. Further, on certain technical aspects of book history and manufacture, few volumes "got it right." Too many authors were not practitioners of the crafts or skills they were writing about. Few had made paper, cut a punch, struck a matrix, or hand-cast printing type; made papyrus or amatl or tapa cloth; or printed on a handpress. Few had run a rare book department or had special training in archives or had worked in the antiquarian book trade. Few had extensive training in the branches of bibliography or had produced a scholarly edition of the work of an important author. Some were collectors or gatherers of books and manuscripts, but not too many had thought deeply enough about these artifacts to say anything useful—let alone accurate—about them.

Many writers turned to the works of others, trusting that the other authors were, themselves, expert in the subjects they were writing about. But many of those authors were as ignorant as their successors. For instance, a myth about the making of papyrus—that the strips cut from the plant must be *pounded* until they fuse—has persisted for at least a century and a half. This error is typical of the lack of scholarship in the field of rare books: writers simply repeat claims without actually testing them. (If the strips of papyrus are pounded, the fibers will separate, and the strips will be mushed out of shape. The strips, arranged in alternating vertical and horizontal layers, must merely be *pressed*, so that the pith fuses, binding all the fibers into a single sheet.) In a similar vein, paper was *not* invented in AD 105, Gutenberg did *not* invent printing, and his greatest achievement was *not* the printing press.

It was one thing to locate texts for my students that covered the topics of my lectures, and another thing altogether to find texts that were accurate and thorough. There are indeed many excellent, accurate, thorough texts available, but none as comprehensive as is needed for a student to become conversant in this wide world of special collections.

I have done all the activities listed earlier. And I have given much thought to all the things one needs to know to be competent—expert—in the rare book world. To be really knowledgeable, one must immerse oneself in an activity, with hands-on experience. Or one must study it and know which experts to study under—the one who would pound the papyrus strips or the one who would put them under pressure.

The basic premise of the present volume is this: a person working in rare books and special collections must know a certain body of information. This book aims to supply that body of knowledge—at least as much as can be recorded in a single volume. Although the primary readers of this book are librarians working in rare book and special collections departments, *anyone* working with rare books and manuscripts should know what this volume imparts. A bookseller, a collector, an archivist, a historian, or anyone working with rare, old volumes or manuscript materials should be able to distinguish a folio from a quarto from an octavo; should be able to recognize antique laid, modern laid, and wove paper; should be able to identify a wire watermark, a three-plane mark, and a shadowmark (also called a light-and-shade watermark); should understand the process of moving a text from writer to reader; should be able to create (and therefore interpret) a professional bibliographical description of a printed piece from the handpress period; should be able to appraise a book or manuscript to determine its monetary worth; should be familiar with legal issues in the rare book world; should understand the differences among preservation, conservation, and restoration, and know how these terms are applied in a collection; and much more.

A bookseller who offers a "second edition" of a book when he is really offering a commercial version of the first edition (as opposed to a deluxe version of the same edition) certainly does not understand the meanings of the terms *edition, printing* (or *impression*), *issue,* and *state,* and, therefore, probably does not know what *points* are. And he would also not know that a book printed from standing type in 1800 is the same *edition* as one printed in 1900 from stereotype plates made from that very type.

The present volume is a compendium of information, terminology, and experience gathered over more than forty years, aiming to make anyone who works with rare books able to speak with authority, using the accepted vocabulary, and not perpetuate the errors that have been canonized over the centuries. Another objective is to gather in a single volume the essential information that practitioners in the rare book field should have, so they will not need to run from book to book or from one Internet site to another (and often to sites with questionable information). This book also looks broadly over the rare book librarian's trade, which is remarkably varied and complex. It tries to cover in some depth what special collections librarians need to know to do their jobs right.

Because no two rare book and special collections departments are alike, no handbook or textbook or compendium of information can fully cover the needs of all who work in such departments. Therefore, along with much specific information that will be useful to anyone working with rare books, this text also offers a general approach to the field.

And while librarians will certainly find information they need here, because the rare book librarian's activities intersect with those of many others—booksellers, archivists, scholars, collectors, students, conservators, and preservationists, for example—it is important that all these people speak the same language, know the same things about books and their makeup and handling, and understand the pressures on each person in the book trade. These pressures include how to handle gifts or sales to libraries; how to treat damaged books and manuscripts; how to undertake fund-raising and outreach activities; how to describe books in such a way that a person who cannot see a particular volume can compare his to the one described; how to make collections secure; what to do when thefts are discovered; how booksellers, archivists, librarians, and collectors can work cooperatively; and so on. These matters affect all in the book world, not just librarians.

■ ■ ■

A scholar goes into a special collections department and is given access to certain materials. She wishes to make copies of them. What should she do? What should the librarians do? Should they allow her to make photocopies or take photographs by herself? Should they make copies for her? Are there reasons for not allowing any copies to be made? What are the legal and fiscal issues involved in such a scenario? In chapter 8 we look at such questions.

Pipes burst in the basement of a library where a substantial number of books are stored. Parts of the collection are getting wet. What should a patron or a librarian do? Who should be notified? And what should be done with the damaged volumes? Preservation and conservation issues are dealt with in chapter 12.

A bookseller in San Francisco is brought a few extremely valuable books. The person who brought them in wants to sell them. The dealer checks the standard bibliographies and discovers that some of these volumes seem to have been stolen. What should he do? Chapter 7 looks at security and theft in libraries.

A public library needs money to repair its leaky roof. It gathers books from its constituents and plans a book sale. But the librarian knows that some of the donated volumes could be quite valuable. She asks a local rare book librarian to help her appraise the sale items so that the library can maximize its take. What should the rare book librarian do? This is actually an issue of ethics, which is dealt with in chapter 2.

Donors want to give their lovingly assembled library to a special collections department. What should the receiving librarian consider? Are there moral, ethical, or legal issues he needs to know about? What considerations should be on the table before the donation is made? How should he direct or advise the donors, especially if the library does not want some of the items being given? This complex situation requires the librarian to know about standard practices in the profession and to be acquainted with federal, state, and local laws, as well as the policies and procedures of her institution, all addressed in the present volume.

These are just a few of the subjects covered in this book. As mentioned earlier, a librarian in charge of a rare book and special collections department must have broad knowledge, including about the nuts and bolts of administration, about issues pertaining to legal matters, personnel, acquisition, preservation and conservation, and about much more of a theoretical nature—all discussed here. But a schooled special collections person also needs to know other kinds of bolts and nuts having to do with the physical materials under her care. This information is here as well. And others in the rare book world should be similarly knowledgeable, not only for their own edification but also to be able to converse lucidly with the special collections librarian about their mutual interests.

Such conversation will necessarily require the use of a specialized vocabulary and a common knowledge about such things as parts of books, binding terminology, famous people in the book trade, practices having to do with theft, mutilation, information dissemination, access to knowledge, selling and buying and donating rare materials, appraisal, ethical standards, and so forth. The present text, while not pretending to be comprehensive (comprehensiveness is impossible), will inform anyone in the realm of rare books and manuscripts about such matters.

In writing this book, I have drawn on a wide range of sources along with my own extensive experience in the rare book field. Many of my examples come from my own life: I have worked in an antiquarian book store, been a head of special collections, been involved actively in the production of books from writing to editing to casting type to making paper to printing by hand, and have taught these subjects for more than forty years. Throughout are sidebars that reinforce or illuminate the theoretical materials of the text with practical experiences. I hope that these personal stories will make the text come alive for you. Anyone working with rare books will benefit not just from learning hypothetical or academic material but also from knowing what goes on in the real world.

■ ■ ■

Chapter 1 is an overview of the fields of special collections and rare books: What do these two closely related, overlapping fields have in common? What do these departments hold? How did those materials get there? What are the responsibilities of those who oversee the items? What is the department's role in its institution? What are the psychological realities of running such a unit? Some basic concepts are covered: rarity and scarcity; the place of first editions in the department; staffing; the importance of knowing the collection, the patrons, the booksellers, and others; the role of the Rare Books and Manuscripts Section in the life of all special collections personnel; and other issues common to the field.

Chapter 2 considers what it takes to manage a rare book department, with an eye toward ethics, professional guidelines, department functions, the creation and importance of a collection development policy, acquisition, weeding and deaccessioning of rare materials, the possibility of using vendors and approval plans, processing and cataloging the collection, transferring books from open stacks to the special collections department, lending books, dealing with patrons, and so forth. Although the bulk of this material is aimed at the librarian in a special collections department, it is important that scholars, booksellers, and collectors understand how these departments work. The chapter also considers the moving of a rare book library, a highly complex and pressure-packed undertaking.

A close relative to the rare book department is the archive—the focus of chapter 3—often overlooked in expositions or discussions about the management of special collections. The Society of American Archivists is an organization parallel to the American Library Association, with its own governing body, regulations, ethical standards, policies, procedures, practices, and responsibilities. Because the operations in archives overlap a good deal with those of special collections, and because most special collections departments are affiliated with (or are inseparable from) archives, chapter 3 gives a brief overview of this closely allied repository, with a look at paper-based and digital materials and how archivists deal with both.

Chapter 4 discusses the physical materials of the collection. In every profession that deals with physical objects, practitioners need to know about those objects: what they are made of, how they are put together, how to identify them, how to describe them, and so on. This entails knowing a vocabulary that has evolved over decades or centuries. People in the discipline need to speak the same language when they write or converse about the materials they use. This chapter looks at many materials that exist in special collections departments: papyrus, parchment and vellum, paper, printing type, presses, bindings, inks, and more. The terminology here overlaps professions: booksellers will bring vellum-bound books to librarians and offer them to collectors. The dealer may say in a catalog, "This volume is quarter bound, has gilt dentelles, and has AEG." Knowledgeable booksellers will know the jargon of the trade, and librarians working in rare books and special collections need to understand this vocabulary. Archivists, too, will encounter bound volumes, broadsides, manuscript materials, and so forth, and they need to understand when a collector or bookseller talks about the shadowmarks and deckle edges in documents, the stab binding of a pamphlet, or the volume that uses amatl in its binding. A knowledge of how paper is made or bindings are created is invaluable in the rare book profession.

In chapter 5 we look at the physical layout of a special collections department. Sometimes these units grow incrementally from a locked closet to a single room to a cluster of rooms. Sometimes they are purpose-built facilities with security and environmental controls in mind from the beginning. What are the optimum ways of laying out the space and creating a congenial and secure facility, given the two kinds of "histories" that are possible for such collections? Layout needs include offices, work areas, public access space for greeting patrons and containing tables for them to sit at when they are using the department's materials, stacks for the collections, storage spaces, areas for the unit's hardware (copy machines, microfilm readers, and so forth), space for the public access terminals, and much more. All through the design of the department there should be a focus on security, environmental conditions, access to collections, satisfactory lighting, and much more.

The following chapter (chapter 6) covers fundraising. No department can ever say, "We have enough (money) (staff) (space)." Like the larger organization around it, the special collections department can be a black hole, sucking in all the resources

made available to it and wanting more. No library wants to remain static; growth is good—for the collection, for the patrons, and for the institution. But growth requires resources, and an active rare book librarian, working with the organization's development staff, can have a strong, positive fiscal impact on the department's resources. Successful fundraising strategies require good people skills, a positive attitude about one's profession and one's collection, and an enthusiasm to better the department's conditions and holdings.

Chapter 7 examines one of the most important aspects of library operations—security. A stolen or mutilated book will be of no use to a patron who needs the information it contains. In the past, many libraries covered up the loss, not wanting to face the humiliation of having been lax in their security measures and not wanting potential donors to know that they were not good stewards of their collections. Today, theft is treated much more responsibly, and libraries have beefed up security in ways that are discussed in this chapter. Because thieves tend to prey on special collections—the institution's most valuable materials—librarians must be particularly aware of thieves' methods of operating and should be on top of the latest security devices and measures.

We live in a world governed by laws, and in the special collections department legal issues often arise. Chapter 8 deals with many situations in which the law affects the management of rare books and manuscripts: Who owns the content of printed matter, manuscripts, correspondence, photographs, audio and video materials, and the like? What are the responsibilities of those in charge of these materials with respect to publication and the granting of permission for the use of intellectual content? What laws govern purchases and the acquisition of gifts and deposits? What should a good Deed of Gift contain? In the acquisition of a gift, what are the responsibilities of the donor? of the librarian? What do booksellers need to know about selling books to libraries or about being the go-between for a gift from a donor to a library? For instance, what is the relationship between the library, the donor, and the bookseller with respect to an appraisal that needs to be done on the materials donated? Who is responsible for the appraisal of donated materials? Who will pay for it? Who gets to see it? What is the "Three-Year Rule"? What are the legal implications of a deposit? What is a Promised Gift Agreement? Is it legal for a public institution to charge patrons fees for the use of library materials? Can a library that receives funding from the federal government refuse to put filters on its computers? What effects has the USA PATRIOT Act had on libraries? And on and on. Much of the information in chapter 8 will also be useful for those outside the department (administrators, archivists, scholars, booksellers, faculty, collectors, donors) who are involved with rare books.

Bibliography, the subject of chapter 9, is an enormous field. By its very nature, it impacts the life of anyone working with special collections materials. We look at enumerative, descriptive, historical, and textual bibliography—each of which impacts the rare book person's life in a different way. People involved with rare books and materials (in special collections departments, archives, bookstores, and private collections) should understand how to use (and compile) bibliographies. They should know the important reference tools in their fields, and they should be able to recognize a reliable and an unreliable bibliography.

Descriptive bibliography is crucial, for it teaches anyone handling books (especially those produced before the nineteenth century) how to describe them in such a way that someone not looking at the copy being described will know what it looks like and how it compares to other copies. When a bookseller lists a rare book in a catalog, the collector or librarian needs to know exactly what is being described: what it looks like, how it is made up, what materials it is made of, what condition it is in, and so forth. The description should indicate the format of the book (folio, quarto, octavo, duodecimo, or another) and whether it is complete. And much more. Rare book catalogers also should understand bibliographic description so that they can populate MARC records with the appropriate information.

Historical bibliography is another extremely broad realm of scholarly inquiry, as chapter 9 explains. What kinds of historical research could anyone working with special collections do? The answer is all kinds. And "all kinds" means delving into just about any discipline in the world. Responsible and well-informed rare book librarians and booksellers will know where to look to educate themselves about books and manuscripts in general and about the specific ones they are doing research on.

And textual bibliography is the discipline in which responsible, reliable, authoritative texts are studied and produced. If two versions of a text exist, which one should the bookseller advise the librarian to acquire and which should the librarian advise the scholar to use as the basis for her research? How can a scholar distinguish between a poorly produced and a reliable edition? Librarians themselves can be textual bibliographers, creating reliable texts for their patrons. How do they go about this? Chapter 9 is a thorough exposition of how this branch of bibliography impacts the world of those working with rare books and manuscripts.

Chapter 10 discusses collecting and handling the materials of a special collections department. We look in depth at collection development, with much information from the perspective of the librarian and the bookseller, and we consider various methods of acquisition, dealing with booksellers (in person, on the Web, through their catalogs), dealing with book scouts, and acquiring books from the Web, book fairs, and auctions. The chapter also examines the antiquarian book trade: What do librarians and collectors need to know? What do booksellers need to let librarians know? Who are the players in the game? And an important section of this chapter is devoted to appraising books and manuscripts: how to do it, the tools of the trade, what to look for, what features raise (or lower) the fiscal value of the item, and so forth. What kinds of value are there beyond the monetary? How should this kind of information influence the purveyor and the purchaser of rare materials? Despite the altruistic nature of librarianship, its practitioners must face the worldly reality that the items they deal with have monetary value. Much of this chapter guides the librarian into thinking about the fiscal realities of his trade, and booksellers and collectors should be as fully aware. For the dealer, such knowledge is essential—her livelihood depends on it.

Special collections departments do not exist in vacuums. They depend on others for their resources, and they are just as dependent on their users, for if the department has no users, it has no reason to exist. The greater the use a department has, the more it can justify its existence and the more resources it has the right to request from its parent institution. To increase use, librarians need to reach out to many constituencies. Chapter 11 provides guidance and presents various forms of this activity, which can be tremendously diverse, depending on the personality of the librarian, the kinds of activities the institution will allow him to perform, and the nature of the community the library serves. Staff levels might allow the rare book librarian to partner with other departments to hold meetings and workshops, offer lectures, and engage audiences young and old.

One essential task for the special collections department is to extend the longevity of the materials in the collection. Chapter 12, "Preservation, Conservation, Restoration, and Disaster Planning" details appropriate actions that must be taken in these realms. The brevity of this paragraph is in opposite proportion to the importance and extent of the information that this chapter presents.

Entire courses are taught on preservation of library materials, preservation management, digital preservation, and the like; conservation is a field unto itself, requiring much specialized training in chemistry, book history, material sciences, bookbinding, paper manufacture, and a great deal more. Chapter 12 presents an overview of the two related fields—with a glance at restoration (more appropriately expatiated upon in the realm of museums). Many a library does not have its own preservation officer or conservator on staff. The importance of these positions cannot be overstated, and chapter 12 makes a case for creating them.

Even if an institution has a preservation librarian and a separate department of conservators, the rare book librarian must understand all the issues, policies, practices, and responsibilities of those in charge of preserving the collections. In fact, with specialized knowledge about the physical makeup of the holdings, and the further knowledge of where information resides in these materials and how they are used, the librarian may be a crucial player in preservation and conservation decisions. At smaller institutions, the librarian himself may be the only one responsible for these activities.

Chapter 13 is about special collections departments today. Traditional materials—paper based, vellum and parchment, items incorporating metals and plastics in their makeup, film, audio, and other analog holdings—remain in special collections departments and continue to be acquired by them. Additionally, the digital age, which began a long time ago, has impacted nearly everyone in the world. Librarians have been eager beneficiaries of and contributors to this revolution. This chapter looks at the traditional activities and all the new opportunities that the electronic world offers. Those working in special collections, as this volume demonstrates, need to know a great deal about many issues (and many kinds of issues) relating to their responsibilities. Digital technologies, while simplifying librarians' lives in many ways and making it possible to serve their clientele to a greater extent than ever before, complicate matters considerably by adding enormously to the knowledge required of anyone employed in the rare book world.

The final chapter picks up a variety of topics that did not fall comfortably in any of the preceding chapters: nonbook collection items, department and extra-department protocols, administrative and fiscal oversight (budgets, annual reports, and such), staffing and human relations issues (hiring, chains of command, searching for and moving to a new job, and so forth), development activities and solicitation of gifts, and special topics (marks in rare books, fine press books, artists' books and altered books, and canvassing books). I review current trends and speculate on future directions, and the text concludes with a brief section on the survival of special collections departments.

■ ■ ■

As I mentioned earlier in this introduction, this text does not purport to be definitive. It cannot be, given the immense complexity of the book world and the equally extensive variety that exists in rare book departments around the world—indeed, just in the United States and Great Britain alone. Instead, I have tried to convey a blueprint for thinking about responsibilities, materials, operations, personnel, activities, and many other areas of rare book and special collections librarianship, bookselling, collecting, and research in the field. The aim throughout is to enlighten all who deal in any fashion with rare books about what they should know.

For me, there is no more exciting, thrilling, and rewarding realm than the world of books—especially rare books and the world in which they live.

The range of topics covered in this text supports my notion that one can never be bored in this field. And it also supports my contention that to be responsible as a librarian, bookseller, collector, archivist, or other participant in this milieu, you must know a good deal about many topics. I offer this volume as one step in the direction of fulfilling that need.

Sidney Berger
Waban, Massachusetts
2013

CHAPTER 1

SOME PRACTICAL REALITIES

Т HIS BOOK IS ABOUT RARE BOOKS AND SPECIAL COLLECTIONS. All those involved in the rare book world must know a great deal about the physical objects in their care, the legal issues relating to these objects, technology, ethics, and much more. But librarians, in addition to all these issues, must deal with the narrower world of the institution they inhabit. For them to be effective at their jobs, some absolutely basic issues must be addressed. Hence, this chapter looks primarily at library practices.

Rare Book and Special Collections Departments

Although a rare book department, in its generic sense, differs from a special collections department, the two terms have come to be used almost interchangeably. Not all items in a rare book department are rare, nor are some of them books. There will also be photographs, pamphlets, maps, drawings, sketches, possibly philatelic or numismatic items, paintings, and a great variety of other genres of materials. Perhaps the term *rare books* goes back to the origin of the department, when certain volumes were segregated from the parent collection because of their value or vulnerability and put into a separate, more secure environment.

But custodians would also have seen, for instance, maps of great rarity, manuscripts that were, by their very nature, unique and irreplaceable, and photographs that were equally unique. And they would have wanted to secure these items as well. It would be only natural to do so in the same place in which the rare books were kept. There might not even have been much intellectual connection between one item and another: a scarce book on medicine; a few first editions of American, French, and British writers; a collection of letters from a Civil War soldier; a political pamphlet that would cause some trouble if it were left in open stacks; a book of anatomy with explicit illustrations of bodies; and so forth. That is, the items in themselves may not have made a coherent collection, the only qualities bringing them together in the first place being their monetary value and their vulnerability to mutilation.

To call it a *rare book* collection would have been strictly inaccurate, but the designation does convey the idea of rarity and the need for protection as well as the notion that this is where research can be done on manuscript and printed sources. So Rare Book Department might be the best way to designate this facility.

On the other hand, a special collections department is the repository of items that are not necessarily monetarily valuable but are distinguishable by virtue of their being assemblages of materials of like kinds or on like topics. In one sense, "special collections" are valuable simply because of the cohesiveness and extent of the items on a particular topic, in a particular genre, or by a particular author. Hence, there can be a special collection on orchids or tobacco, romance novels or science fiction, James Joyce or John Steinbeck, bookplates or binders' tickets, labels or trade cards, or any other focused area or genre of collecting.

So the two kinds of collections are distinct in some respects, but they overlap in a few others.

For instance, they both require heightened security; neither will circulate its holdings; ideally, both will be housed under special environmental conditions, possibly better than those for the open stacks; they require preservation and conservation attention beyond that of the circulating collection; the cataloging of their materials is more extensive than that of the circulating collection and may require special training; methods of obtaining their materials differ from those used by the collection development department; and so forth.

And because it is more expensive to run two separate departments than it is to run a single one, these two functions (rare books and special collections) are usually combined in a single facility, sometimes with both designations as the title of the department, sometimes with one or the other designation in the unit's name.[1]

Finally, it is unusual to find two separate departments because their holdings overlap. Any rare book department will have individual assemblages of materials that are special collections. And every special collections department will hold rare books.

As for the name, it may be common to call such a department Rare Books and Special Collections, but this is rarely necessary because each part of that title

---

WHEN I ARRIVED at the University of California, Riverside, as head of the special collections department, I found some peculiar holdings: a yoke for two oxen, a Nazi knife in its scabbard, polo mallets, large keys to South American cities in fancy presentation boxes, a couple of vials containing tree bark, kids' metal lunch boxes, two massive paintings, a particularly hideous metal sculpture on a pedestal, and so forth. What these objects were doing there was beyond me. I could not see their relationship to the department.

I learned that the ox yoke and polo mallets were part of the campus's heritage, having come from

the days when the school was the Citrus Experimentation Station for the University of California (UC)— long before the second UC campus (UCLA) was established in the 1920s. The Nazi knife and keys to the cities came from the holdings of professors who had retired and left their collections to the library. The Buck Rogers metal lunch box was part of the famous J. Lloyd Eaton Collection of Science Fiction and Fantasy, the department's most renowned and largest special collection. The tree bark came from the first naval orange tree, cultivated at that campus in the early days of the twentieth century. The enormous paintings, which were

leaning face in against a tall wall, turned out to be particularly awful. It was clear why they faced the wall. They were reputed to be too big to be stored in the campus museum, but I suspect their ugliness got them exiled to the library. Likewise, the sculpture was horrible— so it was stuck in the far reaches of the rare-book stacks, down an aisle holding almost-never-used serials, facing a wall so one could not see it when one glanced down that aisle.

Incidentally, the rubber covering of an old auto foot pedal is in a special collection of the Houghton Library at Harvard. Paper decorator Rosamond Loring used it to decorate paste paper.

implies the other part. In the present volume, the terms *rare books* and *special collections* will be used interchangeably, unless the text calls for one particular kind of collection.

Department Holdings

In many special collections departments, one might find a host of things that one would not expect to find there. The department is in a library, so books and manuscripts, prints and drawings, photographs and maps, and many other paper-based items will be on the shelves and in cabinets and files. But what about Native American baskets, a printing press, shoes and socks, handkerchiefs, the rubber covering of an old auto foot-pedal, a special chair, a rolling pin? Articles like this could wind up in a special collections department just as easily as could a book or pamphlet. In any institution, when people find objects that simply cannot be jettisoned, especially because the items are relevant to the history of the organization, they want these things preserved. The only logical place, it is generally agreed, is the library. The reasoning goes something like this: "Libraries hold all kinds of things. They are good at storing important things that someone may wish to know about or consult someday. There really is no other place to house these things. Let's give them to the library."

It is clear that if an institution has something it does not know what to do with and, for any reason, cannot dispose of, special collections is a good dumping ground. Also, people at institutions see the special collections department as not merely the custodian of the standard books, pamphlets, manuscripts, photographs, archives, and so forth. It is also seen as (and therefore becomes) a repository of all kinds of realia, a permanent holding zone for items too "precious" to part with, a storehouse of articles that might someday shed light on something that some researcher might find useful. It is also possible that these nontraditional items came as parts of gifts whose donors stipulated that all the materials donated had to be maintained by the institution. Jettisoning selected pieces was not an option.

One key issue when considering holdings is that all *things* contain information of some kind. The job of the library is to link that information with the patron who needs it. It is sometimes not the librarians' job to say, "This item contains no information—or no information that our users would ever search for. We can discard it." (Although that is exactly what happens in weeding a collection; see later in this chapter.) Keen special collections librarians can see the research potential of the items in their care, and they know which to hold on to. Some things they *must* hold on to; they have no choice.

Department holdings, then, can take many forms. And if the library has a good collection development policy, the holdings should focus properly on the department's collection, mandated by many things: the present needs of the patrons, the history of the collection itself, the different levels of collecting assigned to each subcollection, and so on. (This point will be covered in more detail in chapter 2 when we look at collection development policies.)

As suggested at the beginning of this chapter, the kinds of holdings in the department will differ depending on the emphasis of the collection. If the department is primarily a "rare book" division, the emphasis will be on rare books; if it is a true special collections department, one will expect to find some rare books but also a host of items that might be exceptionally inexpensive or common. The J. Lloyd Eaton Collection mentioned in the sidebar is a true special collection: it contains many thousands of cheap paperbacks that would find their way into mighty few libraries of any kind. However, the Eaton Collection is the world's largest holding of books on science fiction, fantasy, horror, and Utopian literature, and to be comprehensive it must hold thousands of volumes that were issued only in paperback, that were printed in huge numbers, that cost next to nothing when they were published, that can be had for pennies at garage sales today, that may be in poor condition from having been made from cheap materials and having been read over and over and tossed aside, and that would normally be chucked into the trash after years or even decades of abuse. Many volumes in the Eaton Collection fit this description. But they are the only copies of these titles cataloged anywhere in the world. This is a Special Collection in its purest form—exactly what that rubric indicates.

As mentioned earlier in this chapter, there is, of course, overlap with rare book holdings because rare items can themselves be part of a special collection. The Eaton Collection at UC Riverside has a large number of exceptionally costly books, including, for instance, a copy of *Fahrenheit 451* in the asbestos binding, first editions of *Dracula* and *Frankenstein*, seventeenth- and eighteenth-century books on fantastic voyages, and many other treasures. And rare book collections can be special collections, of course, if the special holdings are valuable, rare, or unique.

Naturally, as indicated earlier, we are speaking about many things beyond books: manuscripts, photographs, prints and drawings, maps, trade cards, philatelic items, realia of all kinds, and any number of other genres of materials. This is one of the great appeals of the field for many people: it is varied and filled with riches at all levels of one's budget in a great array of manifestations.

Special collections librarians must familiarize themselves with all the department's holdings—if not volume by volume, at least area by area—and acquire materials in the department's areas of strength and greatest use. And they should be open-minded about what to let into the department. They do not want to bring in junk or items that might never be used, but the sheer breadth of objects that might wind up in the special collections department is prodigious. There are untold numbers of locks of hair of important writers or historical personages; scarves and other pieces of clothing of the famous; other personal effects such as pens and inkwells and desks; pressed flowers; printing plates and woodcuts (the actual engraved blocks); papermaking, bookbinding, and typecasting equipment, and so forth. Think of the rare book department as a museum of the book (and the manuscript), and then it becomes clear that the holdings can be almost anything that will fit in.

The Role of the Department in the Larger Institution

Although rare book departments might like to see themselves as meccas for researchers, occupying a lofty place in the scholarly world, the envy of those around them, the fact is that most such libraries are situated in and beholden to the larger institu-

AS A SPECIAL collections librarian at UC Riverside, I engaged the help of the entire circulation staff to identify books that should have been in special collections. I tutored all who worked in circulation about the criteria that would qualify items for transfer to my department: age, limited printings, certain kinds of illustrations, bindings of various kinds, books signed by their authors, and so on. Not all the items the circulation staff pulled aside for special collections, of course, were admitted into my department, but it was good to have many sets of eyes working for me at a point of great book-viewing activity in the library. Over the years, I did transfer into my department a good number of items that should have been there in the first place. And I made it a point to congratulate and thank the circulation staff for their acuity and diligence.

The same went for Interlibrary Loan (ILL): when items were requested from other institutions, the ILL folks paged them and measured them against the criteria I gave them. Many a volume that would otherwise have been sent out was held back, identified as rare enough that it should not have been circulating, least of all to another institution. Bibliographers and selectors notified me when a particularly expensive item was purchased. Many of these I earmarked for special collections. Reference librarians, catalogers, and even students who reshelved books became allies, finding items for me that were candidates for transfer to special collections, and I reinforced their efforts with hearty and heartfelt thanks.

This was a form of internal outreach, and in the long run the library was better off and the collection was enhanced with the transfer of many items to a more secure department.

tions of which they are a part. This simple statement has some profound implications. To begin with, the department might not exist without the parent institution, and every special collections librarian must remember this. Second, the department must function in the same way that the parent library does, and with the same primary directive: to serve patrons by linking users with the information they need.

Another responsibility is to serve the parent institution in ways that will make the larger body prosper. A rare book librarian, for instance, may wish to contact the chancellor or president of her institution to offer the department for development activities. After all, when an executive officer wants to show off the institution, why not start with the jewels? The library can label itself with the now-trite phrase "the jewel in the crown"—the most intellectually and visually striking venue at the school, whose holdings will impress anyone.

The rare book department runs a risk by its very nature. There may be jealousy from other departments who see what may seem like a disproportionate amount of resources being devoted to expensive books and manuscripts. Think of how many books for the general collection can be had for the price of a single old book or manuscript that maybe no one will ever use. It is incumbent on the librarians in this department to work with all colleagues in a collegial way. This requires much outreach, tact, and insight. And for good reason, for many other departments can be close allies.

It cannot be overstated that staying on good terms with all departments is a must. When you reach out to other departments, asking for their help in strengthening special collections, you must also express a strong appreciation for those who help. This kind of outreach may entail a good deal of training of others, explaining what to look for and why. Once they understand the vulnerability of their library and the cultural heritage they are protecting, colleagues will become increasingly invested in the department by becoming its guardians. It is important that they understand why special collections exists and, far from being jealous, why they should be proud to be at an institution with such treasures and with a reputation based partly on those treasures.

This kind of internal cooperation will make the special collections department no longer a snobby, discrete unit; it will make the department an ally, integrated into the institution. It is important for all your colleagues to see that they are working toward the same end: offering access to our patrons, protecting our cultural heritage, and being responsible.

In holding some of the great treasures of the institution, the rare book department is in a unique position to help the campus at a level above and beyond the library. If the department has a relatively attractive space, it is prime real estate for hosting dignitaries of all kinds. As noted earlier, one form of internal outreach can be to the president or chancellor of the school. The offer is simple: the department is willing to host any gathering that the president or chancellor wishes, and can quickly mount a pointed exhibit focusing on the interests of those who will be in attendance.

It should take little time to prepare a few vitrines with materials from the department, showing the guests some of the treasures of the institution. Even if the library has a no-food-or-drink policy, it may be worth bending this rule now and then for the goodwill such an event could generate for the department and the institution. Just be sure that a well-trained cleanup crew is on hand. Use the opportunity to welcome the guests to the department, and give a short introduction to the items on display. Though the event is not yours, the venue is, and any plug you can get for your department could be useful.

Outreach to others at the institution can be useful as well, as the sidebar about asking for help of the police department shows. This kind of outreach must be done with tact. The goal of such a request is ultimately to improve the department in one way or another.

Not to be cynical, but one thing must be mentioned concerning the psychology of asking for improvements to one's domain. If one goes to a superior and straight out asks for something—an additional staff member, an augmented cataloging budget, physical improvements in the venue, and so on—the chances are that a flat-out no will be the result. An old attitude is common in libraries: You have gotten along thus far without it, so you certainly

A DIFFERENT KIND of outreach can be tremendously valuable. When I began working at UC Riverside, I called the campus police chief to introduce myself and to ask for help: I wanted an expert from the police department to help me do a security analysis for the department. The police are there for just this purpose, and it became clear that they were quite pleased that someone on the campus reached out to them for their assistance. The chief and his best security officer came over to help.

I prefaced our walk-around of the department with a conversation about the importance of the collection, its relationship to the campus and our cultural heritage, its value for scholarship beyond its monetary value, and so on. They got it, and they were wonderfully responsive and immensely supportive. The security officer wrote a superb report, which I was able to use when I wanted various kinds of security upgrades for the department.

don't need it now—whatever the "it" is. (We will see this again and again in the planning for the operations of the department.) Parallel to this attitude is another: I know you are just asking for this so you can get more things for your department; if I give you this, you will just ask for more.

But if the ask comes with a strong corroboration from an outside expert (in the case cited in the sidebar, the top security officer of the campus police force), the administration cannot take your requests too lightly. The request may still be denied, but at least the denial is not a personal "defeat" because it is a rejection of the recommendation of an authority.

As the sidebar explains, one good by-product of having sought the police report was that the officers became part of the special collections "family," and they were thereafter instantly responsive to any security issue relating to the special collections department.

Similar outreach to the fire department of the institution will bring these professionals into this family. One course of action is to ask the fire department to do a fire assessment of the unit. Their response time in an emergency will be improved for two reasons: they will have a greater sense of responsibility to the special collections department after their report is done than they did before it, and they will have had a fresh look at the physical layout of the place, so that they can maneuver effectively in the space if they need to be there.

One way to strengthen this connection between the special collections department and the firefighters is by asking them to give department personnel a workshop in the use of fire extinguishers. Fire department personnel are usually set up to do this

kind of training, and they appreciate the special collections department's taking such an active interest in them and their services. An important by-product of this approach is that special collections staff will become proficient in the use of the extinguishers. Not every institution will have such intelligent, well-trained, helpful colleagues in these areas (security and fire), but do not hesitate to reach out to them. Everyone benefits.

Another target for outreach is the faculty. It is important to seek out the professors on campus to offer the department's services to them. For example, contact a professor who teaches in an area in which the special collections department has strong holdings and offer to host her class in your department to expose her students to primary research materials. It is possible that the professor herself did not know of your holdings. The result could be increased patronage of the department, a desired goal, because increased use is a strong help when asking for augmentations to the staff or for additional resources of any kind.

Becoming familiar with the faculty can have other benefits. If your department has strong collections in the areas of a professor's interests, he can become a selector for you. That is, the professor can notify you of important items that should be added to the collection. If the items he recommends are expensive, faculty research funds may be available that can be shared for the purchases.

One word of caution, however: faculty members can be quite powerful at the institution, and though you want to give them the best service you can— as you want to give all your patrons the best service—you cannot please all people all the time. It is not uncommon to encounter professors who think that because they are faculty, they have special privileges and should be given extraordinary treatment. Professors may demand, for example, that they be allowed to take rare books to their offices. Rules are not meant to be broken. To allow this practice could lead to disaster. Who knows how many other professors, hearing of this arrangement, would demand the same treatment? If the rule is that no book circulates from the department, that rule should *not* be relaxed for anyone.

The department should thus have a written policy that clearly spells out that books do not circulate from the department. A written policy, on paper, that can be handed to anyone requesting this kind of special treatment, carries a good deal of authority. The document makes it clear that the department is not discriminating against one party; it is following a standard policy that applies equally to all. Just be sure that any such policy, in paper form or clearly spelled out on your website, has been shown to and approved by the administration of the library. Policies are subject to review, and certainly they should not be enacted without having been taken through the proper channels. (Appendix 6 reviews the forms you might wish to have on hand in the rare book department.)

So while outreach to faculty will usually eventuate in good relations between them and the special collections department, the friendships that will ensue should not weaken your resolve to maintain the professional practices of the department.

The Psychology of Special Collections; or, The Expectations of Patrons and Colleagues

In running a rare book department, librarians will encounter a variety of responses from their colleagues and patrons. Although specific responses will be considered throughout this chapter and elsewhere, some generic statements are in order.

All libraries have finite budgets. The corollary to this is that there is never enough money to allow a library to do everything it wishes to do. Librarians will almost never say, "We have all the staff, money,

PSYCHOLOGY IN RUNNING the special collections department takes many forms. As a new head of the special collections department at UC Riverside, I made a few changes. My predecessor allowed faculty into the rare book stacks whenever they wanted to get in there. In fact, some of them had keys, and others just walked right in—the door between the public vestibule and the books was always unlocked. One of my first acts, on my first day, was to lock that door, because anyone—faculty, staff, students, researchers "off the street"—could have walked right in. The first time a professor came in, tried the handle, and found the door locked, he complained, rather loudly.

I introduced myself and told him that as the new head of the department, I had made a few changes that would make the collection safer. He immediately snapped back, "Are you saying I am a thief?" I knew I had a problem on my hands. I shall not delve into this case any further. The point is that it takes a good deal of psychology to please as many people as one can, especially when it comes to setting new practices in a department where old practices have been in place a long time.

and space we need. Don't give us any more." The opposite is usually the case: "We could use more money, staff, and space." So when a special collections department acquires an extraordinarily expensive item, responses could be negative: "Why do they need that? Just think of how all that money could be used in the rest of the library." "We could have bought hundreds of Level 3 and Level 4 books for the price they paid for that atlas."[2] "They spent how much on that book? Just think of how much we could be giving to our underpaid staff with all that money." The rare book librarian must counter all these attitudes with tact and patience, with good PR and friendliness, and with an understanding that others see things from perspectives different from hers.

It could be jealousy that prompts such attitudes among those outside special collections. After all, there is a gloss and fame that comes with being part of a rare book department that no cataloger or reference librarian has. It behooves special collections personnel to befriend all those around them to try to defuse that "they think they are better than we are" attitude. The fact is that all who work in the library have the same mission: to link patrons with the information they need. In that view, it does not really matter in what department one works. And that appreciation should be uppermost in the minds of all rare book librarians in their dealings with those around them.

We could take the stance that the customer is always right, but that position would have to be modified when the customer's being "right" compromises the department's security or violates any other reasonable policy.

Another element of the psychology of running the department is the notion that special collections is exclusive—that is, only the elite are allowed inside. Potential patrons frequently say, "I didn't know I could use that department," or "I thought the rare book department was closed to people like me," or "I assumed you had to be a professor to work in there." Some special collections, especially at private institutions, can be as exclusive and excluding as they want to be, but that is not always good. This kind of negative PR might keep the load light on the staff, but it sets up a barrier to research, if only a perceived barrier. There is no way to know what kind of largesse could come the way of the department, or what kind of research might emanate from the department, if it did not turn away people by projecting such an attitude. Rare book librarians must of course screen users carefully, but they should not set up a screen that discourages anyone from asking to use the department's holdings.

Our colleagues and patrons (local and distant) in this field expect from special collections departments some fairly basic things: decent service, courtesy, enthusiastic (or at least uncomplaining) effort, access to information, reasonable explanations for policies that they might not understand, consistency in service from one visit to another and from one patron to another. They expect to be treated well, not as inferior beings, not being given the impression that they are being catered to by an elite staff

which deigns to let them use the institution's precious goods. They should never feel as if the librarians are doing them a favor.

And our colleagues must understand why special collections may seem to get a disproportionate amount of resources, especially for acquisition. Good rare book librarians will command the same kind of respect that they feel for their own colleagues. The whole staff of the library should feel "We are all in this together" and not feel that special collections librarians are "special" or overly indulged.

The Placement of the Department in the Institution, and the Department's Management

Special collections departments may exist in various places in libraries. In many libraries, the departments are located in Collection Development; in others they are under an AUL (Associate University Librarian) for Technical Services or in Reference (under an AUL for Public Services), and in still others they are positioned directly under the administration of the library. If the institution is old and large enough, special collections could be its own unit, as is the case, for example, of the Houghton Library at Harvard.

In one respect it does not really make any difference where in the hierarchy the department exists; its functions and responsibilities will not differ regardless of its position in the institution. In another respect, there is some reputation to be had if the department is a freestanding unit or if it is positioned directly under a library director, or perhaps a president or chancellor.

Chapter 3, "Archives," will address management, but with specific reference to the management of the collection. Here, though, the *concept* of management is crucial because the subject of this section is the department's place in the larger organization.

The department head will often have a staff working under her. This arrangement calls for managerial skills, which do not come naturally to many people. Library schools do have courses in library manage-

THE SPECIAL COLLECTIONS department I managed at UC Riverside kept one huge local-history collection significantly out of call-number order on the shelves. But because it was one of the most used areas of our holdings, it made sense to keep it close at hand for the librarians who paged from it rather than far away in the correct order in the stacks. This simple, rudimentary example shows a fairly modest piece of management, but the staff, and ultimately the patrons, benefited from it in the form of efficiency.

ment, and they could be useful, with much reservation, because the skills they present are not necessarily inherent. We can talk about the X and Y method of management—the stick and the carrot method. We can talk about the Directing style, the Participatory style, the style that encourages teamwork, the paternalistic or autocratic style, and on and on. But this is not a book about the level of management. It is a book about responsibilities, among other things, and regardless of one's style of managing, the rare book librarian needs to manage two completely different kinds of things: the collection and the people around it.[3]

As for the collection, the manager should learn best practices in many areas (covered by the present text): cataloging, security, access, legal issues, marking books, paging and reshelving, cataloging and creating finding aids, and much more. And the department head should do everything in his power to insure that all these best practices are adhered to. Managing the collection means not putting the holdings at risk in any way, no matter the reason. And managing also should be done with an eye to efficiency—which is another way of saying that if the collection is properly overseen, the staff will be operating with maximum productivity and the patrons will be happy to work there, knowing they are well served.

Each department will have its own rules. With rare books, there is no room for the laissez-faire style of management in which the chief leaves the staff to do what they will, observing along the way and making sure that no one gets out of line or slacks off. Because of the nature of the items in the department and the rules about who can bring what into the secure area, who may use pens in what places, who must toe the line with respect to ethical practices, and so forth, there is no room for slack management. It might force the special collections head to be firmer than he likes with the people who work under him, but issues of ethics and access and security trump all others, including the issue of likeability. Being a manager whom people really like or one who is a friend to all staff members is fine, but not to the detriment of the collection or the department's operations or security.

Further, management often means training. A good manager knows the collection and the operations of the department and must often train those under her in what is best for that department. The manager does not need to know *all*. A reference staff will know more about department holdings than does the head of the department. The head will probably not be a cataloger, but she should know good reference service and cataloging when she sees them. Department heads often will have taken classes in these fields and should know when a book or manuscript has been properly cataloged and when proper reference procedures have been used. Department heads should know from the patrons' perspective when they have been well served. This is not to say that you must be glaring at the staff at all times to make sure they are doing their jobs properly. It does mean that you must be observing the staff to make sure they are doing their jobs properly. The distinction is subtle. The key issue here is that the manager must see to it that the department she oversees is operating as well as it can. If it is not, it is a reflection on her.

Access: The Prime Directive

Libraries exist to link patrons with the information they need. I have made this point several times already and shall make it again. Everyone who works in the library has the same objective: increase access to information. And I mean everyone, from the custodians to the director. The cleaning that the custodians do keeps bugs and fire hazards away. Bugs and fire will harm or destroy materials, preventing access to the information those materials contain. The director makes sure that all staff, even the custodians, work toward serving patrons.

There is a perception among many—even among some special collections personnel—that the librarian's first job is to preserve the collection for future generations. And, of course, preservation is key to long-term access to information. But some librarians take this responsibility to an extreme, prohibiting access for any number of reasons—for instance, that the item is too fragile to use, or that a surrogate copy is all a patron needs, or that the potential user is only a high school student.

But there is really no ethical reason to prohibit access. If an item is too fragile to use, get it conserved or reformatted so scholars will have access to the information it contains. Of course, reformatting does remove the patron at least one level from the original item, and some conservation work by its very nature takes away information from the original. In chapter 12 we will look at this in depth. But conservation aims to extend access to the information an item holds.

A good deal of literature exists on the use of special collections by high school students or undergraduates. Most of that literature comes from those who have an open-door policy for such patrons. Many rare book librarians agree with the view that the department should encourage young people to experience the use of primary materials.[4] If the potential user is a high school or even a junior high student, his age and immaturity should not automatically disqualify him from using original or other special collections materials. He is possibly your researcher of the future. Exposure to the department's treasures can make a significant difference in a student's life, especially in terms of his connection to libraries and research. A department should never discourage young readers from using the rare book collection. Naturally, there must be good training and surveillance for students, but so should there be for all users.

Other kinds of patrons deserve equal treatment, though sometimes that intention entails a risk. For instance, some patrons might look shabby and unkempt. The department must, of course, screen potential patrons. Intake sheets (personal information forms) are standard tools for screening. They determine name, address(es), phone numbers, research areas, possibly specific items the patron wishes to use, and so forth. They may include names of references as well. It might be that a homeless person—one without an address—enters the department as a patron. The requirement to obtain an address for all users might have to be waived in such an instance. It must be remembered that even a homeless person pays taxes, and, therefore, in a publicly funded institution, has the same right to access as does anyone else. If the special collections department is in a public institution (a university or public library, for example), it may be illegal for the librarian to prohibit someone from using the collection, no matter the patron's appearance. The librarian should be aware of local, state, and federal laws in such instances.

Private libraries may have similar constraints about use, but they are in a better position to require letters of reference, advanced reservations, and other strictures that may limit access to the collection. But the original stance remains: although the librarian must keep as open a mind as possible about who has access to the department and must try to accommodate as many users as possible—balanced by a keen regard for preservation and security—access must be a prime consideration in deciding who may use the collection.

Rarity and Scarcity

In the world of special collections, the words *rarity* and *scarcity* are bandied about often. In their catalogs, sometimes to get a premium price, booksellers might say, "A scarce book," or "Exceptionally scarce." It is like the word *very*, which has been so overused that it has lost its meaning.

These two words—*rare* and *scarce*—indicate some difficulty in finding an item. Dealers often use the word *rare* for a book that one may find a half dozen copies of on the Web. Such dealers may simply be justifying their hefty asking price. Admittedly, this interpretation is not always true. There are truly rare or scarce books out there—hard to find, beautifully made, significant texts that are essential for important collections and that legitimately command high prices. But not all books described by those two words meet all these criteria.

The point here is that booksellers should use these words carefully and sparingly, librarians should ignore them when they see them in booksellers' catalogs or quotes, and they should purchase books regardless of their rarity or scarcity but on the bases of their appropriateness for the collection and their affordability.

However, we are indeed talking about *rare book* departments, and though such departments may contain a preponderance of items that are not strictly "rare," they do have collections that are characterized by holdings that are difficult or nearly impossible to obtain. The terms, usually used for expensive books, should not make the librarian shy away from an item so described. The attitude should not be, "A rare book. It's probably beyond my budget." It should be, "Let's see what it is, how germane to my collection it is, what the asking price is, and, if I want it for my collection, what I can do to get it."

For many librarians, especially those at non-profit or public institutions, the "we cannot afford it" mind-set has been instilled in them for so long that this attitude is difficult to overcome. But as a professional with a strong responsibility to increase and improve library holdings, the librarian should think about the possibilities, not the impossibilities, of acquiring rare materials. Holding truly rare materials that scholars can use and will seek out will distinguish a library.

First Editions

John Carter's entry for "First edition" says:

> Very, *very* roughly speaking, this means the first appearance of the work in question, independently, between its own covers. But, like many other household words, this apparently simple term is not always as simple as it appears. The question *When is a first edition not a first edition?* is a favourite debating exercise among bibliographers and advanced collectors; and some contributions to the confusion will be found in the present work under

the entries on edition and impression, issue and state, 'follow the flag', serials, secondary bindings, authorised edition, piracy, part-issues, first published edition, advance copies, copyright editions, pre-first, book form, first separate edition.[5]

This note highlights the complexity of issues that surround first editions, and we must not let that rubric attached to a book give it some special aura of value and make us immediately take it into the rare book stacks.

Carter and many others look at most first editions as artificial rarities, made rare by the mere fact of their being firsts, and with no other redeeming, value-enhancing quality. But the fact is that for centuries firsts have been garnering premium prices, and for this reason alone many of them should be handled with a heightened level of security, especially volumes that command seriously high prices.

Some books that were issued in large press-runs could be scarce and valuable, especially if the demand exceeds the supply. However, it is difficult to predict what books in their first edition will eventually merit being housed in the rare book department. If a volume is of a particularly collected, popular author, but the library does not have a special collection of that author's works, even if the book could be valuable, it may not be a candidate for being housed in special collections. And many a book over the years goes from being just another volume on the shelves of a circulating part of the collection to being scarce and valuable by virtue of an author's new-found fame and collectability, because the book wins a prize of some kind, because it is on a topic that suddenly becomes a rage in the collecting world, or for other reasons.

In the end, when librarians are looking for criteria to guide them on selecting what goes into the special collections department and what stays out, the fact that a book is a first edition might have some merit in its favor to bring it in. Obvious other criteria include the present (and potential future) monetary value of the item, who the author is, whether the book is illustrated or not and what kind of illustrations it has, and so forth. (In chapter 8 we will look more at appraisal: what affects the value of books?)

> **I KNOW SOMEONE** who collects second editions. His rationale is that they are abundant and cheaper than first editions. He also says that any book that made it to a second edition is probably a better book than one that never made it past a first edition. Often second editions contain corrections or updated texts that do make them more appealing to a scholar, but they are still second (or subsequent) editions and do not have the aura of a *first edition*.

That a book is a first edition is not enough in itself to make it a candidate for housing in special collections.

And as Carter suggests, what exactly *is* a first edition may need to be elucidated for a particular text. Is it the first appearance of the text in print, bound into covers? Is it the first printing of an author's work in her own country? What about a book that is issued in short numbers for reviewers (that is, "review copies")? These might have many typographic errors in them, or they can be printed on cheap paper with black-and-white illustrations (or no illustrations at all), when the one that is eventually published for general consumption is on fine paper and has color illustrations. Here is another question: Should a librarian, seeing the new collectability of a current author, head for the stacks to pull in the first editions of that author's earlier books, knowing that those early volumes will now be collectors' items themselves? Many a scholar of rare books, including librarians and booksellers, may look at the desirability of first editions as an artificial phenomenon—that is, a foolish obsession of irrational collectors. But the fact is that some of these books can command hefty prices, and thus they should be protected from thieves by having them brought into the safety of the rare book department.

Staffing

In many institutions the rare book department is tiny—consisting perhaps of one FTE (full-time equivalent) position, or even only a part-timer. In others, the staff could number fifteen or twenty or more. Of course, staffing is dependent on many variables: the size of the collection, the nature of the housing institution (public, private, state-run, for profit or non-profit), the size and budget of the parent institution, its mission, the resources available for the department, the recognition (or lack thereof) by the administration of the importance of the department, and other factors.

Also, depending on the size of the host and the department, its functions may vary from mere care-taking of some rare or vulnerable items to a full-service facility with its own acquisitions, reference, development, ILL, cataloging, processing, and other units. If we accept that the primary responsibility of the department is to offer scholars access to information, then the department needs at minimum a staff (of one or more) that can catalog books, create finding aids for manuscripts, page and reshelve books, make the physical objects available to patrons, and keep some kind of record of the unit's activities. Other essential duties may include handling acquisitions, dealing with donors, doing some kind of reference (for local and distant patrons), and creating surrogates (e.g., digitizing, photocopying, or microfilming).

All these functions are essential in a living department—one that is not stagnant or moribund. But in some small institutions, the director of the rare book facility works only a few hours a week in this area and may spend the bulk of her time as a cataloger or reference librarian.

As mentioned earlier, it is the rare (maybe nonexistent) department whose head would say, "We have plenty of space, resources, and staff. We don't need any more of these." No special collections depart-ment could not use additional staffing. It is incumbent upon those in special collections units to do everything in their power to meet the prime directive of access. Because access is provided by employing many kinds of services, as already indicated, the single-FTE department head must try to be as many things as he can to as many patrons as need to use the department. In a tiny unit, it may take continuing education, an understanding administration or supervisor, and extreme dedication to achieve this goal. In a larger unit, access should be an achievable deliverable. Even in tiny departments, imaginative use of volunteers and interns can go a long way in fulfilling the department's responsibilities to its patrons. The unit head must assess the department's needs and create a collection development plan that includes a prioritized listing of optimum staffing for her department—even if there are no resources at present for those listed. (For additional thoughts on this topic, see the section "Personnel Selection and Training" in chapter 14.)

Knowing the Collection

One of the first activities a special collections librarian should do in a new position is to learn the collection. No matter at what level one works in the department, from director to lowest-level pager, a knowledge of the department's holdings is essential.

Learning about the unit's collection can be achieved through talking to others who know it, reading whatever literature there is about it, working on the front line (for instance, in reference), looking at all the department's finding aids, browsing the cataloging records, and simply walking the stacks.

AS A NEW employee at the American Antiquarian Society (AAS), I did all the things mentioned in the text to familiarize myself with the collections. In the process I learned about the society's huge collection of uncataloged pamphlets, and, whenever I could, I would open a box or two and quickly thumb through them to see what topics they covered. I saw leaflets on a huge variety of topics, and I got to know pretty much what was there without memorizing the location and subject matter of more than fifty thousand items. This knowledge was tremendously useful for me when scholars came in, for I would get to know their research areas, and I remembered seeing items they would want to know about among the pamphlets. I was able to supply from that collection important reading matter to many patrons during the time that I worked at AAS.

The higher you are in the hierarchy of a special collections library, the more chance there is that you will be involved in the politics and administration of the institution, and the less you will be dealing directly with the collection and its users. But that is no excuse for not knowing what the library contains. On any number of public occasions the director may be asked what the library contains and what its strengths are. For grant writing, for lectures, for development activities of various kinds and other forms of outreach, for interviews—all employees in the department should be familiar with the unit's holdings.

Similarly, "knowing the collection" implies knowing its weaknesses and knowing the weaknesses of the building in which it is housed. A familiarity with the department's gaps will help you to build the collection. An understanding of its personnel shortages may be useful in fund-raising. A knowledge of its weaknesses as a physical plant may garner support for performing deferred maintenance and possibly raising funds to fix leaky pipes or roofs. The more you know about the collection, the better off you and the collection (and the patrons) will be.

Knowing the Patrons

Librarianship is a service profession. We serve a wide variety of users, from young adults to seniors, from the general public (especially genealogists) to sophisticated scholars. From people ignorant about doing research in a rare book facility to experienced researchers with decades of familiarity with rare books and scholarly practices. Being able to help them all is part of our mandate, but it is also gratifying to know we are fulfilling our primary responsibility.

One excellent way to give the best service to the patrons is to get to know them and their research areas. A top-level administrator in a large special collections department may not have time for such acquaintance. But most others in the department can help patrons through the experience they have with the collection. Although the patrons' primary acquaintance will be with the reference staff,

> **A COUPLE WORKING** on ciphering books came to my library and found a magnificent collection of them in our stacks. They taught our librarians a huge amount about this relatively little-known genre. The staff were enlightened, and the patrons were delighted to have found such a rich collection of materials and such an appreciative staff. Now this couple gives lectures on the genre, and the library is highlighted in their talks. This is an inexpensive form of advertising for us, the public relations benefits have been great, and the staff can now speak with some authority on this genre.

it is important for others in the department to get to know who is doing research there.

At some research libraries, scholars working for an extended time (say, a week or more) in the special collections department are asked to give presentations to the staff about the work they will be doing at the library. All rare book staff should be encouraged or required to attend these talks so that they can bring to the scholars their knowledge of materials in the collection the researchers may profit from. Even if the department is of the one-FTE type, the librarian can discuss in detail what the patron needs and can offer information about the collection tailored to these needs.

This level of service may be difficult to provide, especially for small, overworked, understaffed departments in which each librarian is doing the work of three people. But not providing this service is detrimental to the researcher and will not garner any kind of appreciation or support from the user. Nor do we want poorly served, disgruntled patrons going out into the world and bad-mouthing us to others.

Some patrons can be a chore, difficult to deal with and seemingly impossible to please. But most of them are grateful for our services and willing to impart what they know to our staffs. Most scholars appreciate having an audience to speak to about their work. It gives them an opportunity to articulate what they are working on, as if they are doing a dry run of the scholarship they will be writing up or the lectures they are preparing. The librarians can benefit greatly from this opportunity, for the scholars are working on materials in the library and the staff can learn more about their own materials than they knew before. This increase in their own knowledge will help them to help others in the future.

Naturally departments cannot offer a forum for all researchers who use special collections, as just described, but even a short conversation with patrons about their work, beyond the minimal words exchanged when we are delivering research materials to them, can teach us things we can use in the future.

Library users bring their own interests and passions to their work, often making them experts in the areas of their research. Librarians can share the patrons' interests and learn a great deal from them about the library's collections. A host of benefits can ensue.

Knowing the Collectors

There may be some rare book or special collections departments that are static—that is, ones that exist with no growth. But for the most part, these depart-

ments are alive and developing, with active programs for researchers, acquisition, cataloging, and the like. For many in the rare book field, acquisition is one of the pleasures of the job. It is enjoyable and educational to acquire books and manuscripts, especially the kind that wind up in special collections departments. Making information available to patrons is satisfying to both parties, the giver and the receiver. Making materials available to patrons (and thereby justifying the acquisition of these materials) is equally satisfying. And being able to share one's interests—for some, even one's passions—is another bonus.

As noted earlier in this chapter, rare book departments do not exist in a vacuum. They exist for the purposes already delineated. There is a fraternity and a sorority of participants: booksellers, librarians, historians, archivists, students, researchers, collectors, genealogists, novelists, journalists, casual readers, and many others. The librarian will be enriched by being involved with all these people, and such contacts can lead to the enrichment of his library's collection in several ways.

Many of the finest subject collections in our rare book libraries began as private collections, often the passions of people with no (or little) academic training. George Arents (1875–1960) put together a

I HAVE DONE research in libraries' special collections in which the only exchanges between me and the librarians have to do with regulations I must follow and how I should use the materials and what I may not take into the reading room. This lack of interest does not necessarily reflect an unfriendly attitude, but it does not foster any learning on the part of the staff. If the employee wants to learn about the collection, if she wants to improve her services, one way to do so is to learn about the materials in her care. And even a brief chat about these materials with the people using them will help.

One possible fringe benefit is that a friendship may ensue that could be useful to both parties. At UC Riverside, when I was head of special collections, I met a scholar working on B. Traven, the mysterious author of *The Treasure of the Sierra Madre* and many other wonderful books. The researcher was one of the world's foremost scholars about Traven, and over the months that he was in my department, I learned a vast amount about this shadowy and enigmatic writer. This made me a greatly more informed librarian, and I was able to use this information to help subsequent scholars who visited the department. Later, when a conference on Traven was being held

in Sweden, I was invited to speak about my department's collection. At the conference I met a host of Traven scholars, and eventually my library acquired the research papers of some of them. The benefit to me personally was great; not only did I gain a friend but I became a more responsible and knowledgeable librarian about one of our major collections. And the benefit to the library was equally great, with the notoriety we garnered and the materials we acquired.

This is only one of many such experiences I have had, and it can be a model for others who have similar opportunities to interact with their patrons.

wide-ranging collection of materials on tobacco. In 1942 he deposited this collection at the New York Public Library where it is now called The George Arents Collection on Tobacco. The Rosamond B. Loring Collection of Decorated Papers, now at the Houghton Library at Harvard, is another accumulation put together by a private party and then given to a special collections department. These are just two of many thousands of special collections in rare book libraries, begun outside a library.

One feature of these collections is that, regardless of the academic background of their compilers, these collectors became experts on the topics of their collections, so the holdings they amassed were gathered intelligently and with discernment. Institutions usually cannot gather such collections from scratch on their own. Nor can any librarian, for the most part, become a subject expert on all the areas of the special collections in her care. Collectors are often true subject experts, and they may spend decades and significant amounts of money on their hobbies.

If a library has a special collection in a particular field, one way to augment it quickly is to acquire a fully developed collection from a private party, by gift or purchase. Knowing who these collectors are is not easy, but contacts with booksellers and collecting clubs can be useful. Therefore, it might be valuable for librarians to be involved as much as they can with the book clubs in their areas and even ones in distant places. A list of these can be found at the website of FABS, the Fellowship of American Bibliophilic Societies.[6] Some clubs, like the Caxton, the Grolier, the Zamorano, the Rowfant, the Philobiblon, the Book Club of California, and the Roxburghe, along with the Society of Printers, have been around close to, or more than, a hundred years. Their members are generally collectors with keen interests, deep knowledge, and impressive holdings in the areas of their passions. Rare book librarians can only profit from becoming acquainted with these people, in the knowledge they can glean from them and from the possible collections they can acquire from them.

One way to open a dialogue with a collector about the disposition of his collection is to take him to lunch and forthrightly ask about his plans for it. If the collector is not geographically close enough

for this approach, a formal letter on department letterhead stationery will do. (E-mails are simply too informal and too easy to get rid of with a simple click on the X or the Delete button.)

Many special collections libraries have exhibition or display areas, and arranging an exhibition of a private party's collection, possibly accompanied by a catalog or lectures, or both, shows the library's serious interest in it. Where the relationship goes from there depends on the skills of the librarian and the interests and intents of the collector. The overriding point here is that good things can happen for the library if the head of the department engages the friendship of collectors.

The connection between many a collector and a library has resulted in a sharing of information and resources between the two. A by-product of this collaboration is that collectors and librarians, seeing eye to eye on the importance of the collection, can form strong friendships over their common interests.

IN MY OWN experience, a wonderful Blake collector generously donated items from his own collection, or he bought them for us from dealers and gave them to my library. I notified him of unusual Blake items that came to my attention, some of which he was able to add to his collection. Our friendship was formed over our mutual interest in Blake, and we were both beneficiaries of this connection.

Knowing the Institutional Collections

As service professionals, special collections librarians, as noted several times, have as their prime directive imparting information to their patrons. If the collection she oversees does not contain the information the user needs, the librarian should be able to give the researcher advice on where that information can be found. To be versed in the field of rare books, one should be familiar with the major collections around the country or should be able to find out about them. Before we had the Internet,

MY FRIENDSHIP WITH the head of the UCLA rare book collection led to his transferring to UC Riverside a small collection of science fiction books that UCLA had been given years before. Such inter-institution transfers are not common, but the close knowledge we had of each other's collection made it possible.

this meant immersing oneself in the literature of the field, knowing what reference books would lead one to such information. Now it is easier, for most rare book facilities have websites on which their major and important collections are listed.

Friendships can develop between curators of outside collections, and these relationships, like those with collectors, could result in the enhancement of our holdings.

The point is that the more we know about our profession, the better we will be at helping patrons to find the information they seek. Knowing the holdings of other institutions can be an important tool.

Knowing the Booksellers

Perhaps the most direct friends that rare book librarians have are the booksellers. There is, of course, a commercial relationship between them, and the perception and the actuality of potential conflicts of interest could appear. But specialist booksellers whose expertise is in a library's own areas of specialty will have a line on many items that the library may wish to own.

Rather than listing their goods in catalogs or online, booksellers often first consult us, giving us right of first refusal on choice pieces. They always find material that the library cannot find on its own. This alone is a valuable service. And as experts in their fields, they are often information resources for librarians, who themselves cannot be subject specialists in all the areas of their library's holdings. The booksellers know the intellectual side of their field and know that field bibliographically as well.

Most booksellers love books the same way that many rare book librarians do, and it has been nat-

ural for many of them to become the librarians' friends. But friendships aside, there is still an ethical level of interaction that must be maintained. Chapter 2 takes up the important subject of ethical conduct for special collections librarians. Here it is sufficient to say that the booksellers can be superb resources for librarians, helping them to build collections in many ways.

For instance, dealers sometimes sell special collections departments important items at excellent prices; give the library gifts now and then to keep the friendship alive; and turn collectors on to the department, people whose collections make them instant friends of the library. As "matchmakers," booksellers bring together librarians and others with like interests, for their mutual benefit. Dealers also alert librarians to items at auctions or in other book sellers' holdings. They can bid for the library at auctions and inspect items at auction houses that librarians cannot get to. They will often offer the library good terms for buying expensive items.

There are also stories about fiendish, foolish, greedy dealers, but these tales are few compared to the great number of accounts about the many good ones.

AT UC RIVERSIDE, the special collections department wanted to acquire a hugely expensive archive. The dealer allowed the library to pay it off over several years. One bookseller I knew would occasionally go to a local special collections department and give them an important item. He said to me several times, "This piece really belongs in their department, and they don't have the money for it."

Knowing the Authors

Author collections are common in rare book libraries. And if a library collects the works of particular living authors, those authors might donate or sell their manuscripts and other germane possessions to the library. If the authors are deceased, a connection with their heirs might achieve the same results.

One enterprising librarian conceived the idea of contacting a host of science fiction (sf) writers who were still fairly young. She convinced them that her library was the perfect venue for their archives, and she now has a substantial collection of papers of sf and fantasy writers. Such collections contain first and later editions of works, drafts, digital versions, correspondence, and other papers of the authors. Personal contact with the holders of authors' papers can contribute significantly to a library's ability to acquire important author collections.

Cooperative Collecting

By its very nature, the rare book department collects many costly books. But no department has an infinite budget. Unless one has a vastly wealthy donor, has immense endowed acquisition funds, or works for an institution with a gigantic endowment that allows for nearly limitless buying, the limitation on one's resources will constrain purchases. One way to stretch the budget is to engage in cooperative collecting.

Cooperative collecting means developing one's collection in coordination with other institutions in the neighborhood. When scholars go to a library to do research, they want to have as many of the resources they need as possible in a single collection. It saves them time and money not to have to go from repository to repository to work on materials.

If a special collections department is near other like libraries, the managers may meet to create a plan of cooperative collecting, dividing subject areas among them. Scholars may not be able to see all the materials they need at one facility, but they may be able to use items at libraries close by. This arrangement works well for general collections, but it can be especially economical for rare book departments.

Sometimes, because of the nature of individual collections, it is imperative that geographically close institutions acquire the same books. The special collections librarians at the five southern University of California campuses (UCLA, Riverside, Irvine, San Diego, and Santa Barbara) met to plan to collect cooperatively. Though this plan worked to a small degree, in some respects it would not work. For instance, San Diego has a superb poetry collec-

tion; Santa Barbara has a strong fine press collection. When a fine press book of poetry came out, each library needed a copy of the title for its own collection. Though it was unlikely that two copies were needed for scholars, the collections themselves demanded having a copy in each library. (See levels of collecting in chapter 2.) However, cooperative collecting may be a practical solution for geographically clustered libraries, and it pays to pursue this strategy.

RBMS

The Rare Books and Manuscripts Section (RBMS) is a division of ACRL (the Association of College and Research Libraries), itself a division of ALA (the American Library Association). The section's website says: "RBMS strives to represent and promote the interests of librarians who work with rare books, manuscripts, and other types of special collections."[7] Elsewhere on its website is the following: "From its inception [more than fifty years ago], RBMS has attempted to foster communication between special collections librarians and assist in their professional development."[8] In the *RBMS Newsletter* (No. 12 [November 1989]) is this statement, which, more than twenty years later, holds true:

> The mission of the Rare Books and Manuscripts Section (RBMS) of the Association of College and Research Libraries (ACRL) is to exercise leadership in the local, national, and international special collections communities in order to represent and promote the interests of librarians, curators, and other specialists concerned with the acquisition, organization, security, preservation, administration, and use of special collections, including rare printed books, manuscripts, archives, and graphic, music, and ephemeral materials; to enhance the capability of special collections libraries to serve the needs of users. (p. 1)

In the United States, RBMS is the single most important organization in the rare books and special collections field. Members are mostly librarians, though there are institutional members, booksellers, archivists, graduate students from library schools, scholars, and others. RBMS has many standing and ad hoc committees, discussion groups, a full governing body, and liaisons to other groups. It is a tremendously active, highly professional organization, with decades of experience, extensive knowledge, expertise in a wide range of fields, and a membership willing to reach out to the broad rare book community—beyond the world of libraries.

Library school students interested in rare books and special collections should be encouraged to join RBMS, especially when they are students and the dues are quite low. Each year the organization has a preconference the week before ALA's annual conference and usually in the same city as ALA's meeting (or one nearby). The preconference themes focus on many aspects of rare book librarianship, and other papers are given that range across a broad spectrum of rare book topics.

This preconference is an event for educating younger members of the profession, for meeting friends, and for seeking employment. Formal job interviews may not be held during this meeting, but this is an opportunity to meet others in the field. Further, almost all the committee meetings are open to anyone who wishes to attend, so a person new to the profession or thinking about getting into it can sit in on sessions about all aspects of rare book librarianship. These committee meetings are informative, and they allow attendees to connect actively with others in the profession.

As noted, even some booksellers are RBMS members and attend the preconference—an excellent venue at which to connect with some of their best customers. And in recent years, the ABAA (the Antiquarian Booksellers' Association of America) has been holding small book fairs at the preconferences, creating another opportunity for attendees to meet the dealers.

RBML, *RBM*, and Publishing in the Field

The journal produced by RBMS, begun in 1986, was originally titled *Rare Books & Manuscripts Librarian-* *ship* (*RBML*). Since 2000 it has been called *RBM: A Journal of Rare Books, Manuscripts, and Cultural Heritage*. This journal, the primary voice in the field, publishes original articles and some of the talks given at the annual preconference (and, more recently, book reviews, as was done in *RBML*). Although it is an ACRL publication, *RBM* is not a perquisite of membership—it requires a separate subscription. People new to the profession may do well to look over the full run of the journal from its inception to get a sense of the range of topics it has covered. It is still a good resource for those trying to get up to speed on issues in the profession.

It is important for special collections librarians to think about publishing in the course of their work. They are close to original, valuable, rare materials and can spread the word about their collections through publication. And they lead active lives in the profession and will have much to say about the issues they face in running their departments, dealing with accessions and donors and administrators, learning about the intricacies of particular collection areas, and so forth. By publishing, they will be doing a service to the field, and, in return, publication can only help them in their own understanding of the subject matter of their research, in their advancement in their employment, and in their profession. *RBM* is a good place to get their work into print.

But it is not the only place. Because the subject matter of the broad fields of rare books and special collections is equally broad, there is a host of venues for publication. In chapter 9 we will look at the four main branches of bibliography. Here I will briefly mention only one: historical bibliography. As a study of this field shows, a huge number of disciplines can contribute information to those in special collections. So there is a world of publishing possibilities for those in rare books.

In a syllabus by Anne Welsh at University College London, we find this description of her course on historical bibliography: "By the end of the course, students will have an overview of the history of the book and the materials that make it up (paper, vellum, bindings, illustrations, print, etc.), some practical experience of bibliographic description, and knowledge of the major techniques for research, including provenance research, copy census and reader analysis."[9] Some of the topics this course intends to cover are book history, materials of book construction (several are mentioned), provenance, copy census, and reader analysis. The "etc." covers a vast territory. The point is that in the world of rare books and special collections, one single rubric, Historical Bibliography, covers an exceptionally wide range of topics, not all of which would be appropriate in the pages of *RBM* but which would be appropriate reading for a special collections librarian. The researcher should know what journals would be suitable for publishing articles on various topics. There are scores of journals and newsletters, magazines and online periodicals for librarians to publish in. Being familiar with the publications in one's field and being an active scholar in that field are desirable goals for rare book librarians.

CILIP and the Rare Books and Special Collections Group (RBSCG)

In Great Britain, CILIP, the Chartered Institute of Library and Information Professionals, is "the leading professional body for librarians, information specialists and knowledge managers."[10] One of its divisions is the Rare Books and Special Collections Group, similar to RBMS in the United States. The group's website explains its purpose:

> The Rare Books and Special Collections Group unites librarians responsible for collections of rare books, manuscripts and special materials, with other interested individuals. The group promotes the study and exploitation of rare books, encourages awareness of preservation, conservation and digitisation issues, and fosters training opportunities related to the maintenance, display and use of collections.[11] [Note that "exploitation" is used in the British sense of "to use for profit," with no negative implications.]

The group meets three or four times a year, and it publishes an online newsletter three times a year with news, reviews, and articles, along with some of the papers delivered at the group's conferences.

A professional rare book librarian should be actively involved in his profession. Attendance at the meetings of this group and of RBMS, involvement with committees, and participation in discussion groups will be part of the librarian's growth. Especially early in the librarian's career, there are few better venues for learning about the profession and for networking to meet others in the field. Many booksellers, archivists, and even some private collectors attend these meetings, so the networking is not merely to meet colleagues, it is to meet others outside the library profession who are involved in one way or another with rare books.

Training the Rare Book Librarian

Some areas in the field under scrutiny in this book are constantly changing, while others—especially historical ones—stay the same. The field is so vast that no one can be on top of everything there is to know. In the field of special collections (as in many fields), the notion of "core competencies" is always under scrutiny. What does it mean to be a fully competent rare book librarian? What skills must she have and what information does she need to fulfill the prime directive of supplying information to her patrons? One problem in answering these questions is that there are many kinds of information (practical, theoretical, legal, historical, technological, and so forth). Another problem is that there is certainly more information that could be useful to any given librarian than she could digest or retain. A third problem is that if a librarian wants to augment her knowledge to prepare herself for *all* patron needs, she could spend her entire career in continuing education (CE), taking classes and workshops, going to conferences and lectures, and reading endlessly. This way lies madness. It is more sensible for her to figure out what information and skills she needs *for her particular job.*

Every rare book librarian should assess the collection she works in and figure out what knowledge she needs to be an effective, responsible caretaker for that collection. This might mean becoming a subject specialist—to some degree—for the special col-

WHEN I GOT to UC Riverside (UCR), I knew little about B. Traven, science fiction, the music theoretician Heinrich Schenker, Rupert and Jeannette Costo and their American Indian Historical Society, Sadakichi Hartmann, and other subjects that were the backbones of UCR's special collections. One of the first things I did when I got there was get to know the collection as well as I could—a task I have mentioned previously. By the time I left UCR, I could speak with some authority about these topics, not with the depth of a true scholar in those areas, but I knew the fields with enough expertise that I could help my patrons fairly well, with historical facts and with the bibliography related to the subjects.

The department also had a superb collection on the history of photography. In putting on an exhibition on this collection, I did extensive reading and got to know the collection well, and I got to know the bibliography of this broad field. I took a workshop on the identification and conservation of photographic materials. My aim was, as I have indicated, to become as effective a librarian as I could be. I benefited from this accumulation of knowledge, and, of course, so did the library's users.

Also, the more knowledgeable I became about these areas, and the more I knew about the collection under my aegis, the better I was at selecting items to add to these holdings, so the collection itself also benefited from my continuing education.

lections in the department. And it could mean learning details about some of the most used collections in the library: What physical materials are they are made of? What historical information about the topics of these materials must she know? And what of the provenance of the materials in her care? Is there historical research she can do to make her a more "informational" librarian for her clientele? And on and on. The particular collection and its users will tell the librarian how she must prepare herself to be the optimum caretaker.

Getting to know one's collection, taking workshops, preparing for and then mounting exhibits, and publishing in the field are all forms of CE. Also, it will be useful for the librarian to learn as much as possible about current (and coming) technology to determine if any of it can be helpful in making the department's holdings more available and safer than they are at present. Clearly, CE need not be strictly in the areas of the books and manuscripts in the department.

There are many opportunities for CE, and the first thing one thinks of when it comes to training rare book librarians is Rare Book School (RBS) at the University of Virginia in Charlottesville. Since 1983 RBS has been offering classes on many topics to prepare people for the profession or to increase the expertise of those already in it.

The University of Illinois at Urbana-Champaign also offers a summer program in rare books, with many courses. The program leads to a certificate and is the only program that currently certifies its graduates. Just before leaving UCLA, I started a rare book school there, and it now offers several courses. One can also take courses at the University of Alabama in Tuscaloosa, the University of Utah, the Claremont Colleges in California, and several other institutions that offer courses or workshops in printing, papermaking, bookbinding, and many other topics.

Three universities (Indiana University, Long Island University, and Pratt Institute) have Rare Book and Special Collections specializations in their library schools.[12] Other library schools offer classes in book history or rare book librarianship, the history of libraries, bibliography, medieval codicology, and other courses germane to the education of a rare book librarian. The Northeast Document Conservation Center (NEDCC), The Los Angeles Preservation Network (LAPNet), Lyrasis, the Society of American Archivists (SAA), and other organizations offer workshops useful to rare book librarians.

As emphasized earlier, attendance at scholarly conferences and other meetings is also educational, and librarians and others in the rare book field should try to attend them when time and resources permit and when the pedagogy of the workshops or classes will truly improve their ability to serve their patrons. Especially early in one's career in special collections, attending RBMS meetings and preconferences, and joining committees and working groups, is a valuable part of one's continuing education in the field.

In Britain, RBSCG also offers many learning opportunities, with a liaison with the Antiquarian Booksellers' Association, lectures, the dissemination of information about rare book holdings at various institutions, and more. In 2011 the group held a conference on how to "flaunt" your collections (how to get information out to the world about your holdings), and one on how to develop a major special collections exhibition. And in association with the Antiquarian Booksellers' Association, the group produced the document *Theft of Books and Manuscripts from Libraries: An Advisory Code of Conduct for Booksellers and Librarians*.[13] The opportunities are vast for training in the field.

It is impossible for everyone in rare books to know everything about the field, so the librarian, the bookseller, the scholar/bibliographer, and the collector will have to choose carefully among all the learning opportunities available. A collection strong in children's books might spur its caretaker to learn as much as possible about particular authors, book illustration techniques (especially chromolithography), the history of this field, and where the great children's book collections are. Useful, perhaps, might be workshops on printing techniques, binding, and genres of kids' books. A workshop or class in the making of medieval manuscripts might be excellent, but that was not a period rife with children's books, and such a workshop may be relatively useless for one's job. Of course, such an experience might be personally satisfying, irrespective of one's on-the-job needs, and the pleasure one gets from enhancing one's personal knowledge cannot be discounted. Just because an opportunity to enhance one's knowledge arises in a subject that has nothing to do with one's job does not mean that opportunity should not be taken.

The one area of training that may be useful for all who work in rare books is cataloging, whether the librarian becomes a cataloger or not. To understand special collections cataloging fully one must understand a great deal about books: their provenance, printing, composition, materials, and so forth. Even if the librarian does not go into cataloging, knowing that discipline will increase his abilities as a rare book librarian.

Many institutions have continuing-education funding available for the staff. If the employer does not offer such funding, the librarian may apply to any of a number of private foundations, the federal government, or other funding agencies that support this kind of training. The University of Virginia Rare Book School has fellowships for some attendees. The more the librarian knows, the more his library, his institution, and the scholars he serves will benefit.[14]

■ ■ ■

This chapter has dealt with some of the practical realities of running a rare book or special collections department (or both)—what to do, what to know, how to prepare yourself to do it, what resources are out there, and the like. It is certainly not definitive. Someone once said that your education will teach you about 20 percent of what you need to know for your job. The job will teach you the rest. In the rare book world, this may be true, because it is such a varied realm that one will be facing new challenges and new things to learn every day. In a rare book department it is also true, because each department has its own special collections, its own specific holdings, its own policies and procedures, its own quirks, and its own particular responsibilities, shaped by the parent institution and by the users. A tactic that might work well in one environment might not work in another. Librarians must shape their own educations based on the world around them.

Here we have looked at some overriding concerns and broad areas of operation. More specific, practical concerns will be dealt with in forthcoming chapters.

NOTES

1. As we shall see in chapter 3, archives often fit in with special collections, and a department may have a double title: Special Collections and Archives (or Archives and Special Collections).

2. For levels of collecting, see chapter 2 and appendix 2 in the present volume.

3. No theory of management will work for all people. Clearly, some people have one style of management, others have a different style, and still others were

not meant to manage. Further, a manager may need to use one style of direction for one staff person and a completely different strategy for another. The good manager needs to be flexible and insightful enough to know what kind of treatment to give each person she supervises.

4. On the use of special collections by undergraduates, see Susan M. Allen, "Rare Books and the College Library: Current Practices in Marrying Undergraduates to Special Collections," *Rare Books & Manuscripts Librarianship* 13.2 (Spring 1999): 110–19. See also Ruth Mortimer, "Manuscripts and Rare Books in an Undergraduate Library," *Wilson Library Bulletin* 58.2 (October 1983): 107–10.

5. John Carter and Nicolas Barker, *ABC for Book Collectors*, 8th ed. (New Castle, DE: Oak Knoll Press; London: The British Library, 2004), p. 103. The full text of this book is now available on the Web, free, at www.ilab.org/eng/documentation/29-abc_for _book_collectors.html. [As of the completion of the manuscript for this book (in August 2013), all website content had been checked and verified to be accurate.]

6. See the organization's website at www.fabsbooks.org.

7. See www.rbms.info.

8. See www.rbms.info/history. A great deal more information is available about RBMS on this excellent site.

9. Found at www.ucl.ac.uk/infostudies/teaching/ modules/instg012.

10. See www.cilip.org.uk/about-us/pages/default.aspx.

11. This statement is at www.cilip.org.uk/about/ special-interest-groups/rare-books-and-special -collections-group.

12. Programs come and go, and there is no guarantee that these three schools will continue to offer this specialization.

13. See www.cilip.org.uk/get-involved/special-interest -groups/rare-books/policy/pages/policy_theft.aspx.

14. For one provocative, but discursive, essay on training students for a career in rare books, see William E. Landis, "Personas and Archetypes: Envisioning the 21st-Century Special Collections Professional," *RBM* (*Rare Books and Manuscripts*) 7.1 (Spring 2006): 40–48, http://rbm.acrl.org/ content/7/1/40.full.pdf + html. In the same issue of this periodical is Deirdre C. Stam's "Bridge That Gap! Education and Special Collections," pp. 16–30 (http://rbm.acrl.org/content/7/1/16.full.pdf + html), in which she has a section titled "Education of Librarians" (pp. 25–30). Another article in the same issue is worth looking at: Patricia Fleming, "Education and Training of Special Collections Professionals, Librarians, and Archivists in Canada," pp. 69–72 (http://rbm.acrl.org/content/7/1/69.full .pdf + html).

CHAPTER 2

RUNNING A RARE BOOK DEPARTMENT

ARE BOOK AND SPECIAL COLLECTIONS DEPARTMENTS ARE COMplex and varied in their activities—part of what makes them, for me, the most fascinating unit in a library to work in. The parent library has a full range of functions: selection, acquisition, circulation, interlibrary loan, paying for the books, and so forth. And so does special collections, along with the responsibilities of handling a significant budget and also handling important materials. Running the department poses particular challenges for special collections librarians. This chapter looks at these responsibilities.

Ethical Conduct and RBMS Guidelines

All professions need guidelines to instruct people on proper behavior on the job. In a field in which a good deal of money is involved and when an appearance of a conflict of interest could arise, as is the case in special collections libraries, having codified guidelines is essential.

In the 1980s when RBMS was beginning to work on its code of ethical conduct, some librarians felt affronted: they thought that as professionals they already knew how to act, they understood what was right and wrong, and they did not need to be told by some document. But having the guidelines on paper was important for them as well as for all who came to practice in the field after them. It was also important to those they dealt with, for people working with librarians must see where potential conflicts of interest lie so that they will not put librarians into compromising situations.

The original standards were draconian, and some of its prohibitions were controversial. For instance, no rare book librarian was to receive any personal mail at work. The standards of 1987 were revised in 1993 and again in 2003.[1] It is not the province of the present text to look at the history of these standards. It is sufficient to say that the present ones are practical and clear, sensible and encompassing enough to guide all special collections personnel to fully ethical behavior on the job. And these standards are important enough to cite here in full.[2]

In the most recent (2003) document, the rules are condensed to six fairly concise statements, followed by a brief section called Commentary—passages of expansion and interpretation. Here are the six statements, taken verbatim from the published standards:

I. Special collections librarians must not compete with their library in collecting or in any other activity.

II. All outside employment and professional activities must be undertaken within the fundamental premise that the special collections librarian's first responsibility is to the library, that the activity will not interfere with the librarian's ability to discharge this responsibility, and that it will not compromise the library's professional integrity or reputation.

III. Special collections librarians must not engage in any dealing or appraisal of special collections materials, and they must not recommend materials for purchase if they have any undisclosed financial interest in them.

IV. Special collections librarians must decline all gifts, loans, or other dispensations, or things of value that are available to them in connection with their duties for the library.

V. Special collections librarians may not withhold information about the library's holdings or sequester collection materials in order to further their own research and publication.

VI. Special collections librarians are responsible for protecting the confidentiality of researchers and materials as required by legal statutes, donor agreements, or policies of the library.

For each of these statements, the commentary clarifies the intent. The underlying reason for most of the statements should be clear. For instance, for the first one, the librarian must not acquire items for himself if those items would be perfect acquisitions for the library. If the library for any reason chooses not to get an item, then the librarian is free to acquire it for himself. A wrinkle appears, of course, when the librarian himself is the one who decides whether the library wants the item. If the librarian is the one who decides if the library should get it, then a good collection development policy (see later in this chapter) should help in the final decision making, for it will spell out the criteria that determine acquisitions for or rejections from the collection. The policy, if properly conceived and well written, will determine the feasibility and appropriateness of an acquisition.

But the main points of this first statement are that the library has right of first refusal for any item that might be acquired and that the librarian is in a delicate position if he wants to acquire something first offered to the library. In such a case, the institution should have a policy showing what the librarian should do. For instance, if the library chooses not to acquire an item, the librarian who wants it for his own collection may be required to reveal his interest to his superior and must ask permission to make the purchase for himself. Keeping such transactions aboveboard, fully transparent, removes any hint of a conflict of interest.

The second statement is fairly clear, as is the commentary on it, which states that some kinds of outside employment, like teaching, lecturing, writing, or consulting, might enhance the reputation of the library and could increase the librarian's expertise at her job. It could be seen as a form of professional development. The main idea in this clause is that the librarian's primary responsibility is to her institution, and no outside employment must compromise her ability to satisfy that responsibility.

Statement three, prohibiting the librarian from being a dealer or appraiser, is sensible, but it too can put the librarian into a delicate position. One scenario that came up at the original discussion in 1987 when the first document on ethical standards was being formulated was this: A public library may have an annual book sale to raise money to repair a leaky roof (or for any other reason); only through the book sale will the library be able to raise the money it needs. For the sale, the library will receive a large number of books as gifts. The public librarians are not experts in book appraisal. They do not want to price their books at the common rate (for example, "Hardbound books $2.00; Paperbacks $1.00"). They know that some of the items may be too valuable to let them go at such low prices. These items can be put onto a special table at the book sale with higher prices reflecting their greater value. The rare book librarian should know what adds to (and reduces) the value of books and may be asked to help the public librarians put prices on some of the more special books that will go into their sale. It is a good civic gesture for the special collections librarian to help the under-budgeted public library.

But an appearance of a conflict of interest arises in such a situation, for the rare book expert might price an item quite low and then come back at the opening of the sale and get the book for himself. The possibility exists, so a potential conflict of interest exists. Even in such a seemingly innocent situation, the rare book librarian must avoid appraising. Even if the librarian would never do such a thing, the key is that there could be an *appearance* of a conflict of interest.

This same clause prohibits librarians from profiting from any transaction that has to do with the library. The commentary for this clause makes it clear that the code "recognizes that potential conflicts of interest may arise when special collections librarians profit from the same materials they curate."

A related notion implied by this statement is that it is not inappropriate for librarians to sell books. Many librarians are collectors, and they may have been collecting long before beginning to work in a library. If they own a book—or, indeed, a whole collection of books—that they wish to sell, whether for a profit or not, their books or collections are their own to do with as they please. That they are librarians and that their code of ethics prohibits them from dealing in books does not prohibit them from selling some or all of their own volumes or manuscripts. Statement three specifically prohibits them from "dealing," which means regularly buying books for sale and making continuing profits on them. The line between divesting oneself of one's own holdings and doing so regularly for profit is perfectly clear, and it was not necessary for the authors of this code to spell out that distinction.

Some comment is needed for statement four, prohibiting librarians from taking any gifts or compensation from anyone when those gifts or loans are related to their positions at their libraries. The commentary makes it clear that "[w]hile close relationships between librarians, dealers, and collectors are desirable, it is imperative that conflicts of interest do not arise." May a bookseller or a vendor of library goods or services visit the library to show some of his wares and then take the librarian out to lunch? Is this a gift? a bribe? Could it be seen as a conflict of interest for the librarian to accept such largesse? The commentary does not answer these questions, but it does remind us: "The issue of whether *any* entertainment should be accepted from these sources is problematic, and so librarians must make a judgment in each case as to whether the appearance of improper influence might result. Institutional policies regarding the acceptance of gifts or entertainment must also be observed." Note a keyword in this statement: *appearance*. There are many situations in which an appearance of a conflict could arise, and the librarian must assess each instance individually. Perhaps the best practice is not to let anyone who deals professionally with librarians' institutions (that is, anyone who makes a profit from goods or services purveyed to their institutions) take them to lunch or give them anything. Maintaining this stance rigidly will yield unassailable ethical conduct.

The fifth statement prohibiting librarians from withholding any research materials from patrons is clear: patrons come first. Librarians' prime responsibility is getting information into the hands of their patrons, not publishing their own scholarship (least of all to the detriment of patrons who might have also published scholarship based on the same materials the librarians used). As the commentary says (and as shown in chapter 1), publishing is good for one's career and personal and professional development, but it must not be done to the potential detriment of any patron.

The final prohibition is backed up by the First Amendment to the U.S. Constitution regarding confidentiality. The commentary section of the code says, "The special collections professional must heed all laws and contractual agreements protecting the privacy and confidentiality of researchers and materials in the custody of the repository. Failure to do so can expose the custodial institution to significant legal penalties, as well as undermine confidence that donors and sellers place in the institution."

Librarians are traditional champions of people's rights, and this clause seems fairly obvious because it guards one of the fundamental rights of all our citizens. This code of ethics was published in 2003, two years after the USA PATRIOT Act was passed by Congress.[3] A problem arises when anyone legally challenges a library's desire to keep library records confidential. And that challenge can come from any official who "suspects" that any party might be a terrorist. Even on flimsy evidence, patrons' privacy can be compromised.

The American Library Association, the American Civil Liberties Union, and other organizations challenged this clause in the PATRIOT Act, but they lost in court. This means that a local police officer with a search warrant can require the library to divulge what was once considered private information. To protect the privacies of their patrons, many libraries are now destroying the information they formerly knew to be protected by the First Amendment but which now has become accessible. This practice keeps information about library patrons from falling into anyone else's hands, but it also destroys the information. As we shall see, this data has some important uses in the library. The librarians were forced to choose between keeping the data for future use (and creating a situation in which it could fall into hands the librarians did not want to have it) or destroying it and losing use of it themselves. The PATRIOT Act complicated the lives of special collections librarians who wanted to follow the dictates of this last clause in the ethical conduct document.

This last clause also mentions the ethical issues that arise when donor agreements are in play. This concern will be covered in chapter 8 of this book where we will look at deeds of gift. In summary, librarians must follow the legally delineated restrictions ("strings") that are written into a Deed of Gift, no matter how illogical or inconvenient these strings are. Ignoring them is unethical—and probably even illegal.

The Code of Ethics for Special Collections Librarians cannot be comprehensive. It cannot anticipate every possible situation in which an ethical issue might arise. It offers basic guidelines, with the understanding that an informed, intelligent rare book librarian will know what is right and wrong in any given situation. If he does not, he should be cautious enough and smart enough to consult his superiors or his institution's legal counsel, or both, before acting. As the ACRL/RBMS guidelines say, nothing that a special collections librarian does should reflect badly on his institution.

Department Functions

Employees in the library as a whole will perform a host of functions: selection, acquisition, cataloging, processing, interlibrary loan, reference, and so forth. And in many libraries people performing these tasks are specialists in their areas of activity: bibliographers, catalogers, reference personnel, and others. In the larger library, however, the specialists generally stick to what they are specialists in. In rare book departments many or all of these tasks are necessary too, but unless the special collections department is large and well funded, most of the tasks will be done by the department's own personnel. That is, the tasks of special collections librarians are likely to be more varied than are those of their colleagues in the main library.

It is common for librarians in rare books to select and order items, open the packages when they are delivered, catalog and process the materials, and shelve them. There will, of course, be some specialization: not all rare book personnel will be trained catalogers, for instance. But one of the appealing features of rare book librarianship is the diversity of activities that those in this department do. Of all departments in a library, the special collections unit will have the most widely trained, least bored employees. Much of their activity falls under technical services (acquisition, cataloging, processing), and much falls under public services (reference, circulation, supplying surrogates of department materials). It is a good balance, and it could stave off burnout.

Another by-product of the diversity of the rare book librarian's life is that she is likely to have a good deal of hands-on activity with the collection. Most of us go into the rare book field because we love the objects it deals with: books, manuscripts, photographs, archival materials, ephemera, and lots more. Part of the joy of the profession is the closeness we have with these things: locating them, ordering them, paying for them (with the institution's money), receiving and opening the packages, being able to flip through the items, checking out the bindings and contents, and even smelling and hearing them.[4] The point here is that in carrying out department functions, rare book librarians are offered great opportunities to experience the pleasures of books.

Department functions are many and varied, but one objective should inform the activities and sense of responsibility of everyone working in the special collections department, the same goal delineated several times already: every function should aim at the prime directive—access. Patrons come first, and when a cataloger in rare books who wishes to do nothing else but catalog is forced to work on the reference desk in the absence of reference personnel, he or she should do so without complaint. Certain department functions take precedence over others, and helping clients is at the top of the list.

True, cataloging is helping the patrons, but the results are relatively invisible to them. Reference— face-to-face public service—trumps cataloging when personnel are in short supply and bodies are needed on the reference desk. In general, a patron will not complain if she does not see books being cataloged, but she will complain if she is left waiting at the reference desk, unhelped and unrecognized.

Another caveat should be mentioned under the rubric of "department functions." Some functions are extremely important, but because of a shortage of staff, inadequate expertise on the part of the department's employees, or a myriad of other reasons, some functions simply may not be done. One example is the conservation of the department's holdings. In most collections that contain old or once-popular titles (and this is especially the case with rare book departments), it is likely that a host of items need conservation work. Many special collections departments do not have a conservator on staff, in the rare book department or even in the parent institution. They may not even have a line in the budget for conservation work. But books falling apart on the shelves, with loose covers, rusting staples, leather bindings with red rot, and the like, call out to be cared for. (More on this in chapter 12 on preservation and conservation.) Librarians should do whatever is in their power to get these waifs to a conservator—or at least to someone who can stabilize the items so that they don't fall apart any further. But the reality is that conservation is seldom figured into the rare book department's budget.

One of the rare book librarian's main functions having to do with access is to keep his materials in a condition that will allow access. An item so fragile or in such disrepair that it cannot be handled by a researcher is simply not accessible. Conservation is in order, but without a budget for it, and without the expertise of anyone on the staff to do the work, the item must languish unless its contents can be delivered in a way other than through the item itself. Reformatting (photocopying, digitizing, and—only rarely these days—microfilming) may be the solution. Another possible solution is for the librarian to seek outside resources, through donors or funding institutions. Or perhaps he can divert some other part of his budget for the conservation of a specific item that a patron needs. Creative thinking might yield a way to conserve the item or at least make its information available to those who need it.[5]

Another case in point concerning department functions that will be difficult to perform is the creation of a full disaster plan and a disaster-recovery plan. This task is seldom included in the education one gets for rare book librarianship. But the importance of this activity cannot be overstated. Responsible librarians make sure their institutions have such plans in place, and if the institutions do not, the librarians work with fire and police departments to create such plans. If the library is enlightened enough (and has enough resources), it may have a full- or part-time preservation officer with whom the librarian can work to develop a disaster-recovery plan. The officer may not be an expert in special collections, so the rare book librarian may be greatly helpful in creating a plan that accounts for her department's particular needs. For instance, if there is a water problem, the plan might show a prioritized listing of what to save first. Once such a program is in place, the librarians must familiarize themselves and their staffs with it so that they are all ready to act in an emergency. Also, if funds are available, it may be possible to outsource the creation of the disaster plan. Although disaster preparedness is not the exclusive province of rare book departments, it is certainly a "function" that the special collections staff must be ready to engage in.

Collection Development Policy

Libraries should have collection development policies that help them decide what to put into the collection and what not to.[6] But such a document does much more than that.

As Dora Biblarz says, the policy helps the librarians with selection, planning, and public relations, and it also could help in cooperative collecting if a library is in a consortium or if it is in proximity to other libraries with rare book and special collections departments. The primary function of a collection development policy is to focus the staff on acquiring items that reflect, and performing tasks that support, the main directives of the library. Thus, the mission of the library should be behind every decision (Biblarz).

After general statements describing the library's holdings and audience, the policy should delineate collecting goals vis-à-vis its unique position in its institution, in its community, and in the larger academic world that it serves. A key element of this document is a delineation of the profiles of the subjects that the collection holds (Biblarz). The profiles should be informed by an understanding of the levels of collecting for each subject.

Most collection development policies contain a section in which the levels of collecting are clearly spelled out. Biblarz calls them "collection depth indicators," and she gives the following list:

1 = minimal information level
2 = basic information level
3 = study or instructional support level
4 = research level
5 = comprehensive level

(A sixth level is often recognized, but it is not a "collecting" one: it is level 0—items that the library does not collect and would not put onto its shelves. Hence it is not usually counted as a "level of collecting."[7]) These five levels are, of course, relative to the institution. Whereas a public library in Alaska would probably not need a 1950s guide to cacti in desert climates, this item might be of great interest to an institution in New Mexico.

Level 1 items are almost ready for deaccession. They will offer little information to the library's patrons, they are usually out of scope for the collections, and they have little or no monetary or intellectual value for the library. A good example of a level 1 item is an old *Chilton's Auto Repair Manual* in an academic library at a major university.

Items at level 2 have little research value to the library's patrons but may someday be useful to someone. Arithmetic or literature textbooks of the 1960s might fall under this category depending on the nature of the institution.

Level 3 items are of general interest and should be looked at seriously for acquisition or retention. At an academic library, items that fall under the broad rubric "literature" may be added to the collection, even if the author is obscure and his works are second-rate. It is a judgment call by the librarian.

Level 4 materials are likely to be acquired or maintained because they serve the library's patrons directly. Scholarly books on a vast range of topics, art books, and works of general interest that are likely to have lasting appeal and may receive critical examination are certainly to be retained.

And holdings in level 5 areas are what are called the library's Collections of Record—the world-class holdings that scholars must consult if they are doing work in these areas. The University of California, Riverside's B. Traven Collections; the James Joyce materials at the University at Buffalo and Cornell University; the collection of Mark Twain holdings at the Bancroft Library at Berkeley; and the archive on the history of medicine at the U.S. National Library of Medicine are level 5 collections. When items that fit into a library's level 5 holdings come along, if these are not already represented in the collection, the library is almost obliged to acquire them. Sometimes the price prohibits such an acquisition, but the library does want to offer scholars the most comprehensive collections it can amass. Such holdings add to the library's (and its institution's) reputation, and scholars are served well in that they can do the bulk of their research in one place.

Naturally, all of this—especially level 4 and 5 collections—pertains to rare book and special collections departments. Libraries must usually build to their strengths—"usually" because there are circumstances under which collections can move from one level to another. A library with a small holding in, say, a particular author or on a particular topic may receive a gift or make a purchase of a strong holding of that author or topic. The collection may go from level 3 to level 4 or 5 if the acquisition is strong enough. The Rivera Library at the University of California, Riverside, acquired the J. Lloyd Eaton Collection of Science Fiction, Fantasy, Horror, and Utopia. It had all the foundation items for a world-class collection, so the library began collecting in these areas in earnest, and today the Eaton Collection is its premier level 5 holding.

On the other hand, acquisition for UC Riverside's Godoi Collection on Paraguay, still perhaps one of the best in the world, was fueled by the work of a few scholars teaching at the university and doing heavy research in the history, politics, and culture of that country. When they departed, work dwindled on the materials, and the collection went from a level 5 to a level 4.

Rare book departments should create, as part of the collection development policy, a listing of all their individual collections, giving each a number that delineates its level of collecting. This list should be revisited every few years so that adjustments can be made as to where each collection falls in the hierarchy of prioritization for acquisition.

The policy works, as well, as a guide for deaccessioning materials.

Sometimes an institution may use the collection development policy as a venue for delineating activities other than collecting, for the policy to develop the collection certainly entails the personnel who are needed to do the development. Hence, a collection development policy may contain recommendations about staffing.

As the department and its parent institution change, the collection development policy should be revisited regularly, perhaps every year or so, to bring it up to date. Changes in the economy, in personnel, in donor relations, and so forth can affect the contents of this policy, and a fresh picture of the commitments and responsibilities of the policy can be useful.[8]

Selection and Acquisition

In running a rare book department, the librarian should always be thinking about acquisition. If the prime reason for the library's existence is to offer access to information to its patrons, then adding materials to the collection adds to the information the librarian has to offer.

The library as a whole—outside special collections—will have a collection development department that goes about its selection in a variety of ways. That department's procedures are not germane here, other than to say that bibliographers and selectors, librarians and patrons, administrators and faculty, and even students influence acquisition. The specialized nature of the rare book department's holdings requires a streamlined and specially designed procedure for selection.

Naturally, the librarians will know the collection well and will be able to spot gaps in it, will be able to recognize items that should be added, and will thus do well to get to know the specialists who can help them in finding things to add. The specialists include those just mentioned, including bibliographers and selectors, faculty and students, and researchers.

The librarians should also get to know the specialty dealers in the fields represented by the collections, especially those who sell items for the level 5 holdings. The dealers are often highly trained experts who can help in several ways. They can advise on what kinds of things (or on specific items) to add to the collection. They can search for these and can be an extra set of eyes for the department, always looking out for additional items. Because of their subject expertise, they can help librarians answer patrons' questions, either bibliographical or substantive. There is generally a profit motive for these dealers, but many of them who get to know the librarians give them right of first refusal on items (before they list their offerings in catalogs or online).

> **I HAVE MANY** friends in the world of booksellers. I may see them socially, and our paths often cross at professional meetings of various kinds, most usually at book fairs. Innumerable times in my career I have gotten a call or e-mail from a bookseller notifying me of an item he or she thinks we should have in the library, an item the dealer has for sale or one seen at another dealer's place. I have even had booksellers donate pieces to the collection—part of a goodwill gesture, perhaps. And they can be helpful if the library needs to deaccession things.

As sources for information and books, dealers are some of the rare book librarian's best friends. The only caveat is the one mentioned at the beginning of this chapter: there is an ethical conduct issue here, and though relations between booksellers and librarians are natural and good, there must never be an appearance of (or an actual) conflict of interest.

Worth reiterating is that faculty know their fields well, and librarians should cultivate their assistance in identifying items for the collection. Faculty should also be encouraged to contact the library, either the general or the special collections, if they see books or manuscripts they think should be added to the collection.

Sometimes the faculty suggestions are expensive, and it is possible that faculty resource accounts can be tapped to defray all or some of the costs of the materials they want the library to add. The more faculty members the librarian knows, the better off the collection will be in the long run. These can be friendships well worth nurturing.

Chapter 10 has a discussion about book fairs and auctions, but these are worth mentioning here in passing (along with bookstores) as superb sources for rare books and manuscripts.

One rich source of materials for rare book departments is the bookseller's catalog. Despite the prevalence of the Web, with book sites listing hundreds of millions of books, hundreds or even thousands of paper-based booksellers' catalogs are produced each year. Appendix 3 on booksellers' catalogs will treat these tools in depth. Here it is sufficient to say that librarians should know which dealers specialize in the things their libraries collect and make sure that the dealers who sell through catalogs get theirs out efficiently. Immediately upon the catalogs' arrival, the librarian should go through those that are the most focused on her own special collections and order as soon as possible the items she wants. The kinds of things that go into rare book departments are often hard to find, elusive, and expensive. Get them fast before a rival buyer does.

As I suggested earlier, collectors can offer the same kind of advice that the librarian can get from booksellers. Collectors can be knowledgeable and willing to help. Also, the holdings of many a great collector will wind up as major special collections in libraries. So cultivating the friendship of these people can produce excellent results in terms of advice on selection, acquisition, and collection building.

VENDORS AND APPROVAL PLANS

For the general collection, it pays great dividends to have an approval plan. With such a plan, the library (usually the collection development department) creates a collection profile, listing all areas of the library's holdings and assigning each a number corresponding to its level of collecting, depending, of course, on the strengths of the library and the needs of the patrons. The library then negotiates with a vendor (usually having two or more vendors bid against each other)[9] to get a fixed discount on all purchases. The vendor will take the profile and will identify from the hundreds of thousands of titles in its holdings which ones to send to the library automatically and which ones to send slips for.

Books in levels 4 and 5 of a library's plan will be sent by the vendor; for books at level 3, the vendor will send slips (now doable electronically), and the librarians and others (selectors like staff and faculty who are experts in all the areas of the library's collecting) will select items to keep (from the 4- and 5-level books) and items to order (from the slips).

A well-written contract will save the institution a massive amount of time (in searching and ordering) and money because the vendor and the institution will settle on a discount rate acceptable to both parties for all purchases. This means that the vendor has guaranteed sales, albeit at a discount for the institution. So if a book comes out from a publisher that gives the vendor only a 15 percent discount, and the vendor has a fixed negotiated discount rate of, say, 19 percent with the institution, the vendor could lose money on that volume. But in the long run, the vendor will be getting much more than a 15 percent discount from publishers (perhaps as much as 45 or 50 percent) because the vendor will be buying large quantities of volumes from the publishers to supply all its customers.

The approval plan approach is more complicated than this brief summary indicates, but the point is that such arrangements can be adaptable to special collections departments if the librarian is resourceful. An approval plan may not work for all of a rare book department's collections, but it might work for some.

RECEIVING, PROCESSING, AND SHELVING

We have considered acquisitions from a couple of angles. A few other suggestions about the process are in order.

If the rare book department is in a large institution, it may have the benefit of using the acquisitions department of the library for its ordering. But sometimes, especially with rare books and special collections, time is crucial. Often the items desired are not new and may be in short supply—possibly even unique. The librarian, immediately on deciding on a purchase, should contact the vendor to order the item. Relying on the library's general acquisitions department may result in the special collections department's not getting the item because acquisitions may have a standard method of ordering by e-mail or by post, neither of which is as expeditious as a phone call.

A further benefit of a phone call is that the librarian has the chance to speak with the dealer to learn about the piece being ordered or other like materials the dealer might have. As I have already noted, it is important to establish a relationship with booksellers. This is one reason for it and one good way to do it.

When materials are shipped to a library, they usually come in through a receiving department. One standard practice is that the folks in receiving open the packages and place the books or manuscripts onto trucks, then take the trucks to the appropriate

AT THE UNIVERSITY of California, Riverside, we contracted with a dealer whose specialty was science fiction. Rather than doing the extensive searching that would have been required to locate all sf books published in the United States (and elsewhere), we relied on a bookseller with connections to dozens of publishers in the fields of sf, fantasy, horror, and utopia. The dealer automatically sent us all new titles that he obtained, with an invoice, and with a discount. So many sf and fantasy books came out from so many publishers, the librarians could not keep up with them all. But the bookseller could: it was his business. We did have a curator for this collection, and he sought items the vendor did not get for us—especially unusual titles from out-of-the-way publishers and books from foreign publishers he knew.

We had the benefit, in this instance, of collecting in a genre that had hundreds of authors, producing thousands of titles a year.

What we acquired from the bookseller was not comprehensive, but it was a large percentage of sf titles that came on the market. Using the dealer as a vendor saved us huge amounts of time and also some money, thanks to the discounts we arranged.

Ours was a semi-formal arrangement with a dealer, but the upshot of it was that we created what was essentially an approval plan that benefited all parties involved: the authors, the publishers, the bookseller, and the library.

departments. It is safer to ask dealers to put the librarian's name on the package, along with "Special Collections," and to make it clear to the personnel in Receiving that packages—unopened—are to be delivered immediately to the rare book department. This gets the books directly into a secure area before the packages are opened. Besides, it is a great deal of fun to open boxes containing special collections materials.

As with receiving departments, many libraries have central processing units that remove dust jackets, mark books with rubber stamps and bookplates, and get them ready to be shelved. It is best to do all this in the rare book department for all items going into special collections. This work should be done in the most secure environment available, not in a central processing area that is exposed to less-than-perfect security conditions.

A parallel issue here has to do with the disposition of the dust jackets. Public libraries usually save the dust wrappers of their books, putting them into some kind of plastic cover and affixing the barcodes and call-number labels to the sleeves. The original purpose of the dust jacket was to protect the book, and this method of treatment does just that. It is also expensive (in the cost of the sleeves and the time it takes to do the work), and it takes up additional space on the shelves.

Standard practice in academic libraries is to discard the dust jackets. For special collections holdings, however, in which the aim is to keep the book in "collector's condition,"[10] this almost always means retaining its dust jacket. This wrapper usually contains information the book itself does not have: blurbs from other writers, prices, a biographical sketch of the author, pictures of the author, artwork, advertising information that could someday be of use to scholars, and so forth. One problem posed by these protective sleeves is that they are easily removable, and if the library marks the call numbers on the spines of its books where they are visible to anyone paging the volumes, and if the marking then goes only onto the spine of the dust jacket, a thief could steal the item and throw away the dust jacket, thus removing information about the item's provenance. The book will still need to be marked, beneath the jacket.[11] For special collections books, one practice is to keep the dust jackets on the books, mark the books the way they would be if they had no jackets, and then put the call numbers and barcodes onto the dust jackets for easy location.

As for other elements of processing—rubber-stamping, pasting in labels or bookplates, writing in codes or call numbers at determined places in each volume, and the like—all should be done in the rare book department. Books, manuscripts, photographs, prints and drawings, maps, and anything else that goes into the department should be brought there as soon as possible upon acquisition and, for the most part, should not leave the department for any reason. And all the work that will be done on any materials should be done inside the most secure area of the library: inside the security perimeter of the rare book department. Even the "menial" task of shelving should be done only by department personnel, as will be emphasized in chapter 7, "Security." Also, shelving must be done as expeditiously as possible, for items left on book trucks will not be locatable by a pager. And though I called it a "menial task," it is extremely important that it be done correctly. A misshelved book becomes invisible—impossible to locate if it is not in its proper call-number position.

Cataloging

No cataloging equals no access. An item that is not cataloged may as well not exist, for there is no way for a patron to find it without some kind of record. Because, as I have said, access is the number one desideratum in libraries, cataloging is one of the most important activities.

Most libraries have central cataloging departments. But as I mentioned in the previous section, all activities with special collections materials should be done inside the department, if possible. If an arrangement can be made with the cataloging department, it is good to have the rare books cataloger(s) working inside the rare book department. The rare items need not be outside the secure perimeter, and they will not need to be moved from any less secure area to special collections.[12]

An inexpensive paperback, picked up for ten cents at a garage sale and donated to the library, could cost a good deal to catalog. The science fiction collection at UC Riverside contains thousands of poor-quality paperbacks, but many of them are the only known copies of these cheaply produced books. With no other record in any online database, these orphans need original cataloging, which is costly. Further, cataloging books for special collections entails a special knowledge of rare book cataloging.[13] So the "retail value" of an item heading to special collections has nothing to do with the level of security it should be under. All items destined for the rare book department should be made as secure as possible at all times, wherever they are in the building.

In the 1980s, the RBMS Standards Committee—later named the Bibliographic Standards Committee—created a series of thesauri for rare book cataloging. The aim was to have all people creating online bibliographic records use a controlled vocabulary, so that all main entries in OCLC (and eventually in WorldCat) records would have the same terms for the same phenomena. It would have been counterproductive for a scholar, looking up a particular kind of marbled paper, to seek "French snail" when some of the records used that term and other records used "Dutch curl" for the same pattern.

The Standards Committee eventually published, through ALA, six thesauri of terms for Paper, Printing and Publishing Evidence, Type Evidence, Genre, Binding, and Provenance Evidence.[14] These word lists are reviewed periodically, and anyone can send suggestions for modification to the Bibliographic Standards Committee at any time, so the thesauri continue to morph.

Each thesaurus has a hierarchical list showing where every word falls in its genealogical relationship to other words in the thesaurus. And each has an alphabetical listing, with many of the words having Scope Notes and "Use For" notes explaining what some of the less common terms mean. Despite these aids, a rare book cataloger still needs a great deal of specialized education to be able to use the terms correctly in a cataloging record. For instance, it is unlikely that all rare book catalogers know the differences among (and can therefore accurately iden-

tify) *folio, quarto, octavo, duodecimo, sextodecimo,* and *trigesimo-secundo.*

Because of the extensive special training a cataloger needs in order to use the terms in these thesauri, and also because most rare book catalogers have not had all the training they need, it is unlikely that most rare book records are done to the highest standards, especially for books from the handpress period (before about 1800).[15]

Most catalogers are not fully familiar with the thesauri terminology; therefore, most of the records they create are not as full as they could be. Also, to do a truly in-depth MARC record, the cataloger must handle with care each item under scrutiny, looking for the kinds of things that wind up in thorough bibliographical descriptions.[16] This effort takes a good deal of time, and time is money. Even with extensive training, most catalogers do not have the luxury of spending lots of time on a volume, checking provenance information, collating the book looking for stubs and typographical peculiarities, checking out watermarks, describing binding details, and such. For the rarer (and often the more expensive) items in the collection, however, giving this kind of information is important, as we shall see in the chapter on security. At least, the cataloger should record in a notes field copy-specific information for the item in hand. This task does not require much extensive training; it requires simple observation.

As I noted in chapter 1, continuing education is essential for those in special collections. Cataloging is an essential part of librarianship, and its knowledge will help anyone handling rare books and manuscripts. In special collections, especially, an understanding of cataloging will expand one's knowledge considerably, particularly because rare book cataloging requires so much knowledge.

CREATING FINDING AIDS FOR MANUSCRIPTS AND OTHER NONBOOK HOLDINGS

In librarianship one generally uses the term *cataloging* in connection with printed items. For manuscripts and other nonprint media, one creates finding aids. As with cataloging, a manuscript with no finding aid is essentially "not there" for readers. While we have catalogers, we must also have manuscript processors.

Manuscript "collections" come in all sizes, from single documents to hundreds of boxes of items. Librarians usually distinguish between "manuscripts" and "archives," though often these categories overlap considerably. Chapter 3 will consider archives more fully.

Manuscript collections can contain almost anything that would wind up in special collections: all kinds of documents, photographs, recipes, printed matter of many types, maps and charts, prints and drawings, and even realia (as noted in chapter 1). As with archives, the manuscript processor must assess each item in the collection and decide which to keep, which to jettison. (In archives this assessment is called "appraisal.")

The aim here is not to give a full explanation of the disposition of manuscripts. The aim is to emphasize the importance of their proper arrangement and reporting. Some collections are so central to a department's holdings—that is, they are strongly germane to the kinds of research done at the institution—that they deserve extensive treatment. Such handling could mean going so far as to create an itemized listing of every piece in the collection. But item-level processing is rare because it is extremely time-consuming and hence costly, especially for large collections, and it is seldom necessary unless the collection is composed almost entirely of extremely important documents that individually shed light on the topic of the collection. Item-level cataloging is practically never done for large collections.

Much more common for rich manuscript collections are folder-level or even box-level records. However granular the record-keeping is for manuscript collections, the bottom line is to get into the online record as many of the collection's key words as possible: proper names of people, cities, counties, states, and countries; events; dates; subject headings; and whatever else the individual collection warrants. This information must accompany all the other facts that such records should contain: size of the collection, dimensions of items if appropriate, date of acquisition, provenance, date of processing and the name of the processor(s), descriptions or genres of the contents (e.g., correspondence, hand-colored maps, photographs, busi-

ness records), and so forth, naturally headed by the name of the holding library. And the record should be mounted on the Web on NUCMC (the National Union Catalog of Manuscript Collections) and OCLC WorldCat.[17]

Cataloging and the creation of finding aids, as I have noted, are essential activities, and though many a special collections department will have a full- or part-time cataloger assigned to it, it will not necessarily have a person assigned who deals exclusively with manuscripts. Manuscripts thus often lag behind in processing, or they hardly ever get touched. But by their very nature—because almost everything in a manuscript collection is unique—they deserve to be high on the priority list for processing, depending, of course, on how important they are with respect to the research needs of the department. Manuscript correspondence of a barber may not be as germane to the library's patrons as are the letters of a congressman. Though, of course, a barber from the colonial period may have juicy letters reporting on the news he picked up in his shop. All materials, printed and manuscript, must be assessed and prioritized for treatment.

Transferring Books from the Stacks to Special Collections

One of the RBMS Guidelines is titled *Guidelines on the Selection and Transfer of Materials from General Collections to Special Collections*. As this document points out, "Materials located in a library's general collections may gain, over time, special cultural, historical, or monetary value. Librarians have a responsibility to identify and transfer these materials to a special collections unit to ensure that they remain accessible and that they receive an appropriate level of preservation and security."[18]

As books age, sometimes they gain value depending on the reputation of the authors, the popularity of the subject matter, the collectability of the press or the book's illustrator, or for many other reasons. Items that were properly designated for open stacks at their acquisition may merit being moved to special collections over time.

WHEN I FIRST got to the University of California at Riverside, I asked the rare book cataloger to print out a list of all the books in the collection from particular private presses that I had identified. When she gave me the listing of three hundred or more titles, I searched the shelves and located about three-fourths of them. The rest were unaccounted for. They were not checked out, they were not in a campus bindery, and they were certainly not on the shelves. I had identified these volumes as having come from highly collected presses or publishers who did limited editions of highly collected authors. These were vulnerable books, and I could only assume that a good number of them had been stolen.

Some of these books were produced by presses in universities (Abattoir Editions, Windhover Press) or by printers who worked for universities and whose living came from their professorial salaries, not from the sale of their books (Cummington Press, Stone Wall Press, Perishable Press). So the original selling prices of the books were low enough for the books to have been put into the general stacks. For example, a fine copy of the regular edition of the Stone Wall Press volume of Theodore Roethke's poems *Sequence, Sometimes Metaphysical,* issued in 1963, was priced at $15. A copy of this book today would bring close to $2,000. Its low price on its acquisition, when the book was just off the press, would have put the volume into the circulating collection. (For more on fine press books, see chapter 14.)

According to section 1 of the guidelines,

virtually all libraries acquire materials that, with time and changing circumstances, become rare and gain special cultural and historical value. These materials may also gain significant monetary value in the marketplace. Librarians have a responsibility to identify the rare and valuable materials currently held in general and open stack collections and to arrange for their physical transfer to a library location that provides an appropriate level of access, preservation, and security. For many libraries the preferred transfer location is the special collections unit. (See note 18.)

The guidelines then consider the selection and transfer process, the creation of a formal transfer policy delineating selection criteria and showing what will be brought into special collections, a preservation assessment, and much more.

Rare book librarians should either create such policies for their own institutions or use the RBMS one. In any case, they should have a written policy on the transfer of books ready to show anyone who questions the activity. And they should not create the policy and put it into operation on their own. The transfer document should be created in consultation with others who are involved in the library, including the administration, whose formal approval must be obtained.

Some people in the library or in the institution (or even externally) may be displeased with this project. Patrons used to taking out books from a circulating collection may be frustrated when they learn that the books they want are to be used only in the rare book department. Interlibrary loan people may bristle at not being able to supply titles for distant users. And, of course, catalogers will not be happy when they have to recatalog each item to reflect its new home and its noncirculating status. These objections should not dissuade the librarian from making the transfer.

I repeat, it is essential for the rare book department to have a formal, codified policy—on paper—to show those who are not happy with these transfers that a new order of business is at hand. Access is the bottom line. A stolen book is not accessible.

Weeding the Collection and Deaccessioning

Space is finite in all libraries. Every living library (any library that continues to acquire materials) will eventually run out of space. Areas of great interest shift, heavily used collections lose some of their favor, other collections come to prominence for any of a great number of reasons: increased public or scholarly interest in a person or event, the fading from view of an event or invention, the approaching anniversary of some cataclysmic happening or person's birth, the discovery of a lost piece of art or manuscript that reopens interest in a topic, and so forth.

Collections rise or sink in the levels of collecting. And whole collections may drop out of use in a library over a long enough period. The collection in the Phillips Library at the Peabody Essex Museum was once in an institution with a much more global range of interests, so it had a sizable collection of books on horticulture, gardening, and natural history. The museum has evolved into a great institution focusing on art and culture, and the old library, amassed over three hundred years, now has vast areas that are no longer part of the institution's mission and that practically never get consulted by curators, scholars, or anyone from the general public. What were once level 5 collections have sunk to perhaps level 3 or even level 2. The issue of weeding begins to emerge for these holdings.

As Sam Streit, the former head of special collections at Brown University's John Hay Library, has written: "Although a relatively common practice in the world of Special Collections, deaccession is perhaps the one premeditated activity that is most conducive to controversy."[19] This paragraph continues:

> Among the reasons, I think, are the following: research libraries generally, and Special Collections particularly, have been perceived traditionally in terms of permanence and in correlative terms of the imperative to accumulate, to gather in and preserve forever the product of human intellectual endeavor; deaccession erodes this perception of permanence. Special Collections, virtually without exception, build their collections to a considerable extent through a network of associations with donor/collectors whose collections arrive in the library already developed according to the donor's taste and intellectual construct; therefore, deaccession, no matter how carefully undertaken, can give the appearance of bad faith between the library and its collection of donors. (21)

Weeding and deaccessioning must be handled with great delicacy and forthrightness with the public and the rest of the entire library community.

As I just mentioned, there are many reasons to weed and deaccession, not merely the reduction of holdings from levels 5 and 4 to lower priorities of collecting. Some libraries sell off their duplicates; some get rid of copies in favor of better copies (upgrading a collection is a common strategy for rare book libraries). Many libraries have seen mass reformatting of their holdings, especially of some collections of brittle books and of newspapers. If the papers have been digitized or microfilmed at some point, they are ripe for deaccession.[20] Their texts are (presumably) available on film or online, and disposing of the originals can save huge amounts of space. If, in the reformatting, the items have not been destroyed,[21] it is possible to return them to the shelves, put them into some kind of remote storage, or get rid of them.

If the items are still in good enough condition, they can be given to other libraries, put into book sales, traded to other institutions or to booksellers for materials the library wants, or merely trashed. Disposition depends on institutional policies and practices, the value of the items, state laws, and much more. So if any special collections department wishes to deaccession an item or a collection, the librarian must find out what the institutional and governmental regulations are and adhere to them.

Further, if the items are sold—through auction, to dealers, to other institutions, or to the public in any of various kinds of sales—the standard practice is to put the money generated by the sale back into the collection, usually with purchases of materials in the very areas of deaccessioning, if possible and practical. The sale of objects from the library should never generate money that goes to operating expenses, like salaries, building repairs, or computer upgrades. These uses of the proceeds send a terrible message to past or potential donors, trustees, and others concerned with the appropriate handling and disposition of the collection.

As I mentioned earlier, the public should be part of the procedure—especially for public institutions. If word got out that the rare book department was surreptitiously selling off its treasures, there could be a public outcry, the damage from which could take years to repair. Also, the items selected for deaccession must be carefully scrutinized, with the library considering all the pertinent issues. Is the item truly a duplicate that contains information that can be gleaned from other copies of the item that will remain in the collection? How does this piece fit into the collection development practices and mission of the library? Is the item truly out of scope or in such bad condition that it cannot be repaired or used? Is there any way to conserve the item so that it need not be disposed of? Are there legal reasons the item cannot be disposed of? For instance, was the item acquired (purchased or donated) with a legal document that put strings on it? What might the public's response be to this action? the response of trustees? the response of the library's users—faculty, students, outside or independent scholars (or both), potential donors? Has the public been fairly and openly notified of the decision to deaccession? How will the proceeds of the sale (if an item is to be sold) be used? What could be the long-term ramifications of this action?

One small detail worth mentioning is that when items are donated to a library, they may not be disposed of for three years. The law stems from the possibility that an item could be given by someone who has no right to give it. That is, an heir, or even the ostensible owner of the item, may not be the real owner. It could happen that someone shows up at the library and says, "Those books that you got two years ago from Mr. Smith's estate did not all belong to Mr. Smith. I loaned him some of them and I want them back." After three years, the law assumes, the estate will have been settled and all claims on the ownership of the items in it will have been dealt with. This issue will be revisited in chapter 8 on legal issues.

Although departments should always be ready to weed and deaccession, they may be able to put it off for a long time if they have the space to keep things that would normally be removed from the collection. But eventually, weeding is likely to become necessary. The rare book librarian should be mindful of the issues raised here and should proceed with caution, with a knowledge of the local and federal laws, with an understanding of institutional practices, with a clearly delineated and legally vetted deaccession policy, and with the full support of the institution's administration and legal counsel.

To elaborate about the policy: The department should have a clearly written, fully vetted, and codified document spelling out the procedures one must employ to deaccession items from the collection. Several issues about the removal of things from the collection have already been laid out, but they are worth repeating. The policy should

- describe what kinds of materials may be deaccessioned.[22]
- explain the rationale for deaccessioning, with a statement about what the impact of the deaccessioning will be, and on whom; the decision should consider the interests of all who might use the materials chosen for removal.
- be mindful of the controversy that the deaccessioning will generate and guide those responsible for the action in how to deal with public or other sentiment that disagrees with the decision to deaccession. This recommendation also entails dealing openly and honestly with, and with a good deal of explanation to, the local and regional media, who often create controversy with incendiary headlines based on the ire of a few community activists. (It sells newspapers and makes good sound bites on the evening news.) In fact, dealing with the news media before any information goes public may head off a good deal of bad publicity.[23] Explanations of deaccessioning programs should refer specifically to the stated, clearly delineated, and well thought out written and published policy that allows the deaccession in the first place. And the explanations should also connect the action to the standard professional stance on the removal of materials from collections. (This library is not doing anything extraordinary; it is working within standard professional guidelines and practices.)
- consider all the possible or actual legal restrictions that may be in place on the materials to be deaccessioned. This means looking at the way the item was originally acquired, its reasons for having been acquired, and what strings were attached to its acquisition, if any,

and it also takes into account local, state, or federal laws governing the disposition of institution property. If the donors or donor's heirs are alive, they should be appropriately consulted. In the absence of donors or heirs, state or federal laws should be taken into account.[24]

- mandate the openness of the practice; the actions should not be hidden away from the public.
- delineate the steps one must take to remove items from the collection.
- indicate what will become of these items. They may be given away (to other institutions), traded (with other institutions or with booksellers), sold, or discarded, for instance.
- explain how proceeds (if there are any) from the sale will be used and how this use was decided upon.
- insure that no deaccessioned material becomes the property of any employee or volunteer, unless that person acquires the item publicly and not directly from the institution.
- list (perhaps by office or title) the people who are responsible for the whole operation and what their roles are. Such a draconian measure as deaccession should not be at the discretion of a single person; decisions should be made by a carefully chosen group of experts (e.g., librarians, administrators, faculty). That is, there should be a collection-review committee (or a deaccession-review committee) involved in the removal of items from the collection.
- require that full records be kept of the transaction, no matter what the final disposition of the item may be. Such records may include information on the fiscal impact of the transaction on the library.
- consider that the institution's (and the department's) reputation is at stake, so nothing should be done that could jeopardize the institution's reputation for honesty, translucence, and propriety.
- require that deaccession materials be clearly and indelibly marked to show that they were removed from the collection; a record of all deaccessions should be kept by the institution.

Some librarians may wish to ignore some of these mandates, depending on particular circumstances relative to their own situations. The foregoing is merely a list of suggestions that may guide librarians in weeding and deaccessioning. The deaccession policy is a key document in the arsenal of the rare book librarian, and it should be revisited periodically to make sure it is up to date with current practices in the field.

Interlibrary Loan (ILL)

Books and manuscripts wind up in special collections for many reasons, not the least of which has to do with their vulnerability. Preservation and security are at the root of many decisions to place a book in special collections. Letting an item out of the department is reducing its security and possibly subjecting it to deleterious forces. For this reason, many special collections departments have a standard and fairly solidly adhered-to policy: No circulation.

If a special collections department is geographically close to another, and if the heads of the departments have a close working relationship and a good deal of trust in one another, it might be a good idea to have a limited interlibrary loan practice. But if the libraries are close, any patron needing to use an item can go to the library that holds it. If the department

IN THE DEPARTMENTS I have headed, it was our practice not to loan any materials, and only under the most stringent conditions and overwhelmingly convincing arguments was I forced to let up on this practice of no loans.*

*A cautionary note: At the University of California, Riverside, a person far above me in the hierarchy required that I loan a perfect copy of a valuable first edition of an American author to the University of California, Berkeley so they could make a facsimile edition of it. I protested, but to no avail. When it was returned, despite all protestations by the Berkeley people that they knew how to handle rare books without damaging them, the volume was destroyed, its cover having been nearly ripped off. Do not trust those who claim, "We won't harm it," or "We know how to handle rare books." My response to this latter claim is, "So do I: no loans."

does loan items out, there should be a stringent and clearly written policy that shows all the rules and restrictions on such a loan. For example, items from one special collections department may be loaned only to senior scholars (professors, senior researchers, or graduate students), not to undergraduates or anyone from the public. Books must be used in the borrowing institution's special collections reading room, under proper supervision. A restricted loan period should be specified: one week, two weeks, one month, or whatever time the lending institution decides is appropriate. And, of course, any publications emanating from the loaned materials must be credited by the authors to the proper institution. If the lending institution has a cost-recovery policy for publications created from its holdings, the borrowing institution should be held responsible for conveying the rules and may be responsible for collecting the fees.

The librarian deciding to make the loan should feel comfortable that the piece will be cared for properly in the borrower's library. That is, the borrowing library must have security levels and practices that meet the lender's standards. The borrower should also have environmental conditions that meet the lender's requirements. Further, a secure means of conveying the item to the borrower should be in place. Armored cars, special couriers from one of the institutions, or some other means of safe transport should be in place. Who is responsible for insurance on the item—in transit and in situ at the borrowing institution—should be spelled out, as should costs of the transfer.

As with many areas of rare book activity, RBMS has its own *Guidelines for the Interlibrary Loan of Rare and Unique Materials*. The revised text from 2012 is titled *ACRL/RBMS Guidelines for Interlibrary and Exhibition Loan of Special Collections Materials*. Both documents are valuable, and some of the text of the 2004 version is worth referring to.[25] The 2004 guidelines open with some "basic assumptions," the first of which is, "Interinstitutional loan from special collections for research use is strongly encouraged but must be conducted in a manner that ensures responsible care and effectively safeguards materials from loss or damage." This strong encouragement seems to go against many librarians' views, but there is also good support in the field in favor of interlibrary loan. This stance goes back to the basic premise that access to information is our prime directive, and ILL is one way to effect it.

As for lending for exhibition (see the following section), the lending institution must make sure that items from its collection will be handled in the best conditions possible at the borrower's library. This means that the security and preservation levels must be high, the staff at the borrowing institution must be appropriately trained to handle rare materials, and the materials will be under appropriate surveillance when they are being used.

The 2004 guidelines' second basic assumption is important to understand:

> Institutions may refuse to lend materials of exceptional rarity or monetary value, items in fragile condition, or materials for which size or format creates increased potential for shipping damage or possible loss (e.g. folios, maps, unbound manuscripts). Loans of these materials might be possible with the addition of security measures outside of the normal interlibrary loan procedures outlined in this document such as formal written agreements, insurance certificates or other relevant documentation.

Further, as the 2012 version of the guidelines makes clear, such a transfer of materials should not be done merely through the efforts of the two department heads (at the lending and the borrowing institutions).

> To establish effective policies and practice, staff with responsibilities for special collections, interlibrary loan, exhibitions, conservation, public service and reference, and administration—both within and between institutions—must work closely together. Especially because approaches may vary among institutions, borrowing and lending institutions should take extra care in crafting and communicating their policies and procedures.

This is followed by a suggestion that it might be possible for the borrowing institution to make do with a photocopied or scanned version of the item it wishes to borrow. If a surrogate copy is used, the original is not subjected to the handling and shipping that borrowing entails, and a good deal of expense (and anxiety) might be spared for all parties.

Other assumptions from the 2004 document say that borrowers should go through their own libraries' ILL department, not directly to the holding institution; they should try to locate the piece they want in a circulating collection before going to a special collections department to request a loan; and they should try to find a surrogate copy of some kind before requesting a rare one. Further, borrowers should try to find the item the patron wants at a local library and should ask the patron to go to the other library, if travel does not create a hardship for the user; and they should ascertain that the item the patron is requesting is precisely what he wants and needs. Items should be evaluated individually for loan. "The loan of materials should rest on well-defined interinstitutional commitments rather than on personal contacts. However, personal familiarity and/or direct communications with curatorial staff at other institutions may facilitate the lending process." Finally, as I indicated earlier, the borrowing institution must have proper, secure conditions for handling rare materials. These recommendations, though superseded by the 2012 version, are practical and useful. The 2012 document adds seven additional guidelines, summarized here:

1. Clear and thorough written policies for lending should be in place.
2. Involve appropriately trained staff for all aspects of the transfer. These should include preservation and conservation specialists, a special collections librarian, an exhibition prep specialist, and interlibrary loan people.
3. With requests to borrow, always maintain "clear and consistent communication and decision-making."
4. Fully document all loan transactions.
5. Create and follow a standard work flow for each transaction.
6. Figure into the operation the best security, handling, and environmental conditions for the materials loaned.
7. No matter what is sent to the borrower (originals or surrogates), access to special collections materials is paramount.

Other considerations discussed in the 2012 document concern the care the libraries should take in handling the loaned materials, documentation at all stages of the operation, both parties' following the requirements of the lender's policies and procedures, and returning the borrowed item(s) in at least as good condition as when they were loaned and by the date specified for their return by the lender.

If a rare book library does have an ILL policy, that policy should be especially sensitive to the difference between monographs and manuscripts, the latter being unique and therefore not replaceable. Hence, lending books may be easier to justify than lending manuscripts. And before a book or manuscript goes out, the lender should make sure that a good description of it—its physical attributes and condition—is made so that when it returns, a comparison can be made to verify that it has not been damaged in any way.

Special collections librarians should consult the two ACRL/RBMS Guidelines for ILL (cited in note 25). The 2012 version is excellent, but the 2004 version has features also worth consulting. Copies of the policy should be on the department's website and should be available in paper form. As with any policy that affects any potential department user, a formal, codified statement must be available to all, posted permanently and publicly. And the policy should be adhered to as strictly as possible. Allowing one user to obtain an item through ILL while denying another user could create negative public relations.[26]

Lending Items for Exhibition

Closely related to ILL is lending items for exhibitions. Again, RBMS has its own practices: *Guidelines for Borrowing and Lending Special Collections Materials for Exhibition.*[27]

For at least one good reason, such lending should be encouraged: it is good PR for the lending institution. Also, the goodwill generated by such a loan may be money in the bank if the lender someday wishes to have the favor returned.

The opening paragraph of the 2005 RBMS document says,

> Although this document can offer no specific guidance in the matter, it is assumed that individual institutions will use common sense in applying these guidelines, taking into consideration such factors as rarity, fragility and monetary value of the material being requested for exhibition. For example, the requirements for the loan of a piece of printed sheet music owned in multiple copies by a lending institution may be vastly different from those required for the loan of Thomas Jefferson's autograph manuscript draft of the Declaration of Independence.

The revised 2012 guidelines say this:

> The purpose of these guidelines is to provide a framework for the development of appropriate institutional policies and decision-making criteria to support the interinstitutional loan of special collections materials, to specify the respective responsibilities of borrowing and lending institutions, and to recommend procedures to ensure the security and preservation of loaned materials.
>
> These guidelines are intended for use by libraries, archives, historical societies, and other similar repositories to encourage and facilitate the interinstitutional loan of special collections materials, including rare books, manuscripts, archival documents, photographs, maps, prints, artworks, artifacts, ephemera, and other materials in special formats that are normally consulted under secure, supervised conditions. Although these guidelines are written primarily from the perspective of single institutions, they are also meant to serve the needs of consortial groups in developing policies and procedures for facilitating research and exhibition loans among their members.

The guidelines consider such issues as lead time (how long in advance a lending institution must be notified that a request is being made), the need for written policies and procedures, the need for staff trained in the area of borrowing and lending, the need for extensive documentation at all steps of the operation, the importance of security and proper handling,[28] a request letter, a facilities report, a loan agreement, a condition report, and much more. The 2012 version of the document clarifies the responsibilities incurred by lenders and borrowers, and it distinguishes loans for exhibition from those for research. This document must be consulted by any librarian asked to lend to another institution and by any librarian asking for a loan.

The facilities report mentioned in the preceding paragraph is essential: no one wants to loan an item to a facility with poor security, inappropriate lighting, and an intermittent HVAC system. The lending library should require documentation that all conditions in the borrowing institution meet appropriate standards, with information about security, environment, display cases, security and rare-book-department personnel, and so forth.[29]

The guidelines, which consider many other issues (insurance, references, a loan agreement form, a condition report, packing and shipping, and much more), are excellent, and librarians considering ILL for exhibition must read them. There is even a sample loan agreement form that any institution can adopt or adapt for its own use.

A final word about such loans: As chapter 11 will show, exhibitions are an excellent form of outreach, and every rare book department should consider doing them. The more cooperation a special collections department shows to others, the more likely that it will be to be able to borrow from other institutions.

Dealing with Patrons

Several times these first two chapters have talked about dealing with patrons. At the risk of redundancy, it is useful to revisit some of the key issues because they are extremely important in the running of a rare book department.

There is no excuse for giving poor service. Patrons expect to acquire information and to be treated with dignity and fairness. They do not expect to be ignored, to be left waiting, or to have a distasteful experience. Whether the users are local or distant, they want consistently good service. Rare book departments are service providers, as are all the other departments of the institution.

Bad public relations for the department can be deadly. An administration does not want to field complaints, having either to defend the department or to censure it, or both. Departments that are not living up to the high ideals of the institution can be subject to severe consequences: loss of resources or personnel or other kinds of administrative support.

These generic statements, however, must be served up in the fairly restrictive context of the rare book department. Just because "the customer is always right" does not mean that the department must relax its stringent requirements or flex on its demands of its patrons. There is to be no eating in the department. No one may bring in ballpoint pens, large overcoats, briefcases, or flamethrowers. That is, nothing should be allowed into the department that might damage the department's holdings. Certain items will not be sent out of the department (in fact, almost nothing will be allowed to circulate). The department has strict operating times, and the staff must close the facility and ask patrons to leave when the time comes. Photography and other reproduction policies and fees must be maintained equitably, consistently, and appropriately. Special

dispensations should almost never be allowed for any of the department's operations or policies. And so forth.

As librarians must treat all users with respect, they must also garner the respect of their patrons by providing upright, reasonable, and consistent service, courtesy, and dignity. But faced with the kinds of restrictions that must be placed on rare or unique materials, patrons may not understand why they are not getting instant gratification and special treatment. That is why formal, codified principles and practices must be in place and published, to back up the librarian's stance when patrons ask for materials or services that they cannot have. These practices and policies must be inculcated into all who work in the library, especially those in the hierarchy above the special collections department. Everyone must be trained to support the rare book staff. "We are, indeed, all in this together."

And then there are the seriously difficult patrons. You know who they are. Those in person—in the reading room—are just as much a challenge as those from afar who (by e-mail, post, or telephone) demand services that we think inappropriate or excessive.

Librarians often find themselves in the position of being asked to do much more than they can justify. Researchers may be far from the repository holding the materials they want to use, unable to get there, and eager for the information they need. But the fiscal realities of running a rare book department make

IN MY LIBRARY we have a rule of operation: we will give most patrons about twenty minutes to a half hour of our reference service. For some patrons we might give a bit more. But ours is a small staff—as is the case in many rare book departments. We cannot do the work of the patron. For someone in our reading room, we will guide her to the resources she needs, show her how to use all the finding aids, catalogs, and reference resources, and page whatever she asks for.

But we cannot spend hours doing this—we cannot do the research for her. We do not have the resources.

For patrons at a distance, we cannot do much more, though, of course, we have had requests from distant patrons to page dozens of books and scores of manuscripts, look through them for the information needed, and write it all up (or photocopy or digitize it). We understand how important these resources are for our clientele, how they simply cannot afford to

visit us in person, and how grateful they will be for all the work we do for them. But we must draw the line somewhere. When we see that such requests will be taking a disproportionate amount of time from our staff, we encourage the researchers either to come in or to find a local researcher they can hire to do the work for them. To this purpose, we have a list of local scholars who will do work for hire, and we will send the list of these researchers to the distant scholars.

it impossible for librarians to drop all other crucial work to take on another person's onerous research project. It is useful to have a codified statement—on paper and in digital form—spelling out why department personnel cannot spend excessive amounts of time on patrons' work, delineating how much time staff *can* spend, and offering a list of local researchers who can be employed to do the work.

You can't please all of the people all of the time.

Sign-in Sheets and Identification for Patrons

In chapter 7 we shall dwell at length on security issues related to special collections. Here it is necessary to mention that all kinds of documents that increase security must be used in the rare book department.

Although we may try to remove the notion of exclusivity raised in chapter 1 and attempt to carefully assess all who apply to use the department, we must nonetheless be mindful of the department's security. One of the frontline security measures is screening potential users. And the first order of screening is to have patrons sign in, provide the staff with identification of various kinds, and perhaps even get supporting letters before they show up at the library. References should be checked, and identification cards should be copied and their information recorded.

The specific security issues behind all these procedures will be covered later. Here it is sufficient to say that all patrons must be treated with identical scrutiny. The presence of a printed form, or a formal online version of the form, should convince patrons that they are all being treated with the same level of inquiry, scrutiny, and care.

USE OF CALL SLIPS AND SHELF MARKERS

Again, the use of call slips as security devices will be treated in chapter 7. Despite all our technological sophistication, nothing has adequately replaced the tried-and-perfected call slip for its several uses.

When any user is given anything at her worktable or at the reading room circulation desk, it should be from a request written on a call slip.[30] True, libraries can use online requests to tell staff to page items for readers. But when an item is removed from a shelf, it needs to have a "placeholder" left on the shelf, first, to signal that something has been removed from that spot (with information revealing exactly what that item is and what patron has asked to use it), and second, to advise the shelver where to put it.

Traditionally these slips are in triplicate: a copy for the circulation desk, a copy to stay with the item, and a third copy to be put on the shelf as a place marker and item-return guide. One good tool is a plastic sleeve (sometimes bright red) that holds the third call slip and that is prominently visible from a distance. Call slips in such a sleeve are less likely to blow away or slip out of sight, obscuring the fact that something is missing from the shelf. In a closed, nonbrowsing stacks area, these sleeves are invaluable.

What to do with the call slips is another matter. Whether they should be retained after an item has been replaced on the shelf, disposed of immediately, reformatted (e.g., digitized—formerly they were often microfilmed) and then disposed of, or simply saved in paper form should be determined by the individual library. Disposing of them protects patrons from the invasions of their privacy engendered by the USA PATRIOT Act. But disposal loses potentially valuable information for the library. Saving them engenders other problems. Chapter 7 contains a further discussion of these devices.

The last word here is that call slips should be employed and probably retained in one form or another.

Funding for Incoming Scholars

Budgets are always tight, even in fairly good times. But that does not mean we cannot try to help scholars who cannot afford to visit our repositories. It is good PR for a rare book department to offer scholarships or visiting fellowships to researchers. And it is good for business. The more patrons we can serve, the better we are at meeting our primary directive of linking patrons with the information they need.

Working with the library's top administrators, and possibly also with donors or Friends groups, the head of the rare book department should try to raise some money for an endowed fund to be used to bring scholars in. Even a small stipend can be appealing to young or impecunious scholars, who might not otherwise have the resources to visit a library. Some patrons like the idea of a named fellowship to carry the memory of someone who was once connected to the library in some way. Such support yields good press and encourages the use of the collection. Everyone benefits.

Reference Books in the Department

The issue of providing reference books in the special collections department may have been more germane fifteen years ago when a plethora of reference tools existed in book form only. Today, many reference works are available online, and whether their analog versions belong in the special collections department is no longer a serious discussion.

On the other hand, a host of important reference books exist only in paper form, and whether they should be kept in the special collections department or not can be an issue of debate, depending on whom one speaks to. The aim here is not to list a number of volumes that librarians believe should be in special collections, though a few will be mentioned. Every rare book department is different from all others, so their needs for reference materials will vary.

There are two places in which such reference materials can be shelved: in the closed stacks or on shelves in a reading room (or a room adjacent to it) for patrons' use. What to put out for patrons will depend on the value and vulnerability of each item.

It may be practical to get more than one copy of a reference book to satisfy the needs of the general user and the department personnel. But the decision of where to place a single copy of a book needed by special collections and by patrons who want circulating copies must be made with care. Opting on the side of the rare book librarians could have a serious public relations fallout. Opting for the patrons and putting the books into the circulating collection could yield a good deal of inconvenience for the librarians. As I have noted, each special collections department will have its own idiosyncratic holdings, so it should choose for its own shelves the reference tools it needs to operate. The tools are for the staff as well as for the patrons.

Bibliographies are especially useful if the department has subject or author collections, for often there are no web-based definitive bibliographies for them. And while the Web is filled with dictionaries in all languages and translation sites and a host of other reference materials, many scholars want dictionar-

UC RIVERSIDE HAS a superb Guy Davenport collection. When the definitive bibliography of his writings was issued,* the rare book department ordered a copy. Because many of Davenport's writings were housed in special collections, and because we were trying to find copies of everything listed in the published book (and were comparing the listing in the bibliography with our own holdings), it was logical for us to keep the copy in the department.

But patrons who wanted to consult the book, and who could not get to the library during the hours that special collections was open, wanted to have a circulating copy. We had to decide where to put the copy we had bought. In the end, we bought three copies: one for patrons in special collections, one for the open stacks, and a third into which we entered a host of notes, like call numbers of our copies of items, descriptions of binding variants that the bibliographers had not mentioned, and other information that identified our copies, distinguishing them from the ones used as the basis for the bibliography. It would be impracticable to do this kind of multiple purchase for all our reference guides, but in this instance it made sense.

*Guy Davenport: A Descriptive Bibliography, 1947–1995, compiled by Joan Crane with the assistance of Richard Noble (Haverford, PA: Green Shade and James S. Jaffe Rare Books, 1996).

ies in book form beside them when they do research. Multitasking may be a great boon on a computer, but it can slow down a researcher who wants to look at a reference source or a foreign-language dictionary at the same time as she keys in her text.

Because there is a question about the reliability of the Web as a source of information, and because books usually go through several levels of vetting before they get into print, there might be a level of accuracy in an analog source that is wanting in a digital one. For some scholars this attribute is enough justification for wanting books to work from when they do their research.

The kinds of reference books a rare book department might want other than those related specifically to its collections include comprehensive encyclopedias, pricing guides (some of which are now only in digital form), genealogical materials (depending on the department's area in the country and clientele), domestic and foreign-language dictionaries (though, again, online dictionaries are easily available), appropriate concordances, historical dictionaries (Johnson's; the *OED*; *Merriam-Webster's International, Unabridged*, 3rd ed.; the *American Heritage*), gazetteers and books of historical maps, and national bibliographies.

If the special collections department is in a university, it may want a sampling of the classic texts on its shelves along with some classic guides to various aspects of culture: good editions of the works of Chaucer, Shakespeare, and Milton, among others; catalogues raisonné of artists; Vasari's *Lives*; a *Grove Dictionary of Music*; a classical dictionary identifying the Greek and Roman deities; and a host of other basic reference tools, many focused on the level 5 areas of collecting of the library and covering a broad array of topics likely to be of interest to the library's users. Also common in a special collections department is a section of books published by the faculty of the school (or the curators of the museum).

I have already mentioned pricing guides. In the past, before the Web changed the nature of bookselling, these guides were heavily used, naturally by the staff in special collections, but also by many people in the public who wanted to see if the books they had found in their attics, basements, and local thrift shops were going to enable them to retire early. More about these tools in chapter 10. Today pricing can be done from the Web, and most of these guides have been supplanted by websites like Abe-Books, BookFinder, and AddALL. Nonetheless, many patrons still turn to the special collections staff to ask, "What is this worth?"

We no longer need shelves upon shelves of the huge pricing guides we once needed (*Book Auction Records, American Book Prices Current, Bookman's Price Index*). But we still need to show patrons where they can find out what they are looking for. Librarians cannot appraise anything for patrons, but they can show them where the information is available. Also, sometimes having long runs of these pricing guides can be useful, for not all books offered to a librarian will be listed on the Web, and copies may be listed in the old books. Even finding a price for a copy that sold, say, fifty years ago may be more information than the librarian can find elsewhere. If for no other reason, this shows how uncommon a volume is. And there are ways to figure out what old prices are in today's currency.[31] For decades Peter Van Wingen's little pamphlet *Your Old Books*, published by the Library of Congress, was in print, and many rare book departments kept a stack of copies to give to their patrons. It is now online. This booklet is a good starting place. It is a good idea to have paper copies—freely downloaded from the Web—available in the department.[32]

Scanning and Loading onto the Web Images and Texts from the Collection

Times and technologies have changed considerably over the last twenty-five years, but the principle of what to make available for free to the public has not. In fact, this issue has heated up with the easy ability to capture and use images and texts afforded by computers and the Web. A library has a right to charge for services. (See chapter 8 for a fuller treatment of this subject.) By putting digitized images onto the

Web for all to use, the library is essentially giving them away for free, unless they are mounted in very low dpi (dots per inch) and have a watermark to protect them.

Although the aim of the library, as I have noted several times, is to help researchers of all kinds, the needs of the library must also be considered. Those who require pictures and text for their scholarship will be grateful to have them available digitally and instantly, rather than the old way, by ordering copies to be made and then waiting until the library gets around to making and sending them. The department should, however, weigh the convenience to the patron against the costs to the institution. And those costs can be considerable.

It takes time to select items for digitization and then to digitize them. It takes more time to get the images up on the Web. The long-term costs of maintaining the site must be factored in. And by making these images available, the librarian is alerting the public to the existence of the collection, which could increase reference activities. And finally, publication use of the materials scanned will generate more work from those needing permission to go to press. Granting permission may or may not generate income for the library. Even if the library does not charge for publication, it must send a communiqué to the scholar or publisher releasing the materials for use. If a fee is charged, an invoice must be generated and the payment must be processed. A request is often made at this point for the library to receive a free copy from the author or publisher of the volume in which the library's materials are printed. This request could bring in a copy of the book (or other medium), and that version will need to be cataloged and processed. All of this has costs.

The reward can be as simple as having the library's name acknowledged in the volume, or the publication could generate a good deal of publicity and even income if it promises to become a best-seller or a movie, in which case the library can require, as part of the permission cost, that the publisher or author give the institution a percentage of the profits from the production.

Sometimes patrons will ask for a text or a part (or all) of a collection to be scanned. If there is a good

> MANY YEARS AGO, before I was at the University of California, Riverside, a scholar from another university went to UCR's special collections department and asked to see some of the superb collection of the department's photographs of the Mexican Revolution. He selected many of them and asked for copies. A host of reproduction-quality prints was eventually sent to him, and he later published a book on the subject of the Mexican Revolution, reprinting a good many of the photographs. Nowhere in his book was it mentioned that the originals were at UCR, nor did he thank anyone from there. He presumably profited from the royalties of this publication, and UCR got no return on its "investment."
>
> When this scholar was finished with the prints, he gave them to another university, which put them into its special collections department. Further use of these images, published by other scholars, credited that university. Again, UCR was not mentioned and got no compensation at all from the use of the pictures.

reason to do so, the librarian, considering all the fiscal and copyright issues the particular collection poses, may do the digitization on whatever terms are appropriate, convenient, and agreeable to both parties. But it might be that the material the patron wants is at the bottom of the library's prioritization list for digitization.

In any event, the librarian should be aware of these issues when deciding whether to digitize materials. The initial digitization costs may be picked up by the library, shared by the two parties, or charged to the patron. This last option was not uncommon when microfilms were made. And for the films, many libraries did not "sell" the reels to the patron, they loaned them out as they would have done for a book. The film would go out with a note attached to it: "This film is the property of _____ University and must be returned by _____ [a particular date] to _____ [address]." A due date was included, along with a prohibition from reproducing the film or going to press without the permission of the owning institution. Though there was no way to monitor users to make sure they did not reproduce the film, there was nonetheless a formal contract signed by the borrower that might have been a deterrent.

We are in a new era. Technology has changed radically. If we choose to have a similar arrangement of lending texts and images, it is possible to send out DVDs or send files as attachments to e-mails that do not allow copying. Hence it may be better, for valuable materials that are digitized, to allow their use only from DVDs rather than from having them mounted on the Web. Or we can do as I have already indicated—mount them on the Web, but either not in full or in low resolution versions with watermarks so that users wanting reproducible images must get them from the library, at which time they can negotiate permissions and sign contracts for use.

Librarians, especially those in special collections, are often approached by a patron who says, "I'd like to have such and such a collection digitized. Why don't you just do it?" Patrons, not inculcated into the complexities of the library world, often do not understand the ramifications of what seems to them a simple solution: just digitize. Part of the job of the librarian is to be articulate about such matters and to be able to convey the problems to the patron. Many a scholar has said, "What would it cost? I'll cover the cost myself. I need the information." Researchers seem to believe that because they could digitize a document in a few moments, it would be easy for the librarian to do so, at little cost. But staff time and equipment costs, along with all the other considerations spoken of here, drive the price up and can make digitizing impractical. The goodwill we could generate by digitizing collections must be balanced with all the costs involved. A special collections librarian must be able to explain all the reasons for *not* digitizing and should do so in a way that does not insult or anger the patron.

In recent years, many institutions have given up on the idea that there is money to be made—or at least some costs to be recovered—by charging for

A SPECIAL COLLECTIONS department in which I formerly worked had a perplexing problem about twenty years ago. We owned the manuscript of an unpublished novel by an author who had enjoyed worldwide acclaim. Many movies had been made from his writings. The manuscript was signed with the name of a different author. The scholarly world was divided: was the name on the manuscript that of a different person, or was it an alias of this writer? There seemed to be no real consensus, and voices on both sides were strong and self-righteous. Scholars in both camps wanted us to relinquish the text to them, claiming variously that the author's publisher had given them the rights to his unpublished works and that the author's work should be in the public domain. But no scholar could prove these statements by producing any corroborating document.

Until we could find documentary evidence that Author B was really Author A (or not), we did not want to release the text to anyone. Author A's recently deceased wife had no documents to substantiate either position and probably did not know the truth, anyway. Regardless of whether some document existed that revealed the truth, the work would nonetheless still be under copyright because the author died well within the seventy-year protection window. Scholars on both sides wanted to get their hands on this text so they could publish it. The manuscript could have generated a great deal of interest—even enough to have led to a movie.

My university had spent a fortune to acquire the archive in which this manuscript was found. If there were profits to be made from it, they could have been substantial, and it would not have been inappropriate for the school to have shared in those profits.

We chose not to digitize and not to release the text to anyone until a good contract could be written that protected all parties and that allowed for the benefit of all involved. In this instance, digitizing and releasing the text could have led to the loss of remuneration, or, if we released the text but prohibited publication, we might have been sued because the university did not own the rights outright. And because we did not have control of the text, such a release could have been the equivalent of giving the text away to the first party who could get it into print. The institution would have profited not at all.

The main issue here—for this chapter—is that the library owes its patrons access to information but equally owes itself the rights and opportunities to capitalize on its holdings, especially those that have cost the library dearly and that it is spending resources on to maintain.

the copying of their holdings. If a collection or an item is already in digital form, they just let it go free of charge to the user. This practice is growing, but it is not yet universal.

Two benefits, however, of digitizing a collection are that the information will be available worldwide and that the original documents need no longer be handled. This last, of course, is a preservation issue.

> **MY OWN LIBRARY** is the repository of the original transcripts of the Salem witchcraft trials from the 1690s (most owned by the state, some by my library). They are fairly fragile and should not be handled too much. But they are fully digitized and up on the Web in good images. We almost never need to touch the originals, and the documents are grateful for this.

With the coming of the computer, as long ago as the 1980s, we heard the phrase "paperless society," coined in 1982 by F. W. "Wilf" Lancaster of the University of Illinois, who was talking about the possibility that almost every bit of information we had become used to seeing on paper could now—or in the near future—be storable and accessible in digital form. From the day he created that phrase, the amount of paper in use worldwide has gone up and up. The point for rare book librarianship is that many people have taken this phrase literally and expect that all the department's holdings will eventually be digitized. Even high-level administrators—in their ignorance—say that the library's collection will be digitized soon. What they should be saying is that the catalogs to the library's collections will be online. But word is out, and special collections personnel need to have a handy response for all the patrons who expect digital information to be sent to them immediately. (And we must educate our leaders about what digitization really is and inform them that we will not be digitizing our full collections soon. We will be making our cataloging information available in electronic form.)

The other consideration under the rubric "digitizing our collections" is that scanning is still an imperfect technology. It has its uses, and it can be wonderful for scholarship in many ways, but it is not cheap, nor is it permanent—at least not yet. Determining the costs of scanning is complicated. There are the personnel who must select items for the digitizing and carry out the work. There are hardware and software costs. And there is the cost of maintenance. With the rapid evolution in technology, with constant "upgrades" in speed and miniaturization and storage capacities, no machinery today is guaranteed to be around next week. Texts have to be migrated or emulated or copied from one platform to another. People have to do this, and people cost money.

For this book, it is sufficient to conclude that digitization is a great medium for access to information, especially for rare materials that exist in only one repository or in only a few places. But it is not a preservation medium and should not be looked at as such until we are sure that preservation of digital texts is proven. For special collections materials, librarians should digitize what they can justify copying (and can afford to copy), with the understanding that it is a temporary measure to increase access and that it has long-term costs and many short-term benefits: access, patron satisfaction, preservation of originals, public relations, a message that the department is on the cutting edge of the profession, and more.

Moving a Rare Book Library

Libraries could sit in their repositories for centuries. Or they could outgrow their space and need to be moved. The buildings they are in could become inadequate, get seriously damaged by natural forces, and need repair. A donor could come along and endow a new building (or a renovation of the old one). The institution housing the collection could move from one location to another. It is even possible for an institution like a public library to rethink its mission and decide to close its special collections department. These are just some of the reasons to move a rare book library.

Rather than go into fine detail about moving such a collection, this section will take a bird's-eye view, looking at the main issues that a special collections staff must contemplate.

The librarians must consider the nature of the move: its duration, the distance between the temporary (or permanent) facility and the present one, whether the entire collection needs to be moved or only a part of it, the possibility of shutting down operations completely during a temporary move, the opportunity to put parts of the collection into inaccessible storage, the need to have access to particular parts (or all) of the collection during the move, and so on.

In addition, if the budget can handle the cost, the institution should consider using a project manager to oversee all aspects of the move. This person should have expertise in such things as architecture (planning for the layout of the new space and perhaps for the renovation of the space being vacated, if that is the purpose of the move); bookshelves and other storage devices (cabinets and flat files, for example); HVAC systems; background checks, and other security measures; moving companies; and contracts. He must be good at public relations and staff management. And he must understand budgets—how to create and stay within them.

Of course, the librarians will not be alone in their endeavors; they will need to work with facilities personnel (the physical plant people), the institution's own and local security and police departments, preservation officers, people in the finance department (that is, those who keep the budgets and hold the purse strings), inside staff and outside vendors, and others.

Yet another part of this operation has to do with security. The actual details about the move—when it will take place and the route that will be taken—should be kept confidential. The lack of public knowledge will work to the library's advantage. That is, fine details of the move should be kept as secret as possible, with the staff admonished not to reveal to anyone outside the institution the date or the destination of the move. Sometimes it is not possible to withhold this information from the public. If the destination is a rented facility, the library may be able to write into the lease a confidentiality clause. No one needs to know when the rare materials will be out in the world (during the actual move) or where they are headed. Once the library is moved, open communication with the public is encouraged, especially if the library will be accessible for use while it is away from its home.

No move can be made without planning and preparation. The collection must be prepared for the operation, and teams of people must plan every part of the shift. The preparation is intellectual and physical. The intellectual part includes determining the number of linear feet that will be needed in the new or temporary facility, the configuration of the shelves and ranges, the order on the shelves that the collection will need to be put into, and so forth. The physical planning encompasses preparing items too shabby or weak to move, dealing with red rot and splitting joints, strengthening flimsy pamphlets, and handling other medical cases that need treatment to be given even half a chance to survive the trauma of a move.

SHRINK-WRAPPING

Several methods are available to prepare the collection physically, especially items that are fragile, deteriorating (to such an extent that a move would harm them more), with shaky bindings. Thin items can be put into sleeves of different kinds: paper or Mylar, for instance. Heavier items can be tied with soft tapes. But this approach still leaves them exposed. Phase boxes can be used to house all kinds of materials. A few of them would not take up an appreciable amount of space, but hundreds of them would be expensive, take lots of time to create, and take up significant linear feet on the shelves.

Shrink-wrapping library materials might be the best solution. A number of shrink-wrapping machines, tools, and systems are available, from inexpensive to costly setups, from hundreds to thousands of dollars. If the collection is large and has many items that need special handling for a move, this method of preparation is ideal. The wrapping consolidates all parts of the book—covers, textblock, dust jackets, and so forth. It encapsulates leather covers that have red rot, protecting workers and other library materials that could come into contact with the leather. It allows for safe handling of items: taking them from and returning them to shelves, surviving big moves. The shrink-wrap is easy to remove if an item is needed for a researcher. Most systems place a hole in the film so that no microenvironment forms inside the wrapping. One system inserts a plastic tab (like a pull-string) that facilitates removing the shrink-wrap. Once an item is used, it takes only seconds and costs only pennies to re-shrink-wrap it.

Stiff, thin boards can be used to back an item to be shrink-wrapped. A thin, flimsy, floppy pamphlet, for instance, can be backed by a thin board to keep it upright and make it easily movable.

And the cost to shrink-wrap a piece, even factoring in the cost of the machinery and the film, is only a small fraction of what it would cost to make a phase box for it or to buy archival envelopes or sleeves. After the move, the items can remain shrink-wrapped indefinitely.[33]

SHELF-READS

Every library should do a shelf-read periodically—maybe once every five or ten years, though this task is often put off for financial reasons: most libraries do not budget for it, and the staff is usually so overworked and the shelf-read so time-consuming that figuring it into daily operations is difficult or impossible.[34] A move is the ideal opportunity to do this.

A shelf-read will allow the staff to identify gaps where there should be none, to discover misshelved books, and—because the inventory requires looking at every item—to identify materials that need conservation work. Hence a Collection Condition Report can be a useful by-product of this important activity.

Barcoding of the collection could be added to the shelf-read, once again because both activities require handling every item. Whether, and how, to barcode a special collection must be decided upon. (See the next section of this chapter.) Presumably the move will be done under the scrutiny and with the planning of the department personnel, but by professionals who specialize in such moves. Regardless of who does the move, a pre- and a post-move inventory should be done to make sure that all items identified at the original library wind up in the new facility—and that they are shelved in the proper order.

CLEANING

The close attention paid to the collection at this time will also allow for another task that is often neglected: cleaning. Special collections departments

---

AT UC RIVERSIDE, we had serious earthquake damage to the special collections, especially thousands of heavy, leather-bound eighteenth-century books that came crashing down from top shelves. Red rot had loosened many covers; joints that were starting to split wound up splitting all the way, with covers hitting the floor and flying in one direction while the textblocks they covered flew in other directions. The sewing on many textblocks gave way, creating two or more clusters of fascicles as the signatures flew hither and thither. In one earthquake alone, over 4,500 volumes were seriously damaged, with hundreds of others getting bumped and shaken.

We were able to match up most of the covers with their textblocks. But we couldn't just leave them on the shelves like that. Our preservation officer got a shrink-wrap machine, and we were able to consolidate all the discrete pieces into a single capsule of archival plastic sheeting. In doing this, we also shrink-wrapped other books and pamphlets that were falling apart. By the time the FEMA money became available to do some conservation work on the collection, many months had passed. We were able to identify all the items that were to go for conservation by locating on our shelves the shrink-wrapped pieces. The conservation work took the better part of three

and a half years, and in that time all the shrink-wrapped volumes were happily ensconced on the shelves. If a patron needed to use one of them, we pulled the tab, removed the wrapping in seconds without adding any damage to the book, and re-shrink-wrapped it after use for only pennies.

Further, we were able to put tall, bookmark-shaped, archival paper inserts into the wrapping on the spines (or, for thin volumes, on the covers) of the books, showing the call numbers. Keeping the books on the shelves in proper order was not in the least hindered by the wrapping. Shrink-wrapping may be a good option for special collections, especially departments with many old and damaged books.

have seldom-visited shelves where dust has collected to measurable thicknesses. A cleaning makes sense: the aim is to move the collection, not the dirt.

PROFESSIONAL MOVERS

The selection of a moving company is critical. For any library collection many a good library mover can be employed. But special collections moves will require careful scrutiny. It is imperative to choose movers who have experience with rare books. They should be bonded, and the library may want to conduct an additional background check on all hired workers. They should be required to wear uniforms and badges that identify them as part of the hired moving company. A library-employed guard should check the badges regularly for everyone working in, entering, and exiting the building. (At one library, Stephen Blumberg, one of the most prolific book thieves in history, dressed up like a mover and helped himself, unimpeded, to boxes and boxes of rare books.)

In preparation for the move, all the holdings should be boxed (with the boxes sealed and barcoded) or placed on shelved moving trucks. The company should have the proper book trucks, and the filled trucks should be wrapped in plastic sheeting to keep books from falling off and being removed during the operation. The trucks should obviously not have any materials or be shaped in any way that would harm what is put onto them. It is possible to double-stack books (that is, double-deep) on the book-truck shelf, but this approach should be avoided for rare materials. The trucks should have large casters and should be stable enough not to be top heavy. If a truck falls over, even if its contents are wrapped in heavy plastic, the items on it could be damaged.

Only a library staff member should scan the barcodes when the library's holdings are being moved out. And the staff should also recheck the barcodes when the library is being set up in the destination facility.

COST

One key consideration is the cost of the move. All the activities that the move requires will cost money. The special collections department, volume for volume, will cost more to move than will the general collection because rare materials require special handling, perhaps separate insurance, and certainly more security-based oversight, along with increased staffing during the move (mostly security guards). Any time any part of a collection is out of the protective, secure walls of its home, it is exposed to damage or theft. This is especially so for entire collections. Extra scrutiny and even extra security personnel must be employed until the collection is nestled again into a safe environment.

The parent institution should determine the full expense of the move and should budget for it, not stinting on anything when rare materials are at stake. Cutting corners on the move to save money is asking for trouble.

CONFIGURING THE NEW SPACE

No one knows the department's collections and operations as well as the librarians who work in it. For this reason, the staff must be the central planners of the move from beginning to end. They will know what the new facility should look like: how to lay it out, where to put stacks and offices and workstations, where the most valuable parts of the collection should go, how books move from shelves to patrons and back, which parts of the collection get the greatest use and should thus be situated most conveniently for paging, where the reading room should be and how it should be configured for maximum use and security, where offices should be and how they too should be laid out, and so forth. Librarians should be involved in the selection of the new space and its fitting-out. Experts like fire and police personnel, security companies, and architects and contractors may be involved as well, but all these must work closely with the librarians in all aspects of the move.

Usually, the space to be moved to must have at least as many linear feet of shelving as does the old library. But experience shows that this desideratum is usually not enough. A move will entail a good deal of activity that will necessitate extra shelving and swing space. Further, if the move is to allow a renovation that will increase space for the collection, it makes sense to allow the librarians to get the items onto the shelves, with the added linear feet, at the front end of the move, not when the collection will be returning to the renovated space.

Before the move, the staff should survey the new facility and should mark every empty shelf with a code or designation that shows where every shelf of books from the old library will be placed. If possible, therefore, the shelves in the new library should be at least the same length as those of the library being vacated. Longer shelving is not a problem; shorter shelving is. Also, because of the nature of special collections, the new structure should have swing space built in. Setting up in the new facility will be a challenge, and it will be useful to have about 20 to 30 percent more shelf space there than the old library had. Boxed items, volumes being integrated into the collection, and other materials will need to be put onto shelving somewhere while space for them is created in the new library. This is especially true in rare book libraries with backlogs of uncataloged items. Even with only a small amount of swing space, the librarians should carefully measure the linear and cubic feet of the collection so they will know exactly how much space they will need in the new facility.

One old rule of thumb is that libraries should not use top and bottom shelves. The top shelves are difficult to reach, especially for short people, and the bottom shelves are vulnerable to floods and mops and dust. But most libraries use these shelves. Space is almost always in short supply, and when librarians look at tight shelves and need additional room to add new items to the collection, a shift to a top or bottom shelf is much more convenient and expedient than is a shift of shelves east or west in the collection.

So when the shelves in the new facility are being measured and plotted out for receiving the collection, it may be well to allow for an extra 20 to 25 percent linear feet, if the budget and the new facility allow. This can be accomplished by leaving empty shelves regularly through the stacks in the new facility. Staff members and their successors will appreciate this foresight in the years to come.

AT THE PHILLIPS Library, with a brilliant project manager, I oversaw a move of the entire collection from the buildings that have housed the collection for more than 150 years to a temporary facility off campus. We were able to hire a company to help us with the inventory and barcoding. With a small staff, we would have taken more than a year and a half to do the project, but the vendor was able to do it in about five months—for a collection of nearly a half million volumes and vast manuscript holdings. One decision we made was to barcode each volume—even those from multivolume sets—but not to label every bound volume of serials. Their own volume numbering alone was inventory control enough. Each institution must decide how to do manuscripts (by the box? by the folder? some other way?) and all the department's other media: photographs, ephemera, scrapbooks, glass slides, and so forth. Items with no online record will need a barcode label on the volume and one on the shelf list card (if paper cards are still in place). All the barcoding details must be worked out before this phase of the project begins.

Shelves in the new library must be clearly labeled as to what items will be placed on them. This mapping of the new stacks requires the precision of a mathematician and the foresight of a librarian who does not want to be terribly inconvenienced by a poorly situated collection.

Another consideration may be the furniture and other non-library-collection objects that have to be moved or jettisoned. Maps and charts, broadsides, and prints and drawings, for instance, are likely to have their own cabinets, and the department may have old, important furniture, lamps, carpets, paintings, sculpture, vitrines, and other such things that must be moved as well. All this must be carefully planned for: what to leave behind, what to take, where it will be placed in the new library, and so forth. Also, space must be carefully planned for the library personnel who will move with the collection. They should all have adequate desks, work spaces, and offices. And, as I mentioned earlier, the new facility must have top-quality security and a good HVAC system.

SELECTING A BUILDING SITE

In its selection, the new building, if possible, should be located away from geographical hazards (bodies of water that could overflow, rivers that could flood), or other dangerous places (next door to a facility that is a fire hazard or near a restaurant which could bring infestations of insects or rodents). The neighborhood, the proximity to a fire station and police, the availability of reliable electrical, water, and sewer services, good street lighting at night, street services in the winter, sufficient and affordable parking for all who will be using the facility, convenient public transportation, and other features of the site must be considered. Staff and patrons need to get there, park, and get into the building, and they must be safe, as must the collection itself.

TEMPORARY MOVES

As I noted earlier in this chapter, one consideration in a temporary move is whether the collection will be accessible or out of commission during the time away. If the collection will be closed and no researchers will have access to it, then boxing up everything and putting it into compact storage will save a great deal of money. But the public relations fallout could be disastrous. Further, if there is no access—no library activity—what does the institution do with its staff in the down time? A preferable choice, though more costly, is to put everything on shelves and provide at least curtailed (if not full) access. If there is to be any access at all, planners should consider which parts of the collection will need to be kept closest to the hands of the staff.

If the public-service end of the operation is curtailed, the staff that is released from this activity can be used in a variety of ways during the temporary relocation. After the move to the temporary facility, it might be a good idea to do an inventory to make sure that all items made the trip and that all the collection materials were placed where they were meant to be on the new shelves. The staff who are released from full-time reference work could attend to tasks that are often put off because of a lack of personnel, such as creating finding aids for manuscript collections, processing archival materials, doing simple conservation work that has been put off for decades (putting photographs into archival sleeves, for instance), creating informational pamphlets on individual collections, and similar activities that will increase access, security, and preservation conditions for the department's holdings.

A good map of the present collection must be made and a coordinating map of the shelves and offices and work spaces of the temporary facility must also be drawn up, showing where everything will go. Heightened security must also be worked into the plan. A good moving company must be engaged, and the whole staff should be involved in some way with the selection of this company. Choosing the optimum time for the move—if there is some flexibility—may make the operation go smoothly. Try not to do a move in the dead of winter if the library is in a part of the country in which the weather gets immorally cold.

Growth space (additional space figured into the shelving) must be added into the planning. This is a golden opportunity to help librarians of the future. Shelving in all level 4 and 5 areas of the collection will probably be crowded. This is the time to open up some space for future expansion of the collection.

And there is also a public relations angle. Considering all that must be done, we know that services will be disrupted for some time—possibly weeks, months, or even years. Patrons needing to use the collection will not be happy to have access restricted in any way. The library must do appropriate PR long in advance of the move, putting a positive spin on the operation. Rather than flatly announcing that "the special collections department will be shut for X amount of time," the notice should say something like, "The library is pleased to announce a major renovation project that will improve facilities, increase access, and be of great benefit to our patrons."[35] Patrons who are inconvenienced by the closure will not be any the less disappointed, but at least the library should try to make the best of the situation by preparing users for the disappointment and trouble they will experience at the library's inaccessibility.

Many of the observations in this section about a library move apply to any library, special or not. But rare book libraries are likely to have a particular kind of patron: a scholar who travels from afar to do specialized research in the only place it can be done, given the nature of rare book libraries' holdings. If the department has enough lead time, it should try to contact all the patrons it anticipates might want to use the collection during its downtime. Notices should be sent out, if possible, and certainly a statement should be prominently displayed on the department's website that details the operation and the closure dates, as near as they can be determined. All patrons using the department in person should be given a flyer explaining the situation.

DEALING WITH ANXIETY

One aspect of the move that is left out of many discussions of moving collections, but that should be a serious part of every such discussion, is the anxiety that is generated over such an operation. The project is a test of wills, a challenge to sanity, and a trial of patience. Few people want cataclysm in their lives, and a move of a special collections department is certainly a form of cataclysm, no matter how carefully it is planned for and how many resources are available for the operation. When staff members know that a move is pending, the daunting reality for many is that they must now add to their regular routine of running the library a whole new set of duties related to the move. They will work for months, sometimes for more than a year, in preparation, often with no visible signs of the actual move. They must curtail the services they offer to patrons, at some point closing down the library altogether, for however long it takes to make the move and reopen in the new library. Many librarians are dedicated to the researchers who use the collection, knowing that service is their main responsibility, and being shut down can be psychologically difficult for them to handle. A good manager will know how to get the staff through the project with equanimity and productiveness.

Change is not easy for some people to deal with. And change at the level of such a move can be traumatic to some people. One librarian might take the move in stride and embrace with gusto the entire operation, with an eye on the prize: the renovated space that awaits at the end of the project. Another

might be frozen with fear, troubled by having to shift from a comfortable routine to a realm of activity entirely alien to him, with workloads completely different from and seemingly more burdensome than the one he was familiar with and accustomed to.

This is not overstating the case. Some people handle such a challenge with aplomb and eagerness; some do not. The manager must prepare the staff for the changes, for the increased activity in some realms (preparing the collection for the move, doing a shelf-read, and so forth), and for the decreased activity in others (cutting back on reference or cataloging duties, for instance). One good way to lessen the anxiety is to involve the staff in as much of the process as possible. Meetings with all staff or with key ones for particular parts of the project will engage them and let them know that their concerns are being considered.

Library school courses generally do not prepare students for moves. But with a great deal of logic, foresight, circumspection, compassion, fortitude, and diligence, the staff should be able to get through the move safely, with no mishaps, and without a psychiatrist.

Barcoding the Collection

Barcoding is for security as much as it is for inventory control. Barcoding can be expensive, and it is not for many collections. But if the library is contemplating a move, this may be a good time to use barcodes. As I noted earlier, because a shelf-read should accompany the move, and because the inventory requires handling every item, putting the barcodes on during this operation could be an economical way to improve security and read the shelves. Further, the barcoding will allow a relatively inexpensive inventory assessment just after each move, checking that all items that were moved made it to the new facility and were shelved in the proper order.

Barcodes can be placed onto endsheets, bookplates, or flags (bookmark-like strips) that are laid into the books and manuscripts. Linda A. Blaser, the senior book conservator at the Folger Shakespeare

Library, came up with a system of placing the barcodes onto polyethylene strapping that is wrapped around the rear covers of the books.[36] The library was using this strapping to hold books to mounts in exhibition cases. She mentions that the straps are "quick and easy to make" and that, at the time she wrote her article, "this method has served us well for the past three years. All of the original polyethylene straps are still in place."

Barcodes can be used with great ease on boxes, sleeves, and other kinds of housing for manuscripts and for the kinds of housing used for photographs. They are useful for circulation records (items off the shelves can be tracked as being at a conservation lab, in the reading room, on a curator's desk, in an exhibition, or elsewhere) and for shelf-reads. Regardless of their up-front costs, in the long run they are economical and practical.

Barcodes should, of course, be placed on each item in such a way that does not damage the piece and does not cover up any information the item contains. If they can be placed externally, reading them will save time over those that have to be placed inside a volume or box. Though barcodes are a relatively old technology (they have been around since at least the 1950s), they are still a useful tool for rare book departments.[37]

■ ■ ■

This chapter has looked at many aspects of running a rare book department. More information on this topic will be presented in chapter 7, where security is the focus, and in chapter 12, which deals with preservation and conservation. In fact, the effective running of the department is dependent on the librarians' knowing a great deal of information about all the issues presented here, so the topic will continue to show up throughout this book.

The concentration thus far has been on rare books and special collections, but as chapter 3 shows, archives are a close cousin, maybe even a brother, and must be looked at in some detail.

NOTES

1. The present "Code of Ethics for Special Collections Librarians" can be found at www.rbms.info/standards/code_of_ethics.shtml. It is instructive to look at the first two versions to see how this third iteration has evolved. The present text cannot justify a long historical look at the development of the latest edition of the ethical guidelines. Some of the prohibitions and proscriptions of the first version raised a good deal of ire among special collections people. One statement, for example, did not permit rare book librarians to be collectors because their collecting could be seen as a conflict of interest. Clearly this was too restrictive a prohibition. Later versions reflect much more workable standards of conduct.

2. It is true that particular extraordinary circumstances might arise that are not covered by the RBMS Code of Ethics guidelines, but for the most part, this document is a tremendously useful guide.

3. The full name of the act (hence its long acronym) is Uniting and Strengthening America by Providing Appropriate Tools Required to Intercept and Obstruct Terrorism Act of 2001.

4. One might be reminded of Holbrook Jackson's encomium on the delights book lovers get from books, expressed in his *Anatomy of Bibliomania* (New York: Farrar, Straus and Company, 1950; rpt. New York: Avenel Books, 1981). See, for example, "Part 3. The Pleasure of Books" (pp. 50–61) and "Part 31. The Five Ports of Book-Love" (pp. 608–20).

5. With projects like Google Books, an increasing number of texts are appearing on the Internet. This may relieve the pressure on some special collections departments to get items repaired to a usable condition. But that does not mean that items falling apart on the shelves (those that have been digitized and are available on the Web) should be forgotten about. A comprehensive special collections plan of operation should include the acquisition of resources for conservation. Availability of digital surrogates may influence the librarian's prioritization for conservation, but these surrogates should not remove altogether a damaged volume from a "needs conservation work" list.

6. There is a broad literature on collection development policy. And many institutions' policies are available online. One good source to consult is the *Guidelines for a Collection Development Policy Using the Conspectus Model* issued by the International Federation of Library Associations and Institutions

Section on Acquisition and Collection Development; the text was written by Dora Biblarz with the assistance of other members of the Acquisition and Collection Development Standing Committee in 2001. See http://archive.ifla.org/VII/s14/nd1/gcdp-e.pdf. Citations to this source will be to Biblarz.

7. See appendix 2 in this book, "Levels of Collecting and the RLG Conspectus."

8. One provocative article on collection development is Richard Landon's "Embracing the Flood: Questions about Collecting Twentieth-Century Non-Literary Works," *Rare Books & Manuscripts Librarianship* 2.2 (Fall 1987): 81–93. The full text is available online at http://rbm.acrl.org/content/rbml/2/2/81.full .pdf+html.

9. Getting more than one bid gives the library a choice—usually of the vendor with the best service. It also allows the department to negotiate lower prices (e.g., higher discounts) and other services. The head of collection development at UC Riverside was able to negotiate a good discount rate from a vendor along with a brand new service. When a book came out in paperback and hardbound, if the price difference was great enough, the vendor would sell the paperback to the library, but only after putting a hard cover on it, for far less than the hardbound version of the text would have cost. The practice, devised by the head of collection development, became a standard in the field of librarianship. This shows the power that a good contract between a vendor and a library can have.

10. In chapter 8 we shall look at the notion of the rare book department as collector, and we shall discuss book values. One major component of a book's value is its condition; another is its dust jacket.

11. See chapter 7 on security.

12. Cataloging departments are usually centralized in some technical services area, generally not far from acquisitions and the office that makes the payments to vendors. It may be the cataloging department's policy to do all its work in this technical services department. This puts rare books (and all others) at risk, for such areas are generally not protected with the same level of security as are special collections departments. Rare book librarians should try to convince the head of cataloging to allow the rare book catalogers to work in the special collections department, and they should make a work space just for these catalogers. If this cannot be accomplished, the rare book librarian should at least train those in technical services to be cautious about the rare materials near them. Books from special collections that are in the technical services (i.e., cataloging)

area should be housed with a higher level of security than that provided for books destined for the open stacks.

13. The need for special cataloging of rare materials has been recognized for decades. As Stalker and Dooley point out: "BDRB [the Bibliographical Description of Rare Books] had been compiled and published by the Library of Congress in 1981 as a response to the adoption of AACR2 [*Anglo-American Cataloguing Rules*, 2nd edition] (1978) and the publication of the first ISBD(A) [International Standard Bibliographic Description] (1980)." Laura Stalker and Jackie Dooley, "Descriptive Cataloging and Rare Books," *Rare Books & Manuscripts Librarianship* 7.1 (Spring 1992): 7–23; this statement is on p. 7. See http:// rbm.acrl.org/content/rbml/7/1/7.full.pdf+html. The current standard, DCRM (Descriptive Cataloging of Rare Materials), is beyond the purview of the present text. See http://rbms.info/dcrm.

14. See http://rbms.info/committees/bibliographic _standards/controlled_vocabularies. For more on the thesauri, see appendix 1 of this book.

15. One of the aims of the present volume is to discuss all the areas covered by the thesauri. The overarching question this book seeks to answer is, What do those working with rare books need to know?

16. See chapter 9, "Bibliography."

17. The website to consult is www.loc.gov/coll/nucmc/ about.html. The site says,

> The mission of the NUCMC program is to provide and promote bibliographic access to the nation's documentary heritage. This mission is realized by NUCMC production of cataloging describing archival and manuscript collections held by eligible repositories located throughout the United States and its territories. The program's mission is further realized by the provision of free searching, via NUCMC gateways, of archival and manuscript cataloging in OCLC WorldCat.

18. See www.ala.org/ala/mgrps/divs/acrl/standards/ selectransfer.cfm. This citation is to the most recent (2008) version of these guidelines. The document should be consulted by anyone creating such a policy.

19. Samuel Streit, "Going, Going, Gone: Case Studies in Library Deaccessioning," *Rare Books & Manuscripts Librarianship* 12.1 (Spring 1997): 21–28. This statement is on p. 21. For the full text of this excellent article, see http://rbm.acrl.org/ content/rbml/12/1/21.full.pdf.

20. That, at any rate, is the reasoning of some in the profession. Many librarians believe that digitized materials should be retained for several reasons, not

the least of which is that a digital copy is not a true substitute for the original. Also, the longevity of the digital version is uncertain, and the accuracy of the digitization may be compromised, so the availability of the original is important.

21. It was a long-standing practice to remove textblocks from their covers, discard the covers, chop off the folds at the gutters of the books, and microfilm the books; then the textblocks themselves were sometimes discarded.

22. In some instances the library may wish to make and retain a copy of the deaccessioned material. This possibility may be accounted for in the deaccession policy.

23. With all good intentions, reporters like a good story—and one that generates controversy is particularly juicy. The potential for raising ire and exposing a possibly controversial issue (as deaccessioning is) may lead a reporter to write a story that is not favorable to the library. Also, most reporters have no special training in the library world and may not see the practicality and necessity of deaccessioning. Under the guise of impartiality, many a reporter tells a biased story. Thorough explanations to the media about why weeding is in the best interests of the library may head off bad publicity for the library.

24. These recommendations presume that the materials were part of a gift. They may also apply if the items were acquired by purchase, for, in some purchase situations, sellers may place restrictions on the goods. Some librarians will say that the effort it takes to locate the family that donated materials earmarked for weeding is not worth doing. It opens the possibility that the heirs will be unhappy about the decision, and this could lead to some bad publicity. The alternative is to deaccession silently and hope that the family does not show up at the library asking to see the donated items. In either scenario, the librarian runs the risk of an unpleasant encounter.

25. *Guidelines for the Interlibrary Loan of Rare and Unique Materials*, RBMS, 2004, www.ala.org/acrl/standards/rareguidelines.cfm. This document has been superseded by the new guidelines: *ACRL/RBMS Guidelines for Interlibrary and Exhibition Loan of Special Collections Materials*, approved by the ACRL Board of Directors, January 2012, www.ala.org/acrl/standards/specialcollections.

26. For three thoughtful articles on interlibrary loan, see *Rare Books & Manuscripts Librarianship* 3.2 (Fall 1988): 107–30, http://rbm.acrl.org/content/

rbml/2/2/125.full.pdf+html. The articles are Thomas V. Lange, "Alternatives to Interlibrary Loan," pp. 107–11; H. Thomas Hickerson and Anne R. Kenney, "Expanding Access: Loan of Original Materials in Special Collections," pp. 113–19; and James Woolley, "Special Collections Lending: A Reader's View," pp. 121–30.

27. See www.ala.org/ala/mgrps/divs/acrl/standards/borrowguide.cfm. This site publishes the 2005 version of these guidelines.

28. Chapter 12 of the present text has a section on packing and shipping of rare books.

29. The 2012 guidelines cited in note 25 above contain an excellent appendix (Appendix 2: "AAM General Facility Report"). This American Association of Museums document discusses the elements of a full facilities report that librarians must be aware of. It delineates what librarians must learn about institutions asking to borrow materials. Appendix 4 of the same 2012 guidelines discusses reliable exhibition loan agreements.

30. A small tidbit: have patrons *print* the information on the call slip clearly, including their names. The name of the user can be crucial if an item goes missing. Illegible slips are useless.

31. See, for example, "The Inflation Calculator," which "adjusts any given amount of money for inflation, according to the Consumer Price Index, from 1800 to 2012," www.westegg.com/inflation.

32. See www.rbms.info/yob.shtml. The pamphlet is in the public domain, so no permissions are needed to reproduced it and hand it out.

33. The National Library of Australia had a website titled PRESERconVersATION that included the following statement:

> **Shrink Wrapping: Why Books Love It!**
>
> Imagine . . . if only one book out of every twelve thousand in the Library's collections gets damaged each month, that means over five thousand books would need preservation treatment each year.
>
> The number of items that require treatment of some sort, multiplied by the cost of such treatment gives us a figure of astronomical proportions. So obviously, full treatment of every item by Preservation Services is not possible and we have to find some other solution to this problem.
>
> This is where shrink-wrapping is so useful. It is a quick and cheap way of reducing further deterioration of books that cannot be fixed immediately.
>
> Shrink-wrapping involves surrounding the book in a special plastic and placing it in a

machine that gives it a quick blast of heat to make the plastic shrink without affecting the book. . . . This makes the plastic fit snugly around the book without sticking to it, prevents losing broken pieces and provides some support for the item.

So you can see that we are not neglecting to care for our collections because we use shrink-wrapping. It is helping us to care for as much of them as possible.

Many libraries are using shrink-wrapping as a preservation and conservation tool. The method has been in use for rare books for decades. In 1993, Janice Stagnitto published "The Shrink Wrap Project at Rutgers University Special Collections and Archives" (*The Book and Paper Group Annual* 12 [Fall 1993], http://cool.conservation-us.org/coolaic/sg/bpg/annual/v12/bp12-13.html).

34. Rather than doing a full shelf-read, the library can do it in small, discrete parts, over a period of years.

35. I am reminded of a recent message I got from my credit card company telling me that my interest rates were going up 2 percentage points. When I called to ask about it, the bank representative made a big point, over and over, of saying how great it was that the rates were not going up 5 percent. "The bank considered raising the rates to 12.99 percent," she said with enthusiasm and optimism, "but we decided to keep the customers' interests foremost in our thinking, so we chose not to go up that high." Her message several times was that the bank had the interests of its patrons in mind at all times and that the decision makers were doing us a favor. We should be thanking them. Such a message is hard to convey with a straight face (she was on the other end of a phone conversation), and it was equally difficult to feel as if I were being given a boon and should be tremendously grateful for the bank's kindness.

36. See Linda A. Blaser, "Barcoding at the Folger Shakespeare Library," *Book and Paper Group Annual* 19 [2000], http://cool.conservation-us.org/coolaic/sg/bpg/annual/v19/bp19-28.html.

37. See "Barcode," Wikipedia, http://en.wikipedia.org/wiki/Barcode.

CHAPTER 3

ARCHIVES

Its Relation to the Special Collections Department
and Its Role in the Institution

VERY INSTITUTION HAS A HISTORY, AND THAT HISTORY IS USU-
ally recorded on paper—and, more recently, in digital form.[1] The
record might consist of an actual prose document delineating the
details of the organization's founding and rise, personnel and activities, and so forth, but the history also resides in all the paperwork
that the institution has generated over its existence pertaining to
everything that people thought was necessary to record: personnel records, payroll
information, hiring and firing records, fiscal data of all kinds, records of activities
and events, correspondence, meeting agendas and minutes, proclamations from the
administration, legal papers of many kinds, and a huge range of other materials.
Some things are part of the permanent record of the institution, some are slated to
be discarded after a set period.

These collections, reflecting the history of the establishments, are archives. Also,
when organizations die, they may leave their papers to other institutions. A library
may have its own institution's archives, and it may have the papers of other organizations. These papers could be treasure troves of information. So it behooves the
keepers of these papers to process and organize them and make available the information they contain in much the same way that they handle manuscript collections
or monographs.

Throughout the academic world the terms *archives* and *special collections* are
linked in department names at hundreds of institutions, with the word *archives* preceding *special collections* about half the time. Although the functions of the two
services overlap to a degree, they are really different departments with different
methods of operation. Their primary directives are the same: linking scholars and
other users with the information they need. Both functions achieve this goal by processing information-bearing materials in such a way that patrons can learn of the
existence of the materials through some kind of searchable record. Librarians do
this through cataloging. Archivists do it through the creation of finding aids. Once

MY FORMAL TITLE at the University of California, Riverside, was Head of Special Collections and University Archivist. The library at Northeastern University in Boston has a department called Archives and Special Collections. Virginia Commonwealth University has a library department called Special Collections and Archives. Oklahoma State University's department is called Special Collections and University Archives. At Brandeis University it is University Archives & Special Collections. And so on through hundreds of other schools, which link these two departments into a single entity.

a finding aid for a collection is created, the archivist must then create a cataloging record to put the information about the collection online.

Archives on its very surface denotes the materials that an institution generates in its daily operations—materials that all point to the operation and history of that body. But an archives may also contain collections that are generated by people who are (or were) related to the institution. For example, a professor at a college may have her own files of papers: thirty-five years of syllabi for the classes she taught, copies of exams and quizzes, lecture notes, research materials related to her scholarship and publications, other handouts, copies of excellent essays of former students, and so on. When she retires from the college she gives her cabinets' contents to the institution, and they wind up in the archives. The cabinets may also contain papers other than those relating to her relationship to the college. For instance, there may be folders of personal correspondence, boxes of papers relating to her hobbies of calligraphy and bookbinding, and a collection of political buttons relating to presidential elections. None of these is related to the college except in that she owned or generated them and that they were among her papers. Whether these things wind up in the college archives is a judgment call by the archivist. If they do (and many institutions' archives have just this kind of material), they may be kept in the archives because there is no other logical place to house them, except perhaps in the special collections department,

which, as I noted in chapter 1, often winds up with things that are not "rare books or manuscripts" but that can find no other logical home.

The role of special collections in an institution and for its wider audience has been treated in the preceding chapters. Archives have their own roles to play. As I have noted earlier, the focus here is on the branch of archives that preserves the documentary history of the institution and, perhaps, the papers of its employees. There are also manuscripts and other papers of businesses or families not related to the institution, or materials of any other noninstitutional entity. These last categories of materials belong to the special collections department as part of its manuscript holdings. Archivists are busy enough recording the history of the institution—they do not need the papers of outside bodies to complicate their work. But these kinds of papers must be processed in much the same way that archival materials are, so they may wind up in the archives anyway.

It is clear that one of the primary jobs of the archivist is selection—deciding what to keep and what to jettison when a new collection comes through the doors. The responsibilities of an archivist can be summarized in four words: Appraisal, Arrangement, Description, Delivery.

At some of the larger and better-resourced institutions, the functions of special collections and archives are carried out in separate departments. Most organizations, however, primarily to save money, link the two operations under a single head, eliminating a whole office-full of director and staff,

I KNEW A head of special collections who was a trained archivist, and archives was clearly where his heart was. His department had a smooth-running, fully responsible archival operation, but as a rare book librarian he was less assiduous, and it showed in the way cataloging was not being done and acquisitions were not coming in. Vice versa, I have known many special collections heads whose other title was Archivist but whose activities had little or nothing to do with archives. It is a rare person equally versed in both disciplines who runs his department with a balanced emphasis.

but this structure runs the risk of having the person in charge of the joined department coming from one of these two disciplines, and thus concentrating his efforts on only one of them.

There are administrations at institutions with rare book libraries and archives (every institution has archives) that are not at all interested in one or the other of these important disciplines. This is a shame, because usually both of these units are vitally important to the institution, with an equal vitality, and they both deserve to be as fully functioning as they can be. If only one of them is emphasized, the patrons (internal and external) are the losers. If they are both supported strongly, everyone is the beneficiary.

ADMINISTRATORS ARE COGNIZANT of the bottom line, and they can save money by not having an archives, with its archivists and hardware, software and supplies. But this is shortsighted in one key aspect of the unit's operations: its own legacy. If an administrator wants her accomplishments to be commemorated (or even merely understood) someday, she should understand that such information is recorded in the institutional archives.

No matter how small or seemingly insignificant an organization is, and no matter how little importance the organization (that is, its administration) might place on the paperwork it has generated, in the long run—and that could be centuries—there is likely to be someone doing research who will profit from its archives. The importance of archives to an institution cannot be overemphasized. It is the organization's memory, its explanations for its

being, a record of an enterprise that once flourished in a village or city (and may still be going strong). An organization's historical documents should be maintained with the same intelligence and careful oversight as are the materials we find in special collections departments. And this maintenance should be done—if resources permit—by a trained archivist who understands appraisal, records management, processing procedures, the importance of retention schedules and deaccessioning, the need for access, and other basic preservation and conservation issues. It is almost certain that the institution itself will benefit from having its archives in order, accessible, and in good physical condition. It is likely that others will benefit as well.

Further, although we think about archives in places like universities, museums, historical societies and athenaeums, and religious bodies, for instance, an archive can exist anywhere there are documents being generated by and about any organization. A small commercial business generates papers that show its financial and personnel history. All kinds of profit-making and nonprofit organizations generate paperwork that record their activities over the life of the enterprise. Some of this paperwork may be valueless, or it may contain sensitive information that should not be made public for legal or personal reasons. But some of the papers may contain valuable research information for the present and the future. Law firms, doctors' offices and hospitals, shoe-repair shops, artists' co-ops, and thousands of other kinds of operations will create records that may well be useful to someone someday. This is the province of archives.

Rare books and manuscripts, great photography collections, and the other kinds of things that a

THE PHILLIPS LIBRARY at the Peabody Essex Museum recently bought a seventeenth-century manuscript: an account book from a chandler in Salem, Massachusetts. He was not the purveyor of soaps and candles; rather, he sold provisions to ships. His business papers were kept in this single volume, showing all the things he bought, and—more revealing—all the things he sold, and to whom. To him, this volume was just a record of income and expenses, but to us, it is a treasure house of information about the people (all named in the manuscript) he sold to, the ships he fitted out (also named), the items each bought and the prices paid, the dates of sailing of some of the ships, and so forth. This massive volume may be the only record of his business, but to us it is an archive of extremely valuable information. This is the heart of the archives world.

special collections department might have can be glitzy and bring great notoriety to an institution. This is often not the case with most archival materials. But that does not mean that archives are any less important. They contain the history of the organization and are likely to have wonderful collections in them that scholars will want to plumb the depths of.[2] Susan von Salis says of archives in art museums:

> Archives and special collections may [like special collections] . . . hold . . . published materials, but, unlike libraries, they are primarily responsible for . . . artists' papers, dealers' records, gallery files, and images of everything from works of art and exhibitions to significant individuals and events related to the museum and its collection. Archives also hold documents about a museum's own history, such as exhibition records, administrative files, museum lectures, research notes of curators and scholars, editorial materials related to museum publications, and documentation of museum activities such as expeditions, loans, and collaborative projects with other museums. Archival collections often contain correspondence with colleagues, donors, scholars, and other library stakeholders.[3]

In a talk at the Art Museum Libraries Symposium at the Phillips Library in 2010, Michelle Elligott said that at her institution, MoMA in New York, the archives "is now intrinsically linked to the everyday operation of the institution [as well as providing] one of the world's best centers to conduct original research on the history of modern and contemporary art."[4] Like rare book departments, archives supply information to a wide variety of patrons. Elligott also noted that the archives exists "not only to promote research in the broadest sense, but as an institutional archive, it is constantly in support of the curatorial and business operations of the institution. . . . [T]he Archives is responsible for records management for the entire institution . . . [t]o ensure the proper disposition of records of enduring value." The point to stress here is that the holdings in an archives are not the least bit less valuable than the holdings of the library. Elligott added, "The archives works closely with legal counsel to ensure that [our] record-keeping practices are in compliance with legal guide-

lines . . . [and this is important because] these operations must be maintained even in a time of limited resources and staffing." Archives are indeed worth maintaining.

The holdings in archives are vital to the operation of the institution. They must often be consulted for a wide range of topics having to do with legal and operational aspects of the institution. Elligott pointed out that documents verifying ownership of the institution's holdings, supporting stewardship of the collection, and containing information about the museum's vital records (including all revenues and all purchases and other expenditures "all the way down to every last receipt from the bookstore"; employee files having to do with salaries, benefits, and pensions, among other things; information about the physical plant and building or demolition projects; and much more) are of vital importance to the institution. She said that "the archives [can also feel like] an extension of the museum's press office. Journalists and critics . . . seem to be constantly demanding information, undertaking fact checking, and expecting the answer" in short order so that they can meet their deadlines.

Much of the preceding has to do with internal use of the archives. External users are abundant as well. They do not need to be profiled here because they are just like those who inhabit the reading rooms of special collections departments: scholars and others seeking information of every sort. And all this archival information must be maintained in such a way that it can be retrieved efficiently when it is needed. This is why a trained professional archivist, overseeing the whole department, is essential. And often more than one, if the archives are large and bring in many researchers and donated or purchased collections, or if the institution itself is producing a large number of archival documents (paper based and digital).

Often the papers of other institutions wind up in a company's archives. This may happen if an organization dies and its papers are ceded to another body. Or someone in a company may own the papers of another company and donate her holdings. Or a company can merge with or buy out another organization. Whether the interloping archival materials will remain in the company's archives is the decision of the archivist. The point is that the archives of an entity may contain the papers of another body.

Paper-Based Records

Until the coming of the digital age, almost all archival records were paper based. There were, of course, photographs, some of which were on tin or glass or other material; and there were such oddball artifacts as medals, trophies, and implements of all kinds that were properly housed in an archives. For instance, a company head might have earned keys to a city. A college administrator, in the collection that he willed to a university, may have left all kinds of realia (e.g., trophies and other kinds of awards, desk implements, a special chair, framed paintings or certificates, or other such non-library-like objects) that should remain with the school's archives. Someone in a law firm, in the line of her work, may have received various kinds of honors in the form of trophies or gifts that are all part of the firm's history.

For the most part, however, the focus here is on the common paper-based kind of archival materials that archivists must deal with all the time: employee records (a wide range of these); financial and business records; legal papers of various kinds; (at universities and colleges) student, faculty, staff, and administration records along with copies of dissertations and theses; job descriptions; information about the curriculum (syllabi, copies of handouts); student evaluations; records of personnel actions, such as promotions and reprimands; and much more. There are dozens of categories of things that wind up in archives.

If the archive is in a museum, there are provenance records; information about the acquisition and deaccession of items; records of past events, exhibitions, lectures, other public events, or educational programs; copies of deeds of gift or deposit; statistics of all kinds; information about trustees, overseers, and Friends groups (visiting committees); papers generated in preparation for exhibits, exhibit catalogs, institutional publications and the papers generated in their production; and so forth. Even a single

> **IN MY OWN** holdings, possibly going to an institution someday, are all kinds of things that are not paper based. I have been teaching the history of the book for decades, so I have needed many formats of materials to show my students. My archive will contain texts and images carved into woodblocks or linoleum blocks for printing, copperplates, a lithographic stone weighing about 45 pounds, bamboo scrolls containing Chinese texts, marbled wooden objects, my own dissertation on a huge reel-to-reel film in a heavy metal can, quills and reed and bamboo pens, objects in the shape of books, papermaking equipment, typecasting molds and matrices, and so forth. I hope someone has as much fun processing these things as I have had collecting and using them.

person generates archives—diaries, correspondence, receipts, bills, canceled checks, notes, to-do lists, and so forth. Some of these may not appear to be worth keeping, but who knows! A to-do list from a seventeenth-century schoolgirl could be quite revealing to us today.

As with libraries, archives must manage the materials in their keeping, and the kinds of considerations that apply to books also apply to institutional records. Most things in an archives will be paper based, especially if the collection was amassed before the digital age. Today more and more things will be in digital form: reel-to-reel tapes (often in large metal canisters), 5¼-inch and 3½-inch floppy disks, thumb drives, CDs and DVDs, and other data-storage devices.

Much paper made from about 1875 through about 1975 is likely to be acidic and will probably need conservation of some sort. Even more recent papers can be nonarchival. We will discuss paper from a preservation and conservation perspective in chapter 12, but here we must consider that paper takes up space, it can be shuffled around and reordered, it can be heavy, large quantities of it can become disorganized, it can contain vast amounts of text, and much of that text could be worth saving. Also, paper can be damaged in a variety of ways, and there are methods to preserve it most of the time, if it is worth saving. Archivists, then, deal with the same issues that librarians do with respect to the physicality of the objects in their care. And the head of the department needs to know about the nature of the materials he is responsible for: their physical properties, the intellectual elements that record information, and the best practices to extend their useful life and make them accessible.

As is to be expected, huge caches of archival materials exist with varying levels of importance. Lauren R. Brown says,

> Few would deny that the twentieth century has witnessed explosive growth in the quantity of paper records. Coupled with this phenomenon is the distressing fact that many of these records contain such a low density of useful information that they are for all practical purposes of no use to the research community.[5]

But the papers that do contain useful information must be identified and made available. This is the task of the archivist.

Running an Archives

This chapter does not purport to be a complete course on how to run an archives.[6] Some key concepts, however, are worth looking at in the larger picture of archives management. An archivist must be a manager, not necessarily over people, though that is certainly possible, but over the records generated by people.[7] As I have already noted, there is a good deal of overlap between archivists and rare book librarians—they both are managers over the materials they oversee: manuscripts, correspondence and family papers, other personal papers of authors and scientists, and so forth. In fact, many a special collections department holds records that could well be (and maybe once were) in an archives, perhaps of an entity that no longer exists, or of an organization that can no longer care for its own documentary history.

As with special collections, archives exist in larger entities, and the archivist must conform to the larger entity's regulations and restrictions. Also, in many organizations, archives are treated as a luxury. The archivist must actively strive to show the department's use to the institution, to make the department indispensable. Merely being there to answer questions and to supply information may not be enough. The archivist should be creating new and upgrading older finding aids to increase access; adding new records; letting scholars and the administration know what is new; offering to do exhibitions of archival holdings; working with development people; announcing to the press (within the institution's PR guidelines and working with its marketing department) new, important acquisitions or recently processed and now-accessible collections; volunteering for committee work for the institution (if time allows); and doing as much as possible to keep the good works of the archives in front of the institution, the administration, and the public.

Partly, this kind of activity works to insure the future of the archives once the institution recognizes the value of the department to the parent organization. Also, the public will learn of the institutional records. If a department mandate is to support research, the archivist should do everything she can to let the public know what the department has and how to access it. The greater the number of users, the more justified is the existence of the department. Increased use is a healthy sign. And greater public awareness might be a catalyst for drawing in gifts of various kinds, including papers that should be in the collection. Admittedly, most papers that would come in as gifts would wind up in the special collections department's manuscript holdings. No matter where they wind up, however, the fact that the archives has brought in the gift will be to its credit.

It may also be possible for the department to interact with others outside the institution, for the archivist to cooperate with other archivists in holding meetings or symposia or offering workshops to local or regional professionals. Of course, joining the SAA (Society of American Archivists) or regional organizations that promote the work of archives, and attending their meetings, could do as much for the archivist as being active in RBMS will do for the rare book librarian.

Thomas Wilsted and William Nolte suggest that archivists must understand several points about their departments' placement in the parent organization: "Placement can have a major impact on an archives' program, impinging on such issues as: 1. The ability of the archives to carry out its mission. 2. The level of financial program support for the archives. 3. The commonality of purpose between the archives and the department which supervises its activities."[8] (Naturally, these considerations obtain for a rare book department as well.) Their advice is that archivists (and, by extension, rare book librarians) should try to place their departments as high in the institution's hierarchy as they can, and they should have their own budgets, rather than being a line in the budget of a larger unit.

An archives must also have its own documents relating to use, fees for services, deeds of gift and deposit, photocopying procedures and regulations, and on and on, as does the rare book library. That is, all policies and procedures relating to the conduct of the staff and patrons should be spelled out, along with acquisition and deaccession policies, copyright statements, and much more.

SAA (Society of American Archivists)

The website of the Society of American Archivists explains the organization's purpose:

> Founded in 1936, the Society of American Archivists is North America's oldest and largest national archival professional association. . . . SAA promotes the values and diversity of archivists. We are the preeminent source of professional resources and the principal communication hub for American archivists.[9]

Membership in this organization is almost as important to records managers as is membership in RBMS to a rare book librarian. The mandates for the archivist mirror those of the rare book librarian, with the same focus on making information available to anyone who needs it. In archives, additionally, one will frequently encounter the phrase "to collect, preserve, and protect," core activities of the profession. And the subject of this collecting and preserving is

often "records of enduring value," as in the SAA's vision statement.

What constitutes such records is another question because the definition of "enduring value" is not always clear or universally agreed upon. This is one of the challenges of the profession: in appraising a collection (see the section "Appraisal" later in this chapter), the archivist must be able to distinguish between valuable, useful documents and those with no intellectual use. It takes years of working at this business to make consistently "correct" choices, with the notion of "correctness" always suspect. SAA's website says,

> From the smallest shoe box stored in a hall closet to the voluminous National Archives, documents and memorabilia require special handling and an awareness of the materials' particular value and possible use. Archivists are educated, trained, and experienced to deal with the various questions and problems that arise in the preservation of such material. They are able to bring a specialized perspective and an informed interpretation to decisions concerning the material's worth and usefulness.[10]

One can only hope that "a specialized perspective and an informed interpretation" lead the archivist to the right decisions in processing a collection, but this field is not a science and no two archivists are likely to process a large collection in exactly the same way. The best one can hope for is that the appraisal process produces a well-culled, carefully preserved collection of all items that carry information that scholars might need.

SAA, to this end, has published extensively, held many conferences, and promoted highly professional education in classrooms and workshops across the country. In June 1937, SAA's first president, A. R. Newsome, delineated what he saw as the core function of the organization: "'to become the practical self-help agency of archivists for the solution of their complex problems' and 'to strive to nationalize archival information and technique.'"[11] The attempt to bring uniformity to activities and practices in the profession mirrors the attempts by librarians to follow the same cataloging rules, ethical standards, and policies and procedures in their professional duties. Since the 1970s SAA has published guidelines for the teaching of archives. (For more about the profession and SAA's role, see www2.archivists.org.)

Archivists and Ethical Conduct

As with the rare book world, the world of archives has its own code of ethics. In chapter 1 we looked at the RBMS guidelines. For the most part, the aim of the ethics codes for rare book libraries and for archivists is the same: to guide these professionals in carrying out their duties with no conflicts of interest, within the law, and with a clear view of their responsibilities.

Because of the nature of archival materials, the ethical standards concerning the duties of the archivist are less specific than the prohibitions and strictures we see for special collections personnel. For example, rather than delineating explicit proscriptions (rare book librarians must not compete with their institutions in collection; they must not compete with patrons in availing themselves of research materials; they must not take gifts), the SAA guidelines state flatly what the archivist does (and must do as a professional). The most recent iteration of the SAA ethics document (from January 2012) states, "Archivists endeavor to ensure that those materials, entrusted to their care, will be accessible over time as evidence of human activity and social organization. Archivists embrace principles that foster the transparency of their actions and that inspire confidence in the profession" (www2.archivists.org/ statements/saa-core-values-statement-and-code-of -ethics). The code then elaborates on professional relationships, the exercise of good judgment ("Archivists exercise professional judgment in appraising, acquiring, and processing materials to ensure preservation"), the need to insure "the authenticity and continuing usability of records," the need for security and the protection of the materials in their care, the importance of guaranteeing access to these materials, the mandate of privacy, and the responsibility not to "take unfair advantage of their privileged access to and control of historical records and documentary materials."

These statements are so clear and understandable that they need no commentary. And there is none. All people should know what is ethical and what is not, but the SAA guidelines can be a good starting place for archivists who must decide what to do in possibly compromising situations.

Acquisition

The operations of an archives that is a department unto itself are similar in many ways to the operations of special collections. There is no need to repeat here the statements in chapters 1 and 2 about archivists as custodians, rarity and scarcity, basic mission (access), staffing, the need for continued education, and so forth. But there is a significant difference in one important area: acquisition.

For rare book departments, acquisitions are *decisions*. The selectors in the department choose what they buy or allow in as gifts, and they must balance the budget because their acquisitions can be costly. The department could easily go over budget if the head gets carried away and acquires materials beyond the department's fiscal means. Archives, on the other hand, has a mandate to preserve the institution's historical record and usually does not have an acquisitions budget for buying things. It must seek out all the information the institution generates and deal with it appropriately.

If a rare book department depletes its annual acquisitions budget, it can stop buying. But the information generated by any institution keeps coming, every day, every hour. The archivist sometimes has to run on twelve cylinders to keep up with it, to weed it, to process it, and to make it available to users of all kinds. And even with no archives acquisitions budget, materials will keep flowing into the unit.

This is, of course, an oversimplification. The institution in which the archives exists generates materials, paper based and digital, that in a variety of ways record the history of the entity. This "history" concerns all the activities that happen in the organization, activities such as those mentioned earlier having to do with personnel, financial issues, legal issues, and so forth. The archivist's job is to take it all and then to weed out anything that does not belong there—the process called "appraisal."

The archivist is often surrounded by people who are creating valuable archival materials and are unaware of the value of these things. What is to stop a revered senior administrator at his retirement from discarding into the garbage his old files, not realizing that they could contain important information about his tenure in office? The archivist must go beyond the department to notify all personnel in the institution that they should be saving certain kinds of documents and that they should contact the archives when the mood to jettison comes over them.

This notion needs expansion. The creators of the materials are closest to them, and they will know which documents are most important for the institution. They may also know the best order in which to keep the materials. But they might have an unrealistic view of the importance of *everything* they have generated: "All this is important. We must keep it all." The archivist, on the other hand, will see redundancy within the unit's papers and across the papers of other units and may also see materials of no worth at all for research. The archivist should have the final say on what to keep and what to jettison. Also, the archivist should work closely with all people at the institution, training them on what to retain and what to discard, how the retained materials are best sorted and arranged, and how they should be stored physically to make the archivist's job easy when the documents are transferred to the archives.

Likewise, the institution is constantly creating digital records, many of which have important scholarly and historical value. A regular retention policy should be distributed to all workers showing them what to keep, how to keep it, for how long, and so on, and referring them to the archivist if they have any questions.

Digital Archives

Although the standard image of an archives depicts boxes of papers, technology in the last few decades has allowed institutions to produce records in abundance. In fact, the amount of digital information that institutions produce certainly exceeds the amount of data they create on paper. As the Wikipedia article "Data Proliferation" states,

> Data proliferation refers to the prodigious amount of data, structured and unstructured, that businesses and governments continue to generate at an unprecedented rate and the usability problems that result from attempting to store and manage that data. While originally pertaining to problems associated with paper documentation, data proliferation has become a major problem in primary and secondary data storage on computers.[12]

The challenge for the archivist is to get a handle on all the digital information the organization generates: locate it, appraise it (see the following section), and come up with a plan to archive what needs to be saved—in some form that has a chance of being permanent. Too much information is being generated for this action to be possible for most archivists. The institution should have a policy that will allow it to back up and store all digital information being generated, with the idea that the information creators themselves will be able to designate what is worth

AT MY OWN institution, a curator recently took a position at another museum. In cleaning out her office, she emptied drawer after drawer of her papers into trash cans. One library employee, well schooled in archives, visited the curator almost by chance and stopped the dumping. She coached the curator on what should be saved, and the curator went through the trash cans to retrieve important materials that would otherwise have been recycled or dumped into a landfill. The archivist should hold a tutorial (or create a document) for all personnel at the institution delineating what they should do with their archival materials. At worst, each person at the organization should be told to call the archivist for help in dealing with company records.

saving (with help from the archivist and others at the institution who know what needs to be kept). This solution may not be fully possible for large organizations. But it is clear that born-digital information—that which exists only in electronic form—will contain valuable information that the institution will want to preserve. If the organization has the resources, it should have one person (or a staff) to monitor and save all the digital archival materials, along with the regular archivist who will work on the analog materials the institution generates.

Appraisal

The appraisal of special collections materials will be covered in chapter 10. Such appraisal concentrates on the monetary and intellectual features of objects. In archives, appraisal also deals with value, but of a different kind. The archival appraiser must look at materials with respect to their value to the institution, influenced by the institution's mission, its levels of accountability, and the profession's ethical standards. As one of the core functions of the profession, appraisal must be done with great care, for

one of its purposes is to determine what stays and what goes. For this reason the archivist must have what is the rare books equivalent of a collection development policy, clearly stating the kinds of documents that will have enduring value (and must be kept indefinitely), which have temporal value (certain kinds of records that may be kept for some specified length of time and then discarded), and which have no legal or intellectual importance (and can be discarded immediately).

Given enough time, the archivist may have the luxury of doing the appraisal before the materials come into the archives department. Then there will be no extraneous papers to deal with and the processing can begin.

Retention

The archivist must have on hand a retention schedule for any sort of document that could wind up in the collection. A retention schedule lists all types of holdings for the institution and shows how long each kind must be retained. For instance, information about budgets may need to be retained for

SOMETIMES THE APPRAISAL of archival acquisitions reveals a delicate situation. I once processed a collection of a professor of a major university who was famous in his field and who traveled around the world lecturing about his specialty. After his death his papers came to the school archives as they were found in his office. They contained, along with copies of his publications and lectures, many photographs showing him on the dais before, during, and after his talks, and in casual situations on these lecture trips. He was often, over several years, accompanied by a young, attractive woman, whose visible demeanor and body language, evident in the pictures,

suggested that she was more than just a groupie. But she was clearly not his wife, who apparently never accompanied him on these trips. The dilemma, of course, was what to do with these pictures. Should they be removed from the archive? Should they be left in it, but not be made part of the inventory? Should they be listed along with all other pictures, with no commentary? If they were removed, they would have diminished the collection in that all of them showed the professor in his professional element, often with dignitaries from other schools. If they were left in but not included in the description of the archive, the finding aid would be incomplete, and it

could lead researchers not to pursue images when some of these could be useful to their research. If the pictures were listed as part of the full inventory, they could have caused some embarrassment and possibly some hurt to the family. The decision eventually was to put them into the finding aid but to describe the photographs in general terms: "Photographs of Professor Jones at his lecture in Indiana"; "Photographs of Professor Jones in his award ceremony in Berkeley." Although the inventory lacked specificity, it did give enough information to lead scholars to information about the venues of the professor's professional engagements.

seven years and then discarded. Class syllabi for a school may be discarded after four years. Personnel papers may be discarded after ten years. But papers that reveal historical events or that concern important people may never be discarded. Sometimes legal requirements dictate how long certain papers must be retained. Sometimes it is the institution's own predilections that determine retention time.

The issue of retention raises another question: what kinds of things must be kept? According to the SAA (Society of American Archivists), factors that determine what should be kept are the provenance of the records, their content, their reliability and authenticity, their order and completeness, their condition, what it would cost to preserve them, and their intrinsic value to the institution.[13]

The archivist, then, must look at the historic value of the records, along with their use, and at legal and financial issues. Any of these considerations can lengthen the time the records must be kept—even to perpetuity. With respect to historic value, as I have already indicated, the materials may be significant in recording the history of the institution. They may be used frequently, or often enough that they should be retained at least as long as they continue to be used—and then some. Are there legal requirements mandating their retention? Will the information they contain help the institution avoid legal liabilities? Will they be useful for taxes, budgeting, or other fiscal activities?

The so-called Robek Model of records retention is useful.

1. Avoid the "Every Conceivable Contingency" syndrome.
2. Information should be retained if there is a reasonable probability that it will be needed in some future time to support some legitimate legal or business objective, and the consequences of its absence would be substantial.
3. Retention policies should generally be conservative, in the sense that they should not expose the organization to an inordinate degree of risk.
4. Remember, the presence or absence of information can be either helpful or harmful;

therefore the best way to minimize the risks is to provide for systematic disposal immediately after the expiration of a document's value for legal and business purposes.
5. A retention period is most likely to be valid if it is based on a consensus of the opinions of persons most knowledgeable about the value of the information and the costs, risks, and benefits of its disposal.[14]

The whole topic of appraisal and retention has generated a large literature. A conservative approach, in which everything is kept if it could remotely have some use someday, could lead to an archive that is bloated with much useless material, taking up space on the shelves, costing the institution for its maintenance, and wasting staff time. But it could also be instrumental in the retention of the one crucial document that someone needs with urgency.

A rule of thumb for such decision making is, if possible, to consult the party or parties responsible for the creation of the records who might have some insight into their value. This approach is not infallible, of course, because the records' creator(s) may see great value where there is none. But the insight gleaned from the creator could be useful in appraisal and retention or disposal.

Collection Arrangement

The arrangement of a collection takes special skill and much experience. Once the appraisal is done and unwanted items have been removed from the collection, the remaining items must be arranged into a logical order. The Principle of Original Order sometimes helps the archivist in this task. When the papers are delivered to the archives, they are in some order—logical or not. The archivist should consider carefully what that order is. Because the collection presumably came from the person who generated the papers in the first place, maybe she had some meaningful order in which she kept them. If the archivist can discern no logical order, he might wish to rearrange the pieces into a sequence that makes sense, one that collocates similar items or similar subjects.

For instance, it may make sense to bring together, and arrange in chronological order, correspondence distributed throughout a dozen cartons. Or business records may be pulled out from personal papers and brought together to form a cohesive picture of the business operations of the donor.

Provenance

One other principle may be employed to guide the archivist in arrangement—that of provenance.

> In most fields, the primary purpose of provenance is to confirm or gather evidence as to the time, place, and—when appropriate—the person responsible for the creation, production, or discovery of the object. This will typically be accomplished by tracing the whole history of the object up to the present.[15]

As with all kinds of rare book and special collections materials, where the papers came from, who owned them over time, who produced them, who handled and used them, and so forth could be valuable information for a researcher. It could be useful to know, for instance, if a particular author used certain papers in her writing or if a historian was influenced by the archives of an institution.

Hence it is essential for all papers acquired by an archives to be marked at acquisition with key information: date of acquisition, who produced the papers, who gave them, who used them (if this can be determined), where they were stored and by whom, and so forth. The sooner the papers are so marked after acquisition the more accurate this information is likely to be. So the archivist, if possible, should obtain either orally or in writing whatever information is available from the party giving the papers.

Description and Delivery

Description is akin to the creation of finding aids or cataloging records: items must be accessible through a database, and accessibility means that they must be adequately described, using standard terminology and professional templates of information storage. The level of description depends on the importance of the materials. Some collections that do not hold great quantities of useful information (a value judgment of the archivist) may be given a mere collection-level description: "Steven Phelps Papers: consisting of 23 archival boxes, three manuscript volumes with genealogical records, and one folder of 25 photographs," followed perhaps by a few sentences describing the kinds of materials in the collection. Other collections may warrant much more detailed descriptions, at the box, folder, or item level, this last usually not practical or practicable unless the collection contains extraordinary, important documents, each of which might be used by a researcher. Such a level of description is quite expensive. Throughout the processing of the papers, the archivist must keep foremost in mind the use to which the collection will be put and should produce holdings that do not contain dross, an arrangement that makes sense, and descriptions that lead researchers to what they need.

Of course delivery is the ultimate desideratum. As with rare book and manuscripts librarians, archivists can measure their professional success by how easily the information they have processed can get into the hands of those who need it. Once a good finding aid is prepared for a collection, its record should be put into a bibliographic database like NUCMC (the National Union Catalog of Manuscript Collections). A good finding aid is useful only to those who are in its presence unless we can broadcast its information to the world. Hence the finding aid should be followed up with a reliable cataloging record that is entered into an international database. Libraries and archives will never reach a point of universal bibliographic control—the ability to gain access to *all* information no matter where we are—but such care in handling archives will move us in that direction.

A final note here: The description of the materials in a collection should be delivered with no slant, no bias, no evaluative comments. The text should not read, "James Devereux was a successful ship captain." Success is a judgment. "Jeffrey Dahmer was an evil serial killer." The word *evil* might not take into account madness, which makes a person do things that for a sane person would be considered evil. The aim is to present only facts and let the researchers interpret them.

Outreach

Along with the tasks discussed in the preceding sections (acquisition, appraisal, arrangement, and so forth), the archivist should also be involved in outreach. As with special collections, archives need to let the world know of their existence. As already mentioned, the archivist needs to educate those who are producing archival materials that those materials should be given to an archivist for processing and retention. If the organization has an internal e-mail system that allows a message to be sent to "All Users," for instance, a note should be sent informing everyone that all the materials they produce—e-mails, notes, correspondence, reports, minutes, and so forth—belong to the institution and should be retained as part of the documentary history of the organization. This rule applies to digital as well as paper-based information. If it is possible, and with administrative approval, all online activity of every employee should be captured in the organization's digital archive. The archivist will eventually appraise it for retention or destruction the same way he handles paper materials. But without a message to all users to tell them of the institution's practice, a good deal of information could be lost. Hence the importance of this kind of outreach. And with the right training from the archivist, personnel creating materials could do the appraisal themselves, making their papers almost ready to process by the time they are delivered to the archives.

The outreach should go beyond the institution to former employees, if it is determined that they took with them (unwittingly or not) any documents that shed light on the institution.[16] They must be advised that all work about and done for the institution, generated on the job, belongs to the institution. Further, the outreach should go to potential users and to the public, who, themselves, could be users. Such outreach could raise awareness of the institution's holdings and bring in gifts and additional users. The

outreach can take many forms, which will be the subject of chapter 11.

As Michelle Elligott has cogently said, outreach can bring great fame to an institution and can engage many people in the public arena in the organization's operations.[17] It is good for public image and for fund-raising, so the archivist should work with the public relations and the advancement departments on ways to let the world know of the archives' holdings and availability to scholars. One view in the rare book world is that books and manuscripts are glossier and more attractive than archives, but a clever and imaginative archivist can exhibit a host of materials in exciting, beautiful, and informative ways. Outreach can be a powerful tool.

Policies and Procedures for Archives

As with any functioning body, the archives should have a manual of policies and procedures that guides its staff, from generation to generation. This manual should be revisited periodically to reflect the latest theories on archives management. A key element of this document is a description of staff members' duties, including a list of personnel to be employed in the department and a sharply written statement of each person's responsibilities, something in the nature of job descriptions.

AT THE PHILLIPS Library, a large local history collection is cataloged in a peculiar way, using a system that works well for these holdings. The collection is perfectly accessible under this old system. It is possible to convert the records to Library of Congress cataloging, but there is no reason to do so. No other library in the world uses this cataloging system; it was developed just for this collection. In a huge retrospective conversion project, the librarians decided not to include this collection. So a special page in a procedures manual must be written explaining how these items are arranged and cataloged. Likewise, each archive must create its own operations manual, based on its unique holdings.

It hardly need be said that the policies and procedures of the department must be carefully thought out and codified. That is, the operations manual must delineate the department's practices—all carefully developed following the highest standards of the profession. Each institution should have its own such manual, for the holdings of each department are idiosyncratic and may require a particular approach that would not be taken in other institutions.

Education and Continuing Education

Many graduate schools, mostly in (or in partnership with) library schools or history programs, offer graduate training and advanced degrees in archives. Nearly three dozen academic programs exist in the United States.[18] Also, SAA offers workshops, as do many organizations whose courses will help records managers in the same way as do the courses available to special collections librarians. The program at the University of California, Riverside, is not atypical, with its placement in the History Department and its offerings of such degree-granting courses of study as an M.A. in history, with specializations in archival management, historic preservation, or museum curatorship, and its Ph.D. in history, with a specialization in public history.[19] At Simmons College in Boston, the archives program is in the Graduate School of Library and Information Science. At Drexel University in Philadelphia, the archives program is in the iSchool, College of Science and Technology.[20] In Bellingham, Washington, at Western Washington University, it is in the College of Humanities and Social Sciences. At NYU it is in the Graduate School of Arts and Sciences. At San Jose State in California it is in the College of Applied Sciences and Arts. At SUNY Albany it is in the College of Computing and Information. At East Tennessee State University it is in the School of Continuing Studies.[21] This diversity of placement shows what an orphan archives is—never in its own home, but always part of some other program.

As with the rare book field, anyone wishing to get an education in the field—beyond the standard classroom experience that many schools offer—should join SAA and attend its annual meetings. The talks and committee meetings and networking that one experiences at these conferences are invaluable for sharing knowledge and for learning a great deal about the profession, along with meeting the people who are shaping the profession.

■ ■ ■

No two archives are alike. No single way of organizing and running an archives is "the standard." Archivists can achieve their professional ends in many ways, and even those ends will vary depending on many factors: In what type of institution is the material housed? What are the institution's mandates? How many archivists are employed? What are the resources available (human and fiscal)? Who are the potential (and actual) users of the materials? How extensive are the holdings? How old is the institution? What is the nature of the materials the archives must be responsible for (paper based, digital, photographic, historical or contemporary, and so forth)?

Unfortunately, many institutions undervalue archives or do not recognize them at all as important units, rich with information, with great potential for researchers. If the organization does have an archives (and not all do), it is likely to be underfunded because it is misunderstood. Often librarians with little or no archives training are placed in charge of this unit, and many of them "look the other way," doing their librarian duties and paying little or no attention to archives. It is true that resources often do not allow for the employment of a full-time or even a part-time trained professional to deal with the record of the institution's history. Hence this chapter is a general guide to the operation of archives, with a look at the institution's mandates and the responsibilities of those who are employed to oversee the dissemination of information from the library and its related units. The aim here has been to present an overview of the field, not to delineate "best practices" or the absolute mandates of the profession.[22]

Archives' activities are related closely to those of the library, and so are the physical materials both repositories deal with. Chapter 4 now looks at these materials, for archivists and special collections librarians are responsible for their handling, description, and maintenance. All those who care for special materials must have a common understanding of the physical makeup of the items and the vocabulary required to describe them.

NOTES

1. I wish to thank Tamara Gaydos of the Phillips Library at the Peabody Essex Museum for her sage assistance in shaping this chapter.

2. It is worth noting here that the archives of an organization that "goes out of business" may wind up among the holdings of a special collections department. At this point, the papers, which are truly the archives of an organization, have become just another collection in a larger department with many kinds of holdings and many other special collections.

3. Susan von Salis, "The Role of the Library and Archives in an Art Museum," *Proceedings of the Art Museum Libraries Symposium*, ed. by Sidney Berger and Judy Dyki (Salem, MA: The Phillips Library, Peabody Essex Museum, September 23–24, 2010), pp. 9–10, available at http://pem.org/aux/pdf/library/AMLS2010.pdf.

4. Michelle Elligott, "Serving Various Audiences," *Proceedings of the Art Museum Libraries Symposium*, ed. by Sidney Berger and Judy Dyki (Salem, MA: The Phillips Library, Peabody Essex Museum, September 23–24, 2010), pp. 38–42, available at http://pem.org/aux/pdf/library/AMLS2010.pdf.

5. Lauren R. Brown, review of *Archival Choices: Managing the Historical Record in an Age of Abundance*, ed. by Nancy E. Peace, *Rare Books & Manuscripts Librarianship* 2.2 (Fall 1987): 129–31, http://rbm.acrl.org/content/rbml/2/2/125.full.pdf+html. This passage is on p. 129.

6. For an excellent treatment on how to run an archives, see Laura A. Millar, *Archives: Principles and Practices* (New York: Neal-Schuman, 2010).

7. In chapter 1, I spoke of the need for rare book librarians to be managers. See the section "The Placement of the Department in the Institution, and the Department's Management," for what is said there applies to archivists, too.

8. Thomas Wilsted and William Nolte, *Managing Archival and Manuscript Repositories* (Chicago: Society of American Archivists, 1990), 17.

9. See the society's website at www2.archivists.org/about.

10. See www2.archivists.org/about/introduction-to-saa.

11. See www2.archivists.org/about/introduction-to-saa.

12. See "Data Proliferation," Wikipedia, http://en.wikipedia.org/wiki/Data_proliferation.

13. See the SAA glossary under "appraisal" at www2.archivists.org/glossary/terms/a/appraisal. This glossary is a splendid reference tool for the field, with excellent definitions and links to citations to articles and books that give extensive treatments for the terms.

14. Mary F. Robek, Gerald F. Brown, and David O. Stephens, *Information and Records Management* (New York: McGraw Hill, 1995), www.dartmouth.edu/~library/recmgmt/retention.html?mswitch-redir=classic#3c.

15. See "Provenance," Wikipedia, http://en.wikipedia.org/wiki/Provenance.

16. Chapter 8 on legal issues will touch on the ownership of work produced on the job. Many employees assume that their work is their own, but if the work was produced while the employee is "on the time clock" for the parent organization, it is likely that the organization owns what the employee has produced.

17. See Elligott, "Serving Various Audiences," cited in note 4 above.

18. See the *Directory of Archival Education*, www2.archivists.org/dae.

19. See www2.archivists.org/dae/university-of-california-riverside.

20. See www2.archivists.org/dae/drexel-university.

21. See the list at www2.archivists.org/dae.

22. An excellent treatment of the field with a fine bibliography is Laura A. Millar's *Archives: Principles and Practices* (see note 6 above).

CHAPTER 4

THE PHYSICAL MATERIALS OF THE COLLECTION

I N THIS CHAPTER WE WILL BE LOOKING AT MATERIALS IN THE COL-lection from the stance of their physical makeup. The aim of this book is to answer the question, what do those working with rare books and special collections need to know? And certainly, anyone working with any material objects needs to know about the materiality of those objects.

Items in special collections move through the world in various ways, from their makers to collectors and dealers to other collectors, dealers, scholars, librarians and archivists, investors, and many others. To facilitate movement of items, these people often must be able to describe the objects in their possession, to treat them if they are in any level of disrepair, to house them for protection, to package them for shipment, and so forth. These things will be dealt with elsewhere in this book. Here it is essential that we look at the component parts of the objects in rare book libraries.

A gigantic literature exists on each of the subjects covered here, and the person handling rare materials should become familiar with the bibliography in the field. At the end of the chapter there is a listing of some of the key texts useful for educating oneself about each topic.

Generic Overview

A rare book department contains a host of genres of materials: books, manuscripts, photographs, correspondence, archival materials of all sorts, broadsides and prints of various kinds, diaries, logbooks, sketches and paintings, pamphlets, ephemera in hundreds of manifestations, realia made of many kinds of substances, maps and charts, transportation schedules, menus, bills and invoices, and a vast array of other kinds of things. There are even digital files and the physical "objects" that contain them. For the most part, these all should be handled with the same level of attention to preservation. And, as already mentioned, this responsibility requires

IN A WIDE-RANGING discussion with my students, we explored the qualities that constitute "books." One of those attributes was books' corporeality. When I asked the students, "What is a book?" I got more than a dozen answers, most of which had to do with the physical nature of books. I pointed out that two statements should be kept in mind when one is trying to define what *book* means: (1) I read a book; (2) I bought a book. The first emphasizes the text; the second stresses the object. This second statement is what the present chapter is about.

a knowledge of the raw materials of their composition. Books, for example, are usually made up of paper, inks, and covering materials (more paper, vellum, cloth, leather, adhesives, threads, decorative elements like pigments and metallic foils, and such), not to mention all the kinds of things one might find tipped into the books.

Other materials one might find in a special collections department are bones, wood, metals (in realia and in bindings for staples, bosses, and clasps), palm leaves, pipal leaves, butterfly wings (embedded in some Japanese decorative papers), proto papers (see the following section), plastics, stone and clay, silk, and anything else that someone decided to collect or to put into books. Though each of these elements could fill a chapter of its own, here we will concentrate on the substances most commonly found in special collections.

PROTO PAPERS

The term *proto papers* designates any manufactured surface that looks like paper but is not true paper, which alone among these materials is made from macerated fibers (fibers that have been soaked [and then treated—with beating or some other process] to separate them from one another). That is, to make paper one must macerate fibers and float them in water, then deposit them onto a screen where the fibers mat and become a sheet of paper. This oversimplification is sufficient to distinguish paper from surfaces that are not made by beating and grinding up the fibers, but are composed of fibers treated in other ways.

There are too many of kinds of proto papers to deal with them all here, especially because most of them will not play any important role in the special collections department. They are rare enough in our collections that they do not need any discussion here. Treated here are the most important substances for the dissemination of texts over the millennia.

Papyrus

With the resurgence of interest in papyrus since Hassan Ragab did his experiments and wrote his dissertation on the subject in the 1930s,[1] it is not unlikely that modern special collections departments will have papyrus pieces of one sort or another. Even if we do not have classical, ancient ones, the modern market is flooded with items painted on papyrus made in the last fifty years—mostly painted broadsides with garish images of Egyptian gods and dancers, hieroglyphics and animals. Sheets of papyrus have also been used as tip-ins in books, as parts of book bindings (it actually makes a sturdy book cover), as bookmarks, and in other forms (see figure 4.1).

Because the idea here is to make those handling rare books knowledgeable about the materials in their possession, it is important to look at a couple of the myths about this substance so we will not promulgate the same mistakes that we have seen for some 150 years.

In the late eighteenth and nineteenth centuries, researchers turned their attention to papyrus after its

FIG. 4.1 Papyrus leaf showing the horizontal strips of the sheet; the verso of this leaf is composed of vertical strips, which are visible through the sheet. (Collection of the author.)

discovery in some quantities in Egypt and elsewhere in the Middle East. Especially in the nineteenth century, scholars wanted to offer a history of this wonderful medium and, not having any texts to draw on, simply made up some "facts" to explain its manufacture. Speculation was presented as incontrovertible fact, and, not knowing any better, their followers blindly reiterated the mistakes of their predecessors.[2]

For instance, statements were made that papyrus was a reed or a parchment, that it was cut into lengths of particular, predetermined sizes (when, of course, it was cut into the lengths that the papyrus maker needed), that it was cooked, that it was pounded, that the strips were woven together, and so forth.[3] A simple, clear explanation of the manufacture of papyrus follows, and this is all one in the rare book world needs to know about its manufacture.

The papyrus plant is not a reed; it is a sedge. Some species of it can grow to over twenty feet high, with the diameter of a grown person's wrist. The outer skin of the plant is green, and the shaft is roughly triangular. The plant is cut down and cut into segments of whatever length the maker wishes. The segments are soaked in water until they are hydrated, and then the green skin is pared away from two of the three sides. The segments are sliced into strips, and the little edges of green skin are pared away from these strips. The strips are soaked in water for as long as it takes to get them fully hydrated, perhaps a few days (with the water being changed often to keep mildew from forming and turning the strips brown).

THE FIRST TIME I made sheets of papyrus I soaked it for only a few hours, and the sheets came out fine. But I have heard someone say that it should be soaked as much as a week, with frequent water changes.

Once the strips are as full of water as the soaking will allow, they are laid onto a flat surface in one direction slightly overlapping, and a second layer is put on top at right angles to the first. (The strips are not woven together.) The inner stalk has the pithiness of watermelon and the stringiness of celery.

After the strips are laid out as described, with two layers at right angles to one another, this two-layer entity is placed between blotting materials between flat boards and pressed under heavy weight. The blotting material surrounding the papyrus strips soaks out the water. The strips are definitely *not* pounded, as was once thought. When the blotters are soaked, they are replaced with dry ones. The blotters should be replaced frequently, as they absorb the water, until the leaves of papyrus are dry. The pith, which acts as a "glue" to hold the strips together, gets squeezed powerfully, and the pith in the two layers merges into a single solid layer of binding agent. There is no need to use glue of any kind.

The resultant sheet, or leaf, of papyrus, if it is made properly, will be cream colored and flexible, with rough edges because the strips will not be trimmed at this stage (and may never be). The two sides will look alike, with the exception that the strips on one side will be horizontal, on the other side vertical. To repeat: the final sheet is *not* composed of strips that are woven together, a common error in description. Also, papyrus is definitely not paper, though the terms are often used interchangeably by scholars who even call it "papyrus paper." Paper is made from macerated fibers. In papyrus the fibers are not macerated. It is worth repeating that *papyrus is not paper* and should never be called that.

Scribes or artists would brush their texts onto the papyrus. They did not use quills, presumably not invented (hence not available) in Egypt more than 3,500 years ago when papyrus was being used. Brushes with fine bristles could be used to write a fine line and impart pictograms and characters onto the surface of the papyrus leaves. If a long text were to be written, a second and third and other subsequent leaves of papyrus could be glued together to make a scroll of whatever length was needed. Because the form of text on papyrus was either broadside or scroll, the text would be on only one side of the piece.

Papyrus is a fairly brittle sheet, so it would not be folded. The text would be either in broadside format or rolled, as just noted, and it was perfectly portable because the sheets are quite light. But it was not conducive to the codex form, in which leaves of text are folded in half (or in fourths or eighths or other configurations) and sewn together through the folds.[4]

Thanks to the research of Hassan Ragab, there is a flood of modern papyrus on the market, much of which is of high quality and eminently useful for several kinds of book applications. Rare book people should be able to identify it and know how it is made.

Parchment/Vellum

In the West, papyrus was not an option. The plant needs year-round hot, wet conditions to grow, and it will not survive through Europe's winters. Needing an abundant surface to write on, Western scribes used animal skin. *Vellum* is specifically the skin of calf; *parchment* is a more generic term meaning any skin dried (not tanned, as is leather)[5] to form a flat, thin writing surface. Over the centuries, this distinction has pretty much been lost, and now the two terms are used interchangeably. Some purists still use *vellum* only for skins derived from cows and calves, but they are the exception. It is good for people in the rare book world to be aware of the difference, whether they are purists themselves or not. The two words will be used interchangeably in this text.

The skin of any animal will do. Common are sheep and lambs, cows and calves, goats, pigs, and horses, though other skins will work just as well. There is even a company today making vellum out of the skins of various fish and lizards. These last can be used for bookbinding. If one wishes, even a mouse skin would probably do, though that would produce only enough parchment for a very tiny book.

Another common misconception is that the word *parchment* comes from the fact that the animal skin has been parched (dried). The word actually derives from the city in which the material was supposedly developed, Pergamon (or Pergamum), a city in ancient Greece.[6]

The production of vellum begins in the fields, where the shepherd must keep the sheep away from stone walls and bramble fences that might scrape the pelts and thus weaken the skin. Once the sheep (or other animal) is slaughtered and flayed, the skin

FIG. 4.2 Lunellum and parchment stretched on a frame. (From Christopher de Hamel, *Medieval Craftsmen: Scribes and Illuminators* [Toronto and Buffalo: University of Toronto Press, 1997], p. 12.)

is cooked in a lime solution to soften the hair on one side and the flesh on the other. It is then stretched in a frame and pared down with a lunellum (also called a lunarium), a crescent-moon-shaped knife, that removes the hair and the flesh from the two sides of the skin (see figure 4.2).

The hair side will usually be darker because it was on the outside of the animal, exposed to the oils in the skin, dirt, the sun, and whatever else might have "stained" it. The flesh side is whiter and is often easily distinguishable from the hair side. A good parchment maker will, however, produce a skin that is almost equally white on both sides of the vellum. The final product will be smooth and evenly scraped on both sides, producing a lovely parchment leaf. (Note that the word *page* should not be used here. A page is one side of a leaf. A leaf has two pages, a front and back, a recto and a verso.)

Extremely fine, soft, strong parchment may be *uterine vellum*. (It is also called *slunk*.) Originally this material was thought to have been made from the skin of an aborted or stillborn calf (hence the word *uterine*), but the term was used for any fine skin made from a newborn animal. It may well have been from an aborted fetus, but recent thoughts on uterine vellum are that it was probably made from recently born animals.[7]

In the rare book world we need to know a few fairly simple things. First, vellum is not paper because it is not made from macerated fibers; it is animal skin. (In the nineteenth century papermakers created a paper often called *vellum* that had the look and feel of real animal skin, and, short of tearing a book apart and examining the material under a microscope, it was often impossible to distinguish between a real skin and a sheet of paper that was made to look like vellum.)

Second, its most common manifestation in books in the Middle Ages was for the writing of the texts and for bindings, and, from about 1450 on, mostly for the bindings (and, for many printed volumes, for the printing surface as well). Even some copies of the Gutenberg Bible were printed on vellum. There are serious collectors of things printed on vellum, and such items (books and broadsides) command high prices.

Third, in bindings, goatskin, treated in various ways and dyed many colors, was common. As John Carter says, goatskin "was already in use in Almohavid Morocco and Andalusia and in the Levant from Cairo to Constantinople and as far east as Persia by the 13th or 14th century." He adds that by the fifteenth century, goatskin was in use in Europe. His final warning is that, though various kinds of skins are discernible from one another, designated by their geographical origins (Levant, Morocco, Niger, and so on), "it is fashionable, and certainly safer, to use *goatskin* in preference to the traditional and usually erroneous geographical nomenclature."[8]

Fourth, in the Middle Ages, vellum was by far the predominant surface for writing, and almost all medieval manuscripts are on skins. After the thirteenth century, paper began to take over as the most common surface for writing and, later, printing, but parchment is still in use today by calligraphers and printers creating special texts. Because the inks used for writing in the Middle Ages were oil-based, and because the skin's surface was treated by having a chalk (called *pounce*) burnished over the skin to act as a mordant, the inks sat pretty much on the surface of the skin and could thus be scraped off if the scribe saw an error that needed to be expunged. In fact, so as not to waste whole manuscripts that no longer had a use, scribes could scrape off entire volumes' worth of text and write over the now-blank sheets. With ultraviolet light, the "erased" text can be brought back. Such manuscripts are called *palimpsests*, from the two Greek words meaning "scraped again."

Fifth, vellum, if properly made, is extremely strong and quite flexible, and it has no inherent vice. That is, it is not acidic and has nothing in it that will cause it to deteriorate. Like paper, it can become moldy and turn splotchy black, but it will not disintegrate the way paper will under such circumstances. When it is exposed to fire, vellum will shrink up before it will burn, and some vellum-based texts that have been in fires can sometimes be resuscitated, if the vellum has shrunk, by hydrating and then stretching the material.

Finally, it is still in use, as mentioned earlier, in deluxe printing and for torahs and other ceremonial documents, and also as a binding material. It has been used for more than 1,500 years over boards and in limp-vellum bindings.

Amate/Amatl

Amate (also called *amatl*) is made from the inner bark of trees from the ficus family or from the shrub *Broussonetia papyrifera* (the paper mulberry plant), the same fibers that the Japanese use to make *washi* (their handmade papers). The bark is soaked and then pounded into flat sheets to whatever size is desired (see figure 4.3). Because the fibers are not macerated, just pounded down into leaves, a sheet of amatl is not true paper, though it is often called "Mexican bark paper." It comes in several colors,

FIG. 4.3 Amatl sheet. Shown is a leaf of "marbled amatl." It also comes in single colors, shading from light cream to dark chocolate. (Collection of the author.)

from light cream to dark brown—almost black—and one version mixing light and dark pulps into what is called "marbled amate." Recently available are sheets of amatl that have been dyed pink or light blue.

Amate has a long history, going back more than 1,500 years. It was used for Mayan and Aztec codices, almost exclusively for religious or ceremonial purposes. It is worth mentioning here because for the last thirty or so years its manufacture—mostly in San Pablito, Mexico—has become a full industry, and texts or images written or drawn onto amate or bindings using amate are likely to wind up in special collections departments.

TAPA CLOTH

Like amate, tapa cloth is made from the pounded inner bark of the ficus or the paper mulberry plant and is often referred to as *bark cloth*. It is usually decorated with brown dyes, the decorations being done in many geometric patterns, sometimes with letters of the Latin alphabet incorporated into the design. Tapa cloth may not appear in many special collections departments, but it is prevalent enough to merit being mentioned here.

Pieces range from quite small—for example, a letter-sized sheet—to enormous. Large pieces of tapa have been used as wall coverings, room dividers, and bedspreads. It had practical as well as ceremonial uses, and it was highly prized, especially when affiliated with royalty. It is a sturdy, flexible material, much stronger than amate because the latter goes through much more pounding and fiber breakdown, making it much more easily torn. Modern book makers,

FIG. 4.4 Tapa cloth. (Collection of the author.)

especially those working with limited editions or artist's books, may use tapa cloth in their bindings. (See figure 4.4.)

PAPER

Perhaps the most important substance in the history of the book is paper. It is a complex topic, and anyone working in the world of rare books and special collections must know a good deal about it. Hence this section will treat the subject extensively. To be able to converse with confidence and accuracy about books, manuscripts, photographs, and almost everything else that exists in rare book departments, one must know the terminology of the subject. Hence many terms will be presented here that are essential in this conversation. Only a cursory description of paper's manufacture will be given here, sufficient to allow us to look at all the important terms one must know to be an informed rare book person. (The description is for handmade papers. Those made by machine are beyond the scope of this book.)

Paper—History

Paper was invented in China in the second century BC. Through the misinformation conveyed by a host of "scholars" and poorly informed historians, the myth of the invention of paper in AD 105 by Ts'ai Lun (or Cai Lung, or one of the other transliterations of his name), a eunuch in the court of the emperor Ho Ti, has been repeated over and over again until it has gained, in some quarters, the status of *truth*.[9] But there is no truth to it, and anyone working in rare books should know not to believe (and repeat) the AD 105 error.

The material remained a secret invention in China for more than eight hundred years, but it made its way to the West via Samarkand in the eighth century, and purportedly by 1151 there was a paper mill at Xativa (Jativa), Spain, presumably the first one in Europe.[10]

The oldest company in the Western hemisphere with unbroken production is a paper mill: the one at Fabriano, Italy. It was established by 1276, and it has been producing paper continuously to this day.[11] The range of its papers is wide, and their quality is superb, even the machine-made papers of today.

This feature is worth noting because hundreds of thousands of books and documents used Fabriano papers, and the name of the company comes up in rare book circles often.

As the inventors of watermarks (in the thirteenth century), the Fabriano papermakers have immeasurably impacted special collections and, indeed, the entire rare book world. (See the section "Properties of Paper" later in this chapter.) In 1690, William Rittenhouse established the first paper mill in what is now the United States.[12] Until then, obviously, all paper used on books printed in the colonies was European, and if a dealer in rare books from the period of American incunabula (c. 1639–1700) wishes to know the source of paper of an item, the paper in the piece can sometimes be traced to its European origin by its watermarks.

This extremely brief history will be useful to people in the rare book world, though naturally a great deal more could be said. For more information see the texts in the bibliography at the end of this chapter.

Paper—Materials and Basic Sheet Formation

Most of the paper in the West from the thirteenth century on—until the mass manufacture of it in the middle of the nineteenth century—was made from linen or cotton fibers. In Asia, where paper originated, a few fibers were used, primarily *kozo, mitsumata,* and *gampi.*[13] Experiments were done in the West—especially when a shortage of papermaking fibers loomed with the democratization of education and the expanding need for books—to make paper from various other materials, like straw and esparto grass. These experiments were fairly successful in terms of the final product, but the processes were too costly, and neither caught on to make papermaking from these alternate fibers commercially practicable. The Japanese, however, have continued for more than 1,400 years[14] to use the three fibers mentioned earlier.

Paper is nothing more than matted fibers. The basic sheet-forming process entails gathering and preparing the fibers, macerating them using a stamping mill or a Hollander beater (see below and see illustrations), putting them into a vat with water (about 95 percent water and the rest fibers), and scooping them up onto a paper mold—a screen on top of, or wires drawn across, a wooden frame. When the water drains from the screen or wires, the fibers settle onto the top of the mold's surface, and the fibers mat. A sheet of paper is thus formed. It is transferred from the paper mold to a pile of other newly formed sheets, the process called *couching* (/kooching/). If freshly made sheets are couched atop one another, they will stick together, and enough of them will form cardboard. So each sheet must be couched onto a woven wool felt. Once a sheet is couched onto a felt, another felt is placed on top, and the next sheet is couched onto the next felt. The stack of new sheets, with felt interleaving (called a *post*), is pressed to get the water out and the fibers to mat more strongly than they did on the mold. The sheets are then stacked upon one another, the felts being removed (forming a *white post*), and they are pressed again. Then the sheets are dried in some fashion.

Manufacture—Asian

In the East, two kinds of papermaking were (and still are) practiced: the *Nagashizuki* and the *Tamezuki* methods. The three fibers used in Japanese papermaking—*kozo, gampi,* and *mitsumata*—are well known in the West because the Japanese are some of the most prolific papermakers in the world, and their papers are available worldwide. Hence it is common for the terminology of Japanese papermaking to be used regardless of where in the Far East the paper is being made (China and Korea, for instance).

Stems from the plants are washed and the outer bark is scraped off. The inner bark is composed of long, strong, white fibers, which are stripped off, soaked in water (often in a running stream), cooked, and then pounded to macerate them. The papermakers pound the fibers with sticks, against an anvil, or they use a machine that pounds the pulp in a vessel that looks like a mortar—a pestle is struck into the mortar to smash the fibers and break them up into tiny pieces. There is also a machine that uses sharp blades to cut the fibers apart (a Naginata beater). This fiber produces sheets of great strength and softness, and the papers are often used for conservation as mending tissues.

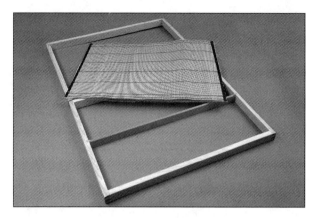

FIG. 4.5 Japanese paper mold (*suketa* or *sugeta*). The hinged *keta* is shown open with the *su* (screen) sitting on top. (Collection of the author.)

In Nagashizuki, the fibers are mixed with a formation aid (the generic term for which is *neri*; one common kind of *neri* is also called *tororo aoi*, made from the gelatinous, oozy material of the roots of the hibiscus plant) that is mixed into the water with the fibers. This formation aid permits the papermaker to dip the mold (see figure 4.5) into the vat several times to add thickness with each dip. In the Tamezuki method no formation aid is used, and the papermaker can dip the mold into the vat only once—as is the case with Western papermaking.

With Nagashizuki, the sheets can be couched (laid onto one another in the growing pile of freshly made

sheets—called a *post*); with Tamezuki the sheets must be couched onto an intervening felt, with a felt alternating with a sheet through the full stack of the post. The sheets are pressed to remove as much of the water as possible, and then they are dried in various ways.

Manufacture—Western

In Western papermaking the fibers are macerated in one of two ways: with a stamper that pounds them in a machine called a *stamping mill* (a series of mortar-and-pestle-like constructs, with the pestles driven up and down into the mortars containing the pulp), or in a Hollander beater that grinds and cuts them down to tiny pieces. The *Hollander*, as it is called, is a large tub with a cylinder containing blades that run across the surface of the cylinder. As the cylinder turns, it pushes the pulp under it and around the tub, and the fibers are ground under the blades against a bedplate. (See figures 4.6 and 4.7.)

Once the fibers are macerated to the proper length, they are put into a vat, and the vatman (the person dipping the pulp out of the vat onto a mold) forms the sheets and couches them onto a *couch* (/kooch/), then covers each sheet with a woven wool felt and couches the next sheet onto the felt. The post (alternating layers of sheet/felt/sheet/felt) is then pressed

FIG. 4.6 (left) Stamping mill. (From *Papermaking: Art and Craft* [Washington, DC: Library of Congress, 1968], p. 34.) **FIG. 4.7** (right) Hollander beater. Shown with its cover up, revealing the cylinder containing the blades that grind the paper pulp against the bedplate. (From *Papermaking: Art and Craft* [Washington, DC: Library of Congress, 1968], p. 45.)

FIG. 4.8 Western paper mold for antique laid paper. Note that the mold has only one layer of wires, so paper made on this mold will have shadows around the chainlines. (Collection of the author.)

to remove the water, and the sheets are dried in various ways. The Western method coincides with the Asian Tamezuki method. (See figures 4.8–4.10.)

This description is, of course, oversimplified, but it gives an idea of the actions one must take to make paper. For rare book librarianship, one must understand the terms of the trade so that certain properties of the sheet can be described. Hence, an understanding of the paper mold is essential.

The Asian paper mold differs from the Western one. In Japan and China the mold was a rectangular frame, originally made of bamboo, with thin bamboo strips tied together to form a "sheet" of bamboo and laid across the surface of the frame. To hold the pulp

onto the surface of the mold during the papermaking process, a second frame was laid over the top of the one with the bamboo screen. Often this second, open frame was hinged onto the frame underneath. The papermaker thus had two items: the top and bottom frames hinged together (called the *keta* or *geta*), and the detachable screen made up of dozens of very thin slats of bamboo sewn together (called the *su*). Hence the whole contraption was called a *sugeta* or *suketa*.

In the West, from the earliest days of papermaking, the mold consisted of two parts: the mold and the deckle. The earlier molds are made of four pieces of wood, joined to form a rectangle, with very thin wires stretched left to right across the longer length of the mold. The four pieces of wood are supported across the short length of the mold by wooden supports, about ¾ of an inch to 1½ inches apart, to which the wires are sewn. The sewing is done with a chain stitch, which appears on top of the wires, right along the full length of each support, and sticking up above the level of the wires. The wires thus run at right angles to the chain stitches. A second frame with no wires in it, called the *deckle*, is placed over the mold when the vatman dips the tool into the vat to form a sheet. The part of the mold that has the wires on it is called the *mold*, though that term is also used for the whole tool.

Because the wires are very close together (there may be as many as a dozen per inch), the paper fibers do not fall through between them. The finely

 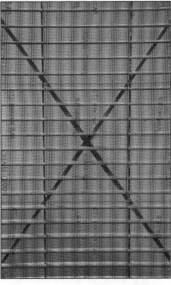

FIG. 4.9A (left) Western paper mold for modern laid paper, showing the mold with the deckle in place. Both layers of wire are visible (see figure 4.9B). (Collection of the author.) **FIG. 4.9B** (right) Western paper mold for modern laid paper. The mold, with its metal cross-bracing bars for stability and strength, has two layers of wires, so papers produced on this mold will have no shadows around the chainlines. This mold is from J. Barcham Green. It additionally has heavy cutting wires on the surface, so a large sheet made on it can easily be torn into nine smaller sheets, each with its own watermark (A and J Walker Ltd / Manchester) and countermark (HAND MADE). (Collection of the author.)

FIG. **4.10A** (left) Western paper mold for wove paper. Note the woven wire screen and the wire watermark of a doe. (Collection of the author.) **FIG. 4.10B** (right) Sheet of wove paper made from the mold shown in figure 4.10A, showing the doe watermark and a vatman's tear. (Sheet made by and in the collection of the author.)

beaten fibers do fall between the wires, but they do not fall through. Hence, the fibers fall over the face of the mold in three different levels: between the wires, on top of the wires, and on top of the chain stitches that go up each of the supports.

To form a sheet, the vatman positions the deckle over the mold and dips the mold (that is, the mold and deckle) into the vat and picks up water and pulp; the pulp settles onto the wires while the water drains off over the edges of the deckle and through the wires beneath the pulp. As the water drains out, the vatman shakes the mold gently left and right, with a torque or two if necessary, to spread the fibers evenly over the surface of the mold. (This is called the *vatman's shake.*) The fibers mat together on the mold and then they are transferred to a felt by couching, as described earlier in the Tamezuki method of Japanese papermaking. The sheet, now on a felt, is covered by another felt, and the process is repeated until there is a post of sheets interleaved with felts, which will be pressed to remove much of the water, and so on. As described earlier, the felts are then removed and the sheets (now forming the white post) are pressed again and then dried.

This process produces a sheet of paper that has three levels of thickness: thickest where the fibers have landed between the wires; thinner where the fibers have landed right on top of the wires; and thinnest where the fibers have fallen on top of the chain stitches, which are sticking up over the surface at right angles to the wires and which are spaced

an inch or so apart. When a sheet made this way is finally dry and held up to the light, less light shines through where the fibers have fallen between the wires. But at the wires themselves, the paper is thinner and more light shines through. This makes a whole leaf-worth of lines that run the full horizontal length of the sheet (when it is held in the landscape format). These are called *wirelines*. All these lines are visible as light shining through the sheet. The sheet is thinnest at the places where the chain stitches were—over the supports. That is, the sheet (still held in landscape format) will show running vertically a series of lines (light shining through the sheet) where each support was, because on top of these supports the chain stitches stand up far enough above the wires to make the fibers fall most thinly there. The lines formed by the chain stitches are called *chainlines*.

Paper made on this kind of mold is called *laid paper*, probably because it is laid onto the felts by hand. Hence laid paper has chainlines and wirelines, running at right angles to one another and visible when the sheet is held up to the light. If the pulp is thick enough, the chain stitches and wires leave a ribbing on the surface of the sheet, which can be seen even without holding the sheet up to the light and which can often be felt if it is pronounced enough and if the sheet has not been pressed in such a way as to iron out this three-dimensional effect.

All the lines visible in a sheet of handmade paper are thus called *laid lines*. This terminology is often

FIG. 4.11A (left) Sheet of antique laid paper, showing the watermark of a decorative crown and the countermark "J Whatman / 1801." Note the shadows around the chainlines, indicating that this is antique laid paper. **FIG. 4.11B** (right) Sheet of antique laid paper, showing four watermarks, one in each corner. This sheet is made by J. Barcham Green, Inc. (Both images collection of the author.)

misunderstood and misused. It is worth repeating: *laid paper is distinguished by its laid lines, of two kinds: chainlines and wirelines*. The wirelines are very close together and are at right angles to the chainlines, which are about an inch apart.[15]

If the mold has only a single layer of wires on it, when a sheet formed on it is couched (pressed against the woven felt to remove it from the mold), the supports under the wires press the fibers firmly against the felt, matting them more densely than are the fibers that are pressed between the supports. When a sheet of paper thus made is held up to the light, one sees the horizontal wirelines and the vertical chainlines. Around the chainlines there will be a shadow—that is, an area running the full length of the chainline—in which less light shines through the sheet than elsewhere where the fibers were not so densely pressed. This shadow will have the chainline right down the middle of it. The sheet thus produced is called *antique laid paper* (see figure 4.11).

To prevent the occurrence of this shadow, mold makers draw a second layer of wires across the mold, above the first layer, and sew them down with the same kind of chain stitch used for the first layer of wires. When the papermaker is couching a sheet of paper made with two layers of wires, the pressure on the felts is from the second layer of wires alone, because the supports are no longer putting pressure on the felts. Hence the fibers beneath the supports are not pressed densely together, and the resultant

sheet does not have the shadows around the chainlines. This kind of mold produces laid paper (with chainlines and wirelines), but with no shadows. The paper is called *modern laid paper* (see figure 4.12). Though the word *modern* implies something relatively recent, modern laid paper is almost as old as antique laid. There is nothing "modern" about it. It is approximately contemporary with the antique laid mold. So there are two kinds of laid paper—antique laid and modern laid, both with laid lines, one with shadows around the chainlines, the other without.

As with the *keta* in Japanese papermaking, the Western paper mold needs a device to hold the pulp on its surface just as it is being pulled out of the vat. Western molds have deckles—rectangular frames

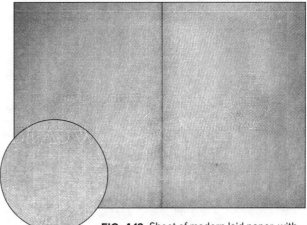

FIG. 4.12 Sheet of modern laid paper, with no shadows around the chainlines, showing the watermark and countermark of the Blauw company. (Collection of the author.)

that fit over the mold. As I have already explained, once the vatman has dipped the mold into the vat and pulled it out, water drains through the surface below, and the fibers mat. The deckle does not fit perfectly onto the surface below, and some of the fibers get beneath it. When the deckle is removed to allow for the couching of the newly formed sheet, the fibers that got underneath the deckle create an uneven edge on all four sides of the sheet. This is called the *deckle edge* (or the *deckled edge*). It is a characteristic of handmade paper.

To make paper Western style, one merely needs the raw fibers and water, plus a means of macerating the fibers. Paper made with only water and fibers, and nothing else in the vat, is called *waterleaf.* (See more about this paper in the section "Properties of Paper.")

In the 1750s, John Baskerville (1706–1775), one of England's great printers, designed a typeface with extremely fine serifs (the little projections off the main stem lines of letters, like the top and bottom cross lines on the capital *I*). The serifs were so fine that when they hit the page right where the chainlines were, they did not print well, because the paper was thin at the chainlines. Baskerville needed paper with fibers more evenly distributed over the whole sheet. The laid lines of laid paper made the sheet too thin to take the full serif.

With James Whatman, one of England's most famous papermakers, Baskerville (or the two in tandem)[16] came up with a paper mold made not by drawing wires in only one direction, but by weaving wires in both directions. The wires were actually woven together to make a screen that did not have any point higher than any other point. The mesh looked like a fine wire window screen. Because the paper was made by Whatman, for over two centuries it has been called *Whatman paper.* But the more

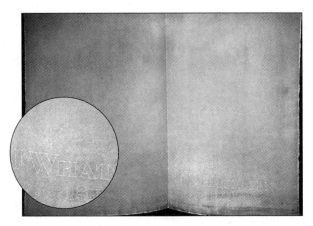

FIG. 4.13 Sheet of wove paper (with no laid lines) and with the watermark "J Whatman / 1839." (Collection of the author.)

generic term is *wove paper,* because it is made from a woven screen. (See figure 4.13.) This is a term, like *laid paper,* that every person dealing in special collections materials must know. The first wove paper appeared in 1757, at the end (the last twenty-eight leaves) of one of Baskerville's books, his edition of *Virgil's Bucolics, Georgics, and Aeneid.* The rest of the book is printed on laid paper.[17]

Paper made on a wove screen the way Whatman made it is still handmade, and it has deckles on all four edges. Until about 1800, all papers in the West were made by hand, most of which was laid, but by the end of the eighteenth century a huge amount of paper was being made on wove molds.

If the paper is waterleaf—made from fibers and water and nothing else—it will have millions of fibers matted together with tiny air pockets around all the fibers. Through capillary action, any liquid on its surface will get sucked into the sheet. A drop of ink dripped onto the surface of a sheet of waterleaf will feather out into the sheet. Modern newspaper, printed on cheap paper called *newsprint,* has the same characteristic. This feature was obviously

IN 1992 A BOOKSELLER in Sacramento called me to tell me he had just bought an incunabulum—a book printed in the incunabula period, from the birth of printing around 1450 to 1500. (The term means "swaddling clothes," and books printed in the fifteenth century are said to be *incunabula,* produced when printing was in its infancy.) He said that the title page was dated 1493. It was a lovely book, and worth a great deal because incunabula are heavily collected. I went to his shop and took the precious tome into my hands. In about ten seconds I saw that it was a fake: it was printed on wove paper. This is information that rare book librarians absolutely need to know, and this instance is a perfect example of why.

not good for printers, for though their inks were oil based, the ink would still feather out. Papermakers solved this problem by putting sizing into the sheets. Sizing is a kind of glue, usually an animal by-product, made by rendering hooves, skin, and bones. After the sheets are made and dried, they are dipped into a tank with the sizing dispersed in water. The sizing fills up all the tiny interstices around the fibers, so there are no air pockets to pull the ink in. This process produces *sized paper*. Because all the fibers are bonded together by this glue, the paper is also called *bond paper*, which merely means paper that has been sized. The method was developed when all paper was handmade, but machine-made paper, from its early manufacture in the nineteenth century on, is almost all sized.

Mold-Made Paper

One other kind of paper must be discussed: mold-made. Sheets of this paper are made in a cylinder machine. They are machine-made papers, but the screen on which they are made has thick "dividers" on them, often made of metal or rubber, so that when the large sheet is formed on the screen, the dividers yield very thin deposits of fibers such that the large sheet can easily be pulled apart into smaller ones. These sheets look like handmade papers because they usually have four deckles. And they can be made of high-quality pulp—all cotton, for instance—so they will have the look and feel of handmade sheets. They will, of course, have a grain, but other than that, they are often indistinguishable from handmade papers.

PROPERTIES OF PAPER

Let's recap: Paper has certain properties that people dealing with rare books must be able to identify and describe. The fibers are important: cotton, linen, or other plant fibers, sometimes mixed to produce papers with particular textures or colors or stiffnesses.

Whether the paper is laid or wove is important; if laid, it could be antique laid or modern laid.

The paper could be waterleaf or bond (unsized or sized).

IN THE 1960s I worked at a private press that used a great deal of handmade papers in its books. Most of the papers were sized, which meant that the surfaces of the sheets were fairly stiff and did not always take the ink well in the handpress. For centuries printers have been dampening their papers before printing on them, softening the size and making the surface of the sheet perfectly receptive to oil-based inks. A dampened sheet needs less ink than does one that is dry, and the ink prints smoothly and thoroughly on the moist surface.

The master printer in the shop used Umbria paper, an Italian sheet made by Fabriano, and he dampened it before printing. From the first impression we knew there was a problem, for fibers from the sheet were pulling out and onto the printing type. We figured out that Umbria was very lightly sized—or perhaps waterleaf—and the sizing that might have bonded the fibers together was not there. We let the paper dry and the printing went along fine. Special collections people should know their papers, not only those in the materials under their care, but also ones they might use for professional purposes, such as for invitations to department events or solicitation brochures to donors.

And the full sheet could be huge or quite small. There were no standard sizes of papers, and from one manufacturer to another—and even within a single paper mill—paper could be made in a great range of dimensions. (See appendix 4, "Paper Sizes.")

Watermarks

In the thirteenth century, the Fabriano mill created the first watermarks. The term *watermark* is a misnomer because it has nothing to do with water (other than the fact that the sheet was made from fibers that were floating in a vat of water). A watermark is an area in the sheet that is so thin that when the sheet is held up to the light, where the paper is thin, the light shines through. The watermark can be numbers, dates, letters, or words, it can be a geometrical or other shape, it can be images of animals or buildings or people, or it can be anything that the papermaker decided to create.

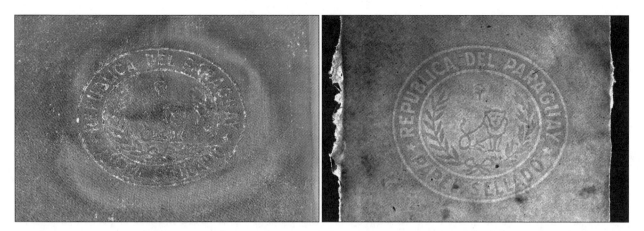

FIG. 4.14 (left) Wire screen showing a three-plane mark: "Republica del Paraguay / Papel Sellado." (Collection of the author.)
FIG. 4.15 (right) Sheet of wove paper with the three-plane watermark made by the screen shown in figure 4.14. Note that the words "Republica del Paraguay" are light; "Papel Sellado" is dark; the rest of the sheet is between these shades. Three different densities of pulp are displayed in this three-plane-watermarked sheet. (Sheet made by the author.)

To make a watermark, the papermaker must put something onto the top of the mold that will stand above the wires (or above the mesh in a wove mold). When the fibers are settling onto the top of the mold as the mold is being pulled out of the vat in the papermaking process, the fibers will fall more thinly over the raised surface than they will on the mold's surface. Imagine a wire clothes hanger bent into the shape of a circle; the circle of wire is then soldered or sewn to the surface of the mold. When the fibers land on the mold, they fall much more thinly over the hanger wire than they do elsewhere on the mold. When the sheet is dry and held up to the light, the light shines through brightly at the circle. (A wire watermark can be seen in figure 4.10.)

The watermark has a vast and varied history, and hundreds of thousands of them have been made through the centuries. Many of them are localizable—that is, they can be traced to a particular papermaker in a particular locale. And thus many of them are datable. In fact, many watermarks have dates in them. So if a book or manuscript or other document lacking information about its provenance (e.g., a date or place of manufacture) is written or printed on a watermarked paper, it is possible, given the correct reference tool, to locate the maker and approximate date of the paper.

Many sheets of paper will have more than a single mark on them. Often in the right half of a sheet there will be one mark, and a second mark will be on the left half. Each would likely be placed in the middle of the half of the sheet.[18] If this is the case, one of them (perhaps the one identifying the paper mill with its name or logo) is called the "watermark" and the other is called the "countermark."

Watermarks are formed in two other ways besides the wire-on-the-surface method. This first ("coat-hanger") method works for all kinds of papers (laid and wove). A second way, for wove papers, is to press the screen between the male and female faces of a die, impressing the screen in some places and maybe raising it in other places. If the screen has a raised area, fibers will fall more thinly there than they will fall on the normal surface of the screen, and the paper will be thinner at those raised areas. Hence a watermark will be visible at those thin areas. But the screen can also be impressed in such a way that depressions are formed, allowing more fibers to collect in those deep areas of the screen than will fall across the normal surface of the screen. The result is a place where the paper is thicker, and when held up to the light, the sheet will let less light through, creating a dark watermark. If the die creates both of these kinds of variations in the screen—embossed (raised) and debossed (indented)—the result is a sheet with three layers of fibers. This is called a *three-plane watermark* (see figures 4.14 and 4.15).

A third method of making watermarks works only for wove paper. The male and female parts of the die can be created to have many shaded layers of surfaces, so when the screen is pressed between the faces of the die, a multilayer screen is formed. This process produces quite amazing "pictures" in the watermark, for the fibers in the sheet are layered gradually from thick to thin (or vice versa), and a real image appears when the sheet is held up to the light (see figure 4.16). Such marks have three names: *shadowmarks, light-and-shade watermarks,* or *chiaroscuro watermarks.* The Fabriano paper mill has been producing these for more than a hundred years, as have many other mills. They are often used in security papers—that is, papers that are almost impossible to forge. Most countries' currencies use this kind of security device. So another property of paper is whether it is watermarked or not, and, if so, what kind of mark it has.

In the paper industry many other properties are tested: tensile strength, burst strength, wet strength, opacity and translucency, and so forth. For the rare book connoisseur, the information here should suffice for professional and scholarly purposes.

Dandy Rolls

As we have learned, the screen on which the paper is made in a machine may have a surface altered by stamping between faces of a die or having something sewn or soldered to it, creating a watermark. Another method of creating a watermark in a sheet uses a dandy roll, a large cylinder covered with a screen out of which protrudes the pattern of the watermark. Imagine a rolling pin with a wire mesh over it; the mesh has the configuration of a checkerboard pattern sticking up from its surface. In the large papermaking machine, when the pulp is being poured over the surface of the moving screen, at the very point when the water begins to drain through the screen, the dandy roll moves over the screen, dispersing the fibers in the still-soaking pulp into the checkerboard configuration that is on the surface of the dandy roll. This procedure creates thinner spots on the sheet where the dandy roll pattern is; and these thinner spots make the checkerboard watermark.[19] (See figure 4.17.)

FIG. 4.16A (top left) Light-and-shade watermark of a crow on a branch in winter, made by the hand-rubbing method. (From Thomas Keith Tindale and Harriett Ramsey Tindale, *The Handmade Papers of Japan* [Rutland, VT, and Tokyo: Tuttle, 1952], "The Watermark Collection.") (Collection of the author.) **FIG. 4.16B** (top right) Light-and-shade watermark of the *Mona Lisa*, from the Fabriano paper company. (Collection of the author.) **FIG. 4.16C** (bottom left) Light-and-shade watermark of the Kremlin, from Fabriano. (Collection of the author.) **FIG. 4.16D** (bottom right) Light-and-shade watermark of a cave with stalactites, from Fabriano. (Collection of the author.)

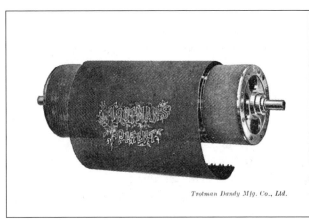 

FIG. **4.17A** (left) Dandy roll for making watermarks in machine-made paper. (From Sheldon Leicester, *Practical Studies for Paper Manufacturers and All Engaged in the Industry* [London: Charles Griffin; Philadelphia: J. B. Lippincott, 1924], p. 150.) FIG. **4.17B** (right) Dandy roll maker, soldering the mark onto the roll. (From *Papermaking: Art and Craft* [Washington, DC: Library of Congress, 1968], p. 76.)

Machine-Made Paper

When we consider the properties of paper, it is also important to discuss paper made after 1800, when the process of papermaking was mechanized. A great many hand papermakers remained in business, especially in the first half of the nineteenth century, but more and more paper was made by machine, made possible by the Baskerville/Whatman invention of wove paper.

Because laid paper was handmade, it had the cachet of a handmade object. Commercial paper mills, using machines in their manufacture, could mimic handmade papers in a number of ways. First of all, a true sheet made on a hand mold would have deckles on all four sides of the sheet. Commercially manufactured papers could be made with deckles, too—all around.

Paper made on a machine must necessarily be made from a wire mesh (that is, a wove screen). But manufacturers devised ways to impart a "watermark" into the paper that looks like the laid lines of modern laid paper. If the sheets were made from good stock (cotton or linen, or both, for instance), the paper could be of excellent quality and look like modern laid paper. (I know of no machine that can fabricate antique laid paper, with the shadows around the chainlines.) In fact, a really beautiful machine-made sheet can look and feel just like a handmade one.

Grain

Grain in paper is easily detectable if one is willing to tear the sheet. Witness the ease with which one can tear a newspaper page vertically, but the difficulty of tearing it straight horizontally. The paper will tear fairly straight with the grain, unevenly across it. In a handmade sheet, the vatman doing the shake is distributing the fibers evenly over the surface of the mold, with no constant motion in one direction, so the fibers do not line up, creating a grain. If you wish to know if the sheet has a grain or not, tear it in both directions. Of course, this test is not an option for books or broadsides or other paper-based library materials. But under a microscope one can see if the sheet is machine made or handmade, because in the machine process the fibers line up in the direction the screen is moving, creating a grain.[20]

The point here—for those in the rare book field—is that just because a sheet of paper has four deckles, laid lines in a modern-laid-paper configuration, and the excellent feel of a fine all-cotton paper, along with any number of kinds of watermarks, it could still be machine made.

PAPER DECORATION

As with all the other subtopics in this chapter having to do with paper, the literature on paper decoration is enormous. The importance of having a grasp of the specialized vocabulary of decorated paper cannot be overstated. In the rare book field, hundreds of millions of books have been adorned with decorated covers, endsheets, or even dust jackets. Presented here is a short overview of the subject, offering the key terminology that anyone dealing with rare materials must know.

From the beginning of the seventeenth century, publishers looked for ways to adorn their books without going to the expense of using tooled or stamped leather or vellum. Paper bindings were common, often as temporary covers put on to protect a volume until the buyer could have the book bound permanently in leather. Paper was a remarkably sturdy binding material, and many collectors, understanding this (and perhaps not in a position to pay for the more expensive leather covering) kept their books in paper.

People working with special collections materials should be able to describe any adornment that could wind up on a book cover or endpaper. As I just mentioned, bindings in paper were often decorated.[21]

Paper decoration is magical in many ways, not the least of which is in its infinite variety. It can be decorated in several ways: on its surface, in the composition of its pulp, and in the distribution of its pulp.

Surface Decoration—Marbling

For centuries marbling has been one of the most common means of decorating books, and it is essential to know its vocabulary. The history of marbling is buried in the distant past, but it seems to have developed in the ninth century in China, though no examples of such old marbles survive.[22] The earliest technique for such paper decoration is from Japan: *suminagashi* (see later in this section).

Marbling is perhaps the most recognizable and prolifically used of the methods of decorating paper. It is done by floating pigments on the surface of a bath and making them adhere to a surface of a piece of paper or other substance. (Marbling can be done to almost any material: cloth, leather, wood, plastic, metal, and just about anything else. For our purposes, we will consider only paper marbling.)

Western marbling was apparently an attempt to copy the paper adornment of the Japanese in their *suminagashi*, a technique that goes back to the twelfth century. The word means "the floating of ink" (*sumi* is "ink" in Japanese). The artists floated ink on the surface of a vat of water, often in concen-

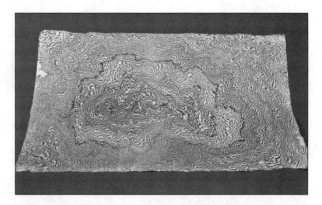

FIG. 4.18 Suminagashi sheet. (Collection of the author.)

tric or neighboring rings, then manipulated the air over the surface with their breaths, hands, or fans to make the inks move in wavy rings. Then they laid a piece of paper onto the surface of the water, and the inks would transfer to the sheets. If the sheet had sizing of any kind in it, the pattern would adhere to the surface of the sheet. If the paper were waterleaf (with no sizing), the pattern would impregnate itself into the paper and be visible from both sides of the sheet. (See figure 4.18.)

Presumably, artists in the West wanted to have a similar product and through much experimentation came up with the kind of decoration we now call *marbling*. The concept of marbling is simple: float colors on the surface of a size, leave them as they are in a random dispersion or manipulate them into a pattern, lay a sheet of paper over the surface of the size, and the pigments transfer to the sheet. The actual implementation is not so easy.

First, if the sheet is not prepared for the pigments, when it is laid over the size the pigments may transfer to it, but the colors will run off unless some mordant (a substance that allows the pigments to adhere) has been put onto the sheet. The sheet must be given a wash of a mordant like alum and then dried. It is now ready to be marbled.

Second, the bath that is to receive the pigments cannot be merely water, for that will be too "runny." That is, pigments dropped onto the surface of water will float hither and thither. The water must be thickened a bit to allow the drops to sit on the surface without floating around. Carrageen (also spelled carragheen and also called *Irish moss*), a similar natural thickening agent called carrageenan (also spelled carragheenan), methyl cellulose, gum tragacanth, sodium alginate, or some other thickener is mixed into the water. Now the size, floating in a shallow tray, is ready to receive the pigments.

For marbling to be successful, the pigments must be prepared in such a way that they float on the surface of the size, expand when dropped onto the surface, and do not blend with one another. That is, for instance, drops of blue dye must be able to sit next to (and touch) drops of green without the two colors mixing together. To achieve this result, the marbler must mix ox gall into the pigments. This putrid-smelling, thick liquid comes from inside an ox's gall bladder. Ox gall must first be mixed with alcohol and then mixed a few drops at a time with the pigments. It allows the drops to sit on the surface of the size and, when the drop hits the surface, to spread out into a circle. If the circle is not big enough (that is, if it does not spread out enough), the marbler adds a few more drops of the ox gall to the color, and it will spread more.

To marble a sheet of paper, the artist drops the prepared pigments over the size—in one or more colors. At this point, the sheet with alum on its surface is laid over the surface of the size, and the colors will transfer to the sheet. The result is a random distribution of droplets on the sheet. If the artist wishes, the drops can be manipulated with a comb or other fine tools into a pattern. Then the pattern can be transferred to the sheet. (See figures 4.19, 4.20, and 4.21.)

Also, if the sheet is not laid down over the size in a smooth movement, but is shaken as it is put over the size, the bath ripples back and forth and causes the pigment to "bunch up and thin out" as the sheet touches the surface. This creates a ripple effect in the final distribution of the pigments; it is called *Spanish marbling* (this can be seen in figure 4.19A).

Patterns can be endless, as can the use of colors. Many common patterns are named: nonpareil, bouquet, peacock, French snail, chevron, and so on. Even the nonpatterned distributions of droplets have names: Stormont, stone, vein, tiger-eye, Gloucester, and others. Turkish marblers were possibly the first to create pictures beyond geometric patterns. Common images are flowers, horses with grooms, and other representational images. Also, using stencils,

---

ONE OF THE great mysteries of marbling is the use of ox gall. Without the ox gall, marbling just won't work. But getting the ox gall is a particularly unpleasant, not to say disgusting, act. One of the world's great marblers, Karli Frigge, has written about her experience obtaining ox gall:

> Ox-gall can be obtained from the slaughterhouse. About once a year I check in with the porter, hoping to leave my bucket with him. But it is never as easy as that.
>
> A tall ashen man in a blood-stained coat comes for me and together we set off on a long journey past all those slaughterhouse sections one would rather not see. I know that this is the price I have to pay for ox-gall.
>
> I try to keep my eyes fixed straight ahead, to look only at where I am going. I jump over pools of blood and yet I am somewhat upset by the time we get to the section where the bladders are cut out. The man selects a couple of big, intact specimens and throws them into my bucket.
>
> At home I cut off all the loose, flabby masses of strange tissue, and pierce a hole into the bladder. Carefully I let the dark brown fluid ooze into a jar, mix it with equal parts of alcohol and put it away in a cool place.
>
> After a few days I pour off the pure liquid and discard the dregs. It is ready for use.*

How did anyone know that this fetid goo from the gall bladder of an ox, when mixed with alcohol, and then mixed with pigment, would allow drops of that pigment to sit on the surface of the size, not blend with other pigment drops, and expand out over the surface of the liquid?

*Karli Frigge, *Marbled Flowers* ([Buren, Netherlands]: Fritz Knuf, [1990]); quoted in Sidney Berger, *Karli Frigge's Life in Marbling* (Newtown, PA: Bird and Bull Press, 2004), 37–38.

---

artists can have a sheet with anything representational or calligraphic marbled onto it.

These methods can be combined, with one pattern marbled over another; with Spanish rippling done on a combed nonpareil pattern; or with three or more layers of pigment marbled over one another.[23]

Another kind of marbling has been practiced for centuries: the oil-on-water technique, in which

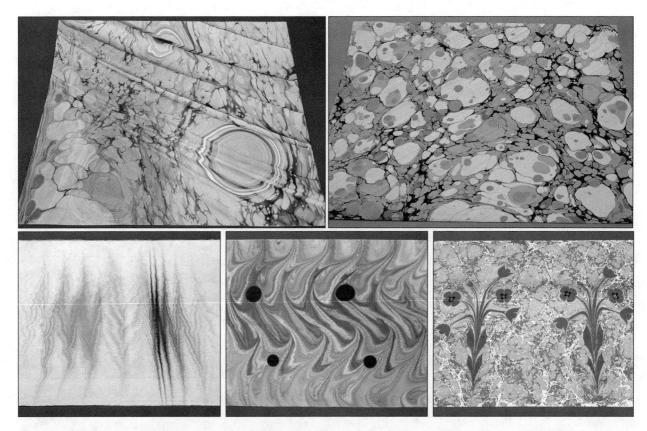

FIG. 4.19A (top left) Random-marbled sheet. (Collection of the author.) **FIG. 4.19B** (top right) Random-marbled sheet, stone pattern. (Collection of the author.) **FIG. 4.20A** (bottom left) Patterned marbled sheet. One of the "landscape" marbles by Karli Frigge. (Collection of the author.) **FIG. 4.20B** (bottom center) Patterned marbled sheet. A sheet of Karli Frigge's "wings" marbles. (Collection of the author.) **FIG. 4.21** (bottom right) Figural marbled sheet. Turkish marbling of poppies. (Collection of the author.)

no thickener is necessary in the water. Because oil floats on water, all one needs to do is drop oil-based pigments onto the marbling bath, and they will sit on the surface, ready to be picked up by the sheet of paper. But because there are no thickeners, the pigments can float any way they wish, so it is practically impossible to comb them into any kind of controlled shape. The randomness of this method mirrors the randomness of marbling on a prepared size when no combing or manipulation of the pigments is done.

Describing marbled paper should not give the scholar any problem, once the fact that the sheet has been marbled is determined. Marbled papers are quite smooth, the pigments sitting flat on the surface. The more familiar one is with the many patterns, paints, and methods of marbling, the easier it is to spot the technique.

Surface Decoration—Paste Papers

Besides marbling, as early as the beginning of the seventeenth century, papermakers began decorating their sheets using colored pastes. Any paste will do, but wheat starch or rice starch paste is a common medium. The paste is mixed with a pigment and is then spread with a sponge or brush over a sheet of paper. While the paste is still wet, it can be manipulated in any of hundreds of ways.

Two sheets with paste freshly brushed over the surface can be put together with the wet pasted surfaces touching one another. They are then pulled apart, and the result is a "pattern" of striations and blotches where the sheets were touching. This is called a "pulled pattern," though there is really no pattern. While the sheets are still together, the artist can press them in many ways to manipulate the paste inside. When they are pulled apart, the pressing leaves the paste shaped in whatever way it was influenced when the wet surfaces were together.

More common is the decorated paste paper. If the wet paste is touched by a fingertip, the result is a little fingertip-shaped dot in the paste. One can touch the paste with a rubber stamp, a potato carving, or anything else that leaves a shaped disruption in the paste. A wood-graining tool can be used to leave a wood-grain pattern. A jar lid can be laid down in the wet paste and pulled a small distance, leaving a circular pattern. And so on ad infinitum. There are no limits to the decoration possible with paste on paper. Paste papers can be monochrome or multicolored, and they can be decorated with any tool one has at hand. A patterned ceiling tile, a pastry-crimping wheel, a potato masher, a patterned pastry roller, a crumpled sheet of paper, brushes, a bookbinder's wheel, or anything else that can disrupt the smoothly brushed-on paste will do.

David Bourbeau describes the process:

> Paste paper is basically a mixture of paste (made from wheat flour or some similar starch) and ground watercolor pigments (or acrylic paint as is more common now), which is applied to dampened paper with brushes, rollers, or sponges. It is then combed, scraped, pulled, or otherwise manipulated into a seemingly unlimited variety of textures and patterns. As the moisture evaporates and the paper dries, light and dark shadows create an interesting three-dimensional effect inherent in this method.[24]

In describing paste papers, one can delineate colors and shapes, pictorial representations, or whatever else one sees. The paste could be on a crumpled or creped sheet, so the substrate might be worth mentioning. (See figure 4.22.)

Some historical paste papers are identifiable, like those by the Moravian sisters in the eighteenth century. Certain modern paste-paper artists have distinctive sheets, identifiable by the patterns they have created or the way they have spread the pigments onto the sheet.

Identifying paste papers is easy: the strokes made by the brush, sponge, or rag should be visible, and the paste has quite a distinct appearance from the look of the pigments in marbling. Describing paste

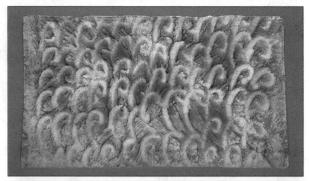

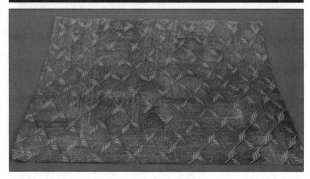

FIG. 4.22A (top) Paste paper, 18th century. (Collection of the author.) **FIG. 4.22B** (center) Paste paper from Susanne Krause, floral pattern. (Collection of the author.) **FIG. 4.22C** (bottom) Paste paper from Susanne Krause, lozenge pattern. (Collection of the author.)

papers is fairly simple: state the color and the decoration. Certain colors and patterns were popular in the eighteenth century and though they have been copied in the last fifty or so years, the older papers have a look to them that is distinct. So an old binding with a paste paper on it will have a certain look that is almost impossible to copy.

Surface Decoration—Block-Printed Papers

Block printing goes back many centuries, but for the decoration of papers it appears commonly in the early seventeenth century. Simple patterns—often geometrics or florals—were printed in one, two, or

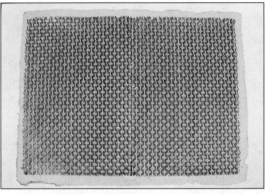

FIG. 4.23A (left) Block-printed paper, late 18th century. (Collection of the author.) **FIG. 4.23B** (right) Wood block used to make block-printed paper, mid- to late 18th century. (Collection of the author.)

three colors. Some Italian companies like Remond-ini (in business in Bassano del Grappa, Italy, from 1634 to 1861) produced hundreds of patterns of these papers, often quite beautiful and charming. They also produced more elaborate patterned sheets, with pictures of flower baskets and court scenes. The papers were used widely as binding materials, usually for the covers, though occasionally one sees them as endpapers. They were used especially for dissertations, almanacs, and copy books, but they could appear covering texts on any topic.

Today hundreds of Italian block-printed (and machine-printed) papers are available in art-supply stores. Some of the old eighteenth- and nineteenth-century patterns are still available from Italy, printed from the original blocks. But the papers they are printed on and the modern, bright pigments they are printed with mark them as new. The Italians today produce many sheets with the old designs or with new designs modeled on antique ones. (See figure 4.23.)

In the world of special collections, one will find books on the market from the eighteenth century with these attractive papers. On many volumes one will see a sheet that covers only half the cover, with a second one with the same pattern glued down right next to the first sheet. That is, binders could use two scraps, neither big enough to bind a volume, but together large enough to cover the boards. One might even see this technique with a geometrical pattern in which, on one piece of the paper, the pattern goes horizontally, and, on the other piece, it goes vertically. Perhaps the binders thought that

the book's owner would have a permanent leather binding put onto the volume, so it was expedient and cost-effective to use up the paper scraps. This is in no way an inferior binding. It shows that the binders were economical with their use of the papers, and it was such a common practice that no one would have commented critically on it.

Surface Decoration—Other Methods

One simple way to decorate a sheet of paper is simply to drop pigments onto its surface. Take a blank sheet and, using a brush, for instance, splatter drops of the color or colors onto it. This technique can be used on sheets already decorated, so that the thousands of tiny spatters cover a marbled or paste paper sheet. For marbling, the spattering can be done in the bath before the sheet is placed onto the size, or it can be done after the sheet is finished being marbled. The technique has several names: spattered, splattered, sprinkled, spotted, and scratted.

With marbling, the pattern is transferred from the surface of a size to the sheet. With this "drip" method, the pigments make their way directly to the surface of the sheet. So although it is sometimes called *bench marbling*, this method is not really a form of marbling.

In the 1920s, Edward Seymour of the Fancy Paper Company devised a machine that automatically dropped pigments onto the surface of a long roll of paper that was unrolling underneath the brushes that delivered the colors. He was not the first to make "machine-marbled papers"—what he called *art marbles*—because they had been done by the French in the nineteenth century. But his papers spread throughout the binding community of English-speaking countries, and hundreds of thousands of books are now adorned with them.[25] The papers are not true marbles because the colors are applied directly to the sheets, but they are distinct and recognizable, and people in the rare book world should know about them because they are likely to encounter books with these papers used for their bindings. (When Seymour used the words *art marbles*, he meant *artificial marbles*.)

As I just mentioned, bench marbling is a form of paper decoration that is not real marbling because the pigments are placed directly onto the sheet. Seymour was adept at this method, too. Standing at a bench, he would place a sheet of blank paper onto a board in front of him. Then he would put the pigments onto the sheet, sometimes by dropping them and sometimes by pouring them on. He could then raise the board and guide where the pigments flowed on the sheet by tipping the board left and right, forward and back. In creating "tree-marbled calf" (see the bookbinding section below), the binder could create similar patterns. So Seymour could produce sheets with a tree-like pattern on them, created with pigments.

Pigments can be sponged onto a sheet, literally with a sponge, or with a rag or paper towel or other material. This technique can produce quite attractive "patterns." Similarly, paper can be decorated by having pigments poured over the surface, somewhat like the way it is done in bench marbling, but on a flat surface that is not raised. One method of achieving this added coloring is not with pigments per se, but with colored pulp. Using some kind of container (think of a restaurant ketchup or mustard squeezer), the artist can pour on colored paper pulp in any pattern desired. It can be poured onto a stencil that is laid over the sheet, with a determined pattern, or it can be poured freestyle. This technique creates "poured-pulp papers," a common Japanese means of decoration.

In yet another variation of paper decoration, batik methods are used, with wax-resist techniques. Similar methods are used to decorate fabrics, and they work well on papers. One artist draws pictures or

IN ECHIZEN, JAPAN, a papermaking village, I saw another composite method of paper decoration in which a sheet of paper is couched onto a table, then the artist, using a stencil-like device, pours colored pulps onto the sheet. The device is removed, and then using a paper mold with no screen but with raised bars of copper shaped in patterns (in this case, the patterns of animals), the papermaker scoops up colored pulp from a different vat, the pulp sitting on the raised bars in the animal shapes, and then couches these animal outlines onto the sheet. This technique creates a lovely sheet with a whole picture on it, made from couched and poured pulps.

shapes over the entire surface of a sheet using crayons. She then soaks the sheet in water, crumples it up, creating thousands of cracks in the crayons' wax, and then paints the sheet with a colored pigment, which tints the paper in the places where the wax is cracked. The sheet is then placed between two other sheets of paper and is ironed flat. (Mindy Dubansky of the Metropolitan Museum of Art in New York City devised this technique.) This process produces a provocative leaf that can be used in book decoration (covers, endpapers, dust wrapper).

Chiyogami

The Japanese are the most prolific papermakers in history, making, by hand, thousands of kinds of sheets, and papers with endless decorations. Here I will discuss only one kind of paper because it is perhaps the best known of the Japanese decorated sheets: Chiyogami.

Originally these papers were decorated with woodblocks, but in the nineteenth century the Japanese began using stencils (called *katazome*), applying anywhere from one to more than two dozen colors through the hand-cut *katazome*. The patterns seem endless: people, children, flowers, wagons, balloons, implements, dolls, water, clouds, scenes from classic literature, trees, towns, umbrellas, toys, geometrics, clothing, and on and on. There are thousands of patterns and subject matters on these papers, printed onto *kozo* papers (though in the twentieth

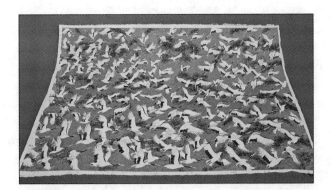

FIG. 4.24 Chiyogami paper with cranes. (Collection of the author.)

century many of the *kozo* sheets have wood pulp in them, and they could be made in Korea or India, or in other countries). (See figure 4.24.) These lovely papers have many uses. Here I will emphasize only bookbinding (covers and endsheets), though they are likely to show up in collections that special collections departments acquire—as paper dolls (among many other paper collectibles), bookmarks, and box coverings.[26] Those in the rare book world should be able to identify these sheets and know how to describe them.

Many other methods of paper decoration are used, limited only by the imaginations of the artists who employ them.

Pulp Composition

Paper can be made decorative by means of what is in the pulp.[27] In the vat, for plain paper, one needs only water and fibers. But a common way to decorate paper is to add leaves or glitter, little pieces of colored threads, or anything else that will show up in the final sheet. The Japanese are masters at this, introducing an endless array of decorative elements into their papers. Sometimes the inclusions are just dropped into the vat. Sometimes a sheet is couched, decorative items are placed over it, and a second sheet is couched over the first to make one sheet with essentially three layers, the top and bottom layers of paper and the middle layer of whatever was sandwiched in. Popular inclusions are butterfly wings, leaves from various trees and bushes, and colored threads. And the Chinese and Japanese also have perfected a kind of paper decorated with metallic gold and silver flakes.

Of course, paper can be decorated when dyes are added to the vat, so the composition of the pulp could include colors. Or it could include such things as sand or other texturizing agents or mica to give the paper a sparkle.

Distribution of Fibers

Paper can also be decorative in the way the fibers are distributed in the sheet. Hence the thinning out or thickening of a sheet to create a watermark of one sort or another can be a form of decoration. Not all watermarks are decorative, but many of them are.

The surface of the sheet can also be adorned. If the paper is made on a mold with a strong three-dimensional texture, the surface of the sheet may exhibit that texture, especially if the paper is not pressed under such weight as to smooth out the surface. (See calendering in the following paragraph.) Paper can also be embossed or debossed (with raised or indented patterns). Some papers—even machine-made ones—are created on a screen with a pronounced laid pattern. The paper that emerges from the mold or the machine will have laid lines (visible when the sheet is held up to the light), but it also may have a laid texture on the surface, palpable with the fingertips and visible under a raking light. This product is not really the same as a "decorated paper," but the technique adds a level of sumptuousness to the sheet because it looks (and could actually be) handmade.

Not directly related to "distribution of fibers," but linked to the surface of the sheet, is *calendering,* the pressing of the paper between rollers to smooth off the sheet. A calendering machine has highly polished cylinders between which a sheet of paper may be pressed. One cylinder can be made to move faster than the other, so that the sheet is polished on one side. The sheet may be turned over and put between the rollers again to burnish or polish it on both sides. In a fourdrinier—a commercial papermaking machine—there might be what is called the *calender stack*, a stack of three or more such cylinders. The newly formed sheet, coming off the machine and eventually to be rolled up, goes through a series of these calendering cylinders, giving the sheet a smooth, almost glasslike surface. If the cylinders are

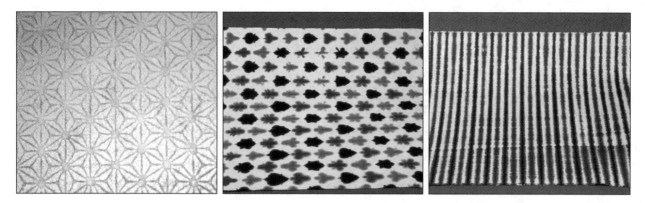

FIG. 4.25 (left) Lace paper, Japan, 20th century. (Collection of the author.) **FIG. 4.26A–B** (center and right) Itajime: Japanese folded-and-dyed sheets. (Collection of the author.)

heated, the paper is termed *hot pressed*. If no heat is used in the calendering, the paper is *cold pressed*. These are terms for artists' papers, the kind that wind up in prints and drawings in rare book libraries. (Calendering can also be done to cloth, and many book cloths are calendered, giving them a bright, smooth finish.)

The pulp can also have clay, calcium carbonate, kaolinite, polyethylene, silicone, or any other such material as part of its composition imparted to the paper's surface. When it is calendered, the surface of the sheet becomes glossy. Magazines and illustrations in books are often on such coated paper. If a glossy sheet with china clay gets wet, the clay in adjoining sheets could fuse if the papers are not pulled apart quickly after the sheets are soaked. If the two wet sheets with their surfaces still touching are allowed to dry, they form a single block of paper that is not repairable.

Lace Paper

From Japan, lace papers are used for bindings or sometimes as flyleaves in books. They are called *lace* because the fibers are distributed in lace-like patterns resembling snowflakes, concentric circles, fans, spider webs, and other traditional motifs. They are produced in white, cream, pink, light blue, and other fairly light colors. (See figure 4.25.)

OTHER KINDS OF PAPER DECORATION

Crepe Paper

Crepe paper was invented in the nineteenth century, possibly in Japan.[28] It was used for prints and to print books, and from the 1880s until the 1920s, the Takejiro Hasegawa crepe paper books, printed in hundreds of thousands, were tremendously collectible. They were done in English, French, German, Spanish, Italian, and other European languages. They are worth mentioning here at some length because many special collections departments have these in their holdings, and there are major collections of them at several libraries.[29]

The paper was called *crepe* because it has the look and feel of the French fabric of the same name. From the noun we get the verb *to crepe*, meaning "to wrinkle up or crinkle" (as in, "Is the paper creped?").

The texts were often aimed at children (there were several fairy tale series), though the books were so beautiful they were collected by adults. They were printed on fine Japanese paper, with multicolor woodblock illustrations done on the paper before the creping. The crinkling reduced the sheets slightly in both directions and intensified the colors in the illustrations. Hasegawa had rivals, who also printed these illustrated books on crepe paper, but he was by far the most prolific and collectible of the publishers of these books.

Itajime

Itajime is Japanese folded-and-dyed paper. It is used in bookbinding, and it is easily identifiable: the folds create lines down the sheet. The paper is dipped into the dye along the folds and, depending on the folding patterns, the resulting sheets are decorated with dyed lines or geometric patterns. The artists usually use rich colors, like deep blue, red and orange, or green. (See figure 4.26.)

Dutch Gilt Papers

About 1700, German bookbinders, wanting an inexpensive substitute for leather, created a decorated paper that was beautiful, even sumptuous in its own way, and quite easy to make, especially when compared to the efforts required to create decorated leather covers.

Dutch gilt paper (from the word *deutsch* meaning "German") was good-quality paper that was decorated in a number of ways. Usually the sheets were brushed with a colored paste (as was done in the first step of creating paste papers), though some sheets are decorated without the color ground. The colored paste would be put on in a single color or in a mottled pattern of several colors. The sheet was then gilded, stamped with a metal plate with a pattern on it using gold foil (or a gold-colored foil). There were dozens of patterns: geometrics, people doing many kinds of things, saints, animals, flowers, rural scenes, and a host of other images. Silver-colored foils were also used, and the gold-colored foils were often mixed with copper or other metals to give the metallic pattern a reddish hue. (See figure 4.27.)

The German word for this paper is *Brokatpapier*, giving us a second English name for them: *brocade papers*. "Sometimes the papers were called 'Kattunpapier' (cotton, calico, or chintz paper), so named because the patterns stamped on them were influenced strongly by the fabrics used for clothes and linens" (Berger, "Decorated Paper," p. 6). Kattunpapier was supposedly produced with woodblocks and stencils, but the term was transferred to what we now call Dutch gilt papers (Wolfe, *Marbled Paper*, p. 22).

A similar-looking paper from the same time, also from Germany, used metallic powders (not foils) that were sprinkled onto freshly printed or stenciled sheets. Where the printed-on or brushed-on mordant was still wet, the gold, silver, or bronze powder adhered. The sheet was raised to allow the excess powder to fall off, leaving the metallic pattern

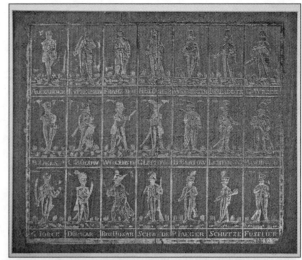

FIG. 4.27A (top) Dutch gilt sheet showing soldiers, 18th century. Note that the pattern is stamped in metallic foil over a paste-decorated sheet. (Collection of the author.) **FIG. 4.27B** (center) Dutch gilt sheet showing alphabet, 18th century. (Collection of the author.) **FIG. 4.27C** (bottom) Dutch gilt sheet with geometric pattern, 18th century. (Collection of the author.)

where the mordant was. The German terms for these papers are *Goldfirnispapier*, *Silberfirnispapier*, and *Bronzefirnispapier* (in English called *gold-*, *silver-*, and *bronze-varnish papers*). They differ from the Dutch gilts in that the latter usually have a pronounced bite into the sheet where the metal plate pressed the gold foil into the paper (unless these sheets have been pressed so much as to remove their three-dimensionality); the ones made with the metallic powder generally lack the impression, the metallic pattern sitting on a smoother surface. From a distance, these two kinds of decoration look alike. Up close, one is distinguishable from the other. And both were extensively used for book and pamphlet covers in the eighteenth century.

These papers were produced for about a hundred years—until the beginning of the nineteenth century. They appear in abundance on dissertations, almanacs, and gift books. And they were used into the first quarter of the nineteenth century, as supplies lasted. One may find a lovely Dutch gilt sheet that is datable to, say, the last quarter of the eighteenth century, but used on a pamphlet dated from 1820. Full sheets are still obtainable, but rarely, and some modern artists have tried their hand at making comparable papers, with varying levels of success.[30]

PAPER—DESCRIPTION

One thing about paper that is nettlesome for those in the rare book field is its description—specifically having to do with its colors, but also with respect to its bulking, its watermarks, its surface, its opacity, and any of its other physical properties.

Some features are easy to describe: Does it have deckles? Is it antique laid, modern laid, or wove? How big is it? (Physical measurements are tricky in any book that has had its leaves trimmed.) How far apart are its chainlines? Does it have watermarks and countermarks? What do they look like, how big are they, and where are they placed in the sheet? Other features are more difficult to deal with, the most problematic being color.

G. Thomas Tanselle addresses this problem in two landmark essays, "A System of Color Identification for Bibliographical Description" (Tanselle, "System")

and "The Bibliographical Description of Paper" (Tanselle, "Bibliographical"), in which he writes,

> One of the peculiarities in the historical development of descriptive bibliography has been the small attention paid to paper. Since paper and inked type-impressions are the two principal physical ingredients of a book and since paper is the one which gives a book its most obvious physical characteristics (shape, size, weight, bulk), it would seem natural for a description of paper to occupy a prominent position in any description of a book. Yet the majority of descriptive bibliographies of the past make no mention of paper, except the indirect references afforded by an indication of format or leaf measurement. Those that do include some description of paper generally provide no more than a few words, such as "Wove paper, unwatermarked" or "Printed on white wove paper." ("Bibliographical," p. 27)

In his essay on cloth bindings, Tanselle says that there is a "dichotomy in the verbal presentation of visual data: one may either use a precise, technical term, which often has little immediate meaning for the uninitiated reader, or else a more readily visualized term, which often is less exact and which breaks down when fine discriminations are needed" ("System," p. 204).

These essays present the bibliographer (and others wishing to describe items in their libraries) with a challenge: how does one delineate clearly what one is looking at? If a bookseller offers a rare book librarian a copy of one of William Morris's multi-volume works and describes it as covered with blue cloth, what does the word "blue" refer to? How many shades of blue are there? Morris had his books bound in various shades of cloth. Which shade of blue is this particular set bound in?

This is also a problem with paper, of course. Today we have the good fortune to have technology that can accompany our verbal texts, so it is possible to have an image attached to a bibliographical record (or to have a picture accompany a quote from a bookseller to a librarian) that shows the item in hand. But how accurate is the camera that took the image? How accurate are the monitors we are using to show us the colors?[31]

When Tanselle wrote his essay on the description of paper (in 1971), he could accurately conclude,

> It should go without saying, in other words, that a descriptive bibliography, if it is adequately to describe certain books as physical objects, is obligated to include some description of the paper used in those books. But bibliographers have no place to turn for detailed instructions about which features to record, how to present them, and how to vary the treatment so as to preserve the overall proportions of the description. A standard procedure for these matters is desirable, both to insure balanced coverage in the recording of information and to facilitate later reference to the information. ("Bibliographical," p. 31)

He discusses at length chainlines, sizes, watermarks, and other physical features, such as thickness, color, and finish. His essays are excellent guides for special collections people, and they should be studied with care. For our purposes, however, here are a few simple guidelines for those working with rare books who wish to describe papers:

- If possible, state whether the paper is antique laid, modern laid, or wove. (If the paper is tipped in or pasted down to covers, it may be impossible to determine whether it is laid or wove.)
- If possible, give the dimensions of the full sheet or of the leaf if the paper is a broadside or in a book.
- State if the sheet has deckles or not.
- Describe any watermarks or countermarks, if possible.
- Give at least a generic statement of the paper's color (e.g., bright white, off-white, cream, gray, light [or pale] blue, etc.).
- If it is determinable, name the maker (sometimes revealed in the watermark or, for some private press books, in the colophon).
- Describe any decoration: marbled (if the pattern is nameable, name it); paste paper; block-printed; with inclusions (describe the inclusions); Dutch gilt; and the like.
- Describe any defects (e.g., with a hole, torn, wrinkled).

Ink

Those in the rare book world do not often need to speak of the ink used to print the books in their care. But a cursory knowledge is essential, for ink is ubiquitous in the world of books.

Basically, black ink has been made for centuries out of lampblack and linseed oil. Other oils have been used, and colored inks do not use lampblack, of course. This simple formula produces an alkaline ink that will not damage paper or other substrates.

Another source of the black, however, was a problem: oak galls. Ink made with these was sometimes called "iron gall ink" because it contained iron salts. The galls were small, marble-sized "pods" that were formed when a gall fly laid its eggs in a tree and the tree formed the galls as a kind of protection.

Lois Fruen says,

> Iron-gall ink was the most important ink in Western history. Leonardo da Vinci wrote his notes using iron-gall ink. Bach composed with it. Rembrandt and Van Gogh drew with it. The Constitution of the United States was drafted with it. . . . And, when the black ink on the Dead Sea Scrolls was analyzed using a cyclotron at the Davis campus of the University of California, it was found to be iron-gall ink (Nir-el 157). (Fruen, "Iron Gall Ink")

If the documents on which the ink was used are stored properly—away from high temperatures and humidity—the documents have a chance of lasting a long time.

> The ink was generally prepared by adding some ferrous sulfate ($FeSO4$) to a solution of gallotannic acid, but any iron ion donor can be used. The tannic acid was usually extracted from oak galls (also known as "oak apples" or more correctly Oak marble galls), or galls of other trees; hence the name. Fermentation or hydrolysis of the extract releases gallic acid, which yields a darker black ink. The fermented extract is combined with the ferrous sulfate and a binder such as gum arabic. ("Iron Gall Ink," Wikipedia)

As the Wikipedia entry explains, this ink was quite acidic, and it could have seriously deleterious effects on paper and other substrates. The ink may have looked black when it was new, but over time it could turn brown and eat through the paper beneath it. Where this ink was used, many a manuscript page is extremely fragile or eaten away. Likewise, if the ink were used in fountain pens, it would corrode the metal inside them.

Ink received some serious press when a group of scientists and humanists got together to analyze the inks in the Gutenberg Bible. Using a cyclotron, they were able to distinguish one batch of Gutenberg's ink from another. (See Cahill, Kusko, and Schwab, "Analyses of Inks," and Schwab et al., "Cyclotron Analysis," in the bibliography at the end of this chapter.) Hence, the analysis of ink has been exceptionally valuable in rare book scholarship in recent years, and rare book librarians should be familiar with the literature in this field.

Printing Type

Thousands of volumes have been written about printing type. Those in rare books need to know a good deal about this subject because almost everything they handle in this field will have some form of printing.

Cylinder seals and stamps were in use more than five thousand years ago in Mesopotamia to transfer "text" from the seals into clay. The Chinese invented printing in the third century AD, using woodblocks that were carved with the text in reverse (i.e., mirror writing), inked, and covered with a sheet of paper or cloth, which was pressed against the block. "The oldest confirmed printing remnant is a Korean sutra from about AD 750; a printed Buddhist charm from Japan dates to about 768–770" (Berger, "Reconsidering Gutenberg," p. 14).

For our interests here, we shall look at printing type in the West, not at the other methods of printing that the Japanese and Koreans borrowed from the Chinese. The historical and technical information here may not have a direct application to the day-to-day activities of everyone in the rare book field. But a skeleton history of this topic is absolutely essential because just about everything in the hands of anyone in this field is impacted by this history. Also,

IF WE ASSUME, as most people do, that Johannes Gutenberg invented the tools that made Western printing possible,* then we owe him our gratitude for three major achievements. *Note:* Gutenberg did not invent printing. Gutenberg did not invent the printing press. And Gutenberg is not the "Father of Printing," though he may be given that title if we add "from movable type in the West." These are errors perpetuated for generations, akin to the one about the invention of paper in AD 105. People in the rare book world should never make these mistakes.

*"There . . . is evidence that the Dutch printer Laurens Janszoon Coster (c. 1370–1440) developed a method of printing from movable type before Gutenberg perfected his techniques and equipment" (Berger, "Reconsidering Gutenberg," p. 14).

those in rare books are targets for questions from laypeople who want to know about printing, type and typefaces, and other book-arts topics, and an ignorance of this information is embarrassing and unprofessional. One should not perpetuate long-standing errors, guesses, and incorrect information.

Asian characters were logograms, characters representing whole spoken words. To print from movable type, the Chinese and Koreans needed to cast one piece of type for each logogram in their language. In the West, writing was done using alphabets in which individual characters represented sounds, not words. The Chinese needed thousands of different pieces of type; in the West printers needed only as many as were necessary to express each sound and combination of sounds, plus other pieces of type for numbers, punctuation, and special characters (e.g., parentheses, brackets, asterisks, daggers, and the like). To be knowledgeable about books and broadsides, ephemera, and other printed materials, one must understand the method by which printing was originally done.

Gutenberg's three developments changed the course of the book and, to be sure, the course of civilization. His first and most important invention was the adjustable type mold. Gutenberg's crowning achievement was a type-casting mold that created individual pieces of type (called *sorts*) that were uni-

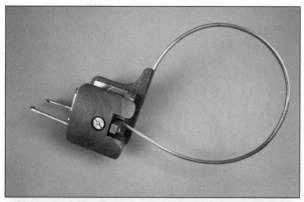

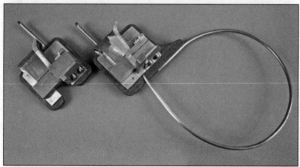

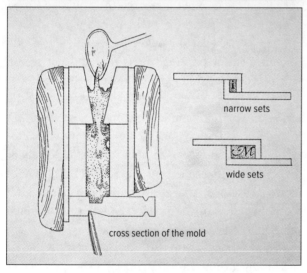

narrow sets

wide sets

cross section of the mold

FIG. 4.28A (top) Type mold for hand-casting printing type, closed; made by Stan Nelson. (Collection of the author.) **FIG. 4.28B** (center) Type mold for hand-casting printing type, open; made by Stan Nelson. Note that in this view, a copper matrix shows at the bottom of the mold's funnel; the large metal loop is the spring that holds the matrix into the mold during casting. Also visible is a sort with its jet attached (cast by the author), protruding from the matrix and still in the mold. The prongs sticking up from the top of the mold, called "hags," are used to pull the hot, recently formed piece of type from the mold. (Collection of the author.) **FIG. 4.28C** (bottom) Type mold; drawing of a cross-section, showing the type metal being poured into the mold's funnel and through to the matrix at the bottom of the mold. (Drawing by Stan Nelson.)

formly high and deep, but the mold was adjustable "left to right" to allow for the varying widths of the characters in the Roman alphabet. It was a brilliant piece of engineering. (See figure 4.28.)

TYPECASTING

As a metallurgist—he was a goldsmith—Gutenberg knew how to cast metal in matrices. To envision a matrix, picture a Jello mold. Pour the liquid into the mold, let it set, and when it comes out, it is in the shape of the mold. In this case, the mold is a matrix—the little container that contains the shape that is to be molded.

The challenge for Gutenberg was to create a matrix for each character he wanted to print. That meant one matrix for each of the twenty-three letters in the Roman alphabet (there was no "J," "U" or "V" [there was only one of these, "V" being equivalent to "U"], or "W"). First he designed an alphabet and the other needed characters. Then he transferred one character onto the flat end of a square metal shaft called a *punch*. (See figure 4.29.) He filed or gouged away everything other than the character he drew onto the end of the shaft, leaving in relief on the end of the punch the shape of the character. Taking proofs as he worked, he reached a point of perfection and stopped filing down the punch. He put it into a flame and when it reached a particular red color, he plunged it into cold water to harden it.[32] The hardened punch was then hammered into a softer piece of metal, probably copper, and the matrix was thus formed.[33]

Gutenberg needed one punch for each character—letters, numbers, punctuation, common abbreviations, and special characters. And all this for only one size of type. He needed a set of punches for capitals, one for lowercase, and a set for any other sizes of type he wanted to print. Scholars estimate that he needed to cut 288 punches to print the Bible.

It was essential that every sort was exactly the same height and depth. When set into a page, they all needed to be perfectly squared up, left to right and front to back, so that they could be locked into a metal frame (the *chase*—see more in the section "Printing Practices and Essential Terminology" later in this chapter) without moving around. And they all had to be the exact same height from foot to face

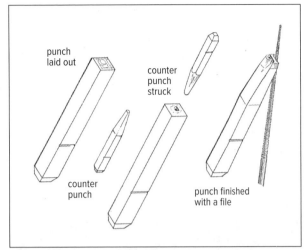

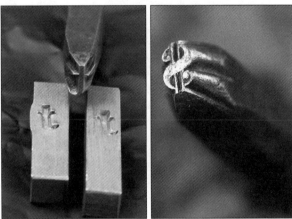

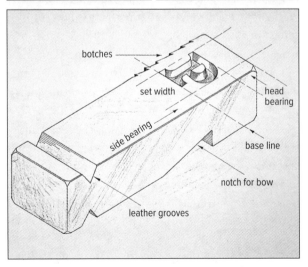

FIG. 4.29A (top) Drawing of punch, counterpunch, and file. (Drawing by Stan Nelson.) **FIG. 4.29B** (center left) Punch and matrices. The punch of the lower-case "T" is shown, along with an unjustified matrix (on the left) and a justified matrix, with the bulge of copper filed off. (Collection of the author.) **FIG. 4.29C** (center right) Punch of a dollar sign. (Collection of the author.) **FIG. 4.29D** (bottom) Drawing of a matrix with the parts delineated. (Drawing by Stan Nelson.)

so that when the printer applied ink to them, none stood up too high or was too low. If one was too high, it would cut right through the sheet that was pressed into the type; if one was too low, it would not receive ink when all the other sorts around it did, and it would thus not print. The adjustable mold allowed for the variations in width of the letters, and it also cast sorts of exactly the same height and depth. (See figure 4.30.)

The second of Gutenberg's inventions, no less ingenious and the one that probably took the greatest amount of time to formulate, was the composition of his printing type. No single metal would do because he needed a metal that (1) would take ink in the inking process and give it up to whatever was to be printed on, (2) would melt at a temperature lower than that of the copper (he could not cast a type metal that required a melting temperature greater than that of the matrix), (3) would solidify in a split second once it hit the face of the matrix, (4) would be strong enough to withstand the pressure of the press without being crushed, (5) would cast up with a perfectly smooth face for printing, and (6) would not shrink when it cooled. No single metal met all these criteria.

It must have taken him a decade to come upon the proper mixture of metals. We do not know what that mixture was because none of his sorts survives. Later types were made from an alloy consisting of about 80 percent lead, 10 percent tin, and 10 percent antimony (these percentages are variable depending on the application of the type). Though often unsung, the type metal was the result of no less genius and persistence than was the adjustable mold.

The third thing that Gutenberg developed that is also not much praised is his ink, which is as bright and black and beautiful today as it was when he printed it. The ink was oil-based, not water-based as were most of the pigments used to write out manuscripts. Also, the sheen of his inks came from the small amounts of metal (lead, copper, and titanium) that he used in their formulation. (See Cahill, Kusko, and Schwab, "Analyses of Inks," and Schwab et al., "Cyclotron Analysis," in the "Ink" section of the bibliography at the end of this chapter.)

Let's return to the making of the type. The matrix was put into the bottom of the type mold, which

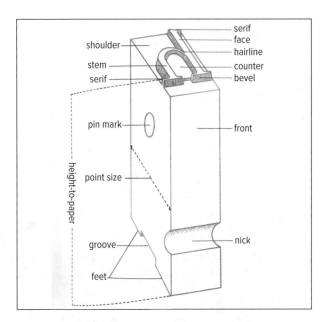

FIG. 4.30 Drawing of a sort with parts labeled. (From Alexander Lawson, *Printing Types: An Introduction* [Boston: Beacon Press, 1971], p. 23.)

formed a little funnel from the opening in the top of the mold to the bottom of the funnel where the matrix sat. The type caster poured molten metal into the funnel, it filled the matrix, forming a sort, and it also filled the rest of the funnel above the sort. Hence, when the sort was removed from the mold, it had extra type metal stuck to it, called the *jet*. The jet had to be broken off from the bottom of the sort, leaving a rough spot where it had been attached. The rough spot was filed or planed away, making a shallow groove on the bottom of the sort and forming what is called the *feet* of the sort, on which it stands. The distance from the foot to the face of the type is called the *type height*, and in the United States, it is .918 inch.[34]

The type founder had to cast one sort at a time, so if one thousand *E*s were needed, the type caster had to perform the casting that many times. And this was for just a single letter. The whole font consisted of all the characters cast, as mentioned earlier: alphabet, numbers, and so forth. Once a full font had been cast and prepared, it was sorted into a type case,[35] ready for the compositor to set.

Over the centuries thousands upon thousands of typefaces have been created. And they are still being designed, especially with the coming of the digital age when companies want to present as legible a face as they can for the computer screen. This is not the place for a dissertation on type. Some basic terminology is in order, however.

THE TERMINOLOGY OF PRINTING TYPE

The following terminology is taken from several sources, with many terms coming from Alexander Lawson's *Printing Types: An Introduction* (Boston: Beacon Press, 1971), 22–29.

Terminology Describing the Characters and Their Component Parts

apex. The point in a character at which two straight lines join, as at the top of the capital A, the bottom of the capital V, and at the points of juncture of the capital M and W.

arm. The short horizontal stroke of letters, such as the horizontal strokes in the capital E or F; or the angled strokes of letters as in the capital Y and the upper- and lowercase K.

ascender. A stroke of a lowercase piece of type that projects above the x-height of the sort as in a lowercase b or h. See also **x-height.**

base line. The invisible line delineating the bottom of serifs for all letters that have serifs on their bottom; the base line would run beneath the lower serifs of such letters as A, E, F, f, H, h, I, i, K, k, and so on.

beard. See **bevel.**

bevel. "The space in the physical type [i.e., on the actual sort] between the face, or printing surface, of the letter and the shoulder. This is often referred to in the United States as the beard" (Lawson, *Printing Types*, p. 24).

bowl. The round, closed part of a letter, as in the closed part of the letters B, b, D, d, O, o, Q, q, and others.

TYPES HAVE THE printing surface in relief—that is, the part of the type that presses the ink onto the paper sticks up from the sort. This is called *letterpress printing*. A relatively new material, photopolymer, has been used in printing for about twenty-five years. A photopolymer plate is covered with a negative or positive stencil and then exposed to light. The light eats away the plate where it is exposed, leaving the rest of the plate in relief. Computer-generated text and images can thus be transferred to the stencil and can then be printed in relief, leaving the same kind of impression in the paper as is left with metal type. Purists do not like to think of this as letterpress printing, but it *is* relief printing and looks like printing from type, though no metal was involved in the process.

bracket. Same as **fillet.**

counter. The part of a letter that is fully or partly enclosed, as in the letters A, a, B, b, C, c, P, p, R, and others. (A punchcutter, creating a punch with a counter, can more easily remove the metal where the counter is by "punching" it out than by removing the metal with tools; for this purpose, he makes a counter punch; see the section "Typecasting" earlier in this chapter.)

crossbar. Sometimes called a **cross-stroke.** A horizontal line connecting two lines in a piece of type, like the stroke on the A and H, or a stroke like that in the lowercase f and t.

descender. A stroke of a lowercase piece of type that projects below the x-height of the sort, as with the lowercase p, q, and y.

ear. In some fonts, the small projection from the top bowl of the lowercase g.

face. The surface of the sort that receives ink and prints onto the surface that is placed over it.

feet. The two small areas at the bottom of the sort, formed by the removal and filing down of the jet in typecasting; the sort sits on the two small feet thus formed (if for any reason a sort is off its feet, it will not print properly).

front. The bottom side of the sort.

groove (*pl.* **grooves**). The small, filed-down part at the base of the sort where the jet was attached; when the jet is removed and its point of attachment is filed down, feet are formed on either side of the groove.

hairline. An extremely fine line on a piece of type (e.g., the thin "crossbar" on the lowercase "e").

jet. The extra type metal that is poured into the type mold when sorts are being cast in their matrices; see the section "Typecasting" earlier in this chapter. See also **groove.**

link. The small connecting stroke between the upper and lower bowls of the lowercase g.

loop. The lower bowl of the lowercase g.

nick. The indentation at the part of the sort that coincides with the bottom of the letters and numbers and other characters; when type is being set into the composing stick, the nick for each sort should be visible, indicating that the bottoms of all the letters are where they should be—that is, that each sort is being placed into the composing stick in the right direction, with the bottoms of each letter facing out in the stick.[36]

pin mark. In machine typecasting, the machine ejects the sort from the mold by means of a pin; this pin makes a mark on the side of the sort—a little circular depression—that indicates that the type is not hand-cast.

point. In the United States and England, a quite thin measurement in printing, approximately 1/72 of an inch.

point system. The system of designating the size of the printed characters in a font of type, as in 12-point type, 18-point caps, and so on.

serif. The little projection that sticks out of the basic shape of a character, like the horizontal lines at the top and bottom of a capital I; serifs are beaked, bracketed, hairline, hooked, slab, spur, or wedge.

shoulder. "The non-printing area on the [sort] between the base-line [sic] and the front of the [sort]. In certain styles capitals may be shorter than ascending lower-case letters, creating a shoulder between the face of the letter and the back of the [sort]" (Lawson, *Printing Types*, p. 27).

sort. A single piece of printing type. (If the printer runs out of these, he is "out of sorts.")

stem. The vertical strokes of a letter and angled strokes that run the full height of a letter, as in the upright strokes of B, D, F, H, T, V, and W.

tail. On the capital K and capital R, and also at the bottom of the capital Q, the short downward stroke, the one on the Q usually being curved.

x-height. The height of the lowercase letters that have no ascenders or descenders: a, c, e, m, and the like; so called because of the height of the lowercase x.

Terminology Describing Typefaces

antique. "In the United States, a boldface, rather monotone letter with solid serifs, exemplified by Bookman. In Europe antique is the term applied to roman type, in its secondary meaning as an Italian-derived letter, not as simply an upright letter" (Lawson, *Printing Types*, p. 27).

bastard (bastarda). "[A] Gothic script used in France and Germany during the 14th and 15th centuries. These scripts were designed to provide a simplified letter that was appropriate for the copying of books or documents of minor value or importance" (http://en.wikipedia.org/wiki/Bastarda).

black letter (sometimes spelled as one word). A term used to denote type designs that are modeled after medieval manuscript scripts, with broad counters and thick ornamental serifs; also called **gothic** or *Old English Text.*

boldface. As the name indicates, a typeface that is heavy, with strokes much thicker than those in the face's regular lightface manifestation.

brasses. One of the thins—small, thin pieces of spacing material, made from brass, that are used to fill out a line of hand-set type; equal to 1 point in thickness.

Civilité type. "[A] typeface invented in 1557 by the French engraver Robert Granjon. These characters imitate French cursiva letters of the Renaissance" (http://en.wikipedia.org/wiki/Civilité); because the Civilité types were modeled after handwriting, fonts are filled with many swash characters with elaborate strokes, and often with variant designs for single characters.

coppers. One of the thins—small, thin pieces of spacing material, made from copper, that are used to fill out a line of hand-set type; equal to ½ point in thickness; hence, two coppers make up the thickness of one brass.

display type. Type in large sizes, perhaps 24-point and larger, used for headlines, posters, and titles in broadsides.

Egyptian type. Also called *slab serif type*. Typefaces with squared-off serifs.

ems. Also called *em quads* (from *quadrats*). A square sort cast with no part of the sort that is type-high; hence, when ink is spread or dabbed over the forme, this quad, being much shorter than the sorts receiving the ink, gets none; it is a space that is the same width as it is deep.

ens. Also called *en quads*. Similar to *ems*, only half the thickness.

family of types. All the typefaces based on a single design; for instance, there is Bembo Roman, Bembo Italic, Bembo Condensed, Bembo Condensed Italic, Bembo Bold, Bembo Semi-Bold, Bembo Heavy, Bembo Titling.

fat face. "An offshoot of the moderns, intended for display purposes (that is, to be attention-getting for use in large sizes, particularly in advertising). The first such types appeared from 1810–1820. They further exaggerated the contrast of modern typefaces, with slab-like vertical lines and extra emphasis of any vertical serifs, which often acquired a wedge shape. Bodoni Ultra, Normande and Elephant are all examples of fat face types which are closely based on early to mid-19th Century originals, and are available in digital form" ("Foam Train Fonts," www.foamtrain.com/glossary/fff.html#.UtnETF7TmUl).

Fraktur type. A font of black letter type used in German printing, mirroring the hand of early German scribes; millions of books were printed in Fraktur type in Germany.

Gothic. "Traditionally a term describing the lettering style of northern Europe during the period when Johann Gutenberg developed movable type, adapted as the first type. In the United States, since the 1830s, the term [has] applied to sans serif types issued by European typefounders after 1820" (Lawson, *Printing Types*, p. 27).

groove. A filed- or planed-down area on the base of a sort where the jet was once attached; once the jet is broken off, the sort is filed down where it was attached, creating the feet on which the sort stands.

Grotesque. "[A] style of sans-serif typeface from the 19th century" [http://en.wikipedia.org/wiki/Grotesque_(typeface_classification)].

hair spacing. See **thins.**

height-to-paper. The height of a sort from its feet to its face; in the United States and England, this distance is .918 inch.

inferior. A piece of type on which the printing surface is cast low on its body so it prints beneath the line; also called a *subscript*.

italic type. Typefaces with slanted or sloped characters.[37]

kern. A part of the printing surface of a sort that protrudes beyond the body of the sort, as with the upper and lower swash strokes of an italic lowercase *f*.

leaders. "A row of dots to lead the eye from one point to another on the page; a poor practice."[38]

ligature. An instance in which two or more characters are cast on a single sort, and are joined, as with the commonest ones: ff, fi, ffi, fl, and ffl; some typefaces, especially italic or cursive fonts with steeply leaning upright strokes, have many ligatures, such as ft, st, ct, gg, gy, and zy.

lightface. The regular showing of a font of type, with no heavy strokes, as opposed to boldface or italic.

logotype. An instance in which two or more characters are cast onto a single sort, but they are not joined, as they are with ligatures.[39]

long S. The letter S that looks like a lowercase *f*, but without a full crossbar as the *f* has; the crossbar on the S, if it has one, goes only up to the upright stroke, but not through it and out onto the right side of the upright stroke.

oldstyle type. Early printing types that mimicked the handwriting of the manuscript scribes.

pica. A measurement, in printing, of 12 points; there are 12 points to a pica and 12 picas to an inch.

roman type. "[T]he alphabets of capitals and lowercase letters usually designed upright, as against italic alphabets which are usually sloped."[40]

sans serif types. Fonts with no serifs.

script types. Typefaces that mimic handwriting.

serif types. Fonts that have small strokes protruding off the main stems of the characters; on the capital T, for instance, the two downward strokes at the ends of the crossbar at the top of the letter and the horizontal stroke at the bottom of the upright stem are serifs.

slab serif type. See **Egyptian type.**

steels. One of the thins—extremely thin pieces of spacing material, made from steel, that are used to fill out a line of hand-set type; equal to ¼ point in thickness; two steels are the thickness of one copper. It is difficult to squeeze a thin piece of spacing material into an almost perfectly tightened-up line; the thinnest of the "thins" needs to be made from a sturdy metal that will not easily bend when it is being inserted between other sorts.

superior. A piece of type where the printing surface is cast high on its body so it prints above the line; sometimes called a *superscript*.

swash types. Also called *swash characters*. Italic types with fancy, extended strokes to add to the character's elegance.

thins. Also called *hair spacing*. See **brasses; coppers; steels.**

transitional type. Fonts from the late seventeenth century that were modeled on earlier faces, but which had elements of later design; they came before "modern types."[41]

WOOD TYPE

A brief statement is in order about wood type, because untold numbers of items in rare book departments were printed with it.

Type metal is heavy. In the larger sizes—say 20-point type and larger—a forme of metal type could be quite hefty. Wood had been used for printing for centuries in woodcuts. So printers knew that it was a usable material for alphabetical printing as well. Boxwood, some mahogany, and rock maple were strong enough to withstand the pressures of the printing press, and these woods weighed a fraction of what the metal type weighed. By the 1820s wood type was in use. It was used for headlines, broadsides, posters, and any other kind of printing that called for large type. Thousands of typefaces, many of them quite hideous, were cut into wood.

OTHER INVENTIONS

Gutenberg's inventions had a gargantuan impact on the world of books. Also of great impact on book history was an invention that changed the world of typesetting and printing.

The history of the book is marked by massive inventions (paper, printing, the composition of the perfect type metal, the codex), and then by attempts to speed up the process, make it cheaper, and make it better.

For books, type was invented to speed up book production from the world of manuscripts. The maceration of pulp was sped up with the invention of the Hollander beater.[42] Papermaking was mechanized by the beginning of the nineteenth century (Hunter, *Papermaking: History and Technique*, 341ff.). Printing presses run by steam were in use by 1814, and "[t]he steam powered rotary printing press, invented in 1843[43] in the United States by Richard M. Hoe, allowed millions of copies of a page in a single day. Mass production of printed works flourished after the transition to rolled paper, as continuous feed allowed the presses to run at a much faster pace" ("Printing Press," Wikipedia, citing Meggs, *History*).

IN THE WORLD of industry (and printing is an industry) there is a saying: "Better, Faster, Cheaper: Pick two." If you make something better and faster, it will not be cheaper. If you make something faster and cheaper, it will not be better. And if you make something better and cheaper, it will not be faster. In the history of the book, all innovations—variations on all the acts that must take place to produce a book—strove, never with full success, for all three results. It is debatable that any machine-printed item matches the beauty and three-dimensionality of a letterpress-printed page.

Mechanical Typesetting

The one thing slowing down the production of books was typesetting, which, from Gutenberg forward, remained a handcraft for 425 years. As early as 1822, William Church attempted to mechanize typesetting with his composing machine. Anyone interested in this subject must consult Richard Huss's informative *The Development of Printers' Mechanical Typesetting Methods, 1822–1925*. For the present text, we must look at four major developments in printing, two having to do with typesetting.

THE LINOTYPE The first important development to consider is the Linotype machine. In fact, there were several Linotype machines because their inventor, Ottmar Mergenthaler, began working on mechanical typesetting in the early 1880s, and he produced his Band Machine No. 1 in 1884. Rather than give an exhaustive and exhausting account of all of Mergenthaler's accomplishments and machines and their evolution, what we need to know is that the Linotype machine that evolved from the inventor's constant work over several decades was a fantastic creature with innumerable moving parts. It contained hundreds of matrices in a large magazine above the machine. Each time the operator hit a key, one matrix was released from the magazine, and it lined up next to those that came before and after it. The full line of text was set in matrices, then it was shifted into the machine where type metal was cast into the line of matrices, producing a full line of type in a single slug of metal. If the slug had a typo or needed to be replaced for any reason, the operator (called the *compositor*) could just keyboard another group of matrices to compose another line of text and replace it for the one with the error. The one replaced could be dropped back into the pot to be melted down for reuse.[44]

If Gutenberg's inventions brought millions of volumes into being, Mergenthaler's brought even more—and at a much faster rate because the necessity for hand composition was now a thing of the past, replaced by machine composition at vastly faster rates. Now, with the Linotype machine, newspaper companies could put out more than one daily paper: a morning and an evening edition, filled with more pages than ever before could have been conceived. Millions upon millions of books and newspapers, not to mention vast quantities of documents and ephemeral material, were created from text set in the Linotype machine.

MONOTYPE A second invention that anyone working in special collections should know about is Tolbert Lanston's Monotype machine. From experiments in the late 1880s, Lanston developed the first commercially successful Monotype machine in 1897 ("Tolbert Lanston," http://en.wikipedia.org/wiki/Tolbert _Lanston). That should actually be "machines," for with Lanston's inventions typesetting was made possible through a pair of related apparatuses. The first was a keyboard with a roll of paper on it. When the compositor struck a key, the machine punched a series of holes in the roll of paper, each combination of holes creating a different sort. Where Mergenthaler's machine cast text in slugs of type metal, Lanston's cast individual sorts.

Lanston's second machine was the caster into which the roll of punched paper was inserted. As the paper unrolled, the configuration of punched holes directed the machine to move a small rack of matrices forward, backward, or from side to side, so that the designated matrix was positioned beneath the casting machine's "funnel" into which the molten type metal was squirted, creating a single sort. Whole pages of text would be built up from single sorts (hence the word *mono-type* and the name of the machine, the Monotype). (See figure 4.31.)

The Linotype machine could produce slugs of text, and errors could be reversed with the removal of a

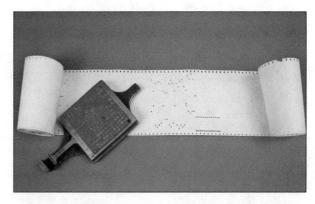

FIG. 4.31 Monotype punched roll and matrix holder. (Collection of the author.)

slug (a full line of text) and its replacement with a new slug, cast without the error. The Monotype machine produced what looked like handset type because each line consisted of individual sorts. If the printed text of Linotype looked bad (for instance, if it had rivers in it),[45] it could not be fixed as easily as it could in Monotype-set text, which can be reset by hand.

Before the invention of Monotype, printing type had to be ordered from foundries in which type was set in casters or by hand. The Monotype machine, to this day, is used to cast up fonts of type for printers who like to set their type by hand. Hence, printers who buy type today are almost certain to get "Monotype," not "foundry type." The two are indistinguishable in the text that is printed from them, but foundry type is harder and more durable than the other.[46]

STEREOTYPING A third invention, going back to the eighteenth century, had a huge impact on book history: stereotyping, in which a page of set type has papier-mâché pressed into it, creating a mold of the text. The papier-mâché mold, called a *flong*, was like a copper matrix: type metal was poured into it, and it made a perfect copy of the page of type, cast in type metal, but on a flat plate, called a *stereotype plate*. Type metal in the form of sorts was more than five times as thick as a stereotype plate, so the plates (called *stereos*) could be stored in much less space than type needed. Also, once the printer had the stereotype plates for a book, he could distribute the type back into the cases for reuse, mount the plates type-high, and print from them in a standard press. The plates could be stored and then pulled out in a year or in two decades and be reused. A typo in a plate could be fixed by simply cutting it out and soldering in a correction. If the publisher sold the text (i.e., all the stereos for a book) to another company, the plate with the title page could easily be modified (to reflect the new issuer) in the same manner: the old publisher's name and other information could be cut out of the plate and the new publisher's information could be soldered in; or a new plate could easily be made for a wholly new title page.[47] (See figure 4.32.)

A book printed from standing type and another copy printed from stereos cannot be distinguished from one another, the process is so good at reproducing the look of the original. Millions of books were printed from these plates, and sometimes one can put two copies of a text side by side and see how the plate that produced one was fairly fresh and uncorrupted while the same plate, after much use, was worn and printed not as sharply (or with broken serifs or lighter illustrations). Often, however, a book printed from plates will have a tiny logo of the stereotyper somewhere on its pages, sometimes on the very last printed leaf.

As we shall see later (in chapter 9 on bibliography), one of the definitions of *edition* is "all of the books printed from the same setting of type." The first edition of a book may be printed from standing type; then stereo plates are made from that type. If, one hundred years after the first printing, a publisher uses those plates to print another run of the book, the newer ones are still part of the first edition because all copies were printed from the same setting of type. (The fact that the stereotypes were made from that same setting of type makes all items printed from those plates of the same edition as are those books printed from the original type.) If the stereotype-printed text was the second time the text was printed from that one setting of type, it would be designated "First edition, second printing," with the possible addition (if the information that it is printed from plates is known) of "stereotype version," or something akin to this.

ELECTROTYPING The fourth important invention, closely aligned with stereotyping, is electrotyping. The *American Dictionary of Printing and Bookmaking* gives this explanation of "Electrotyping":

> The art of taking one metal, and, after placing it in a state of solution, causing it by electric or galvanic action to spread itself over the surface of a mold of whatever design, and there be deposited in a film or sheet. . . . in reference to printing, . . . it has proved of incalculable value. Small particles of metal penetrate the most remote recesses, and the finest lines are reproduced by it with accuracy and delicacy. It has almost entirely superseded stereotyping, as wood-cuts can be much better copied by it than by the older process. (p. 157)[48]

An electrotype plate (called an *electro*) looks just like a stereo, with the exception that it has a copper coating on it. (See figure 4.32; see also figure 4.33.)

Stereotyping and electrotyping belong in this section because both methods of printing derive directly from set type. The literature on printing type is monumental. The bibliography at the end of this chapter will lead to a host of good books on the subject. Those in special collections will profit from and be able to use this information in their dealings with the materials of a rare book department.

FIG. 4.32 Electrotype plate (left) and stereotype plate. The electrotype plate has a copper surface. The stereotype plate shown has had a correction soldered into it (the seventh line from the bottom at the right side of the line in the illustration). (Collection of the author.)

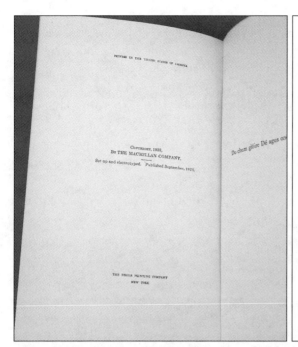 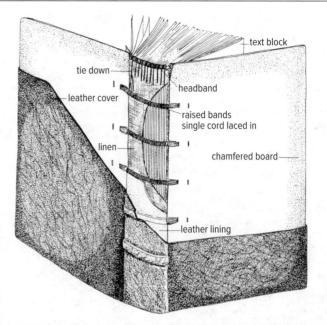

FIG. 4.33 (left) Electrotype notification on copyright page. James Stephens, *Deirdre* (New York: Macmillan, 1923), p. iv. The notice says, "Set up and electrotyped." (Collection of the author.) FIG. 4.34 (right) Drawing of the binding elements of a sewn textblock. (Drawing by Margaret R. Brown. In Matt T. Roberts and Don Etherington, *Bookbinding and the Conservation of Books: A Dictionary of Descriptive Terminology* [Washington, DC: Library of Congress, 1982], p. 29. All further references to illustrations from this volume will be cited as "Brown.")

Bookbinding

Everyone handling rare books must know about bindings. They hold the book together, and they are the first things we see in a book (other than a dust jacket, perhaps). They are prominent in a bibliographical description. They can carry a great deal of information, and they can add significantly to the value of a book.[49]

As with all other topics in this chapter, the text will be limited to the bare essentials, but it will be sufficient to give people in rare books enough of a vocabulary to speak with some enlightenment about bindings.

The two "stages" of binding are forwarding and finishing. The former is the process of affixing all the signatures together. They can be sewn or glued or spiral-bound; the result of forwarding is that the book is essentially bound but not necessarily adorned in any way. Finishing is the aesthetic part of binding, in which the decoration is applied.

FORWARDING

Several basic categories of bindings must be discussed: laced in, cased in, perfect, stab bound, and other.

Laced In

The form of the book we have today—leaves of text bound between covers—goes back to perhaps the fourth century, possibly earlier. The manuscript (and later the printed) leaves were folded and then sewn to one another through the folds to create the textblocks.[50] The textblocks were attached to the covers with sewing. (See figure 4.34.)

The covers could have been vellum, paper, or boards (either cardboard—made from couching several sheets of paper on top of one another—or wooden boards). The boards were often covered with vellum, leather, or paper.

The textblock was sewn, on a sewing frame, to tapes, thongs, or cords[51] that ran at right angles to the upright spine and extended beyond the textblock

FIG. 4.35A (above) Exposed sewing on a volume that is laced in. The volume is Mika Bar-Chaim et al., *Manuscript* ([Claremont, CA]: Scripps College Press, 2011). (Collection of the author.) FIG. 4.35B (right) Drawing of lacing-in for binding. In this illustration the text block is sewn, and the ends of the cords are drawn out, ready to be laced through holes in the cover boards. (Brown, p. 149.)

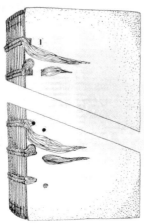

leather, vellum, or paper, leaving what are known as *raised bands* over the spine. Such bands were originally a sign of a hand-bound book and meant that the volume was sturdily constructed. Later, when cased-in bindings were invented (see the following section), binders could put three or five cords (or even thin strips of cardboard) across the spine, and when the volume was covered with leather, there was a raised band at each of these strips—essentially looking like hand-binding but really a cheap and not very sturdy binding.

THE PRACTICE OF creating fake raised bands was common in the nineteenth century when there was a craze for deluxe versions of books. The fake raised band under cheap (but attractive) leather implied the high quality of hand-binding. No purchaser would rip apart a "deluxe" book to verify that the raised band was genuine. The practice continues today.

It was possible, as well, to do a full hand-binding on a book and not have the raised bands. The binder would put all the signatures together, before sewing, and would saw a groove into the spine at each place that a cord would be pulled across the spine. If the binder wished to use, say, four sewing stations, she would saw four grooves into the folded part of the signatures where the cords would be. The cords, then, nestled into the grooves, and when the sewn textblock was covered with leather or vellum, the cords and the sewing around them would not be sticking up, but would be flush with the folds. This is called a *sawn-in* binding.

Another feature of a hand-bound book, the headbands, is optional, but most binders created them. The very top and bottom of the spine would receive stitches for each signature, and the binder could use a cord drawn across the top and bottom of the signature and sew this cord to the signatures. (The generic term *endbands* is used to designate the bands at the head and the foot of the binding.) The result was an extra level of sturdiness, because the so-called *headbands* added strength to the binding. The sewing around the cord of the headband was often done with two threads of different colors, or the cords or

for an inch or more. The extensions were drawn into holes in the covers, attaching the textblock to the boards. (See figure 4.35.)

This explanation of the process is greatly simplified. Some fine details need to be added. The thongs, tapes, or cords were attached to the top and bottom of the sewing frame, and each signature (a folded leaf, or several folded leaves nested) was sewn to the previous one with the thread going through the fold at the spine of the book. The stitch that went around the cords was called a *kettle stitch*. It left a raised ridge on the back of the book standing up from the spine. If the signatures were sewn with three or five tapes, there would be three or five raised areas over the spine. Eventually the sewing was covered over with thongs were wrapped with two different-colored cloths, so many headbands look as if they are made up of a striped cloth wrapped around a tiny cord.[52] Later, when case binding was invented, a piece of cloth—monochrome or striped—could be pasted onto the top of the spine before the covers went on. Once the covers were affixed, the cloth looked like a real headband, though it was merely pasted on, not created from the reinforcing stitches that were part of a real headband. It was a fake (like fake raised bands), and it did not add appreciably to the quality (i.e., the sturdiness) of the book. But again, a consumer would not pull a new book apart just to see if the headband were real. Today there are companies that sell these headbands by the hundreds, in all kinds of colors and color combinations, several kinds of cloth, and many widths.

W. J. E. Crane, in 1888, wrote, "The headband is an ornamental appendage, formed in thread and silk of various colors, which is placed at the back of a book at the head and tail. Besides its ornamental appearance, it serves to support that part of the cover projecting above the back of the book in consequence of the square of the boards."[53] Talas, the artists' supply company, says, "Headbands are the decorative element found at the head and tail of the textblock on a bound book."[54] Hollander's, a binding-supply company, says, "Headbands are used as a decorative element on the head and tail of the book and are often added as the finishing touch."[55] As Crane and these two suppliers show, headbands have reached the point of being merely decorative; but they once were structural and made the bookbinding sturdy.

Cased In

William Tomlinson and Richard Masters begin their opening chapter of *Bookcloth, 1823–1980* with this statement:

> The bookcloth used for covering books during the nineteenth century and widely employed until recent years consists of a bleached, woven base-cloth (almost always cotton) that has been "filled" several times with coloured starch and then calendered to give a smooth finish. The introduction of such starch-filled bookcloth in the 1820s not only provided a new material for binding books but precipitated a revolution in publishing. (p. 1)

This revolution was the case binding.

For about 170 years cloth has been the favored binding material. Before that, leather and vellum for better books and paper for cheaper ones (or ones intended to be rebound—the paper was supposed to be a temporary cover) were the main binding materials to cover the boards. Bernard Middleton writes, "[C]anvas was used in the middle ages in Europe, principally as a base for embroidered bindings, and in England in the second half of the eighteenth century publishers sensibly issued school books bound in canvas" ("Foreword," p. vii). Later he notes that

> by a fortunate chance the development of a suitable filler for the more humble calico and the use of casing, which facilitated gold blocking of the spine, coincided with the beginning of the rise of the book-reading middle classes as Britain prospered industrially. And so, within a short time was born a great industry. (pp. vii–viii)

A DISTINCTION MUST be made between "sewing" and "stitching." According to Cloonan (*Early Bindings in Paper*), "Using the records of Stationers' Hall, Foxon has demonstrated that the *stitching* of books has sometimes been differentiated from the *sewing* of them. In the sixteenth century, stitching referred to the types of sewing that did not require the use of a sewing frame, while in the seventeenth century the term *stitched* became synonymous with *pamphlet*, and denoted the practice of stitching over the covers rather than through the folds. The differences between sewing and stitching were of some consequence to the British book trade; ultimately, the amount of duty imposed on an item depended on its format" (p. 84). She then discusses the two ways pamphlets can be stitched: "*saddle-stitching* (through the folds), and *side-stitching* (over-sewing through the text and covers, also known as *whip stitching*)" (p. 84). The complexities of bookbinding methods are far beyond the province of the present text. The bibliography at the end of this chapter includes several texts that expatiate on and elucidate some of these complexities.

FIG. 4.36 Cased-in binding. Shown is the case ready to receive the textblock. (Collection of the author.)

Until this kind of fabric was invented, books could not be bound in cloth because that material was not sturdy enough to withstand the rigors of the frequent opening and closing of the covers, and the cloth was not stiff enough to hold the boards in place.

From about 1820 on, this new material allowed for a whole new kind of binding, not using vellum, leather, or paper. Publishers, searching for ways to cut expenses in book production, took advantage of this material to reduce the costs of binding. It was now possible to create a case for the book, sew up the textblock, and simply glue the two parts together. In other words, with a laced-in binding, the boards were attached to the textblocks with cords or thongs, making them a solid unit. But with cloth to cover the boards, the cases could be made separately and the two parts just glued to one another. The final product is called a *cased-in binding*. (See figure 4.36.)

The pastedown endpaper was (as the name indicates) glued to the boards; the free endpaper was attached to the first leaf of the textblock. This is what held the cover on. Because the boards were held in place basically with glue only, the binding was quite weak. It eventually became the practice to paste mull (also called *super* or *crash*—a gauze) around the spine and onto the first and last leaf of the volume. The tiny holes in the gauze held much more adhesive than the flat paper could, and this extra glue slightly strengthened the binding, but not

a great deal. Cased-in bindings are still nowhere near as strong as laced-in ones. However, the decorations that had to be tooled onto leather covers could be applied by stamping them onto the cloth. So hundreds of attractive cases could be assembled in one place, an equal number of textblocks could be prepared in another, and they could be quickly joined with adhesive. Money was saved in the cheaper cloth (over leather or vellum), in the speed with which the decorations could be put onto the cloth, and in the physical act of attaching covers to textblocks.

The bindings could be beautiful because multicolor and blind-stamped images could be applied to the cloth in endless patterns or pictures, even using gold- or silver-colored metallic foils that mirrored the decorations of fancy leather bindings. For leather, the decoration was generally applied by hand (though it could be stamped from metal dies); for cloth it was seldom hand done. It would have almost always been stamped using metal dies. But despite their beauty, cased-in bindings were structurally inferior to laced-in bindings because they were nowhere near as sturdy, as the shoddy condition of thousands of nineteenth-century cloth-bound books attests. One reason is that cloth is just not as strong or resilient as leather. Also, the adhesives used in the nineteenth century are not as good as are today's, and many of the glues dried out under the cloth, making the bindings brittle at their joints, outside, and also inside between the two leaves of the pastedown and free endpapers.

For those in rare books and special collections, a few things stand out. First, as just noted, cloth bindings should be handled with some care because they are not as sturdy as leather-bound books. Second, they have become tremendously collectible, primarily because they are quite attractive. Also, about twenty-five years ago, there were many of them on the market at fairly low prices because the texts they covered were hardly read. In fact, almost all the cheap fiction and nonfiction books of the nineteenth and early twentieth centuries were bound in cloth, and to make a beautiful cover did not add much to the original price of the book, so many publishers adorned their books by the thousands with attractive cloth bindings. Further, because the decorative covers were designed to catch the eye of the reading public, the books seldom had dust jackets, so some of the decoration on most of these books has abraded off. With the increasing use of the dust jacket in the twentieth century, publishers' decorated bindings came to be less and less used. It was cheaper to print up a decorated paper jacket than it was to create a decorative cloth cover. Also, the jackets could increase sales because they could contain advertisements and other selling points.

Perfect Bound

If ever there was a misnomer in the book world, "perfect binding" is it.

To save time and money, binders cut off the fold at the gutter of each signature, creating individual leaves, not attached to one another. At the spine, they dipped the whole textblock into glue and let it dry. The leaves were now attached to one another with as much glue as would attach to the edge of the sheet. That is, there was as much glue as the paper was thick—which was not much. The textblock was then glued into a case. Sometimes *mull* (the gauze that was used in cased-in bindings; also called *crash* or *super*) was affixed around the textblock at the spine and then the textblock was glued into a case (or even into a stiff paper cover). The mull not only wrapped around the textblock for some additional strength, but its tiny holes held more glue than

would be there without it, so the binding had more strength with the gauze.[56]

This is not to say that the result was a sturdy binding. It was not. The fact was that only a hairline of glue touched each individual leaf in the book. To add a small amount of additional adhesive, binders would fan out the leaves in one direction, exposing a very thin strip of the printed surface of the sheet, dip the spine into the glue, and then fan it in the other direction, exposing another strip on the opposite side of the leaves. This operation would more than triple the amount of glue on the spine, even gluing the leaves together from their surfaces, not just from their edges. This process was called *double-fan adhesive* perfect binding. (It is also called the *millennial binding*.)

When this technique was developed in the nineteenth century, the adhesives were fairly poor. They dried out, turned white or brown, stained the sheets, and often flaked to dust, allowing the leaves to fall out. Sometimes the adhesives turned brittle, and the book would crack at the spine when the book was opened, and the textblock would break into pieces.

Today there are long-lasting glues that retain their flexibility, that will not dry out, and that will hold the leaves with some sturdiness. But this kind of binding is nonetheless a "perfect" binding, and it will not have the longevity of a volume that is sewn. Most commercial paperback books today are perfect bound.[57] (See figure 4.37.)

FIG. 4.37 Perfect binding of a paperback book. (Photo by Zepfanman/Flickr.com.)

I HAVE SEEN "deluxe editions" bound in fancy leather, with raised bands and headbands and gold-stamped decorations, fall apart and reveal perfect bindings. The raised bands were false, as were the headbands, the leather was cheap, and the adhesives were extremely poor quality. But when the book was issued, these things were not visible, and they could not be detected unless the book was pulled apart, which no one would do to a "deluxe edition." This was a deceptive tactic on the publishers' part, because no one knew until years after the purchase that the book was cheaply made. It took several years for the symptoms to appear, and by that time the buyer had no recourse to return the books. This kind of binding was often used in large sets of books: *The Complete Writings of* _____. And in many cases, these sets sat on shelves looking beautiful and sumptuous while the materials they were made with ate them to death from inside. If they were read at all it would have been while the sets were fairly new, and when the materials had not yet begun their slide to oblivion.

Stab Bound

In the Orient, for centuries, the papers used for books were fairly translucent. That is, there is a good deal of show-through from one side of the sheet to the other. So it was impractical to print on both sides of the sheet. If the leaves were folded and then sewn through the folds, the result would be an opening of a two-page spread of printed matter followed by an opening of a two-page spread of blank pages. The solution was to fold the sheets in half, naturally with the printed pages on the outside, and then sew the textblock at the edge *opposite to* the fold. This technique sews the leaves in such a way that the blank pages are permanently on the inside of the fold and only printed surfaces are exposed.

To achieve this kind of sewing, the binder must punch or drill holes through the entire textblock along the edge opposite the folds. This process is called *stab binding*. (It has also been called *side sewing* or *Japanese sewing*.)[58] The Roberts and Etherington description of Japanese sewing is worth quoting:

> A method of sewing leaves or sections which, despite the name, was actually developed in China. The method involves gathering and jogging the leaves, and then drilling a hole through the entire thickness of the pile in the center anywhere from ¼ to ¾ inch from the edge of the spine, or more depending on the size of the book, the nature of the paper, and the extent of the binding margin. Additional holes are then drilled on either side of the center hole at uniform distances, the total number, including the one in the center, being an odd number. The sewing proceeds from the center hole to the head of the book, over the head and then down over the spine past the center hole to the tail and then back to the center. When the sewing is completed, the ends are tied in a flat knot on the outside. An alternative method is to begin at either end, in which case the number of holes may be even or odd. Thread, cord, string, yarn, tape, or rope fibers can be used. Japanese sewing may be considered as a form of side sewing (or stabbing) and, although it does not allow much flexibility, especially with small books, it is an extremely strong method of sewing, possibly one of the strongest ever devised. (*Bookbinding*, p. 143)

It should be added that many Oriental papers, made primarily from *kozo*, *mitsumata*, or *gampi* fibers, are quite flexible, so the stab binding does not necessarily yield a book that does not open well at the spine. Also, an accomplished binder winds up the sewing at the same hole he began with, ties off the string, and then trims it down to a short piece. The tiny ends of loose thread at the knot can be pushed into the hole they emerged from, and the knot can be made fairly invisible. The concept and execution are quite simple, and the result is an elegant binding. (See figures 4.38 and 4.39.)

Often the top and bottom corners of the book at the spine are covered with a glued-on cloth that is decorative and protective. Also, the papers for the cover can be decorated in any number of ways, though usually when there is decoration on the covers, it is subtle and understated.

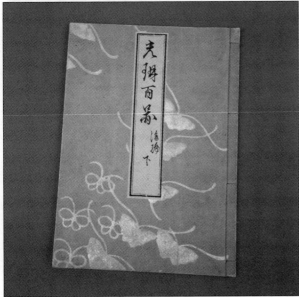

FIG. 4.38 (top) Stab (or Asian) binding. (Brown, p. 143.)
FIG. 4.39 (center) Stab-bound book. (Collection of the author.)
FIG. 4.40 (bottom) Girdle book from Kungliga Biblioteket (Royal Library) in Stockholm.

Other Kinds of Bindings

With a continuing interest in fine printing today, and with ongoing fine-press, artist's-book activities, there has been a concomitant interest in fine binding. Artists and bookbinders are experimenting with new forms of binding, and they are also turning to old ones.

One structure that has persisted is the *Coptic binding*, produced by the Egyptian Christians, known as the Copts, from about the fourth century on. These bindings usually had wooden boards and were sewn through the folds with an exposed chain stitch on the spine. The boards could be left uncovered, or they could be covered with leather. The leather could be unadorned or decorated. The boards were often attached to the textblock, in which case they were a form of laced-in binding.

The girdle book was a structure invented in the Middle Ages. Its intent was to allow someone to carry a book without having to hold it in his hands. A horseback rider could reach down to the volume that was attached to his girdle (sash or belt) and swing it up, open it, and read it. The binding itself formed a little bag over the bound pages. (See figure 4.40; for more information, see "girdle books" in the section "Additional Binding Terminology" later in this chapter.)

In the twentieth century one of the most common (and least expensive) bindings is the *spiral binding*. The textblock, with the folds trimmed away, was punched through with a series of holes from the top to the bottom of the spine, and a spiral coil—of metal or plastic—was wound down through the holes. There are also books that have holes punched in them at the inner margin, and plastic prongs, held by a plastic spine, are inserted in the holes. Some people refer to this structure as a "spiral binding," though the binding "mechanism" is not really a spiral.

Bookkeepers and accountants had *post-bound* books; heavy covers had metal posts screwed into them—usually two or three—and sheets with holes punched in them were dropped over the posts. The posts came in varying lengths (1-inch, 2-inch, 4-inch, and so forth), and they could also screw into one another. So someone with a volume with posts 4 inches high, needing to add more sheets to the volume, could open the book, screw an extension into the existing post, and add one or more inches of post to the height of the book.

Workshops in binding structures often begin with one of the simplest of all: the *accordion binding* (also called *concertina binding*), in which a long strip of paper (or a series of pasted-together leaves making a long strip) are folded into an accordion pattern, with a cardboard or other heavy material affixed to the first and last leaf as a cover.

In the late nineteenth century, bookbinding was mechanized in many ways with the development of sewing machines and case-making machines for case binding. One fast form of binding used staples. In a *stapled binding*, the textblock had its folds trimmed away and the entire block of leaves was stapled at the spine, at two or more stations, right through the whole textblock (not through folds). The process produced a tight binding, so that the text would not lie flat when it was opened, and, indeed, the volume had a tendency to pop shut if it were not held open. Cloth or paper would be glued over the spine and front of the boards, enough, at least, to cover the staples so that they could not be seen. A drawback to this binding method was that if the book got damp, the staples would rust, with the discoloration showing through the cover material.

As we shall address in chapter 12 on preservation and conservation, one type of preservation is deacidification, one form of which uses aqueous (water-based) solutions to deacidify large quantities of books at once. This is not a good treatment for books bound with staples because adding water to the volume will cause the staples to rust. Hence, before such treatments are undertaken, the collection must be examined carefully to remove any stapled books from the group undergoing treatment. The problem is, of course, that in stapled bindings, the staples are fairly well hidden, in the tight spines and under the covering materials. (See the entry for "side stitching" later in this chapter.)

Other kinds of binding exist, but they are often idiosyncratic to a single volume or artist. Those discussed here are the most likely to be found in rare book and special collections.

FINISHING

Finishing[59] is the addition of decorative elements to a binding after the forwarding is done.[60] In some respects, forwarding is the more important activity because it is the operation that yields the binding—that holds all the signatures together. But because finishing often yields beautiful objects, the number of books published showing elegant bindings (that is, concentrating on the result, the finishing) far exceeds the number showing the how-to of binding. Books and pamphlets by the thousands have been published showing the aesthetic work of single binders or that of binders in different countries, at different times, using different materials, and so on.

It is important for those working with rare books and special collections to know how books are made, their parts, the tools used, and the structures the binders create. For this reason, the figures in this section show some of the tools and operations used

IN ONE OF the classic manuals on bookbinding, James B. Nicholson warns us that if we are to have our libraries bound in our own bindings, we must not choose an ugly style:

It is of the utmost importance to a young workman that he have correct ideas in regard to taste, and be able to distinguish it from caprice or mere fancy. . . . Taste may be said to be a perception and an appreciation of the principles of beauty and harmony as revealed by Nature through Art. Nothing contrary to nature, no violations of any law of proportion or fitness, can be in good taste. The amateur and book-collector, in commencing the foundation of a library, will do well to pause before they adopt a species of binding that will in after years create a feeling of annoyance, and perhaps lead to pecuniary sacrifice.

This is the opening statement in his chapter on Finishing.*

*James B. Nicholson, *A Manual of the Art of Bookbinding* (Philadelphia: Henry Carey Baird, 1856; rpt. New York and London: Garland, 1980), p. 186.

in bookbinding. The information is drawn for the most part from the excellent text of Matt Roberts and Don Etherington, *Bookbinding and the Conservation of Books*, with Margaret R. Brown's superb drawings. Librarians, booksellers, archivists, collectors, and others dealing with books should know the terminology and the tools. This volume supplies that information in abundance. Figure captions explain each term and tool.

In some binderies, the forwarding is seen as a mechanical activity, the finishing as an aesthetic one, so the apprentices and journeymen do the sewing and the master adds the artistic embellishments later.

The Faheys describe finishing in a nutshell: "The finisher must decide what lettering and decoration are to be put on the book. This includes tooling of the patterns in blind or with metal, onlay and inlay work, polishing and varnishing" (*Finishing in Hand Bookbinding*, p. 7). They conclude this paragraph by saying, "The process of finishing is the means by which designs are put upon covers to echo the spirit of the story and what the binder thinks will further express that spirit" (p. 7). This optimistic statement does not account for the innumerable books whose decorated covers have nothing at all to do with the books' contents. The Faheys' text, however, begins with an understanding that "[t]here are two schools of thought on bookbinding design": one that holds that any decoration, not ugly or in "conflict with the spirit of the book," is acceptable; the other holding that "the binding design must harmonize with the subject of the book" (p. 9).

The Terminology of Finishing

For the present purpose, finishing yields a few terms that people dealing in rare books should know, for they are descriptive of binding features and should be used in delineating the appearance of a book. Many terms refer to tools that are heated and then blind-pressed into the cover material; these tools then can be pressed again into the depressed pattern with foil to impart colors or metallic materials.

allover designs. Designs that completely cover the outer boards of a binding.

blind tooling. See **tooling.**

blocking. The impressing of a pattern into a cover of a book by means of a block—that is, "[a] piece of metal, without a handle, bearing an engraved or etched design."[61] The block is made of a sturdy metal that is usually heated before the impressing is done. This way, an entire pattern—a full cover—can be adorned at once, without the binder's having to use individual tools to build up the decoration. Often the impression made by the block is filled with gold or another color, though blind stamping is possible. Booksellers and others trying to market handmade books will often refer to the sumptuousness of a volume by saying it is "Blocked in gilt." This is an error in terminology in which two terms are combined. The correct wording is "gilt blocking" or "blocked in gold." (*Gilt* is an adjective; the locution calls for a noun.) See also **tooling.**

diaper pattern. Refers to a "gold- or blind-tooled decorative pattern, consisting of a motif constantly repeated in geometric form. The pattern may consist of figures such as diamonds, lozenges, or flowers, separated only by background, or by constantly repeating compartments, each filled with designs."[62] The same website adds, "A publisher's cloth with a cross-hatched effect of minute lozenges or squares."

fillet. A wheel (usually made of brass) on a handle, with a decorative pattern on its edge. The heated fillet is used to impress its pattern into the leather cover and sometimes also to press a colored foil into the first impression. It can have many kinds of patterns, but lines and double lines are common. (See figure 4.41.)

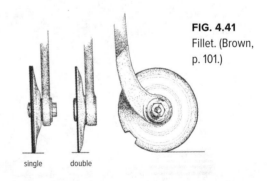

single   double

FIG. 4.41 Fillet. (Brown, p. 101.)

gold tooling. See **tooling.**

gouges. Tools that impart curved lines to the leather. They are sometimes called *curved line tools*.

inlays. Materials that are laid into openings that have been cut into the binding surface. For instance, a book may be covered with brown leather; the binder cuts out the title of the book from the cover leather, making little "wells" or holes where the title has been cut. Then letters are cut in a different color of leather to fit into these holes, and they are laid into the little holes to spell out the title. Inlays can be of the same or different materials. Inlays sit flush with the surface of the cover. This practice is opposed to **onlays** (q.v.).

lettering pallet. A tool that enables the binder to impress full words into the leather or other cover material. Pieces of type (usually of brass, though printing type can also be used) that will print letters and words are placed into the lettering pallet and then heated to the proper temperature for stamping. (See figure 4.42.)

line pallets. Binding tools with brass at the end of a wooden handle, the brass patterns shaped like straight thick or thin lines; used to tool the spines of books.

onlays. Decorative or textual elements attached to the surface of the binding material. See also **inlays.**

ornamental tools. Tools with decorative ends that can be pressed into the leather. There are countless ornamental tools, with every kind of decorative element: flowers; calligraphic swashes; leaves; representational images like animals, insects, and buildings; and on and on.

roll. A small, thick wheel, like a fillet only much smaller (i.e., with a much shorter circumference), containing on its edge a design that is pressed into the cover as is the pattern on a fillet. (See figure 4.43.)

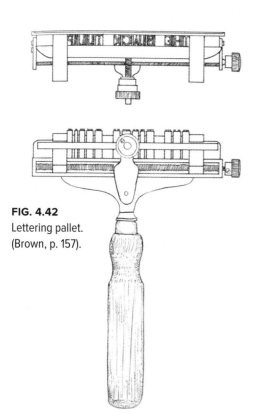

FIG. 4.42
Lettering pallet.
(Brown, p. 157).

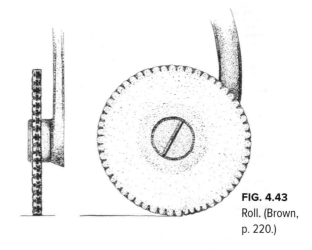

FIG. 4.43
Roll. (Brown, p. 220.)

tooling. The impressing of patterns onto a cover using straight, curved, or ornamental tools. The tooling can be *blind* (that is, with no color or foil impressed into the surface), or it can be gilt, silver, bronze, or colored. See also **blocking.**

"THE GREAT OMAR." There are many stories in the rare book world, and anyone working in the field should know many of them. This one has to do with finishing, perhaps the most famous "finished" book in history. The grand illustrated edition of *The Rubaiyat of Omar Khayyam,* often called "The Great Omar" (Boston: Houghton Mifflin, 1884), illustrated by Elihu Vedder, was even more sumptuously bound in 1912 by Francis Sangorski of the well-known bindery Sangorski and Sutcliffe. It has been called the greatest binding of all time. It had, besides spectacular tooling and ornamentation, inlays of ivory, mahogany, satinwood, and silver, and about 1,050 jewels on its cover, including the ones mentioned in the poems: rubies, turquoises, topazes, garnets, and others. The tale of the book is a story of loss in many ways, not only in what the firm lost in the low price it got for its work but also in the fact that the book went down on the *Titanic.* A later copy was made, but it was destroyed in World War II.

ADDITIONAL BINDING TERMINOLOGY

The language of bookbinding is vast. In this section are just a few additional terms of binding that must be mastered by anyone in the rare book field. (For clarity, a few terms reappear in this alphabetical list.) Other terms will be presented later in this chapter in the section "Parts of the Book."[63]

AEG. The standard abbreviation in the rare book world for a volume with All Edges Gilt. This common decorative technique adds to the beauty or sumptuousness of a volume, and it protects the outer edges from dust and pollution. See also **TEG.**

alum-tawed. Refers to "[a]nimal skins—usually goat- or pigskin—prepared with aluminum salts. Alum-tawed skins tend to be white, but they sometimes yellow with age" (Cloonan, *Early Bindings in Paper*, p. 56). Tawed skins are flexible, strong, and soft.

back. Refers to the spine of a book. Roberts and Etherington say that the term *backstrip* is "[a] term used incorrectly with reference to the spine of a book" (*Bookbinding*, p. 16); however, the term has been used with that meaning for so long and so widely that it is probably no longer incorrect. People's tendency to pull a book from the shelf using an index finger has led to the tearing off of many backstrips. Many a dealer's catalog will say "Backstrip missing" or "Top 2 inches of backstrip loose."

back cornering. "The process in bookbinding of cutting away a small triangular piece of the head and tail edges of the boards of a book at the joints . . . to relieve the strain on the joints of the book when the covers are opened" (Roberts and Etherington, *Bookbinding*, p. 14). (See figure 4.44.)

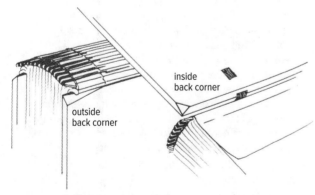

inside back corner

outside back corner

FIG. 4.44 Back cornering. (Brown, p. 14.)

backing. A convex curve in the spine of hand-bound volumes; the binder will often shape the signatures at the spine to give the book this curve (see the explanation in figure 4.45).

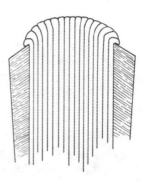

FIG. 4.45 Backing in bookbinding ("shaping a ridge or shoulder on each side of the spine of a text block"; Brown, p. 15.)

bands. The thongs or cords on the spine of a volume that are formed when the book is sewn; they are often raised (hence the term *raised bands*; see the section "Laced In" earlier in this chapter). Bands that are formed by stitching at the top and bottom of the spine are called *headbands* and *tailbands*, respectively. They can be decorative, and they are also functional in that they give the binding extra strength. Fake ones can be glued on, while genuine ones are formed from stitching over leather or vellum bands or cords.

barrier sheets. See **manifold paper.**

beaded bindings. Covers with elaborate beadwork on them; very scarce.

binder's ticket. A small label the binder adheres to the binding, usually on the front or rear pastedown, to identify him and perhaps give an address. See also **ticket.**

binder's waste. Any old piece of paper, cloth, or vellum that was trimmed away from the binding material and cannot be used for any further binding operation. Sometimes it winds up inside books, inside spines, or under pastedown endleaves.

blind stamping. Also called *blind tooling*. The imprinting of the cover (or other part) of the book by pressing text or image (or both) into the cover (often leather, though the process can be used for vellum, paper, or cloth as well) with no gold or other colors impressed. Strictly speaking, stamping and tooling are different from one another. Stamping is done from blocks or type; tooling is done with hand tools. See also **gold stamping.**

boards. The cardboards used over the textblocks of books; originally it could also have meant actual wooden boards. When booksellers say that a book is "in boards," they mean that it is in a hardbound binding, as opposed to a paperback or a limp cover.

book cloth. A wide range of cloths that are used in binding. In libraries, a common type of cloth is buckram, a sturdy material covered or impregnated with acrylic to make it water resistant. Much has been written about book cloths. (For example, see Tomlinson and Masters, *Bookcloth, 1823–1980*, in the bibliography at the end of this chapter.)

book sizes. See chapter 9, "Bibliography."[64]

bosses. Metal "knobs," often decorative, that are attached to the upper and lower covers—generally in the four corners (though sometimes also in the centers of the covers)—of books in boards; when set on a flat surface, the volume sits on the bosses, not on the cover. They were most often used on large books with heavy wooden boards, and they kept the tooling on the cover from being rubbed by the flat surface the book lay on.

buckram. See **book cloth.**

calf. Perhaps the most commonly used leather for binding. True calfskin is quite smooth and usually shows no sign of grain. It is excellent for stamping and other forms of decoration.

chained books. Books from libraries of the Middle Ages that were literally chained to their shelves to prevent theft. (The precaution did not always work because innumerable chained books "traveled" from one place to another despite the bolts placed in their covers for the connection of the chains.) Such bindings were in use from the fifteenth to the eighteenth centuries.

clasps. Used at the fore-edge of the front and back boards of a binding (usually with wood boards) to snap the binding together and hold the boards in place. They were typically used for heavy volumes, but they appear on smaller ones as well. (See figure 4.46.)

FIG. 4.46 Clasps on a leather binding. (*Das neue und verbesserte Gesangbuch, worinnen die Psalmen Davids* . . . [Germantaun: Michael Billmeyer, 1807].) (Collection of the author.)

Concertina. A binding structure created in repairing a volume when original signatures are taken apart and washed or mended. They can then be resewn back into a textblock. But the original folds might be too weak to hold the sewing thread. So guards (thin folded strips of paper, called *Concertina guards*) can be tipped onto the leaf along the fold, and the sewing threads will go through these guards, creating a Concertina. (See figure 4.47.)

cords. Used in binding, the cords go around the gatherings (or signatures) of folded sheets of the book at the outside of the spine; the binding threads are stitched around the cords to form the raised bands. (Tapes and thongs are also used.)

deluxe binding. See **edition binding.**

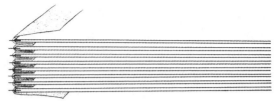

FIG. 4.47 Concertina guards in bookbinding; folded edges of the leaves onto which individual leaves can be pasted. (Brown, p. 63.)

dentelles. The lace-like patterns that appear on the turn-ins—that is, stamped, almost always in gold, on the boards, often around the front and rear pastedowns. (The word is from the French word for "lace.")

diced leather. Leather that has been impressed with a diamond or square pattern, often gilt, and used over boards.

disbound. Term describing a volume that was once bound and has been removed from its binding. See also **in sheets; unbound.**

doublures. Decorated materials—usually leather or vellum, but also possibly silk or paper—that are found where pastedown endpapers are usually placed. They can be extraordinarily ornate, and a sign of a valuable book is sometimes its elaborately decorated doublures. They are not attached to the flyleaves.

edition binding. Also called *publisher's binding* or *trade binding*. The binding done for most or all of the volumes published at the same time of that edition. That is, whether a publisher produces an edition of five or a million copies of a title, most or all of them are bound in the same binding, sanctioned by the publisher. Often a number of copies in a larger edition are not given the edition binding but are clad in a special cover ("all leather," for instance) as the deluxe version, commanding a higher price. The truly maniacal collector, wanting a copy of a book in each of its manifestations, will want copies in each binding variant. (See chapter 10, "Book Collecting and Handling.") As Cloonan points out, "Edition bindings were usually done for publishers or distributors rather than for booksellers or individuals, though it is important to keep in mind that for books published before the nineteenth century it is not always possible to make a publisher/bookseller/distributor distinction" (*Early Bindings in Paper*, p. 74).

embroidered bindings. Volumes bound with embroidery on their covers. The term is also used when embroidery is not actually done, as when needlepoint or other kinds of stitched decoration different from embroidery are present. The work can be fairly crude or exceptionally splendid, with gold and silver threads, sequins, beads, and other elaborations worked into the patterns.

endband. See **headband.**

fascicle. A single group of folded leaves, usually nested together, as in a signature of a book. Often books are issued in parts over time, each part being one fascicle. Sometimes called a *gathering*.

finishing. Essentially the decoration of the binding after the book has been bound. Roberts and Etherington define finishing as "The art or process of polishing, lettering, and embellishing the spine, covers, inside of the covers, and sometimes the edges of a book, as well as inlaying, onlaying, varnishing, and otherwise decorating and/or protecting the finished bookbinding" (*Bookbinding*, p. 102).

fore-edge. The edge of the volume opposite the spine.

full binding. Binding that uses a single material—all leather, cloth, paper, or vellum. See also **half binding; quarter binding; three-quarter binding.**

gathering. See **fascicle; signatures.**

gauffered edges. Also called *goffered edges* or *gouffered edges*. The three edges of the book decorated with carving, stamping, or tooling into various kinds of patterns, usually geometrical, and then usually covered with gold, though some were covered in colored pigments.[65]

girdle books. Produced in the late Middle Ages and early Renaissance as protective bindings; they were so called because the volume was covered not only with the normal binding but also with a long, projecting piece of leather (often doeskin or deerskin) that covered the volume and that allowed the book to hang upside down from a girdle (that is, a belt that was girded around the waist), so that the reader could pull the book up and turn it upright to read it without detaching it from the girdle. (See figure 4.40.)

gold stamping. Also called *gold tooling*. The imprinting of the cover (or other part) of the book by pressing text or image (or both) into the cover (often leather, though the process can be used for vellum, paper, or cloth as well) using gold foil. For the distinction between *stamping* and *tooling*, see **blind stamping.**

half binding. Binding that uses one material on the covers and another over the spine and corners. The boards, for instance, can be covered in one color cloth while the spine and tips (corners) are covered in another cloth, paper, vellum, or leather. See also **full binding; quarter binding; three-quarter binding.**

headband. "A functional and/or ornamental band at the head and tail of a book between the sections and the spine covering which projects slightly beyond the head and the tail. Originally, the headband consisted of a thong core, similar to the bands on which the book was sewn, around which the ends of the threads were twisted and then laced into the boards of the book" (Roberts and Etherington, *Dictionary*, p. 129). Headbands have a long history and an extensive literature. Some scholars distinguish between real and fake headbands—the "real" ones containing a core of a thong or some other material around which

the sewing thread goes, the "fake" ones merely pieces of colored cloth pasted onto the top (and bottom) of the spine of a textblock and protruding above the block. The old term *tailband* was used for the one at the bottom of the textblock, but nowadays they are both called headbands. The term *endbands* has also been used. The Roberts and Etherington entry "Headband" is worth reading in full (*Bookbinding*, pp. 129–30). (See figure 4.48.)

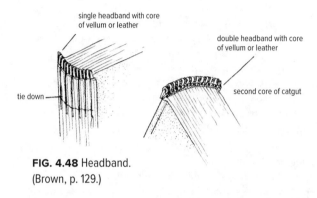

FIG. **4.48** Headband. (Brown, p. 129.)

headcap. The part of the spine at the top and bottom that is just outside the headbands. It was originally designed to protect the headbands, but, thanks to the ignorance and carelessness of many a user, books are often pulled off shelves by their headcaps, which are then torn from the spine. "Headcap torn" or "headcap wanting" are defects often noted in booksellers' catalogs.[66] (See figure 4.49.)

FIG. **4.49** Headcap. (Brown, p. 130.)

hinge. A cloth or paper strip between the endpaper and the first leaf of the textblock (either the flyleaf or the first leaf of the text), pasted in to add strength to the binding. The hinge receives a great deal of activity because it is the part of the book that flexes whenever the cover is opened. In many a volume the hinge is "starting" (beginning to crack) or has completely torn its whole length, with the consequent separation of the boards from the textblock. If mull (super or crash) were used, the split hinge would reveal it, and the mull itself may have torn. To repair the book, one can rehinge it—that is, take it apart and replace the old hinge with a new one.

hollow back. A binding style in which the spine of the book reveals a little tunnel from the top to the bottom of the spine when the book is opened. That is, the binding materials are not glued to the textblock spine, but are attached at the joints. See also **tight back.**

in boards. Refers to a book that is hardbound.

in parts. Refers to books that were not issued in full text but were issued in fascicles over time. Especially in the nineteenth century, many books were issued in parts over many months or even years, and then the parts were brought together and bound into a single volume. Such items are sometimes referred to as *part-books.*

in sheets. Refers to a full textblock of a book with no binding. Often books were issued in sheets so that the purchasers could put their own bindings on them. The term *in sheets* usually implied that the sheets were unfolded, though I have seen many books in sheets that have been folded and gathered, ready for binding. See also **disbound; unbound.**

in wrappers. Refers to a book that is not hardbound, but is in a flexible (usually) paper cover.

joints. The parts of the binding at which the boards connect with the textblocks. As the term implies, the cover swings open and shut at the joints, so a great deal of movement takes place here. Joints are some of the most vulnerable parts of a binding.

laced-paper case. "A paper book cover made off [i.e., separate from] the textblock, but then laced onto it" (Cloonan, *Early Bindings in Paper*, p. 77, citing Gary Frost, "Historical Paper Case Binding"; see the bibliography at the end of this chapter). Cloonan adds, "*Laced-paper cases* are attached only by lacing and therefore do not require gluing or *casing-in*" (p. 77).

limp binding. Binding in which the covers are not thin paper, nor are they stiff. They are made of leather, vellum, or cloth (or, rarely, paper), and they are quite flexible. One common style is the limp vellum binding, about which a good deal has been written.[67] See also **suede.**

manifold paper. Also called *offset sheet.* A thin sheet often used as an overlay for engraved or other illustrative materials in books, designed to keep the pigments and inks of the illustration from offsetting onto the facing sheet. Ironically, in many books the pigments and inks did not have any offsetting properties and the manifold papers were not imprinted with any offsetting text, but they themselves were made from papers that were acidic; hence, they yellowed or foxed and damaged the very papers they were designed to protect. (In printing, slipsheets are sometimes used to keep freshly printed pages from offsetting onto the neighboring page. These are sometimes called *barrier sheets*.)

marbled calf. See **tree calf.**

Mauchline bindings. Wooden boards onto which images (often the silhouettes of ferns) have been stenciled or dyed. The boards are usually dark brown or black, and the images show the brown boards or a color that looks like wood. Sometimes photographs are also pasted onto the boards. The Online Dictionary for Library and Information Science (ODLIS) gives this definition: "A decorative technique that originated in the 1830s in the Scottish town of Mauchline in which a transfer print of a wood engraving, often a color design (tartan or floral motif), was applied to a lacquered wooden object, such as the boards of a bookbinding. In the 1860s, photographs and stencils began to be used in the design process" (www.abc-clio.com/ODLIS/odlis_m.aspx).

morocco. One of the designations for goatskin used in bindings; morocco has a "pinhead grain pattern developed either naturally or by means of graining or boarding, but *never* by embossing. . . . [L]eather made from vegetable tanned goatskin having a grain pattern resembling that of genuine morocco, but produced other than by hand boarding, is more properly termed 'morocco grained goat' or 'assisted morocco'" (Roberts and Etherington, *Bookbinding*, p. 172).

offset sheet. See **manifold paper.**

overcasting. "A method of hand sewing in which groups of single sheets are sewn together using a single length of thread which passes through the paper and over the back edges of the leaves" (Roberts and Etherington, *Bookbinding*, p. 182). (See figure 4.50.)

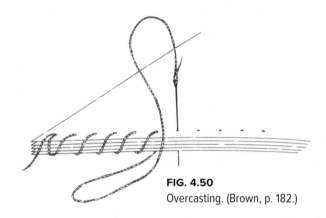

FIG. 4.50 Overcasting. (Brown, p. 182.)

pamphlet bindings. Stiff covers into which pamphlets, issues of magazines, or other thin texts are sewn, stapled, or glued; for decades in the twentieth century they were made of cheap, unattractive, acidic cardboard.

panels. The little square or rectangular areas on the spine of a book, formed between raised bands. Panels are often gold stamped with information (author's name, title, publisher, date) or with decorations.

paperbacks. See **soft cover books.**

part-books. See **in parts.**

polished calf. Cover leather that has been burnished until it shines.

primary binding. The first binding a book is given. The term implies that the volume was issued in an inexpensive cover with the intention that its owner would then rebind it into something more sumptuous and permanent.[68]

printer's waste. Any piece of paper or vellum (possibly also cloth) that is discarded from the print shop. It may wind up inside the binding of a book, as a lining for the spine or boards. Some printer's waste can be historically important, as is the case for a leaf from a hitherto unknown printing of a text.[69]

publisher's binding. See **edition binding.** Although the concept of "edition binding" does explain what *publisher's binding* means, it is worth adding that a large literature has emerged on publishers' bindings, with a narrower meaning: that such books are cloth-bound (or paper-bound) with decorated covers. The Ruari McLean books cited in the bibliography at the end of this chapter are just two of many such studies.

quarter binding. A term denoting a cover that has the spine and a little part of the covers bound in one material and the rest of the boards covered in another material. The spine, for instance, can be cloth or leather, and the rest of the book is covered in cloth. The strip at the spine can be one kind of paper and the boards can be covered with a different kind of paper. That is, the two covering materials could be different (cloth spine, paper over boards; vellum spine, cloth over boards) or just different manifestations of the same material (plain paper over the spine and marbled paper over the boards). See also **full binding; half binding; three-quarter binding.**

rag board. A kind of cardboard made from rags and used as binder's board. If properly made, it is alkaline and acid-free, and it is stiff and smooth.

rebacked. Refers to books that have been repaired by having their spines replaced.

rebound. Refers to books that have had their original bindings removed and replaced by newer ones. The term implies that the sewing has been redone as well, though this is not always the case.

recased. Refers to books that have had their cases replaced.

red rot. The powdery stuff that rubs off leather bindings that have become deteriorated from the acid left in the leather during the tanning process. The development of the red rot is accelerated by exposure to damp conditions and air pollution. The damage caused by red rot cannot be reversed, but the leather can be treated with a powder called Klucel G (mixed with alcohol or with water, it can be brushed on and left to dry), and the leather can then be coated with a microcrystalline wax (one brand is called Renaissance wax).

rehinged. Refers to books whose hinges have been replaced.

rolls. See **scrolls.**

rounded and backed. Refers to books that have had their textblocks literally hammered (sometimes pushed) into a convex form so that the spine protrudes in an arc. This produces a concave fore-edge in the volume.

According to Roberts and Etherington, "A book is rounded to help prevent the spine from falling in, i.e., assuming a concave shape (and a convex fore-edge), which would result in severe strain on the hinges of the book. It also facilitates the outer sections being knocked over to form the backing shoulders, and, in conjunction with this backing process, helps accommodate the swell in the spine resulting from the bulk added by the sewing threads" (*Bookbinding*, p. 222). This process can now be done with a rounding and backing machine.

Russia. Also called *Russia calf*. "Originally, a leather produced in Russia from calfskin, vegetable-tanned with tannin obtained from the bark of willow, poplar, or larch trees, curried from the flesh side with a mixture containing birch-bark extracts—which gives it the characteristic odor for which it was famous—and dyed red or reddish brown. It was often given a grain pattern of latticed lines" (Roberts and Etherington, *Bookbinding*, p. 224).

saddle stitching. Accomplished when a signature of the book is folded in half and then stapled through the fold; the most common form of binding for magazines or small pamphlets.

scrolls. Also called *rolls*. Texts in the form of rolls. There is no actual binding in the simplest scroll; all one does is roll up the papyrus, parchment, or other material. But many scrolls have a board of some kind on the outside for protection, with perhaps some kind of string to tie the scroll so it will not roll open. Scrolls were usually written on only one side, so the text would be rolled on the inside.

sewing frame. "A frame or press on which books are sewn by hand. It consists of a flat baseboard, two uprights threaded on both ends, a crossbar and two supporting wooden nuts. Tapes, cords, or bands are stretched from the slotted baseboard, where they are secured by keys, to the crossbar, where they are attached to loops (laycords)" (Roberts and Etherington, *Bookbinding*, p. 229). One signature at a time is placed onto the baseboard with its fold against the suspended cords or thongs or tapes. The binder sews through the

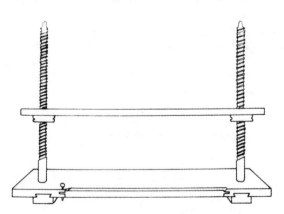

FIG. 4.51 Binder's sewing frame. (Brown, p. 229.)

fold, around the tapes, moving from one sewing hole to the next until the signature is secured, and then places another signature in the frame to continue the operation. (See figure 4.51.) The sewing can be done in many different ways, as can be seen in figure 4.52, which shows some traditional sewing patterns.

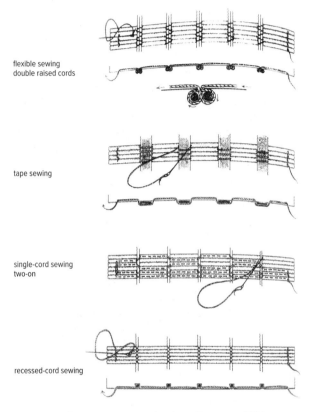

flexible sewing
double raised cords

tape sewing

single-cord sewing
two-on

recessed-cord sewing

FIG. 4.52 Sewing patterns in binding. (Brown, p. 230.)

side stitching. "A method of securing the leaves or sections of a book with wire staples, from front to back of the entire thickness of the textblock" (Roberts and Etherington, *Bookbinding*, p. 235). Because the textblock is pierced all the way through, the gutters inside the book are narrowed, and the volume will not open well.

signatures. Sections or gatherings in books, made up of all the leaves that are folded and then sewn through the fold in one sewing operation. The volume can have one or a hundred or more signatures.[70] A signature can be made of a single sheet folded into two leaves, or many sheets, folded and nested into ten or twelve leaves. Sometimes called *fascicles*.

signed bindings. Bindings that can be identified by the signature or other identifying mark of the binder somewhere on the binding. The identification can be a name stamped somewhere on the book, a cypher particular to the binder, or even on a binder's ticket. The signature can be anywhere on the volume, but it is most often somewhere on the bottom of the rear inner board. See also **binder's ticket; ticket.**

single-section books. Pamphlets or magazines bound in only one section. (This is a redundant definition, but necessary because the name of the structure is self-explanatory.)

skiver. Thinly pared leather (usually from sheep or goats). Because it is quite thin, it is excellent for spine and cover labels, but it is fairly weak and not good for binding.

slipsheets. See **manifold paper.**

Smyth sewing. (Roberts and Etherington call it *Smyth-Cleat sewing*.) "A method of machine sewing or lacing adapted from an earlier European method by the Smyth Manufacturing Co. in the late 1960s and early 1970s. It combines thread and adhesive to secure the leaves of a book. In a separate machine, the back[s] of the sections are planed off leaving the spine as smooth as possible. This is a very critical part of the operation, because if the cut spine is not smooth and even, subsequent operations are affected detrimentally. The block of leaves is then placed spine down in the Smyth-Cleat machine and is moved into position where a circular saw cuts a number of cleats completely across the back from head to tail (the number depending on the long dimension of the book). The sawn leaves then move into the sewing position where a single hollow needle laces thread around the cleats in the manner of a fiddle or figure-eight stitch" (Roberts and Etherington, *Bookbinding*, p. 240). This strong method of binding is used in millions of books today and is probably second only to perfect binding in the amount of its use.

soft cover books. Paperbacks; the great majority from commercial presses are perfect bound, but they can also be Smyth sewn for extra strength. The distinction is that a "paperback" has the connotation of cheapness—as being printed on poor-quality paper and also as being little more than ephemeral—while the term "soft-cover book" connotes a higher quality product, on better paper and possibly with a sewn binding.

Solander box. An enclosure devised to protect books and manuscripts; one of the most popular of the many kinds of enclosures that have been developed. The box was "invented by Dr. Daniel Charles Solander, a botanist, during his tenure at the British Museum (1773–1782)" (Roberts and Etherington, *Bookbinding*, p. 243). (See figure 4.53.)

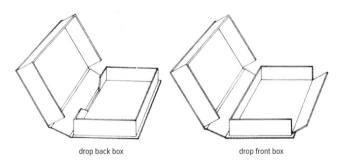

drop back box   drop front box

FIG. 4.53 Solander box. (Brown, p. 243.)

squares. The parts of the upper and lower boards in a binding that stick out beyond the textblock. If the book lacks squares—that is, if the textblock is flush with the boards, the leaves of the book will be scuffed by anything touching the edges of the book. To prevent this from happening, many a careless binder, in rebinding a volume, trims the textblock down so much that the margins are reduced, sometimes to the point of actually cutting off top lines of the printed pages.

suede. "A leather finished on the flesh side by buffering so as to raise a velvet-like nap" (Roberts and Etherington, *Bookbinding*, p. 253). This was a popular material for binding in the late nineteenth and early twentieth centuries, and thousands of volumes were bound in "limp suede" covers. Suede leathers were easy to use in binding, and they took decoration (blind and foil-stamping) beautifully. Their main drawback, which did not become manifest for many years after their production, was that many of them were tanned with acids that remained in the skins. The acids eventually led to the deterioration of the skin, and innumerable limp suede bindings developed red rot, the flaky, powdery material that rubs off bindings at the slightest touch. See also **red rot.**

tailbands. See **bands.**

tapes. Binding strips made of cloth. See **cords.**

TEG. The standard abbreviation in the rare book world for Top Edge Gilt. See also **AEG.**

textblock. In binding, refers to all the leaves of the book that are bound into covers other than the ones the binder uses (endleaves [also called *endpapers* or *endsheets*] and doublures).

three-quarter binding. A term denoting a volume with one material over the boards and a good deal of other material used for the spine (and some of the front cover) and large areas over the corners. A three-quarter binding is like a half binding, but with a good deal more material used on the spine and corners. See also **full binding; half binding; quarter binding.**

thongs. Thin strips of leather or vellum. See also **cords.**

ticket. A small label pasted into volumes, usually at the bottom of the rear pastedown, showing the name of the binder, the bookseller, or possibly someone else responsible for the production or sale of the book. Hence, there are binders' tickets and booksellers' tickets. (See figure 4.54.)

ties. Tapes, cords, or ribbons that protrude at the fore-edge of a volume (sometimes at the head and foot of the volume as well) that are used to tie the binding shut. They can be threaded through holes made in the covers, and they can even be extensions of the tapes or cords that were used in the binding (the ones that wrapped around the spine and formed the raised bands).

tight back. A binding style in which the materials covering the spine have been glued down to the textblock. When the book is opened, the material on the spine

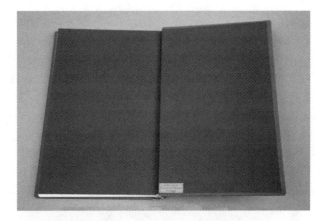

FIG. 4.54 Bookseller's ticket on Henry Aldous Bromley, *Outlines of Stationery Testing: A Practical Manual* (London: Charles Griffin; Philadelphia: Lippincott, 1913). The ticket (label) is at the foot of the rear paste-down endpaper. This is also where you might find a binder's ticket, especially in finely bound books. (Collection of the author.)

stays closed (that is, stuck to the textblock). See also **hollow back.**

trade binding. See **edition binding.**

tree calf. Calfskin that has been treated with an acid that runs down the skin and creates a pattern that looks like a tree trunk with spreading branches. It is a common form of binding decoration. One problem with it is that if the acid is not washed off after the pattern is formed, it will remain on the skin and will eventually cause the calfskin to be eaten away. Not uncommon are books with tree calf bindings on which parts of the tree pattern have been eaten away down to the board beneath it. The acid can also be applied in such a way as to simulate marbling, producing *marbled calf*.

turn-ins. The inner corners of bindings, inside the covers, at which the book's cover material has been folded from the front onto the inner boards and pasted down.

unbound. Refers to a textblock that has never been bound. See also **disbound; in sheets.**

wrappers. "Usually defined as the temporary covers for books which were intended to last only until the books could be bound" (Cloonan, *Early Bindings in Paper*, p. 88). Wrappers were usually paper, and they were sometimes decorated. And though they were not as sturdy as hard bindings, "many of them from the seventeenth century on have survived intact" (p. 88).

Yapp edges. "A style of binding featuring a cover (leather, or other material, but customarily leather) that overlaps the three edges of both upper and lower covers continuously. The covers are always limp or semi-flexible, and are sometimes fitted with a zipper, which was a later refinement" (Roberts and Etherington, *Bookbinding*, p. 286). Roberts and Etherington point out that books of devotion or of poetry were often bound in this manner. Yapp edges protruded from the edges of

FIG. 4.55
Yapp edges.
(Brown, p. 286.)

the book and had folded-down strips the full length of the side of the book. (See figure 4.55.)

yellowbacks. Volumes that were covered with yellow paper and contained cheap fiction. "Yellowbacks were cheap, 19th century British literature sold at railway book stalls, with colorful, sensational covers to attract buyers. While some were well-known books such as 'Sense and Sensibility,' many of the yellowbacks were obscure titles by authors unknown today."[71]

Illustrations

The vast topic of book illustration, as with others in this text, has been treated extensively in hordes of publications. For this volume, intended to help those in the rare book world, the following sections will concentrate on the book before printing, looking at the three main methods of book illustration over the centuries (relief, intaglio, and planographic), and finally at other kinds of illustration.[72]

Rather than rehearse this sizable topic, we will look at medieval manuscript illumination in only the most cursory way, with references to many readings that will help the rare book librarian, the bookseller, and the collector. A close examination of pigments, tools, styles of illustration, evolving techniques, gilding, and so forth is beyond the scope of this book. Here we will concentrate on the vocabulary of the trade rather than on the extremely complex, extensive history of the subject and the methods of illustration used in the Middle Ages. After all, for the most part, those involved in the rare book world usually need to talk about, describe, and know the terminol-

ogy of the items in their care more than they need to know how a particular pigment was made or how the techniques of painting the page evolved. That kind of information will be available in the volumes cited in the bibliography at the end of this chapter.

The illumination of manuscripts was done by hand, as the word *manuscript* indicates. For the work done in medieval manuscripts, consult, in the bibliography, the items by Alexander, Brown, Cennini, De Hamel, and others.

RELIEF

Printing in relief is printing from a raised surface. Printing from metal type is relief printing. So is rubberstamping because the surface that creates the impression sticks up from the rubber beneath it.

Five thousand years ago cylinder seals were used to impress a pattern (words, numbers, or images) into clay.[73] The seal contained a relief image that appeared "right reading" when it was rolled into soft clay. I mention it here as a kind of relief printing because the surface that made the images was raised.

More germane for our purposes is woodblock printing, invented in China. It appears on fabric in the fourth century AD.[74] In a woodcut, the image or text was drawn onto the smooth surface of the block and then everything else was carved or filed away. Also, "[w]ood engraving is a technique in printmaking where the 'matrix' worked by the artist is a block of wood. It is a variety of woodcut and so a relief printing technique, where ink is applied to the face of the block and printed by using relatively low pressure. A normal engraving, like an etching, has a metal plate as a matrix and is printed by the intaglio method [see the following section]. In wood engraving the technique for working the block is different from woodcut, using an engraver's burin to create very thin delicate lines, and often having large dark areas in the composition, though by no means always" (http://en.wikipedia.org/wiki/Wood_engraving).

Printing from relief can be done from metals, wood, plastics, and even rubber erasers and potatoes. Any solid surface that protrudes in relief can be used to print.

INTAGLIO

Intaglio printing is done from beneath a surface. The image or text is carved (or possibly etched with acid if the surface is metal) into the surface of a plate (with gravers and burins, sharp tools with wooden handles), in grooves and dots of varying sizes and depths. Originally wood and copperplates were used, though other materials have been developed for this purpose. For instance, a synthetic material called Resingrave has been in use for at least twenty-five years, replacing boxwood and other woods for artists working in intaglio illustration.

Once the surface is prepared with dots and grooves, ink is squeegeed over the surface and forced into the areas beneath the surface of the plate or block. The surface is then cleaned, leaving the ink in the areas beneath the surface. A damp piece of paper is laid over the plate, a wet, thick felt is laid over the sheet, and then a roller is forced over the top of these layers of materials, pressing the paper down into the grooves and dots, where it picks up the ink and transfers the image to the sheet.

In etching, the plate is coated with wax, which acts as a protective covering for the plate. With a fine metal tool, the artist scratches through the wax, exposing the plate beneath, in the pattern that will eventually be printed. Once the text or image is "revealed" through the wax, the plate is either exposed to acid that drips across it or the plate is immersed in an acid bath for as long as the artist wishes. The longer the plate is exposed to the acid, the more depth will be etched out of the plate and the more ink it will take, yielding a darker impression.

A related method—strictly speaking not intaglio, but closely related in its method of design—is drypoint printing. With burins and gravers, the artist cuts into the copper plate, leaving a burr of metal along the edges of the incised grooves. Rather than squeezing the ink into the grooves beneath the plate's surface, the artist puts ink onto the raised burrs, which are sticking up above the plate's surface. Hence, this is a form of relief printing. The paper is pressed against these inked burrs to print the image. The burrs are not strong, and the pressure can be great, so the burrs do not last long. Hence,

only a few prints can be made from this drypoint method.

Incising can be done in wood, creating a wood engraving. This is an intaglio method of printing, as opposed to woodcuts or woodblock prints, which are relief methods.

Usually with copperplate engravings, the plate is smaller than the sheet that is being printed, so the margins of the plate are pressed into the paper and leave an impressed border around the image or text. Later steel-plate-printed images do not leave this border, but sometimes a fake one is pressed into the sheet to make the image look as if it were done from a copper plate. Also, the image in true intaglio is three-dimensional because the wet paper receiving the print is forced into the grooves, creating a place where the paper stands up in relief where it has been pressed into the grooves and dots. The result is a raised surface where the ink is.

A fairly modern method of faking this kind of raised printing was developed in the twentieth century: thermography. As the name indicates, heat is used to activate a particular kind of ink, which thickens and stands up above the surface of the sheet, giving the look and feel of truly engraved text. But with engraving, a debossing effect occurs on the back of the sheet, while with thermography the back of the sheet is flat. This kind of raised printing is popular (because it is far less expensive than intaglio printing) for letterheads and business cards.

PLANOGRAPHIC

From the fifteenth century until the end of the eighteenth, relief and intaglio were the two basic methods of printing. In 1798, the Bavarian actor Alois Senefelder, looking for a way to print music cheaply, discovered another method, which used the flat surface of stones. By chance, he lived near a quarry from which a special kind of limestone was mined. It had a couple of properties that made his discovery one of the most influential methods of printing in the nineteenth century. The first property was that it held oil-based ink well. The second was that when it was covered with water, the water would pool over the whole surface, not bead up into drops.

Knowing the basic principle that oil and water do not mix, Senefelder figured out a way to draw onto the surface of a polished, flat stone the image or text he wanted to print. The text was applied with tusche, an oil-based ink, which lay flat on the surface of the stone. He then covered the stone with water, which covered the entire surface except where the tusche was. He inked the stone, which took the ink where the tusche was, but not where the water was on the stone's surface. When a sheet of paper was laid over the stone and pressed (with a press like that used for intaglio printing), the ink transferred to the paper. Because the printing surface was flat, the method was called *planographic* printing.

The artist uses crayons or fine pens to draw onto the stone, and exceptionally fine lines can be achieved, allowing for great variations in shading and density of ink. Of course, anything could be put onto the stone's surface: pictures, drawings, text in any language, and so forth.

Another way to create the image was developed. The text, pictures, or both were drawn onto a sheet of paper—right reading—with an oil-based or wax-based ink. The sheet was then turned over with the "text" pressed against the surface of the stone. Under great pressure, the oil- or wax-based image transferred to the surface of the stone and was ready for printing. One advantage of this transfer method was that the artist need not work "in reverse"—that is, in "mirror writing"—to produce the image that was to be printed.

Planographic printing is done with no form of abrasion, so none of the tusche is removed; hence, a huge number of impressions can be made from a stone with no deterioration of the image. When the printer no longer needs what is being printed, the tusche can be rubbed off and the stone reused. Because the lithographic stone is quite thick (and quite heavy), and because in the removal of the tusche only a very tiny amount of the stone gets rubbed away, stones can be used over and over for decades.

The practice yields a print of a single color. In the early 1820s the French developed a method of printing more than one color, one on top of another,

ONE OF THE fascinating phenomena in the world of books is Extra Illustration, the practice of taking a text, often disbinding it and rebinding it with extra blank sheets, and then tipping in illustrations, ephemera, photographs, and other things, usually relevant to the topic of the book. A single-volume text can be extended to a dozen volumes with extra illustration. One of the things about this practice that angers many is that to extra-illustrate a book, one must sometimes take pictures from other books. The practice is also called *grangerizing*, after the English clergyman James Granger (1723–1776), whose *Biographical History of England* (1769) "included areas for readers to illustrate the pages" (Wiktionary, http://en.wiktionary.org/wiki/grangerize).

to create a multicolor image. The method is called *chromolithography*. A picture is created in color and then the artist (or a professional lithographer) does a color separation into all the shades that will be overprinted to achieve the final image. It requires great skill to do the color separation, knowing what colors to separate the original into, how much of each color to use, where to place them on successive stones, how to get perfect registration, and so forth. Millions of children's books in the nineteenth century were printed from chromolithography (the prime company being McLaughlin Brothers), usually using three or four colors. Some artists adopted lithography and produced pictures in a dozen or more colors. There were even prints using as many as twenty-five colors. The method was sometimes combined with relief printing—for instance, with the images done from stone and the text from type.

One additional note: when an illustration is used in a book, regardless of its method of manufacture, it is sometimes (often inaccurately) referred to as a *cut*. One might, for example, see, "The book has cuts on every page," when the writer means "illustrations" on every page. So many illustrations were produced by woodcut, linocut (linoleum illustrations), or some other hand-cutting process that the term *cut* has often been used to designate any illustration.

OTHER KINDS OF ILLUSTRATIONS

Those working in rare books and special collections must know about the three printing and illustration methods thus far described. More modern forms of illustration, using offset printing, photography, stencils (pochoir) and silkscreens, photocopying, and the many other kinds developed in the digital age are beyond the scope of the present text. The bibliography at the end of this chapter includes source materials for this broad field.

Related to illustration in its methods of production is another kind of decoration: the *fore-edge illustration* (sometimes called *fore-edge painting*). The principle is simple: when a volume is closed, the edges of the pages at the fore-edge are visible. When the textblock is fanned out, more than just the very edges of each leaf is exposed. What becomes visible is a thin area of the surface of the pages themselves. An artist secures the fanned-out leaves of a volume in a press, holding the textblock in this position and revealing the thin surface of the face of the leaves. Working on this fanned-out textblock, she paints a picture of some kind on the fanned-out sheets. Once the painting is dry, the book is taken out of its press, and the edges of the pages disappear as the textblock returns to its normal shape. Usually the edges of the volume are gilt (or marbled), hiding the picture even further. (See figure 4.56.)

A good fore-edge artist must be a good miniaturist because there is not much space to work. Also, some books have one painting when the book is fanned out in one direction and another when it is fanned out in the other direction: a so-called double fore-edge. Roberts and Etherington even mention "[a] triple fore-edge painting [that] has a visible scene in addition" to the other two, "in which case the edge is not gilded or marbled."[75] And sometimes a fore-edge painting extends to the fanned-out edges of the head and tail of the volume.

Parts of the Book

Although it may be obvious what a cover or a dust jacket is, a title page and a half title, there is nonetheless a broad terminology, describing the parts of the book, that all people in rare books and special collections should be familiar with; some of the terms are not as familiar as others. "Parts of books" can refer to the intrinsic elements of the book, such as covers and title pages; it can also refer to things that are added to the book and become part of it, like labels of various kinds. Key terms appear in boldface.

Because much of this chapter has focused on physical aspects of the book, many of the "parts" have already been delineated (especially so in the section on binding). This section will pick up other terminology that is essential for those in the rare book world.

Before looking into any volume, anyone holding a book must look at the binding structure and the

FIG. 4.56A (left) Fore-edge illustrated book with the pages unfanned. Thomas Campbell, *The Poetical Works* (London: Edward Moxon, 1843). (Collection of the author.) **FIG. 4.56B** (right) Fore-edge illustrated book with the pages fanned, exposing the illustration. This miniature was painted in 2007 by Martin Frost. Note that this binding has gilt dentelles (the gold-stamped lacy pattern on the inside edges of the boards—around the rear pastedown endpaper).

elements of the binding. Of course, there are the covers, either boards or paper (**wrappers**—sometimes referred to as *wraps*); sometimes a **dust jacket** (or dust wrapper); the turn-ins (on the inside of the covers, at the corners of the boards and under the endpapers); the **endpapers** (or *endleaves* or *endsheets*), comprising the pastedown (sometimes hyphenated) and the free endpaper; **doublures** (as noted earlier, the fancy material affixed to the inner front and rear boards); **flyleaves** (sometimes called *blanks*); and then the printed pages.

Under the subject of printing, Roberts and Etherington say this about "Parts of the Book": "The different segments of a book, gathered in the following order: half title page, frontispiece, title page, printer's imprint and copyright notice, dedication, preface, acknowledgments, table of contents, list of illustrations, introduction, errata, text, appendices, author's notes, glossary, bibliography, index, and colophon. Publishers sometimes vary the order of inclusion, and not all works contain all segments indicated" (*Bookbinding*, p. 192). This is a good summary of some of the parts, if one looks at the book from a bird's-eye view.

HALF TITLE

The half title (sometimes called the *bastard title*) may reappear on the leaf immediately preceding the main text and after all the other prelims.[76] That is, there may be a second half title. It usually contains only the title of the volume—or an abbreviated version of the title.

FRONTISPIECE

Usually the frontispiece is some kind of illustration or printed page that faces the title page. But some books have the frontispieces positioned so that they are on rectos, not versos. (Two key terms with respect to parts of the book are **recto** and **verso,** the two sides of a leaf in a book. When a two-page spread is open, the page on the right is called the *recto* (the Latin word for "right"). The reverse side of the leaf is called the *verso*. Generally, rectos are odd-numbered pages, though I have seen books laid out by novice designers with all rectos being even-numbered pages. Many frontispieces are printed on paper different from that of the text of the book, and they are therefore tipped in rather than bound in. They are thus not part of the bibliographic record as part of the printing of a book—that is, they do not figure into the original printing of, say, an octavo or a quarto.[77] In a bibliographic description, they may appear in a notes section, not part of the collational formula.[78]

PRELIMS

After the title page but before one gets to the other prelims, one may find the **imprint.** John Carter defines the imprint as

> [a] notification to the reader (and to the legal authorities) of the person or persons responsible for the production of a book. Some of the earliest printed books bore no such note; but from about 1465 till late in the 16th century the *printer's imprint* was generally placed at the end of the book (and there properly called the colophon). It normally comprised the place of printing, the name of the printer and the date. (*ABC for Book Collectors*, p. 129)

In modern books this information is often given on the title page, and it will certainly be on the copyright page (though finding a copyright page in some books—especially those printed in languages other than English—can be tricky).

Roberts and Etherington mention that the errata page(s) could be part of the prelims, but it is often found at the end of the volume. In the handpress period, however (that is, up to about 1800), the prelims were almost always printed after the main text was, primarily so that the table of contents and other lists designating the location of pages in the text could reflect accurate page numbers. So errata would then be in the prelims.[79]

Robertson and Etherington list the "printer's imprint and copyright notice" together. This juxtaposition is odd, because the printer's imprint generally appears on the title page while the copyright notice (mostly for books from the late nineteenth century on) is likely to appear on the verso of the title page. That is, they are usually not together. Nowadays, the two pieces of information will often appear on the copyright page, along with the ISBN.

THE INTERNATIONAL STANDARD Book Number was first used in 1966—as a unique number for every book copyrighted. On the binding, the dust jacket, or the copyright page (or all three, or any combination of two), one might find the ISBN. ISBNs are sought before books are published so that they can be printed on the volume. Sometimes a fine press book or one for which the author does not seek an ISBN will lack the number, though it can be obtained at any time after the book is published. The U.S. publisher R. R. Bowker is officially the company that assigns ISBNs, and because it does so, it can keep an accurate count of all books published in the United States (other than the ones lacking the number). The total of new books published in the United States each year, given in the first volume of *Books in Print* every year, is calculated from the number of ISBNs that Bowker assigns. Periodicals have an equivalent identifier: the ISSN (International Standard Serial Number). Originally ISBNs contained nine digits; today they have thirteen.

DEDICATION; PREFACE; ACKNOWLEDGMENTS

The dedication, preface, and acknowledgments, if all three appear, are usually in this order, though many volumes lack prefaces and many an introduction contains acknowledgments.

ERRATA

Depending on the kind of book one is looking at, the volume may lack **errata,** appendices, author's notes, glossary, bibliography, index, and colophon. Most mass-market books, especially fiction, will lack all these. If the publishers notice an error in the volume before the printing has been completed, they may wish to acknowledge the mistake by printing, at the end of the text, a note called an *erratum* for a single mistake they want to correct or *errata* for more than one. It is better to do this than to issue the book to the public with the mistake(s) unacknowledged. But if the errata notice is at the end of the text, the reader has no clue of its existence at the point of reading and may never spot it. If the book is to be used for scholarship, the scholar may quote the error without ever having seen the errata list. (The errata,

in older books, might be called *corrigenda*—corrections.) An errata slip might be laid in or tipped into the volume, if it is not printed along with the text. If this approach is used, the publishers can do so near the beginning of the volume—as, for instance, on the verso of the half title—to alert the reader of the intended changes.

COLOPHON

In many books printed in the last hundred years, the **colophon** may well appear at the front of the book, just after the title page. Colophons can differ (in placement and content) from one volume to another depending on a number of factors, such as, the purpose of the book, whether it is handmade or commercial, and the audience. A mass-market paperback will probably not have a colophon. A fine press volume, printed in, say, one hundred copies or fewer, is likely to have a colophon showing who the printer is, where and when the book was printed, how many copies were done, the number of the present copy, the typeface and paper used, and so on. Some printers take the colophon as an opportunity to wax poetic, to reveal all kinds of information to their readers.

From the early manuscript period, books had colophons, the final flourishes of writing by the scribes, sometimes stating when the work of copying was completed, possibly the city in which the work was done, and, rarely, the name of the scribe. The word comes from the Greek, meaning "acme" or "summit." Before title pages were a standard part of a book, the colophon might have been the only place at which one could find the title of the work. In modern press books (from the end of the nineteenth century on), colophons have been used to offer many kinds of information: number of copies printed, the paper used, the typeface(s) the book was printed in, sometimes a brief biography of the type designer, the binder and binding material, the date of the conclusion of the printing, the name of the illustrator, the method of printing, the weather and the other hardships the printer faced during the production of the book, and much more.[80]

ADVERTISEMENTS

One thing Roberts and Etherington do not mention is **advertisements.** It was a common practice in the nineteenth century for publishers to bind into their books advertising "fliers." That is, a pamphlet of a few pages—or one of dozens of pages—could be bound in after the book's text, advertising other items for sale from the publisher. In modern books, especially fiction, the equivalent to this feature is a page, often on the verso of the half title or on a separate leaf preceding the title page, which lists "Other Works by This Author." Presumably the other works were published by the same company, so the list is an advertisement for other books one could buy from this publisher.

In earlier books—those with the advertising leaves or pamphlets listing other books from the publisher bound in—these lists can be useful to librarians and scholars. For instance, they are like little bibliographies of books available at the time of the publication of the volume they are added to, so they may establish a date or the priority of issue of a volume listed therein. They will also be guides to titles that were supposedly published, though it is possible that books will be listed in these advertising pieces that never actually made it to print: ghost books (ones for which there is a record, though no known copy exists). Another advantage of the advertising add-ons is that they usually give the original selling price of books, information that is not easily obtainable from other sources. As Carter points out, some of the advertising is on leaves that were printed right along with the text of the book and are thus on the same paper as the original text and are "integral to the gathering" of the volume (*ABC*, p. 20); and other advertising is printed separately from the text (usually on different paper) and bound or tipped into the book.[81]

DUST JACKET; DUST WRAPPER

Parts of the book related to binding have already been mentioned, though we might want to add **dust jacket** (or **dust wrapper**).[82] For hard-cover bindings, to protect the volume and to advertise, publishers will often put a dust jacket onto a book. Naturally, a well-designed wrapper can call attention to itself on a bookshelf and could draw a potential buyer to it. The jacket can have text or images that are enticing to a customer. Also, dust jackets contain information that could be lacking anywhere else on the volume, like blurbs of critics, photographs and biographical notes of the author, plot summaries, ISBNs, and information about whether the book exists in other media, if it has been made into a movie, if it has won a prize, or if it has been on a "best-seller" list.

Public libraries often keep the wrapper, covering it with a protective sleeve and putting the call number on the sleeve (as well as onto the volume). Academic libraries usually discard the jacket for books that go into the circulating collection; special collections departments will generally keep the jackets. Each library has its own practices, but special collections personnel should always keep in mind that researchers will want as much information as they can get from the materials they use in the reading room, and discarding the dust jacket is usually discarding information.

John Carter claims that the use of dust jackets dates to 1832 (*ABC*, p. 85), though Mark Godburn pushes that date back to 1829.[83] That early, and through the next three or four decades, jackets were fairly scarce, though growing in popularity. A book issued with a dust wrapper is more desirable to a collector if the jacket is present than is one lacking the wrapper. So these protective coverings have a fiscal relationship to a book as much as they have an informational one. In fact, maniacal collectors insist on the dust jacket when the book originally had one, and the lack of this piece of paper could affect the book's value significantly—by thousands of dollars, pounds, or euros.

BOOKMARKS; REGISTERS

Some books have bound-in **bookmarks,** sometimes called **registers,** often a thin, silky, shiny, colored fabric. Although these amenities could be nice, many have dyes that transfer to the leaves, or they are acidic and leave marks on the sheets. If a book comes with one of these, it probably is anathema to many an owner to cut the thing out, but this approach might be best for protecting the volume. Naturally, a collector would rather have the bookmark there, transferring its dye to the neighboring sheets, than have the thing removed.

LABELS

Labels of various kinds get affixed to books. The obvious kind is the bookplate (sometimes called an **ex-libris** because those two words often head such a label; they mean "from the books [of]"). As will be discussed later in the section "Appraisal and Book Evaluation" (in chapter 10, "Book Collecting and Handling"), the value of a volume is affected, positively or negatively, by the presence of a bookplate. If negatively, an owner might wish to remove it, but at the risk of leaving signs of its former presence. And such signs can reduce the value of a book as much as the bookplate itself did. Bookplates themselves can be printed on inferior, acidic paper and can harm the books they are in. If the plate is of a famous person, showing the provenance of the volume, the value of the book could increase. But it is possible that the bookplate of a well-known person was pasted into a book that the person never owned. Further, some bookplate designers are themselves collectible, so the book may be worthless, but the plate may have some value.

Bookbinders' labels (usually quite small and pasted onto the rear pastedown) have been collectible for decades. They are usually called "bookbinders' tickets." (See **ticket,** under "Additional Binding Terminology" earlier in this chapter.)

BOOKPLATES

Another kind of label is the bookplate, for which an enormous literature exists. These tipped-in labels identify the owners of the books, and there is a rich history of bookplate research in the world of historical bibliography. The scholarship focuses on many areas of bookplate research: owners (personal, library, institutional, etc.), heraldry, illustrators, printing processes, subject matter (bookplates show readers, books, libraries, erotic scenes, animals, coats of arms and family crests, particular subjects like beekeeping, horseback riding, and dozens of others), and an endless array of other topics. They often have the words "ex libris" (from the books of _____); for this reason a bookseller might say, "This volume contains the ex libris of John Doe," using that phrase as a synonym for "bookplate." Roberts and Etherington say that these plates "can be dated back to at least as early as 1516" (*Bookbinding*, p. 34). A vast world of bookplate collectors exists, and booksellers and librarians should be particularly wary of the bookplate collector, who might wish to soak off the plates of books, depriving the volumes of a key element of their provenance.

PAGINATION; FOLIATION

Page numbers are called *page numbers*, but in the terminology of medieval manuscripts and early printed books, page numbers are sometimes referred to as **folios** (a possibly confusing term because it also means a book format in which the signatures are made up of full sheets that have been folded only once). Used in context, however, there should be no confusion: "Throughout the text the folios are written in the same hand as is the text." Many books from the manuscript period and printed in the incunabula period (up through and including 1500) had no page numbers; they had leaf numbers. The leaf was sometimes called a *folio*, and, properly speaking, because the leaves were numbered, not the pages, it is common to refer to "folio 77r" (i.e., recto—the page on the front of leaf 77) and "folio 77v" (the verso, or back, of that leaf). Such numbering was not "pagination" (in which each page is numbered), but **foliation.**

A few terms from the early book world will be useful if the special collections or rare book librarian is dealing with medieval manuscripts. These terms designating the book's format will be seen again in chapter 9, "Bibliography," but as terminology delineating the parts of a book, they belong here as well.

MEDIEVAL MANUSCRIPT TERMINOLOGY FOR LEAVES

When a sheet of vellum or paper, being prepared for use in a manuscript, is folded in half, forming two leaves and four pages, and then gets sewn into a volume in this form, it is called a **folio,** or a **bifolium.** If two leaves are folded in half, with the second nested into the first, this structure is called a **folio in fours** (or **folio in 4s**); the resultant format is a folio, each signature containing four leaves. If three such sheets are folded in half and then nested into one another, this format is called a **folio in sixes** or a **ternion.** Four such sheets nested the same way creates a **folio in eights** or a **quaternion.** It takes a full sewing operation to sew a simple 2-leaf folio into a volume. It takes two such operations to do two of them. But by nesting the folded leaves (2, 4, 6, 8, or 10 of them), it takes only one sewing operation to attach all of them into the bound book. Hence, the nesting reduces the labor of the sewing. Some common formats, then, for manuscripts and printed books are folios in 8s and folios in 10s. When the individual leaves are folded and brought together, the resultant group of sheets is called a **gathering** or a **quire.** It is also called a **signature.**

BLANKS

Blanks are sheets of paper or vellum that are inserted into the binding of the book usually between the free endpapers and the printed text. (Sometimes they are called *flyleaves*.) The more the publisher wants to save money, the fewer blanks will appear in a book, because paper can be one of the most expensive elements of a book. But sometimes, wanting to add some bulk to a thin volume, or wanting to add a feeling of sumptuousness to a finely made book, the publisher will add blanks. They are much more common in fine press books than they are in commercially made, mass-market volumes. Because they are almost always added by the binder, they are not properly part of the printing of the book, so they do not deserve to be considered in a bibliographical

IN WILLIAM MORRIS'S Kelmscott *Chaucer,* one of the front leaves between the endpaper and the printed text looks at first glance like a flyleaf. On careful examination, however, one will find a small printed *a* at the foot of the page, designating the first leaf of the first printed signature of the book. It looks like a blank, but it definitely is not. The lowercase *a* is the only thing printed on the page, but it is part of the printing and should be included in the part of the bibliographical description that covers the printed book. (See chapter 9.)

description in the section describing the printed part of the book.

Blanks can be inserted anywhere through the book other than at the endsheets, as at the end of a chapter or section, before a major part of the book (e.g., the table of contents, index, or appendix), or facing illustrations or plates. Blanks can go missing in books for any number of reasons, and when a person is doing a collation of a volume (that is, examining it carefully for completeness and condition), one might find a blank "wanting" (that is, "missing," in the bookseller's and bibliographer's terminology). A related term is *called for*, which means that a part of the book which should be there (like a blank, a tip-in of some sort, or a bookmark) is missing. "The blank between chapter 3 and chapter 4 called for" means that a blank leaf should be there. This is, as noted, a bookseller's term, and it implies that the person using the term has it on good authority that something should be there (which, by implication, is now not there). One must know the jargon of the trade, as these examples attest.

NOTES

On some printed pages one will find **footnotes** (as opposed to **endnotes,** which follow the text and do not appear on the page on which the endnote number appears). But one may also find **side-notes,** those printed in the outer margins of a page beside the text that they refer to, or **shoulder-notes,** printed at the outer margin but usually at the top of the page.

HEADLINES

The top of the page is called the **head,** so **headlines** or **running heads** (sometimes **head notes**) are printed at the top of the page, indicating various kinds of things: authors' names, book titles, chapter titles, the subject matter covered on that page, and more. Sometimes these are at the foot of the page, but they are still called *head lines* if they serve the same functions that running heads would. (Amusingly, these are also sometimes called *running feet.*)

PRINTERS' DECORATIONS

At the opening of a chapter or section of a book, especially at the top of the page before the text begins, one might find a decorative item printed: a flower, a **dingbat** (called a **fleuron**—similar to a *printer's flower*), or a picture of some kind; this decoration is called a **headpiece.** Similarly, at the end of a chapter, especially on a page on which the text ends high on the page and leaves a good deal of blank space beneath it, one might find a similar such decorative element, here called a **tailpiece.** A printer's **logo** or trademark can be anything, from letters to numbers to images of any sort. They are sometimes called **devices.** Some famous ones are instantly recognizable. The one used by Gutenberg is a branch holding two shields with a Greek lambda (looking like an inverted *V*) on one shield (representing the word *logos,* "the word"), and a Greek chi (looking like an *X,* the first letter of Christ's name) on the other.[84] The logo of Aldus Manutius, the great Italian printer of the incunabula period, is an anchor with a dolphin wrapping around it—copied by many printers who followed him.

In chapter 7, "Security," we shall see a discussion of marking books; here it is necessary to discuss briefly a "part" of a book that does not fall conveniently anywhere else: marks in books. For a variety of reasons (for security, to identify books that have been recovered after having been lost, to claim or prove ownership, to deter theft), books will receive marks: rubber stamps, pencil marks, hole-punched or embossed information (usually showing the name of the owning institution or party), or signatures of owners. Of course, library books will have call numbers and possibly pockets on the rear pastedown. How these affect the value and salability of a volume will be taken up in chapter 7.

Printing Practices and Essential Terminology

The vocabulary of the world of printing is massive. The aim of this section of the chapter is to present terminology that a person working in rare books needs to know. Some of the terms have been used earlier, and some will be repeated later on. But they need to be gathered here under the rubric "Printing Terminology" because they figure into book descrip-

tion, and they will reveal information about how books are put together. Key terms appear in boldface.

Earlier in this chapter we covered the making of printing type, which, of course, includes **sorts** (individual pieces of type) for the alphabet, numerals, punctuation, and other characters to be printed, like **asterisks, percentage signs, slashes** (also called **virgules**), the **paragraph sign** (also called the **pilcrow**), **ampersands, circumflexes, accents grave** and **ague,**[85] **plus** and **minus signs** (the latter of which can be delineated with a simple hyphen—along with the single character ±, which is a **plus-and-minus sign**), **arrows, fists** (these are the pieces of type that depict a pointing hand; they come in all sizes and many designs, pointing right or left), **kerns** and **ligatures,**[86] **superscript** and **subscript sorts, fractions,** and so forth.

There are also **fleurons,** decorative elements like little flowers (fleurons are also called **printer's flowers,** or **dingbats**), calligraphic squiggles, or other decorations. The number of fleurons is seemingly endless, and because there are so many of them, they are often housed in their own type case—or several type cases.

Type cases over the centuries, and from country to country, language to language, have differed in hundreds of configurations. This is no place for a dissertation on them. But people in the rare book world should understand that until the late 1870s, all printing type was set by hand from sorts sitting in type cases. The **compositor** takes individual sorts (pieces of type) out of the type case and puts them in proper order into a **composing stick.**[87]

The type could have been put into the wrong case (mixing fonts), or it could have been put into the correct case but misdistributed so that the sorts are not in their correct receptacles. This is called a **foul case,** and it accounts for many a typographical peculiarity—when books or pamphlets are printed with mixed fonts or with upside-down lowercase *n*'s used for *u*'s.[88] For people describing old books that have mixed fonts, the term *foul case* explains what has happened.

Once the compositor has set as much type as she can into the composing stick for a single line, she must then decide if the line is to be **justified** (that is, set with the last printed sort at the right margin—also called **flush right**) or **unjustified** (set without hyphenating the last word of the line and stopping the setting of the type with the last full word that will fit into the composing stick—also called **ragged right**). On a computer it is easy to decide which one wants: justified or not. But in typesetting, the compositor has to set every line the exact same length, whether it ends in printed text or blank spaces. So justifying the line in the stick, to tighten it up at the same length as all other lines, must take place whether the printed text is justified or ragged right.

With the composing stick holding as many lines of type as she wishes, the compositor transfers the type to a **galley,** a flat metal tray with three raised sides. The compositor would continue to set the type and transfer lines of type until the galley was as full as she wished it to be. This could mean that she would put into the galley enough lines for a single page, or for two pages, more or less, until the galley held as many lines as was desired. Eventually the type would be broken down into pages. Galleys came in several sizes, so it was possible to have two or three or more pages' worth of type in a single galley. There are tiny ones used for small texts and huge ones large enough to hold enough type to fill a newspaper page.

In early printing it was customary to proofread the text from a printing of the type while it was still in the galley; hence **galley proofs.** It was much easier to make corrections in the text while it was still in the galley than it was once it had been locked up in a press. The term *galley proofs* has stuck, and often when a modern author gets the first proofs from a publisher, they are called galley proofs (or **galleys**), though the entire text has been set and printed by computer. The term has come to mean something like the first proofs generated for the author to read.

After the galleys were proofed and corrected, the type was broken down into the number of lines desired for each page. Proofs were then taken again: **page proofs.** Once again, in the modern world, this term could designate the second level of proofs, sent to editors or authors for corrections—with all the text broken up into pages. But in the handpress period this was a literal designation: the text to be proofread was now set into pages. Sometimes the page proofs were printed from galleys, but usually the fact that the texts were at the page-proof level meant that the type was already in the press.[89]

If the type was set one line upon another (called **set solid**), it could be printed this way; but to add some space to the page, thin strips of lead (actually made up of type metal, which is mostly lead) could be slipped in between the lines of type. This is called **leading,** a term that is still used in the computer world. It means **interlinear spacing.** Leads are 1 or 2 (sometimes, but rarely, 3) points thick.[90]

To get the type into the press, the printer moved it from the galley into the **chase.** Remember that the galley had only three sides, against which the loose type could lean, so that it would not fall over. The fourth side was open so the type could be slid out of the galley into the chase. The chase is a four-sided metal frame that holds the type and the pieces of wood (or other material—sometimes metal or some kind of plastic, for instance) that go around the pages of set type. Thick pieces of wood are called **furniture;** thin ones are **reglets.** They surround the type to hold it in place, and **quoins,** wood or metal wedges, are placed into the chase. When a **quoin key** is used to tighten up the quoins, they squeeze the type tightly together and against the four inner sides of the chase.[91] Everything inside the chase is called a **forme.** In chapter 9, "Bibliography," this term will come up again. Anyone dealing in rare books and most people working with special collections materials must know this word. To repeat: the forme is composed of everything that is inside the chase that will go into the printing press, including printing type, any illustration to be printed (e.g., linoleum blocks or woodcuts), a numbering device that might print a number onto each page, furniture, reglets, **slugs** (strips of type metal, usually 6 points thick), **leads** (1, 2, or sometimes 3 points thick),[92] quoins, and anything else the printer puts in there.

The act of putting everything (especially the type) into the chase is called **imposition.** When we speak of the printer "imposing the type," this means that he is putting the type into the chase. A **misimposed** page could lead to a page's being printed upside down or, more commonly, in the wrong sequence.

Once again, these are key terms that will appear again in chapter 9, with a more extensive discussion of what the type "looks like" in the press—how it is placed with respect to the pages that will be printed.

When the type is in the press, it is ready to be printed. Modern high-speed printing (developed at the beginning of the nineteenth century with the mechanization of the craft and made greatly more complex as technology has evolved) can be done on any of myriad kinds of presses—all beyond the scope of the present text. Useful for the world of special collections, however, is a discussion of printing in the handpress period. Again, there are scores of kinds of presses, and the practices from one printing house to another may vary. Presented here, then, are only the bare bones of the craft, reviewing basic concepts and practices, with crucial terminology, again printed in boldface.

In the **handpress period** (from the beginning of printing in the middle of the fifteenth century until about 1800), presses had some basic parts. The type had to be placed somewhere where it could be printed; it sat on the **bed of the press,**[93] inside the chase. Hinged over the bed of the press was a **tympan,** a metal frame covered with vellum or paper, stretched tautly (hence the name, which comes from the Latin word for "drum"). The piece of paper or other material to be printed was set onto the tympan, which would be folded down over the inked type. If the tympan with the sheet of paper were folded down, the paper would fall off before it settled over the type. So another metal frame, called a **frisket,** attached to the tympan, hinged down over the tympan. It was covered in vellum or paper (usually the latter), and it folded down onto the tympan over the sheet to be printed. The frisket had holes cut in it to expose the sheet of paper beneath it where that sheet was to be printed.

The type sitting on the bed of the press was inked with **inkballs**[94] or a **roller** (also called a **brayer**); the sheet of paper was placed onto the tympan; the frisket was folded down over the tympan holding the sheet in place and covering the sheet completely except where holes were cut in the tympan; the tympan and frisket were folded down over the inked type. Then the bed of the press was pushed

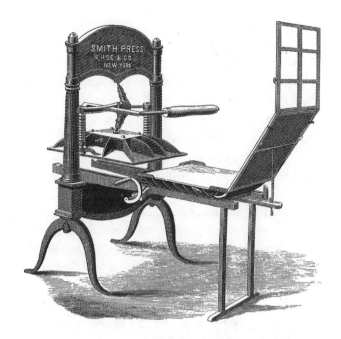

FIG. 4.57 An iron handpress, showing the bed (where the type will be placed in a chase). To the right, hinged and open, is the tympan. Hinged to the tympan is the frisket. The operation goes like this: The sheet is laid onto the tympan, the frisket is folded down over that, the tympan and frisket are folded down over the inked type in the bed of the press, and the bed is rolled under the platen when the printer turns the handle (called a rounce). The bar is pulled, and the platen descends over the type, pressing the sheet against the inked type; the bar is then released. The rounce is turned in the other direction, pulling the bed out from under the platen, the tympan and frisket are opened up, the printed sheet is removed, and the process is then repeated. (From Harold E. Sterne, *A Catalogue of Nineteenth Century Printing Presses* [Cincinnati, OH: Ye Olde Printery, 1978], p. 191.)

into place under a **platen** (hence the delineation of the **platen press**—one with a flat bed and a flat slab of metal over it); that is, the platen is a flat metal plate on the press that hovered over the tympan and frisket ready to be lowered to press the paper against the type.[95] A bar was pulled, and a screw or toggle mechanism forced the platen down over the type, pressing the sheet of paper onto the type where it picked up the ink. (See figure 4.57.) To get the bed of the press underneath the tympan, on most presses, there was a large cylinder underneath the press to which were attached leather belts. A handle (called a **rounce**) protruded from this cylinder.[96] When the rounce was turned, the carriage was pulled under the platen. After the printing, the rounce was turned in the other direction to get the bed of the press out from under the platen.

At this point the tympan and frisket were hinged back open from the bed, the frisket was hinged back open from the tympan, and the sheet of paper, now printed, was taken off the tympan and hung up to dry. Then the process was repeated.

When a sheet is printed as just described, it receives ink (and therefore text or images or both) on only one side of the sheet. Once the ink is dry, the printer now has to **perfect** the sheet: that is, print the other side. In printing, a sheet that is **imperfect** is one that is printed on only one side and is waiting for the other side to be printed. (In chapter 9 we will look at a format [*half-sheet imposition*] that allows a sheet to be printed on both sides before the ink has dried on the first side printed.)

If a sheet were placed on top of another one on which the ink was still wet, it might leave an impression of the text on the underside of the top sheet. This is called **offsetting.**

All the sheets printed at one time or in one single operation is called the **pressrun.** So one could say, "The pressrun was four hundred sheets." The term is also used for the number of copies of a book or pamphlet (or broadside) that is produced in a single printing: "The latest Harry Potter book had a pressrun of 12 million copies."

During the pressrun, the printer could spot a typographical error or could be asked by the author to add something to (or change something in) a text. The printer would stop printing and make the change. This is called a **stop-press correction,** though the change is not always a correction.

The time a printer works without pausing is a **stint:** "He had a six-hour stint at the press."[97]

When all the sheets are printed and perfected in a single pressrun, they are set aside, the type is removed from the press and can be distributed back into the type case(s),[98] and the compositor can begin setting more type for subsequent pressruns.

Once all the pressruns are complete, the book now exists **in sheets.** That is, the entire text is fully printed on both sides of the sheets and is now ready for the binder. Books were often kept in sheets at the publishing house for at least two reasons. First, many customers wanted to put their own bindings on the books, so they would not want to buy bound copies, only to have to remove the publisher's binding to replace it with one of their own. This was an added expense. Also, binding was a considerable expense to the publisher. If the entire pressrun were bound and, say, only half were sold, the publisher would have spent a good deal of money for bindings on volumes that were never sold. It was more economical to bind as many books as the publisher could reasonably expect to sell, and then bind up more once the first group of bound books was (about to be) sold out.

This practice led to a bibliographical phenomenon: books of the same edition (as noted earlier, this means all the books set from a single standing of type), all printed at the same time, but issued in variant bindings. Between the time of the binding of the first books issued from the press and the binding of the second issued volumes, the binder could have run out of the leather or other binding materials used for the first batch and may have used a different kind of binding material (or bound the second issue of books with a different binding style or even additional inserted signatures). It might be difficult or impossible to distinguish which was the earlier one to be issued.

This discussion is getting beyond the subject of printing, but it is a key element in the world of rare books, and anyone working in the field must know about such things. As mentioned earlier in the section on binding, special collections and rare book people must understand how the items they deal with came into the world and must also be able to describe them.

■ ■ ■

This chapter has looked at a wide range of subjects having to do with books as physical objects. It has demonstrated that the vocabulary of the book is extremely broad, emanating from all the elements from which books are made and all the processes books go through to become objects in our collections. To be competent in this field, the person in rare books must understand a great deal about all the topics this chapter has presented.

Not covered here, however, are the many formats in which books are printed and the sizes of books. These will be covered in detail in chapter 9 on bibliography.

Once the books exist, in their myriad manifestations, they must be kept somewhere. Chapter 5 will look at how to lay out a special collections or rare book department.

NOTES

1. Hassan Ragab, *Le Papyrus* (dissertation, L'Institut National Polytechnique de Grenoble, 1934). See also the three citations to Ragab's work in the bibliography at the end of this chapter.

2. In a classic essay that all people in the rare book world should know—"Printers of the Mind: Some Notes on Bibliographical Theories and Printing-House Practices," *Studies in Bibliography: Papers of the Bibliographical Society of the University of Virginia* 22 (1969), pp. 1–75—Donald McKenzie warns all scholars not to write definitively about any process or practice that they have not observed in person or, even better, that they have not tried themselves. He also advises scholars not to take as fact the assertions of others who are writing about any ancient or complex practices that the writers may never have done. Such acceptance merely compounds and memorializes the errors and makes it difficult for future scholars to know the truth. An insidious and prolonged error about the invention of paper will be debunked later in this chapter.

3. Wikipedia has this: "the sticky fibrous inner pith is cut lengthwise into thin strips of about 40 cm (16 in) long" (http://en.wikipedia.org/wiki/Papyrus#Manufacture_and_use). The pith is not sticky, and the length is completely variable, depending on the needs of the maker. To compound this error, the website continues: "It is also possible that the two layers were glued together. While still moist, the two layers are hammered together, mashing the layers into a single sheet." Both of these assertions are absolutely wrong, and they are typical of the kind of misinformation one will find in "scholarly" writing about papyrus.

4. See chapter 9, "Bibliography," for a discussion of book formats.

5. This point must be emphasized. Vellum or parchment is definitely not leather. The latter is tanned and takes on the colors of the tanning medium or whatever other color is used to dye it. One should never refer to any parchment as "leather," a common error.

6. "Today, the main sites of ancient Pergamon are to the north and west of the modern city of Bergama in Turkey." See "Pergamon," Wikipedia, http://en.wikipedia.org/wiki/Pergamon.

7. The Wikipedia article on vellum says, "The best quality, 'uterine vellum', was said to be made from the skins of stillborn or unborn animals, although the term was also applied to fine quality skins made from young animals" (http://en.wikipedia.org/wiki/Uterine_vellum).

8. John Carter, *ABC for Book Collectors*, 8th ed. (New Castle, DE: Oak Knoll Press; London: The British Library, 2004), p. 115. The full text of this book is available on the Web at the ILAB website: www.ilab.org/eng/documentation/29-abc_for_book_collectors.html.

9. Another example of the perpetuation of misinformation is this: "Paper as we know it, was invented in China, AD 105, by the Chinese Eunuch Ts'ai Lun" (http://users.stlcc.edu/nfuller/paper). Nowhere in this article on the Web is there the slightest hint that the date and other information are in doubt. And why is it always pointed out that Ts'ai Lun was a eunuch? It sounds as if his having been castrated has something to do with his invention—which he did not invent. Similarly, the opening statement of the Wikipedia article on "History of Paper" states, "Paper was invented by the [sic] Ts'ai Lun by 105 AD during the Han Dynasty and spread slowly to the west via the Silk Road" (http://en.wikipedia.org/wiki/History_of_paper).

10. See W. Turner Berry and H. Edmund Poole, *Annals of Printing* (London: Blandford Press, 1966), p. 4.

11. See Dard Hunter, *Papermaking: The History and Technique of an Ancient Craft* (New York: Knopf, 1943; rpt. New York: Dover, 1978), p. 474.

12. See Horatio Gates Jones, Claus Rÿttinghousen, and Will Bradford, "Historical Sketch of the Rittenhouse Papermill; The First Erected in America, A.D. 1690," *The Pennsylvania Magazine of History and Biography* 20.3 (1896): 315–33, www.jstor.org/stable/20085701?seq=2.

13. Timothy Barrett, *Japanese Papermaking: Traditions, Tools, and Techniques* (New York and Tokyo: Weatherhill, 1983).

14. Papermaking came to Japan in AD 610. See Hunter, *Papermaking: The History and Technique*, p. 53.

15. The distance between the chainlines is purely the whim of the paper-mold maker. There are no set measurements, and a mold maker can vary this distance as she or he wishes. Some molds have these supports quite close together, perhaps no more than a half inch apart. Some molds have them spaced three or more times that distance.

16. The identity of the inventor of wove paper is still a matter of debate. John Baskerville and James Whatman are the primary suspects. Baskerville, many scholars believe, was a papermaker and might have been responsible for it himself. Dard Hunter says,

    The "wove" mould-covering is thought to have originated in Europe by John Baskerville (1706–75), and the date of his rediscovery is usually given as about 1750. John Baskerville has long held the honour of having invented and used for the first time in Europe paper of the "wove" type. In late years, however, this distinction tendered the great Birmingham printer has been disputed in favour of the Balston paper mill, Maidstone, Kent, an establishment originally purchased by James Whatman and a Mr. Brookes in the year 1731. In 1759, two years after the Baskerville Virgil was issued, the Whatman mill manufactured genuine "wove" paper for a book by Edward Capell. . . . In this book the "W" of the Whatman watermark has been found. . . . In a thorough examination of various copies of the Baskerville Virgil of 1757 it has not been possible to discover any watermark whatever, but the paper may have been made in the Whatman mill, as it is now generally accepted that John Baskerville did not operate a mill of his own. It was probably Baskerville who suggested the use of woven wire moulds and the paper was actually fabricated in the Whatman mill. (*Papermaking: The History and Technique*, pp. 125–26).

17. See "The Whatmans and Wove Paper," www.wove paper.co.uk/baskerville.html. The site says, "The first specimen of wove paper to appear in the West was used by John Baskerville for printing his famous edition of Virgil in 1757 (the discovery of an earlier example is an eventuality discussed in the Ephemera Section of the book). Only part of the Virgil (28 unmarked sheets) was printed on the new wove paper and the rest on an unusual laid paper." Thomas Balston says, "There can be little doubt that Whatman was the first European maker of wove paper, but it is possible that he made it at the suggestion of Baskerville." See his *James Whatman, Father and Son* (London: Methuen, 1957), p. 15.

18. The placement of watermarks is carefully planned. A full discussion of watermarks would take many pages. Suffice it to say that when sheets of water-marked papers are folded for printing, the marks usually do not wind up in the center of the printed area; they wind up in margins. (For folios the watermarks may wind up in the center of each leaf.) This simplification is not definitive, for papermakers can put watermarks anywhere they want into sheets. Many watermarks are along the edges (often the "bottom" edges) or in other places in the sheets. The literature on this subject is huge; the bibliography at the end of this chapter offers a few sources to consult.

19. If the dandy roll is covered with a watermark in the pattern of laid lines (chainlines and wirelines), it will produce a sheet that looks from its "water-marks" like handmade laid paper. Papermakers have been producing such fake laid paper for decades.

20. Under the entry "Fibre direction, Grain direction," E. G. Loeber says, "In the ideal paper the fibres are felted in such a way that they point equally in all directions, but owing to the flow on the machine wire [in machine-made paper], the major part of the fibres will settle in the same direction as the machine direction, i.e. lying parallel to the Deckle straps and the sides of the machine-reel/mill-roll" (Loeber, *Supplement*, p. 24). He explains why a knowledge of this process is important, especially for printers, binders, and "wrapping machines."

21. The best book on this subject is Michèle V. Cloonan's *Early Bindings in Paper* (London: Mansell; Boston: G. K. Hall, 1991).

22. For an informative history of marbling see http://en.wikipedia.org/wiki/Paper_marbling. Precise dates and countries of origin of marbling cannot be determined.

23. Most marbled sheets have only one layer of pigment, though many marblers have perfected over-marbling with two or more layers of pigment imparted to the sheet. Karli Frigge has produced a sheet with ten distinct layers of marbling, each layer dated in pencil along the edge of the sheet. Although most marblers are content with one or two layers, after which patterns begin to blur, Frigge planned this sheet carefully, working from darker colors to lighter ones. The layers are distinct: a tour de force of artistry.

24. David Bourbeau, *Paste Papers of the Pioneer Valley, with Brief Biographies of Their Makers* (Northampton, MA: Catawba Press; Cambridge, MA: Kat Ran Press, 2011), [7].

25. See Sidney Berger, *Edward Seymour and the Fancy Paper Company* (New Castle, DE: Oak Knoll Press, 2006).

26. Two publications may be useful for those interested in pursuing these attractive papers: Ann G. Herring, *The World of Chiyogami: Hand-printed Patterned Papers of Japan* (Tokyo, New York, and San Francisco: Kodansha International, 1987); and Sidney Berger, *Chiyogami Papers* (Newtown, PA: Bird and Bull Press, 2011). Many other books exist showing (and explaining the manufacture and use of) the *katazome* stencils.

27. Everything that is in the vat ready to be made into a sheet is called the *furnish*—which includes water and pulp, sizing materials, dyes, scents, texturizing agents, and anything else. This section is called "Pulp Composition," which means all the materials in the vat that are placed "into" the sheet during its formation.

28. Despite extensive research, I have been unable to determine when and where crepe paper was invented. The Japanese were prolific users of it from at least as early as the 1870s, but there is some evidence that it comes from the United States, England, or France.

29. The best source of information on these books is Frederic A. Sharf's *Takejiro Hasegawa: Meiji Japan's Preeminent Publisher of Wood-Block-Illustrated Crepe-Paper Books* (Salem, MA: Peabody Essex Museum, 1994).

30. In England, Susan Doncaster in the 1980s made some passably nice copies of Dutch gilts. The Swiss bookseller Thomas Laurentius made some papers that were attractive, but nowhere near copies of the original Dutch papers. And more recently, John and Jane Jeffreys in Scotland have made lovely copies, done on old papers. None of these rivals the originals, but the interest is strong in some circles for these wonderful sheets.

31. In a department store's electronics department, one may see thirty or more TV screens lined up, all showing the same pictures. It is instructive to see how the pictures on the monitors differ in color and quality from one another—even two of the same brand. Such variations make suspect any picture printed in a catalog.

32. This description of the process of making a punch is a simplification. Other steps had to be taken, and the tools Gutenberg used are more than merely burins, gravers, and files. For instance, the counters of letters (enclosed areas like the bowls of the letters *P*, *Q*, *D*, and *B*) had to be removed as well, but a file was not suited for this. He had to make a second punch just for the counter (called a *counter punch*), which he hammered into the end of the punch to displace the metal where the counter was. Then he could file away this displaced metal and have the counter on the end of the punch perfectly "gouged out" and the punch cleanly prepared.

33. As with other elements of this description of printing type, the making of the matrix is more complicated than can be fully explained here. One of the best descriptions of punch cutting and the making of matrices is Joseph Moxon's *Mechanick Exercises on the Whole Art of Printing (1683–4)*, ed. by Herbert Davis and Harry Carter (London: Oxford University Press, 1958), pp. 99–119 (on punch cutting) and pp. 150–61 (on making matrices). This volume was issued in facsimile by Dover (New York: Dover, 1978).

34. Type height was 0.916 inch until 1886, when the United States Type Founders Association "adopted a new type height when it adopted the point system. Having decided that the pica would be defined by 83 pica = 35 centimeters, it decided to let 15 type heights = 35 centimeters. So type height became 23.333 . . . millimeters, approximately 0.918 inches. Although only 0.002 inches higher than the old standard, this difference is great enough that old and new type could not be mixed in the same line" (see www.sizes.com/tools/type.htm). See also Richard Hopkins in the bibliography at the end of this chapter.

35. A type case looks like a shallow drawer that has been divided into many little boxes, one for each kind of sort. Compositors wanted easy access to the small letters, the ones they set much more than the capitals. So they kept the small sorts in front of them at an easy level to retrieve. Capitals were put into a second type case above the other one. Hence our terms *uppercase* and *lowercase* letters.

36. The nick on the bottom of the sort serves at least two functions. (1) It tells the compositor that the sort is being put into the composing stick in the right direction; if a line of type is set, the compositor can glance over it and see that all the nicks are visible. If a sort does not show its nick, the sort is probably in the stick upside down. (2) The nick is not necessarily in the exact same place on sorts from different fonts. So if a sort is set into the composing stick and its nick is higher or lower than that of a neighboring sort, there are at least two typefaces represented by the two differently positioned nicks. Some fonts are cast in molds that create two or even three nicks on the edge of the sort. Types cast in the last few decades, however, will rarely show this

difference if they are cast in the same molds, because it is the mold, not the matrix, that imparts the nick into the sorts, and many matrices from various faces can be used to cast fonts in a single mold, thus giving many fonts of varying designs with nicks in identical positions.

37. This definition, though serviceable, is an oversimplification, of course. Lawson says of italic, "A sloped or cursive variation of roman. In many cases this represents a complementary style of the upright letter, although some of the lowercase letters may change form slightly, and the serif construction is different" (*Printing Type*, p. 27). Early computer roman typefaces could be automatically slanted to produce an italic, but many of them were quite ugly and not terribly legible. Designers of digital faces now understand this problem, and they create roman faces with perfectly complementary, legible italics.

38. John Ryder, *Printing for Pleasure* (Chicago: Henry Regnery, 1977), p. 126.

39. About logotypes Lawson says, "The linecasting machine firms have developed many standard logotypes such as Ta, Te, Va, Vo [in which the vowels are positioned underneath the right-hand stroke of the top of the *T* rather than beyond the sort of a normal capital *T*], to eliminate what might be an unsightly gap of space under the overhang of an arm. In advertising terminology, logotype is simply the name or trademark of a business firm" (*Printing Type*, p. 29).

40. Ryder, *Printing for Pleasure*, p. 128.

41. Perhaps the best, most succinct text on type is Alexander Lawson's *Printing Type: An Introduction* (Boston: Beacon Press, 1971). This is the text to consult for concise definitions of the various stages in type design: Black letter, Oldstyle, Transitional, Modern, Square Serif, Sans Serif, Script-Cursive, and Display-Decorative (pp. 47–119).

42. "A Hollander beater is a machine developed by the Dutch in 1680 to produce paper pulp from cellulose-containing plant fibers. It replaced stamp mills for preparing pulp because the Hollander could produce in one day the same quantity of pulp it would take a stamp mill eight days to prepare" (http://en.wikipedia.org/wiki/Hollander_beater).

43. The date given by Wikipedia (1843) is contradicted by Frederick G. Kilgour: "In 1846 in the United States Richard Hoe invented the first rotary press" (Kilgour, *The Evolution of the Book* [Oxford, New York, etc.: Oxford University Press, 1998], p. 8). Kilgour also says that "two double-cylinder presses, each powered by a two-horsepower steam engine, . . . went into operation on November 29, 1814" (p. 102). This book is not listed in the bibliography because there are more important ones to cite.

44. Two good biographies should be consulted on Mergenthaler and his Linotype machine: Carl Schlesinger, *The Biography of Ottmar Mergenthaler, Inventor of the Linotype* (New Castle, DE: Oak Knoll Press, 1989); and Basil Kahn, *Ottmar Mergenthaler: The Man and His Machine: A Biographical Appreciation of the Inventor on His Centennial* (New Castle, DE: Oak Knoll Press, 2000).

45. Rivers are white spaces that line up vertically or diagonally (or in curves) on a page where spaces between words—in successive lines—link up to form a long channel of space that is not printed on. It is distracting to the reader. In hand-set type, compositors do what they can—for example, they can reset the type for several lines—to get rid of this white line. The resetting of a line or two does the trick. But that cannot be done with text in Linotype because all the spaces are in a fixed slug of type metal. Another typesetting phenomenon that is unsightly occurs when descenders of one line almost touch ascenders in the line beneath—especially if the long stems are doubled letters. These can be adjusted in Monotype, but not in Linotype, without a full resetting of a line or two or more.

46. Richard Huss (*The Development of Printers' Mechanical Type*) gives a good description of these typesetting methods, and he shows the other machines invented for this purpose by Mergenthaler, Lanston, and dozens of others. Monotype contains 74 percent lead, 16 percent antimony, and 10 percent tin. Foundry type contains 54 percent lead, 28 percent antimony, and 18 percent tin, making it much more durable than Monotype (http://en.wikipedia.org/wiki/Type_metal).

47. For a good description of the stereotyping process and a compact history, see *American Dictionary of Printing and Bookmaking*, pp. 526–29. Also see the two volumes on stereotyping in the bibliography: Charles Brightly, *The Method of Founding Stereotype*, and Thomas Hodgson, *An Essay on the Origin and Progress of Stereotype Printing*.

48. The article on electrotyping in the *American Dictionary of Printing and Bookmaking* is exceptionally thorough, running from pages 157 to 166 in 6-point type.

49. A good copy of a first edition of Mark Twain's *The Celebrated Jumping Frog of Calaveras County* (New

York: C. H. Webb, 1867) can bring about $5,000 if the frog on the cover is in the lower-left corner; if it is in the middle, the price is about three times that much. Also, a book in a simple publisher's binding could be greatly enhanced in monetary value with a sumptuous cover from a famous binder. But it should be added that sometimes the simple, unadorned original binding of a book could make the book retain its value whereas a sumptuous rebinding, lovely as it is and even done by a well-known binder, might lower the value of the volume. Collectors are usually inclined to want their books in a condition as close as possible to the way they were issued from the press.

50. The term *textblock* has two meanings: (a) all the leaves of the book between the covers and (b) the printed text on the page, not counting the margins. So one can say, "The covers were ripped off the volume, but the textblock remained intact." And one can also say, "The margins were filled with the scholar's notes, but the textblock on the page was not written in."

51. Binders used cord, wide cloth tapes, or leather or vellum thongs over the spine of the book. The sewing threads went around these, and then back into the folds. I will use the three terms interchangeably, though they are, of course, different from one another.

52. One website, Bookbinding.com, gives the following:

> The simplest head-band is made as follows: Two strips of vellum are cut (using very sharp knife and rule) slightly longer than the round of the back [i.e., the width of the rounded spine]. The height of the strip should be a shade less than the width of the squares at the head and tail. These strips are made to assume the curve of the back [of the book] by drawing them between the finger and a rounded surface, such as a lead pencil. The silk used for covering these strips of vellum is usually of two colors, though more colors may be used as one becomes expert. For the purposes of explanation, however, we will assume that two colors, red and white, are used.

And so forth. The long explanation that follows includes a section on double headbands. The result of this extra operation is that the binding is strong at the head and foot, and there is an extra touch of adornment as well. See http://bookbinding.com/practical-bookbinding/headbands.html.

53. W. J. E. Crane, *Bookbinding for Amateurs: The Various Tools and Appliances Required and Instructions for Their Effective Use*. See www.aboutbookbinding.com/Amateur/Headbands-and-Registers.html. By the

time Crane was writing, cloth bindings had had more than fifty-five years of "perfection." The original purpose of headbands, as features that added strength to the binding, was on its way out with the extensive use of fake ones.

54. The Talas website offers many colors and widths of headbands and sewing threads to choose from (at http://talasonline.com select "Bookbinding Tools & Supplies" and then select "Threads, Tapes, Headbands").

55. See the Hollander's website at www.hollanders.com.

56. See the entry for "Spine lining fabric" in Matt T. Roberts and Don Etherington's *Bookbinding and the Conservation of Books: A Dictionary of Descriptive Terminology* (Washington, DC: Library of Congress, 1982), p. 245. This superb, informative text has been a standard reference tool in the field for decades and is often cited for its authoritative descriptions and definitions.

57. See Roberts and Etherington, "Adhesive binding," *Bookbinding*, pp. 5–6.

58. Roberts and Etherington (*Bookbinding*) prefer the terms *side sewing* where the technique is explained (p. 235) and *Japanese sewing* where they give another definition and a good illustration (p. 143).

59. Because forwarding is a complex subject closely tied with the decoration of the book, some of the act of decoration has already been presented. Finishing, however, is a topic unto itself, and must be dealt with separately, albeit with some overlap of information.

60. Herbert and Peter Fahey write, "The term 'finishing' is applied to all work done after the book has been forwarded." See *Finishing in Hand Bookbinding* (San Francisco: Herbert and Peter Fahey, 1951). Roberts and Etherington are more thorough in their explanation. Finishing is "[t]he art or process of polishing, lettering, and embellishing the spine, covers, insides of the covers, and sometimes the edges of a book, as well as inlaying, onlaying, varnishing, and otherwise decorating, and/or protecting the finished bookbinding" (*Bookbinding*, p. 102). They then add, "The purpose of finishing is to identify (letter) and beautify the book, but, at least in the latter case, in such a manner as not to interfere with the strength of the binding. The degree of finishing depends upon the nature of the book, the craftsmanship of the binder or finisher (gilder, as he is traditionally called), whether another craftsman did the forwarding, and, at times, the wishes of the customer" (p. 102).

61. Roberts and Etherington, *Bookbinding*, p. 26.

62. See http://cool.conservation-us.org/don/dt/dt1014. html. This site is particularly strong on conservation and preservation issues. It is CoOL (Conservation Online). The Faheys say: "If the finisher is doubtful about making a good, allusive design he could resort to the old favorite—a diaper pattern. These may be made with lines six units one way and six units the other, or six units wide and nine units deep, arranged to fit the size of the tools used" (p. 17).

63. Perhaps the most thorough and certainly one of the best compendia of information about bookbinding terminology is Julia Miller's *Books Will Speak Plain: A Handbook for Identifying and Describing Historical Bookbindings* (N.p.: The Legacy Press, 2010). The glossary alone runs more than sixty-five pages of small type, and the bibliography contains nearly four hundred items. The text is excellent, and so are the wonderful photographs throughout the volume. The abundant illustrations in the volume are all black and white, but they are all in color on the accompanying CD. Anyone wishing to see what all the terminology of bookbinding is about must refer to this superb text.

64. The Roberts and Etherington charts on book sizes are useful, but they must be carefully interpreted (*Bookbinding*, p. 35). More on this in chapter 9 of the present volume.

65. For excellent images of gauffered edges, enter "gauffered edges" in Google's image search tool (www.google.com/imghp).

66. "Wanting" is a common bookseller's term for "missing." See appendix 3, "Booksellers' Catalogs and the Business of Selling."

67. See, for instance, Pamela Barrios, "Notes on the Limp Vellum Binding," *Bonefolder* 2.2 (Spring 2006): 24–27. This journal is available online at http:// digilib.syr.edu/cgi-bin/showfile.exe?CISOROOT = /bonefolder&CISOPTR = 67&filename = 68.pdf. See also Christopher Clarkson, "Limp Vellum Binding and Its Potential as a Conservation Type Structure for the Rebinding of Early Printed Books—A Break with 19th and 20th Century Rebinding Attitudes and Practices," ICOM Committee for Conservation, 4th Triennial Meeting, Venice 1975, 153: 1–15; rpt. Hitchin: Red Gull Press, 1982.

68. Michèle V. Cloonan, in *Early Bindings in Paper*, notes that innumerable books were issued in primary bindings and then stayed in them. She says,

> Some paper covers are important as the first manifestation of the complete book, affording some protection and ready for purchase, a half-way stage between books in sheets and bound books. . . . Although previously book collectors, dealers and librarians have generally assumed that such covers were intended to be temporary, the survival of paper-covered books proves that they were on the contrary often remarkably sturdy and enduring. (p. 4)

69. Perhaps the most famous piece of printer's waste is an indulgence printed by England's first printer. See Paul Needham, *The Printer and the Pardoner: An Unrecorded Indulgence Printed by William Caxton for the Hospital of St. Mary Rounceval, Charing Cross* (Washington, DC: Library of Congress, 1986).

70. In chapter 9, "Bibliography," the term *signature* will reappear with other meanings.

71. The term *yellowbacks* is included here because it designates a particular kind of book recognizable by its binding. The definition comes from Emory University, "Download 19th Century Books from Emory Libraries Website," news release, May 24, 2010, http://shared.web.emory.edu/emory/news/ releases/2010/05/download-19th-century-books -from-emory-libraries-web-site.html#.TpOieqhfIs8.

72. A sidebar in Wikipedia lists the following methods of printing and the years in which they were first used (dates in brackets are my own corrections): Woodblock printing (200); Movable type (1040); Printing press (1453 [1440s]); Etching (ca. 1515); Mezzotint (1642); Aquatint (1772); Lithography (1796 [1798]); Chromolithography (1837 [1823]); Rotary press (1843); Hectograph (1869); Offset printing (1875); Hot metal typesetting (1884); Mimeograph (1886); Screen printing (1910); Spirit duplicator (1923); Inkjet printing (1951); Dye-sublimation (1957); Phototypesetting (1960s); Dot matrix printer (1968); Laser printing (1969); Thermal printing (ca. 1972); 3D printing (1984); Digital press (1993). See http://en.wikipedia.org/ wiki/Woodblock_printing.

73. "A cylinder seal is a cylinder engraved with a 'picture story,' used in ancient times to roll an impression onto a two-dimensional surface, generally wet clay. Cylinder seals were invented around 3500 BC in the Near East, at the contemporary site of Susa in south-western Iran and at the early site of Uruk in southern Mesopotamia" ("Cylinder seals," Wikipedia, http://en.wikipedia.org/wiki/Cylinder _seals, citing Edith Porada, "Why Cylinder Seals? Engraved Cylindrical Seal Stones of the Ancient Near East, Fourth to First Millennium B.C.," *The Art Bulletin*, College Art Association 75.4 [December 1993], pp. 563–82). See also Tsuen-Hsuin Tsien, "Inscriptions on Seals and Sealing Clay," chap. 3

in *Written on Bamboo and Silk: The Beginnings of Chinese Books and Inscriptions* (Chicago: University of Chicago Press, 1962), pp. 54–58. Tsien says that the cylinder seals were made from "metal, jade, stone, earthenware, ivory, and horn" (p. 54).

74. "The earliest woodblock printed fragments to survive are from China and are of silk printed with flowers in three colours from the Han Dynasty (before AD 220)" (Shelagh Vainker, in *Caves of the Thousand Buddhas*, ed. by Anne Farrer [British Museum Publications, 1990]); see http://en.wikipedia.org/wiki/Woodblock_printing.

75. Roberts and Etherington, *Bookbinding*, p. 107. The literature on fore-edge illustration is not extensive, though a few books are well known on the subject. The first to treat the method in a single volume was Carl J. Weber in *A Thousand and One Fore-Edge Paintings: With Notes on the Artists, Bookbinders, Publishers, and Other Men and Women Connected with the History of a Curious Art* (Waterville, ME: Colby College Press, 1949). This volume was updated by the same author and published as *Fore-Edge Painting: A Historical Survey of a Curious Art in Book Decoration* (Irvington-on-Hudson, NY: Harvey House, 1966). Weber's grandson, Jeff Weber, has become the reigning expert on the subject and has published *Annotated Dictionary of Fore-edge Painting Artists and Binders, with a Catalogue Raisonné of Miss C. B. Currie* (Los Angeles: Jeff Weber Books, 2010). See also his article "A Collector's Primer to the Wonders of Fore-Edge Painting" at the ILAB website (www.ilab.org/eng/documentation/35-a_collectors_primer_to_the_wonders_of_fore-edge_painting.html).

76. "Prelims" (or "preliminary leaves") refers to all printed matter that precedes the main text of the book. They include the half title, the title page, preface, introduction, acknowledgments, table of contents, list of illustrations, dedication, and any other things that are not part of the main text.

77. For a definition of *octavo* or *quarto*, see chapter 9, "Bibliography."

78. For a full explanation of the collational formula, see chapter 9, "Bibliography."

79. The subject of errata is quite complex; only a brief explanation of it is given here. For a more in-depth explanation of it, consult John Carter, *ABC for Book Collectors*, pp. 93–94. In his entry on Errata, he brings up the added complication of things inserted into a text after it has been printed ("addenda").

80. Some printers are famous for their colophons, which go on for paragraphs or pages. Walter Hamady of the Perishable Press is one such. In one of his long colophons, he talks about the paper the book was printed on: "The book serves several functions, [among which are] to use up all the different papers that came from trying to reduce our supply of old towels, ties, jeans, sheets & shirts—so you could say our friends have slept on & worn this book" (Hamady, *In Sight of Blue Mounds* [Mt. Horeb, WI: Perishable Press, 1972], colophon).

81. Advertisements in books have a complicated history. Where most of John Carter's entries in his *ABC for Book Collectors* are quite short, the entry for this topic runs two and a half pages. Carter covers one of the subjects to which I have alluded—the issue dates of books:

> As it has been a common practice since the early 19th century for such publishers' catalogues to be dated, their evidence in assessing priority between two observed variants of a book is sometimes useful. (It is obvious, for example, that copies of Trollope's *The Warden* 1855 with an 1858 catalogue cannot have been among the earliest issued.) But it is evidence that must be used with great caution; and the classification of one copy of a book as preceding another because, though otherwise identical, its inserted catalogue is dated a month earlier than that found in the other, is no more valid, without strong support from other arguments, than the proposition that a third copy is incomplete without any advertisements at all. (p. 21)

The presence or absence of advertising, and what exactly the advertisements look like, can lead a bibliographer or other scholar astray because of the many possibilities that lead to their existence. As Carter observes,

> . . . others besides the publisher whose name is on the title-page may in certain cases have been responsible for the wholesale binding, whether in boards, half cloth or (less often) cloth, of a part of the edition. A wholesaler for the provincial trade, an exporter to the colonial market, an Edinburgh or Dublin agent, a jobbing publisher who had bought a "remainder" of the edition—any of these might buy in quires, order his own binding, and insert his own catalogue. (pp. 20–21)

82. John Carter points out that the term *dust wrapper* (for a dust jacket) can be confused with the term *wrapper*, which means a soft cover on a book (as opposed to stiff boards). That is, a wrapper is part of the binding of a paperback, while the dust wrapper is a separate piece of paper that wraps around the book for protection. They are not the same thing. Hence, Carter prefers the term *dust jacket* because it cannot lead to confusion.

83. See Mark Godburn, *Nineteenth Century Dust Jackets*, at http://earlydustjackets.blogspot.com. Godburn says,

> Anyone who bought or sold books in the nineteenth century would have been astounded to know that publishers' dust jackets would one day be valuable objects and that collectors would search the world for them and pay a premium—often far more than the value of the books themselves—to own them. Throughout the first century of their use, roughly the 1820s to the 1910s, dust jackets were issued as temporary covers meant to protect books only until they were sold. Most people discarded the dust jacket as soon as they bought a book, and booksellers often removed them as books were put out for sale. The bindings of nineteenth century books were almost always more attractive than their jackets—this was the golden age of decorative bookbinding in cloth—and few people wanted their books covered in paper on the shelf. It was not until dust jackets became generally more attractive than bindings—a sea change that occurred for economic reasons around the time of the First World War—that people began to save jackets and keep them on their books. By that time, more than ninety-nine percent of all dust jackets issued in the nineteenth century had been lost.

Perhaps the most intense study of jackets is that by G. Thomas Tanselle, *Book Jackets: Their History, Forms, and Use* (Charlottesville: The Bibliographical Society of the University of Virginia, 2011), a reprinting of Tanselle's three essays on the subject from 1971, 2006, and 2010.

84. Whether Gutenberg actually intended the lambda and the chi to refer to "word" and "Christ" is speculative.

85. "Grave" rhymes with "Slav"; "ague" rhymes with the sneeze sound "atchoo."

86. Kerns are elements of sorts that will print, and they protrude beyond the sort itself—like the projection on the bottom of a swash lowercase *f*. Ligatures are sorts composed of two or more letters. Common ligatures are "fi," fl," "ff," "ffi," and "ffl," though some swash or italic typefaces have many more of these.

87. In informal language, the person setting the type was sometimes called the *sticker* or *typesticker*, and he was said to be *sticking type*. More formally, he was the compositor composing the text.

88. Upside-down letters would not be a problem if the lowercase *n* and the lowercase *u* were cast in the center of the body of the piece of type. But if the letter were cast above or below center, the incorrectly set sort would print too high or too low in the line. The same goes for other letters that can be turned upside down (*O*, *S*, and *X*), along with the numerals 1, 6, 8, and 9. In many typefaces not all of these can be used for one another by merely inverting them.

89. Printers never liked getting heavily marked-up page proofs back from anyone, author or editor, because it is difficult to make changes in standing type that is in the press. Today printers feel the same way, despite how easy it is to make changes in computer-generated text and computer-set "type." There is usually no charge to the author when he makes changes at the galley-proof level; but sometimes publishers charge a fee to make changes over a certain number when the book is in pages. If the changes alter the number of lines on a page, the proofing can force the printer to redesign subsequent pages.

90. The point system is too complex to expatiate upon fully here. Most know that the term *points* refers to the size of the type, because we see on our computers, accompanying the name of the typeface, a designation of the size of that face delineated in points. Ten- or 12-point type is a standard size for a book face—that is, a good size for reading a text. We can refer to a text "set in 12-point Baskerville, leaded two points." This last means that there are two points of space between lines of type. It is typical in the modern age for people to adopt the language of earlier times for modern phenomena. Hence, we use the term *leading* to mean interlinear spacing, though the little strips of metal do not exist in modern printing.

91. One could write a (small) chapter on quoins. The original ones were merely pairs of wedges of wood that were tapped together with a mallet and a "shooting stick," a stick that rested against one of the quoins and forced it against its mate, tightening up the contents of the chase. Modern ones are made out of metal and are turned by a quoin key, as the text indicates. In the twentieth century, **high-speed quoins** were invented that were not wedge-shaped, but rectangular. The quoin key would be inserted into a hole in the top of the quoin, and the two faces of the quoin would move apart as the key was turned. As the faces moved away from each other, they tightened the type in the chase.

92. Slugs and leads are often used along with furniture and reglets to fill up the chase, tightening the pages of type against the inner walls of the chase. Leads, as indicated earlier, are also used between lines of type.

93. The bed of the press was also called the *coffin*. Printing was called the Black Art. (In fact, there is even a journal about printing with that title, published in London by the Furnival Press, 1962–1965.) It was so named presumably because any time two identical items existed, it must have been the work of the devil—and printing produced identical items. Hence, much of the terminology of printing has to do with the Black Arts. The printer's assistant was called the *printer's devil*. Broken and unusable pieces of type were thrown into a box to be melted down and reused; the receptacle was called the *hell box*. Pulling the bar on the press to lower the platen was called *pulling the devil's tail*.

94. Inkballs (sometimes called *dabbers*) are tools made of soft leather stretched over batting and attached to a handle; they came in pairs, and they were used to pick up ink from an inking surface and impart it to type; the person inking with inkballs was said to be "beating the type."

95. From the fifteenth to the end of the eighteenth century, presses were made of wood, so this description of the printing process needs to be adjusted for this early printing. In the nineteenth century another kind of press was invented: the **clamshell press,** so called because it opened and closed like a clamshell. When the press was open, the type, locked into the chase on the bed of the press in a relatively upright position, was automatically inked by a roller. The paper was placed on the tympan, which formed a V shape with the bed of the press. Once the rollers inked the type as the V closed up, the rollers would rise out of the V, and the V would close together, allowing the type to press against the paper.

96. Sometimes the term *rounce* is used to refer to the whole mechanism, the handle and the cylinder to which it is attached. In Los Angeles a book collectors' group is called the Rounce and Coffin Club. Those familiar with the jargon of printing will understand immediately what the interest is of those in the club.

97. An old printer's poem says, "I must confess, / I love my Press; / For when I print, / I know no stint, / Of Joy" (punctuation and capitalization as in the original; Edwin Roffe, 1861). I found this little rhyme on Google Books in Roffe's *Bibliomaniac Babblings*, in a section titled "Platten Pleasures or Hours of Rest," p. 5 (after twelve roman-numeral–numbered pages). This volume was dredged up during a Google search for Roffe's *A ryghte goodlie booke of frisket fancies set forth for bibliomaniacs!* (To see the poem, enter this title in the Google Books search box at http://books.google.com.) Roffe was a private-press printer (under the imprint Rochester Press) in London.

98. If a single font is used on a page, then the person distributing the type need use only a single type case for the lowercase sorts and one for the uppercase sorts. But many pages will have one font for the text, another for the headlines (or running heads), perhaps another for the page number, and maybe even a fourth or fifth for italics or boldface printing on the page. So distributing the type after a pressrun is done could entail using more than two type cases.

Works Cited and Bibliography

A vast literature exists on all the topics listed here. Only a few important texts are cited. This selection is my own, and it does not pretend to be "complete" or to list every important book on the subjects covered in this chapter. As Mark Twain wrote: "It were not best that we should all think alike; it is difference of opinion that makes horse-races" (see Twain, *Pudd'nhead Wilson*, p. 97). For a more thorough bibliography see *The Reader's Adviser*, edited by David Scott Kasten and Emory Elliott (New Providence, NJ: R. R. Bowker, 1994), Volume 1, Chapter 1, "Books about Books," compiled by Sidney Berger, pp. 1–57. Also noteworthy is the output of Oak Knoll Press in New Castle, Delaware, which has produced scores of excellent texts on books, their history and production.

AMATE (AMATL)

Amith, Jonathan D., ed. *La Tradición del Amate / The Amate Tradition.* Chicago: Mexican Fine Arts Center Museum; Mexico: La Casa de las Imágenes, 1995.

Christensen, Bodil, and Samuel Marti. *Brujerías y papel precolombino / Witchcraft and Pre-Columbian Paper.* Mexico: Ediciones Euroamericanas, [1971]; 2nd ed. 1972.

Hunter, Dard. *Primitive Papermaking: An Account of a Mexican Sojourn and of a Voyage to the Pacific Islands in Search of Information, Implements, and Specimens Relating to the Making and Decorating of Bark-Paper.* Chillicothe, OH: Mountain House Press, 1927.

Lenz, Hans. *Mexican Indian Paper: Its History and Survival.* Mexico: Libros de México, 1961.

Sandstrom, Alan R., and Pamela Effrein Sandstrom. *Traditional Papermaking and Paper Cult Figures of Mexico*. Norman and London: University of Oklahoma Press, 1986.

Starr, Frederick. "Mexican Paper." In *The American Antiquarian and Oriental Journal* 32 (Jan.–Nov. 1900): 301–9.

Valentini, Ph[ilipp] J. J. *Mexican Paper*. In *Proceedings of the American Antiquarian Society*, New Series 1 (October 1880): 58–81.

Von Hagen, Victor Wolfgang. *The Aztec and Maya Papermakers*. New York: J. J. Augustin, 1944.

BOOKBINDING

Barrios, Pamela. "Notes on the Limp Vellum Binding." *Bonefolder* 2.2 (Spring 2006): 24–27. http://digilib .syr.edu/cgi-bin/showfile.exe?CISOROOT = /bone folder&CISOPTR = 67&filename = 68.pdf.

Bosch, Gulnar, John Carswell, and Guy Petherbridge. *Islamic Bindings and Bookmaking*. Chicago: The Oriental Institute, The University of Chicago, 1981.

Brenni, Vito, comp. *Bookbinding: A Guide to the Literature*. Westport, CT, and London: Greenwood, 1982.

Breslauer, B. H. *The Uses of Bookbinding Literature*. New York: Book Arts Press, School of Library Service, Columbia University, 1986.

Burdett, Eric. *The Craft of Bookbinding: A Practical Handbook*. Newton Abbot, London, and Vancouver: David and Charles, 1973.

Clarkson, Christopher. "Limp Vellum Binding and Its Potential as a Conservation Type Structure for the Rebinding of Early Printed Books—A Break with 19th and 20th Century Rebinding Attitudes and Practices." ICOM Committee for Conservation, 4th Triennial Meeting. Venice 1975, 153: 1–15; rpt. Hitchin: Red Gull Press, 1982.

Cloonan, Michèle V. *Early Bindings in Paper: A Brief History of European Hand-Made Paper-Covered Books with a Multilingual Glossary*. London: Mansell; Boston: G. K. Hall, 1991.

Cockerell, Douglas. *Bookbinding and the Care of Books: A Text-Book for Bookbinders and Librarians*. 5th ed. Rpt. London, Toronto, et al.: Pitman, 1973.

Crane, W. J. E. *Bookbinding for Amateurs: The Various Tools and Appliances Required and Instructions for Their Effective Use*. www.aboutbookbinding.com/ Amateur/Headbands-and-Registers.html.

Davenport, Cyril. *English Embroidered Bookbindings*. London: Kegan Paul; New York: Dodd Mead, 1899.

Diehl, Edith. *Bookbinding: Its Background and Technique*. New York: Rinehart, 1946; rpt. New York: Dover, 1980.

Duncan, Alastair, and Georges de Bartha. *Art Nouveau and Art Deco Bookbindings, 1880–1940*. New York: Harry N. Abrams, 1989.

Fahey, Herbert, and Peter Fahey. *Finishing in Hand Bookbinding*. San Francisco: Herbert and Peter Fahey, 1951.

Foot, Mirjam. *Pictorial Bookbindings*. London: The British Library, 1986.

Foxon, David F. "Stitched Books." *The Book Collector* 24 (Spring 1975): 111–24.

Frost, Gary. "Historical Paper Case Binding and Conservation Rebinding." *The New Bookbinder* 2 (1982): 64–67.

Gibson, Strickland. *The Localization of Books by Their Bindings*. Read 20th February, 1905. *The Library* 8.1 (1906): 25–38.

Gnirrep, W. K., J. P. Gumbert, and J. A. Szirmai. *Kneep en Binding: Een Terminologie voor de Beschrijving van de Constructies van Oude Boekbanden*. Den Haag: Koninklijke Bibliotheek, 1992. Though the text is in Dutch, this volume is included here for its superb illustrations.

Ikegami, Kōjirō. *Japanese Bookbinding: Instructions from a Master Craftsman*. Adapted by Barbara B. Stephan. New York and Tokyo: Weatherhill, 1986.

Johnson, Pauline. *Creative Bookbinding*. Seattle: University of Washington Press, 1963.

McLean, Ruari. *Victorian Publishers' Book-Bindings in Cloth and Leather*. London: Gordon Fraser, 1974.

———. *Victorian Publishers' Book-Bindings in Paper*. London: Gordon Fraser, 1983.

Middleton, Bernard. Foreword to *Bookcloth, 1823–1980: A Study of Early Use and the Rise of Manufacture . . .*, by William Tomlinson and Richard Masters, pp. vii–viii. Cheshire, England: Dorothy Tomlinson, 1996.

Miller, Julia. *Books Will Speak Plain: A Handbook for Identifying and Describing Historical Bindings*. N.p.: The Legacy Press, 2010.

Miner, Dorothy. *The History of Bookbinding, 525–1950 A.D.* Baltimore: Trustees of the Walters Art Gallery, 1957.

Morris, Ellen K., and Edward S. Levin. *The Art of Publishers' Bookbindings, 1815–1915*. Los Angeles: William Dailey Rare Books, 2000.

Needham, Paul. *Twelve Centuries of Bookbindings, 400–1600*. New York: Pierpont Morgan Library; London: Oxford University Press, 1979.

Nicholson, James B. *A Manual of the Art of Bookbinding*. Philadelphia: Henry Carey Baird, 1856; rpt. New York and London: Garland, 1980.

Nixon, Howard M. *Five Centuries of Bookbinding*. London: Scolar Press, 1979.

Roberts, Matt T., and Don Etherington. *Bookbinding and the Conservation of Books: A Dictionary of Descriptive Terminology*. Washington, DC: Library of Congress, 1982. This volume contains a superb bibliography of further readings, pp. 289–96.

Smith, Keith. Smith has published a series of well-illustrated books on binding, too numerous to list here. His series of texts on nonadhesive bindings is worth examining. The first three of them are listed here.

———. *Exposed Spine Sewings: Non-Adhesive Binding Volume III*. Rochester, NY: Keith A. Smith Books, 1995. This volume contains exceptionally complex sewing patterns, with excellent illustrations.

———. *Non-Adhesive Bindings: Books without Paste or Glue*. Fairport, NY: Sigma Foundation, 1990 (date at colophon).

———. *1- 2- and 3-Section Sewings: Non-Adhesive Binding Volume II: Decorative Sewing Patterns*. Rochester, NY: Keith A. Smith Books, 1995.

Szirmai, J. A. *The Archaeology of Medieval Bookbinding*. Aldershot, Hants, England: Ashgate Publishing Ltd.; Burlington, VT: Ashgate Publishing, 1999; rpt. 2000. With superb illustrations of binding structures and sewing patterns.

Tomlinson, William, and Richard Masters. *Bookcloth, 1823–1980: A Study of Early Use and the Rise of Manufacture* . . . . Cheshire, England: Dorothy Tomlinson, 1996.

Wakeman, Geoffrey, and Graham Pollard. *Functional Developments in Bookbinding*. New Castle, DE, and Kidlington, Oxford: The Plough Press, 1993.

Watson, Aldren A. *Hand Bookbinding: A Manual of Instruction*. Bell Publishing, 1963.

BOOKPLATES

Allen, Charles Dexter. *American Book-Plates: A Guide to Their Study with Examples*. New York: Macmillan, 1894; rpt. New York and London: Benjamin Blom, 1968.

American Society of Bookplate Collectors and Designers, www.bookplate.org.

Arellanes, Audrey. *Bookplates in the News, 1970–85: A Collection of Sixty Issues of the Newsletter of the American Society of Bookplate Collectors and Designers,*

Including a General Index and an Illustrations Index to Bookplate Artists and Owners. Detroit: Gale, 1986.

Castle, Egerton. *English Book-Plates, Ancient and Modern*. London: George Bell and Sons, 1894.

Johnson, Fridolf. *A Treasury of Bookplates from the Renaissance to the Present*. New York: Dover, 1977.

Jones, Louise Seymour, and Lawrence Clark Powell. *The Human Side of Bookplates*. [Los Angeles]: Ward Ritchie Press, 1951.

Lee, Brian N. *British Bookplates: A Pictorial History*. London: David & Charles, 1979.

———. *British Royal Bookplates and Ex-Libris of Related Families*. Aldershot, England: Scolar Press, 1991.

DUST JACKETS

Carter, John. *ABC for Book Collectors*. 8th ed., rev. by Nicolas Barker. New Castle, DE: Oak Knoll Press; London: The British Library, 2004, pp. 84–86.

Godburn, Mark. *Nineteenth Century Dust Jackets*. http://earlydustjackets.blogspot.com.

Heller, Steven, and Seymour Chwast. *Jackets Required: An Illustrated History of American Book Jacket Design, 1920–1950*. San Francisco: Chronicle Books, 1995.

McMullin, B. J. "Precursors of the 'Dust-Wrapper.'" *Bibliographical Society of Australia and New Zealand Bulletin* 24 (2000): 257–66.

Mulley, Jessica. "Evolution of the Dust Jacket." July 2005. Internet Archive: Wayback Machine. http://web.archive.org/web/20080705035328/http://www.readingbooks.info/Dustjackets.htm.

———. "Jackets Require Reading Too: A Guide to Identifying Fake Dust Jackets." December 2005. Internet Archive: Wayback Machine. http://web.archive.org/web/20080623230639/http://www.readingbooks.info/FakeJackets.htm.

Pauli, Michelle. "Earliest-Known Book Jacket Discovered in Bodleian Library: Friendship's Offering, Dating from 1830, Found among Forgotten Book-Trade Ephemera." April 24, 2009. The *Guardian* and *Observer* Books Season. www.guardian.co.uk/books/2009/apr/24/earliest-dust-jacket-library.

Rosner, Charles. *The Growth of the Book-Jacket*. Cambridge, MA: Harvard University Press, 1954.

Struik, A. S. A. "The Dust-Jacket: Cloth of Gold in the Auction Room." *Quaerendo* 28 (1998): 185–214.

Tanselle, G. Thomas. *Book-Jackets: Their History, Forms, and Use*. Charlottesville: The Bibliographical Society of the University of Virginia, 2011.

ILLUSTRATION

Alexander, Jonathan J. G., ed. *The Painted Page: Italian Renaissance Book Illustration, 1450–1550*. Munich: Prestel Verlag, 1994.

Benson, Richard. *The Printed Picture*. New York: Museum of Modern Art, 2008.

Bland, David. *A History of Book Illustration: The Illuminated Manuscript and the Printed Book*. 2nd ed. Berkeley: University of California Press, 1974.

Brown, Michelle P. *The British Library Guide to Writing and Scripts: History and Techniques*. Toronto and Buffalo: University of Toronto Press; London: The British Library, 1998.

———. *Understanding Illuminated Manuscripts: A Guide to Technical Terms*. Los Angeles: The J. Paul Getty Museum; London: The British Library, 1994.

Cennini, Cennino d'Andrea. *The Craftsman's Handbook / Il Libro dell'Arte*. Trans. Daniel V. Thompson Jr. New York: Dover, 1960.

Daniels, Morna. *Victorian Book Illustration*. London: The British Library, 1988.

De Hamel, Christopher. *A History of Illuminated Manuscripts*. Boston: David R. Godine; London: Phaidon Press, 1986.

———. *Medieval Craftsmen: Scribes and Illuminators*. London: The British Museum; Toronto and Buffalo: University of Toronto Press, 1992.

Dyson, Anthony. *Pictures to Print: The Nineteenth-Century Engraving Trade*. London: Farrand Press, 1984.

Friedman, Joan M. *Color Printing in England, 1486–1870*. New Haven, CT: Yale Center for British Art, 1978.

Gascoigne, Bamber. *Milestones in Colour Printing, 1457–1859*. Cambridge: Cambridge University Press, 1997; rpt. 2010.

Harthan, John. *The History of the Illustrated Book: The Western Tradition*. London and New York: Thames and Hudson, 1981.

Hodnett, Edward. *Five Centuries of English Book Illustration*. Aldershot, England: Scolar Press, 1988.

James, Philip. *English Book Illustration, 1800–1900*. London and New York: King Penguin Books, 1947.

Katz, Bill, ed. *A History of Book Illustrations, 29 Points of View*. Metuchen, NJ: Scarecrow Press, 1994.

Muir, Percy. *Victorian Illustrated Books*. London: Batsford, 1971; rpt. 1985.

Pitz, H. C. *A Treasury of American Book Illustration*. New York and London: American Studio Books and Watson-Guptill, 1947.

Thompson, Daniel V. *The Materials and Techniques of Medieval Painting*. New York: Dover, 1956.

Wakeman, Geoffrey. *Graphic Methods in Book Illustration*. Leicestershire: The Plough Press, 1981.

Ward, Gerald W. R., ed. *The American Illustrated Book in the Nineteenth Century*. Charlottesville: University Press of Virginia; Winterthur, DE: Winterthur Museum, 1987.

INK

Bloy, C[olin] H. *A History of Printing Ink, Balls and Rollers, 1440–1850*. London: The Wynkyn de Worde Society; New York: Sandstone Press, 1967, rpt. 1980.

Cahill, Thomas A., Bruce H. Kusko, and Richard N. Schwab. "Analyses of Inks and Papers in Historical Documents through External Beam PIXE Techniques." *Nuclear Instruments & Methods* 181 (1981): 205–8.

Fruen, Lois. "Iron Gall Ink." http://realscience.breckschool.org/upper/fruen/files/enrichmentarticles/files/irongallink/irongallink.html. Fruen cites Y. Nir-el and M. Broshi, "The Black Ink of the Dead Sea Scrolls," *Dead Sea Discoveries* (March 1996): 157–67.

"Iron Gall Ink." Wikipedia. http://en.wikipedia.org/wiki/Iron_gall_ink.

The Iron Gall Ink Website. http://ink-corrosion.org. Perhaps the most thorough treatment available on iron gall inks.

Schwab, Richard N., Thomas A. Cahill, Bruce H. Kusko, and Daniel L. Wick. "Cyclotron Analysis of the Ink in the 42-Line Bible." *The Papers of the Bibliographical Society of America* 77 (1983): 285–315. The information in this piece, and in the one headed by Cahill, was published under a number of titles in the journals of several disciplines.

PAPER

The Paper Publications Society in Hilversum, Holland, has published more than a dozen volumes of tracings of watermarks. Only a few of these volumes are listed here, but they should be consulted by anyone doing research on watermarks in specific countries and during certain centuries.

Balston, Thomas. *James Whatman, Father and Son*. London: Methuen, 1957.

Barrett, Timothy. *Japanese Papermaking: Traditions, Tools, and Techniques.* New York and Tokyo: Weatherhill, 1983.

Berger, Sidney. *Chiyogami Papers.* Newtown, PA: Bird & Bull Press, 2011.

———. "Decorated Paper." *Hand Papermaking Newsletter,* no. 81 (January 2008), 6–7. An article on Dutch gilt papers.

———. *Edward Seymour and the Fancy Paper Company.* New Castle, DE: Oak Knoll Press, 2006.

———. *The Handmade Papers of Japan: A Biographical Sketch of Its Author and an Account of the Genesis and Production of the Book, with a Reprint of the Original Text.* Newtown, PA: Bird & Bull Press, 2001.

———. *Karli Frigge's Life in Marbling.* Newtown, PA: Bird & Bull Press, 2004.

Bidwell, John. *American Paper Mills 1690–1832: A Directory of the Paper Trade with Notes on Products, Watermarks, Distribution Methods, and Manufacturing Techniques.* Hanover, NH: Dartmouth College Press; Worcester, MA: American Antiquarian Society, 2013.

Bourbeau, David. *Paste Papers of the Pioneer Valley, with Brief Biographies of Their Makers.* Northampton, MA: Catawba Press; Cambridge, MA: Kat Ran Press, 2011.

Briquet, C. M. (Charles Moise). *Les Filigranes: Dictionnaire Historique de Marques du Papier.* 4 vols. Geneva: 1907; rpt. Leipzig: Verlag von Karl W. Hiersemann, 1923. This is the grandfather of books on watermarks. It shows tracings of more than sixteen thousand watermarks, reproduced from the more than sixty thousand that he collected. See also www.journalsandbooks.com/support/terminology/watermark.html.

Byrne, Alexander. "Chirimen-bon or Crêpe Paper Books." *Daruma, Japanese Art & Antiques Magazine* (Issue 47) 12.3 (Summer 2005): 12–27.

Churchill, W. A. *Watermarks in Paper: In Holland, England, France, etc., in the XVII and XVIII Centuries and Their Interconnection.* Amsterdam: Menno Hertzberger, 1935; rpt. New Castle, DE: Oak Knoll Press, 1990.

de Bofarull y Sans, Don Francisco. *Animals in Watermarks.* Hilversum, Holland: The Paper Publications Society, 1959.

———. *Heraldic Watermarks: Or La Heráldica en la Filigrana del Papel.* Hilversum, Holland: The Paper Publications Society, 1956.

The Dictionary of Paper: Including Pulp, Paperboard, Paper Properties and Related Papermaking Terms. New York: American Paper and Pulp Association. This excellent text has appeared in several editions, with varying titles: 1st (1940); 2nd (1951); 3rd (1965); 4th (1980); 5th (1996, ed. by Michael Kouris).

Easton, Phoebe Jane. *Marbling: A History and a Bibliography.* Los Angeles: Dawson's Book Shop, 1983.

Gravell, Thomas L., and George Miller. *A Catalogue of American Watermarks, 1690–1835.* New York and London: Garland, 1979.

———. *A Catalogue of Foreign Watermarks Found on Paper Used in America, 1700–1835.* New York and London: Garland, 1983. This volume and the preceding one have been reissued, with Elizabeth Walsh, in a single volume: New Castle, DE: Oak Knoll Press, 2002.

Haemmerle, Albert. *Buntpapier.* Munich: Callwey, 1961; 2nd ed. with same title and publisher, 1977. A tremendous source of information about decorated papers. A classic often cited by scholars, especially for European papers of the seventeenth and eighteenth centuries. In German.

Herdeg, Walter, ed. *Art in the Watermark / Kunst im Wasserzeichen / l'Art du Filigrane.* Amstutz and Herdeg, Graphis Press, 1952.

Hills, Richard L. *Papermaking in Britain, 1488–1988: A Short History.* London and Atlantic Highlands, NJ: Athlone Press, 1988.

Hughes, Sukey. *Washi: The World of Japanese Paper.* Tokyo, New York, and San Francisco: Kodansha International, 1978.

Hunter, Dard. Hunter was a prolific writer on paper, its history, manufacture, tools, and distribution in the world. He wrote many books on the topic. A few are listed here.

———. *Chinese Ceremonial Paper: A Monograph Relating to the Fabrication of Paper and Tin Foil and the Use of Paper in Chinese Rites and Religious Ceremonies.* Chillicothe, OH: Mountain House Press, 1927.

———. *My Life with Paper: An Autobiography.* New York: Knopf, 1958.

———. *Papermaking by Hand in America.* Chillicothe, OH: Mountain House Press, 1950.

———. *Papermaking in Pioneer America.* Philadelphia: University of Pennsylvania Press, 1952.

———. *Papermaking in the Classroom.* Peoria, IL: Manual Arts Press, 1931; rpt. New Castle, DE: Oak Knoll Press, 1991.

———. *Papermaking: The History and Technique of an Ancient Craft.* New York: Knopf, 1947; rpt. New York: Dover, 1974.

———. *A Papermaking Pilgrimage to Japan, Korea, and China*. New York: Pynson Printers, 1936.

Labarre, E. J. *A Dictionary of Paper and Paper-Making Terms, with Equivalents in French, German, Dutch and Italian*. Amsterdam: N. V. Swets & Zeitlinger, 1937. This and the following item are essential sources of information on paper.

———. *Dictionary and Encyclopaedia of Paper and Paper-Making, with Equivalents of the Technical Terms in French, German, Dutch, Italian, Spanish and Swedish*. 2nd ed., rev. and enl. Amsterdam: Swets & Zeitlinger, 1952.

Loeber, E. G. *Supplement to E. J. Labarre, Dictionary and Encyclopaedia of Paper and Paper-Making*. Amsterdam: Swets & Zeitlinger, 1967.

Loring, Rosamund. *Decorated Book Papers: Being an Account of Their Designs and Fashions*. Cambridge, MA: Harvard University Press, 1942; rpt. Cambridge, MA: Harvard University Press, 2008.

Mason, John. *Paper Making as an Artistic Craft: With a Note on Nylon Paper*. London: Faber and Faber, 1959.

———. *Paper Making as an Artistic Craft*. 2nd ed. Leicester: Twelve by Eight, 1963. No subtitle; no essay on nylon paper.

Sharf, Frederic A. *Takejiro Hasegawa: Meiji Japan's Preeminent Publisher of Wood-Block-Illustrated Crepe-Paper Books*. Salem, MA: Peabody Essex Museum, 1994.

Shorter, Alfred H. *Paper Making in the British Isles: An Historical and Geographical Study*. New York: Barnes & Noble, 1972.

Spector, Stephen, ed. *Essays in Paper Analysis*. Washington, [DC]: Folger Books, The Folger Shakespeare Library; London and Toronto: Associated University Presses, 1987.

Stevenson, Allan H. *The Problem of the Missale Speciale*. London: The Bibliographical Society 1967.

———. "Watermarks Are Twins." *Studies in Bibliography* 4 (1951–1952): 57–91.

Stone, Douglas B., and Hardev S. Dugal. *The Dard Hunter Collection at the Institute of Paper Chemistry*. Appleton, WI: The Institute of Paper Chemistry, 1984.

Sutermeister, Edwin. *The Story of Papermaking*. Boston: S. D. Warren, 1954.

Tanselle, G. Thomas. "The Bibliographical Description of Paper." *Studies in Bibliography* 24 (1971): 27–67.

———. "A System of Color Identification for Bibliographical Description." *Studies in Bibliography* 20 (1967): 203–34.

Tindale, Thomas Keith, and Harriett Ramsey Tindale. *The Handmade Papers of Japan*. Rutland, VT, and Tokyo: Charles E. Tuttle, 1952. The text of this book is reprinted in Berger, *The Handmade Papers of Japan* (Newtown, PA: Bird & Bull Press, 2001).

Voorn, Henk. *The Paper Mills of Denmark and Norway and Their Watermarks*. Hilversum, Holland: The Paper Publications Society, 1959.

Wolfe, Richard. *Marbled Paper: Its History, Techniques, and Patterns*. Philadelphia: University of Pennsylvania Press, 1990. The most extensive treatment of decorated papers in English.

PAPYRUS

Parkinson, Richard, and Stephen Quirke. *Papyrus*. London: The British Library; Austin: University of Texas Press, 1995.

Ragab, Hassan. Foreword to *The Nature and Making of Papyrus*. Yorkshire, England: Elmete Press, 1973.

———. *Le Papyrus*. Cairo, Egypt: Dr. Ragab Papyrus Institute, 1980.

———. *Papyrus, Its History and Methods of Sheet-Making by the Ancient Egyptians*. [Egypt]: Ministry of Culture and Information, Culture Centre for Diplomats, [1972].

Wallert, A. "The Reconstruction of Papyrus Manufacture: A Preliminary Investigation." *Studies in Conservation* 34 (1989): 1–8.

PARCHMENT/VELLUM

Bigus, Richard, Colin Franklin, and Decherd Turner. *The Mystique of Vellum*. Boston: Bromer, 1984.

Clarkson, Christopher. "Rediscovering Parchment: The Nature of the Beast." *Paper Conservator* 16 (1992): 5–26.

Mowery, J. Franklin. "Parchment: Its Manufacture, History, Treatment, and Conservation." *Guild of Book Workers Journal* 32.2 (Fall 1994): 13–73.

Reed, R[onald]. *Ancient Skins, Parchments and Leathers*. London and New York: Seminar Press, 1972.

———. *The Nature and Making of Parchment*. Yorkshire, England: Elmete Press, 1975.

Ryder, Michael L. "Parchment: Its History, Manufacture and Composition." *Journal of the Society of Archivists* 2 (1964): 391–99.

PRINTING

Of all the areas covered by the bibliographical entries here, this topic is probably the widest, for by itself it covers an enormous range of subtopics, including history, techniques, design, geographical variations, presses and other tools, inking practices and equipment, historic printers and their books and practices, printers' manuals, lexicons of the trade, descriptions of printing through the centuries, printing on the handpress and on commercial machines, the printing of newspapers, design in printing, the bibliography of the field, the work of particular printers, printers' devices, printing and censorship, the economics of the trade, advances in printing over the centuries, publishing, and so forth, each subdividable by country and era. The present listing is merely suggestive.

Berger, Sidney. "Reconsidering Gutenberg." *Biblio* 3.2 (February 1998): 14–15.

Chappell, Warren. *A Short History of the Printed Word.* New York: Knopf, 1980; Boston: Godine, 1984.

Eisenstein, Elizabeth L. *The Printing Press as an Agent of Change.* Cambridge: Cambridge University Press, 1980.

Gascoigne, Bamber. *Milestones in Colour Printing 1457–1859.* Cambridge: Cambridge University Press, 1997.

Gaskell, Philip. *A New Introduction to Bibliography for Literary Students.* Oxford and New York: Oxford University Press (Clarendon Press), 1972 (and later editions).

Ing, Janet. *Johann Gutenberg and His Bible: A Historical Study.* New York: The Typophiles, 1988.

Kapr, Albert. *Johann Gutenberg: The Man and His Invention.* Trans. by Douglas Martin. Cambridge: Cambridge University Press, 1997.

Krummel, Donald, and Stanley Sadie, eds. *Music Printing and Publishing.* Norton/Grove Handbooks in Music. New York: W. W. Norton, 1990.

Lawson, Alexander. *The Compositor as Artist, Craftsman, and Tradesman.* Athens, GA: Press of the Nightowl, 1990.

Lewis, John. *Anatomy of Printing: The Influences of Art and History on Its Design.* New York: Watson-Guptill, 1970.

McKerrow, R. B. *Introduction to Bibliography for Literary Students.* Oxford: Oxford University Press (Clarendon Press), 1927 (and later editions).

McLean, Ruari. *The Thames and Hudson Manual of Typography.* New York and London: Thames and Hudson, 1980 (and later printings and editions).

Meggs, Philip B. *A History of Graphic Design.* 4th ed. New York: John Wiley, 2006. First published 1998.

Moran, James. *Printing Presses: History and Development from the Fifteenth Century to Modern Times.* London: Faber, 1973.

Moxon, Joseph. *Mechanick Exercises on the Whole Art of Printing.* Ed. by Herbert Davis and John Carter. London: Oxford University Press, 1958; rpt. New York: Dover, 1978. First published 1683.

Needham, Paul. *The Printer and the Pardoner: An Unrecorded Indulgence Printed by William Caxton for the Hospital of St. Mary Rounceval, Charing Cross.* Washington, DC: Library of Congress, 1986.

Norman, Jeremy. "The First Printing from the First Steam Powered Printing Press at 800 Impressions per Hour (April 1811)." *From Cave Paintings to the Internet: Chronological and Thematic Studies on the History of Information and Media.* www.historyofinformation.com/index.php?id=514.

Oswald, John Clyde. *Printing in the Americas.* New York: Gregg Publishing, 1937.

"Printing Press." Wikipedia. http://en.wikipedia.org/wiki/Printing_Press.

Ringwalt, J. Luther. *American Encyclopaedia of Printing.* Philadelphia: Menamin & Ringwalt, 1871 (and later reprints).

Romano, Frank J. *The TypEncyclopedia: A User's Guide to Better Typography.* New York: Bowker, 1984.

Saxe, Stephen O. *American Iron Hand Presses.* Council Bluffs, IA: Yellow Barn Press, 1991; 2nd ed. New Castle, DE: Oak Knoll, 1992.

Silver, Rollo. *The American Printer, 1787–1825.* Charlottesville: University Press of Virginia, 1967.

Steinberg, S. H. *Five Hundred Years of Printing.* Middlesex, England, and Baltimore, MD: Penguin Books, 1955 (and later printings).

Twyman, Michael. *The British Library Guide to Printing History and Techniques.* Toronto: University of Toronto Press, 1999.

———. *Printing 1770–1970: An Illustrated History of Its Development and Uses in England.* London: Eyre and Spottiswoode, 1970.

Winship, George Parker. *Gutenberg to Plantin: An Outline of the Early History of Printing.* Cambridge, MA: Harvard University Press, 1926 (and later printings).

———. *Printing in the Fifteenth Century*. Philadelphia: University of Pennsylvania Press, 1940.

Wroth, Lawrence C. *The Colonial Printer*. Portland, ME: Southworth-Anthoensen Press, 1938 (and later editions).

Printers' Guides

A host of printers' guides were published in the eighteenth and nineteenth centuries (as well as in the twentieth century, though not as many), all of which have extensive information on the practices of printing. They were fairly consistently based on Moxon's superior work (*Mechanick Exercises on the Whole Art of Printing*), and many of them unabashedly stole from Moxon, verbatim in places, without giving any credit. Following is a listing of the more famous of them, with no bibliographical details. They can all be found on OCLC WorldCat. Many of these were reprinted in facsimile as a series by Garland Publishers in the 1970s. Even these reprints are now difficult to obtain because they were done in small numbers.

Jack Abbott, *The Harper Establishment* (1855)

Theodore Lowe De Vinne, *The Practice of Typography* (1900–1904 in several volumes, each with a different title)

Joseph Gould, *The Letter-Press Printer* (1876 and later editions)

Edward Grattan, *The Printer's Companion* (1846)

Thomas Hansard, *Typographica* (1825)

Charles Thomas Jacobi, *Printing: A Practical Treatise on the Art of Typography as Applied More Particularly to the Printing of Books* (1890 and later editions)

John Johnson, *Typographica* (1824)

Thomas MacKellar, *The American Printer* (1866)

Richard-Gabriel Rummonds, *Printing on the Iron Handpress* (1998)

William Savage, *A Dictionary of the Art of Printing* (1841)

———, *Practical Hints on Decorative Printing* (1822)

John Smith, *The Printer's Grammar* (1755)

John Southward, *Modern Printing* (1899–1900)

———, *Practical Printing* (1882 and later editions)

Caleb Stower, *The Printer's Grammar* (1808)

C. S. Van Winkle, *The Printer's Guide* (1818)

PRINTING TYPE

Brightly, Charles. *The Method of Founding Stereotype*. Bungay: Printed by Charles Brightly for R. Phillips, 1809; facs. ed. New York and London: Garland, 1982. Bound with the facsimile of Thomas Hodgson, *An Essay on the Origin and Progress of Stereotype Printing* (see below).

Carter, Harry, and H. D. L. Vervliet. *Civilité Types*. N.p.: Published for The Oxford Bibliographical Society by the Oxford University Press, 1966. Oxford Bibliographical Society Publications, New Series, Volume 14.

Eason, Ron, and Sarah Rookledge. *Rookledge's International Handbook of Type Designers*. Surrey, England: Sarema Press, 1991.

Fine Print on Type: The Best of Fine Print Magazine on Type and Typography. Ed. by Charles Bigelow, Paul Hayden Duensing, and Linnea Gentry. San Francisco: Fine Print, Bedford Arts, 1989.

Goudy, Frederic W. *Typologia: Studies in Type Design and Type Making*. Berkeley and Los Angeles: University of California Press, 1940.

Hodgson, Thomas. *An Essay on the Origin and Progress of Stereotype Printing: Including a Description of the Various Processes*. Newcastle: Printed by and for S. Hodgson, 1820; facs. ed. New York and London: Garland, 1982. Bound with the facsimile of Charles Brightly, *The Method of Founding Stereotype* (see above).

Hopkins, Richard L. *Origin of the American Point System for Printers' Type Measurement*. Terra Alta, WV: Hill & Dale Press, 1976.

Huss, Richard E. *The Development of Printers' Mechanical Typesetting Method, 1822–1925*. Charlottesville: Published for the Bibliographical Society of the University of Virginia, University Press of Virginia, 1973.

———. *Dr. Church's "Hoax": An Assessment of Dr. William Church's Typographical Inventions in Which Is Enunciated Church's Law*. Lancaster, PA: Graphic Crafts, 1976. On Church's invention of a typesetting machine.

Hutchinson, James. *Letters*. New York, Cincinnati, et al.: Van Nostrand Reinhold, 1983.

Jaspert, W. Pincus, W. Turner Berry, and A. F. Johnson. *The Encyclopaedia of Type Faces*. 4th ed. New York: Barnes & Noble, 1970.

Johnson, A. F. *Type Designs, Their History and Development*. 3rd ed. London: Andre Deutsch, 1966.

Kahn, Basil. *Ottmar Mergenthaler: The Man and His Machine; A Biographical Appreciation of the Inventor on His Centennial.* New Castle, DE: Oak Knoll Press, 2000.

Kelly, Rob Roy. *American Wood Type 1828–1900: Notes on the Evolution of Decorated and Large Types and Comments on Related Trades of the Period.* New York: Van Nostrand Reinhold, 1969.

Kubler, George A. *A Short History of Stereotyping.* Brooklyn, NY: Brooklyn Eagle Commercial Printing Department, 1927.

Lawson, Alexander. *Anatomy of a Typeface.* Boston: Godine, 1990.

———. *Printing Types: An Introduction.* Boston: Beacon Press, 1971.

McGrew, Mac. *American Metal Typefaces of the Twentieth Century.* 2nd ed., rev. New Castle, DE: Oak Knoll Press, 1993.

Perfect, Christopher, and Gordon Rookledge. *Rookledge's International Typefinder: The Essential Handbook of Typeface Recognition and Selection.* New York: F. C. Beil, 1983.

Reed, Talbot Baines. *A History of the Old English Letter Foundries: With Notes Historical and Bibliographical on the Rise and Progress of English Typography.* London: Faber and Faber, 1887; rpt. 1952.

Schlesinger, Carl. *The Biography of Ottmar Mergenthaler, Inventor of the Linotype.* New Castle, DE: Oak Knoll Press, 1989.

Silver, Rollo G. *Typefounding in America, 1787–1825.* Charlottesville: Published for the Bibliographical Society of the University of Virginia, University Press of Virginia, 1965.

Tracy, Walter. *Letters of Credit: A View of Type Design.* Boston: Godine, 1986.

"Type Metal." Wikipedia. http://en.wikipedia.org/wiki/Type_metal.

Updike, Daniel Berkeley. *Printing Types: Their History, Forms, and Use.* 2 vols. 2nd ed. Cambridge, MA: Harvard University Press, 1951.

Wallis, L. W. *A Concise Chronology of Typesetting Developments 1886–1986.* London: The Wynken de Worde Society in association with Lund Humphries, 1988.

TAPA/BARK CLOTH

Arbeit, Wendy. *Tapa in Tonga.* Honolulu: Palm Front Productions, n.d.; Honolulu: University of Hawaii Press, 1995.

Brigham, William T. *Ka Hana Kapa: The Making of Bark-Cloth in Hawaii.* Honolulu, HI: Bishop Museum Press, 1911; rpt. Millwood, NY: Kraus Reprint, 1976.

Buck, Peter H. *See* Te Rangi Hiroa.

Einfeld, Linda. *Pygmy Drawings: A Collection of Rare Drawings on Bark Cloth by the Mbuti Pygmies of the Ituri Forest of Zaire.* Chicago: Linda Einfeld, 1980.

Hiroa, Te Rangi (Peter H. Buck). *Arts and Crafts of Hawaii.* Section V: Clothing. Honolulu, HI: Bishop Museum Press, 1957; rpt. 1992.

Kapa: Hawaiian Bark Cloth. Honolulu, HI: Boom Books, and Bernice Pauahi Bishop Museum, 1980.

Kooijman, Simon. *Polynesian Barkcloth.* Aylesbury, Bucks, UK: Shire Publications, 1988.

———. *Tapa in Polynesia.* Honolulu, HI: Bishop Museum Press, 1972.

Neich, Roger, and Mick Pendergrast. *Tapa of the Pacific.* Aukland, New Zealand: David Bateman, in association with Aukland War Memorial Museum, 2001.

———. *Traditional Tapa Textiles of the Pacific.* New York: Thames and Hudson, 1998; rpt. *Pacific Tapa,* Aukland, New Zealand: David Bateman, 1999, 2001, 2004.

Pritchard, Mary J. *Siapo: Bark Cloth Art of Samoa.* American Samoa: Council on Culture, Arts and Humanities, 1984.

Rose, Roger G., Carol Turchan, Natalie Firnhaber, and Linnea O. Brown. "The Bishop Museum Tapa Collection: Conservation and Research into Special Problems." *Bishop Museum Occasional Papers* 28 (February 1988): 2–34.

Tapa, Washi and Western Handmade Paper. Papers Prepared for a Symposium Held at the Honolulu Academy of Arts, June 4–11, 1980. Honolulu, HI: Honolulu Academy of Arts, 1981.

Troxler, Gale Scott. *Fijian Masi: A Traditional Art Form.* Greensboro, NC: Charles-Frederick Publishers, 1977.

Waltz, Nathan. *A Specimen of Cubeo Indian Bark Cloth.* Los Angeles: Dawson's Bookshop, 1969.

Wright, Margot M. *Barkcloth: Aspects of Preparation, Use, Deterioration, Conservation and Display.* London: Archetype, 2001.

OTHER

American Dictionary of Printing and Bookmaking, Containing a History of These Arts in Europe and America. New York: Howard Lockwood, 1894; rpt. New York: Burt Franklin, 1970.

Carter, John. *ABC for Book Collectors.* 7th ed. New Castle, DE: Oak Knoll Press, 2004. All editions of this classic reference tool are excellent, especially those from the 6th edition on, with some revisions by Nicolas Barker (London, Toronto, Sydney, and New York: Granada, 1980; New Castle, DE: Oak Knoll, 1992).

Clair, Colin. *A Chronology of Printing.* New York: Frederick A. Praeger, 1969.

Glaister, Geoffrey Ashall. *Glaister's Glossary of the Book.* 2nd ed. London, Boston, and Sydney: George Allen and Unwin, 1979.

CHAPTER 5

PHYSICAL LAYOUT
AND OPERATIONS

RARE BOOK DEPARTMENTS WANT THEIR STAFF TO UNDERSTAND everything that makes the department function effectively. Sometimes the department's physical evolution affects its operation. That evolution may have forced a configuration that is less than ideal for the department's needs, including offering the staff comfort and efficiency, giving the collection the best possible environment (especially with respect to heat, humidity, and air quality), and protecting the collection.

In this chapter we will consider, among other things, operations and physical space, and we will take up the challenge of deciding whether to create a new facility from scratch or to work on a global scale on an old one. We'll also discuss such specific operations as library tours.

The Evolution of the "Rare Book Department"

Many rare book departments are formed over several decades, starting from a librarian's recognition that some of the books in the circulating collection are valuable, rare, vulnerable, or, for whatever reason, in need of special handling. These books are segregated from the rest of the collection and put into a secure place: a locked cabinet, the office of the director, a special room—someplace that keeps them out of the hands of the "general user." They no longer circulate, they are made available only by special arrangement, and their use is monitored.

As the number of items in this little collection grows, it fills a room, and at some point the components are recognized as a separate collection, large enough to merit having a designated caretaker, either full- or part-time. The room soon becomes inadequate, so a larger space is located, or perhaps two rooms. As the collection grows, it becomes a department in itself, and a specialist is appointed to be its custodian: the special collections librarian.

Patrons need to use the books and manuscripts and other materials in this collection, so a secure reading room is carved out of the library's space. Perhaps someone in the cataloging department is trained to do special cataloging to a higher level than that used for books in the general collection (see chapter 1). A work space is designated for processing manuscripts and archival materials. Patrons, unable to check out these books because they are now part of a noncirculating collection, demand photocopying services. The department must have supplies, so a storeroom or storage cabinets are added. And so forth. Eventually the burgeoning collection takes over more rooms, usually contiguous to the original spaces, and these new facilities grow in strange directions.

Areas that were once public spaces need to be refitted to be inside the secure perimeter of the department. This retrofitting requires special walls, special ceilings, carefully designed window treatments, and other devices that involve security and environmental controls along with storage and human habitation.

This is one way that special collections departments are born and grow. Their growth is "historical," and their configuration is haphazard, emanating from the space that was first available for them and how they expanded, accruing and adapting additional space for shelving, security, access, and other factors.

After such departments have been on the scene for some time, they might have expanded significantly, again outgrowing the space they have taken up for years. At this point, a whole new department may be carved out of the library space, or, in some instances, a whole new building is built for the express purpose of housing the rare book department. This is the second way that special collections departments are formed. If this is the situation—that a rare book facility is created from scratch just for that department—the library staff is in the fortunate position of having some say in what the working space will look like.

Operations and the Space They Take

The physical shape of the department is necessarily linked to its operations.[1] That is, what goes on in the department will guide the librarians and architects in determining how much space must be created for offices, a reading room, stacks of various kinds, storage cabinets, processing, restrooms, and other essential functions. If the department is of the "historical growth" kind, the operations are often shaped by the space that is available.

(Along with all the basic operational considerations that go into the shaping of a department are a concern for security and an allowance for preservation and conservation, topics of later chapters. But these factors must constantly be in the purview of those working in special collections.)

A good deal of what needs to be said of operations was presented in chapter 1. Here we will look at these tasks again with respect to the space they require. A prefatory note is in order: chapter 7 will cover security. For our purposes here, however, it is assumed that once patrons enter the department, they are in a secure environment. The entry space or room may be a public area, but even here a raised level of security is in place. The public space within the department is nonetheless inside the department's perimeter, and security begins at the door.

WHEN I FIRST got to UC Riverside as head of special collections, there was no office space for the department head. There was one long closet (perhaps 8 by 24 feet) that had been used for storage of uncataloged materials, brooms, department supplies, and the like. It was cleared out and a handsome desk and some shelves brought in. In this case the operation was clearly shaped by the extant space. Later, when a new facility was built for the department, I was given the great opportunity to design it, and I put in a fine, purpose-built office for the department head, with everything I needed: space for a big desk and computer table, shelving, proper lighting, many electrical outlets, a table for meetings, space for filing cabinets and chairs for guests, and so forth. This was the purpose-built space that I didn't have in the "historically grown" facility.

Space Requirements

Operations are carried out by the personnel of the department. Each person will have a space, and each space will have characteristics that mark it as allowing certain functions, within the secure perimeter of the larger department.

OFFICE OF THE DEPARTMENT HEAD

The department head will need an office that provides confidential space for phone conversations and meetings with staff. Because fund-raising is often a duty of the department head, the office should have a look of prosperity. Donors want to back winners; a shabby office is not the sign of a winner. If the department head does any kind of research (as should be so), her office should reflect the intellectual activity that she conducts and that the department and parent institution encourage. So the office should have bookshelves that are not empty.

I KNOW OF a university librarian who was deeply into digital librarianship, always working away at his computer. But he sat in a lovely office with beautiful empty bookshelves. He called the special collections librarian and asked him to bring books to his office. When asked "Which books," he said, "Any ones. They just have to look good. You know, with leather bindings. Hardbound books. Ones that look scholarly." He got several shelves of "scholarly looking" volumes—nineteenth-century sets of the writings of obscure authors, books that would never have been used by any sane patron. And he was happy. He understood that the look of anti-intellectualism that empty shelves conveyed was not good for his image. He even said this. Ten years later the books were in the same places on his shelves, probably never having been touched. But the message they conveyed was worth their weight in donations.

The head of the department must also have an office not too far from the entryway, where patrons come into the facility, because he will often entertain scholars, potential donors, faculty (if the library is in an academic institution), administrators, vendors of various kinds (including booksellers who want to purvey their goods), and others. Convenient access to the department head's office is desirable partly so that no others are disturbed by the visits and partly for security, so that the visitors are not taken through secure areas. Further, the office itself should have good security because the research the director does and the vendors he works with will bring valuable materials into the space.

Another consideration with respect to the placement of this office is that the head should be fairly close to the staff, if possible. The sense of teamwork that this proximity engenders, along with the mere convenience, makes for a good working environment. Also, if the department head's office is near the reading room, she can deal with patrons who need to consult her.

TECHNICAL SERVICES

As noted in chapter 1, in many institutions, rare book catalogers are apart from the department, situated in technical services departments among other catalogers. If the unit is fortunate enough to have room for the cataloger, and can convince the institution that that person should be in special collections, a measure of security is added to the operation. In such a case, the cataloger's office should be far from the entry vestibule of the department, deep in secure territory, because his space will be filled with books and manuscripts of value. Before these materials are cataloged, they are fairly vulnerable (it is difficult to retrieve a stolen item that has not had its record properly entered into the institution's database and that has not been properly processed with identifying marks).[2]

The cataloger's office should be close to a receiving area, if possible, and also to a processing area because the books will need to be processed in various ways before being shelved. Proper rare book cataloging requires the addition of many details to the MARC record that need not be entered into the records of items for the general collection. So the cataloger can save a good deal of time if his office contains shelves full of reference books helpful in his work: the RBMS thesauri for rare book cataloging, subject bibliographies, LCSH, AACR2r, an RDA manual,[3] and so on.

Further, it is a rare special collections department that does not have a backlog of items waiting to be cataloged, so the office in which the processing is done should have lots of shelves for the backlog. It is safer and more convenient to have these materials in the cataloger's office inside the secure perimeter of the rare book department than to have them in a technical services department (or stored in Special Collections and brought in truckloads to technical services for cataloging).

In the past, before computers and before OCLC WorldCat, rare book catalogers often needed access to the major international bibliographies: NUC, BLC, BN, GW, and others.[4] These volumes are filled with vast amounts of bibliographical information, and they can help catalogers and scholars identify particular editions, individual copies, bibliographical peculiarities, and other useful data. The problem was that they took up huge amounts of space. The NUC, first series alone, ran to 754 giant volumes. Equally important was NUCMC, the National Union Catalog of Manuscript Collections, originally published in large volumes, one volume a year. Although much of the information in these monumental sets of reference volumes is now on the Web, they are still valuable for consultation, and some rare book catalogers still resort to them. So it might be useful to have these giant sets inside, or situated near, rare book rooms (or at least near where the catalogers are working).[5]

Individual special collections departments will have their own specific needs with respect to reference resources, and space must be available to accommodate these needs—for the catalogers working there and for the patrons using the facility.

PUBLIC SERVICES

Public services personnel will be face to face with patrons or will interact with them by post, phone, or e-mail. The librarians, of course, need a public space (with some degree of privacy) to conduct a reference interview, and patrons need a reading room to work in. A reference desk in the reading room large enough to seat at least two people is also necessary. If one librarian is paging materials, the other will be at the desk maintaining surveillance and conducting other services.

Reference work for distant clients can be done in a fairly modest space, though in some departments reference librarians are inundated with requests for information and should have a good-sized desk and enough tables and shelves to hold a large amount of reference materials.

The reading room requires much careful planning. It will see a good deal of activity, and it is a place of some vulnerability for the department's holdings because books, manuscripts, photographs, and all kinds of other materials will be in the hands of the patrons. As just noted, there must be a desk—with secure access—from which staff can hand out the reference materials to the patrons. Patrons naturally need generous work surfaces with good lighting and outlets for power cords. If the department allows photography, perhaps the reading room should have a mobile cart with a light to allow for this activity. And the tables in the room must be situated such that staff can observe the patrons and the materials they are working on.

> **WHEN I FIRST** got to UC Riverside as head of special collections, the reading room tables were lined up in front of the service personnel, but configured in such a way that a patron could be sitting in a chair, working on a manuscript, with his back to the librarian and his body between the staff and the manuscript. Simply turning the tables at right angles to the reference desk allowed the staff person to see all that was on the table. It was a mystery to me why that had never been done before.

Because many scholars spend whole days, weeks, and more at the library, the room needs holding shelves for the research tools the patrons are using and similar shelves inside a secured area near the reading room for overnight storage. There should also be department computers for users to search the local catalog, shelves of reference tools for the patrons and staff, card catalogs (if the library has saved its old ones),[6] and perhaps a table or other display area (tabletop racks, for instance) for disseminating flyers about the department and its collections.

As mentioned, reference interviews should be conducted in an area that is far from other patrons to avoid disturbing them and to maintain the confidentiality of the interviewee.

Though the practice varies from one library to another, ideally the reading room should be accessible only with the approval of a librarian, often through a locked door that only a staff person can open. Egress should be equally restricted: no patron should be able to leave the reading room without being let out by a librarian. This practice, of course, emanates from the need for security, which is a global operation of the rare book room.[7]

As for security, many rare book facilities have a special vault inside the department that holds the most valuable pieces of the collection. One may, of course, think that everything should get the same top level of security, but clearly some items will merit special treatment: a particularly scarce manuscript collection, individual volumes with exceptional value, unique photographs or ephemera that would bring extraordinary prices on the market, and so on. The vault should be in as remote a place as possible in the department so it is not easily approached if anyone breaks in.

Further, having the special collections department in a basement or on the first floor of a building is not as safe as having it on the second or third, or even the fourth floor if possible. Ground-level access is much easier than is entrance from above the ground. Department personnel should also be cognizant of the locations of the water pipes (for drinking water, sinks, or sewage). A leaky or broken water fountain or toilet can wreak havoc on the collection on the floor(s) beneath it. Personnel should do frequent walk-throughs of the entire collection on a regular schedule, looking specifically for anything out of the ordinary. This vigilance is part of operations and part of an awareness of the department's proximity to other spaces. If the operations of the department include receiving packages, a room or area should be set aside for this purpose, naturally well within the secure perimeter. And, of course, there must be an area of lockers for patrons' bags, coats, overshoes, and umbrellas. The department may have its own toilet facilities, but if others are conveniently available outside, this might not be necessary.

Much of what has been presented thus far seems fairly obvious, especially to anyone working in a rare book department. The basic layout and furniture are relatively standard for special collections departments, though not all operations can supply everything mentioned here. One of the crucial elements guiding much of this advice is work flow. Librarians wish to offer the best service possible for their patrons, and high-quality service usually goes hand in hand with creating the most convenient layout.

> **WORK FLOW CAN** be affected by the department's layout. At UC Riverside, if we had shelved the local history collection where it would normally have gone in the sequence of Library of Congress cataloging, thousands of frequently paged books would have been at the far end of a long aisle, perhaps fifty yards from the staff doing the paging. We put the entire section of local history just inside the door leading to the stacks, only a few steps from the librarians' desks, saving ourselves much time in fetching these items.

The smoothness of the operation of any special collections department depends on how carefully the collection is arranged with respect to the physical movement required of the staff. And that movement has to do with transporting research materials to desks and patrons; it also has to do with security and with the way the department is shaped.

STAFF OFFICES

In special collections departments there never seems to be enough space. A frequent problem is a shortage of proper office space for the staff. Ideally each employee should have an office that affords all the space needed for privacy and for efficient work. Each office should have an adequate workstation and desk, shelves, storage spaces, a worktable, good lighting, adjustable climate control, a window to the outside, and a dedicated phone line. But what is ideal is often not attainable, and many a department has only shared interior offices or even shared cubicles, offering no privacy, shared phone lines, and the constant opportunity to chat. In such circumstances productivity can be low and tensions high. The manager of the department should do everything in her power to create that ideal space for each employee, possibly by having staggered shifts or working with the administration to locate extra space for the staff.

Also, the staff offices should be located strategically in the department. For example, they could be located between the patron-accessed and the secure areas of the department, acting like a line of security. Or they could be situated such that the staff could have a view of the reading room, allowing for an extra pair of eyes for surveillance of the patrons. The offices can be located close to copy machines and work areas with large tables should the staff need to spread out materials they are working on. And at least one office—presumably that of the department head (or a larger conference-type space)—should have a table large enough for staff meetings, which should be held regularly.

What Can Be Done for a "Historically Shaped" Department: Reconfiguring an Old Space

Much as librarians would love to have brand new buildings created for them, the reality in almost all cases is this: if money is secured for improvements, the best the librarians can expect is the renovation—and in some cases the reconfiguration—of their old spaces. It is extremely expensive to build new buildings. Further, new construction requires either the destruction of the existing facility or, with luck and at great cost, the location of a new piece of land and the wherewithal to build something completely new. Most librarians can only hope for the "fix" that will cost the least. Especially in a tight economy (and it always seems, to libraries, that they are in a tight economy), any improvement must be looked upon as a boon.

As with all areas of library operations, the librarian must be in the middle of the action if renovation is being planned. She must be in the forefront of the discussions, particularly because she is more familiar with the rare books part of the building than will be the library's administrators, architects, designers, contractors, electricians, plumbers, or anyone

else. She knows the good, the bad, and the ugly of the department: what works, what does not; where improvements could be made and where they *must* be made. The administration will have its fingers on the purse strings for the project, but the librarian must be privy to the budgetary constraints and must be informed at all stages of the project—especially the planning stage—about the cost of all recommended changes. She should work with all who will have an impact on the facility, and she should be making the recommendations, but she should also be listening to the wisdom of the professionals who have worked with library buildings and know what is possible and what is not, what things will cost, what might look good but could be a disaster, and what is simply beyond budget and should be off the table.

If the building is old—and this is likely because relatively new buildings usually do not need renovation—there may simply be nothing that can be done to remedy some of its problems, short of spending vast amounts of money. A nineteenth-century brick building with no environmental controls presents a typical series of problems. Can the windows be double-paned and sealed properly to keep out insects and winter cold? Can the building be retrofitted with a good HVAC (heating, ventilation, air-conditioning) system? Can the building contain a good air-filtration system? (This is especially important in cities and in areas with much air pollution.) Can skylights be sealed so that they do not leak and so that they admit a minimum of UV light? Can basements be sealed and kept dry year round, especially in rainy seasons? Can bricks and stone decoration be solidified and kept from deteriorating?

Many of these issues will be revisited in chapter 12 on preservation and conservation. They are worth noting here because they are key features in the renovation of buildings, and they are costly. It is the lucky library that will have enough money available to treat the physical plant to all the care and nurturing it needs. But fund-raising can go only so far; available funds from the institution's coffers are finite. Sometimes even the bare minimum—deferred maintenance—is beyond the fiscal scope of the project (hence the word *deferred*). Those involved in the renovation must realistically prioritize the building's needs and opt for the most practical plan, which must include keeping the facility as secure as possible and making the building as functional as possible to the greatest level of protection for the collections and staff as possible.

> **DURING ANY KIND** of construction work, the collection is quite vulnerable, so especial security should be in place during the renovation operations. Stephen Blumberg stole thousands of books from libraries when they were in construction mode.

Especially nettlesome in projects with tight budgets is that, most often, after the renovation, there will be no more space for the collection and for work and office space than there was in the old facility. Space is expensive to create, and, in many facilities, it is impossible to carve out additional space. Even compact shelving is not always possible because it requires increasing the load-bearing capacity of the floors, and this upgrade could cost far more than is in the budget. Building out, or up, or down—that is, adding additional square footage to the present facility—is equally (or even more) expensive. Whatever problems are prompting the renovation, the librarian must work closely with those who are generating costs for the work (architects, contractors, shelf suppliers, and many others) and must be given information about the incremental costs of the project.

The matter of operating costs often falls through the cracks during the planning process. A renovated facility, especially one with new HVAC and electrical operations, will cost more to run than did the old building. Basic library operations will generate greater costs than were created by the old facility. The institution must figure this increase into the new operating budget, for these expenses are permanent and ongoing. These costs are part of doing business. Although not directly the responsibility of the rare book and special collections librarians, these costs will clearly have an impact, possibly forcing cutbacks in some parts of the department's operations. This unpleasant result is particularly conceivable if a certain dollar amount is allotted to the department as part of the institution's line-item budgeting and the cost of running the department exceeds this amount. Can resources be siphoned off from other parts of the institution to cover the added costs of the renovated rare book department? Do not count on it.

It should be acknowledged that not all renovations of special collections are done on a shoestring. Sometimes a good deal of money is made available for the renovations. Nonetheless, the librarian should have a list of needs in hand, prioritized from the most to the least important. If the resources can handle all of them, that is excellent. But if they cannot, at least the most needed improvements should be attended to before the department head's desired spa with Jacuzzi.

When prioritizing needs, librarians must consider the following (along with a parallel consideration of the funds available): (1) the safety of the collection (security and environmental issues), (2) space for the present collection and for its growth, (3) the ease of use by the staff and patrons, and (4) certain creature comforts for all who will be working in the facility. The collections do come first, but the people working with the collections must be taken care of, too. Poor physical conditions (cramped quarters; poor, practically inaccessible shelving; dim lighting; uncomfortable temperatures; uneven floors; carelessly designed storage; badly laid-out offices, work spaces, and reading rooms; inconveniently placed collections and elevators; truly ugly work areas; and many other things which are physically inconvenient and aesthetically repulsive) should be acknowledged as almost as important as leaky roofs, drafty windows, and loose bricks.

During the actual renovation phase of the project, either the library will need to shift from area to area inside the building's envelope or it will have to move out completely. In a carefully laid-out department, the staff can work efficiently. In a situation dictated by the building, nothing can be done to smooth out operations. And in the exigencies of a renovation project, working conditions can become abominable.

Sometimes inexpensive measures can be taken to improve the working conditions of the staff.

THE LIBRARY INITIATIVE of my own library forced us to close the department completely for over a year. The building needed so much work that the entire collection had to be moved to a temporary facility. More about moves later. The point to make here is that it goes against the serious librarian's conscience and desire to help patrons to cut them off from all services for any length of time. But sometimes there is no other choice.

Moving furniture around, reconfiguring offices, increasing lighting, adjusting temperatures, locking doors and so on can make the operations more secure and ease the labor of the staff. A good brainstorming session with all who work in the collection can reveal the holdings that get the most use and the best way to reshelve materials to make the most used the most accessible. But with a renovation project under way, all such measures might have to be put on hold so that the staff can relocate to areas not being worked on. With a move or without one, the department must operate within the fiscal restraints granted by and negotiated with the parent institution. If the facility lacks a vault, if it does not have appropriately designed space for maximum security and work flow, if it does not have enough shelving or work space for processing collections, or if it has the collection shelved in an inefficient way, these things might be remediable with some expensive reconfiguration. The key word here is *expensive*. A fix for each of these scenarios may be achievable if there is enough money in the budget: build a vault; reconfigure the shelving, aisles, and work spaces; build more shelves; move collections around. But such resources are usually lacking, and the staff must continue to make do with an inadequate situation.

The head of the department should work with the administration (and possibly with donors) to create a plan that will allow for the changes that need to be made. Patience is key. Nothing happens overnight, and marshaling the resources to make the necessary alterations can take years. But a constant pressure to adjust the department may produce fruit someday. Prioritizing the needs and costing them out is essential. A well-written plan to improve operations and increase security, with a justifiable, reasonable budget, can get results, especially if the plan emphasizes these two considerations: efficiency and security. Think of the extra expenditure as a way to save money through efficiency and as a form of long-term insurance.

No matter whether the renovation allows the staff to stay in their facility or forces them to move from side to side or out of the building, all who are involved should recognize that the Project (now with a capital letter!) will create stress of many kinds. The entire staff, at all stages of the operation, should be apprised of what *will* be happening, what *is* happening, and how much more of this they must endure before the project is completed.

SOUTHERN CALIFORNIA IS a great place to live, despite its faults. This old joke came into play for me when I was at UC Riverside, thanks to the facts that we were in a giant earthquake zone and that the building housing my special collections department had been built in the 1960s, before strict building requirements were established for structures in earthquake zones. A federal mandate made it possible for me to completely rebuild my department, because the entire building had to be upgraded to protect it and its collections from seismic activity.

At my present library, thanks to the institution's development department and some donors' careful considerations of the needs of my collection and its facilities, a complete rethinking of the facility is under way, with the result that the building will be given a facelift, inside and out, and major work will be done on collections over the next few years. Again I find myself in the fortunate position of creating my spaces anew. Rare as this is in a librarian's career, it does happen, and a discussion of what to do is useful.

Creating a New Facility from Scratch

The possibility exists that a librarian will be able to create a whole new department—even a whole new building. That is, he will be in a position to work with administrators and architects, designers and engineers, and others to reconfigure the existing facility completely or to build a totally new one. Many of the observations made in the preceding section will shape this project, including moving furniture and moving collections, looking at pipes and putting bars onto windows, marshaling resources and accounting for all the spaces needed by employees and patrons, with the overarching considerations of security and work flow.

Although this chapter is basically about the physical plant—the building inside and out, its roof, its façade, its "envelope" (the architect's word for the exterior walls that protect what is inside), rooms, work spaces, offices, public and private zones, air, heat, and humidity and the delivery systems for them, and much more—the librarian must also keep in mind that all work done on the building will have a great impact on the work that can (and will) be done inside the building and an equal impact on the people who occupy the building. Poor planning of the structure modifications can yield an attractive building with a seriously flawed environment and a disgruntled staff. I have heard one staff person at a distant institution, when a poorly thought out renovation was completed, say, "If they spent all this money, why didn't they get it right? I hate this place." She also said about the architects and designers, "They should have talked to the librarians more." More on this later.

The librarian must recognize that outside vendors like architects and designers will be brought onto the project with varying levels of expertise with respect to libraries. They do not know every library, nor can they be expected to know the needs of each facility. It cannot be overemphasized that they must be taught what they need to know about your collection's history and its evolution; the quirks and excellences of the present facility; the staff and their activities and needs; the patrons and their needs; the expectations of all involved in the new facility; the budget and how inflexible it is; and so forth.

> **THE TEXT MENTIONS** "the budget and how inflexible it is." This phrase could have been "the budget and how flexible it is," but that wording could give the architects the wrong message. Usually budgets are fixed; they cannot be stretched too much, if at all. On both projects in which I have been involved with architects, they came up with figures that exceeded what they were told was our limit. Although the librarian is usually not working at that level with the builders—the money is usually coming from or through the administration— the librarian, like the architect, must be realistic about how much is available for the project, and therefore must not present requests that would take the project beyond its budgeted figure.

It is essential that the librarians work closely with all who are planning the project, because the staff know more than does anyone else about what works and what does not for their own facility. Although the librarians' voices are not always listened to and their advice not always heeded, at least they have a better chance of coming up with a well-designed facility if they speak up than they do if they are silent during the process.

> **AT UC RIVERSIDE** I had a strong voice in the layout of the new space the special collections department was given, but in the end several of my urgent recommendations were taken off the table. In fact, with my son, who has a degree in architecture, I was able to draw up excellent plans for the new space. Massive areas of my work were deleted from the architects' plans, to the detriment of the final "product." An administrator at the school told me that the architects wanted to earn their keep, so they did plans as if my own did not exist. They couldn't take the ones my son and I had designed. The department is lovely, but it lacks some things that should have been there.

The following features must be considered in the plans:

- Work space
  - Offices
  - Tables for processing collections
  - Staging areas to hold materials for later treatment and cataloging
  - Work space for the creation of finding aids for manuscript collections
  - Copying facilities (for cameras and for photocopying and scanning machines); fax machines
  - A staff room for eating and work breaks
  - A work area for in-house conservation and minor repair work (optional)

- Public space
  - A greeting desk (optional)
  - Circulation/Reference counter
  - Reading room tables
  - Computer workstations
  - Private areas for reference interviews
  - Places for coatracks, lockers, and umbrellas
  - Exhibition spaces—rooms or just vitrines to show department holdings
  - Tables or shelves for flyers about the department and its collections
  - Shelves for reference books that should be available for patrons
  - Shelves of the publications of those at the institution (optional)
  - A seminar room or meeting room (optional)
  - An area for small receptions (optional)
  - Photo stands

- Stacks and other kinds of storage
  - Shelf height and materials specifications
  - Rooms, closets, and cabinets for supplies
  - Vaults
  - Holding shelves for patrons' research materials

Other things to consider:

- Security
- Work flow—how the staff and visitors actually move through the department
- Wi-Fi accessibility
- Lighting
- Environmental controls
- Outlets

Some departments may need places to store realia: statuary, paintings, objects from archival collections, and the like. Others might have different kinds of special storage needs: unused desks, chairs, lamps, and so on. And the department might need to house special equipment like stereopticon readers, old computers, sound equipment, podiums, slide and glass-slide projectors, other kinds of projectors and cameras, viewing screens, and audio equipment. The idiosyncratic nature of each department will dictate what the final layout and facilities of the new (or newly reconfigured) department will look like.

Though I have already made this point, it is worth repeating: the librarians should work as closely with the architects and designers as possible. They should strongly voice their opinions about things in the plans that are workable and those that are not. It is frustrating and irritating to enter a newly created place and have to face, for the rest of one's career at the library, something that was poorly thought out, that impedes smooth operations, or that compromises security. You have only one opportunity to get it right. If you do not, you must live with the consequences. But if you do, you will be happy to live with the results.

Services and Physical Layout

Rare books and special collections departments in general look alike with respect to the basic services they provide. Two final issues should be stressed—reference services and library tours.

REFERENCE SERVICES

In chapter 2 we looked at the many functions of a special collections department, one of which was reference service. Because reference is a library operation, we will revisit it briefly here. A sidebar in chapter 2 explained one way to figure out how much time to give patrons who need reference assistance. Each department must figure this out for itself, depending on the patron's distance from the library, the size of the staff, the amount of time the staff can offer each user, the availability of local researchers who can be employed by distant scholars, the mandate of the library (is it primarily for employees as in a museum or narrowly focused academic institution?), or other factors.

Staff must remember that reference is perhaps the number one way that the public is engaged with the library, and poor reference service can be a black eye to the institution.[8] Word gets out when patrons are unhappy. For this reason, the better the reference service a department can give, the happier will be the patrons, and the better off the library will be in the long run. But this does not mean that librarians have all the time in the world to spend with difficult patrons, or with those who have great amounts of work they would like to have done for them. So it might be useful to have a form to give patrons that spells out the reference-service policies of the library, showing time limits, limits on materials that may be consulted at one time (e.g., for manuscripts, one folder at a time may be used; for books, up to five at a time), reference strategies that the patrons might employ themselves, a description of the reference tools that are available in the reading room, and so forth. This form should be on the department's website as well so that distant patrons get the message. If it is all spelled out in codified form, there should be no complaint.

Further, the reading room and the rest of the department must be set up with reference—that is, with access to information—in mind. Tables at which patrons work should be in sight of the shelved reference books they might need. The private space delineated for the reference interview should be close to the reading room and should not be accessible only through staff or secure space. The reading room and the reference interview room should have computer terminals linked with the Web and the library's online catalog, and they should also have some of the basic department forms just described,

especially one listing the unit's reference services and policies.

LIBRARY TOURS

As will be noted in chapter 11, "Outreach," one of the optional operations activities is giving department tours. A constant goal of the library is to increase public awareness of the collection and, as a consequence, to expand use. The more use the department has, the more it can justify its existence, and the more it can justify its requests for additional resources.

The administration and others in the organization may not understand what a superb resource the rare book department could be for the institution. Notifying faculty and students of what the department holds—especially showing them on tours some of the treasures or, more to the point, the items in the collection that have to do with their areas of interest—will likely increase use. The public, groups of potential donors whom the development people want to impress, scholars, and anyone else the department wants to reach out to will profit from and be entertained by the tours, each of which could be tailored to the specific interests of the visitors.

As noted in chapter 1, the rare book library should strive to boost an awareness of and a connection with special collections by the administration and the development staff. In few other places at the institution can these people wow potential donors with materials chosen to reflect the donors' special interests.

Naturally, visitors may not be taken into the rare book stacks or any other restricted area. But a tour should include a visit to the reading room and any other area open to the public, and the librarians should have a selection of impressive items to show, held on a special shelf and easy to get to in case the library head or some other high official from the institution comes in unannounced with a visitor.

■ ■ ■

The physical layout of the building, with all its systems (security, HVAC, plumbing, electricity, and so forth), will have a strong impact on operations, partly in how the staff feel about their working conditions, and partly in how suitable the space is for all the functions it can permit, for staff and for patrons. Although for the most part staff inherit the space they have, they can do some things to modify it to their benefit, and perhaps they will be able to do a major reconfiguration, if the opportunity arises.

NOTES

1. Chapter 2 presented much information about library operations. In this section the focus will be on operations related to the physical layout of the department.

2. As with other issues concerning operations, cataloging is related to security. And all this has to do with access to information because securely cataloged books that have not been stolen are accessible for users. As noted already a few times in this chapter, security will be dealt with in more detail later, but it is so inextricable from other topics that it must also be dealt with throughout this book.

3. LCSH, *Library of Congress Subject Headings*, though available online, is still often consulted in its paper version. No cataloger can memorize all the thousands upon thousands of headings that delineate preferred terms for rare book cataloging. AACR2r, *Anglo-American Cataloguing Rules*, 2nd edition, revised, is still the cataloging system of choice in the English-speaking world, and it is essential to have a copy of it at one's elbow when one catalogs rare books. Its complexities are so numerous that no one will have memorized it in its entirety. RDA (Resource Description and Access), a new wave of cataloging, will be dealt with later in this volume.

4. The abbreviations NUC, BLC, BN, and GW designate, respectively, the National Union Catalog (American and Canadian), the British Library Catalog, Bibliothèque nationale de France, and the Gesamtkatalog der Wiegendrucke (German). Other national bibliographies were often at hand for catalogers, but for Western languages, these were the most important and most consulted. The NUC volumes, listing books printed before 1956, displayed photocopies of millions of catalog cards, all copied onto large pages. The set was published by Mansell, so it is sometimes referred to as "Mansell." One might hear a librarian or bookseller say, "Is this book in Mansell?" The set had over 528,000 pages, took up 130 linear feet of shelf space, and weighed over six thousand pounds. See http://en.wikipedia.org/wiki/National_Union_Catalog. There were also sixty-nine supplementary volumes, and the entire set contained

more than 13 million entries. After the printed volumes, more such information was made available in microfiche. The set was often hailed as one of the greatest bibliographical endeavors ever to have been produced. See Jeffrey Beall and Karen Kafader, "The Proportion of NUC Pre-56 Titles Represented in OCLC and WorldCat," *College & Research Libraries* (September 2005): 431–35, http://crl.acrl.org/content/66/5/431.full.pdf. Parenthetically, NUC contained so many records that booksellers took advantage of this to claim for many of the volumes they were trying to sell, "Not in NUC"!—as if that fact meant the item for sale was exceptionally scarce and could therefore command a high price. I recall seeing, many years ago, a whole bookseller's catalog titled "Not in NUC." This designation does not really mean much beside the fact that at the time that NUC was published, the item in question was not listed. Hundreds of thousands of volumes are not listed there, nor did the compilers of NUC claim that it was anywhere near "complete" or comprehensive.

5. Joel Silver, one of the most prolific writers about rare books and prominent in the field, teaches a whole course titled "Reference Sources for Rare Books" in the library school at Indiana University. He covers nearly four hundred volumes, not an astonishing number because every special collection has its own specialties and each of these specialties has its own bibliographical literature. At UC Riverside, for example, we needed in our special collections stacks the bibliography of the work of Guy Davenport (Joan Crane, comp., *Guy Davenport: A Descriptive Bibliography, 1947–1995* [Haverford, PA: Green Shade, 1996]); not all libraries need that volume.

6. On April 4, 1994, Nicholson Baker published an article in the *New Yorker* (70.7, pp. 64–86) that he called "Discards," about the practice of throwing away catalog cards after librarians had digitized their paper-based bibliographic catalogs. A large literature, a backlash to Baker's views against the practice, emerged soon after his diatribe. See, for instance, Nancy Douglas, "Debating 'Discards': A Response to Nicholson Baker," *Rare Books & Manuscripts Librarianship* 9.1 (Spring 1994): 41–47.

7. As with much else in this chapter, some of the points made about library operations will be treated again in greater detail in chapter 7, "Security."

8. Poor cataloging would also be an affront to patrons if they knew about it. Great catalogers work in the dark as far as patrons are concerned. Users do not see the great help they receive from catalogers who do their job well. But if a reference person falls down on the job, it is right in the face of the patron.

CHAPTER 6

FUND-RAISING

APOLEON PROBABLY DID NOT SAY, "AN ARMY TRAVELS ON ITS stomach." Whoever did say it, however, did not get it exactly right. If the army needs food, it requires something even more basic: something to exchange for the food. There is no such thing as a free lunch. These clichés and old axioms get to the nub of this chapter: money is the driver. Without it, no one gets paid, books and manuscripts cannot be bought or cared for, library holdings will not be cataloged or processed, there will be no access to research materials, and nothing will get done in the library. Although fund-raising is usually part of the standard job description of a department head (and often even some of the staff), not all departments have the personnel or the time do to it.[1] In fact, many special collections departments take the funds available to them from the institution's rare book department budget line and do not spend much time on development. But it is incumbent on rare book librarians to work with the development department and the administration in creating a plan to help the institution and the special collections department financially.

This notion of engaging the administration and the development personnel in the department's activities is a natural lead-in to fund-raising. I should point out, as well, that development for the special collections department is not necessarily the only aim of this activity, for the department can be used to raise funds for the entire institution. This chapter focuses on some of the key issues in fund-raising and concentrates on tactics for rare book libraries.

Basic Principles

There are a few basic principles of fund-raising. First, development is not a solo endeavor. Although it is possible for a librarian to identify and cultivate a donor, it is always best to work with the institution's advancement unit, who have at their fingertips all kinds of databases that allow them to determine who is a likely candidate for philanthropy and at what level. Different institutions have different configurations with respect to development, but there is usually a central office in charge of it. At larger organizations, there may be a development officer assigned just for the library. If the rare book department is significant enough, it too may have its own fund-raiser. No matter the configuration, the head of the rare book department should work closely with development personnel. The aim is to show off the institution at its best, and rare books and special collections are in a unique position to be shown off. People like to see and be associated with fine things, and special collections departments are filled with them.

Second, the rare book facility is just one small part of the parent body, so librarians should be sensitive to the fact that the larger institution's fund-raising success could well have trickle-down effects—especially if the library has been instrumental in raising the funds in the first place. Also, it is better for the parent organization to get larger gifts than for the smaller rare book unit to get smaller ones.

There are, of course, situations in which the donor has no interest in the parent body and is solely interested in supporting the rare book library. If this is the case, with the institution's permission and help from its development team, the librarian may pursue the donor for whatever initiative seems the most promising. The library should never be in competition with the institution. And even when acting on behalf of the rare book department alone, the librarian must still work with development personnel for guidance and to keep them informed of the department's progress.

Third, librarians should rely on development personnel to determine the nature and level of the donation they seek from any potential donor, whether from government agencies (local, state, or federal), foundations, corporations, or private parties,[2] and they should also rely on advancement to determine the best method and timing of the ask. Additionally, almost all gifts come with strings. This is not necessarily unreasonable. A donor to a library wants to know that the money is put to the use the donor specifies. So most grants and deeds of gift have clear statements showing exactly what the resources are to be used for. It would be foolish, and possibly in some cases illegal, to use the gift for anything other than its original stated purpose. (More on this later in this chapter.)

Fourth, most donors want an accounting, after a reasonable period, of how the gift was used. This is especially true for government grants, some of which have extremely complicated applications and rules for qualification and equally complex reporting requirements. It is extremely important to make these accountings regularly, on a schedule required by the grant or in such a way as to keep the donor happy.

Funding Sources

All sources of funding carry subsidiary issues. For government grants, the efforts one must go through

---

AT MOST INSTITUTIONS, anyone outside the development department who does fund-raising work must submit a contact report to the development department. It is crucial that this kind of information flow be established. There is nothing worse in advancement than having a single potential donor be approached by two representatives from the same institution who are not communicating with one another. The report should explain thoroughly the nature of the contact and what transpired. In fact, no employee should be contacting any potential donor without the express permission of and guidance from the development personnel.

Long ago when I was at a large academic institution, I wanted to raise money for my unit, but I was required to go through the organization's advancement department. I did extensive research about what parties to approach for support and passed along a list of about 150 prospects to advancement. A week later I was told that the institution had asks out to about 140 of them and that I was prohibited from going to them. This is a possible drawback of working at a large organization.

just to apply can be daunting. Also, government agencies increasingly require cost sharing from the institution. That is, the institution may have to contribute a significant amount of resources to match some or all of the amount granted. This contribution is usually made in in-kind resources, such as the percentage of time an employee devotes to the work the grant covers. The library must figure out whether it can come up with a sufficient amount of cost sharing before it applies for a grant.

Foundations may have their own requirements. For instance, the grant application may be for a symposium that will entail feeding the attendees and giving honoraria to speakers. The foundation may require that their largesse may not be used for food, drink, or honoraria. Information about the strictures inherent in any foundation's or agency's gift giving is usually spelled out in the literature the entity publishes.

Many books on fund-raising—even those directed toward libraries and other nonprofit institutions—exist. (A cursory search on the word *fundraising* through AbeBooks.com revealed over 10,800 volumes for sale with that keyword in their titles.) In the past, directories of funding sources were published yearly in large volumes. There was the comprehensive *Foundation Directory* (New York: Foundation Center, various years), and the two directories published by the Taft Group in Washington, D.C.: *The Taft Foundation Reporter* and *Taft Corporate Giving Directory*. Today the *Foundation Directory Online* is available by subscription.[3] The most recent *Corporate Giving Directory* from Taft seems to be the 2007 version (they do not seem to have an online version). Changes take place in corporations often, so this source might not be as up to date as the *Foundation Directory*. It is best to locate the institutions you wish to go to for support and then get up-to-date information about them directly from their websites. The Web contains a host of sites to help fund-raisers. And there are private for-profit companies that offer their fund-raising services to anyone willing to pay for it. Even if you find information in an online directory, it is wise to check out the website of the agency you intend to approach. Foundation and corporate websites are likely to have the most up-to-date information about their philanthropic activities.

> **ONE LIBRARY WAS** considering applying for a grant that offered a lot of money, but when the director figured out all the work an entire team would have to do to get the grant, and all the effort that would be required to report their progress, plus the vast amount of matching funds they would need to come up with, she figured that the resources the library might get through the grant were hardly worth all that.

Usually, dealing with donors is a pleasure. It is refreshing to be involved with people who love books and libraries and who wish to support collections and the people who maintain them. Occasionally, however, potential donors can be demanding of one's time and can dangle gifts before the institution just to have their favor curried. And the dangling can go on for years with no gift in sight. Private parties or family trusts often want their donations to go for specific projects, like cataloging of papers or conservation of particular kinds of materials, and they may wish to dictate to a stringent or unreasonable extent how they are to be involved in the management of the gift. In 1995 Yale University had to return a gift of $20 million from a donor who wished to be involved in the appointment of the faculty who were to be hired by his gift.[4] Sometimes the strings attached to a gift make it impossible for the institution to accept the donation.

It is difficult to turn down gifts, and it has to be done with great sensitivity, to avoid hurting the feelings of the donors and to insure that they understand how much the institution appreciates their generosity. Diplomacy may win the day in the long run, for an "appropriately rejected" philanthropist may remain a philanthropist to the institution.

Giving money is usually a transaction with legal implications. Often there are tax consequences for the donor. So it is essential that legal counsel be brought in (or development people highly trained in the legal requirements and implications of the gift) to oversee the paperwork. It is critical that the terms of the gift be clearly spelled out: what the money is to be used for, who has the right to decide on its use, if it is to be used as an endowment or if it can be

A KIND DONOR at the University of California, Riverside, had a substantial collection of materials about the Panama Canal, a subject the special collections department was strongly interested in. The donor, however, also had a collection of bottles that had been dredged up when the canal was being dug, and he wanted the two groups of items to be kept together. My department wanted the papers, but we were not a museum, and we had no interest in, and had no place to store, the bottles. We had to turn the gift down. About two years later the donor returned and said that the position we took was the same as that taken by all the other places he offered the items to. He saw the impossibility of placing both of his collections in the same library, so he split the gift: papers to Riverside and bottles to a museum.

spent immediately, and if there are any restrictions on it.

Naturally institutions want unrestricted funds, but if that is not the intent of the donor, the receiving body must assess whether the gift meets its mandates and mission. Receiving a cash gift that must be spent in ways the donor dictates but that does not meet the mission of the institution or that compromises the institution's integrity in any way can make the money more of an embarrassment than a boon. For this reason, it may be wise to create a department form—an acquisition policy—that can guide the institution in its procurement of gifts; this form may be shared with prospective donors to inform them of what is acceptable and what is not.[5]

AT THE PHILLIPS Library an endowed fund was set up almost a hundred years ago for the purchase of books and manuscripts in an area in which the library has not collected for perhaps seventy-five years. The fund sits there decade after decade accruing money that cannot be touched. The original donors are long gone. It may be possible to have the restrictions on this fund changed, but it will involve legal activity that takes time and resources.

Gifts Other Than Funds

Naturally, the special collections librarian wants the holdings to increase. One way to do so is to increase the acquisitions budget, and that could come through the kind of fund-raising just spoken of. Another way is through the acquisition of whole (or major parts of) collections from donors. A topic collection from a well-heeled and keen collector can put a library on the map in an area in which it was particularly weak. Some collectors, over a lifetime of acquisition, amass what would be a level 5 collection at any institution. When they are ready to part with the collection, the institution that receives it could instantly become preeminent in that subject. So although it is often best to get cash as a donation, the gift of a library, possibly holding unique or exceptionally hard-to-find items, could be far better.

Collectors

Collectors can be experts in the things they collect. Their libraries can be brilliantly assembled and filled with rare and important items. Chapter 1 presented a case for getting to know the collectors: they can be subject experts in the areas of their holdings, they may have spent many years amassing superb collections, they understand the importance of their books and manuscripts, they are usually friends of libraries and librarians, and so forth. It is wise for librarians to get to know them and befriend them. The argument need not be rehashed here.

What is important here, however, is that the librarian encourage the collectors with holdings the librarian is interested in to keep in mind the disposition of the collection. Some fairly obvious issues are at play. No one lives forever. Collectors often want to see all their efforts appreciated and perhaps even recognized in the form of some kind of immortality—the kind that is imbued in a collection's permanence in a prominent institution. Two alternative views are possible for the collector. First, "I have had great fun putting this collection together. If I put it up for auction or sell it to a bookseller, my holdings will be dispersed and others will be able to have the same kind of fun that I have had." Second, "I have invested a great deal of my resources in this collection. I would like my heirs to reap the fiscal rewards of my efforts." Both of these views are reasonable, and a librarian must honor them with no complaint when a collection she was eager to get for her library winds up on the market. All the librarian can do is make the best case to the collector that the books should go to a (her) library, and then let the collector decide what he will do. The final decision is obviously out of her hands.

But there are some strong arguments for not dispersing the collection, and whether the books and manuscripts are given or sold, the librarian may be able to get them for her collection. For instance, the librarian may take the position that such a magnificent collection could never be accumulated again. It is a monument to scholarship and to the glory of the person who was keen enough to assemble it. This sounds as if it is playing on the ego and pride of the collector, but it is a fact in many cases. It would be a shame and a blow to research to disperse the items.

Also, the collector must realize that if the books are dispersed, scholars who wish to use them may have to go to several institutions to do their work. If the dispersal is through a bookseller or auction house, there will be no way for anyone to go to all the places the items will wind up in—which could be all over the world, given the way books are now sold on the Web and the far-reaching influence of auction houses.

If finances are at the root of the collection's breakup, the librarian can explain that booksellers will offer perhaps 25 to 30 percent of the retail value of the materials and that auction sales are unpredictable and a gamble. Items could go for more than their normal market value, they could go for less, and they might not sell at all. On top of this, auction houses have been raising their seller's premiums over the years, and the consignor will have to pay up to 25 percent of the hammer price just to sell an item at auction. That is, if the item sells for $1,000, the consignor gets only $750. It is true that consignors can negotiate the seller's premium, but whatever the final figure is, the items will bring much less than the final bid indicates.

Another argument is that the owner may have to pay capital gains if the collection sells for a profit. Depending on the owner's tax bracket in the United States, the taxes on profits could be substantial, cutting even more into the consignor's take. Other tax implications may be quite appealing to a collector. If the collection is donated to a nonprofit institution, the donor can take a tax write-off for the value of the collection. This will be examined in more detail in chapter 8, "Legal Issues." (In chapter 8, we will also look at the appraisal of the collection, which could be costly.) The tax write-off may net much less "profit" to the collector than if the collection is sold, so selling the collection might still be appealing. But this situation, combined with the other factors just mentioned, could convince the collector not to sell.

A related strategy is to have the collector sell part of the collection to the institution and donate the rest. Going through a bookseller, the collector will get perhaps as much as 30 percent of the holdings' retail value. Selling directly to an institution at, say, 60 percent of retail value is good for both parties: the seller gets more than he would have from a dealer, and the institution pays 40 percent less than if the books were bought through dealers. Further, the institution can get all the items at once rather than having to locate, order, and deal with numerous items individually. It is a good savings. By bequeathing part of the collection, the collector can take a tax break for the donated part.

Another strategy to convince the collector to donate the items to the library is to have the library put on an exhibition featuring the collection. This tactic is common in the museum world, and there is no reason that the library cannot adopt it, too. If the library has exhibition space and an exhibition program, it can easily mount an exhibit of the collector's treasures. Such an event could flatter the collector, but, more important, it shows her that the library is serious in promoting the materials she has amassed, which suggests that the library will continue to treat the collection right: cataloging it, promoting it, making it available to others. Of course, the library can call it "The John Smith Collection of _____," and can put bookplates on all items, showing who donated the collection.

In all these activities, the library must let the donor know that the institution is serious about the donation, that it will treat the materials and the collector with respect and care, and that the collection, though out of its former owner's hands, will still be available in the library. This last is a key point: many collectors get powerfully attached to their books and manuscripts, thinking of them as "part of the family." They have lived in proximity with these things for years, maybe decades. For the collections to be taken from them, even under the most happy and congenial circumstances, is still a cataclysmic event for the owners. It is like the empty-nest syndrome.

> **I HAVE FIRSTHAND** experience with the loss of a collection. Over the decades I have had to part with major sections of my collections, and though they went for good causes (e.g., to help us raise the money to pay for out-of-state tuition and books), I felt their loss for years. My recompense was that I loved my son dearly and was happy to do this for him, and I am still happy I did. But that does not fill the gap of those empty shelves (which, by the way, got refilled quickly enough).

The point is that the library owes a great deal of thanks to the donor and his or her family and should express these thanks often. The librarians and staff should maintain good continuing relations with the donors, and the library should make its appreciation known as publicly as the donor is comfortable with. The donor must know that his library is available to him during business hours, so he can still have the thrill of touching the items that he so lovingly assembled. It may encourage him to continue to find items for the collection and continue to contribute them to the library—as many a donor has been known to do. Here, of course, I am describing the situation for a major gift. Small ones, of some books or some modest amount of cash, also deserve the same kind of treatment and showing of appreciation, but scaled down to an appropriate level.

Acquiring a Collection

Four issues arise when an institution acquires a collection through donation. First, it costs practically nothing to name the collection. That is, the collector is honored when the library is able to advertise—publicly to the world and in cataloging records—that the _____ Collection has just been acquired. This information can also be put onto bookplates in each volume acquired. Naming the collection may also be a good incentive to donors.

Second, some collectors want their books to be kept together, preferably in one room. Unless the collection is truly extraordinary and would fill a whole room (and unless the library has a room available), this request is seldom honored. It is impractical and usually impracticable. And it may add considerably to the institution's costs.

Third, some donors wish the collection to remain intact. The reason the institution wanted the collection in the first place could be that it was building to its strengths. If this is the case, then it is certain that the library already has many items that are in the collector's holdings. It is costly and usually not feasible to keep, catalog, process, and shelve duplicates. This practice is not only expensive, it also takes up valuable shelf space, and it does not add anything new to the institution's research offerings. The librarian should try to negotiate for the freedom to deaccession any item from the acquisition that the library does not want. This point could prove nettlesome in the negotiation between the donor and the library, but the librarian must explain in as conciliatory a way as possible why such deaccession is necessary. She could say that if the donor's copy is in any way different from the one already on the shelf, the new copy will be kept.[6] And if the donated copy is in better condition, it may be swapped into the collection for the library's less good one. But if the two copies are identical, the library should be able to keep the one it has on the shelf and discard the donor's copy. If the donor is adamant, and if the collection is rich enough, it might be necessary to accede to this demand, but normally the librarian should try to avoid such a stricture. The donor should be told that even swapping out identical copies is costly: there are cataloging and processing costs and deaccessioning efforts that take time, and the copy that must be deaccessioned has library marks on it, so it will not bring a premium price on the market.

There are, of course, other reasons for not wanting to take a whole collection. Though the collector has put all these objects together and sees them as a unified lot, the holdings might contain things that are truly outside the scope of the library's collection. There also might be conservation problems: items that are in such disrepair that they cannot be used without costly repair work. It is possible, too, that the collection is simply too massive for the library to accommodate.

The fourth issue is fiscal: acquiring even a single book is expensive, even as a gift. There are cataloging, processing, shelving, and storage costs. A common tactic is to ask the donor for funds to catalog the items transferred. This again falls under the "Fund-raising" rubric, and collectors should understand how much books cost once they have been acquired. If they have the means, generous and thoughtful donors might be in a position to pay for the handling of their collections. However, sometimes they take a more negative stance: "I have given you the books; isn't that enough?" Once the costs associated with the gift are manifested, donors should see the reason for the additional cash request. So it seldom hurts to request an additional cash gift with the donation of the objects.

THE DEED OF GIFT

One key element in the acquisition of a collection is the Deed of Gift (or the Deed of Sale, if the collection is to be sold; in such instances the sale may have restrictions just as with a gift). The document should have some standard features: (1) the date; (2) the name, address, and other contact points of the donor(s); (3) a description of the gift; (4) the terms of the gift; (5) a statement about intellectual property rights (especially important for manuscript materials); (6) appropriate signatures (donor, recipient, witness); and (7) the date signed.

The first date indicates when the contract was drawn up; the second date, when it was signed. If the gift is not from a single person, then all who are involved in its transfer must be delineated. The gift must be described so the contract is clear about what is being given. In some instances, especially when the entire gift is not tremendously valuable, it may be sufficient to say: "Collection of manuscripts" or "Collection of fifty-five (55) manuscripts." For books it is the same: "Collection of two hundred (200) books." If the collection is substantial, this brief description may not be enough. Again, in chapter 8 we will look at legal issues with reference to gifts. Here it is sufficient to say that when a donation reaches a point at which serious tax implications are involved, it is probably a good idea to be much more explicit as to what the gift contains. This might mean creating an itemized bibliography of everything, or at least a listing of all the most valuable volumes—say, anything over $250 (£150)—with an added gathering list like this: "Also, four hundred (400) books valued between $25 and $250; average value $75."

Serious collectors may have made listings of their books, so this kind of enumeration may not be difficult to produce. It can be appended as an addendum to the Deed of Gift, stapled or clipped as separate sheets. If such a listing does not exist, it may be good to have one made. And because this document is obviously prepared before the transfer of the gift, the donor is responsible for making this list (just as the donor is responsible for any appraisal that may be done before the transfer). It could happen that the library, eager to get the collection, offers to make the listing, makes it, and then, for whatever reason, the gift is not made. (The donor could see the extent of the collection from the inventory and change his mind; he could give the listing to an appraiser who gives him a huge figure, and the donor now sees gold at the end of this rainbow; the donor's family may convince him not to give the collection away; or the donor could die before the gift is transferred and the heirs decide to sell the books instead of giving them away.) The library is out all of its efforts. Thus all activities having to do with the items to be given (e.g., inventorying, conservation, appraisal) should be the responsibility of their owner.

It could be—before the signing of the final Deed of Gift—that some preliminary document exists which makes the gift a certainty and that includes wording which shows the library as responsible for creating the inventory of the donated materials. If this is the case, and the library is assured of getting the materials, then it may be necessary for the librarians or staff to do the listing. But this is an extraordinary case.

One other clause may be in the Deed of Gift showing how items the library does not wish to retain may be dealt with. It could look something like this: "The library may keep any and all of the books/manuscripts in the donated collection. If it wishes, it may sell any items from the donation, and the money realized from this sale should be used to acquire more books for the collection." The wording can be different, depending on the intent of the donor.

Further, the librarian can promise that a bookplate showing the name of the donor will be put into every volume given and that a bookplate, also showing the donor's identity, will be placed into every volume purchased from the money raised by the sale of the donor's books. The latter plate will read, "This volume purchased through the generosity of _____," or similar wording.

APPRAISING THE GIFT

For large gifts, or small ones that have high value, donors often get appraisals for tax purposes. The actual value of the items is not germane to the library in the transfer, and the appraisal, presumably done by a professional appraiser or qualified bookseller, is the property of the donor, who must pay for it. (As mentioned in chapter 2, ethical standards of the profession prohibit librarians from placing values on library materials.) The donor need not share the information of the donation's value with the librarian, though there are no legal issues if that information is given. It may be useful to the library to have a copy of the formal appraisal, and the librarian is within her rights and is performing ethically to ask for a copy of it. But it is not necessary for the donor to give it over, and the librarian should not expect to get it.

For internal use, the librarian (whether she gets a copy of the formal appraisal or not) may wish to make her own evaluation of the gift. Many institutions need this kind of information for tax, insurance, or statistical purposes. The librarian's appraisal should be kept strictly confidential. It is not for broadcast beyond the library. If the institution wishes to announce to the public or to the professional world the acquisition of the gift and wishes to put a monetary value on it, the institution may ask the donor to give this information. If the donor refuses to give the amount, any announcement may just have to say, "A major collection of . . ." without giving a figure. Also, it is good for relations between the institution and the donor to ask the latter for permission to go public with the announcement. Some donors may not wish to have the publicity. Some donors even specify in the Deed of Gift that if an announcement is to be made, they want to see it (and approve of it) before it is made public. This request is perfectly reasonable, and the library should not complain about it.

UNRAVELING THE STRINGS

The fourth area of the Deed of Gift, Terms, can lead to problems. Gifts often come with an open-ended statement to the effect of, "Do what you wish with what we are giving you. It's up to you." This unencumbered donation is the ideal, for the library can indeed deal with duplicates, items out of scope, and so forth any way it wishes. But for some donations, the strings that are attached could create great headaches down the road. The Terms of the Gift may include such fairly straightforward statements as, "The library promises to catalog the books in this collection and mount the cataloging records online," or "The library will make these materials available to all scholars." These "strings" are what libraries do, so complying with such requirements is not a problem.

But when the strings border on the difficult, the untenable, or the ridiculous, there may be a problem. Here is an example of the difficult: "The library shall maintain these manuscripts with no access to anyone for fifteen (15) years after the death of the donor." There might be a good reason for this restriction having to do with the sensitive nature of the manuscripts' contents. But holding onto things for fifteen years beyond the donor's death (especially if the donor is young) so that no one has access to them is difficult: the library is taking up valuable shelf space for essentially dead materials. Perhaps fifteen years is reasonable, but longer than this might not make any sense.

> **I ONCE ACQUIRED** a large collection of wonderful materials pertaining to an important scholar/actor/writer. The person from whom we were buying the collection (note that this was a sale, not a gift, and that the transfer of the material came with a Deed of Sale that had its own Terms clause) insisted on putting into the deed a restriction that the diaries in the collection were to be sealed for one hundred years. I made it clear that this was simply not possible and that we might allow fifteen years of closure. The seller said that there were extremely sensitive materials in all the volumes of that diary, but I held firm. We would not put items on our shelves that were inaccessible for a century. It would take up a lot of shelf space for no return on our expense of housing them, and in a century the diaries would have much less value to scholars than they would in the short term. She finally saw the light and acceded to the shorter term.

An untenable string might be that the library put a vase of fresh flowers once a week in front of the donor's portrait in the library. Fresh flowers in libraries are trouble: they could house pests that could damage the collection. They could run into a huge expense over time. And their purchase and maintenance can be costly as well. One can only imagine what ridiculous demands might be: closing the collection for one hundred years, keeping items in the collection on permanent display, or hiring a curator of the donor's choosing just for the collection. This last is not unreasonable if the donor provides all the funds for such a hire (which would mean a substantial endowment) and if the institution has space and other resources to make it happen. Allowing the donor to select the curator, however, is a problem. The chosen curator could be the donor's nephew, who has no training for the job, is unreliable, and has been arrested for theft a half dozen times. This scenario is obviously exaggerated for effect, but the point is that the donor should have no say in hiring anyone for the institution. The fewer the strings the better.

One thing to remember is that often strings are for life. That is, the contract's restriction may be permanent. The library must be certain that it can adhere to this restraint to perpetuity. It is always best if the librarian can convince the donor to apply no strictures to the gift, or at least ones that are reasonable.

Another matter concerning the Deed of Gift has to do with intellectual property rights. This will be covered in detail in chapter 8, but in a nutshell, the donor should be encouraged to sign rights over to the library.

Other Fund-Raising Issues and Strategies

Many kinds of giving are extant, as Lisa Browar and Samuel Streit explain, from "planned giving and

> **ONE INSTANCE OF** a restriction that falls under the "ridiculous" rubric is Sir Thomas Phillipps's demand that if the British Library bought his vast collection of books and manuscripts, the institution would refuse access to the collection to his son-in-law and to all Catholics.* The library of course turned down the purchase.
>
> *See Philippa Levine, *The Amateur and the Professional: Antiquarians, Historians and Archaeologists in Victorian England, 1838–1886* (Cambridge, England, and New York: Cambridge University Press, 1986). She says about Phillipps, "His violent hatred of Catholicism was matched by his loathing for his son-in-law, James Orchard Halliwell" (p. 21). John Michell, in his chapter "Bibliomaniacs," says of Phillipps, "Catholic scholars were barred from his library" (*A Passion for Books,* ed. by Harold Rabinowitz and Rob Kaplan [New York: Three Rivers Press, 1999], p. 119). Nicholas Basbanes says in *A Gentle Madness* that Phillipps was maniacal about the disposition of his books, pointing out that no scholar or bookseller should be allowed to rearrange them in any way and that Roman Catholics and Halliwell should be forbidden from looking at them (*A Gentle Madness: Bibliophiles, Bibliomanes, and the Eternal Passion for Books* [New York: Henry Holt, 1995], p. 122).

investment vehicles to donor-advised giving instruments" (see Browar and Streit, "Mutually Assured Survival," in the bibliography at the end of this chapter). Sam Streit was something of a role model for fund-raising for special collections in the 1980s when he was head of special collections at Brown University. He devoted 20 percent of his time to the development department, not specifically for the library, but for the university. The liaison became a successful partnership, and Streit worked in development for many years. The university certainly benefited from his efforts, and in the long run the rare book library did, too. This strategy may be useful for other special collections librarians.

Streit expatiates on some of the issues and strategies for fund-raising in his article, "All That Glitters: Fund Raising for Special Collections in Academic Libraries" (*Rare Books & Manuscripts Librarianship* [Spring 1988]: 31–41), in which he shows that there are different kinds of sources for fiscal support: private donors, government agencies, corporations, foundations, and so forth (pp. 35–38). Further, Streit points out that the rare book librarian can adopt various strategies for fund-raising: for budgetary support, for acquisitions, for conservation, as seed money for larger funding initiatives, and so on (pp. 34–36). The department may even go to the institution for special resources outside its regular line-item support.

Under the rubric of "Strategies," Streit writes,

It is at this point that special events, mailings, campus visits and personal contact begin to bear fruit; but the type and extent of the cultivation techniques to be employed should be determined by the nature of the fund raising goal, the pool of potential donors, and institutional custom. It is important also to have a realistic understanding of what cultivation can and cannot accomplish. In and of themselves, glossy brochures, elegant dinners and special events do not usually result in a spontaneous return in the form of significant contributions, and the librarian who expects to conclude a successful fund raising effort through such subtle means is doomed to disappointment. (p. 38)

Streit advises that a well-designed campaign should be mapped out and publicized so potential donors know what the library's needs are. The actual solicitation from a donor should be made by the best person to do it—the special collections librarian, the head of the library, an institution administrator, someone in development, or perhaps someone else altogether (p. 38). Streit points out, however, that if someone other than the rare book librarian is designated to make the ask, the librarian is thus removed from the picture, and that librarian may have been the one who created the possibility in the first place (p. 39). Donors may enjoy their time with the librar-

---

HOW MUCH TIME a librarian should give to cultivating a particular donor can be problematic. I once spent an inordinately immense amount of time with a donor. Over more than two and a half years I had scores of phone calls from him, some lasting two hours or more. He would call me at 11 p.m. to talk about his books, to ask me for advice about potential purchases, to brag about a new acquisition and describe it to me, to discuss with me the disposition of his collection, and on and on. He visited me at my home and I saw him at his. His collection was truly spectacular, and almost any institution in the world would have wanted it. He needed someone to listen to him about his passion, and because his family did not satisfy that need for him and I did, I was the one he turned to. He had given a large cash gift to the institution, and my supervisors wanted me to continue to cultivate him because he had the means to give substantially more. But this donor was eating up a great amount of time from my professional and private life, and he showed no signs of giving. Much as I liked him (he was truly a wonderful person) and his collection, and much as I enjoyed his enthusiasm for collecting, he became a burden. Librarians should guard against such incursions on their time. Working with the administration and development, the librarian should develop a strategy to end the relationship or to shift it to development, where, presumably, people have tactics for avoiding such a waste of time.

ians and dislike time with development people. This dynamic underscores the importance of a well-coordinated approach.

Streit also makes the point that when the request for funds is made to a private donor, the representative from the institution should not beat around the bush and leave the level of the gift up to the donor. A specific figure should be requested, and if, in strategizing, the institution comes up with an appropriate range of funds, the request at the higher end is better than that at the lower end. A donor is more likely to be flattered than offended at a higher figure, and asking for a lower one might net that amount when the donor was willing and able to give more (p. 40).

Finally, Streit says that

[m]uch of the success, or failure, of a fund raising campaign is determined by how well the development office and/or the library follows through on administrative details. Keeping accurate records of incoming cash, monitoring pledge payment schedules, properly assigning account numbers so as to ensure that gifts do not stray from their intended purpose, and the prompt and accurate acknowledgement of gifts, are all matters of major importance. (p. 40)

There is a simple "courtesy" level of operating with a donor, who should be kept in the loop about many things pertaining to the donation, whether it be cash or in-kind.

Another key issue is relevant here: when the donor does come through, it is essential that the Deed of Gift specify exactly what the donation is to be used for. This point was mentioned in the earlier discussion about Terms of the gift. But it needs to be emphasized again. The wording in the deed must make clear the donor's wishes for the gift in such a way that the statement cannot be reinterpreted and the gift used for something else. It may be good to add into this part of the deed what the donation may *not* be used for. A donor who has specified that his gift be used only for acquisition of books may be upset to learn that it has paid for travel for the librarian—even if that travel is ostensibly for a book-buying trip. The trip is, indeed, for acquisition, but the actual use of the money was not for buying books.

Responding to the Gift

Almost all agencies (governments, corporations, or foundations) require an accounting of how the money given was used. It is a common courtesy (and it could actually be written into a Deed of Gift) to let the private donor know how her largesse has been used. Regular updates will engender goodwill and may please the donor so much that she is willing to continue to offer support. Keeping a good relationship with the donor is essential. This is accomplished through appropriate thank-you letters, frequent updates on the use of the donation, invitations to library functions, notifications about how the donation has impacted a library user, occasional lunches, and in many other ways.

Fund-raising is clearly more complex than the discussion here can show. Rare book librarians should always have development on their minds because special collections departments always can use extra resources for a host of things (budget relief, acquisitions, conservation, exhibitions, and much more). Successful fund-raising pleases all parties involved: the librarian, of course; the donor, who knows that the donation will be for a good cause—one she is happy to support; the institution; and the patrons, because almost all raising of resources makes the department better and, in the long run, provides more service or research materials for the users.

Friends Groups and Visiting Committees

In libraries we often have friends groups. In museums such groups are called "visiting committees." No matter what they are called, these organizations can have a great deal of influence on the department's success or no influence at all. Victoria Steele and Stephen Elder discourage the formation of friends groups.[7] But some librarians find their groups quite useful.

Elaine Smyth and Robert Martin responded to the Steele and Elder proposition in an article that proved that friends groups can be boons to special collections ("Working with Friends of the Library to Augment

AT THE PHILLIPS Library at the Peabody Essex Museum, the Library Visiting Committee is composed of extremely devoted, insightful, and generous members who understand the needs of the library, see the library's importance to the institution and the academic world beyond, and enthusiastically support the library's endeavors. They offer advisory, moral, and fiscal support and have made a huge difference in the success of the library. They are a living testament that friends groups can make a significant difference in the achievement of the institution as a whole and the library in particular.

Staff Resources: A Case History," *Rare Books & Manuscripts Librarianship* 9.1 [Spring 1994]: 19–28). Steele and Elder said that such groups can take up great expanses of librarians' time, can be pushy and intrusive, and will seldom raise enough money to make a significant difference for the department. Smyth and Martin's experience proved that these objections are not always true. They held two successful auctions, with most of the work done by the friends, and were able to raise a significant amount of endowment support for a position in their department.

One point Smyth and Martin make is that the volunteers group they had at Louisiana State University (LSU) was fairly autonomous and did not encroach much on library staff, though group members did use the staff for advice and some direction for and input into the auctions. Their advice is that a good working relationship with the friends group could be such that the friends do most of the work and the library is the beneficiary. They say, "Only rarely do members [of the friends] donate substantial amounts of cash. Instead, a core group of active members makes very substantial contributions of time and effort. . . . Although the Friends of the LSU Library has not been managed as a straightforward development-oriented group according to Steele and Elder's model, its development efforts are nonetheless successful in its context" ("Working with Friends of the Library," p. 26).

Smyth and Martin also recommend that, if the library is to use a friends group, it should do so using a model that creates a specific goal—based, perhaps, on a single project—rather than a model that looks for long-term cultivation. They say,

If time and staff for development efforts are severely limited and the library must rely heavily on a Friends group for energy and initiative, taking a project-oriented approach is preferable to a long-term approach that is unpunctuated by the achievement of goals. It is important for volunteers to be rewarded by seeing the effects of their efforts. (p. 27)

The effect of the effort is the completion of a particular project—in their case the raising of a specific amount of money for an endowment.

In short, whether one uses a friends group depends on the circumstances of the library, what kind of community surrounds it, the enthusiasm of the volunteers, the careful handling of the group by its head and by the head of special collections, and so forth.

■ ■ ■

This chapter has examined some of the issues pertaining to one key operation: fund-raising. The treatment here is more provocative and informative than it is comprehensive because even the broadest generalizations cannot cover all the realities of every rare book department.

And though the main focus of the text is on libraries, anyone in the world of rare books should be aware of the issues raised here. Library operations influence not only the librarians, they also have an impact on those who deal with rare books in general. How the library operates, how it is structured, how it deals with resources—all these issues impact librarians, users, administrators, and the philanthropic world beyond the library.

NOTES

1. In this chapter the terms *fund-raising, development,* and *advancement* are used interchangeably, as they are in this field. This chapter focuses primarily on raising funds, not the acquisition of gifts in-kind: books, manuscripts, or other collections materials. Of course, many of the recommendations and observations about dealing with donors are applicable to this latter kind of resource raising as well.

2. Some foundations represent families, so the distinction between "private parties" and "foundations" blurs.

3. To subscribe to the *Foundation Directory Online,* visit http://fconline.foundationcenter.org.

4. See Jacques Steinberg, "Yale Returns $20 Million to an Unhappy Patron," *New York Times,* March 15, 1995, www.nytimes.com/1995/03/15/us/yale-returns-20-million-to-an-unhappy-patron.html?pagewanted=all.

5. A sample acquisition policy is appended to the Steven Cox article cited in the bibliography at the end of this chapter. The policy has a list of six bullet points showing when *not* to take an item or a collection from a donor:

   - Donations which present a financial drain due to conservation or preservation needs
   - Items which the special collections staff is unable or unqualified to maintain and store
   - Items and collections which may require a large amount of space for storage
   - Items or collections in formats which might require constant updating, reproducing, and/or duplicating
   - Donations which come with particular conditions, stipulations or legal encumbrances which might make their access and use too restrictive or impractical, or which may cause an overemphasis to that particular collection
   - Duplications of items already held in the Special Collections ("Libraries and Donors," p. 40)

   This list is, of course, in reference to items for the collection rather than cash.

6. G. Thomas Tanselle has said that there are no true duplicates. See *A Rationale of Textual Criticism* (Philadelphia: University of Pennsylvania Press, 1989) in which he states, "There can be no identical copies of printed books or of any other objects; but the differences in some cases may be such that one will consider them insignificant for the purpose at hand. (They may not, however, seem insignificant to another person, with other interests or greater perceptiveness.)" (p. 51). Similarly, Tanselle has observed, "No two physical objects are ever identical, even if they are intended to be, so in the strict sense there are never any duplicates. The crucial question, of course, is to decide what differences are significant enough to pay attention to—a question made particularly difficult by the fact that one can never know what details now regarded as insignificant may be shown in the future to be important" ("Bibliographers and the Library," *Library Trends* 25.4 [April 1977]: 745–62; this statement is on p. 756).

7. See Victoria Steele and Stephen Elder, *Becoming a Fundraiser,* in the bibliography at the end of this chapter. Their book caused some consternation on this point because many libraries have relatively successful friends groups.

Bibliography on Fund-raising

Benedetti, Joan M., ed. *Art Museum Libraries and Librarianship.* Lanham, MD: Scarecrow Press; [Ottawa]: Art Libraries Society of North America, 2007.

Bostic, Mary J. "Gifts to Libraries: Coping Effectively." *Collection Management* 14.3–4 (1991): 175–84.

Bradbury, D. J. "Seven Strategies for Effective Fund Raising." *Bottom Line* 2 (1988): 11–14.

Breivik, Patricia Senn, and E. Burr Gibson, eds. *Funding Alternatives for Libraries.* Chicago: American Library Association, 1979.

Browar, Lisa, and Samuel A. Streit. "Mutually Assured Survival: Library Fund-Raising Strategies in a Changing Economy." In "Special Collections in the Twenty-First Century." Special issue, *Library Trends* 52.1 (2003): 69–86. http://findarticles.com/p/articles/mi_m1387/is_1_52/ai_111853139/.

Burlingame, Dwight F., ed. *Library Fundraising: Models for Success.* Chicago: American Library Association, 1995.

Cox, Steven. "Libraries and Donors: Maintaining the Status Quo." *Southeastern Librarian* 52.3 (2004): 34–41. http://digitalcommons.kennesaw.edu/seln/vol52/iss3/7.

Cullingford, Alison. "Influencing and Fundraising." In *The Special Collections Handbook,* Section 10. London: Facet Publishing, 2011. http://specialcollectionshandbook.com/10-finding-funding-and-friends.

Dewey, Barbara I. *Raising Money for Academic and Research Libraries: A How-to-Do-It Manual for Librarians*. New York: Neal-Schuman, 1991.

Grendler, Marcella. "Beyond the Guidelines, or Better Access to Access Projects." *Rare Books & Manuscripts Librarianship* 1.2 (Fall 1986): 107–15.

Hughston, Milan. "Fundraising for the Library at the Museum of Modern Art." In *Art Museum Libraries and Librarianship*, ed. by Joan M. Benedetti, pp. 172–74. Lanham, MD: Scarecrow Press; [Ottawa]: Art Libraries Society of North America, 2007.

Huston, Kathleen Raab. "How to Look a Gift Horse in the Mouth: Saying No to Donations." *Bottom Line* 3.1 (1989): 14–17.

Lapsley, Andrea R. "Major Donors, Major Gifts." *Bottom Line* 9.2 (1996): 40–43.

Little, Paul L., and Sharon Saulmon. "Gifts, Donations and Special Collections." *Public Libraries* 26 (Spring 1987): 8–10.

Mahurter, Sarah. "Charging for Reproduction Services: University of the Arts London." Look-Here! Project Case Studies. www.vads.ac.uk/lookhere/UALCase Study.pdf.

Nelson, Veneese C. "Buried Alive in Gifts." *Library Journal* 113.7 (1988): 54–56.

Norris, Janice G. "A Subject-Oriented Approach to Gifts Management and Donor Relations." *Collections Management* 27.1 (2002): 41–57.

Paustenbaugh, Jennifer F. "Fundraising for Special Collections." *Bottom Line: Managing Library Finances* 15.4 (2002): 186–89.

Smith, Amy Sherman, and Matthew D. Lehrer. *Legacies for Libraries: A Practical Guide to Planned Giving*. Chicago: American Library Association, 2000.

Smyth, Elaine B., and Robert S. Martin. "Working with Friends of the Library to Augment Staff Resources: A Case History." *Rare Books & Manuscripts Librarianship* 9.1 (Spring 1994): 19–28.

Spyers-Duran, Peter. "Revitalization of Academic Library Programs through Creative Fundraising." In *Austerity Management in Research Libraries*, ed. by John F. Harvey and Peter Spyers-Duran. Metuchen, NJ: Scarecrow Press, 1984, pp. 105–8.

Steele, Victoria, and Stephen D. Elder. *Becoming a Fundraiser: The Principles and Practice of Library Development*. 2nd ed. Chicago: American Library Association, 2000.

Streit, Samuel A. "Acquiring Rare Books by Purchase: Recent Library Trends." *Library Trends* 36 (Summer 1987): 189–213.

———. "All That Glitters: Fundraising for Special Collections in Academic Libraries." *Rare Books & Manuscripts Librarianship* 3 (Spring 1988): 31–41.

Swan, James. *Fundraising for Libraries*. New York: Neal-Schuman, 2002.

Townsend, Allen. "Three Experiences in Museum Library Development and Fund-Raising." In *Art Museum Libraries and Librarianship*, ed. by Joan M. Benedetti. Lanham, MD: Scarecrow Press; [Ottawa]: Art Libraries Society of North America, 2007, pp. 170–72.

CHAPTER 7

SECURITY

**S HAS BEEN NOTED A NUMBER OF TIMES IN THIS VOLUME, ONE** of the premises of the rare book and special collections world is that all who work in these departments have as their prime mission giving patrons access to information. Nothing cuts off access more effectively than a book or manuscript that is not there. Close behind is a book or manuscript that has been defaced in some way. Stolen or damaged items are the bane of librarians and the patrons they serve. This chapter looks at ways to protect collections.

As chapter 5 stated, of the many operations performed in the rare book department, security is one of the highest priorities. In fact, security is a series of operations, activities, and attitudes. It goes without saying that an insecure department exposes itself to loss, through theft and mutilation, and it thus prevents librarians from carrying out their prime directive, access, because stolen or mutilated items are no longer usable by the department's patrons.[1]

Special collections and rare book departments have always been recognized as areas that need heightened security—higher than elsewhere in the library. This is practically part of the definition of a rare book department. And since the inception of such departments, many measures that increase the safekeeping of the collection have been devised. Further, since the depredations of Stephen Blumberg were revealed in 1990, libraries have increased security in a number of ways.[2] How Blumberg operated and what he got away with were shocking revelations in the wake of his crimes, and rare book libraries throughout the country (maybe throughout the world) reacted in many ways to safeguard their collections.

It is worth noting, however, that Blumberg is not alone. He is part of a long history of bibliokleptomania (book theft) that is still going on. It may seem defeatist to say, but where there is money to be made by stealing things (and money is not the only catalyst for theft), those things will be stolen. And special collections departments are particularly vulnerable because of the kinds of things they hold.

I HAVE KNOWN two heads of special collections who have been demoted because of thefts that have taken place in departments for which they were responsible. Whether the thefts were their faults is moot. They were at the helm, and security was lax enough in their departments to have allowed for the robberies. They have become examples in the profession of how blame is assigned and what the consequences are for lax security.

Hence there is a touch of paranoia in many rare book librarians that their own collections will be hit.

An old statistic has been making the rounds for decades in the library community: 80 percent of library theft comes from within. This statistic is certainly apocryphal, partly because there is practically no way to measure book theft and thus to verify this figure, and partly because, for all anyone knows, thousands of books have been stolen and their theft has not yet been detected. But it stands to reason that it is easier for an employee in a library to steal a book or manuscript than it is for someone not employed there to do so.[3]

Theft is not the only problem. Every year untold numbers of books get mutilated for many reasons: political motivations, censorship, perversity, prurience, and who-knows-why. Heightened security may reduce these kinds of ravages, but no level of security will stop them all.

Mark McComb, with the assistance of Edward Dean, wrote "Library Security," an important publication to be read in conjunction with the RBMS guidelines that will be discussed later in this chapter. They say that security should be not just for the collection but also for staff members and patrons. McComb states, "The goal of the security system should be to provide a safe and secure facility for library employees, library resources and equipment, and library patrons"; he emphasizes "the physical safety of the staff and patrons" along with the safety of the collections.[4] Hence, a "security" device to protect an employee is a "panic button" or some other device that the librarian can activate if she feels she is in physical danger. The device activates an alarm in a security office or other location, notifying someone that the employee feels she is in danger.

McComb's first recommendation is for the library to do a risk assessment. He says, "ASIS International, the leading international organization of security professionals, has published a guideline entitled, The General Security Risk Assessment Guideline." This policy outline contains a seven-step approach to risk analysis that assesses the people and assets at risk, vulnerabilities, probabilities of loss, the impact of loss, means of mitigating possible losses, and "the feasibility of actual implementation of options," along with a cost-benefit analysis weighing the cost of a variety of loss-prevention measures against the cost of undoing the effects of the loss (pp. 1–3).

Librarians face a number of issues here, not the least of which is determining what books are likely targets of attack. Certain categories are obvious:

- extremely valuable items that could fetch money on the rare book market
- items with sexual content—especially pictorial texts
- books with content that espouses particular political positions
- books that treat any emotional topic and that take sides on charged issues (religion, birth control, the death penalty, immigration reform, any kind of persecution, capital punishment, and the like)
- volumes that are beautiful (especially ones with fancy bindings or color plates—and especially hand-colored illustrations)
- banned books or books that have raised controversies
- books on highly collected topics (children's books, books on the book arts, cooking)
- handmade items (e.g., fine press books done in limited editions)

The problem is that no one can predict just where a thief or mutilator will strike. It could be anywhere in the library, and it is impossible to have surveillance everywhere.

Many libraries recognize these areas of vulnerability and create a semisecure place for those parts of the collection. That is, the library may not be able to justify housing all items in these areas in a special collections department—it just does not make sense to put fairly inexpensive, easily replaceable books into a rare book facility. So they create a browsing area that requires special access but little other special treatment.

> **UC RIVERSIDE HAD** an area called the Cage in which several thousand at-risk volumes and periodicals were housed. Users had to show an ID to get in and—because it was a circulating collection—had to check items out at the controlled exit point when leaving, but once inside, the patrons were free to browse at will. The system was imperfect, because damage could have been done by patrons in the Cage, but the idea was that it made the users feel watched, and it recorded what left the area and who the borrower was. Many libraries resort to this intermediate level of security.

Another solution is to make the entire collection nonbrowsing—that is, to have closed stacks, accessed only by staff, who page books for patrons. There are many such libraries throughout the world. Patrons look up the books or manuscripts they wish to use, fill out call slips, turn them in at a circulation desk, and have the items delivered to them after the materials have been paged. This system raises two main issues: it costs the library more to supply books to patrons than it does to allow patrons to fetch their own things, and it makes browsing next to impossible. Of course, there is a way to "browse," if patrons have access to the shelf list—either online or in a card catalog. Once an item is located in a catalog, the researcher can look to the right or left of it on the shelves (using the catalog). But this is not true browsing, because the researcher cannot page through each item to see if it contains information he is looking for. Closing the stacks to patrons is a form of security, but its drawbacks are great. The biggest drawback, as just suggested, is that all books

that wind up in patrons' hands have to be paged. This could add significantly to the number of personnel required.

If the librarians can figure out what books are likely to be mutilated or stolen, they may be able to place them in a semisecure area. The problem here is that there are too many things that might require this heightened level of care. In one library thousands of illustrations from a nineteenth-century set of *Harper's Weekly* magazine were razored out, along with thousands more illustrations from books throughout the art-books section of the open stacks. When the plates were discovered to be missing, the periodicals and the rest of the section were surveyed to reveal still other losses; by then it was far too late to do anything. Librarians also found bindings that were sitting on the shelf with their entire textblocks removed. All that was there was the binding. There was no way to know over how long a time this mutilation had been taking place and no way to catch the perpetrator(s).

Chapter 2 dealt with the transfer of books from the general stacks to the special collections department. The procedures need not be rehashed here, but the practice is one form of security in that vulnerable books are being removed from an area of particular exposure (the open stacks) to a place of higher safekeeping. As noted, however, it takes a careful analysis of the collection, and a recognition of where in the stacks threatened books are shelved, to allow for the identification of the items that should be transferred. Such diligence is security in action.

Removing vulnerable books from open-access areas is one form of security. The next question to ask is, what criteria do items have to meet to merit being transferred to the special collections department? Understanding the ubiquity of this problem for all libraries, RBMS appointed an ad hoc committee to create a code for this transfer. It was published as an RBMS Standard—*Guidelines on the Selection and Transfer of Materials from General Collections to Special Collections*, 3rd ed. (2008). Libraries may use these guidelines as their own, or they may create their own, perhaps based on those of RBMS. But however they go about it, such transfers should be "justified" and fully rationalized in a document the department can produce showing its practices. This transfer policy has already been discussed at length in chapter 2. Some of the categories of books that fall under the provisions of this transfer policy are listed earlier in this chapter. The main point to reiterate here is that this transfer is a form of security.

The Library Security Officer

The library should have an LSO, a Library Security Officer, charged with doing a careful analysis of the department for weaknesses in security, monitoring staff activities that could lessen or heighten safety, and for taking the lead if a security breach is discerned. (More about this in the following section, "Security Measures to Reduce Theft.") This can be a full-time position in larger, well-resourced institutions, but usually this person does security perhaps 20 percent of the time and does her primary job the rest of the time. (At UC Riverside the head of preservation was also the LSO.) The LSO should work closely with the department's, the library's, and the institution's administration, and she should make sure that a library security policy is kept up to date, addressing the kinds of things this chapter covers. Such a plan requires a good deal of work up front, but updating it, and then following the plan's dictates, should not be difficult. As a formal document, this security policy should be reexamined periodically. It may need to be updated depending on changes in the institution: the addition of highly valuable items or collections, a change in personnel, growth in the institution's rare book department and its acquisition budget, physical changes in the building, and so forth. The policy should be produced by the LSO and all other stakeholders: administration, institution security personnel, attorneys who may need to look at the legality of some of the mandates in the policy, librarians close to the collection who can advise on certain kinds of vulnerabilities, and others. Small libraries that do not have an LSO may wish to bring in an outside consultant to assess the weaknesses of the department, make recommendations to increase security, and write up a library security policy. The institution's own security personnel should be able to assist in writing the policy.

Security Measures to Reduce Theft

A series of steps may be taken to reduce the possibility of theft. One key issue is access to the collection. Only authorized staff should be allowed in. At some academic institutions, faculty were given keys to the rare book stacks. In recent years this privilege has generally been revoked, but it reminds us of the power of the faculty, and it warns us to be on the alert for the entry to the rare book stacks of *anyone* beyond the immediate department. In libraries in museums, likewise, curators may have access to the rare materials. In some cases, these faculty or curators have been instrumental in building the collection, and they know the materials, in their areas of expertise, as well as, or better than, the librarians do. A head of the rare book library will know who is trustworthy among those professionals, so some limited access may be justifiable for some people beyond the department. The department head, in consultation with the administration, should decide who should have access to the stacks. All others must have their privileges curtailed.

To keep the department as secure as possible, the staff must monitor all human movement there. If patrons are seated in the reading room, and then they get up to use reference materials, to go to the reference desk, or to take a break of any kind, the materials they have been using should be returned to the reference desk and held for them. This requirement could mean that they have to gather their own and the library's papers and undo all the physical laying out of those items that they had done. But leaving all the papers out is asking for trouble if there are other patrons in the room. If the patron is the only one using the room, maybe the librarian can keep an eye on the research materials for a few minutes while the researcher is absent.

This advice goes, as well, for the staff. If they need to be relieved from their surveillance and reference duties for a while, they should be replaced before they depart. "I am going to the bathroom; I will be just a moment" is no reason to allow the staff to be short at the points of surveillance. It takes a thief only a few seconds to remove a plate from a book or a document from a folder. There is practically no such thing as too much surveillance.

A second security measure seems obvious: background checks for all who are allowed in.[5] But these take time and are not inexpensive, and many units have employees who have worked in the department for decades, before the need for such security checks became mandatory in many institutions. Whether background checks of these older employees should be done is at the discretion of the individual department head or administrator. On the other hand, if the library decides to do these checks, they should be done for *everyone*. There should be no exception.

The so-called CORI[6] checks are criminal reports that reveal records of criminal convictions, misdemeanors, felonies, and other criminal offenses, and they should be performed for current and prospective employees, contractors and subcontractors, other laborers, volunteers, interns, and anyone else who will be given access to the special collections. If the policy is that *everyone*, even the department head, is to be given this check, then no one should feel singled out and everyone must comply.

If someone fails this test, he should be told why he is not being considered for access (that is, why he is not being hired or kept on), but he must be given the right to challenge the decision. There might be some mitigating circumstance or some explanation why he failed. An applicant for a job could be flagged by his CORI check as having a blot on his record. He may claim that it is because someone stole his identity and that he is working to straighten out the record. The institution should not employ this person until he has gotten the record straight with the CORI reporting agency.

A third measure is also obvious: the use of sign-in sheets for patrons. New users should be asked to fill out all the forms necessary to identify them, locate them in the world, and learn of their research areas. This was discussed in chapter 5. It should be reiterated that all use statistics and patron information should be gathered and kept for a set period, determined by the library.

Another security measure is key control. Staff tend to come and go, and a policy of having departing employees turn in their keys may not be strictly enforced. It may be a good idea to have the keys changed on a regular schedule. This process is not terribly costly if the "key" is an electronic or magnetic swipe card that can be adjusted without the institution's literally having to change the locks.

The electronic keys can also be used to monitor staff movement through buildings and their attendance on the job, and can be combined with photo identification cards. The card can be programmed for several levels of security, allowing the bearer into some areas but restricting her from others. And they can be combined with systems that read irises, palms, or fingerprints (see McComb, "Library Security," http://libris design.org/docs/LibrarySecurity.pdf, p. 17).

Changing the locks and thus excluding from the department people who have had access for years may engender some discontent. But a written policy—on paper—should take some of the heat off and should show everyone the reasons for the decision. The policy should be clearly written, explaining the

AT UC RIVERSIDE, as one of my first acts as head of special collections, I changed all the locks and issued keys only to those who needed access to the department—which meant employees of the department. I convinced the head of the library that he did not need one, though a key was kept in a special locked box in the administration suite for emergency purposes. I had a long discussion with the head of the campus police department, and he was convinced that his department did not need a key. If something were discovered to be missing from special collections, no one on his staff would be a suspect if there were no key available to the police. If they needed to get into the department, a telephone tree told them whom to call, with a few people only a few minutes away. Likewise, the head of the fire department, accepting the same logic, said his unit did not need a key. If there were a fire, they would not spend any time trying to hunt up a key. They had more expeditious ways of entering the department.

decision to close the stacks to "outsiders," and it should be firmly and consistently applied.

As I noted earlier, staff are often the thieves, and sometimes not much can be done about it. Some measures, however, are helpful. First, all staff should be trained to look for signs that security has been compromised: missing items; department records that seem to have been tampered with;[7] furtive actions of colleagues, who may be in areas that they do not need to be in. The staff should also be counseled on how to notify their superiors when they spot something suspicious. It must be impressed on them that this is not "tattling" or "ratting on a colleague"; it is security, similar to the U.S. government's policy for confidential revelation of crimes.[8] Many institutions have what they call a "silent witness" form on which the suspicious activity is delineated and the person reporting remains confidential. People are often nervous or reticent about fingering their colleagues or friends, but they should be schooled in how to do this and trained that such theft or mutilation is a crime not merely against the library and its patrons but also against our cultural heritage.[9] It may also be useful to tell the employees that anyone knowledgeable about the crime who does not report it is a confederate to it and can also be found guilty if he remains silent about it.

Security for Patron Access

A CORI check combined with good staff training will go a long way toward reducing internal theft. But just as staff must be checked, so must patrons. A careful check of bags and coats should be done on the entrance to and departure from the department of everyone, even the staff and the department head.[10] The required use of lockers and coatracks (outside the secure area of the department where the collection is stored) for all staff—especially for containers or garments large enough to hold any library materials—is essential. And as mentioned earlier, all patrons should be carefully screened, and records of their use of department materials should be kept. At each visit, a patron must present photo identification, which should be matched with the picture(s) already

on file. This procedure may take the staff a little extra time, but it is a good means of increasing security.[11] And letters of recommendation from scholars may be required of researchers, though for libraries that serve a large public, this is impracticable.

When anyone enters or exits the library, a security staff person should record each movement. At the entrance, all bags should be checked, and all who enter should be required to sign in, giving their name and time of entry, and should be required to hang up their coats; lockers should be provided for their bags. At their exit, bags should again be checked, and patrons must sign out. These movements must be recorded in a security register, which should be kept in a security office for future consultation, if necessary. If the library requires identification badges for visitors, the use of these badges should be recorded, and the security staff must make sure these badges are returned when the visitor checks out. Also, some institutions require all staff to wear a photo-identification badge at all times when they are in the building. Guards checking in patrons should make sure each party signs his or her name legibly. The guard may be instructed to have the patron who signs an illegible name also print that name beside the signature.

It is essential that there be no places in the department to which a patron can go that are not under surveillance by a staff person. Every patron must always be where she can be seen. When a scholar requests the use of materials for the reading room, only a set number of books (maybe from one to five, depending on the library's policy) should be allowed at a time. If the patron is using manuscripts, only one folder at a time should be given out, even if the folder contains only a single item. (This regulation may be modified if a large number of folders all contain only one thing.) Every volume and every folder must be inspected before and after the patron uses it. If a volume has a defect of any kind, that should be noted, either in the cataloging record or on the call slip. If the book comes back with a defect that was not there when it went to the patron, the department head or some senior official should be notified, and perhaps the patron's papers should be checked. But if a librarian looks carefully through a book and notes defects before the patron gets it, then already-noted defects spotted when the book is returned cannot be blamed on the patron. The cataloging record should show what these defects are (broken spine, missing plates, writing in the volume). It takes time to do this, but it is a good security measure. This is why the rare book librarian must work closely with the catalogers to instruct them about what to put into bibliographic records for items in special collections. There is a place in the records for copy-specific information. A well-trained rare book cataloger will know what information belongs in the database. Good cataloging is part of good security.

If a folder has many manuscript pieces in it, they should be counted before and after use. In the last few years a method of checking has been written about: the use of sensitive scales to weigh manuscript materials before and after use.[12] Many scales on the market are sensitive to a fraction of a gram. If a patron removes anything from a folder, that folder will weigh less when it is returned than it did when it was given out. Even trying to replace a piece of paper with another will be detectable if the two pieces are not exactly the same weight. This method applies to books as well as to manuscripts. Also, when a librarian is checking the materials that a patron has used, the patron should not be let out of the reading room until the checking is done.

When a department is born and grows in the "historical" way described at the opening of chapter 5—one room is taken over and then other spaces are added on to it—the secure areas were originally not secure. The aim of high security is to protect these areas from the kinds of crime that this chapter is

about. To do so will entail a careful assessment of the physical structure of the department.

Making the Building Secure

Any point of entrance must be assessed: doors, transoms, windows, skylights, ducts, areas above dropped ceilings, dumbwaiters, elevator shafts, loading docks, and so forth. Every possible entrance to the department must be secured at all times and monitored when any (doors to the department, for instance) have to be accessible. Grates can be put over air conditioning vents, windows can have "decorative" metalwork placed over them,[13] ceilings can have metal plates put above tiles, and so on. Stephen Blumberg was a cat burglar, among other things. He knew how to hide in elevator shafts and above ceiling tiles. He was also an expert locksmith, and when he was caught, the house in Ottumwa, Iowa, where he stowed all his booty had shelves of books about lock-picking and all the tools and key blanks he needed to get through almost any locked door. He taught librarians and other institution security people that any space—big enough for a human being—that led into the rare book area needed to be secured and that key control was essential. Additionally, as I stated earlier in this chapter, it is a good idea to have all the locks changed periodically. It is worth repeating that if the keys are metal, changing locks can be expensive, but if a magnetic or electronic swipe card is used, this security measure can be relatively inexpensive.

Walls themselves can be points of entry. If the "historically" grown space has developed by the mere addition of a neighboring room, then that added room may be adjacent to a public area, and the wall between safe and public space could be no more than wallboard, easy to get through. Walls in rare book departments should be reinforced in some way, and all the aisleways in the department should be under surveillance when the facility is closed.

The physical space should have a vault area in which especially valuable materials are secured. If an intruder gets into the department, it might be impossible for him to get into a specially safe-

> **AT UC RIVERSIDE** a public reading room and the special collections department shared a wall that could easily have been breached. Also, in the basement of the library was one of several rooms that were commandeered to house rare materials because the department did not have enough space. When I took over the department, we found that the basement room, which of course had a locked door, was accessible from nonsecure sections of the basement via the space above the dropped ceiling tiles.

guarded area before a response team shows up. Further, entrance to the vault should be allowed only for personnel who must get into it. And entry should be by a means that allows the library to identify who was in there. In a department of, say, ten or fifteen staff, perhaps only two or three should have access to the vault. If a staff person who has the combination (or a key card that allows entrance) to the vault leaves the department permanently, the combination or electronic/magnetic code should be changed.

The department should have the minimum number of entry and exit ports. The fewer there are, the easier it is to monitor what comes in and goes out. Of course, fire exits must be available, but they should be carefully monitored, and they should have an exit-delay on them so that someone wanting to get out through an emergency exit will be detained for a set length of time before the door will open—with good planning that length of time will be enough to allow a staff person or guard to get to that exit.

The LLAMA (Library Leadership and Management Association) security guidelines discuss crime prevention through environmental design—the actual physical laying out of the facility in such a way as to enable detection of criminal behavior. The guidelines' list of recommendations is worth quoting in full:

a. Place windows overlooking sidewalks and parking lots.
b. Leave window shades open and partial interior night security lighting on.
c. Use passing vehicular traffic as a surveillance asset.
d. Create landscape designs that provide surveillance, especially in proximity to designated points of entry and opportunistic points of entry.
e. Use the shortest, least sight-limiting fence appropriate for the situation.
f. Use transparent weather vestibules at building entrances.
g. When creating lighting design, avoid poorly placed lights that create blind-spots for potential observers and miss critical areas. Ensure potential problem areas are well-lit: pathways, stairs, entrances/exits, parking areas, ATMs, phone kiosks, mailboxes, bus stops, storage areas, dumpster and recycling areas, etc.
h. Avoid too-bright security lighting that creates blinding glare and/or deep shadows, hindering the view for potential observers. Eyes adapt to night lighting and have trouble adjusting to severe lighting disparities. Using lower intensity lights often requires more fixtures.
i. Place lighting along pathways and other pedestrian-use areas at proper heights for lighting the faces of the people in the space (and to identify the faces of potential attackers).
j. Natural surveillance measures can be complemented by mechanical and organizational measures. For example, closed-circuit television (CCTV) cameras can be added in areas where window surveillance is unavailable. It is also suggested that CCTV cameras should also be placed in areas of vulnerable attacks that

THE SPECIAL COLLECTIONS department at UC Riverside's Rivera Library moved to a temporary facility during a renovation. The temporary facility had been a library that had open stacks and a fire escape door at the rear. Because the building had a fairly open floor plan, it would have been remotely possible (but doable) for someone to pass the secure barrier and get into the protected stacks, behind which was the fire escape door. We consulted with the fire department and were told that the fire door was required to be unlocked when the stacks were open to browsers. But state law said that the door could be locked and not be available for egress if the public were not allowed into that area of the library and if the area were never populated by more than five staff members. We were able to lock that door. Sometimes local laws determine the use of space and the security measures one can apply. In fact, librarians should know all local laws regarding how patrons must be treated, how buildings must be made safe, how theft is to be handled, and related issues.

are not near windows. Selection of the appropriate cameras and lenses is important and exterior cameras should be day-night cameras and in extremely dark areas it would be suggested to use cameras equipped with infrared lighting.

k. Use caution when planting shrubbery so as not to provide or obstruct the view of customers or staff by providing an opportunity for criminals to hide.[14]

This document also recommends that security system signage be prominently displayed to announce that the building is carefully secured (LLAMA, *Library Security Guidelines Document*, p. 22). Good security, it is clear, requires a careful analysis of all the physical features of the building and its site. Architects, designers, librarians, police and fire personnel, contractors, and others should be brought into this process.

Other elements of security, as Mark McComb points out, have to do with lighting, the placement of shrubbery around the building, and signage, all meant to make people safe. He says, "Landscaping elements should enhance security by deterring unwanted entry while not allowing criminals to conceal themselves from security personnel and CCTV systems" ("Library Security," p. 4). Signage warning drivers outside the facility as to where pedestrians walk is also a security measure. He adds,

> Vehicle control is important; a specified distance from the library building to unscreened vehicles and parking should be appropriately set. Various types of buffers and barriers should be evaluated to enhance the landscape design while still providing the appropriate protection. These buffering features could include walls, fences, trenches, plantings, trees, static barriers, sculptures, and street furniture. Vehicular entrances should be designed to prevent high speed approaches. ("Library Security," p. 4)

One common feature of a security system is a series of alarms. These can be excellent, though the response time for an alarm could be long enough to give a thief plenty of time to snatch and flee. And that could be a short time indeed. It could take a criminal under a minute to grab some treasure and be out of the facility. Some security systems have a timer on them to lock building exit doors for a few minutes once an alarm is set off. So if a thief grabs a book from the special collections department and gets to a back staircase that leads to a floor that can be exited from, the doors in that stairwell can be made to stay locked for, say, five minutes before the thief can get out of the building. In that time, someone checking monitors for all the stairwells might be able to see the culprit and notify the police. This sounds like a scene from a game of Cops and Robbers, but it could be an effective way to prevent a thief from escaping.

Alarms and ancillary surveillance systems can thwart theft. The alarms should be audible in the area that has been invaded and at the station to which the pictures are broadcast. Break-ins can be detected through sound, heat, light, and movement.

THE SPECIAL COLLECTIONS department at UC Riverside, many years ago, had motion detectors that spotted any movement throughout the department. When the department alarm was set for the night, the alarm system was activated, and movement activated a VCR (now it can be done using digital cameras) that captured on tape anything that was moving in the department. When we shut off the alarms in the morning when the department was reopened, we could check the numbers on the VCR recording machine to see if the tape had moved forward. Prominently placed cameras can also deter theft. I was once in a library that had large cameras in conspicuous places, with little blinking red lights on them. The librarian told me they were dummies—not real cameras, but big enough to fool your average thief. What about your above-average one? For only a small amount of additional resources that library could have had real cameras.*

*Mark McComb's publication has a section on dummy cameras, with no statement on whether they are effective or not ("Library Security," pp. 10–11).

Someone breaking a window, moving in a secured area, or even giving off body heat should be observable. For small investments, cameras and detectors can monitor huge areas. Pressure-sensitive mats and light beams that set off alarms if they are stepped on or broken may also be employed in areas that are hard to monitor with cameras and other detection devices.

Some libraries have video monitors at the reference desk—that is, at the desk where librarians sit to monitor patrons. The screens are linked to a system of closed-circuit cameras placed throughout the facility, and the person watching the screens is able to select any area she wishes to focus on, or she may allow the pictures to cycle from one camera to another. The system can also be broadcast to a central monitoring office—campus or city police, for example—if desired. How long the pictures should be kept is up to the librarians, but with the ability to store huge amounts of data in fairly small devices, it might be good to store these images for years.

McComb discusses the nature and types of cameras that are useful for surveillance. They can be fixed or able to pan, high-resolution or not, able to record in dim areas or requiring good lighting, sensitive to movement or not, wide or narrow angled (able to cover a large room or a narrow aisleway), with zoom or fixed lenses, in color or black and white, clearly visible in the room or fairly well hidden, covered with a plastic dome or not, and so on; and he also discusses the various kinds of monitors a library might get ("Library Security," pp. 18–20). A careful analysis of the physical plant, with respect to the placement of staff, patrons, stacks, work areas, and such, will help the staff decide what is best for each facility.

The cameras and other detectors should not be wired into any system; they should be wireless, run by batteries, so that if there were a power failure in the building, the system would still work. Batteries should be replaced regularly. Also, the system should be hooked up to the local police department so the notice of a breach in security could reach the right people, instantly. And if the librarians have been diligent, the police should already have been brought into the equation as allies, as described in chapter 1. During off hours, when the department is closed, the police and other security personnel in the library should be asked to walk past the department regularly to see if there is any activity taking place within. Any activity should be questioned, and the legitimacy of anyone's presence in the department when it is scheduled to be closed should be carefully checked.

> **ONE OF STEPHEN** Blumberg's tactics was to carry a folder containing handwritten notes. If he were apprehended in a rare book room, he would claim to be the professor whose ID he had stolen (and he would gladly show the ID) and say that he had been doing research in the department in the afternoon. He would say he had left his folder in the department and was there to retrieve it. He would show the folder to the person who caught him and make it clear that he had nothing belonging to the department with him. What he would not say was that he had already tossed rare materials out a window that he was able to open, that those materials were in nearby bushes, and that he would fetch them later that night.

With alarms, the department must of course have a good system that goes into effect when it is activated, usually from a keypad. Some systems are integrated with fingerprint readers. The keypad requires the entering of a code to set and to deactivate the system. Each person in the department who is authorized to set this system should have his or her own code number so that the individuals entering and exiting can be identified. In some libraries, there are security doors from one inner room to another, fully inside the secure perimeter of the library. Each door must be accessed by a card, so that each person's movements can be recorded. Further, if the keypad requires, say, a five-digit code, the pad itself should not have the numbers in the same position at all times. For instance, if the number a person enters is 1–2–3–4–5, someone observing may be able to see which numbers are pushed. The keypad should be shielded by little "walls" so that only the person hitting the keys can see which ones are being pressed, and the numbers should come up in random order so that the 1 may be in the lower center position one time and elsewhere the next. Such random-display keypads have been in use for decades.

Some companies today are touting Radio Frequency Identification (RFID), a method using small computer chips with signals that can be detected with the proper sensing device. McComb discusses their benefits:

> RFID solutions are being designed to improve library operational efficiency. This enhanced capability is provided by RFID tags which do not require line-of-sight to be read, so that books are actually handled less. The tag combines book identification and book security into one label, minimizing labeling time and cost. More than one book can be read at a time, speeding circulation. The tags can be placed on any type of media, including CDs, DVDs, and videocassettes. The RFID tags are read/write, providing flexibility in what is encoded. They can also be put into the patron cards, speeding up the process even more. Library staff can check out and check in several items simultaneously without having to locate and scan individual bar codes. ("Library Security," p. 15)

What McComb does not mention is that these chips have a short life. Simon Edwards and Mick Fortune, in their *Guide to RFID in Libraries*, skirt the issue. They say, "The 'chip' will normally have a projected life expectancy: usually measured in 'cycles' this will indicate how many read/write operations can be expected to be completed successfully before failure. Libraries should ask suppliers about chip life expectancy to ensure that their solution provides adequate cycles."[15] The website Technovelgy.com says that there are passive RFID tags that do not contain sources of power, but even these have limited longevity.[16] One salesman at an RFID firm told me that even the longest-lived tags have a life expectancy of about forty years. This will certainly not do for a special collections department that presumably will have many decades of life beyond that time. RFID is not the way to go for rare book departments.

One system used in many open-stacks libraries is "tattle tape"—a plastic, magnetic strip affixed to items (usually books, CDs, and DVDs) that sets off an alarm if it is not deactivated before being taken through the tattle-tape readers at the exit doors of the library. For the most part, this kind of detection system works well for a public or nonsecure library, but it would be tremendously costly to affix these tapes to hundreds of thousands of books in special collections. Also, they are bulky and could disfigure slender pamphlets. And theoretically, no book should be taken out of a rare book department, especially when staff are around to hear the alarm. So these tapes would not be effective most of the time. If the item is stolen after everyone has left the department, the alarm would rouse no one. They are simply not a good choice for a rare book department.[17]

Though not strictly a "security measure," a telephone tree is a useful tool for immediate action when a theft is discovered—especially if there is a break-in. First responders can call others to survey the scene to determine if anything has been taken. It might not be immediately apparent if the intruder has been successful, but someone familiar with the scene should be on hand as soon as possible after an alarm is activated. And it may be possible to have a security guard on duty all the hours the department is open. This coverage, of course, is a great expense, but it may be a fairly good form of security because of the psychological factor associated with the presence of a guard.

Sightlines should all be monitored, electronically when the building is open or closed, and as much physically when the building is open. That is, staff should be situated such that they can always see what all readers are doing in the reading room and what movement is taking place anywhere other people might be. Cameras monitoring all aisles and rows in the stacks and everywhere else should be observed by someone on the staff. Tying up equipment and staff to do such surveillance sounds expensive. And it is. But it is cheaper than replacing stolen or mutilated materials. It also sounds paranoid. And it is. But a healthy dose of paranoia can keep a collection safe.

Another security "action" previously mentioned, but worth restating here, is to keep all rare books and manuscripts in the department before and after they are cataloged. It is essential to keep unprocessed materials in the secure area of the department and have them cataloged there, if the cataloging unit allows for such a placement of one of its personnel.

Closely related to security is inventorying the collection—sometimes called "shelf reading." This activity is time-consuming and therefore expensive, but it must be done. Its two purposes are (a) to make sure every item has been properly shelved, for a mis-shelved book is nearly impossible to locate and is therefore practically unusable, and (b) to identify missing books and manuscripts. The department must keep an up-to-date shelf list, in call-number order, registering every item that should be on the shelves.

Security during Construction, Renovation, and Moving

Moving a special collections department is a complex business, as we saw in chapter 2. I wish to expand on the advice given there by looking particularly at security during the move.

Libraries are at their most vulnerable during construction, remodeling, or moving. Stephen Blumberg was keenly plugged into library literature, and he knew which libraries were bringing in outside workers for these activities. At one institution he reportedly hired students to dress like workers; he paid them to load up boxes of rare books and carry them out to his van. Whether this is apocryphal or not, it could happen, especially if the special collections department is being moved from its present secure place to anywhere else or if workers are in the vicinity to do reconstruction work. When a library is planning for any kind of cataclysmic activity like the moving of a collection or remodeling of the facility, extra security should be figured into the budget. Also, the library will want to announce good news to the public—that the library has been given such and such a gift or has raised money to do a certain activ-

ity. But in the announcement, the library should be careful not to reveal too much information, such as when the activity will take place, what companies will be (or have been) hired to do the work, whether the library will need to move and to where, and so forth. It is like announcing, "We will be exposing our rare materials on this date." Knowledge that the library will move is fine to announce, but the actual moving details should be kept secure. Even the staff need not be told all the information, or, if they are, they should be told how confidential such information should be kept. Some institutions may even go so far as to have the employees sign confidentiality agreements.

When the move or the construction is under way, staff should be augmented by the extra security personnel just mentioned, and staff themselves, not able to perform their regular duties during the disruption, should be on hand for the undertakings and should be trained to look for security weaknesses during the operations. In the selection of vendors to help with the move, the library should do background checks on the companies who apply for the job. Librarians should consult former customers of these companies and should analyze carefully the techniques these movers will use, all of which should be spelled out in their proposals. A simple thing like using locked plastic crates to transport the books or large book trucks that are securely plastic-wrapped for the move will be important. Insurance for the project should be carefully worked out: Who pays for it? What does it cover? How long is it in effect? A full inventory should be done before and immediately after the move to see if everything that was identified as being on the shelves before the move is still there after.

Architects or project designers should also be carefully screened. Most will understand why such stringent security measures must be in place. The staff should work closely with the architects to show them where the collection needs the greatest security and may offer advice on how to achieve it. Responsible architects will let such information guide them in their planning. Some will want their buildings to be monuments to their brilliance as designers. But security of the collection, in the long run, is far more important than a fabulous monument that is porous to theft.

If the library is moving to a temporary facility, this space should be designed with security foremost in mind. What the interim facility looks like while the library is in it temporarily is far less important than how safe it is. And again, detailed information about the move—when and to where—should be kept fairly confidential.

When Stephen Blumberg was actively plying his trade, he was not the only book thief on the market. In fact, there is almost always one of them out there, or more, and librarians must be constantly on the alert. By checking with RBMS, librarians can generally be informed about what to look for (or, perhaps more properly, whom to look for) with security in mind. Photographs of known book thieves are available from the FBI or local police. Many a rare book department will get these photos and post them for staff. When Blumberg was nearing release from prison, many rare book departments posted pictures of him in sight of the staff. It is good that the staff be familiar with the faces of those who can do them harm.

Marking Books for Security

In the original RBMS discussions about marking books, one significant issue arose, as it still does when

> **IN THE 1980S** I was chair of the Curators and Conservators Discussion Group for RBMS. One of the topics the group considered at length was marking books for security. A number of issues were raised, and the results of that long meeting had repercussions in RBMS. Eventually the section issued a statement on marking books, which is an appendix to the *Guidelines for the Security of Rare Books, Manuscripts, and Other Special Collections.* The appendix was approved at the American Library Association's Midwinter Meeting in January 2006, but it had been in front of RBMS members for several years before this.

such a discussion begins: if you mark up a book, you are reducing its value. The logical response is fairly straightforward: when a book is on a library shelf, its monetary value is immaterial. Its value to the library lies in the information that the item can offer to a user. Libraries are not in the business of bookselling. They acquire items not to sell them for a profit (certainly not for a loss!), but to add to the store of knowledge their patrons can access. So the moment a book enters a library collection, the only value it has is intellectual.

Certainly, the item could be worth a great deal of money, but if the library does something to the book to reduce its monetary value, that should not be an issue. If the library does something to it to reduce its intellectual value, that is wrong.

A pristine copy of a library book, with no markings, if stolen, may be sold for whatever its intrinsic value is. But a copy that is marked, indelibly, with the name of the library and other information (a) will trigger suspicion on the part of anyone to whom it is offered for sale and (b) will have lost a considerable amount of its monetary value. A thief will also know, presumably, that an honest bookseller or collector will question the institution whose name is on the book to determine whether the book has been legitimately withdrawn from the collection. So marking books in an obvious way can deter theft.

There is also the marking that is undetectable—that is, marking that cannot easily be seen and that can be used to facilitate the return of stolen items. Invisible marking can be done with invisible ink or by putting ownership information in the volume or on the manuscript in a place known only to the librarian. For instance, the library may use its initials as a marking scheme. So John Smith University might place a small pencil dot under the last printed *J* in a book, followed by another nearly invisible pencil dot under the next *S*, and another dot under the next *U*. Librarians can designate other places to put the marks or other letters or numbers that only the staff know of. If a stolen book is recovered, these secret marks will confirm ownership.

Other libraries use a microstamp, which costs little and creates an impression on the page that is truly invisible. The impression is so small that only a high-powered lens can reveal it. The stamp, made of steel, can carry the logo and name of the institution on its tip. The image can be impressed into paper, leather, vellum, wood, and other such surfaces, but it will not work on glass or cloth. If the library chooses to put fifty such stamps onto the title page, no one will see them because they are so small. They can be placed in some determined spot in every volume (e.g., under the number on page 5 of every book, or inside the bowl of the first lowercase *b* on page 3). This kind of marking, like the pencil dots, is invisible and will assist in retrieving books that have been stolen once they have surfaced and the librarian has been informed.[18] (Making the librarian aware is part of the reporting system discussed in the following section, "Dealing With and Reporting Theft.")

Hence, two kinds of marking are possible: blatant and secret. The first deters theft, the second helps in recovery. Both should be employed. The key to effective marking is that no information should be obscured by it. Naturally, the invisible marks will not cover up anything a researcher needs to discover in a book or manuscript. But the obvious marks may cover information if they are carelessly applied. The visible marks can be done tastefully: in the lower margin of the title page and selected other pages in the volume; in the gutters of certain pages; on the backs of plates, which are particularly vulnerable; and so forth.

If there are plates in the book, marking them on the front or back in a lower margin may not be enough, because a thief can remove the plate and then cut off the stamp without damaging the image in the plate. One standard practice for many libraries is to stamp plates on the rear in the middle of the image. There is no way to remove the stamp without damaging the plate. Unscrupulous thieves may steal valuable pictures or maps, mat them or back them with paper or cloth or put them into fine frames (or do both), making the library's marking fairly inaccessible. If a dealer or private party offers the rare book department such a framed piece, the librarian must insist that it be removed from its frame to determine whether it has a library stamp on it. A pasted-down lining could obscure the stamp and would make the item suspect. Buying such a piece—any valuable image or map, chart, or broadside—without being able to inspect it to see whether it has been taken from a library book or collection is tantamount to encouraging such depredations. If librarians and collectors refuse to buy such pieces, the market for them could dry up. But this is not likely to happen because serious collectors could look the other way if they are offered something they strongly want for their collections.

The point here is that all plates in books, especially those with high monetary value, should be indelibly marked in an area that makes it impossible to remove the mark without ruining the piece. And it is possible to mark just about anything such that the marking does not obscure information a scholar might profit from. So perhaps marks should not conceal watermarks, inscriptions in the book, text of any kind, pictures, or decorative elements such as one might find on endpapers. Stamps along the edges of books are difficult to remove, identify the institution or collection they are from, are easy to see, and deter theft.[19]

One practice that some libraries use, rather than stamping the books themselves, is to insert a long bookmark into a volume and put the call numbers and library's name onto that. But that is asking for trouble, because once these bookmarks are removed, the book has nothing to deter a thief from taking it. The practice of marking books on anything that is removable is foolish. This goes for bookplates as well as bookmarks, for the plates can easily be soaked off, leaving no trace of the identity of the former owner (though a trace of a removed bookplate may be left). It is worth repeating that all marks should be done with indelible and nonacidic ink, should identify the owning institution, and should reduce the monetary value of the item. This last is obviously not the primary aim, but it is a useful by-product of the marking.

Again, the marks should clearly identify the institution; they should not be generic like "Rare Book Room." The RBMS security document recommends using the Library of Congress institution-identification symbols, which consist of three elements: (1) the abbreviated name of the state the library is in, (2) an abbreviation of the city, and (3) an abbreviation

ONE OF THE strange and infuriating practices that Stephen Blumberg employed was to remove all traces of ownership from all the books he stole. He soaked off bookplates, scissored off rubber-stamped names, abraded book edges to remove edge stamps, and erased all penciled-in marks that identified the original owning institution. When the FBI set up a warehouse in Omaha, Nebraska, to which all the books from the Ottumwa, Iowa, house were moved, agents were determined to return as many of the items as they could to the former owners. But hardly a single identification mark remained on any of the books. And the frustrating thing was that investigators knew many of the institutions that Blumberg hit because he saved the bookplates. Bookplates are removable. Relying solely on them to identify ownership is practically senseless.

of the institution's name. For instance, the American Antiquarian Society's code is MWA (Massachusetts, Worcester, American). Not everyone knows how to read these codes, and there are thousands of them, most of which are not user friendly. They will work, but any other means of identifying will also do. "U of I" can refer to the University of Illinois, Iowa, or Idaho. This abbreviation is too generic.

A point made earlier is relevant in this context: cataloging records for books in special collections should contain copy-specific information—notes that distinguish the very copy the cataloger is creating a record for. This kind of information is just as valuable as are library markings, for it can help a librarian retrieve a stolen item.

If the department deaccessions a marked item, staff should leave the identification marks where they are and add another, at whatever place is appropriate, that says, "Withdrawn from _____," possibly with a penned-in date of deaccession as well. Records of deaccessioned books should be kept in an accessible file. An unscrupulous thief could have such a rubber stamp made up. If a librarian is offered a book with a "withdrawn" stamp on it, he would be courteous and wise to contact the former owner of the volume to verify that the stamp is legitimate and that the book was truly deaccessioned from its

former home. Also, a document from the deaccessioning library may accompany the volume. If this document remains with the book, the next institution to which it is offered may not have to contact the former owner. Also, the RBMS guidelines suggest that (a) an item should be marked immediately upon acquisition, not during later processing, which takes place after cataloging (unmarked items sitting in unprocessed backlogs can be stolen with little or nothing to prove that they are from a particular library's collection), and (b) if the volume has any removable parts (plates, illustrations, broadsides in a portfolio, bookmarks), each should be marked.

Dealing With and Reporting Theft

The Association of College and Research Libraries (ACRL), in conjunction with the Rare Books and Manuscripts Section of ACRL, published its *ACRL/ RBMS Guidelines Regarding Security and Theft in Special Collections.*[20] The section on theft is excellent, and every library—especially rare book departments—should have in place a document that mandates for the institution what the ACRL/RBMS document suggests. Or each department should use the ACRL guidelines. However the library plans to deal with theft, its guiding document should spell out what steps are to be taken. As ACRL/RBMS says, "An institutional plan for dealing with a theft will ensure a quick and well-organized response."

When an item in the collection cannot be found, even after a sustained, thorough search, the librarian should suspect theft. And the librarian should not spend a lot of time trying to verify this suspicion. The longer the time spent verifying the loss, the more time the thief has to sell the stolen item. It is better to report a theft and then find the item that was missing than to wait until it is too late to notify potential buyers of the loss. Unfortunately, learning that a book is missing is not usually a soon-after-the-theft occurrence. If no one requests the use of a book, its absence may not be known for decades. That is why an important activity in all special collections is shelf reading, as explained in chapter 2.

ONE LIBRARY BOUGHT a collection of manuscript pieces (leaves and fascicles) at auction. When the lot arrived, the librarians realized that it contained several pieces that had been stolen from their department about fifty-five years earlier. A few of the recovered pieces had shelflist cards on which were penciled notes explaining that pages from particular manuscripts were missing, and one shelflist-card note was dated in the 1950s. But other items in the lot also came from the same library, and there was no record at all, anywhere in the online or paper catalogs, that the items were known to be missing. A shelf-read would have revealed decades earlier that the items were not where they were supposed to be. The importance of regular shelf-reads cannot be overstated.

At the point of learning of the theft, the librarian must quickly notify the book world of it. ACRL/RBMS lists the following organizations to contact:

- Antiquarian Booksellers' Association of America
- ACRL/RBMS Security Committee
- Art Loss Register
- DeRicci Project
- International League of Antiquarian Booksellers
- International Antiquarian Mapsellers Association "Missing and Stolen Map Database"
- Interpol
- Museum Security Network
- Professional Autograph Dealers Association
- Society of American Archivists

One might add to this the list for the ABA (the Antiquarian Booksellers' Association in the United Kingdom).

Most of the addresses and contact points listed at the ACRL/RBMS website are still current, but all the organizations on the list have current information on their own websites. Rare book librarians should keep an up-to-date listing of these sites handy for quick dissemination of information. And "quick" is one of the keys to success in locating stolen books and manuscripts. These organizations and people can effi-

ciently spread the word of a theft, but the librarian should also contact all local dealers—perhaps within a one-hundred-mile radius. These are where a thief wanting to make a sale expeditiously will go. So it is useful to have handy a list of all local dealers with current phone numbers. In chapter 1 I discussed "knowing the dealers." Here is a good reason to do so: if they are the librarian's friends, dealers will do whatever they can to help the institution get back its lost materials.

As all this indicates, one absolutely essential thing should be done: notify the world as soon as possible. It might even be appropriate, with the assistance of the institution's administration, attorney, and public relations department, to go to the press. The more people who know of the crime, the more eyes are out there looking for the stolen goods. A single person at the institution should be designated to speak for the library, so all queries from outside go to one person with a consistent story. The institution may wish to issue a press release. If so, it should be carefully written, revealing only the information that the public needs to know.

With the loss of items from the collection, insurance policies may come into play, so it will be useful—maybe essential—to have an appraisal done of the loss. If the items are valuable enough, bringing in a professional appraiser or an expert bookseller is important. The librarian can do her own appraisal, of course, but having an outside expert corroborating her judgment may be required by the insurance company.

Naturally, the librarians will want to unravel the mystery. That is, they will want to know who the culprit is. Good circulation records may help, as noted earlier in this chapter. All paperwork regarding library users should be consulted to see if the stolen material can be linked to a particular patron or patrons. Checks should be done quickly on the security system and the holders of keys or swipe cards (or both). Any video revealing the aisle in the stacks where the missing book was should be checked. The staff should be interviewed, individually and together, about the missing item and potential thieves. Everyone should be suspect, and though this stance is draconian, such suspicion may prove fruitful if the theft is from within. Staff should be

ONE CAN UNDERSTAND a library's reticence at revealing that rare books have been stolen from its collection, especially from one that relies on the largesse of donors. Who would give money to an institution that spends it on expensive books, only to have those volumes disappear with thieves? One famous case of a library's not revealing to anyone that some of its great treasures had been stolen—and not responding to those who tried to notify the library— is that of the John Crerar Library in Chicago. The story is too long to recount here, though it has been admirably recorded by Jennifer S. Larson.* It is a good story, and it is instructive in that it reinforces to all in the rare book profession the importance of expeditious notification of stolen books.

*See Jennifer S. Larson, "An Enquiry into the Crerar Library Affair," AB/ Bookman's Weekly (January 22 and March 12, 1990); rpt. in Traditions and Culture of Collecting: Articles by and about Collectors, Librarians, and Booksellers, available at Jeremy Norman's History of Science.com (www.historyofscience.com/articles/ howell-larson-crerar.php). The story is worth reading in its entirety, along with the follow-up pieces at the same site by Jake Chernofsky and others, commenting on Larson's article. The present volume is about the rare book world. Those in it should be familiar with the great tales of that world; they should know the Warren Howells / Crerar Library story. Along with the Blumberg tale that has appeared throughout this chapter, the Crerar Library experience is an education in itself.

reminded of the importance of colleague surveillance and the existence of a confidential reporting policy. The staff should be kept abreast of all activities and any progress that is being made in the investigation. And a full record should be kept of all the efforts that are put forth in the process.

ARCL/RBMS also has a section on what to do if someone sees a theft in progress. That witness should immediately get another witness, call the library's LSO or the institution's security office (if the institution permits such a notification), try to capture the theft or mutilation on camera (many cell phones have this capacity), and keep the suspect in the library until appropriate backup personnel arrive. According to the guidelines,

> If there is probable cause that a theft has occurred, the appropriate library staff should request that the police officer place the suspect under arrest. (Laws regarding grounds for arrest vary from state to state, and library staff should know the relevant state laws.) If there is evidence of theft, (e.g., materials hidden on the suspect's person), one should not agree to the suspect's release in return for the suspect's assurances that he or she will return to face charges. If the officer will not make an arrest, attempt to persuade the officer to detain the suspect until the officer can verify his/her identity and place of residence.

One additional bit of advice comes from the Blumberg arrest at the University of California, Riverside: if it is possible, the officer in charge of the situation should arrange for the suspect to be fingerprinted. Through fingerprinting Blumberg was recognized at the University of Washington to be the same person who had been caught at UC Riverside. Also, all who are involved in the event should be asked to write out a record of what they saw and heard while it is still fresh in their minds. These documents "may be needed later, especially if the case is prosecuted. Any materials the suspect has already turned back in should be immediately retrieved and inspected for loss or damage" (ACRL/RBMS).

If a case of theft does make it to the courts, the institution and its attorneys should be as closely allied to the prosecution as they can be. ACRL/RBMS says,

> After the perpetrator is apprehended and brought to trial, the institution should establish lines of communication with the prosecution throughout the process of adjudication. This is particularly important if a plea-bargain and restitution are involved, since the institution may need to submit an account of damages. It is advisable for a representative to be present during the trial and especially during the sentencing phase, at which point the institution may wish to make a statement. This

statement should refer to the seriousness of the crime, the damage to the cultural record, and its impact on the institution and its users. Such statements have been known to influence judges to impose harsher punishments.

And the institution should ask the prosecution to seek the harshest possible penalties. The prosecution should be given a full accounting of the efforts that the library personnel have expended in learning about the theft or mutilation, what activities this investigation triggered in the department and the institution, what monetary loss was sustained, if any (especially if the items were never found or were returned damaged in some way), and so forth. The penalties imposed may reflect a great deal of staff time and the monetary value of the losses (e.g., if conservation work needs to be done or if a replacement copy must be obtained), and any other outlay of efforts and resources. It may be useful to have a professional appraiser or specialist bookseller offer an appraisal of the goods in question. There can hardly be too much punishment for the perpetrator and too much compensation for the institution.

If the damaged or stolen items must be confiscated for the trial, the library should make sure they are kept in a secure place and are returned as soon as possible after the trial. If the items have been sold, all efforts should be made to find out who possesses them, and legal paths should be opened for their return to the library. Finally, ACRL/RBMS states, "Careful records of the stolen and returned items and all other aspects of the theft should be kept in perpetuity."

There can hardly be too much security. Librarians and all others in the rare book world should know how to identify breaches in security and know what to do about them—before anything untoward happens and after. They should be familiar with all kinds of security devices and activities and should adhere as closely as possible to the recommendations made here. Our cultural heritage needs to be protected, and security in our rare book libraries is one way to do so.

Forgeries, Fakes, and Facsimiles

In the realm of security, one overarching concept is that libraries—especially special collections—must not be stolen from or taken advantage of to their detriment. They must be ever vigilant so that their resources are not sapped by illegal or unethical actions. This applies, of course, to the kinds of things this chapter has dealt with thus far, but it also applies to ways that people with criminal intent might try to cheat the department out of its money. Purveying forgeries and fakes could be a means of foisting on a rare book department—for a high price—something that is not what it purports to be. Librarians must always be on the lookout for these things.

FORGERIES

Forgeries are copies made to look like genuine items, usually with fraudulent intent. A pricey broadside can be forged using photographic reproduction, paper that looks like that of the original, and basic carbon-and-oil–based ink. Forgeries can also be made by hand, especially of written texts but also of ones that were originally printed. And, of course, forgeries can be in manuscript form if the original was also a manuscript. Even engraved texts can be forged, either with another engraved plate or by hand if the forger is skilled enough. The problem with this is that an engraving produces a raised text, with debossed reverse, and a forgery done by hand will be planographic unless a way can be devised to make the forged surface the same as the engraved one.

The art of forgery has been around for centuries, and people in the rare book world should know about forged materials: what ones are "out there," what signs to look for that indicate that an item is not genuine, what things are likely to be forged, what tests can be done to corroborate suspicions of spuriousness, and so forth. As with all other topics in this book, a vast literature exists about forgery and its detection. One often-heard maxim is that as the forgers get increasingly sophisticated, those working on detection must keep pace.

Forgers have many motives, a few of which are to receive monetary gain, to discredit an enemy, to carry out a prank, or "to support or refute complex philosophical and religious doctrines."[21] Whatever their motives, their methods have become more and more sophisticated as technology has offered increasingly sophisticated methods of copying and printing. Even in letterpress printing, photopolymer plates can be generated from images created on computers and printed in relief, leaving a three-dimensionality in the sheet that perfectly mimics that of printing from metal type. And thanks to sophisticated photocopying machines, some forgeries are so close to the originals that they are exceptionally difficult to detect. Anyone working in the rare book field should be suspicious of any item (broadside, letter, pamphlet, book, drawing, or anything else that comes through the door) that could be forged.

It is easier to forge a document or broadside than it is to forge a book—primarily because of the length of the book. In the time it takes a forger to make a two-hundred-page book, he could make two hundred broadsides (and not have to fake the binding), so if the reason for the forgery is monetary, the shorter the piece, the easier it is to make, and the more money the forger can bring in.

Detecting Forgeries

Several red flags should go up for a bookseller, a collector, or a special collections librarian when a possible forgery appears. Lack of provenance is one flag. Also, as W. Thomas Taylor warns,

> The first piece in the pattern is a realization that an item that has been, and by rights should be, extremely rare is suddenly, shall we say, less rare. It is a matter of instinct and judgment to determine where the line should be drawn between the merely unusual and the highly improbable.[22]

That is, if an exceptionally rare item appears, the potential buyer should require the dealer to provide incontrovertible and tangible provenance information on it. According to Taylor, forgery should be suspected because "(1) the number of copies able to be located will have increased in recent times, with no convincing explanation for this increase; (2) they will bear no direct evidence of prior ownership; and

(3) the first traceable owner of those copies able to be located will be the same" ("Provenance," p. 4). He points out how difficult it is to learn these facts about any item, but calls to specialist dealers, searches in auction and other book-sale records, and consultations with librarians and collectors may reveal one or all of these circumstances.

Forgeries, of course, can be detected in many other ways, including by using microscopes (to examine paper, for instance), cyclotrons (to examine ink), and handwriting experts (to identify false handwriting), by trying to determine printing methods, and so forth. Forgeries made on color copiers may be detectable if the machines used are manufactured by particular companies. As Wilbert de Vries explains, "Although modern printers are distinguished by the label their manufacturers give them, the insides aren't that different from one another. This is because their print engines are made by only a few companies, such as Toshiba, Canon, and Ricoh. It is the engine that has its own identity that can be traced." De Vries also says,

> Sources familiar with the printer industry confirm this built-in security is in fact a unique number that is printed on every color page. The code, in yellow, can be printed on a line as thin as 0.1 millimeter.
>
> With help from manufacturers like Canon, authorities can gather information about the printer used in counterfeit crimes. The number tells them in which country a specific printer has been delivered, and to what dealer. The dealer then can lead them to the local computer store where the printer was sold.[23]

Bibliographic evidence of various kinds can be used to detect forgeries, as John Carter and Graham Pollard proved with their examination of textual evidence and typefaces (among other things) in their exposure of Thomas Wise and Harry Buxton Forman (see sidebar below).[24]

The present text is not the place to expatiate on the larger world of forgeries and detection. The main point here is that people dealing with library materials should approach certain kinds of items with some skepticism and a cautious mind, and should consult experts if a suspicious item is offered to them.

FAKES

If an existing book or broadside, pamphlet, or illustration is forged, there is an original to copy from. If there is no original, but a spurious piece is created, the result is a fake, not a copy of anything. The so-called Salamander Letter discovered by Mark Hoffmann, which exposed Mormonism to ridicule,[25] was a fake, not a forgery, in that no original existed. It was a fabrication by Hoffmann. Likewise, Konrad Kujau's famous fake, the Hitler Diaries, was not based on an original, but was his own creation.[26]

And James Macpherson's "translations" of the Scots Gaelic poet Ossian turned out to be Macpherson's own creations—quite imaginative and literarily adept fakes.[27] Everyone in rare books should be on guard for these kinds of materials.

A collector or librarian eager to get an important piece may be blinded by the fact that the item has no logical provenance, may be poorly produced, or may not stand up to any other kind of scrutiny as to its genuineness. As Larry McMurtry writes, "The urge to collect—or, more basically, to *acquire*—is deeply

---

AS I HAVE previously mentioned, those in the milieu of special collections must know about the great stories in this field. We have already explored the tale of Stephen Blumberg and his thefts. The story of Thomas J. Wise is equally appropriate here, not only as part of the lore of the profession but also, and more important, as a means of elucidating some of the now-classical methods of detection. The case, presented in brief here, should be part of the education of everyone dealing with rare books.

Wise (1859–1937) was one of the most revered bibliographers of the nineteenth and early twentieth centuries. He published excellent bibliographies on "Tennyson, Swinburne, Landor, Wordsworth, Coleridge, Ruskin, the Brownings, the Brontës, Shelly and Conrad,"* and was the scholar to consult with respect to these and many other authors.

The collection of first editions hit a feverish peak in the nineteenth century, with firsts of the great authors commanding "collectors' prices." When a new first was discovered—an item that preceded what up to then had been considered the first edition of a work— a sensation was created, and

collectors and booksellers avidly sought copies of these new finds. When certain nineteenth-century pamphlets began to turn up in the late 1920s and early '30s—pamphlets that were quite early printings of the works of well-known writers—a good deal of suspicion was generated on the rare book market.

The long and fascinating story boils down to this: Wise and an accomplice, Harry Buxton Forman, had fabricated a long series of fakes that purported to be "pre-firsts"—that is, pamphlets containing the texts of important and eminently collected authors and dating before the known dates of the works' true first-edition appearances. Two young scholars, John Carter and Graham Pollard, through extensive research, in 1934 revealed the hoaxes to the public in their overly modestly titled exposé, *An Enquiry into the Nature of Certain Nineteenth Century Pamphlets* (see note 24 at the end of this chapter).

Carter and Pollard looked at the paper Wise used for the pamphlets and found that much of it was made from esparto grass—not commercially available at the time of the dates on many of the fakes. They also determined that the typeface used for many was Clay's Long

Primer Number 3, a proprietary font created after the date on many of the pamphlets. And they studied the texts themselves. Some of the pamphlets had versions that matched later, revised editions of the authors, so they couldn't have been printed *before* the date on the true firsts. Finally, the lack of clear provenance on all the pamphlets threw the whole lot under suspicion. This thoroughly and scientifically researched study proved beyond a doubt that many of the pamphlets were fakes. And in every instance in which a source could be determined of the appearance of the pamphlets, Wise's name came up. Carter and Pollard's work was the death knell for Wise's prominence as a trusted bibliographer, and though at first he denied the charges, he soon went silent, dying in ignominy in 1937.

To anyone dealing in rare books, the story is educational in its revelation of the world of fakes and forgers, its scientific examination of the objects in question, and its lucid presentation of the research methods and the exposé of the hoax. It is a story well worth reading.

*See "Thomas James Wise," Wikipedia, http://en.wikipedia.org/wiki/Thomas _James_Wise.

atavistic and almost always overrides rationality. Few of those afflicted with the need to acquire want to slow things down by asking awkward questions when a chance to get something [extraordinary] comes along" (italics in original).[28]

I have just mentioned that many fakes have no provenances. That is, there is no accompanying information that shows them as having been around for as long as purported. That is the case with almost all the Thomas Wise and Harry Buxton Forman fakes. But librarians should be doubly wary when an item comes along with too much provenance. Forged signatures and dates, fake bookplates, and even contrived correspondence could seem to corroborate the authenticity of an item, when the proof itself is fake. Fakes live in a slippery world, with slippery fakers, and caution, suspicion, and scientific forensics may be our best protections. We must not become maniacal about such things, but a solid level of thoughtful *mistrust* can never hurt.

FACSIMILES

As Wikipedia explains,

> A facsimile (from Latin *fac simile* ['make alike'], a spelling that remained in currency until the late 19th century) is a copy or reproduction of an old book, manuscript, map, art print, or other item of historical value that is as true to the original source as possible. It differs from other forms of reproduction by attempting to replicate the source as accurately as possible in terms of scale, color, condition, and other material qualities. For books and manuscripts, this also entails a complete copy of all pages; hence an incomplete copy is a "partial facsimile."[29]

As this definition says, the aim of a facsimile is to be a copy that looks exactly like the original. Sometimes the creator of this copy can even find paper or vellum that mimics the original. With photography and scanning, quite accurate images can be reproduced for written or pictorial, black-and-white or colored texts. Generally such reproductions are identified as such in their own pages, but it is possible to create a facsimile of such accuracy that it could pass as an original, right down to the binding—in which case it

could be passed off as genuine and would merit the status of a forgery. People in the book world should be keen to this possibility and should try to ascertain the authenticity of any item presented to them.

■ ■ ■

There cannot be "too much" security. People with evil intentions are "out there," and when they get "in here," librarians need to do everything in their power to protect their collections. It should be added that booksellers are just as vulnerable as librarians are— even more so if they have open shops with books available for browsing on their shelves. Even private collectors, especially those who like to share their holdings with others, are exposing their collections to various kinds of depredation and should be aware of the issues this chapter has covered. Also, the lessons to be learned from close scrutiny of potential purchases are themselves important for anyone dealing with special collections materials.

Some of the issues raised in this chapter involve asking people to obey regulations, reveal information about themselves, show the contents of their bags and purses, and so forth. Many may see these actions as invading their privacy or making them act in ways they may not wish to. These and many other legal issues are raised in the operation of a special collections department. Chapter 8 looks at these.

NOTES

1. Because security is gained through a broad scope of actions, some of what will be presented in this chapter will overlap with information given elsewhere in this book. This duplication is fine because the material presented in this chapter must all be said here, and one cannot hear too much about security. One way to protect the collection is to keep it in good condition. Although not traditionally considered a form of security, physical preservation is, in fact, a way to make the collections "secure" from damage. The actions to prevent the deterioration of the collection are commonly considered under the rubric of preservation and conservation, activities that will be addressed in chapter 12.

2. An extensive literature on Stephen Carrie Blumberg's thefts exists, so much, in fact, that it is superfluous to list them. A look at any search engine on the Web will turn up enough information for days of reading. The main point here is not so much what he did as it is what the outcome was from what he did and how to prevent such depredations from happening again.

3. See David Zeidberg, "'We Have Met the Enemy . . .': Collection Security in Libraries," *Rare Books & Manuscripts Librarianship* 2.1 (Spring 1987): 19–26.

4. Mark McComb, "Library Security" (N.p.: Libris Design, 2004), http://librisdesign.org/docs/Library Security.pdf. "The publication is provided through the Libris Design Project [www.librisdesign.org], supported by the U.S. Institute of Museum and Library Services under the provisions of the Library Services and Technology Act, administered in California by the State Librarian."

5. "Allowed in" refers to those who are employed at the institution. One can simply assume that *no* outside person would be allowed into the stacks.

6. The acronym CORI stands for Criminal Offender Record Information. The Massachusetts website explaining this check says, "It is a record of your Massachusetts criminal history, including any time you were arraigned in court on a criminal charge, no matter what the final outcome of the charge was" (see www.masslegalhelp.org/cori/applying -for-jobs).

7. At a university in the Midwest, a night manager whose job it was to close the library at 2 a.m. took not only the books he wanted but also their acquisition records, the catalog cards if they had been cataloged (this was before computer databases), the records of the library proving that the items had been paid for, and so on. He left nearly no trace of the items he stole. He was caught only when a professor and a librarian consulted with one another about a book the library had ordered for the professor and the librarian remembered having received. It is possible that a canny employee could tamper with online records in the same way that the manager tampered with the paper ones.

8. The federal government has what it calls "Confidentiality of Suspicious Activity Reports" (see www .federalregister.gov/regulations/1550-AC26/ confidentiality-of-suspicious-activity-reports), implemented especially for banking activities, but revelatory of the fact that a system of colleague surveillance is important. Although the federal government has implemented these Suspicious Activity Reports to "identify individuals, groups and organizations involved in fraud, terrorist financing, money laundering, and other crimes" (see http:// en.wikipedia.org/wiki/Suspicious_activity_report), libraries should have their own formal policies— perhaps on paper—to advise employees of what to do if they see suspicious activities in their departments.

9. When Stephen Blumberg was being prosecuted, book theft had traditionally been looked on as not much of a crime, and many a book thief was lightly punished and let off with a small fine or a warning. Blumberg's prosecuting attorney, appropriately named Linda Reade, took a stance that changed book theft prosecution henceforward: she said that Blumberg was stealing our cultural heritage.

10. The LLAMA guidelines say, "The program should . . . include everyone using the library, including staff of every category, board members, volunteers, contract and construction workers, interns, researchers, maintenance staff and office visitors, without exempting any library user from security controls." See Library Leadership and Management Association (LLAMA), *Library Security Guidelines Document*, June 27, 2010, p. 15, www.ala.org/llama/sites/ala.org .llama/files/content/publications/LibrarySecurity Guide.pdf.

11. One of Blumberg's ploys was to show the campus identification card of a professor from the Midwest. He had stolen the card, and he used the professor's identity innumerable times on his theft spree.

12. Everett Wilkie Jr. has written an article on the use of scales in rare book rooms. See "Weighing Materials in Rare Book and Manuscript Libraries as a Security Measure against Theft and Vandalism," *RBS* (*Rare Books and Manuscripts*) 7.2 (Fall 2006): 146–63, http://rbm.acrl.org/content/7/2/146.full.pdf + html. The article also appears as a chapter titled "Weighing Materials in Rare Book and Manuscript Libraries to Prevent Theft," in *Guide to Security Considerations and Practices for Rare Book, Manuscript, and Special Collection Libraries*, ed. Everett Wilkie Jr. (Chicago: ACRL, 2012). ACRL is the Association of College and Research Libraries, a division of ALA.

13. Mark McComb says, "There are many types of window security including locks, guards, grilles, bars, screens, and films" ("Library Security," p. 8). He describes all these in detail. He also looks closely at door protection, display case protection, and electronic security (pp. 8ff.).

14. Library Leadership and Management Association (LLAMA), *Library Security Guidelines Document*, June

27, 2010, pp. 20–21, www.ala.org/llama/sites/ala .org.llama/files/content/publications/LibrarySecurity Guide.pdf. The LLAMA document also has an excellent appendix delineating "Suggested Security Staff Qualifications" (p. 23) and another on "Staff Pre-Employment Screening Guidelines" (pp. 24–28).

15. Simon Edwards and Mick Fortune, *A Guide to RFID in Libraries* ([London]: Book Industry Communication, 2008), p. 6, www.bic.org.uk/files/pdfs/ 090109%20library%20guide%20final%20rev.pdf.

16. See www.technovelgy.com/ct/Technology-Article .asp?ArtNum = 47.

17. See Arthur T. Hamlin, "The Technological Revolution," in *The University Library in the United States: Its Origins and Development* (Philadelphia: University of Pennsylvania Press, 1981), pp. 211–25, cited at http://libraryhistory.pbworks.com/w/page/ 16964569/%27tattle%20tape%27. For a historical approach, see Alice Harrison Bahr, "Electronic Collection Security," in *Encyclopedia of Library and Information Science*, ed. by Allen Kent, vol. 44, *Technical* (New York: Marcel Dekker, 1989), pp. 95–133, http://books.google.com (enter "tattle tapes in libraries drawbacks" in the search box).

18. The RBMS security document (www.ala.org/acrl/ standards/security_theft) has links to sites that offer "microtaggants" and "microdots." See www.micro tracesolutions.com and www.datadotdna.com/us.

19. The ALA guidelines on security say, in the appendix on marking books,

> Given the varying nature of special collections materials and the varying nature of beliefs and sentiments concerning what is proper placement for a visible mark, it is probably futile to overly prescribe placement of marks. It is recommended, however, that no position for a mark be rejected outright. Some repositories might, for example, be comfortable stamping the verso of a title page or the image area of a map; others might reject those options. However, no matter where the visible mark is placed, it should not be in a position that it can be removed without leaving obvious evidence of its former presence.

This advice is in *Guidelines for the Security of Rare Books, Manuscripts, and Other Special Collections*, Appendix 1, "Guidelines for Marking Books, Manuscripts, and Other Special Collections Materials"; see www.ala.org/acrl/standards/securityrare books#ap1. See this appendix for advice on marking pages of medieval manuscripts, tightly bound books, and leaf books. Note that this website shows the 2009 iteration of these guidelines. Like all RBMS standards and guidelines, this version will

be revisited—and possibly revised—in the next few years, so readers should check the RBMS website for updates. Further, this site has an important Appendix 3, listing "Addresses for Reporting Thefts." (See the next section of this chapter.) See note 20 referring to the document that has replaced this one. The newer document, among other things, blends into the original guidelines on security the companion document on reporting thefts. Another document to consult is that produced by LLAMA (Library Leadership and Management Association, a division of ALA): *Library Security Guidelines Document*, Prepared by LLAMA BES Safety and Security of Library Buildings Committee (June 2010), www .ala.org/llama/sites/ala.org.llama/files/content/ publications/LibrarySecurityGuide.pdf.

20. See www.ala.org/acrl/standards/security_theft. According to the note at the end of this document, "This version was completed by the RBMS Security Committee in 2008 [and was approved by ACRL in 2009]. It replaces the separate 'Guidelines for the Security of Rare Books, Manuscripts, and Other Special Collections' and 'Guidelines Regarding Thefts in Libraries.'" Many of the suggestions in this chapter about dealing with theft come from this ACRL/RBMS document, referred to here as ACRL/RBMS.

21. Anthony Grafton, *Forgers and Critics: Creativity and Duplicity in Western Scholarship* (Princeton, NJ: Princeton University Press, 1990), p. 18.

22. W. Thomas Taylor, "Provenance and Lore of the Trade," in *Forged Documents: Proceedings of the 1989 Houston Conference*, ed. by Pat Bozeman (New Castle, DE: Oak Knoll Press, 1990), pp. 1–6; this statement is on p. 3.

23. Wilbert de Vries, "Dutch Track Counterfeits via Printer Serial Numbers," https://engineering .purdue.edu/~prints/articles/itworld.shtml.

24. The vast literature on Thomas Wise's and Harry Buxton Forman's forgeries begins with John Carter and Graham Pollard's exposé, *An Enquiry into the Nature of Certain Nineteenth Century Pamphlets* (London: Constable; New York: Scribner, 1934; reprinted several times). This work was followed by Wilfred Partington's *Forging Ahead: The True Story of the Upward Progress of Thomas James Wise* (New York: Putnam, 1939); Nicolas Barker and John Collins's *A Sequel to an Enquiry* (Hants: Scolar; New Castle, DE: Oak Knoll Press, 1983); John Collins's *The Two Forgers: A Biography of Harry Buxton Forman and Thomas James Wise* (New Castle, DE: Oak Knoll Press, 1992); and many other treatments.

25. See "Salamander letter," Wikipedia, http://en.wiki pedia.org/wiki/Salamander_letter. See also the three books that came out in the wake of Hoffmann's capture: Linda Sillitoe and Allen Roberts, *Salamander: The Story of the Mormon Forgery Murders* (Salt Lake City, UT: Signature Books, 1988); Robert Lindsey, *A Gathering of Saints: A True Story of Money, Murder and Deceit* (New York and London: Simon and Schuster, 1988); and Steven Naifeh and Gregory White Smith, *The Mormon Murders: A True Story of Greed, Forgery, Deceit, and Death* (New York: Weidenfeld and Nicolson, 1988).

26. See "Hitler Diaries," Wikipedia, http://en.wikipedia .org/wiki/Hitler_Diaries.

27. See "Ossian," Wikipedia, http://en.wikipedia.org/ wiki/Ossian. See also John Whitehead, "Ossian and Fingal," in *This Solemn Mockery: The Art of Literary Forgery* (London: Arlington Books, 1973), pp. 74–92; and Joseph Rosenblum, "'Ossian' James Macpherson," in *Practice to Deceive: The Amazing Stories of Literary Forgery's Most Notorious Practitioners* (New Castle, DE: Oak Knoll Press, 2000), pp. 19–54.

28. Larry McMurtry, introduction to *Texfake: An Account of the Theft and Forgery of Early Texas Printed Documents*, by W. Thomas Taylor, p. xviii (Austin, TX: W. Thomas Taylor, 1991).

29. See "Facsimile," Wikipedia, http://en.wikipedia .org/wiki/Facsimile.

CHAPTER 8

LEGAL ISSUES

EGAL ISSUES PERMEATE OUR LIVES, NO LESS SO IN RARE BOOKS and special collections than in any other realm of our activities. In fact, because this field deals with valuable things, with personal materials that reveal the privacies of people's lives, and with personalities, special collections can be especially law influenced. The intellectual and monetary value of the materials in the rare book world make them subject to various kinds of legal control. Likewise, information is a commodity, subject to local, regional, national, and international regulation, whether it is entering, remaining in, or leaving a collection, or is being used for commercial or noncommercial purposes.

In the special collections department, the law certainly plays a role, because it is there that monetary and privacy issues exist. In this chapter we will look at several of these issues, with an eye toward suggesting to those who deal with these materials where they must be particularly scrupulous in their activities, and what the best practices are for preventing them from breaking the law, for warning others how not to break the law, and for avoiding controversy. I should point out, however, that although it is important for librarians—especially those in rare books—to know about the laws concerning intellectual property, they are in no legal position to enforce these laws with their patrons, nor are they in a position to counsel their users. As will be noted more than once in this chapter, the ultimate responsibility concerning the use of intellectual property and copyright is in the hands of those who will be using the library's materials, not in the hands of the librarians. Librarians do not have an obligation to inform users about copyright *except* for the standard reproduction notices required by Section 108 of the copyright code. In fact, even law librarians, who have degrees in both law and library and information science, when acting as librarians, should not give out legal advice.

Many legal issues surround special collections departments. That is, libraries and workplaces in general are subject to various kinds of legal constraints that are not specific to rare book departments but that those working in these departments must be aware of. This chapter focuses on some specific special collections issues and examines a few others that are applicable to the wider world of librarianship.[1]

Copyright in the United States

Perhaps the first thing that comes to mind when one thinks of legal issues in the library world is copyright. The obvious and most evident concern has to do with the simplest form of copyright infringement: stealing someone else's words and passing them off as your own. This is called *plagiarism* and also *copyright infringement* if the quoted work is still protected. Willful copyright infringement may be criminal, but it usually involves piracy or out-and-out copying of marketable goods such as CDs or T-shirts. It is a form of theft, like taking someone else's car or jewelry without permission. Copyright infringement could deprive the victim of income that he could make from the material he created. People have a right to profit from their creations, and taking those creations without permission can inhibit that profiting.

Some key terms, then, from the preceding paragraph are *stealing* and *theft, plagiarism, victim,* and *without permission.* These terms need no definition because their meanings are clear. Some fine points must be observed, however. First, copyright protection applies to a wide range of materials. The U.S. Copyright Office lists eight categories of things that are protected:

1. Literary works
2. Musical works, including any accompanying words
3. Dramatic works, including any accompanying music
4. Pantomimes and choreographic works
5. Pictorial, graphic, and sculptural works
6. Motion pictures and other audiovisual works
7. Sound recordings
8. Architectural works[2]

Works that are not copyrightable are

1. Works that have not been in a tangible form of expression (for example, choreographic works that have not been notated or recorded, or improvisational speeches or performances that have not been written or recorded)
2. Titles, names, short phrases, and slogans; familiar symbols or designs; mere variations of typographic ornamentation, lettering, or coloring; mere listings of ingredients or contents
3. Ideas, procedures, methods, systems, processes, concepts, principles, discoveries, or devices, as distinguished from a description, explanation, or illustration
4. Works consisting entirely of information that is common property and containing no original authorship (for example, standard calendars, height and weight charts, tape measures and rulers, and lists or tables taken from public documents or other common sources) (*Copyright Basics,* p. 3)

A work does not need to have been published for it to be under copyright protection. In fact, it is the unpublished materials that can cause the greatest problems for scholars.

As *Copyright Basics* explains,

Section 106 of the 1976 Copyright Act generally gives the owner of copyright the exclusive right to do and to authorize others to do the following:

- To reproduce the work in copies or phonorecords
- To prepare derivative works based upon the work
- To distribute copies or phonorecords of the work to the public by sale or other transfer of ownership, or by rental, lease, or lending
- To perform the work publicly, in the case of literary, musical, dramatic, and choreographic works, pantomimes, and motion pictures and other audiovisual works
- To display the work publicly, in the case of literary, musical, dramatic, and choreographic

works, pantomimes, and pictorial, graphic, or sculptural works, including the individual images of a motion picture or other audiovisual work; and

- In the case of sound recordings, to perform the work publicly by means of a digital audio transmission. (p. 1)[3]

The text adds, "In addition, certain authors of works of visual art have the rights of attribution and integrity as described in section 106A of the 1976 Copyright Act."

All the materials delineated here are likely to be in special collections departments, even the notations for choreography. Whatever is in the department's holdings is subject to copyright protection. For those working in rare book libraries, the details here and in the rest of this circular are often not directly applicable because the librarians themselves will not be using the materials—they will be supplying them to their patrons. But scholar librarians who use the materials themselves are subject to the laws as much as are others. So for two reasons they must know the law. In fact, if a patron plagiarizes from papers (say, unpublished correspondence) that were in a special collections library, the librarians themselves are not liable to punishment. Only the patron is. But it is incumbent on the staff to let patrons know the copyright status of the materials, if they know it. If they do not know it, the patron is responsible for finding out who owns the copyright.

To help scholars, librarians may wish to do their own research on the materials they hold to find out who owns rights to them. This could be a huge task, and most departments, understaffed and under-resourced, probably cannot do this research for all their holdings. Items in print, even when they delineate intellectual property rights holders on the copyright page, are not always up to date. A publisher could own the rights to a book, then sell those rights to another publisher or back to the creator.[4] And for unpublished works—likely to reside in rare book departments[5]—the situation is tricky. A living author probably still retains rights to anything she has produced, published or not, though she could have sold those rights to a publisher (or to anyone else—like a

film studio)[6] or given them to a relative or friend, a library or charity.

> **MANY YEARS AGO** I had a cluster of original letters from prominent authors from 1930, writing on how to become a great author. I wanted to print the first edition of these letters, but because they were recent enough to be under copyright protection, I needed permissions for them. For Ellen Glasgow, this proved to be a headache, for at first I could not find out who owned rights to her unpublished writings. After much (pre-computer) research, I learned that she had willed her royalties to the Richmond, Virginia, Society for the Prevention of Cruelty to Animals, and I was able to get permission to print her letter from them.

Sometimes searching for copyright holders can be maddening. There is, however, a website, jointly sponsored by the Harry Ransom Center at the University of Texas at Austin and the University of Reading Library in England, that might be a good place to begin a quest. It is called WATCH: Writers, Artists, and Their Copyright Holders.[7] The website says that its patrons must be advised that "United States copyright law protects unpublished materials as well as published materials. If you wish to make more than fair use of an unpublished manuscript in a publication, you must determine whether the work has passed into the public domain and is no longer under copyright protection or find the copyright holder and get permission to use the manuscript."[8] And the site offers a list of actions that people searching for copyright holders can take:

Step 1. Ask the owner.
Step 2. Ask the Copyright Office.
Step 3. Ask other scholars.
Step 4. Examine acknowledgments and notes sections.
Step 5. Ask the author's publisher.
Step 6. Ask an author's society.
Step 7. Use genealogical sources.
Step 8. Write to the author's last known address.

Step 9. Ask your librarian to search national
databases.
Step 10. Search published references.
Step 11. Publish a notice in the newspaper.[9]

The WATCH database will help, but if the creator of the item being researched does not appear in its list, all these actions are sensible, though time consuming, and could be futile. That is, librarians and other scholars may be unable to determine who owns the rights to a work. Such items are called *orphan works*. The Copyright Office has been pushing for copyright legislation to reduce infringement liability for uses of orphan works, and the library, archives, and museum communities have been actively involved in the legislative efforts.[10] The U.S. government's website says about these works,

> The Copyright Office is reviewing the problem of orphan works under U.S. copyright law in continuation of its previous work on the subject and to advise Congress on possible next steps for the United States. The Office has long shared the concern with many in the copyright community that the uncertainty surrounding the ownership status of orphan works does not serve the objectives of the copyright system. For good faith users, orphan works are a frustration, a liability risk, and a major cause of gridlock in the digital marketplace.[11]

And the Copyright Advisory Office of Columbia University says, "Congress has considered legislation to address the problem of orphan works, but statutory protection is not yet forthcoming."[12] This office suggests four avenues of action if the researcher cannot find the copyright owner of an orphan work: (1) Assess whether the use you wish to put the material to falls under fair use; (2) "Replace the materials with alternative works"; (3) "Alter your planned use of the copyrighted works"; and (4) "Conduct a risk-benefit analysis" (balance the benefit of using the material against the risk that the owner of the material will surface and will want some kind of compensation from you). The best advice is to move with great caution, with an emphasis on options two and three.[13]

In Great Britain, a new law, passed in 2013, called the Enterprise and Regulatory Reform Bill, allows for the relatively painless use of orphan works. The website DIYPhotography explains,

> Images on the net are not up for grabs, even if you don't know who they belong to. This means for example that if a newspaper found a photograph online, it has to locate its copyright owner (sometimes it's easy, if it was found on a Flickr gallery, but sometimes it's harder, it was on that newsletter-you-subscribed-to-when-they-offered-free-Cheetos). Nevertheless, no one could have used your work if they could not obtain permission from you. Last night [this piece is dated April 29, 2013], a new act in the UK, called the "Enterprise and Regulatory Reform Bill" received Royal Assent which basically means that it is on its way to becoming a law. Basically that act changed the UK copyright laws to allow commercial use of orphan works including photographs.[14]

Though the bill had not been implemented at the time of this writing, and there was still opposition to it, it would simplify free access to orphan works.

The 1978 U.S. copyright law states that works go into the public domain (that is, they lose their copyright protection) seventy years after the death of their authors. The USGPO brochure says that if a work was created in a fixed, "tangible form for the first time on or after January 1, 1978, [it] is automatically protected from the moment of its creation and is ordinarily given a term enduring for the author's life plus an additional 70 years after the author's death" (*Copyright Basics*, p. 5). A work by two or more authors gets the same protection, the seventy years beginning on the first day of the last surviving creator's death (p. 5). This law is operable whether the work is published or not, and it applies to such things as notes someone writes down, a drawing he makes on a napkin, or a photograph on a smart phone. The *Copyright Basics* paragraph adds,

> For works made for hire, and for anonymous and pseudonymous works (unless the author's identity is revealed in Copyright Office records), the duration of copyright will be 95 years from publication

or 120 years from creation, whichever is shorter. (p. 5)

Similar protections operate for works produced before January 1, 1978. There are, of course, many complications to this, and I encourage you to seek out this pamphlet, in print or online, for the fine details. For the purposes of this book, these facts are sufficient with respect to duration of copyright protection.

One excellent, succinct source of information on this subject is Peter Hirtle's chart "Copyright Term and the Public Domain in the United States."[15] It was last updated on January 3, 2012, and was as up to date as possible at the time of this writing. Hirtle covers several areas of materials that are copyrightable:

"Never Published, Never Registered Works"
"Works Registered or First Published in the U.S."
"Works First Published outside the U.S. by Foreign Nationals or U.S. Citizens Living Abroad"
"Works Published Abroad before 1978"
"Works Published Abroad after 1 January 1978"
"Special Cases"
"Sound Recordings"
"Unpublished Sound Recordings, Domestic and Foreign"
"Sound Recordings Published in the United States"
"Sound Recordings Published outside the United States"
"Special Cases" with respect to sound recordings
"Architectural Works"

This chart is an invaluable resource, and it should be at the librarian's fingertips (as an icon on her computer's desktop or in printed form), to be shown to researchers for their own benefit, to help them know what is protected, by whom, under what conditions, and for how long.

One thing to note here is that the laws of copyright are "local." That is, they apply only to the countries in which the infringement took place. Anyone working in rare books and manuscripts should know the term "Rule of National Treatment" that concerns what law governs a copyright infringement claim. Simply stated, it is the law of the land where the alleged infringement took place. Law of domicile

or citizenship governs copyright ownership. As the Wikipedia article on "National Treatment" explains,

National treatment is a principle in international law vital to many treaty regimes. It essentially means treating foreigners and locals equally. Under national treatment, if a state grants a particular right, benefit or privilege to its own citizens, it must also grant those advantages to the citizens of other states while they are in that country.[16]

Wikipedia adds that the rule applies to a product or service and also to intellectual property.

WORK FOR HIRE

"A work made for hire is a work prepared by an employee within the scope of his or her employment, and a work by an independent contractor specially commissioned for an employer" (Crews, p. 133). Additionally, an editor of a reference book or a book with many chapters may wish to hire out the writing of parts (most or all) of a text, securing the services of experts for each of the chapters or entries of the book. He could do it by letting them write under their own names but paying them for their work. Then the editor can go to press at will, owning all these mini-texts. This is called "work for hire." The editor need not give the writers credit, and he can publish all the pieces under his own name, if he wishes. He has paid for a product, and the producers take the money and give up all ownership in the texts they have sold to the editor. So the ownership of the intellectual property in a work for hire is not in the hands of the creator, but in the hands of the one who has paid for it.

A related issue specifically pertinent to rare book departments, because many special collections librarians are encouraged to (and actually do) publish, is this: Can the work that they do on the job be considered work for hire? At academic institutions, especially in fields in which inventions and writings can bring in large amounts of money (medicine and engineering, for example), does the employer own the products or does the scientist or writer have exclusive control of intellectual property? In medicine, for instance, if a professor at a university invents a medicine that is destined to be a block-buster in the pharmaceutical field, does she have the right to reap the rewards of her efforts, or is she under a work-for-hire situation? Contracts in fields in which such profits can be made spell out the division of labor and the equitable division of profits. It is important that scientists, for instance, have attorneys look over their contracts with potential employers before signing.

No such clause is likely to be in a contract in the library field. But it is incumbent on librarians who hope to reap some rewards for their writing to do this writing on their own time. Unless the publication is being done expressly for (and with the sanction of) the institution, there should be a separation of time commitments—the writing to be done on the librarian's time, not taking time away from his professional duties.

OWNERSHIP OF A WORK

The *Copyright Basics* pamphlet points out that copyright is the same as personal property and that the rights can be sold or given away at the holder's dis-

cretion, or they can pass into the hands of heirs if the creator dies without having specified what is to be done with the rights. In the realm of transferred property, the original copyright holder no longer controls the content of the work, and the researcher begins to get headaches in trying to locate the new rights holder(s).[17] The waters get muddier if the original owner has passed along copyright to two or more parties. If a writer wants to use some of the copyrighted work in her own writing, she needs to get permission from only one of the joint owners. As Beth Dodd in the "Copyright Crash Course" at the University of Texas says, "joint owners can grant non-exclusive rights to others without the agreement of their co-owners; however, in the absence of agreement from all joint owners, no owner can assign or exclusively license the copyright in the jointly owned work."[18]

PUBLIC DOMAIN

The phrase "public domain" means the realm of the status of works that no longer are protected by copyright. To say that a work is "in the public domain" is to say that anyone can quote from it to any length,

---

FINDING COPYRIGHT HOLDERS, as I have said, can be a challenge. And even when they are found, the outcome is not always rosy, for they can control rights any way they see fit. In about 1977, for the first edition of my Norton Critical Edition of Mark Twain's *Pudd'nhead Wilson* (PW) and *Those Extraordinary Twins*, I wished to print for the first time about ten long passages—in Mark Twain's hand—that had been removed from the original *PW* manuscript. The manuscript was in the J. Pierpont Morgan Library in New York, so I asked the library for permission to quote the passages. The librarians replied that the library owned the manuscript but not the rights to it. They did not know where to send me. I contacted the Mark Twain

Papers at the Bancroft Library at the University of California, Berkeley, thinking that the librarians there would know who held the rights. And they did. They directed me to Chamberlain, Willi, and Ouchterloney, a New York law firm, which informed me that when Twain's last relative—his daughter Clara Langhorne Clemens—died in 1962, all her possessions, including rights to all Twain's unpublished words, reverted to the firm. I asked for permission to quote the ten passages, and they refused. They said they had an agreement with the University of California Press that it was to be the first to publish any of Twain's hitherto unpublished work. I appealed to the editors at the Mark Twain Papers, who were working with the UC Press to

publish the works of Mark Twain, but they refused to give me permission. Then I asked the law firm about this, and they said that Clara had "renewed copyright" and that they had an agreement with UC Press. I was out of luck. I had to go to press with the first edition of my Norton *PW* with brief summaries of the ten passages and a note explaining why I could not quote the original prose directly. When the second edition of the Norton volume was issued in 2005, Twain had been dead for ninety-five years, and the editors at the Mark Twain Papers told me I was free to use the passages verbatim. I could not go to press with these passages without permission. By waiting more than twenty-five years, I got it.

can use it as much as she wants, without having to get permission to do so and without having to pay anyone for that use. As Crews says,

> The concept of public domain applies to a work that has no copyright protection. This label is often mistakenly applied to works that are publicly available, such as on websites, without any apparent condition on access or use. Most materials that are freely available on the Internet are in fact protected by copyright, but the owners have simply permitted them to be openly available. Even open access works are usually copyrighted, but the owners again have chosen to make them publicly available. They are not necessarily in the public domain. (Crews, p. 19)

A key point that Crews makes must be reiterated: just because a work is publicly available does not mean that it can be used without permission. It may still be under copyright protection.

TRANSFERS OF COPYRIGHT

As *Copyright Basics* points out, "Transfers of copyright are normally made by contract" (p. 6). There are no USGPO forms for such transfers, but they can be formally recorded in the Copyright Office. The transfer "does provide certain legal advantages and may be required to validate the transfer as against third parties" (p. 6). Also, "There is no such thing as 'international copyright' that will automatically protect an author's writings throughout the entire world. Protection against unauthorized use in a particular country depends . . . on the national laws of that country" (p. 6).

The *Copyright Basics* pamphlet has a good deal more information about the subject, including sections on how to register for copyright, effective dates of registration, "Mandatory Deposit for Works Published in the United States" (p. 10), fees, and other things relating to the creation of texts and the obtaining of protection for them. Most of this information is not germane to librarians in that they are usually dealing with others who wish to use the library's materials. But librarians themselves might be the creators, in which case they should be familiar with the contents of this pamphlet.

> IN 2001, I PUBLISHED a book titled *The Handmade Papers of Japan* (Newtown, PA: Bird & Bull Press). In an article that referred to that book, I wished to describe the original book of that title that I wrote about (Thomas Keith Tindale and Harriett Ramsey Tindale, *The Handmade Papers of Japan* [Rutland, VT, and Tokyo: Tuttle, 1952]), so I found a bookseller's description of it on the Web and decided that it was good enough to use for my purposes. But at the end of his description, the bookseller had a warning that his description was under copyright protection and that it could not be used by anyone without his permission. Even the description of a book, filled with mere facts about what the book looks like and why it is important, can be covered by copyright.

RULE OF NATIONAL TREATMENT

One rule that will affect patrons using copyrighted materials (and the librarians who serve them) is called "National Treatment," which is "a principle in international law vital to many treaty regimes. It essentially means treating foreigners and locals equally."[19] That is, for copyrighted materials, the prevailing laws in any given country will be the operative guiding principles in deciding what is copyrighted and what is not. "National treatment only applies once a product, service or item of intellectual property has entered the market." So a book under copyright in the United States will have its text protected, and no one can use it without obtaining permission. Foreign nationals *residing in the United States*, even if the laws in their country would permit use without permission, are governed by U.S. laws.

PATRON NOTIFICATION

Also important, and probably more directly relevant to the librarian's duties, is the need to notify patrons about the laws. It might be useful for librarians to have a few copies of the *Copyright Basics* pamphlet on hand in their reading rooms for patrons' use. Many departments have copyright statements on their copying machines (if patrons are allowed to make their own copies), notifying the users about the need to follow federal laws in their use of other people's words. If a patron misuses someone else's words, the patron can get into trouble; the librarian will not. Nonetheless, such warnings can be a blessing to ignorant scholars (and there are plenty of them in the world).[20]

Two main points are worth reiterating. First, libraries may own the original materials, but they do not necessarily own the intellectual content of these materials. Second, librarians owe it to their patrons to provide access to original texts, but if those texts are under copyright protection and are used by the scholars without authorization, the librarians are not at fault, the users are.

FAIR USE

The term *fair use* has been used previously in this chapter. It means

the right to use copyrighted material without permission or payment under some circumstances,

---

MANY CASES OF plagiarism have been reported over the years. Whether intentional or not, it still happens and often winds up in the headlines. "Ian Hamilton's unauthorized biography of Salinger was rewritten, when the author did not accept extensive quoting of his personal letters. The new version, *In Search of J. D. Salinger*, came in 1988" (see the "books and writers" web article on this case at http://kirjasto.sci.fi/salinger.htm). This was an important case, for it put before the public (not just the scholarly public) the key issue that even if an institution owns an author's letters, it does not own the contents. That is, physical ownership is distinctly different from ownership of intellectual content. Hamilton never got Salinger's permission to quote from the writer's letters, and Salinger—one of the most reclusive and sequestered writers of all time—was angry that the privacies of his life, revealed in the letters, were made public. This is a lesson for librarians and the researchers they serve: ownership is of two kinds, physical and intellectual. Although the libraries that made the letters available to scholars were acting perfectly legally, they apparently did not warn the users of the copyright issue (nor

should they have). The researcher should have known that the copyright in the letters belonged to the copyright holder (in this case, Salinger). It is a basic copyright principle. It is not the job of the librarian to warn the user about what copyrights are owned by whom. Research libraries should provide an online copyright or intellectual property law reference guide that gives users information about copyright and possibly other subjects such as privacy, publicity, patents, and trademarks. Librarians should not be the direct conduits of legal advice, but they should have that information available for their patrons.

Other notorious cases of plagiarism were those of Stephen Spender, who "sued author David Leavitt for allegedly using his relationship with Jimmy Younger in Leavitt's *While England Sleeps* [New York: Viking, 1993] in 1994." Leavitt apparently stole some text, plot, and characters from Spender's *World within World* (London: Hamish Hamilton, 1951). "The case was settled out of court with Leavitt removing certain portions from his text" (Wikipedia, http://en.wikipedia.org/wiki/Stephen_Spender); see also Stephen Spender, "My Life Is Mine: It Is Not David Leavitt's," at the *New York Times* site, www.nytimes.com/books/98/04/26/specials/leavitt-spender.html. There is also the well-publicized case of Kaavya Viswanathan's novel *How Opal Mehta Got Kissed, Got Wild, and Got a Life* (New York: Little, Brown, 2006); "the book was withdrawn after allegations that portions had been plagiarized from several sources. Viswanathan apologized and said any similarities were 'completely unintentional and unconscious.' All shelf copies of *Opal Mehta* were ultimately recalled and destroyed by the publisher, and Viswanathan's contract for a second book was canceled."*

*The Wikipedia article quoted here cites David Zhou, "Student's Novel Faces Plagiarism Controversy," Harvard Crimson, April 23, 2006, at TheCrimson.com, www.thecrimson.com/article.aspx?ref=512948. It also cites "Harvard Novelist Says Copying Was Unintentional," New York Times, April 25, 2006, at NYTimes.com, www.nytimes.com/2006/04/25/books/25book.html. The Wikipedia article cites parallel passages in Viswanathan's book and in the works of other writers. Despite her protests to the contrary, this young writer seems to have been appropriately skewered for literary theft.

especially when the cultural or social benefits of the use are predominant. It is a general right that applies even—and especially—in situations where the law provides no specific statutory authorization for the use in question. Consequently, the fair use doctrine is described only generally in the law, and it is not tailored to the mission of any particular community.[21]

The "Fair Use" pamphlet from which this statement comes says that "fair use is an essential component of copyright exemptions for librarians" (p. 2), and it points out that often librarians who do not understand this doctrine err on a side of stricture—that is, librarians

> [overestimate] the level of conflict between the strictures of copyright law on the one hand and their respective libraries' missions on the other. The cost of this uncertainty [is] amplified because many research and academic librarians routinely act as the de facto arbiters of copyright practice for their institutions and the constituencies they serve. (p. 2)

That is, fair use gives librarians a wider latitude in using copyrighted materials than the librarians realize. The text also points out that, regardless of where in the world the rights to a text are held, if the use is in the United States, then U.S. laws permitting fair use prevail. The text notes, however, "Under some circumstances, fair use rights can be overridden by contractual restrictions. Thus, these principles may not apply if a library has agreed, in a license agreement, donor agreement, or other contract, to forgo the exercise of fair use with respect to some set of collection materials" (p. 4).

There are several circumstances under which fair use applies to library situations. The "Fair Use" pamphlet lists these eight:

1. Supporting teaching and learning with access to library materials via digital technologies
2. Using selections from collection materials to publicize a library's activities, or to create physical and virtual exhibitions
3. Digitizing to preserve at-risk items
4. Creating digital collections of archival and special collections materials

5. Reproducing material for use by disabled students, faculty, staff, and other appropriate users
6. Maintaining the integrity of works deposited in institutional repositories
7. Creating databases to facilitate nonconsumptive research uses (including search)
8. Collecting material posted on the World Wide Web and making it available (pp. 13–27)

The pamphlet explains all these in detail and is worth perusing. For the present text, it is sufficient to say that librarians in special collections should be conversant with the fair use doctrine and should have information (perhaps in the form of this pamphlet or a reference to an online guide) available for patrons.[22]

The foregoing discussion shows how stern and protective the copyright laws in the United States are. But as already noted, they do not prohibit some use of others' materials without permission. If a scholar wants to copy a text for his own private use (not to make any money on it, but simply to have access to the text in his own home, for instance), he need not pay for copying another's work—up to a point. Similarly, short passages can be quoted in a book or article without the author's permission. But these instances are clearly delineated. The U.S. Copyright Office website on fair use says,

> One of the rights accorded to the owner of copyright is the right to reproduce or to authorize others to reproduce the work in copies or phonorecords. This right is subject to certain limitations found in sections 107 through 118 of the copyright law (title 17, U.S. Code). One of the more important limitations is the doctrine of "fair use." The doctrine of fair use has developed through a substantial number of court decisions over the years and has been codified in section 107 of the copyright law.
>
> Section 107 contains a list of the various purposes for which the reproduction of a particular work may be considered fair, such as criticism, comment, news reporting, teaching, scholarship, and research.[23]

Use of copyrighted materials is fair (that is, can be employed without permissions or payments) under four conditions. The first concerns whether the use is for commercial or for nonprofit, educational purposes; the second considers the "nature of the copyrighted work"; the third looks at "[t]he amount and substantiality of the portion used in relation to the copyrighted work as a whole"; and the fourth considers whether the use will affect the market value or profitability of the original (see www.copyright.gov/fls/fl102.html).

This information is followed in the Copyright Office document by a key statement:

> The distinction between fair use and infringement may be unclear and not easily defined. There is no specific number of words, lines, or notes that may safely be taken without permission. Acknowledging the source of the copyrighted material does not substitute for obtaining permission.

If the researcher wants to quote a sentence from another writer's work, that probably falls under the rubric "fair use." What about two sentences? three? a paragraph? At what point does fair use turn to infringement? It is always best to err on the side of caution. That is, scholars would do well to consult an attorney or the copyright holder before going to press with a "substantial" amount of another writer's words or ideas. Deciding what "substantial" means can be tricky. And as this extract reminds, just giving a clear citation of the source is not the same thing as having gotten permission.

Hence, it is important for scholars to be aware of what level of use—what kind of use—might be interpreted as infringement (especially if there is no citation of a source). Again, the U.S. Copyright Office, on the same site, offers this:

> The 1961 Report of the Register of Copyrights on the General Revision of the U.S. Copyright Law cites examples of activities that courts have regarded as fair use: "quotation of excerpts in a review or criticism for purposes of illustration or comment; quotation of short passages in a scholarly or technical work, for illustration or clarification of the author's observations; use in a parody of some of the content of the work parodied; summary of an address or article, with brief quotations, in a news report; reproduction by a library of a portion of a work to replace part of a damaged copy; reproduction by a teacher or student of a small part of a work to illustrate a lesson; reproduction of a work in legislative or judicial proceedings or reports; incidental and fortuitous reproduction, in a newsreel or broadcast, of a work located in the scene of an event being reported."

Note the gray areas: "quotation of short passages," "a portion of a work," "a small part of a work." These phrases do not specify amounts. What is a short passage? a portion? a small part? The quoted passage is followed by a warning that it is always best to get permission from the copyright holder before using a protected work. The document then says, "When it is impracticable to obtain permission, use of copyrighted material should be avoided unless the doctrine of fair use would clearly apply to the situation." And it concludes that when the copyright holder cannot be located, it is best to consult an attorney.[24]

Section 108 of the Copyright law gives libraries and archives the right to provide users with individual copies of certain works for private study, scholarship, and research; to make digital copies of certain published and unpublished works; and to make them available on the premises of the library. For these purposes, the library could provide low-resolution digital copies. Section 108 applies mostly to text works and excludes many other categories of works such as images that are not adjunct to a print or text publication. The library is not responsible for guaranteeing that the user has obtained permission for a publication before it provides the high-resolution image. The library can provide that high-res image and trust that the user knows of (or can instruct the user about) the necessity of obtaining third-party rights. The only rights the library can grant are those that it owns. The library can police the rights situation, but it is a better strategy to simply get the user to agree in writing that she has the responsibility to clear rights and that she accepts the liability for not doing so. It should also be pointed out that practices at institutions vary.

FAIR USE HAS been a boon to scholars for decades. But as already noted, what constitutes fair use has not always been crystal clear. In an issue of *Art Newspaper* (No. 232, February 2012, p. 4), an article on origami use has brought the fair use problem to light. The article by Charlotte Burns, "Origami Artists vs Abstract Painter: The Legal Battle Continues," concerns an artist who used in her paintings patterns that were created by origami artists. The origami artists claimed that the painter had stolen their original art—had unlawfully appropriated their creations for her commercial use and had infringed upon their copyright protection. Her response was that her work was transformative, perhaps inspired by the original origami patterns, but in no way stealing from them. Burns writes:

> These cases all centre on the question of what constitutes "fair use," a legal concept intended to mediate between the First Amendment (which defends individual freedom of expression), and copyright law (which protects the rights of the creator of an original work).
>
> Fair use is determined by four factors: whether a work is derivative or transformative; the nature of the copyrighted works; the amount of the original used overall; and the effect on the "potential market or value" of the source. (p. 4)

The fact that case after case appears in court, month after month over many years, proves that "fair use" is not easy to define or demonstrate. Artists and writers do not want their works plagiarized from, for they may claim that this kind of theft could affect their ability to sell their own work. When money is at the root of the issue, contentiousness will often ensue.

The ARL document on Fair Use (cited in note 21) points out that what constitutes fair use is not made explicit in copyright law and that

> Because copyright law does not specify exactly how to apply fair use, the fair use doctrine has a useful flexibility that allows the law to adjust to evolving circumstances and works to the advantage of society as a whole. Needs and practices differ with the field, with technology, and with time. Rather than following a prescriptive formula, law-

yers and judges decide whether a particular use of copyrighted material is "fair" according to an "equitable rule of reason." In effect, this amounts to taking all the facts and circumstances into account to decide whether an unlicensed use of copyrighted material generates social or cultural benefits that are greater than the costs it imposes on the copyright owner.

Because the fair use doctrine allows for many kinds of use of otherwise protected materials, authors wanting to use copyrighted materials may be able to do so for free under the right circumstances. It may take a consultation with a copyright attorney to determine what is fair game and what is not. The author wanting to use protected materials should proceed with caution but not with despair that the materials *must* be paid for or that permission *must* be granted.

The complications of copyright law could yield extensive discussion far beyond what is presented here. It is important that librarians understand much of this, that they be able to guide their patrons to the proper tools to prevent them from breaking the law, and that they do not give out legal advice themselves. Although thousands of books and articles are available for consultation, the Internet has become a gold mine of often excellent information, and librarians should be able to guide their users to appropriate websites, cautioning their patrons to take what legal information they get from the Web with great care.

PERMISSIONS

In a nutshell, if a scholar wants to use the protected words of someone else, he must get permission from the copyright holder. As already explained, finding out who that holder is might be difficult. It should be obvious that if an author sells a work to a publisher, most often the publisher takes ownership of the intellectual content. But it is possible that the author retains ownership or vests it in another party. So determining ownership is key to getting permission.

Once ownership is known, the scholar wanting to use the material must ask for permission to use it. Many possibilities could materialize. The owner (a publisher of books, a magazine or journal publisher, the original author, or anyone else—remember the SPCA ownership of Ellen Glasgow's works!) may say, "You may use as much as you want, no charge." Or he may impose a fee of anything he wishes: 10 cents a word, a flat fee of $500, $50 a page, or anything else. The owner of the material has full power over the holdings and can ask for any fee he wants.

Copyright in Great Britain

Basic current U.S. copyright laws, always evolving with new cases being heard in courts regularly, came into use in 1976. In Great Britain the Copyright, Designs and Patents Act 1988 is the British equivalent.[25] Its second paragraph states in simple terms one of its basic principles:

> Essentially, the 1988 Act and amendment establishes that copyright in most works lasts until 70 years after the death of the creator if known, otherwise 70 years after the work was created or published (fifty years for computer-generated works).

Wikipedia then offers links to copyright information in all the lands under the rubric "Great Britain" (including Bermuda, Gibraltar, Isle of Man, Antigua, Dominica, Gambia, Grenada, Guyana, Jamaica, Kiribati, Lesotho, St. Christopher-Nevis, St. Lucia, Swaziland, and Tuvalu).

As with the U.S. act, the British one explains what works are subject to copyright. They include "literary, dramatic and musical works . . . artistic works . . . sound recordings and films . . . broadcasts . . . cable programmes . . . [and] published editions." The act then explains,

> The 1911 Act provides that an individual's work is automatically under copyright, by operation of law, as soon as it leaves his mind and is embodied in some physical form: be it a novel, a painting, a musical work written in manuscript, or an architectural schematic. This remains the legal position under the Schedules of [the] 1956 Act and of the 1988 Act.
>
> Once reduced to physical form, provided it is an original work (in the sense of not having been copied from an existing work), then copyright in it vests automatically in (i.e. is owned by) the author: the person who put the concept into material form. There are exceptions to this rule, depending upon the nature of the work, if it was created in the course of employment.

As in U.S. copyright, there is also the notion of Work for Hire, in which one party hires another to create an "original work," and the person who does the cre-

---

IN 1979, I FOUND a chapter of a Yale University Press book that I wished to use in my Norton Critical Edition of *Pudd'nhead Wilson* (*PW*). I contacted the press and they said, essentially, "No problem. Go ahead. But we want $3,500." This was more than thirty years ago, when that was a bundle! Norton would pay up to $1,000 in permissions; the rest came out of my pocket. That $3,500 would have eaten up my royalties for decades to come. And that was just for one piece; I wanted to have at least twenty other essays in the Norton edition. I declined the press's offer to use the chapter. Interestingly, I notified the author, who was disappointed because it would have been good for him to be so prominently quoted—in a Norton Critical Edition that was destined to be a textbook and to be in print long after his own book went out of print. But the author had no say in the matter. (Parenthetically, the Norton *PW* is in its second edition more than thirty years later.* The scholar's book has been out of print for decades.) Perhaps Yale University Press was worried that the use of one chapter would reduce the sales of that volume, but it was possible, too, that it would have been a form of advertising for that book and might have increased the sales.

*Incidentally, for the PW volume, I wound up incurring about $3,600 for permissions. The publisher paid for them up front, but $2,600 of that came out of my royalties, and it was not until about seven or eight years later that I received my first royalty check. Permissions can be expensive, but a scholar cannot go to press safely without obtaining them.

ation is paid for her service. Then the work belongs to the one who paid for it, and the actual creator, having signed a Work for Hire contract, has no further interest in the work. Additionally, if someone is paid on the job for doing work for her employer, any work she produces belongs to the employer.

> THE LINES OF ownership can blur if the writer is, for instance, a professor of creative writing, and he writes a short story, novel, or poem "on the job" and has it published by a publisher. Ownership is just as tenuous for a professor of history who writes a book on his subject of expertise or a mathematics professor who creates a textbook "on the job." How is "on the job" defined? Who owns the rights to these texts? Is it work for hire or an original work that the writer has a right to own? Also, what if the creator of a work is not in the teaching field but works, for instance, in a law firm or in a medical practice, and she writes a novel based on personal (professional) experience? Or a CPA who writes a how-to book on personal finances or on orchid cultivation? Has he done this on company time? Does that make any difference? Ownership of intellectual property can be difficult to substantiate.

The British copyright law then discusses the ownership of computer databases.

UK copyright law recognises the element of labour and skill used in compiling them, even though they are not in truth original works (being entirely derived from existing records), applying a principle sometimes called the 'Sweat of the Brow' doctrine; they are also protected by database right. The term 'Unfair Use' is sometimes applied in that context, to refer to the use of a work into which someone has invested a lot of skill and labour, but where little or no originality is present. This is mainly in the case of reproduction photography, or the retouching of artistic works that are out of copyright, or for simple computer databases, such works not being original.

In Great Britain a work can qualify for copyright protection in two ways: "by the nationality of the author, or by the country of first publication." From here the act details the many features of copyright that obtain in Britain, including discussions on "First Publication," "Printed Works," "Other Works" (e.g., sculpture, carvings, statuary, architecture), "International Copyright" (works produced by non-British authors, published outside Great Britain, are protected by the laws in their countries of origin), "Extension of Copyright," "Broadcasts," "Sound Recordings," and so on.

Under the rubric "Authors and Owners of Copyright," the British law states,

> Under the 1988 Act, the first owner of a copyright is assumed to be the author of the work. If a work is made by an author in the course of employment then the author's employer is the first owner of copyright.
>
> Unlike American copyright law, the duration of the copyright term does not (after the commencement of the 1956 Act) vary depending on who owns the copyright.
>
> The author of a work is:
>
> - The creator of a literary, musical, dramatic or artistic work.
> - The publisher of a published edition of a work.
> - The producer of a sound recording.
> - The producer and principal director of a film.
> - The maker of a broadcast.
> - If a work is computer generated, the person who made the arrangements necessary for the creation of the work.

And the document adds that if there are two or more creators of a work, they all share in the ownership.

What is called Fair Use in the United States is called Fair Dealing in Great Britain—conditions under which a writer may use the protected work of another without breaking the law (as in book reviews, for some scholarly purposes or other non-commercial use, news reporting, and other uses). And this section concludes that "[e]ducational establishments, libraries and archives have many exceptions that are applicable only to them, which enable them to do their work. However, most people do not have to worry about these exceptions in everyday life."

A feature of the British law not in the U.S. document concerns Moral Rights:

Moral rights were introduced into UK law by the 1988 Act. They come from the alien civil law system, not from the common law tradition. The 1988 Act introduced moral rights for authors of literary, dramatic, musical and artistic works and the directors of films. The moral rights include the right to be identified as the author or director of a work as appropriate, the right to object to the derogatory treatment of a work and the right to object to false attribution of a work. The rights to object to derogatory treatment and not to be falsely attributed as author operate automatically. However, the right to be identified as the author or director of a work must be asserted. Works of joint authorship have separate moral rights for each author. Each author or director must separately assert the right to be identified as the author or director of a work.

Moral rights cannot be transferred to heirs or to anyone else who is a subsequent owner of copyright. The British code then discusses Privacy, Performance, and Resale rights, and other issues.

The article cited in note 25 is a good place to begin a study of British copyright laws. Though these laws touch on databases, they otherwise shy away from the complications engendered by the digital world. Laws in this area are being formulated as more and more texts (including photographs, sound and video recordings, and so forth) are created in digital form.

Dealing with Donors

Although dealing with donors is a part of running a rare book department (especially the subtopic of ethical conduct—subjects of chapter 2), this dealing does expose librarians to certain legal situations worth mentioning here. In fact, a fine line can exist between whether an issue is an ethical or a legal matter. The ethical guidelines warn librarians not to take gifts from anyone who could profit from her relationship with the library. If a librarian is the recipient of any kind of personal gift from a donor

(e.g., a painting, a book, a trip, a fancy dinner, a piece of jewelry) and then is asked to sign off on a gift to the library that is manifestly appraised at far more than its true value, has the personal gift to the librarian been of such influence that she will keep quiet about what amounts to fraud? (A donor might claim a tax write-off of, say, $25,000 for a gift, when the librarian knows the gift was worth one-fifth that amount.)

> **CHEATING WITH REGARD** to donations puts a librarian in a delicate position. What if Donors A and B, individually, give gifts to a library, with Donor A appraising the gift of Donor B at far above the donation's value, and Donor B doing the same thing for Donor A? They are both cheating the government by claiming more of a tax rebate than they deserve. Neither is a professional appraiser or an expert in rare books. They are old friends, and they do this year after year for the tax break. The librarian may take the stance, "I merely sign off on this gift. I am theoretically not privy to the donation's claimed value. My signing is only to tell the tax man that I have received these gifts, not that I corroborate or confirm the value these donors are claiming." The librarian also knows that if he becomes a whistleblower, the gifts would stop, and he does not want that to happen. The librarian's position is technically correct. He does not necessarily know the true value of the claimed gift. But if he *does* know, what must he do?

A whistleblower's basic impetus is to reveal fraud or other illegal dealings. A fraudulent claim of the high worth of a donation to a library is essentially a crime. Should a librarian who is aware of this crime let authorities know? Will that revelation hurt the librarian or the library in any way? Is a whistleblower subject to retaliation, and if so, are there protections for him? The laws are extremely complex on these issues.[26] The RBMS guidelines for ethical conduct for rare book librarians is silent on this topic. As the sidebar indicates, a generous donor over the years who consistently overevaluates her gifts will nonetheless continue to be a donor. The librarian who knows of the donor's crime may not want to blow the whistle and thus lose the continued largesse of the donor. But he could be accused of breaking the law himself if he sees the crime and says nothing about it. He would be complicit in it.

THE DEED OF GIFT

The document of conveyance for donations is called a Deed of Gift. It is a legal instrument, and it must be created with great care, sometimes with the assistance of an attorney who specializes in such matters.

THE RIVERA LIBRARY at UC Riverside did not have a Deed of Gift when I got there, so I wrote one, which had to go to the director of my library, who sent it to the legal counsel of the university. In its final form it served the library well, for it covered everything we needed to protect ourselves and the donors. It was not elaborate, but it left open spaces for all contingencies, including a field for the donors to place any restrictions they wanted on the materials given. This clause closed the deal of the donation in many instances. But before the donors filled out the form, I had a long discussion with them about why we discouraged strings.

The typical Deed of Gift identifies the donor or donors, states their contact points (address[es], phone number[s], e-mail address[es], and so forth), and then has a clause for the description of the materials donated. Depending on the nature of the gift, this section can be as simple as "One photograph," it can describe the photograph ("One photograph of Aunt Tillie Coburn on her porch, Springfield, Missouri, 1877"), it can list a number of items ("One photograph, seventeen books, two long-play phonograph records, and a lock of hair"), it could say "Twelve cartons of books," or it could be a gift of an entire library with five thousand volumes and a host of manuscripts. This part of the Deed of Gift can be crucial to a donor who wants to get a tax deduction for the donation, because specificity may be necessary to corroborate the value of the gift. For this

reason, the rubric "Description of the Gift" usually includes a statement such as "See Attached Inventory," in reference to a full inventory at the end of the document.

The inventory, for a collection of books, could be dozens or even hundreds of pages, naturally depending on the size of the gift. The donor may wish to have an itemization of "Books of $300 and up," followed by a statement, "Also, 2,755 volumes with average value of $15." For donations that are valued at $5,000 and above (even if the gift is only one or two books), this kind of listing should be done by a professional appraiser. (See the section "Evaluation and Appraisal" later in this chapter.)

The next part of the Deed of Gift can be titled something like "Terms of the Donation."[27] This is the area of "strings," the constraints the donor wishes to put onto the items given. As noted earlier, no librarian should accept any gift of any kind that puts unreasonable constrictions on access to the materials or that forces the library to retain *all* the items given if some of them would not be advantageous for the library to own (that is, they would be evaluated as level 1 or level 2 items; see chapter 2). On the other hand, the gift could contain some spectacular material that the library would dearly love to have, and it may be worth living with some strings to get the prized pieces. This could be a delicate balance, and each librarian should assess the pros and cons of the terms before accepting any gift.

Certain strings should be avoided: anything that would damage the collection (a requirement, for instance, that the books be kept in a room with open windows or that fresh flowers be delivered each week), a requirement that the library take massive numbers of pieces that it does not want and that would take up huge amounts of time and resources (not to mention shelf space), strings that border on the unethical or illegal (like Sir Thomas Phillipps's desire that his son-in-law and all Catholics be barred from his books), a demand that the collection be closed (that is, unavailable for use) for an inordinately long time (twenty-five years or more), a request that the books be kept together in a single room, the donor's insistence that the books not be rebound or conserved when many of them are falling apart and cannot be used without rebinding or some other conservation treatment, and so forth.

The librarian should work closely with the donor when the terms of the deed are being filled in. Before the document is signed, the librarian should read it carefully and perhaps ask the donor to change some of the terms. Most donors, because they are kind enough to make the donation in the first place, and if they are properly consulted and advised, will understand why certain restrictions are unacceptable to the library and will modify their requests accordingly. Ideally, the deed will have no terms delineated at all. Or the librarian can ask the donor to write in specifically the terms that the library would like to see, such as, "The library is free to keep or dispose of the volumes in this gift as it sees fit."

However, a librarian may find herself saddled with a donor who is intransigent about putting into the Deed of Gift conditions that are extremely difficult to adhere to, or she may be equally saddled with an old deed with such intractable conditions. She is constrained by the legal document to uphold the terms of the deed (or will) as near as possible to the original intent of the former owner. The term for upholding the terms as near as possible to this intent is *cy pres*, coming from Old Norman French and meaning "as near as possible."[28]

It is possible, also, to have a Deed of Gift that does not have a clearly delineated Terms section at all. That is, the donor is not encouraged (or clued in) to add terms to the gift. Such a document would help the librarian immeasurably if the donor does not even think of any restrictions at the time of the signing.

The last feature of the Deed of Gift is the signature of the donor. In community property states both spouses must sign the form. In fact, even in states that do not have community property laws, it would be a good idea to have both spouses sign. And the receiving institution should have one person as a designated recipient who also signs—but only after the donors' signatures are on the document.

The Quit Claim

Under some circumstances a donor may sign over rights to the intellectual property of materials in a gift, but the librarian later learns that the donor did not own those rights in the first place. It may be useful for the librarian to ask the donor at the time of the donation to sign a Quit Claim. "The Quit Claim transfer shows that the grantor or owner of the property is releasing the property. This release proves nothing else."[29] The Quit Claim may transfer only the property itself, or the property and its intellectual rights as well. The *Communications Journal* says,

> The grantee must perform all of the due diligence to understand that the grantor has the right to sign the Quit Claim.
>
> Since the Quit Claim is considered "final" it is a good idea to get it notarized if possible. Notarizing only proves that the signature of the person is the same as that on the agreement.[30]

An inexperienced librarian might read the Quit Claim and think that her institution owns the rights when the library actually has none because the donor had none. Hence, the recipient (the grantee) must not assume that it owns the intellectual rights; if it wants to use the materials in such a way that might infringe on someone's copyright, it must find out who actually owns that copyright.[31]

Provenance

Closely related to the Deed of Gift is the issue of provenance. When a librarian is in the process of acquiring any item, by gift or purchase, it is important for him to check the provenance of the piece. The obvious questions are these: Does the donor or seller own the piece outright? Does she have the right to transfer the ownership to the library? If the item is stolen, or if it belongs to someone else (as with a book borrowed from another person), the seller or donor is not the rightful owner and does not have the right to transfer it to the library.

Rare book librarians want to know the provenance of many of their books and manuscripts. One reason is for pedagogical purposes: to learn the ownership history of the item may help a researcher in some way. Another reason is that the librarian does not want to be bringing in stolen property (or property owned by someone other than the donor or seller). It might be impossible for a bookseller or donor to have documentary evidence that he owns the item to be transferred to the library. In most cases the librarian must take it on faith that the dealer or donor has the right to make the transfer. But for extraordinary items—especially quite expensive ones—provenance information is extremely important.

EVALUATION AND APPRAISAL

One of the legal aspects of the donation, especially in the United States, concerns the tax implications of the gift. IRS laws for books allow a donor to claim up to (but not including) $5,000 for a write-off. If the gift is $5,000 and up, and the donor wishes to claim the value for tax purposes, she must get a formal appraisal from a bookseller or professional appraiser. The donor must pay for this. The institution is not responsible for the tax implications of the gift and should not be involved at all in the appraisal. For this reason, too, the donor is not obligated to share the appraised value with the institution. So the librarian should not expect to see a copy of the final appraisal. The IRS publication (No. 561) titled "Determining the Value of Donated Property"[32] says of books,

> The value of books is usually determined by selecting comparable sales and adjusting the prices according to the differences between the comparable sales and the item being evaluated. This is difficult to do and, except for a collection of little value, should be done by a specialized appraiser. Within the general category of literary property, there are dealers who specialize in certain areas, such as Americana, foreign imports, Bibles, and scientific books.

As already mentioned, it is good for the library to get a copy of the appraisal, but it is not a requirement of the gift, and the library should not expect to see the final appraisal or to know what the appraised value is.

The IRS stipulates,

Generally, if the claimed deduction for an item or group of similar items of donated property is more than $5,000, you must get a qualified appraisal made by a qualified appraiser, and you must attach Section B of Form 8283 to your tax return. There are exceptions, discussed later. You should keep the appraiser's report with your written records. Records are discussed in Publication 526.[33]

The donor should keep the appraisal handy in case she needs to show it later on.[34] The librarian should know these things, should be knowledgeable about current laws, and should notify the donors about this requirement because many donors do not know what do to in such circumstances. (The Deed of Gift should have another clause about ownership of the intellectual rights of the materials given. See the section "Ownership of Holdings and Control of Original Materials" later in this chapter.)

A formal appraisal must include the following features:

- "A description of the property in sufficient detail for a person who is not generally familiar with the type of property to determine that the property appraised is the property that was (or will be) contributed"[35]
- A description of the property's physical condition
- The date the item or collection is to be donated
- "The terms of any agreement or understanding entered into (or expected to be entered into) by or on behalf of the donor that relates to the use, sale, or other disposition of the donated property, including, for example, the terms of any agreement or understanding that: a) Temporarily or permanently restricts a donee's right to use or dispose of the donated property, b) Earmarks donated property for a particular use, or, c) Reserves to, or confers upon, anyone (other than a donee organization or an organization participating with a donee organization in cooperative fund-raising) any right to the income from the donated property

or to the possession of the property, including the right to vote donated securities, to acquire the property by purchase or otherwise, or to designate the person having the income, possession, or right to acquire the property"

- Full identification of the appraiser with his Taxpayer Identification Number
- The appraiser's qualifications along with her signature and TIN (Taxpayer Identification Number)
- A statement of the reason for the preparation of the appraisal (if it was for tax purposes, for instance, this should be noted)
- The dates on which the appraisal was done
- A statement of the fair market value of the materials to be donated (keeping the date of the transfer of property in mind)
- A statement explaining how the fair market value was ascertained
- "The specific basis for the valuation, such as any specific comparable sales transaction"

This document makes it clear that neither the donor nor the donee may be the appraiser. Other restricted parties are listed as well, such as

[a] party to the transaction in which the donor acquired the property being appraised, unless the property is donated within 2 months of the date of acquisition and its appraised value is not more than its acquisition price. This applies to the person who sold, exchanged, or gave the property to the donor, or any person who acted as an agent for the transferor or donor in the transaction, anyone employed by or related to these parties, and others.

The IRS also makes it illegal for the appraisal to be paid for on the basis of a percentage of the total appraised value.[36] In all, the appraiser faces the possibility of a penalty "for aiding and abetting an understatement of tax liability by providing inaccurate appraisals."[37]

Another important issue arises if the donor allows the library to sell or otherwise part with any item or items in the gift at the librarian's discretion. If appropriate, the donor may wish to stipulate that if

books are sold from the donated collection, the proceeds of the sale must be used strictly for the benefit of the library. In fact, the donor may wish to be more explicit than that: that the proceeds be used for buying books for the special collections department, or that the proceeds be used for conservation, or whatever else the donor wants the proceeds to be used for. This kind of explicitness can be worked out between the donor and the librarian, if the opportunity arises for such arrangements, and it may work to the benefit of the library because without such precise designations the income from the sale of gifts could be used for salaries or the physical plant, depending on the way the parent institution deals with such income.

Once the gift is received, the librarian may wish (or may be required by the institution) to do an appraisal of his own. In annual reports, institutions often give statistics on gifts received, and having a dollar figure for the gift of books may be mandated for this report. This appraisal should in no way be made public; it is for internal purposes only, and the figure the librarian comes up with may vary widely from that of the professional appraiser.

One last thing about appraisals must be mentioned: The Tax Reform Act of 1984 introduced a protection for the IRS to prevent people from lying about the value of materials. As Payne points out, "New penalties are levied on donors and appraisers for the over-evaluation of gifts."[38] Before this 1984 act, donors could claim a deduction that was thousands of dollars more than the donated item merited. Librarians should notify their donors of the chances they take if they lie about the value of their donations.

THE ISSUE ABOUT inflated appraisals and Form 8283 raises serious concerns. Perhaps the best way to handle a gift with an overstated valuation (if the librarian learns of this, which he might not) is simply to sign Form 8283 acknowledging the receipt of the gift and then contact the donor with a gentle comment that the appraised value seems high. The donor should be advised to discuss this possibility with the appraiser or tax person, or both.

Librarians should be able to direct their donors to the right people to do the appraisal. If the librarian suggests a bookseller, which is the obvious route to go because specialized dealers can be true experts in their fields, the donor should be given at least three names to choose from. If the donor is given only one bookseller's name, there could be an appearance of a conflict of interest. The donor may think that that one dealer has an "arrangement" with the librarian: You send me customers to do appraisals for and I will share the proceeds with you. Even if that is *not* the case (and it probably is not), there is the possibility of an appearance of collusion. Better for the librarian to give the donor at least three names and have her contact them on her own.

If the librarian, for whatever reason, recommends a professional appraiser rather than a bookseller, it is probably best to suggest a few from the professional appraiser societies, like the Appraisers National Association, the American Society of Appraisers, or the International Society of Appraisers.[39] Most rare book librarians, with a knowledge of the field, will know booksellers who specialize in whatever area a collector may have focused on in his collecting, and they will thus prefer a bookseller to a more general "professional appraiser." Auction houses offer "free" appraisals for collectors, but they have a conflict of interest in that they are definitely interested in selling in their auctions the materials they appraise (thus making money on the books). So it is possible that they will give the collector an inflated evaluation to entice him to give the book up for auction.

Appraisals are not always done for tax purposes. They might be for insurance, or "replacement," value, though, of course, many items headed for special collections are irreplaceable. The appraisal could be for what is called "forced sale," as in a bankruptcy or estate liquidation. The owner may just want an informal appraisal, with no monetary reasons in mind. Or the appraisal could be a by-product of a listing of a collection's holdings for estate purposes, with no immediate goal of using the appraisal for tax purposes. The basic aim of an appraisal is to determine the fair market value (FMV) of an item or a collection. This value is the basis of gifts to libraries—that is, when a donor gives a book to a library, the appraisal should be of that volume's FMV. And the owner must understand that the figures the appraiser comes up with are subjective—based on that person's experience and knowledge—and that just because a book's FMV is a particular figure (as determined by the appraiser) does not mean that the owner can sell the item for that amount. (For more information about this, see the section "Appraisal and Book Evaluation" in chapter 10.)

Finally, and to reiterate, if the total value of the item to be given to the library is under $5,000, there is no need for a professional appraisal, and the librarian can guide the donor to the appropriate websites and price guides so that the donor can make her own appraisal.

BILLS OF SALE

Most of the rare book department's acquisitions will be from booksellers or the Internet. However, sometimes a private party will not be in a position to give his collectibles to the library and will wish to sell them. Another tactic for the librarian wishing to convince the owner of the materials to part with them is to negotiate a combination of gift and sale. That is, the librarian may ask the owner to sell a portion to the library and to give the rest. The gift portion may offset any capital gains taxes the donor may have to pay.

LIBRARIANS KNOW THAT a gift will cost a good deal of money, in personnel time and in the processing of the gift. It is fairly common for the recipient to ask the donor to offer some money to catalog and process the materials. This is not a legal issue, and it has been mentioned elsewhere, but it is worth repeating here.

It is possible that the seller will ask for restrictions on the materials as part of the transaction. As with a Deed of Gift, librarians should discourage such strings, but it may be necessary to accept some restrictions if the sale is to be consummated. The comments about such matters in the preceding section apply here as well.

Ownership of Holdings and Control of Original Materials

Special collections departments contain manuscript materials that scholars want to use. As mentioned in the preceding sections, and as the copyright laws show, ownership of a physical item is one thing; ownership of the rights to its intellectual property is another altogether. The J. D. Salinger case is a good reminder that anyone using original materials (or even using published texts, done in multiple copies) must diligently seek permission to use any words or ideas that are still under protection. Rare book departments, then, would do well to seek both kinds of ownership of all materials they acquire (by sale or gift).

For several reasons, it is ideal for the special collections department to own the intellectual rights to the materials in its possession, though only in rare cases is such ownership actually held by the library. For printed books, copyright is almost always in the hands of publishers, authors, or authors' assignees (heirs or institutions that are specifically given those rights by the former copyright holder). On rare occasions a copyright holder will give rights to a library.

Because rare book departments often collect the papers of writers, it is common for libraries to possess manuscripts of published or unpublished works, the rights of which could be in the hands of the donor. When a gift of this kind comes in, a legal document (the Deed of Gift) should be given to the donor because the transfer raises a few legal issues: Who will own the physical item(s)? Who will own the intellectual property of the items?

The Deed of Gift, then, should contain two options for the donor: the materials given will become the physical property of the receiving party, and the recipients will be given full control over the intellectual property rights of these materials; or the physical items will become the property of the recipient, but the intellectual property rights of the copyrightable materials will be retained by the donor. From the library's perspective the former of these two arrangements is preferable. It would seem that the latter of these options would be preferable to the donor, but the librarian has a strong argument to counter this view. If the donor has specific wishes for the use of the given materials, he will have control of them according to his desires and wishes until his death. At that point the rights revert to whomever he assigns them to, and whether that person carries out his wishes is not guaranteed. Also, the farther down the inheritance chain the materials pass, the more likely will it be that someone along the way will decide to go against the original copyright holder's wishes. And, the more the protected materials pass from one holder to another, the more likely will it be that the materials will be used in ways contrary to the original donor's wishes, especially if the user cannot locate the copyright holder.

To prevent these things from happening, the library can tell the donor that the library will hold the rights and will maintain the donor's wishes to perpetuity. One owner, one copyright holder, one place to find the materials and who owns them, and one rigid adherence to the donor's original requirements may convince the donor to check off the box

AUTHOR HARRY LAWTON, a resident of Riverside, California, wrote a popular children's book, *Willie Boy: A Desert Manhunt* (Balboa Island, CA: Malki Museum Press, 1960), based on a true story about a Native American boy (a Paiute) who, in 1909, supposedly shot and killed a white man in self-defense, and then shot some of the posse sent out to capture him, and was hunted down for it. In 1969, the book was turned into a movie starring Robert Redford, *Tell Them Willie Boy Is Here* (Universal Pictures). As a friend of the University of California, Riverside, Lawton gave his papers to the university, and he also gave it the rights to the book. To this day, the university library gets royalties on the sale of the book.

in the Deed of Gift that conveys ownership of copyright to the institution. This, of course, makes things easier for the library, because it does not have to try to keep up, over the decades, with the current rights holders for all the library's collections.

The Three-Year Rule

There is one thing that librarians must be aware of with gifts, though it does not affect the library that receives the gift. It affects the donor, and, though most donors are unaware of this rule, the librarian may wish to notify them of it. It is called the "Three-Year Rule," and the law states,

> Estate taxes are imposed on the amount of assets that a person owns at his/her death. In order to reduce the amount of estate taxes, many people will make gifts during their lifetime in order to reduce their assets as much as possible before their death. However, the tax law may pull back some of these gifts and impose estate tax on them if they are made too close to the date of death.[40]

To be more specific,

> Section 2035 of the tax code, which stipulates that assets that have been gifted through an ownership transfer, or assets for which the original owner has relinquished power, are to be included in the gross value of the original owner's estate if the transfer took place within three years of his or her death. If gifted assets do not meet the necessary requirements, the value of the assets is added to the value of the estate at the time of the original owner's death, increasing its value and the estate taxes imposed on it.[41]

The only exception to this rule is as follows:

> The three year rule does not apply if the grantor (maker) of the revocable trust makes a gift of the trust assets to another person. The gift will not be pulled back into the calculation of the estate tax of the grantor even if it is made within three years of his/her death.[42]

Hence, a donor who gives books to a library within three years of her death, thinking that she will get a tax write-off for them, will leave her heirs with a situation in which the tax write-off is denied because the gift was given too soon before the donor's death.

Another rule with a three-year limit concerns a library's acquisition of gifts. If a donation consisting of several or dozens of books comes in, many of which the library does not want to keep, it should do two things: (1) the books should not be formally accessioned, because it is easier to get rid of items that have not been accessioned than to part with materials that have become documentarily included in the institution's holdings; and (2) all items that will be discarded must be retained for three years. "IRS rules require that the Libraries retain for a minimum of three years each item for which the donor claims a tax deduction."[43] This rule protects the donor in that if there is any question about the accuracy of the appraised value of the items given, they can be looked at by an expert to corroborate the amount the donor has requested for a tax break.

Further, any party can approach the library and claim that particular item(s) donated did not belong to the donor, who had no right to give the pieces away in the first place. The library's three-year retention of unwanted items gives interested parties time to request the return of particular pieces. Of course, they must be able to prove their ownership of these things or the libraries need not hand over anything claimants wish to have.

Though not strictly a legal issue, the topic of donor relations is extremely important in the rare book world. What is germane, however, is the need for the librarian to know the complexities of the laws that relate to donors and booksellers and to be able to advise them on the matters discussed here.

Deposits

Closely related to gifts are deposits—materials coming into a rare book library that must be handled in a variety of ways and presumably be made available to patrons. The big difference, of course, is ownership:

anything on deposit is not owned by the institution taking the materials in. Most special collections librarians strongly discourage deposits for several reasons, not the least of which is that the materials could take up lots of space. They are not owned by the holding party, so that party feels a strong reticence to invest any resources in the materials. That means that most often the items will not be cataloged and will thus remain fairly inaccessible. In taking up space, the deposited materials ultimately cost the holding institution money in physical plant and staff costs—especially when moves of collections must be made.

There are possible liability issues as well. If the materials are damaged in any way, the holding institution is responsible because it was the caretaker of the items when the damage happened. But should the library be responsible for costly conservation treatments, or should the owner be asked to cover some or all of the costs? Are the materials insured? by whom?

For many reasons, some of which are hinted at in the sidebar, deposits should be discouraged. What would a library do if a deposited treasure were sto-

len? or damaged beyond repair by a burst pipe or a fire? Who pays the insurance on deposited materials? Who pays for repairs or replacement (if these are even options)?

On the other hand, there are times when taking a deposit may be either unavoidable or in the best interests of the institution. If a major donor has a relationship with an outside entity (a church, a civic organization, a local club that has been in existence for a century, a historical society, a public library that has housed local historical materials for 150 years), and that entity finds itself in a position—for whatever reason—of being unable to care for the materials anymore, and if the governing board of that entity refuses to divest itself of its archival holdings, it may be good PR with the donor or with the organization holding the materials (or both) to offer to take them on deposit. It is always preferable, as mentioned earlier, to receive the collection as a gift, but if this arrangement is not possible, a deposit may be the only alternative. Better to have the materials stored in a responsible library than languishing in deteriorating conditions, inaccessible, in an institution that cannot care for them and cannot make

AT UC RIVERSIDE, my department had vast holdings that were owned by Riverside City and County, who deposited the massive volumes at the offer of a professor who wanted to do research in local historical papers. The offer came when the city and the county, independently, were pressed for space in their own facilities and needed to do some work on their buildings. A librarian took all the books into the special collections department, partly as a gesture of goodwill to the professor and the volumes' owners, and partly because he had no idea of the long-term implications of this "generosity." When I got there, one massive area of shelving was clogged with these giant, leather-bound volumes, many

of which had red rot, and by this time—perhaps fifteen or twenty years after their acquisition— the books were taking up much-needed space in a department that had run out of shelf space years before. Then all heck broke loose when a giant earthquake sent hundreds of these volumes cascading to the floor in tight aisles. Covers broke loose, corners were severely bumped, and many other kinds of damage resulted. The department staff, along with others from the library outside special collections, were charged with getting all the volumes back onto the shelves. We tied many with string and shrink-wrapped many more. I vowed to do all in my power henceforth to reject deposits if it was at all possible.

A second case at Riverside is also instructive. A professor of English had a valuable Milton collection. Many years before I arrived, he made overtures to the library, suggesting that he would give his collection to the campus someday. After he stored his books in the library vault for close to twenty-five years, he notified the head of collection development that he was in negotiations with a bookseller, who was going to buy the collection, and he wanted it returned to him. He had essentially gotten a quarter of a century's free secure storage. These two cases militate against accepting anything on deposit, no matter what the materials are, and no matter what promises the depositor makes.

them available to scholars. Another benefit is that the library receiving the deposit can offer its patrons this much more information. If one of the main reasons for taking the deposit is to please the donor, it might be possible for the receiving library to ask for resources to catalog, process, and house the collection. But as already mentioned, most libraries have large enough backlogs that they could not justify diverting their own staff to the processing of a collection on deposit.

Also, if a major donor to an institution insists that his family papers be held on deposit for an unspecified length of time, the nature of his relationship to the institution may make it imperative that the library go along with the deposit. There are other situations in which deposits should be sought out and embraced. It might be a good way for a rare book department to engage an author who is looking for a good home for his papers. If two institutions are vying for the manuscripts of someone whose works the institutions' libraries collect, the one which first presents an appealing package that begins with housing the writer's papers on deposit may well have a foot in the door to get them.

Sometimes an administrator of an institution offers to take a collection on deposit to help out a colleague, not realizing the implications for the library. This is another situation in which it might be impossible to avoid taking a deposit. It is useful, then, for rare book librarians to explain to their superiors the plusses and minuses of such arrangements.

THE PROMISED GIFT AGREEMENT

One document that might make a deposit more palatable is the Promised Gift Agreement. A promised gift is similar to a deposit in that the materials are deposited into the library or are held by the donors in their own possession, but the agreement stipulates that after a determined period (often at the death of the donors) the materials will be given to the institution. With an agreement like this in place, heirs have no recourse to pull back into their ownership the items promised.[44]

THE DEED OF DEPOSIT

If a deposit is mandated for any reason, and accepting it is unavoidable, the library should have a good Deed of Deposit on hand. This document should have many of the same features as the Deed of Gift, with information about the owner and a description of the materials to be deposited. It should delineate restrictions if there are any. It should have a clause about what steps must be taken to have the materials returned to their owner, and so forth.

Clauses like those mentioned in the sidebar—with provisions for the institution's acquisition of deposited materials or compensation for storage—may well find a place in most deeds of deposit. It must be added, however, that in some circumstances accepting a deposit is in the best interests of both parties, and in some cases such arrangements cannot be avoided.

At any rate, though deposits can be more of a headache and a liability than a blessing, it is important to have a good Deed of Deposit form on hand in case this is the only way for the library to get possession of the materials. Good stewardship, continued friendly relations between the parties, and a carefully drafted deed can mitigate the liabilities for the library.

THE DEED OF Deposit used at the University of California, Riverside—which had to go through the same legal channels as did the one for gifts—contained two important clauses. The first said that after _____ years of stewardship, ownership of the deposited materials would revert to the university (the number of years should be negotiated between the depositor and the library, and it should not be a great length of time), and the second clause stated that if the materials were removed before they became the library's property, the depositor would pay the library _____ dollars per linear foot for storage charges. Needless to say, the number of deposits offered dropped to zero.

Cost Recovery and Fees for Services

Running a library is costly, what with staffing, overhead, acquisitions, cataloging and processing, and much more. Hardly a library is a cost-recovery unit in a larger institution. That is, libraries do not pay their own way. Nor are they expected to. The parent organization generally looks at libraries as line items in the institution's budget. Freestanding libraries, like the FAHN libraries (Folger Shakespeare; American Antiquarian Society; Huntington Library, Art Collections, and Botanical Gardens; and also the Newberry Library—along with other independent research libraries like the J. Pierpont Morgan in New York City),[45] must pay their own way. That is, for

---

UC RIVERSIDE'S RIVERA Library holds the world's largest collection of documents by and about B. Traven, the mystery man who wrote many wonderful novels, short stories, political pieces, and much more, and published under at least thirty-two known names. From 1915 to 1919, Traven wrote a newsletter called *Der Ziegelbrenner* (The Brickburner), under his name and that of Ret Marut.* Traven's wish to be as anonymous as possible, in the light of his antigovernment publications and to protect himself from retribution, led him to glory in his anonymity and to maintain it throughout his life. This led to the great difficulties scholars have had in trying to figure out who owns rights to the Traven texts.

The Riverside collection contains unpublished fiction by this writer. Several scholars would like to publish first editions of these unpublished works. When I left that department in 2000, the campus was holding off giving anyone permission to go to press. The campus did not own the rights, but it did own the documents, for which it had paid vast sums of money over the decades. It was only right for the campus to earn back some of its expenditures by being allowed to share any profits that could have been made by the sale of Traven's writing. The campus's reticence in granting permission had to do with legal matters,

the main one of which was who owned copyright. As the footnote indicates, two camps were slugging it out with respect to the identity of the writer. The unpublished short stories were typed under the name Ret Marut. If Marut was indeed the same as B. Traven (and no one apparently knows what the "B" stands for—not even Traven's wife, who went to her grave not able to reveal anything about him), then the rights to his writing belonged to a German publishing house that has now gone out of existence, the Büchergilde Gutenberg. (Who now owns the rights to the Büchergilde's holdings?) One professor claimed that that publishing house had full rights to publish all Traven's writing. But he had no documentary evidence to prove this. And he also claimed that the Büchergilde had given him exclusive, complete rights to publish any hitherto unpublished Traven writings. Again, he had no documentary evidence to prove this assertion. Could UCR allow him access to these papers, as he claimed he had a right to, lacking any documentary evidence that he had a right to them?

But another complicating factor was that a camp of scholars with strong arguments claimed that Traven and Marut were not the same person. If this group was right, then the ownership of Traven's unpublished (and published) texts was thrown into fur-

ther shadow. Then scholars had to find out who Ret Marut was and whether his works were owned by anyone, and this proved even more murky.

Two major issues arise in this case pertinent to the legal issues discussed in this chapter: (1) Did the university have a right to prohibit anyone from using (and eventually publishing) the papers? and (2) Did the university have a right to proceeds from any work published from the papers it owned, even though it did not own the intellectual property in those papers? Because many of Traven's novels were made into movies, including *The Treasure of the Sierra Madre*, the stakes could be high.

*To this day, despite extensive research by dozens of great scholars, Traven remains much in the shadows. Two camps of researchers exist: those who think that Traven and Ret Marut were one and the same, and those who think they were two people. Though the former camp has more adherents, the latter is not convinced. For a good place to start reading about this brilliant writer, many of whose novels were turned into movies, see the UCR website: http://library.ucr.edu/view/collections/spcol/travensite. A point made in chapter 1 of the present text is that those in the rare book field should know the collections of record of important writers. Here is a good example. The UCR collection is the place to begin any research into the life and writing of Traven.

most of these, there is no parent organization footing their bills.

Some of them may survive on large endowments (like the Getty), but most must raise their own money to keep alive. They can get grants from the government and from private foundations, support from any number of organizations, gifts from private donors, and income from some of the services they render. This last falls under the rubric "Fees for Services." With the widespread existence of free public libraries over the past 150 years, people have gotten comfortable thinking that they should be able to go into a library and use its resources for no fee. But most independent research libraries, and even those in public-supported institutions, have expenses far beyond what they bring in to cover their operating costs, and they are often looking to any income stream they can find to offset their expenditures.

This raises the question, is it legal for these libraries, which hold vast amounts of materials that are in the public domain, to charge for the use of these materials? The answer is yes. Hence, some of the libraries have entrance fees for scholars, though the trend is to do away with these, and they charge for several kinds of services, some of which are expensive, like extensive reference work, digitization of texts and images, photography, microfilming, and the like. It is perfectly reasonable for rare book departments to charge for their services.

One practice that has been changing recently is that of giving permission to patrons to use their digital cameras and phones to photograph materials from the collection. Some departments have strict rules against this practice, others allow it with certain limits and with a fee for the patrons, and still others allow it with practically no restrictions. Limits include such things as, no more than five images from a particular source; a fee of $__ for each image made (along with a list of each picture taken); a fee of $__ for a certain number of pictures and an additional fee of $__ for any pictures over that first number; a fee of $__ for one whole session of pictures; and the like.

If a library has manuscript materials that are in the public domain, these could generate income for the department. For instance, the library may own a batch of a Civil War soldier's letters, with vivid details about encampments, battles, uniforms, field hospitals, and such. The family has been gone for a hundred years, and the intellectual property of the letters does not rest in any known hands. The library, too, does not own copyright in the letters. But it may require a scholar wishing to go to press with an edition of this correspondence to pay a fee for copying them and to share the royalties with the library.

One way or another, the library that owns papers that could be published for profit does have a right to profit from these papers. Librarians could sign a contract with a scholar stating that anyone who goes to press with a publication that yields profit must share the profit (with the percentages stated) with the papers' holders. For the unpublished works of a popular writer, when no copyright holder can be found, it is best to err on the side of caution and not go to press. But this could tie up publication of important works indefinitely. The institution should work with the scholars and with attorneys to come up with a mutually agreeable arrangement.

A last word about fees in libraries: the operating budget of any rare book or special collections department will be vast compared to the small amount of money that any department fees can generate. The librarians might take the stance that collecting those fees costs more than the amount taken in. The trend is away from fees, but they are a legitimate operating option and whether to collect them or not should be carefully considered.

Watermarking Digital and Other Images

Libraries that choose to put restrictions on images they do not wish patrons to use can supply these images with watermarks (for digital images) or with overprinted text for works on paper. To help scholars who are working under fair use, the library will usually supply digital images in a resolution low enough that they are not reproducible for commercial purposes, or the library can supply photocopied sheets

AT UC RIVERSIDE the special collections depart-ment had a policy that images, microfilms, or other copies sent out to scholars were done on a tem-porary arrangement. For instance, the department made microfilms of an important collection (at the patron's expense), and then required the return of these films after a stated period. The films and the boxes containing them were marked some-thing like, "Property of the Rivera Library, Univer-sity of California, Riverside; must be returned to the library." That way, copies of our rare materials were not floating around outside our reach. It was, of course, impossible for us to monitor whether the users made their own copies, but that was prohibited in an agreement we had the patron sign before we sent out the films.

that might have printed in gray right across the text or image, "Property of the University; Not for Repro-duction," or wording similar to this. Then, for publi-cation, the scholar who wants to use the original will have the library supply reproducible images at what-ever terms the library's policy sets—that is, for what-ever fee the library chooses to assess.

Filtering Web Access; The ALA Code of Ethics and Bill of Rights

The American Library Association takes a strong stand on Freedom of Information, and librarians are expected to follow suit. The association has two pub-lished documents that are not exactly legal docu-ments, but that fall under the rubric "Legal Issues" because, by following the dictates of the profession, a librarian will be acting in accordance with—or in opposition to—cases of law that have set precedents for library practices.

FILTERING

Because of a number of legal issues (including the Children's Internet Protection Act—see later in this section—and the demands of many patrons who wish to "protect" the youth of their communities), librarians are often asked to filter their computers such that certain words cannot be accessed. The

American Library Association and other civil rights groups see filtering as a form of censorship and also see this as an impediment to the free access to infor-mation they believe is the right of all citizens.[46] The ethics of the profession, and the specific issue here strongly advocated by the ALA, seriously frown on any kind of curtailment to information. Those in the rare book field should know about the pressures and the ALA response to them.

THE ALA CODE OF ETHICS

The first document to look at for the ALA's stance on legal issues is the American Library Associa-tion Code of Ethics. This needs little comment here because the Ethical Standards document of RBMS has already been examined in detail in chapter 2, and the two documents overlap a good deal. For the purposes of the present chapter, one key statement to note is in clause 2: "We uphold the principles of intellectual freedom and resist all efforts to cen-sor library resources."[47] The manifestation of this stance is evident in legal cases all over the coun-try in which anyone (usually a private citizen with his or her own view of public morality) challenges a library (usually a public library) for having on its shelves items that the person does not approve of. Here is not the place to expatiate on how such chal-lenges (cases of censorship) are the results of indi-vidual assessments of texts (that the challengers often have not even read) done in the name of pub-lic morality and "for the greater good"; these chal-lenges are usually the results of personal prejudices. Often public libraries give in to this kind of pres-sure, but sometimes these cases come to court as tests of intellectual freedom.

Clause 3 of the ALA Code of Ethics is about pro-tecting library users' right to privacy. This, of course, is a basic right in the United States guaranteed by the Bill of Rights. How that right of U.S. citizens has been eroded has already been covered in chap-ter 2 in the discussion of the USA PATRIOT Act. Officials wishing to learn of the private informa-tion that libraries keep on patrons (their identity information, the books and manuscripts they have used, and so forth) can circumvent the U.S. Bill of Rights and obtain whatever information they want that the library holds. It is, of course, a major legal issue that went to the U.S. Supreme Court, with the ALA, the American Civil Liberties Union, and others fighting on the side of privacy. The ALA lost, and now total privacy of library records can no longer be guaranteed. Those working in rare books, as chapter 2 explained, must decide what records they wish to keep (because it is important to have information about past library use) and which to discard or destroy. It is a difficult choice to make.

The ALA Code, clause 4, states, "We respect intellectual property rights and advocate balance between the interests of information users and rights holders." This, of course, follows on the discussion at the opening of this chapter. As disseminators of information, rare book departments have a mandate to get research materials into the hands of their patrons, but they are not unmindful of the rights of holders of intellectual property. This, again, is a delicate balance, but in all activities, librarians must fall on the side of the law.

The next clause talks of safeguarding "the rights and welfare of all employees of our institutions," clearly a legal issue when it comes to employee rights. Most libraries have formal channels for grievance by employees who think they have been unfairly or illegally treated. Other clauses talk about separating personal from professional beliefs, maintaining open access to information, and striving for excellence, not strictly legal issues, but worth mentioning here as part of the expected mind-set of those working in special collections and rare books.

THE ALA BILL OF RIGHTS

The American Library Association Bill of Rights is short enough to quote in full:

> The American Library Association affirms that all libraries are forums for information and ideas, and that the following basic policies should guide their services.
>
> I.   Books and other library resources should be provided for the interest, information, and enlightenment of all people of the community the library serves. Materials should not be excluded because of the origin, background,
>
> or views of those contributing to their creation.
>
> II. Libraries should provide materials and information presenting all points of view on current and historical issues. Materials should not be proscribed or removed because of partisan or doctrinal disapproval.
>
> III. Libraries should challenge censorship in the fulfillment of their responsibility to provide information and enlightenment.
>
> IV. Libraries should cooperate with all persons and groups concerned with resisting abridgment of free expression and free access to ideas.
>
> V.   A person's right to use a library should not be denied or abridged because of origin, age, background, or views.
>
> VI. Libraries that make exhibit spaces and meeting rooms available to the public they serve should make such facilities available on an equitable basis, regardless of the beliefs or affiliations of individuals or groups requesting their use.

It is beyond the scope of the present text to comment at any length on these concerns. It is clear, however, that private parties can challenge any of these mandates, with the result that the library could wind up in court defending its decisions to act in accordance with these professional principles. A liberal court should uphold all cases in the library's favor; a conservative court may not do so. Likewise, libraries not following these principles can be challenged in a court of law, for failure to follow them could be breaking federal laws. For instance, if a library chooses not to keep on its shelves a book the head librarian deems "immoral" or "not in the public interest," a patron could challenge the library on the grounds of free access to information.

In such a situation, however, when a library does not supply a book a patron wants, it could be because of financial exigency. That is, the library could claim that it has not purchased a particular item because it has a small, finite budget and that other books took precedence over the one not purchased. It may not have anything at all to do with censorship; it is merely a matter of priorities. This might not placate a patron, but it could be the truth.

The last clause of the ALA Bill of Rights says that the library should allow groups to use its spaces "regardless of the beliefs or affiliations of individuals or groups requesting their use." Librarians can expect public outcry if the space is offered to incendiary groups advocating radical views. Local politics and political and moral differences of opinion can wreak havoc in a library that is trying to follow this mandate.

Such matters certainly have to do with the library as a whole, not merely with special collections, but they still may have an impact on the rare book department for assaults could be leveled at that department as well as at the larger library.

CIPA

One particular act is worth singling out, for it obliquely influences the special collections department: the Children's Internet Protection Act (CIPA). The Federal Communications Commission's (FCC) website explains,

> The Children's Internet Protection Act (CIPA) is a federal law enacted by Congress to address concerns about access to offensive content over the Internet on school and library computers. CIPA imposes certain types of requirements on any school or library that receives funding for Internet access or internal connections from the E-rate program—a program that makes certain communications technology more affordable for eligible schools and libraries. In early 2001, the FCC issued rules implementing CIPA.

The federal government provided funds for schools and libraries to get deep "E-rate discounts for Internet access or internal connections."[48] When CIPA was passed, it required libraries and schools to put filters on their computers to protect the young from inappropriate content that could be accessed from the Web, and it threatened to cut off funding for the E-rate discounts for Internet access to all institutions that did not filter their computers. Such implementation, according to the ALA, was tantamount to censorship and to blocking free access to infor-

mation. The ALA objected, and, with the backing of other organizations, it sued the federal government to strike down CIPA. The Supreme Court upheld the act by a close decision. Now any library that receives federal funding (especially public libraries) must filter its computers.[49]

Many public libraries have rare book departments, and many special collections departments are in academic institutions that get federal funding. Although there are provisions for shutting off the filters for adult patrons, such action still takes a special request, and it places in a delicate position those who ask for the filters to be canceled. All people working in libraries—and that certainly includes rare book librarians—should know about CIPA and its implications.

Endowed Funds

Over years, decades, and (for some libraries) centuries, a number of endowed funds may be formed, especially in rare book departments where it is likely that well-heeled donors have showered their support in areas of their own interest. These are funds the principle of which cannot be touched, but the earned income of which can be tapped for whatever the fund was designated for. And this is where the legal issues enter.

If the donor has said, "Proceeds of this fund are to be used for the acquisition of books printed in the Renaissance," then that is how the interest from the fund *must* be spent. The document that conveyed the funds to the library in the first place is a legal instrument with its own mandates, and even if the collecting areas of the library have evolved over the decades, the endowment stipulations have probably not evolved equivalently. They are fixed at the time of the endowment. Librarians should point this out to the donors and perhaps get them to word the stipulations in such a way that there is some flexibility in the terms of the gift. For instance, "Proceeds of this fund are to be used for the acquisition of books printed in the Renaissance, for books about the Renaissance, or for conservation of books and manuscripts in the special collections department."

THE PHILLIPS LIBRARY currently has two narrowly designated funds, one for Canadian maritime materials and one for medical materials. The first of these is a problem because the library has been collecting maritime items for over two centuries, and practically nothing in that area with a connection to Canada comes on the market that we do not already have. The second fund is a problem because the library has not had an interest in medical books for a century. An item would have to come on the market that fits into our other collecting areas but that has a medical connection in some way. This is quite unlikely, so the fund continues to grow.

It is frustrating for a rare book librarian to have an old fund, with a narrow designation of how that fund can be spent, in a library that no longer collects in that area, or in an area in which practically nothing comes on the market. The fund continues to grow, and could reach significant proportions, but not be accessible at all.

If the heirs of the original donors who endowed the fund are still alive, the library may appeal to them to change the designations in the fund. If they are not, it is possible to go to court to change the fund's strictures. But this is costly and time-consuming, and unless the fund is truly gargantuan, it might not be worth the effort.

Another issue arises with endowed funds: If the payout rate of the fund, set by the institution, is fixed (at, say, 5 percent) and the fund earns much more than that, the extra money the fund earns is then put back into the fund, to let the principle grow. But if there is no set payout rate, the librarian will be able to spend whatever the fund generates in a given year (sometimes 5 percent, sometimes more, and possibly nothing at all if the fund has a down year). These two possibilities should be worked out with the donor, and how the money is to be accruing and spent should be stipulated in the endowment document.[50]

The final word on endowed funds is this: do not spend the earned income from the fund for anything that the fund does not permit you to spend it on. That is breaking the law. Look for innovative ways to interpret the wording in the endowment document such that the expenditures can be fully justifiable, and look for items on the market that fit the fund's strictures.

Weeding and Deaccessioning

Collections grow, age, and evolve. Eventually many of them run out of shelf space. One of the librarians' mandates is to weed collections to get rid of items that have slipped to level 1 priority and to make room on shelves for new acquisitions. The main point here is that weeding can raise a legal issue if it is not done properly.

To begin with, donors may, in their deeds of gift, specify that certain books in the gifts may not be deaccessioned, but must be kept to perpetuity. This places a lifetime restriction on such items and forces the library to keep on its shelves volumes that it would love to get rid of. There may be some legal way to break the restriction, but this takes a lawyer and judges, and the cost of such proceedings could be prohibitive—far more than getting rid of the

AS THE TEXT mentions, one fund at the Phillips Library is strictly for medical books or manuscripts. That fund had not been used in decades when a bookseller offered us a ship's log (which we collect in abundance) written by a ship's physician. We have a fund for buying maritime materials, but for this purchase I was able to tap the medical fund without breaking the terms of that fund. A careful examination of the terms of the document made it imperative that such a use of the money had to be sanctioned by a particular state medical group. The group is still in existence after more than a century, and when I called its president to ask permission to make the purchase, he was astonished and amused. But he had to run it by his board for their approval. The message is that the librarian must be familiar with *all* the terms of the deed of transfer of funds. The use of the money is a legal activity when it is governed by an endowment, controlled by someone who might have been dead for two hundred years.

volume is worth. On the other hand, if the weeding comprises a large number of books in the collection, such proceedings may be worth the effort.

Weeding is difficult and unpleasant, but it sometimes must be done. If the collection is owned by a private organization, the institution can usually draw up its own procedures and follow its own mandates and practices. But thousands of collections are part of public—or publicly funded—entities, in which case the weeding must be done within the boundaries of the laws that govern each institution.[51]

The problem can be acute in special collections in which a good number of items will likely have been acquired through gifts, with their concomitant deeds.[52] It is essential for the department (or the institution) to keep good, thorough records of all acquisition transactions and to make sure that these records can be easily accessed. It is equally important for the acquiring library to discourage any form of restriction on the donated (or purchased) items. And finally, it is imperative that the institution scrupulously adhere to any restrictions on materials. Not doing so could lead to serious litigation a generation or three down the line.

Deaccession is the step beyond weeding. It is one thing to pull the book from the shelves (weeding), but another to get rid of it. If a library has a policy of accessioning—taking an item formally into its collection, often signified by creating a cataloging record for it—it should have a policy for deaccessioning as well. As already noted, in the rare book department deaccessioning can be especially problematic.

To avoid such problems, it might be a good idea (to circumvent the institution's mandates about accessioned materials) for the library to take things in but not formally accession them. A library cannot formally deaccession a book that has not been formally accessioned in the first place.[53] The main issue here is that all activities related to disposing of items in the collection must be done with a clear understanding of the strings attached to the original acquisition and of the laws of the institution, city, or state that govern such activities.

Digitization Agreements with Vendors

With the growth and expansion of digital tools, an increasing amount of material may be disseminated to a wider audience than ever before in history. Vendors for decades have contracted with libraries to print and publish copies of their holdings. The publisher does most of the work (making facsimiles of original materials, for instance) and then publishes the text, sharing the royalties with the holding institution. This model has been successful for libraries to a great degree since digital copying came onto the scene.

WHEN I WAS head of special collections at UC Riverside, I contracted with Gale/Cengage Learning to digitize the finding aid for one of the department's most important collections, the holdings of the American Indian Historical Society. Gale digitized the finding aid, and it is now on the Web.*

Likewise, at the Phillips Library at the Peabody Essex Museum, I worked with Adam Matthew, another company putting together superb packages of original materials—not just the finding aids, but full-color images of original documents. Adam Matthew locates the materials it wants to package, arranges for the digitization, cleans up the text, writes the introduction, does the indexing, and markets the product. The library gets a royalty for each copy that the company sells. And scholars all over the world can have access to important collections, provided that a library near them buys the package.

*See http://microformguides.gale.com/Data/Download/9022000C.pdf.

The point is that a world of information exists that people want, companies exist that can make that information available where libraries are not able to do so, and rare book departments, with their vast holdings of original materials, stand to engender resources while fulfilling their mandate to get information into the hands of as many users as need it. All this activity must be governed by carefully crafted contracts that protect the rights of the commercial companies and the libraries. This is the wave of the present for rare book departments. It is generating income, organizing and digitizing and getting cataloged important collections, and helping the world of scholarship. The documents that make it all possible—the contracts between the rare book departments and the commercial vendors—must be scrutinized by legal experts so that both parties will be satisfied.

The companies implementing these projects have been at it for decades, and their contracts have been scrutinized by the many institutions they have worked with. So the contracts have fairly standard contents. The librarian and her institution's counsel should peruse this document before signing (of course), and they may be in a position to change some standard stipulations. For instance, the company may have exclusive rights to the package of digitized materials for five years, but the library may be able to negotiate for a shorter period. It may also be able to negotiate for more remunerable terms (e.g., 12 percent for the first eight packages sold rather than 10 percent for the first ten packages). But for the most part, the companies' contracts are reasonable and offer the library a service and an income it could not have generated on its own.

Licensed Databases

Another legal issue that those in the rare book world should be aware of pertains to the use of licensed databases. For the purposes of this volume, two kinds are germane: public databases such as Flickr, Wikimedia, Twitter, and the like; and commercial or nonprofit ones available by subscription that offer reference materials to the library, like those from companies like Adam Matthew or the Ship Index (ShipIndex.org).

Special collections departments are increasingly using their fiscal resources to acquire online databases for their patrons and their reference staff. The Ship Index, just mentioned, is one of hundreds available. As Tomas Lipinski and Andrea Copeland point out, the use of such sources entails the signing of a contract.[54]

Two main questions arise when the department agrees to the terms of a licensed service: (1) Does the licensor (the provider of the database) warranty the accuracy and legal integrity of the product? and (2) If the database provider changes any of the terms of use, must it notify the licensee of this change? A change could lead a user into improper use of materials, possibly resulting in the user's being sued. If this happens, is the licensee indemnified (protected from harm)? That is, does the licensor promise to cover expenses if the licensor is the source of the problem?

The ramifications of these issues can be great. For instance, using the Ship Index as an example, if the owner of the index claims that the materials this index offers are in the public domain (but are in fact protected by copyright) and the institution (or one of its researchers) uses such materials, what will happen if the rights holder sues for copyright infringement? Who is responsible? In special collections and in any other realm of endeavor (for a rare book dealer may find herself in a similar circumstance), those agreeing to the use of a service must know all the potential pitfalls. It may be a good idea to have a specific special collections librarian consult an attorney before the department signs a legal document for the use of a vendor's product.

As Lipinski and Copeland say, "A licensee of a database of articles desires to have the vendor warrant that the content is non-infringing and indemnify the licensee in case it turns out the vendor was wrong and the content supplied turns out to be infringing" (p. 77).

Because libraries are acquiring by license more and more databases, they must observe copyright laws with respect to the dissemination of the information that these databases contain. The website Licensing Digital Information[55] is a good guide to preventing the library from breaking the law if it wishes to use information contained in licensed databases. The site, maintained by Yale University, has a document titled "Analysis of Licensing Agreements for Digital Information." The document points out that just because the library has a contract to use (and disseminate) the information in the digital databases it has contracted for, librarians must not assume they have full rights to disseminate that information as they wish. This document states,

> Because of several unique properties of digital information, agreements that govern the acquisition and maintenance of traditional paper collections are inadequate in the digital information context. Unlike paper materials, digital information generally is not purchased by the library; rather it is licensed by the library from information providers. A license usually takes the form of a written contract or agreement between the library and the owner of the rights to distribute digital information.

The site gives a model of a standard licensing agreement that should help all who wish to contract with publishers to use their databases.[56] Inasmuch as special collections departments have an increasing number of databases available to them, it is useful for librarians to familiarize themselves with this document.

Another issue that Lipinski and Copeland treat at length has to do with what happens when the licensor changes the terms of agreement after the library (or other customer) has subscribed to the product. Must the licensor notify the licensee of the change? Or does continued use of the product constitute approval of the change? Or can the licensor merely tell its customers, "We have changed the terms of use; click here to accept this change"? The issue can be quite complex, and because so much of this is new in the digital world, there are no national or international laws in place as yet to regulate such things. Anyone using licensed databases—libraries, booksellers, collectors, private scholars, archivists— must be aware of these issues and may need the services of an attorney versed in the complexities of this emerging field.

Employees

The observations offered in this section apply to all employees, not just those in special collections.

These are legal issues, however, and it is appropriate to bring them up here.

HIRING

Bringing into the department a new employee entails several legal issues. To begin with, many positions require broad national searches, and, even if there is a front-runner inside the institution, the library may be required to do the wider search. Needless to say, the hunt must be done with no bias, for any kind of discrimination can be a cause for legal action. Bias in a hiring decision is often difficult to prove, but certainly an unsuccessful candidate for a position can charge bias in such obvious areas as race, age, sex, sexual preference, marital status, familial background, and so forth. It is essential that bias not be part of any decision making for a special collections position (or for any position).

As with all jobs, those in special collections require a number of skills, and one way to eliminate unqualified candidates is simply to assess the applicants for the abilities they have. For this reason it is critical that all the skills required of the successful candidate be spelled out clearly in the job advertisement. And skills are not the only requirements that must be delineated. The ad may also say, "Must be able to work weekends and evenings," "Must be able to lift 40-pound boxes," "Must be able to travel midweek" (if the person is being hired to develop donor prospects or to look at distant collections), "Must be able to begin work full time on September 1," and so forth.

Among the job requirements to spell out are computer proficiency, language capabilities,[57] experience running conferences or symposia, familiarity with development activities, editing skills, a record of publications, and much more. The more explicit the job description, the more it weeds out potential applicants who do not measure up to the department's needs, and the better (though much smaller) the applicant pool will be. If one of the requirements of the position is that the successful candidate have an MLS degree from an accredited academic institution, it is essential that the person hired does have that degree. Candidates will send in application letters that say, "I am in my last semester in my Library School program and I will have the MLS in two months." This candidate may have all the skills listed in the job ad and may look superb on paper—exactly the right combination of qualifications that the department is looking for—but there is no guarantee that the applicant will indeed have that degree by the time he is scheduled to begin the work. If the degree is not already in hand, it is a gamble to offer the position to this person. If he is offered the job, accepts it, and then does not complete the degree by the stated beginning date of the job, the institution is open to challenges from untold numbers of possible candidates who could say, "If we knew you would hire someone without the MLS degree, we would have applied." So it is not enough to spell out in minute detail what the successful applicant must be able to do, it is equally important to find someone who can do what is asked for and who meets all the job requirements delineated in the job ad. Failing that, it may be necessary to extend the application deadline or change the job description.

In chapter 7, CORI (Criminal Offender Record Information) checks were discussed. This check produces what is not strictly speaking a legal document, but the document may contain information that is inaccurate or outright wrong. Being denied a position on the basis of an inaccurate, suspect, or damning CORI check can lead to legal repercussions. People have the right to get copies of their CORI checks and to fix errors in them, and possibly the right to get them sealed if the offenses they record are old enough. From the library's perspective, it is important that these checks be done, especially in a rare book environment.

DISCIPLINE AND TERMINATION

Certainly, disciplining or terminating an employee is not strictly a rare book department issue, but it is indeed a legal matter that could wind up in the courts, so it should be looked at briefly here. These acts must be undertaken with great care and only after a long and documented case of inappropriate conduct has been monitored and recorded in performance appraisals. Camila Alire and G. Edward Evans

say that discipline should be carried out in cases in which an employee's objectionable activities are the result of true poor performance. They say that "letting problems 'slide' only hurts everyone in the long-run."[58] Carefully and honestly done appraisals will record long-standing behavior (good or bad), and if the behavior has not been satisfactory, the recorded appraisals can be a solid legal basis for discipline or termination or both.

Hence, performance appraisals must be carried out with a constant set of standards, not ones that shift from week to week or project to project. The supervisor must weigh her own personal biases to make sure the assessment is fair. It is beyond the present text to delve deeply into reasons for and methods of discipline and termination. The key point here is that these actions are legal issues, and a disgruntled employee on the receiving end of one of these actions may create a legal problem for the institution by going to court. It is important to have good documentation over time to support the decision to discipline or terminate.

The Americans with Disabilities Act

The Web page "25 Important Legal Issues Every Librarian Should Research"[59] has a link to Mary Minow's article, "Does Your Library's Web Page Violate the Americans with Disabilities Act?"[60] This piece begins with a comment from a blind user:

> "When blind people use the Internet and come across unfriendly sites, we aren't surfing, we are crawling. . . . Imagine hearing pages that say, 'Welcome to . . . [image].' 'This is the home of . . . [image].' 'Link, link, link.' It is like trying to use Netscape with your monitor off and your mouse unplugged. See how far you'll get."

The article is about how libraries must adapt to the digital world—in this case, how people with disabilities seek digital information, and how libraries must accommodate them. If the library does not allow for "equal access," it could be violating the rights of the disabled—in this instance the blind. Minow points out that the Americans with Disabilities Act of 1990 "prohibits discrimination against persons with disabilities, and provides a private cause of action to patrons to enforce its provisions." She then quotes "Section 12132 [which] states that 'no qualified individual with a disability shall, by reason of such disability, be excluded from participation in or be denied the benefits of the services, programs, or activities of a public entity.'" And finally, she points out, "In a policy ruling dated 9/9/96, 10 NDLR 240, the Department of Justice stated that state, local governments and the business sector must provide effective communication whenever they communicate through the Internet. The effective communication rule would apply to libraries using the Internet for communication regarding their programs and services."

This clearly applies to rare book departments, though the problem of how they are to accommodate the blind is not always solvable. Minow summarizes the ten means of accommodation that the City of San Jose, California, has come up with.[61] Special collections departments often have excellent websites, listing their strong collections and showing images of many of their holdings. In constructing these sites, each department should do all it can to make its information accessible to the blind.

■ ■ ■

This chapter has looked at many of the key (and some of the less central) legal issues that rare book librarians face. Librarians—even those with special collections and rare book training—are generally not lawyers, but their familiarity with the legal issues dealt with in this chapter is essential. Legal dilemmas raise many questions in the rare book world. If librarians don't "have all the answers," they should at least know what the questions are and should know where to turn to get the answers.

NOTES

1. The extent to which libraries and legal issues are intertwined is evident if one searches on the Web under the term "libraries and legal issues." A giant number of hits results. The present chapter deals with only a few of the more prominent ones.

2. *Copyright Basics* (also designated Circular 1) (Washington, DC: U.S. Copyright Office, Library of Congress, 2008). This twelve-page pamphlet, the source of some of the information in the present chapter (cited as "*Copyright Basics*"), is available from the United States Government Printing Office (USGPO), and it is also on the Web at www.copyright.gov/circs/circ01.pdf. Another informative publication from the USGPO is *Publications on Copyright* (designated Circular 2), www.copyright.gov/circs/circ02.pdf. The American Library Association has also published an excellent volume directly germane to readers of this book: Kenneth D. Crews, *Copyright Law for Librarians and Educators: Creative Strategies and Practical Solutions*, 3rd ed. (Chicago: American Library Association, 2012), further cited as "Crews." Another ALA publication to consult is Carrie Russell, *Complete Copyright: An Everyday Guide for Librarians* (Chicago: American Library Association, 2004).

3. The wording of this passage on the PDF version on the Web is slightly different.

4. Note that the word *creator* is used consistently in copyright explanations because *author* does not describe the work of an artist, a photographer, an architect, or a musician, whose work is equally protected by the laws.

5. Libraries with important collections of writers will often have manuscripts that are not in the public domain and that are still under the protection of the 1976 Copyright Act.

6. The studio may have been sold only the film rights, or it may have rights to all public releases of the text.

7. See http://norman.hrc.utexas.edu/watch. This is the U.S. site for WATCH.

8. See http://norman.hrc.utexas.edu/watch/us.cfm#Q1.

9. See http://norman.hrc.utexas.edu/watch/uk.cfm. This is the British site for WATCH; it has additional information on the project at its home page.

10. According to Wikipedia,

An orphan work is a copyrighted work for which the copyright owner cannot be contacted. In some cases the name of the creator or copyright owner of an orphan work may be known but other than the name no information can be established. Reasons for a work to be orphan include that the copyright owner is unaware of their ownership or that the copyright owner has died or gone out of business (if a company) and it is not possible to establish to whom ownership of the copyright has passed.

See "Orphan works," Wikipedia, http://en.wiki pedia.org/wiki/Orphan_works.

11. See www.copyright.gov/orphan.

12. See http://copyright.columbia.edu/copyright/ permissions/if-you-cannot-find-the-owner.

13. On October 22, 2012, the U.S. Copyright Office issued its "Notice of Inquiry Concerning Orphan Works and Mass Digitization." For the implications of this notice for libraries, see the document issued by the Library Copyright Alliance (LCA) titled "Comments of the Library Copyright Alliance in Response to the Copyright Office's Notice of Inquiry Concerning Orphan Works and Mass Digitization," www .librarycopyrightalliance.org/bm~doc/lca-orphan works-comments-14jan13.pdf. The LCA "consists of three major library associations—the American Library Association (ALA), the Association of College and Research Libraries (ACRL), and the Association of Research Libraries (ARL)."

14. See www.diyphotography.net/new-uk-may-allow -free-usage-orphan-works. There will be a backlash to this bill. As the BBC News Technology site explains,

> Photography groups have reacted angrily to new legislation passed in Parliament over the use of copyrighted material when the owner cannot be contacted. Photographs or other creative works can be used without the owners' explicit permission as long as a "diligent search" has taken place. Campaigners said the new act paved the way for the exploitation of images posted on the internet. But the government said the act made 'copyright licensing more efficient' (www.bbc .co.uk/news/technology-22337406).

15. See http://copyright.cornell.edu/resources/public domain.cfm. Peter Hirtle, in his first note to this chart, cites other charts that were influential to him in compiling his own, and also charts with different foci. His note says,

> The chart is based in part on Laura N. Gasaway's chart, "When Works Pass into the Public Domain," at http://www.unc.edu/~unclng/ public-d.htm, and similar charts found in Marie C. Malaro, *A Legal Primer on Managing Museum Collections* (Washington, D.C.: Smithsonian Institution Press, 1998): 155–156. A useful copyright duration chart by Mary Minow, organized by year, is found at http://www.librarylaw.com/ DigitizationTable.htm. A "flow chart" for copyright duration is found at http://www.sunstein

law.com/practices/copyright-portfolio-develop ment/flowchart.htm, and a "tree-view" chart on copyright is at http://chart.copyrightdata.com.

16. See "National Treatment," Wikipedia, http:// en.wikipedia.org/wiki/National_treatment.

17. An author or playwright, for example, may bequeath a work to three nieces. The intellectual property rights "holder" could be a cluster of people. If one of the nieces dies or passes her property to others, and they, eventually, divide and pass on their percentages of the rights to yet others, the person seeking permission is really in a bind, trying to get permission from many rights holders, of different generations, perhaps across the country or around the globe. The more generations that pass, the more invisible become the rights holders.

18. This item from the "Copyright Crash Course" is titled "Getting Permission to Use Archival Materials Related to Architectural Works" (http://copyright .lib.utexas.edu/architec.html).

19. See "National Treatment," Wikipedia, http:// en.wikipedia.org/wiki/National_treatment.

20. This assertion does not imply that ignorant scholars are stupid. It merely means that they do not know the law. (Ignorance of the law is no excuse.) Young scholars, from junior high school to professorial ranks, could be ignorant of these laws.

21. *Code of Best Practices in Fair Use for Academic and Research Libraries* (N.p.: Association of Research Libraries; Center for Social Media, School of Communication, American University; and Program on Information Justice and Intellectual Property, Washington College of Law, American University, January 2012), p. 1. This twenty-nine-page text was endorsed by the American Library Association and the Association of College and Research Libraries. This excellent pamphlet also states, "Feel free to reproduce this work in its entirety. For excerpts and quotations, depend upon fair use" (p. 29). The discussion in the present volume about fair use relies heavily on this text, which is cited parenthetically as "Fair Use." The justification for "Copyright and Fair Use" is clearly spelled out in this pamphlet (pp. 5–10). And the notes lead the reader to many important writings on the subject, pertinent to the present text. An extensive treatment of this subject can be found in Patricia Aufderheide and Peter Jaszi's *Reclaiming Fair Use: How to Put Balance Back in Copyright* (Chicago and London: University of Chicago Press, 2011). A key passage in this volume explains,

Law provides copyright protection to creative works in order to foster the creation of culture. Its best known feature is protection of owners' rights. But copying, quoting, and generally reusing existing cultural material can be, under some circumstances, a critically important part of generating new culture. In fact, the cultural value of copying is so well established that it is written into the social bargain at the heart of copyright law. The bargain is this: we as a society give limited property rights to creators to encourage them to produce culture; at the same time, we give other creators the chance to use that same copyrighted material, without permission or payment, in some circumstances. Without the second half of the bargain, we could all lose important new cultural work. (p. 158)

And Aufderheide and Jaszi point out that fair use is the principle feature of the copyright law that allows for such free use.

22. One website to note, titled "Fair Use" and posted by the U.S. Copyright Office, is at www.copyright.gov/fls/fl102.html. The Wikipedia article, with the same title, is at http://en.wikipedia.org/wiki/Fair_use; it is extensive and excellent. Another excellent site is that of the Association of Research Libraries, "Code of Best Practices in Fair Use for Academic and Research Libraries" (January 2012), www.arl.org/focus-areas/copyright-ip/fair-use/code-of-best-practices.

23. See the U.S. Copyright Office website at www.copyright.gov/fls/fl102.html.

24. This discussion of copyright can offer merely basic regulations, advice, and cautions. For perhaps the most thorough treatment of the subject, one work stands out as authoritative and about as current as possible: *Nimmer on Copyright* (New York: Lexis Publishing, in continual production). This revered, most-often-cited text is bound in post binders so that it can be constantly updated, with updates issued every four months. The original publication was authored by Melville Nimmer; its present incarnation is carried on by his son, David Nimmer. (See "Melville Nimmer," Wikipedia, http://en.wikipedia.org/wiki/Melville_Nimmer).

25. The extensive and thorough Wikipedia article gives great detail on this act (http://en.wikipedia.org/wiki/Copyright,_Designs_and_Patents_Act_1988). All material on British copyright is taken from this site.

26. See "Whistleblower," Wikipedia, http://en.wikipedia.org/wiki/Whistleblower#USA.

27. This section of the deed could be called "Restrictions," but that is a term to avoid, for it gives the donor the idea that she can restrict the library's disposition or use. The generic word "Terms" does not convey this.

28. The etymology is from "Cy-près doctrine," Wikipedia, http://en.wikipedia.org/wiki/Cy-pr%C3%A8s_doctrine.

29. *Communications Journal*, http://thecommunicationsjournal.com/quit-claim-agreements.

30. *Communications Journal*, http://thecommunicationsjournal.com/quit-claim-agreements.

31. Contracts for digitized materials can be exceptionally complicated. Some issues relate solely to digitization, but most contracts are merely contracts, and librarians should be comfortable reading and understanding them, writing them, negotiating them, and terminating them.

32. See www.irs.gov/publications/p561. Besides the quoted paragraph, the IRS guidelines discuss books' conditions, signatures in books, and other things that affect value. The site opens with a good discussion of fair market value.

33. See www.irs.gov/publications/p561/ar02.html#d0e139. This document clarifies that gifts of "similar items" means "property of the same generic category or type," and it warns that

> if you give books to three schools and you deduct $2,000, $2,500, and $900, respectively, your claimed deduction is more than $5,000 for these books. You must get a qualified appraisal of the books and for each school you must attach a fully completed Form 8283, Section B, to your tax return.

Most librarians and donors do not know these fine points of U.S. tax law, and rare book librarians should be able to enlighten their donors about these complications of giving.

34. One example of how these regulations are employed can be found in George Mason University's "Gifts-in-Kind Policy," which states,

> Under current tax law for gifts over $500 but less than $5,000, donors must file a completed IRS Form 8283 which must be signed by the George Mason University Foundation. Gifts exceeding $5,000 require a formal appraisal, which must be secured by the donor, to accompany filing IRS Form 8283. The value of the gift should be determined by the donor prior to transfer to the Libraries. If possible, a copy of the appraisal should also be submitted to the Libraries.

This site adds,

IRS law prohibits librarians and staff from appraising materials or the Libraries paying for or arranging for appraisals. Pertinent information is available in IRS Publication No. 561 "Determining the Value of Donated Property." Because tax laws change frequently, it is advisable that donors seek professional tax or estate counsel prior to making a gift. (http://library.gmu.edu/libinfo/giftpolicy.html)

To repeat, the institution is not automatically given a copy of the appraisal, and the donor need not supply one.

35. These criteria are summarized or quoted from the IRS document cited in note 32. Note that the appraisal described here is specifically for tax purposes (this is, after all, an IRS document), but appraisals for insurance or replacement purposes can also be done, and the owner should explain the reason for the evaluation to the appraiser before the assessment is done.

36. See John R. Payne, "A Closer Eye on Appraisals," *College & Research Library News* 46.2 (February 1985): 52–56; this information is on p. 53.

37. Payne, "A Closer Eye," p. 52.

38. Payne, "A Closer Eye." This statement is followed by another warning: "Appraisers who have performed work unacceptable to the IRS in the past are prevented from submitting subsequent appraisals for income tax purposes" (p. 52).

39. See Appraisers National Association, www.ana-appraisers.org. See also "New IRS Rules Relating to Non Cash Contributions" at a site that lays out laws concerning the responsibilities of appraisers: New England Inventory & Appraisal Services, www.newenglandinventory.com/irsrules.html; www.appraisers.org/ASAHome.aspx; and www.isa-appraisers.org. These are but three of many professional appraiser societies.

40. See www.legalmatch.com/law-library/article/gifts-made-within-three-years-of-death.html.

41. See www.answers.com/topic/three-year-rule.

42. See www.legalmatch.com/law-library/article/gifts-made-within-three-years-of-death.html.

43. See http://beta.library.miami.edu/gifts-policy.

44. A sample such agreement for the J. Paul Getty Trust can be found at http://files.ali-aba.org/thumbs/datastorage/skoobesruoc/source/CR005_16A_Adelson-Promised_gift_agreement___2pg_thumb.pdf.

45. The Independent Research Libraries Association (IRLA) is composed of those mentioned, along with the American Philosophical Society; the John Carter Brown Library; the Canadian Centre for Architecture; the Getty Research Library; the Hagley Museum and Library; the Historical Society of Pennsylvania; the Library Company of Philadelphia; the Linda Hall Library; the Massachusetts Historical Society; the New York Academy of Medicine; the New-York Historical Society; the New York Public Library, Astor, Lenox, and Tilden Foundations; the Virginia Historical Society; and Winterthur Museum, Garden and Library. Some of these, like the Getty, are connected with other institutions, but most are free-standing institutions that must raise their own funding for their operations. The Herzog August Bibliothek is a German Affiliate Member of IRLA (www.hab.de).

46. The generic freedom to information discussed in this section is distinct from that delineated in the Freedom of Information Act, which pertains to information contained in government records. For the latter, see "Freedom of Information Act (United States)," Wikipedia, http://en.wikipedia.org/wiki/Freedom_of_Information_Act_(United_States).

47. Card-carrying members of the American Library Association will have this full text in their wallets: it is printed on the back of their ALA membership cards. It is also available at the ALA Web page, www.ala.org/advocacy/proethics/codeofethics/codeethics.

48. See the ALA Web page, www.ala.org/advocacy/advleg/federallegislation/cipa.

49. One problem created by the passage of CIPA was that the government mandated the Internet filtering, but it did not provide funding for this. Libraries needed the E-rate discounts because they were already short of funds. The hardware and software to do the filtering had to be paid for by the libraries, not to mention the long-term monitoring and upgrading of the filters. Some libraries refused to do the filtering and found ways to pay for Internet access on their own. Joseph Anderson, in an article published at WebJunction, says,

> Libraries in other cities and towns across the country are wrestling with the costs and implications of complying or not complying with CIPA. But in San Francisco, the decision has already been made—a city ordinance passed two years ago explicitly bans the filtering of Internet content on adult and teen public access computers. (www.webjunction.org/cipa/articles/content/432255).

This decision—not to put filters on their computers—cost the San Francisco Public Library an estimated $225,000. The article also refers to Susan Hildreth, the San Francisco city librarian, who points out that each community must figure out on its own how it will deal with CIPA. "'We have a fairly unique community,' she says, 'and our community doesn't want filtering.'"

One reason the ALA opposes the CIPA (and other forms of censorship) can be seen in one of the by-products of this act. A young girl who has pain or a lump in a breast may want to look up "breast cancer," but *breast* is a filtered word, and she would be unable to find a site she could access through that route. For an analysis of CIPA, see the article by Bob Bocher, "Answers to the Most Frequently Asked Questions about the Supreme Court's June Ruling That Upheld the Filtering Requirement in the Children's Internet Protection Act," *Library Journal* (August 15, 2003), www.libraryjournal.com/lj/ljinprint/currentissue/874577-403/a_cipa_toolkit.html.csp.

50. One rule of thumb in the investment world is that about 3 percent of a fund's earned income is "lost" in merely keeping up with inflation. Accurate or not, this assumption should not influence the institution to want to keep the spendable part of the endowment at a lower fixed rate and put the profits above that fixed rate into principle. All this needs to be worked out with the donors and their attorneys.

51. ALA has a bibliographical fact sheet on weeding that should be consulted: *Weeding Library Collections: A Selected Annotated Bibliography for Library Collection Evaluation*, ALA Library Fact Sheet 15, www.ala.org/tools/libfactsheets/alalibraryfactsheet15. This Web page opens with Will Manley's statement, "Next to emptying the outdoor bookdrop on cold and snowy days, weeding is the most undesirable job in the library. It is also one of the most important. Collections that go unweeded tend to be cluttered, unattractive, and unreliable informational resources" ("The Manley Arts," *Booklist* [March 1, 1996], p. 1108).

52. It should be added—as has been commented upon elsewhere in this volume—that even individual items or whole collections that are purchased may have deeds of sale with their own restrictions, one of which may be a prohibition on deaccessioning purchased items. It is clear that full ownership of books or manuscripts does not necessarily allow full freedom to dispose of them at will.

53. Deaccessioning does not merit a full discussion here. See the 1992 version of the RBMS Standards for Ethical Conduct, 2nd ed. (see chapter 2 in the present volume and www.ala.org/Template.cfm ?Section=speccollections&template=/Content Management/ContentDisplay.cfm&ContentID =8969); and Richard W. Oram, "Current Professional Thinking on the Deaccessioning of Rare Books in Academic Libraries," *Rare Books & Manuscripts Librarianship* 9.1 (Spring 1997): 9–18. Two other articles are worth consulting: Daniel J. Bradbury, "Barbarians within the Gate: Pillage of a Rare Book Collection?," *Rare Books & Manuscripts Librarianship* 9.1 (Spring 1994): 8–16; and Samuel Streit, "Going. Going, Gone: Case Studies in Library Deaccessioning," *Rare Books & Manuscripts Librarianship* 12.1 (Spring 1997): 21–28.

54. Tomas Lipinski and Andrea Copeland, "Look before You License: The Use of Public Sharing Websites in Building Co-created Community Repositories," *Preservation, Digital Technology and Culture* 42.4 (November 2013): 174–98. These authors are writing about implied agreements on social networking sites, but the principles apply for rare book and special collections libraries using any online database by subscription.

55. See www.library.yale.edu/~llicense/intro.shtml.

56. The model agreement may be seen at www.library.yale.edu/~llicense/standlicagree.1st.html. Other sources of information are "Licensing, Contract Management, End-User Education, Copyright, e-Books, Consortial Licensing, Software, Legalities, and Much More," ed. by Karen Rupp-Serrano, special issue, *Journal of Library Administration* (*JLA*) 42.3–4 (2005). See also "Digital Images and Art Libraries in the Twenty-First Century," ed. by Susan Wyngaard, special issue, *Journal of Library Administration* 39.4 (2003). Another issue of this periodical worth looking at is "Libraries and Electronic Resources: New Partnerships, New Practices, New Perspectives," ed. by Pamela L. Higgins, special issue, *Journal of Library Administration* 35.1–2 (2001).

57. A special collections department is likely to have foreign-language collections and may need people conversant with these languages for research or cataloging purposes.

58. Camila A. Alire and G. Edward Evans, *Academic Librarianship* (New York and London: Neal-Schuman, 2010), p. 284.

59. See www.bestcollegesonline.com/blog/2008/09/29/25-important-legal-issues-every-librarian-should-research.

60. See www.librarylaw.com/ADAWebpage.html; reprinted from *California Libraries*, 9.4 (April 1999): 8–9.

61. See www.librarylaw.com/ADAWebpage.html.

BIBLIOGRAPHY

S STEWARDS OF INFORMATION, LIBRARIANS AND OTHERS IN the rare book field need to know how information is gathered and stored. The broad field of bibliography reveals a host of ways. Those dealing with rare books and manuscripts, as shown in chapter 4, must be conversant with the vast vocabulary of books, a good proportion of which is encompassed by bibliography in its several branches.

Most people, when they hear the word *bibliography*, think of a list of books—or, more generically, a list of sources in many media: books, manuscripts, pamphlets, online sites, interviews, ephemera, audio and visual formats, and so forth. This is perhaps the most common view of the field, but bibliography is much more than this. This chapter looks at the four basic branches of bibliography with the goal of presenting all the concepts and terminology a person in special collections needs in order to speak knowledgeably about books and manuscripts and other items in rare book collections.

As with other topics in this book, there is a large literature on all areas of bibliography. This chapter will look at these areas from a bird's-eye view, with the rare book world in mind: what must those in the field know, and what may they do in the bibliographical realm to help scholars?

Enumerative (or Distributive) Bibliography

> . . . *without good bibliographies, the world would resemble a library without catalogs: a hodge-podge of inaccessible ideas and knowledge.*
>
> —*Sharon Tabachnick*[1]

"This book has a bibliography." "This book is a bibliography." The first of these statements shows that some books use information drawn from sources and that those sources are listed somewhere in the volume. The second statement indicates that the whole volume is a list of sources, presumably on some defined topic. In either case, what is spoken of here is enumerative bibliographies, which are lists of citations telling readers where to go for information or where the author of a text has gone.[2] Anyone working in special collections helping patrons gather information needs to know the standard bibliographies in the fields of their users' research—the key reference tools that scholars who use their libraries need—whether they are full volumes or lists in the backs of books or articles. Also, because many who work in the rare book field are experts in their own areas, they themselves may also wish to do research, create scholarship, and compile bibliographies of their own.

A bibliography emanating from someone's scholarship is fairly easy to compile: just list every source you got your information from. It is essential to do this, because if sources are not shown, the writer could be breaking the law.

> THE NEED TO credit sources cannot be emphasized enough: if a scholar uses information from others and does not show where that information came from, he is plagiarizing, possibly committing a crime with serious consequences. Appendix 7 shows how plagiarism can be avoided.

The aims of the entries in a bibliography are (a) to lead a scholar to exactly where the information comes from so she can check to see if the use is accurate, and (b) to see what else that source has to say about the topic. So it is important to get the citations correct, with accurate information about authors' names, titles, publication information, editions, and so forth. Specific page numbers are important. If a fact comes from page 355 and the author, in the bibliographical entry, says it is from page 35, the reader will probably never be able to find the full context of the cited information. Accuracy of citation is crucial. Any error in the citation can lead a reader astray.

THE CONTENTS OF BIBLIOGRAPHICAL ENTRIES

Like cataloging records, bibliographies have many possible data fields, depending on the needs of the users and those compiling and recording the data. Also like a library catalog, the amount of information in any entry depends on the aims and nature of the bibliography. At minimum, an entry needs enough information to lead a reader to the source of the cited or listed matter: author, title, and publication data (city, publisher, date, and page numbers), when these are available.[3] Other data fields in bibliographies could contain the edition or printing (see later in this chapter), dimensions of the item described, number of pages, breakdown of contents for books (e.g., where appropriate: preface, dedication, introduction, acknowledgments, table of contents, list of plates or illustrations, translator, the writer of the introduction if different from the author, the illustrator, appendices, glossaries, indexes, and so on), the number of copies printed, information on the binding or the binder (or both), or other data. If the bibliography comes at the end of a chapter in a book or at the end of an article, the cited item clearly relates to the piece that the bibliography follows. If the bibliography is a volume by itself—that is, if it is a reference tool revealing source information for scholars studying in the area the volume covers—the compiler may add annotations to all (or most) entries. This requires a good deal of work, for it entails getting copies of items to be annotated and reading enough of each to write the annotation. A standard style of writing annotations uses sentence fragments: "Reveals the reasons for the economic downturn. Explains the difference between the performances of stocks and bonds." There is no need to say, "This

> IF BIBLIOGRAPHER A is compiling a list of sources relating to feminism in French drama, he might annotate a volume or an article with a focus strictly on that topic. But Bibliographer B may be giving general annotations about the entire content of the books or articles, and thus may hardly mention feminism for the same source.

book (or "This author") explains. . . ." It is clear that the annotation refers to the contents (or the author) of the item being cited.

Two pieces of advice: (1) Do not rely on citations compiled by anyone else; you could be perpetuating other people's errors. If Compiler A lists an article as coming from *Italian Studies* Volume 7, Number 4, and it really comes from Volume 17, a reader using that bibliography will be lost trying to find the original. Copying other people's entries without checking on their accuracy is flirting with disaster. And (2) Never rely solely on another's annotations. Compiler A may be looking for something in a text completely different from what Compiler B is looking for. Hence, they will create radically different annotations.

An unannotated bibliography is like a book's cataloging record that lacks subject headings. The user of the bibliography has to intuit from a title what the book or article contains. With many a writer using cutesy two-part titles, their subjects are not always apparent. The aim of a bibliography is to be as useful as possible for a reader. If the reader cannot deduce from the author, title, and publication data what a book or article is about, he will have to find that source to assess for himself its relevance to his work.

> **WHEN I DECIDED** to annotate every entry in my bibliography, I did not count on a concomitant phenomenon: the extra time it took me to locate, get copies of, read, and annotate each entry was enough time for additional titles (books and articles) to be published. The topic was popular and broad, so more articles came out month after month than I could keep up with. I would "finish" all outstanding items that I had located, look one last time in the latest issue of a journal, and find two new items, often with citations in their notes to other quite recent pieces. At that rate, I could have gone on forever. I decided to simply cut off the work at a particular date. This decision was my salvation. The message here is that the compiler must set particular limits and stick to them.*
>
> *R. C. Alston said, "[T]he newcomer to research, whatever his discipline, can be forgiven dismay at the sheer bulk of the sources at his disposal, sources which seem to multiply with undisciplined rapidity. The threat to enlightenment lies less in the insufficiency of information than in its overwhelming flood." ("'The Grammar of Research': Some Implications of Machine-Readable Bibliography," *British Library Journal* 11.2 [Autumn 1985]: 113–22; this statement is on p. 113).

> **IN MY BIBLIOGRAPHY** *Medieval English Drama*,* I listed all sources I could find on the topic. One item was a children's book, but I listed it anyway because the title was ambiguous as to its audience. If I had not annotated all entries, a user of my bibliography might have seen just the title and taken the trouble to seek out this item, only to be disappointed. By citing this book and annotating it simply "Children's book," I saved her the trouble.
>
> *Medieval English Drama: An Annotated Bibliography of Recent Criticism,* Garland Reference Library of the Humanities (New York and London: Garland, 1990).

Compilers owe it to their readers to guide them to works they need and to help them avoid sources that would be a waste of time. But the temptation to simply list sources and not to annotate is powerful because this kind of minimal presentation requires only a fraction of the work. The bibliographer must weigh the convenience to the user with the practical realities of compiling the listing. Annotating may double the time it takes to create the bibliography, but it produces a far more useful tool.

DESIGNING THE BIBLIOGRAPHY— ORGANIZING THE DATA

In designing the bibliography, the compiler needs to consider (a) what data will go into each entry (its intellectual content) and the organization of that data (the order the information will be presented in), and (b) the physical presentation of the information on paper (or on the screen).[4] The compiler's choice of the contents of entries (described earlier) will vary from one bibliography to another depending on various considerations, as explained. The order of the information in the entries may well depend on the audience for whom the bibliography is being compiled.

If the listing is being done for a publisher—say, for an article in a scholarly journal—the publisher is likely to have its own preferred style, and the author or compiler will usually be required to conform to that style. Many journals, especially those in the humanities, rather than having their own style sheet or stylebook, will require authors to conform to the *MLA Style Manual and Guide to Scholarly Publishing.* The other major style books are from the University of Chicago Press (*The Chicago Manual of Style*) and, in the social sciences and sciences, the *Publication Manual of the American Psychological Association* (usually referred to as the *APA Guide*).[5] Because of the breadth of the field—especially historical bibliography—scholarship falling under all these styles will be published, so anyone writing about rare books in all their manifestations should be familiar with all three styles in the rare book world.

Additionally, many publishers have their own unique style, and they will have, either online or on paper, a guide for writers who wish to publish with them. If a writer using the APA style submits a text for publication to a publisher that uses Chicago, the editor might think, "This writer is so ignorant about us that he does not even know to use Chicago. This manuscript is probably not for us." Many editors are swamped with submissions, and such reasoning may lead them to eliminate the article or book without having to waste any time on it. It is in the author's best interest to know the preferred style of the publisher before submitting a manuscript.

DESIGNING THE BIBLIOGRAPHY—THE PHYSICAL PRESENTATION OF INFORMATION

However the data are organized in each entry—that is, depending on what style the author adopts—that organization should be applied consistently throughout the bibliography. That is, titles should always be in the same place in each entry, as should cities of publication, publishers' names, dates, and so forth. Users of the bibliography should be able to glance at a page and know exactly where entries begin and end and where to find authors' names, dates, and the

other data in each entry. There are two ways to distinguish data fields from one another: typographic and spatial.

Typographic Coding

To code a text typographically, the compiler chooses various elements of printing types to distinguish data fields. Type can vary in its size (for instance, the first words of an entry may be in 14-point type and the rest of the entry in 10- or 12-point), in upper- or lowercase usage (last names can be printed in all caps), or the designer can use roman, italic, boldface, sans serif, or some other variation to make data fields differ from one another. Further, the designer can use a dingbat or printer's flower between data fields or between entries to signal the movement from one element to the next.

> HOWARD, Frank. • *"What Was the Question?": My Best Post-Game Interviews.* • Cooperstown: Homer Press, 1983.
>
> ଧ
>
> AUTREY, Gene. • *We're No Angels.* • Los Angeles: Diamond Press, 1988.

In these examples, caps signal a new entry, a black dot separates data fields, and a dingbat separates entries. This example may not be elegant, but it demonstrates how typographic coding works.[6]

Spatial Coding

The entries can also be distinguished by the way they are spaced on the page (or on the screen). Herbert Spencer, Linda Reynolds, and Brian Coe, prolific writers on the layout of bibliographic entries (see note 6 of the present chapter), show these six spatial variations:

1. Copy runs on (that is, where an entry ends, the next one begins on the same line).
2. The first element of each entry begins on a new line, while subsequent elements run on.
3. All elements begin on a new line.
4. All elements begin on a new line, with the first element full out from the left margin and

all other data fields successively indented (so line two is indented, say, three spaces; line three is indented five spaces; and so forth).

5. A line space is inserted between entries, and subsequent data fields run on with no line break.

6. A line space is inserted between entries, and each new data field begins a new line.

Differentiation, then, is achieved with line spaces and indentations, combined with line breaks between elements within entries and between entries. Many of these variations, combined with typographic ones, are easily achievable on a word processor, which can also add variant fonts, small caps, fleurons, variations in leading (e.g., partial interlinear spaces, like 1.5 lines between entries), italics, and even color printing to distinguish data fields.

All this borders on information overload in a book on rare books and special collections, but it shows how scholars in this field can present the results of their research bibliographically in a field that cries out for bibliographies. Anyone working with rare books should know how to use and how to compile good bibliographies. Booksellers' catalogs themselves are bibliographies, and a good catalog will be carefully composed and written up, designed and printed. It should be legible and informative, and it should not obfuscate information in its compilation and design. (Appendix 3 is a study of booksellers' catalogs.)

FORMAT

A knowledge of book formats is essential for anyone working in the rare book world.[7] Variations in format between two volumes could indicate different editions and could signal huge differences in price. They could also distinguish between a reliable and a seriously flawed text. The topic of format is complex, and it is not surprising that many people in the rare book field—librarians, collectors, booksellers (even experienced ones), scholars—do not understand it fully. Anyone working with rare books—especially books of the handpress period—absolutely must understand the meanings of the key terms of format: *broadside, folio, quarto, octavo, duodecimo* (often called *twelvemo*), *sextodecimo* (called *sixteenmo*), and so on.[8]

To determine a book's format requires an understanding of papermaking and binding. Refer to chapter 4 of the present text to review papermaking methods and terminology. A quick overview will be useful here.

A PATRON IN a rare book department once asked me, "Can you tell a book's format by looking at the title page?" The answer is no. The title page may reveal the dimensions of the book, but size is not an indication of format. In fact, it usually has little to do with format. Other characteristics of a book are much more important in determining its format.

A sheet of handmade paper, produced on a laid mold, held in landscape format (that is, with the wide dimension running horizontally and the narrow dimension vertically), will have hundreds of wirelines running horizontally and many fewer, widely spaced chainlines running vertically. It is likely to have four deckles (uneven edges), and a watermark in the center of each half of the leaf. A laid-paper sheet will have three levels of fibers, depending on where they fall in the papermaking process: thickest between the wires, thinner on top of each wire, and thinnest where the fibers settle on top of the chainlines. When the sheet of paper is held up to the light, the wires and chain stitches are visible, as is the watermark, if the sheet has one.

There are many formats in printing. Only the most common ones will be delineated here. A glance at a printer's manual will show the many formats that a printer may use and how he is to impose his type into the bed of his press for printing. The bibliography in chapter 4, under "Printing, Printers' Guides," gives a list of some of the better known manuals. Their sections on format can run dozens of pages because the imposition schemes can be quite elaborate, especially for the smaller formats.

Broadside

The format of a book is a function *not* of the size of the volume, but of the number of times the original sheet was folded in the making of the volume.[9] If the original sheet remains unfolded and printing exists on only a single piece of paper, the format is called **broadside,** and the text is most often printed with the sheet vertical—in the portrait format. Strictly speaking, a broadside is a full sheet printed on one side only, but the term has come to mean any sheet of paper, even one trimmed down to a fraction of the original full sheet. In the portrait layout, the chainlines in a broadside are horizontal.

Folio

Books—that is, codices, formed from folded sheets that are sewn together through the folds—are obviously not made up of broadsides. If the original printed sheets of a volume are folded once, with the crease at a right angle to the long side of the sheet, the resultant format is a **folio.** Each sheet, with one fold, creates two leaves and thus four pages, because there are two pages to each leaf: a recto and a verso. To create a folio, the printer must rotate the original sheet 90 degrees from the broadside layout, so the chainlines are vertical in a folio. The larger the original sheet, the larger the volume produced. If the original sheet is quite large, the resultant format is sometimes called an *elephant folio*.[10]

The folio volume could be made up of a cluster of simple folios, as just described: large sheets, each folded once, and then laid one on top of the other, folds all aligning at the left. The binder would sew the first folio signature (a *signature* is all the leaves sewn into the volume with one sewing operation) to tapes or cords, as described in chapter 4. Then the next pair of leaves would be sewn, and the next, and so forth, until all the signatures are sewn and the textblock is formed. In the handpress period, the standard practice was to put a letter at the bottom of each leaf before the fold to alert the binder to the order in which the signatures needed to be sewn. The binder did not have to be literate, but he had to know the alphabet. So the letter "A" would be at the bottom of the first page in a signature of a simple folio. That letter is also called a "signature," and the pair of leaves that constituted the first signature of the text was said to be "signed." That is, leaf one of this signature would have a signature (the single letter) on the recto (the front of the leaf), equivalent to page 1 (if "A" were the first page of the text).[11] The letter "A" (or any other letter designating later signatures) indicates leaf one of the signature, and can be called "A1," though the numeral is almost never printed for the first leaf of a signature. Subsequent leaves in the signature are A2, A3, A4, and so on, depending on the number of leaves in the signature.

AS WITH ALMOST all assertions in bibliography, the statement, "There will always be an even number of leaves in a signature," should be taken cautiously. There are so many variations in the way books are designed, printed, and bound that such generalizations are not perfect. There are certain to be innumerable books with an odd number of leaves in each signature. In my own library I have a volume with 6 leaves in the first three signatures and 9 leaves in all the others in the volume. This is an exceptionally unusual phenomenon, but there it is. The book is James Thatcher, *An Essay on Demonology, Ghosts and Apparitions, and Popular Superstitions. Also an Account of the Witchcraft Delusion at Salem, in 1692* (Boston: Carter and Hendee, 1831). I doubt that the book's being on demonology and witchcraft influenced its printer to choose such an unusual format. Another assertion that must be taken with caution is that only leaves before the fold will be signed. In some signatures, and in some idiosyncratic volumes, there might be an unsigned leaf before the fold, or, more likely, a signed leaf after it. That is why I will often use the word *usually* when describing "general" practices in bibliography. If a person collates a volume—that is, if she examines it carefully to see if it is complete or if it has leaves missing or damaged—she might discover a signature with an odd number of leaves. This usually means that a leaf has been removed, but in the case of the demonology volume, nothing is missing; the text is complete. If a leaf is missing, there is almost always a stub where it was once attached. If the leaf is removed right at the fold, not leaving a stub, the conjugate leaf would be loose because there is no fold through which the sewing holds the attached leaf. See the section "Cancels" later in this chapter.

A simple folio volume as described, if it has, say, 20 signatures (20 sheets folded in half to produce 40 leaves and therefore 80 pages), requires 20 sewing operations to sew all the signatures into the textblock. It saves a great deal of effort to interleave the first 2 folio signatures, nested one into the other, creating a signature of 4 leaves, not 2, and thus halving the sewing operations. This produces what is called a **folio in 4s**—that is, a folio with 4 leaves in the signatures. More common still is to nest three, or four, or even five simple folios into one another, producing a **folio in 6s**, a **folio in 8s**, or a **folio in 10s**, respectively. There are even **folios in 12s,** though this is not as common as is a folio in 10s. The more sheets that get nested, the less time it takes to bind the book. Such books are sometimes said to be composed of *gatherings*, in this case a synonym for *signatures*, because the individual folded sheets are gathered into a signature.[12] And the term *quires* can be used, also, to designate signatures or gatherings.

Another thing to observe is that usually all leaves before the fold will be signed; that is, they will have signatures at the bottom of each recto: B, B2, B3, B4, and so on. (A volume signed this way—B, B2, B3, B4 for the first 4 leaves of an 8-leaf signature—could be a folio in 8s.) There will always be an even number of leaves in a signature because each gathering is formed from the folding of the original sheets. (But see the sidebar.) The signatures are there to help the binder get all the signatures in the proper sequence for sewing. Hence, there is no need to sign any leaf past the fold. In a folio in 8s, the B tells the binder to let this simple folio precede the B2, and so forth. Once the 4 simple folios are gathered (nested) in proper sequence, they are sewn into the volume, and the binder moves along to the C signature. B5, B6, B7, and B8 are attached to (conjugate with) B4, B3, B2, and B1, respectively, so they automatically fall into place in the correct order. They do not need to be signed.

Quarto

If the sheet is rotated 90 degrees again and a second fold is introduced, the result is a format with four leaves, eight pages, and horizontal chainlines. This is a **quarto.** A full handmade sheet folded once yields a folio that is relatively tall and slender compared to the proportions of a quarto, which are more squat and closer to square. From a distance, if a folio and a quarto are held up next to one another, the two formats are usually distinguishable by their proportions: taller and thinner = folio; shorter and squatter = quarto. If the sheet of the quarto were trimmed in such a way that it became "thinner" left to right, it is possible that the two formats could look alike, but such trimming was seldom done, and the two formats are generally distinguishable from one another. The quarto is still a fairly large format because it is formed from a sheet that is folded only twice. And some folios are printed on sheets that were relatively small, so a folio could be fairly small. That is, it is not uncommon to have a folio volume that is smaller than a quarto. As noted in the "Broadside" section, size is not the issue. The crucial determiner of the format of a book is the number of times the original sheet has been folded. Quartos were often the preferred format for "large-paper editions," versions of a text that were printed on large paper with extremely generous margins, part of an edition that may also have been printed on smaller sheets. The large-paper editions[13] would be bound in a more sumptuous cover and sold as a deluxe version.

A quarto is usually (almost always) signed only on the first two leaves ("C" and "C2," for instance).

> **A FRIEND OF** mine, a papermaker in Hawaii, makes sheets from a tiny paper mold, producing "full sheets" the size of business cards. That is what the mold was made for. Theoretically, she could fold the tiny sheets in half and print a miniature book on them. It would be a folio, because the volume was made from original full-sized sheets that were folded in half.

Also, it has a fold at the gutter (on the left side of the signature where the book's spine will be) and at the top. The folds are called *bolts*, and through the bolts C1 is conjugate with C2 and C4; C3 is conjugate with C2 and C4.[14] And again, it has horizontal chainlines. So to distinguish a folio in 4s from a quarto (they both have 4 leaves in the signature), look at the direction of the chainlines and the proportions of the volumes, because the folio will have vertical chainlines and the quarto's will be horizontal, and because the quarto will be squatter than the folio. Also, for a folio, if the original sheet had a watermark and a countermark (traditionally placed in the center of each half of the sheet), each of the two leaves would have the mark in the center of the leaf, whereas in a quarto, the marks would be in the upper inner corners. It is tricky with quartos (as it is with all formats) because papermakers did not always use a watermark, or they used one but not two, or they placed the marks not in the center of the two halves of the sheet. For instance, the watermark may be at the bottom corner of the sheet, or the bottom center. Again, generalizations do not apply consistently in statements about the way books are put together. The more books that librarians and dealers look at, the more they will learn about bookmaking techniques, and the more they will see variations from the "standard" practices.

The bolt at the gutter is the fold through which the sewing is done. All other bolts will need to be opened for the book to be readable. And depending on the format, there can be bolts at the top, foreedge, or bottom—or even all three. There are two ways to cut the bolts: with a knife, slitting each bolt one at a time the way an envelope is opened with a letter opener, or by using a paper cutter (the guillotine type) that chops off all the folds. Anyone using the latter method can cut off a good deal of the margin, and thousands of books have been butchered in this way, sometimes having their running heads or page numbers cut in two or slit away completely. This is often the sign of a rebound book.

One other thing that is extremely common in the handpress period is that the main text of a book—the part that follows the prelims (see chapter 4)—usually gets the standard uppercase letters for the signatures, while the prelims get some other means of signage, most often lowercase letters, but sometimes Greek characters, sometimes some unusual squiggle made up by the printer or type founder,[15] or sometimes some other typographic peculiarity. The alphabet consisted of 23 letters, *A–I*, *K–T*, *U* or *V* (but not both), and *X–Z*. (There was no *J*, the *U* and *V* were interchangeable, and there was no *W*.) Hence, the prelims could run a–i, k–t, v, x–z; though it would be unusual (but not unheard of) to have so many signatures of prelims. If the main text exceeded 23 signatures (that is, if the printer ran out of letters for signing the signatures), she could do a number of things past Z. Most common was Aa, Aa2, Aa3, Aa4, and so on, followed by Bb, Bb2, Bb3, Bb4, and so forth. Or the printer could do this: 2A, 2A2, 2A3, 2A4, or this: AA, AA2, AA3, AA4. There was no standard practice, and the printer could designate signatures any way she wished. The only thing needed was that the system be clear enough to guide the binder in getting the gatherings in the proper sequence.

The prelims would almost always be printed after the main text was done. The most compelling reason for this is that the preliminary text contains the table of contents (and perhaps also a table of illustrations or plates), and there was no way of assigning page

---

MY WIFE AND I have a book that has the following at the bottom of the colophon, above the printer's logo: "Registrum. / a b c d e f g h i k l m n o p q r s t v x y z [a character that looks something like a small deformed 7] [a character that looks like a deformed, large-topped question mark, lacking the dot beneath it] [a character that looks something like a number sign {#} or a crooked 4, with a slightly bulging stroke dropped down from its underside] A B C D E."* The three odd characters are like nothing I have ever seen elsewhere in print. They were almost certainly created by the printer just to designate these three signatures. And, of course, the corresponding signatures in the book are signed with these odd characters. No binder would have known what order they were to be in, so the register was provided at the colophon to guide him.

*The book is Cassiodorus, [Flavius Magnus Aurelius], *Cassiodori Clarissimi Senatoris Romani in Psalterium Expositio* (Venice: Octaviani Scoti Medoe, 1517). The register is on f. 227v.—that is, leaf 227, verso. The pages are not numbered, the leaves are foliated—numbered on the rectos of each leaf, so that pages are designated by leaf (folio) number and whether the page is recto or verso. (See note 10 at the end of this chapter.)

numbers for that table until the text of the book had been printed.

In assigning signatures to the signatures, if the printer used unusual characters, ones that were not alphabetical, or if she adopted an unusual lettering practice, the binder would be notified about the proper order of the signatures at the back of the volume—usually somewhere in the colophon—in a data field called a *registrum* or *register*, that would literally print out the signature pattern of the book.

Octavo

An **octavo** is a book format in which the original sheets have been folded in half three times, creating 8 leaves and 16 pages. (The Latin word *octavus* means "eighth," and, from quarto on down, the number in the name of the format indicates the number of leaves in the printed signature.) To go from a quarto to an octavo, the printer turned the sheet another 90 degrees, so the chainlines now are again vertical, as they are with a folio. Also, the proportions of the octavo are those of the folio, with the octavo exactly one-quarter the size of the folio, and with both formats having the same upright proportions, as opposed to the squat proportions of the quarto.

An octavo has 8 leaves and 16 pages, vertical chainlines, and bolts at the spine (of course), at the top, and in the leaves behind the centerfold. The feet of the sheets in the book do not have bolts, so they should retain their deckles unless the book has been trimmed. Remember that a volume that still has its bolts (where the folds have not been slit open) is called *unopened*, and a volume that still has its deckles is called *uncut* or *untrimmed*. The octavo will have (1) the same number of leaves as will a folio in 8s, (2) vertical chainlines, and (3) an upright proportion that is distinctly different from that of a quarto. One can distinguish the octavo from the folio in 8s by the placement of the watermarks (if there are any, and if they are visible) and by the size of the volume, because octavos are usually much smaller than folios.

In chapter 4 the section "Printing Practices and Essential Terminology" explained that a sheet printed on only one side has not yet been "perfected." To perfect the sheet, the printer prints the text on the side opposite the side printed first. In the printing,

type set into the chase will print either the surface of the sheet that will be on the outside of the sheet or the surface that will be on the inside of the sheet after folding. All the type and furniture and other things (quoins, illustrations, numbering devices, and so forth) in the chase in a single pressrun is called the *form* (or *forme*). The form that prints what will be on the outside of the sheet after it is folded is called the *outer form*. The other form, which prints what is inside the folded sheet, is called the *inner form*.

All this is repeated here because in the rare book world, bibliographic description requires a knowledge of the concepts and terms, and they all run a close parallel to the discussion of formats. For instance, in laying out the type in the press to create a particular format of a book, the printer must remember that the lowest page number of the signature will be on the outer form of the sheet, and the leaf containing the lowest number will be conjugate with the leaf (also in the outer form) that will have the highest number page. The octavo is a format with 8 leaves and 16 pages. Page 1 of the first signature will be on the recto, facing the reader when the signature is closed, but with the first page of that signature showing. Page 16 will be the last one in the signature (on the verso of the last leaf).

Octavo in Half Sheets

One common format in the handpress period is called **octavo in half sheets** (sometimes called *octavo in 4s*). The original sheet is folded the same number of times as for the standard octavo (three folds), but in this case, the printer duplicates pages 1–8 on both sides of the sheet. That is, in a standard octavo, the outer form will have pages 1, 4, 5, 8, 9, 12, 13, and 16; the inner form will have pages 2, 3, 6, 7, 10, 11, 14, and 15. The signature has 16 pages. In an octavo in half sheets, all pages 1–8 appear on both sides of the sheet, still yielding 16 pages, but when the sheet is torn or cut in half, two small identical signatures bearing pages 1–8 are formed. (See figure 9.1.) It is called *octavo in half sheets* because each smaller signature is formed from half of a regular octavo signature.

This format will produce signatures with only 4 leaves in them, though of course they are still octavos because they were originally part of an 8-leaf,

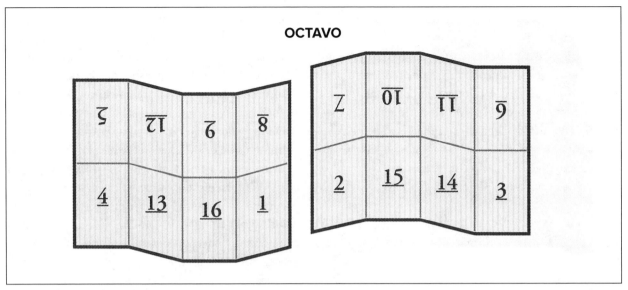

OCTAVO

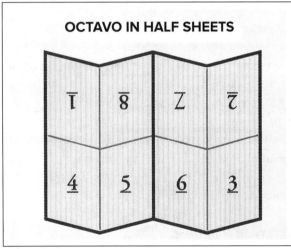

OCTAVO IN HALF SHEETS

FIG. 9.1 Octavo and octavo in half sheets. In the octavo format, eight pages are arranged on the outer form (left) and the remaining eight pages on the inner form (right), creating a sixteen-page signature. Note the vertical chainlines. In the octavo in half sheets format, pages one through eight are duplicated on both sides of the sheet. The sheet is then cut in half before folding, creating two identical eight-page signatures. (From Sidney E. Berger, "Book Format, Part Two: Octavo, Duodecimo, and Sextodecimo," *Biblio* 2.6 [June 1997]: 50–53.)

16-page format. And because they are still true octavos, they will have vertical chainlines and the same proportions as the folio: upright and not squat. So if a pamphlet has four leaves in each signature, it could be a folio in 4s, a quarto, or an octavo in half sheets. To distinguish which it is, look at the direction of the chainlines, the placement of the watermark (if there is one, and if it is visible), the proportions of the item (upright or squat), and its size. Because the signatures will have only 4 leaves, only the first two are likely to be signed (e.g., C, C2), but this is the same as for a folio in 4s and a quarto. So signatures on the leaves will usually not help in determining format. The other features will.

Sextodecimo

A **sextodecimo** (also called *sixteenmo* or *16mo*)[16] is the result of yet another rotation of the sheet 90 degrees. It produces, as the name indicates, a signature with 16 leaves or 32 pages, and with horizontal chainlines. The format yields a fairly small book, though, again, it depends on the size of the original sheet. Signatures will appear at the foot of the first 6, 7, or, more commonly, 8 leaves of the signature, though the page is quite small, and sometimes books in this format will have no signatures. Printers may also create 16mos in half sheets, with each signature containing 8 leaves. A book with 8-leaf signatures could be a folio in 8s, an octavo, or a 16mo in half sheets. They are distinguishable from one another by the direction of the chainlines, the placement of the watermark, the proportions (a 16mo will be more squat than will an octavo or a folio), and the overall size of the volume.

Duodecimo

One other—extremely common—format is worth mentioning: the **duodecimo** (also called *twelvemo* or *12mo*). Up to here, all formats were produced by folding sheets in half. In a duodecimo, the original sheet is folded into thirds and twice into halves. It yields signatures with 12 leaves (thus 24 pages), it has vertical chainlines, and anywhere from 4 to 6 of its leaves are signed. Different folding patterns are possible, but the more common ones produce a printed sheet that is torn into two parts after printing. One part has 8 leaves, the other has 4 leaves, and these two parts are bound with the 4-leaf part preceding, following, or nested into the 8-leaf part. The format was extremely popular for it produced

small volumes that contained substantial texts, and the books were easy to put into a pocket.

FORMAT IDENTIFIED

As has been shown in the preceding sections, it is usually not difficult to determine the format of a book printed in the handpress period. The method is fairly simple. Begin by looking for the beginning of one of the interior signatures (after the prelims and perhaps after the A signature). Count the number of leaves in each signature. This should be done for several signatures because it is possible that not all of them will have the same number of leaves. Look at the direction of the chainlines. Look for the position of the watermark(s), if the paper is watermarked. Look at the proportions of the book—tall and thin or squat. Look at the signatures at the bottom of the leaves before (and occasionally after) the fold. All these are clues for identifying a book's format. And, for the most common formats, accounting for perhaps 95 percent or more of early books, table 9.1 should be useful.

TABLE 9.1

Table of Formats

Name of Format	Abbreviations	Number of Folds	Number of Leaves	Number of Pages	Direction of Chainlines
Broadside		0	1	2	horizontal
Folio*	F, f, f°	1	2	4	vertical
Quarto	Q, qto, q°, 4°	2	4	8	horizontal
Octavo†	Oct., 8vo, 8°	3	8	16	vertical
Duodecimo‡	12°, 12mo	4	12	24	vertical
Sextodecimo	16°, 16mo	4	16	32	horizontal

*Remember that folios in 4s, 6s, 8s, or 10s are still folios; the original sheets are still folded only once, and the chainlines are vertical. The only differences here are the number of nested sheets, producing 4, 6, 8, or 10 leaves per signature.

†An octavo in half sheets, while producing two small, identical 4-leaf signatures, is nonetheless an octavo because it is printed the same way a regular octavo is, with 8 pages in the press at a time.

‡One folding pattern of duodecimo produces a short, squat (almost square) volume with horizontal chainlines, but this is quite rare.

CANCELS

When something has been removed from a printed book—part of its original printed text—the removed part is called a **cancel**. Also, if the removed part is replaced, the replacement is also called a *cancel*. So there are two phenomena here—the piece taken away (the **cancellandum**) and the piece replacing it (the **cancellans**). (As implied, there can be a cancellandum—a piece removed—with no cancellans.) Cancels were created for a number of reasons. A part of a printed text could be identified as having a serious typographical error, a blasphemous passage, a political hot-potato, or anything that could bring embarrassment or punishment to the printer or others involved with the creation of the text.

The removed piece could be a single word, a line, a paragraph, or even a whole chapter. As noted, sometimes the piece taken out is not replaced, leaving just a gap in the text or in the page.

Cancels comprise changes that range from the correction of small errors to the addition, alteration, or deletion of large blocks of text before or after the publication of a book. They also signal the (potential) existence of prior, uncorrected states or issues of books that usually have greater value or significance, depending on the nature of the changes and the reasons behind them. On a purely personal level, cancels can present a challenge to discover just what happened—and why.[17] The Cassiodorus volume mentioned earlier has a cancel on the opening page: a small rectangle cut out of the leaf, with a blank piece of matching paper pasted over to fill the hole completely. As is typical, there is no way to tell what was excised. An examination of other copies of this edition may reveal what was lost (if another copy exists without the cancel).

The easiest way to fix a mistake in a book is to cut it out, but that often means that text around it—perhaps all the text on the same leaf—must be excised as well. If a whole leaf had to be removed, the binder (who was often given this task) would leave a stub onto which to paste a replacement leaf. And as mentioned, the leaf could not be removed at the very fold for it was the fold that held the sewing that connected the conjugate leaf and kept it from falling out. Hence, the printer may have been forced to print up, on both sides, a leaf to replace the one that had the offending text that was removed. This could entail the resetting of the type, and it is possible that textual variants could have been introduced on the cancellans. (As already noted, it is also possible that the offending leaf was removed and not replaced.)

When a librarian or anyone else in the rare book world collates (carefully examines) a volume, she should look for cancels, though they may be difficult to spot if the replacement is skillfully done or if the binding is tight. Often, it is also challenging to determine when the cancel was done—before or after the book was issued to the public. "If done before, virtually every copy of the book would contain the cancellans. . . . If done after, however, presumably a number of copies lacking the cancel remain; copies without the cancel are said to be the first issue, those with it a second or later issue" (Berger, "Stop," p. 57).

In the nineteenth and twentieth centuries it was not uncommon for a publisher to sell to another publisher a text it had issued under its own imprint. The second publisher would buy the standing type (or, more likely, the stereotype or electrotype plates), and would reissue the book with a new title page with its own name on it. This new title page is called a *cancel title leaf*, though it is not the standard "cancel" if a new leaf were printed and bound in, having been printed along with the rest of the text (which came from the plates). That is, rather than having the original title page (from the first publisher) cut off and the new one replace it, a title page showing the new publisher is printed along with the rest of the text. If the volume were printed with the first publisher's name on the title page and that page is removed and replaced with the second publisher's title, that is a true "cancel title." The "cancel title leaf usually indicates only a straightforward and planned substitution, not an error, addition, change of thought, or suppression" (Berger, "Stop," p. 57).

EDITIONS, IMPRESSIONS (PRINTINGS), ISSUES, STATES, AND POINTS

Before moving on to descriptive bibliography, the reader must be familiar with a few key terms in the rare book world: *editions, impressions* (*printings*), *issues* and *states*, and *points*. These words are bandied about by many booksellers and even librarians, often used loosely and therefore with imprecision. They have precise meanings that people in the field must understand. Because modern printing practices, with high-speed presses and enormous rolls of paper, in many instances obscure the concept of "edition," the terms are used with some precision for books produced in the handpress period and with a bit less precision for books printed later. Nonetheless, specific editions are distinguishable for printing in all eras.

Editions and First Editions

The complex concept of "editions" has led to endless confusions in the rare book world. For example,

a book is published in a regular paperback copy, a second version with a hard cover, and a third, bound in leather. The bookseller's catalog says, "This title can be purchased in the regular edition, the hardcover edition, and the deluxe edition." That designation—"deluxe edition," "special edition," "limited edition"—can be a bibliographical misrepresentation. "Limited edition" may be accurate, but even that term is subject to misunderstanding.

Strictly speaking, an edition of a text is composed of all copies of that text printed from the same setting of type. Although this is a simple concept, it is complicated by the fact that a text can be set into type and printed, and then the author revises two of his twelve chapters. The next printing is done from the "same setting of type" for ten chapters, but from a different setting for the other two. Is this still the same edition? The answer is that it is the same edition for the first ten chapters. How this is designated bibliographically is up to the bibliographer, scholar, bookseller, or library cataloger.

In the example just cited, all the versions delineated—"regular paperback," "hardcover," and "deluxe"—if they are printed from the same setting of type, are the same edition, regardless of how they are bound and presented.

As mentioned in chapter 4, a book can be printed from stereotype or electrotype plates. These plates were created from standing type. Hence the printing of the text, done from type, is identical to the text printed from the plates. They are all the same edition. It is not strictly accurate, then, to call one the "first edition" and the other the "stereotype edition," because there is no difference in edition. That is, they are both first editions. More accurate would be to say that one is the "first edition" and the other is the "stereotype version (or printing) of the first edition."[18]

Likewise, a publisher can sell the standing type or the plates of an edition to another publisher and company number two can print a text, from the same type or plates, one hundred years after the first edition was printed. The publisher can even change the title page to reflect the new ownership of the work. If the rest of the volume is printed from that same setting of type, it is still the same edition.

It is clear than an edition can have varying typography in some instances: a new title page, some typos corrected in later-printed versions, an added preface, or some other change in the original typesetting. But if the bulk of the second or subsequent printing of a text is from the first setting of type, the volume is essentially the same edition. How much change can be done that will yield the designation "same edition" is up to the bibliographer. Maybe if half the book is printed from the original setting of type, the two copies will be of the same edition. Perhaps some scholars would say that that much resetting constitutes a new edition. There are no "industry standards" for such a decision on terminology.

Summing up, John Carter says,

> Strictly speaking, an *edition* comprises all copies of a book printed at *any* time or times from one setting-up of type without substantial change (including copies printed from stereotype, electrotype or similar plates made from that setting of type).[19]

So the printing of the text is the only thing that constitutes an edition, not the binding, the date of printing, the release of the text to the public, or the number of copies printed.

First editions[20] are just what that phrase denotes: the first time a text is printed. But, of course, it is much more complex than this. A novel can be published serially in a magazine, say, over a year. Bibliographers generally do not call this the "first edition." Such a designation is usually reserved for the first printing of a text that is bound into covers. Of the term *first edition*, Carter says,

> Very, *very* roughly speaking, this means the first appearance of the work in question, independently, between its own covers. But, like many other household words, this apparently simple term is not always as simple as it appears. The question *When is a first edition not a first edition?* is a favourite debating exercise among bibliographers and advanced collectors. (p. 103)

He then points out that to understand the whole idea of first editions, the scholar must also understand other terms: "edition and impression, issue and state, 'follow the flag,' serials, secondary bindings, autho-

rised edition, piracy, part-issues, first published edition, advance copies, copyright editions, prefirst, book form, first separate edition" (p. 103). The complexities raised by these terms show that the idea of a first edition is not as simple as it sounds. Some of the terms are self-explanatory or have been (or will be) dealt with here.

ADVANCE COPY An *advance copy* has been printed up by the publisher and sent out before the book is published in its final form (with its finally edited text and its binding). These copies are sent out to reviewers at newspapers, magazines, television shows on which books are reviewed, book clubs, and others, with the hope that (1) they will give the book a good review before (or soon after) it is issued to the public, thus generating sales, or (2) the reviewer will write a complimentary blurb that the publisher can use on the dust jacket or in its own advertising. These copies are thus also called *review copies* or *reviewer's copies*. Sometimes they are the final versions, fully edited, printed and bound as will be the regular editions, and with the same dust jackets. Some, however, are really just proof copies, not fully edited, printed on cheaper paper, possibly bound in paper wrappers, and with no jacket. Millions of these exist, for advance copies have been a staple in the book-publishing industry for at least 75 years. Many of them represent an early stage of the book's development, and for this reason they are sought after by collectors—especially those of popular authors. Because they are produced in relatively short numbers, they do not constitute a true "edition" of their own (or a different "issue" of the edition they are a part of).

AUTHORIZED EDITION An *authorized edition* is presumably sanctioned by and given the blessing of the author, thus giving it an aura of authority (how is that for pleonasm!). That is, any other printing of that text by another publisher, it is hinted, is full of errors and is unreliable. Carter explains, however, that the phrase is often preceded by the word *first*, and thus brings the whole enterprise into question:

> When the collector of first editions is called upon to explain or defend his pursuit, he often emphasizes

the importance (as well as the sentimental appeal) of the earliest authentic text. But when he sees "first authorized edition" in a catalogue description, that argument is apt to yield to his preference for chronological priority. For he will infer that this authorized edition was preceded by an unauthorized one; and even though he may take this opportunity of acquiring the former, he will nevertheless probably continue to covet the latter as well (and even more violently). (Carter, *ABC*, p. 33)

In the early decades of the twentieth century, publishers like Harper's would buy the rights to the works of an author and might publish the "complete works" or the "collected works" as an "author's edition" or something similar. Harper & Brothers Publishers, in 1907, issued a large set in uniform bindings of Mark Twain's novels and other writings. They called it the "Author's National Edition: The Writings of Mark Twain," and they had the author write "This is the Authorized Uniform Edition of all my books. Mark Twain," which, in his handwriting, was printed before the frontispiece of each volume. The texts were not "edited" in any way. They were taken (and reset) from some earlier printing, and they had no authority.

COPYRIGHT EDITION A *copyright edition*, as Carter explains,

> has one specialised use which concerns the collector. In order to safeguard copyright by formal publication (whether of a poem printed in a magazine, or to comply with American or British law, or for some other reason), a small number of copies of a pamphlet or book may have been printed before the regular edition, and formally 'published' but not distributed or sold in the ordinary way. (Carter, *ABC*, p. 74)

Carter's explanation is fine, but he needed to explain that most of the time the "edition" sent in to gain copyright was not really a different edition at all; it was a printing of the very edition that would eventually come out that the "copyright edition" was protecting. A more accurate term would have been *copyright version of the edition*.

For serious collectors (and, of course, this could mean special collections in libraries that have strong author or subject collections), the value of a book is often linked to whether it is an acknowledged first edition or not. But what constitutes a first edition could be hazy. One point of contention in the rare book world is when a work of an author from country A is published in a country other than her own. If a writer from Germany publishes a novel that appears in print for the first time in Sweden, some scholars believe that that book does not count as a first; only the first volume of that title published in Germany is the first edition, according to this way of thinking. This is the meaning of the phrase "follow the flag."[21]

AN EXCELLENT EXAMPLE of a copyright edition is the first edition of Mark Twain's *Pudd'nhead Wilson* (Hartford: American Publishing Company, 1894). To secure copyright, Twain had his publishers send two copies of the book—before it was issued to the public—to the Library of Congress (LC). The LC copy* looks exactly like the regular first edition from this publisher: same paper, same binding, same title page, and identical illustrations and text—until the last chapter. In collating the Library of Congress version (and the copy at the Houghton Library at Harvard), I noticed that all the many copies of the regular edition that I had seen had 432 pages, while the LC and Harvard copies had 433. It was clear that (1) the LC copy was printed slightly earlier than were all other copies, (2) it had been deposited at LC for copyright, and (3) after it was printed and sent to LC, the editors at the American Publishing Company decided to trim it back by one page to save the cost of printing a full octavo signature for just that 433rd page.

*The Library of Congress made it mandatory, for publishers to get copyright, to send in two copies of each book. When the Library of Congress sold off its duplicate copies, the second *Pudd'nhead* copy went to Harvard. For a fuller explanation of this "copyright edition," see Sidney E. Berger, "Editorial Intrusion in *Pudd'nhead Wilson,*" *Papers of the Bibliographical Society of America* 70 (1976): 272–76.

SERIAL PUBLICATION AND PART-ISSUES From the late eighteenth through the nineteenth centuries (and even into the twentieth), a common way to publish books was to print one or a few chapters at a time in a serial. Magazines loved to do this because, if the work was captivating enough, buyers would want to get all issues of the publication containing the text. It was a way to guarantee sales. The work published serially could also have been issued "in parts"—hence the term *part-issues*; that is, the subscriber would receive a fascicle or two in the post periodically. In either case, the first printings were not in covers. That is, they were not issued as a bound volume, so for many bibliographers these copies, even if they were later bound into covers, were not true "first editions," though they *were* "first printings." Because of the nature of the publication of the *Oxford English Dictionary*, in fascicles over many decades, subscribers got one part after another (not always in alphabetical order), and kept them as separates or had them bound into volumes when they had enough fascicles to constitute a volume. Whether this constitutes a "first edition" is debatable, because the work would not have been issued as a book unto itself. Once it got to be issued fully, in its own cover, it might be called the "first separate edition." Carter has a long entry in his *ABC* on this (pp. 162–64) and another on "Part-Issued Books in Volume Form" (p. 164).

"PRE-FIRSTS" Another "first" term needs clarification. If an author printed a few copies of her work for private distribution to friends and family, before the commercially issued text was printed, these *pre-firsts* might also be called *first printed edition*, as distinguished from *first published version*, because the notion of "published" implies release to the public. As for the bizarre term "pre-first," Carter has this to say:

> This self-contradictory term, having no proper meaning of its own, is put to various uses, many of them dubious, but all symptomatic of the chronological obsession. It alleges that the edition, issue or copy referred to precedes the commonly accepted first edition; and *pre-first* may be found applied to trial issues, advance copies, copyright editions, privately printed editions, pirated or unauthorized editions, extracts, offprints, and even magazine appearances. (*ABC*, p. 172)

I HAVE AN aversion to the airplanese term *pre-boarding*. When a passenger boards the plane, he boards it. What goes on before (pre-) boarding? How can anyone board the plane before boarding the plane? What does pre-boarding look like? It looks like boarding. It *is* boarding. Many professions have terminology that borders on the ridiculous. "Pre-first" is one of those words, but it sounds impressive and rare and exclusive. So collectors and booksellers like to use it to enhance the aura and the value of their books. Librarians should be particularly sensitive to such silliness and not be influenced to pay more than an item is worth just because a slick term is added to its description.

OFFPRINTS An *offprint* is a small piece of a larger volume—usually a single essay or chapter, given to the author for distribution to his friends or other scholars. It is not uncommon today for some professional journals to send the author of an article a clutch of offprints, sometimes just sheets from the original journal pulled out and stapled, sometimes in a heavy printed cover from the original publication. A more elaborate presentation would be the same text, even in the same edition as that in the journal, but with the pages numbered from 1 on, and with a cover and title page that made the essay look like a separate publication in pamphlet form. It has been a courtesy of the academic world to trade offprints with others working in the same field. If the work was a short story from an anthology, written by a well-known (hence, a collected) author, collectors would be happier to have the offprint—as a single-volume publication of their idol—than they would be to have the anthology in which their author's precious text was besmirched by the detritus around it.

ONE FAMOUS CASE of "pre-firsts" has been extensively documented in the practices of Thomas Wise and Harry Buxton Forman and their notorious forgeries. A series of pamphlets containing literary texts with dates preceding those of the known first editions came on the market over many years. Wise, an honored and respected bibliographer, explained them as pamphlets printed by the authors for distribution to their friends before the commercial editions hit the world. Almost every one of them was a proven forgery. The same John Carter who authored the *ABC for Book Collectors*, along with Graham Pollard, unmasked the perpetrators of these crimes.* These pamphlets were not "genuine pre-firsts." Another early printing of a text was called the "trial issue" or "trial edition," a text that an author had set into type before going to press with it. The idea was to show it to friends or others for their assistance with proofreading. Whether these texts were proofread or not, the authors usually had the final text reset and printed as the first edition. These looked like "pre-firsts," but their reason for being was to help the author, not as a gift to friends of what the pre-first was ostensibly: a finished copy of the text. Carter distinguishes them from "proof copies" in that they were aimed primarily at the author's close circle, not at the media (*ABC*, p. 221).

*For more about Wise and Buxton Forman, see the section "Forgeries, Fakes, and Facsimiles" in chapter 7.

EXTRACTS Carter also mentions *extracts*: "As a noun, this is used of papers, articles, stories, etc., taken out of periodicals, transactions of learned societies or the like and listed individually. Sometimes called excerpts" (*ABC*, p. 98). This definition does not clearly distinguish extracts from offprints. It seems that the difference lies in intention, the offprint being created in multiples for its author and deliberately presented as a separate entity, while the extract is merely pulled out of the original publication. What Carter means by "listed individually" is unclear. In scholarly terms, an extract is a passage pulled from a larger piece and quoted in another text.

THE HINMAN COLLATOR, OTHER MACHINES, AND THE IDENTIFICATION OF DIFFERENT SETTINGS OF TYPE Sometimes printers ran out of copies of a text and had to reset the text into type to print another batch of copies. Even if they used the same type and even if every line matched every line of the first printing, the two settings would constitute two different editions. It may be difficult to see a reset text with the naked eye, but there are a few ways to discern reset type. The first uses a Hinman Collator, a machine developed by Charlton Hinman in the late 1940s. During World War II, Hinman learned of a way to observe enemy encampments from the air and determine whether they were moving or changing. This was done by optically superimposing aerial photographs of enemy positions. Hinman adapted this technology to create a machine that optically superimposes an image of a page over an image of what purports to be an identical page. By lighting the page on the left and leaving the one on the right in darkness, then reversing the lighting (lighting the right leaf and plunging the other into darkness), over and over again, the person collating the two pages will pick up motion if there has been any resetting of type or changing of text.

A second machine, the Lindstrand Comparator, invented by Gordon Lindstrand, and a third machine, invented by Randall McLeod, working on yet another principle, were also used to examine texts to see if they were reset. The Hinman was the best of the three, but the other two did work, and they were portable while the Hinman was huge and unwieldy. (See the sidebar below for references.)

Another method, crude but fairly accurate, and performable by anyone with a straight edge and a pencil, also works. Take a photocopy of the two pages in question and, for both supposedly identical pages, draw a diagonal line from the top leftmost stroke of the first printed letter on the page to the bottom rightmost printed character in the last line on a page. The line should pass through characters, line after line, in exactly the same spots on both pages. If type has been reset, the line will pass through different letters or different parts of equivalent letters.

All this discussion about collating machines and resetting of type is essential knowledge for the librarian or bibliographer who wishes to test a pair

AS A GRADUATE student in the University of Iowa's Center for Bibliographic Study, and then as a professor at the University of California, Davis, I used a Hinman Collator for more than fifteen years. It was an unreal experience, sitting in a dark room with two texts in front of me, each purporting to be the same. With the darkness around and the lights flashing on the machine, I was able to detect, over the years, hundreds of variations in typography that revealed all kinds of changes that had taken place in printed texts. Rather than reading a page out loud to another reader, who was comparing his copy of the text with mine, I could do the work by myself in a fraction of the time (only a few seconds per page versus however long it took to read the text out loud), and with vastly more accuracy. The two "identical" pages were set into the machine, one on the left, the other on the right, and then, through a series of mirrors they were observable through a binocular eyepiece, superimposed, one over the other till they looked like one page. Lights blinked first onto the left sheet then onto the right, and any changes in typography would show up as movement on the page. If a dot over a lowercase *i* were present on the page on the right, but missing on the page on the left, the blinking lights, showing first one page then the other, would make the dot seem to blink off and on, appearing and disappearing. The eye can spot this kind of "movement" in a couple of seconds, so a full page could be collated in a few seconds. In an oral reading, there was no way to "show" the other reader where the type sat on the page, so all kinds of resettings could have been missed using the oral method. But with the Hinman, even the slightest resetting of type could be detected in a moment. It is an amazing machine; it saved bibliographers untold hours of work, and it produced results far more accurate than could have been produced by oral reading.*

*See Stephen Escar Smith, "'The Eternal Verities Verified': Charlton Hinman and The Roots of Mechanical Collation," *Studies in Bibliography* 53 (2000): 129–62. Other collating machines, based on different principles, are those made by Gordon Lindstrand and Randall McLeod. See Gordon Lindstrand, "Mechanized Textual Collation and Recent Designs," *Studies in Bibliography* 24 (1971): 204–14 (in which Lindstrand describes his own inventions, the Mark I and Mark II Comparators); and Randall McLeod, "A New Technique of Headline Analysis with Application to Shakespeare's Sonnets, 1609," *Studies in Bibliography* 32: 197–210. See also Vinton A. Dearing, "The Poor Man's Mark IV or Ersatz Hinman Collator," *Papers of the Bibliographical Society of America [PBSA],* 60 (1966), 149–58; and Gerald A. Smith, "A Collating Machine: Poor Man's Mark VII," *PBSA* 61 (1967): 10–13.

of volumes to detect separate printings, if they are detectable.

Impressions (Printings)

All copies of a text that were printed at one time, without the printer's taking the type out of the press, are of the same *impression* or the same *printing* (in this context, the two words are interchangeable). Thus, a copyright page for a modern book (or a bibliographer with information about the printing history of an older book) may say, "First edition, second impression." In many books printed in the twentieth century, the copyright page may even give more specific information: "Second edition, fifth impression; August 1945"; "Second edition, sixth impression; December 1945." (The text may also say, "First edition, second printing.") A bibliography might have an entry which contains this information: "This impression of the book was of 2,000 copies"; or "There were 1,500 copies in this printing."

Determining what printing a book is within an edition is not easy, though in recent years the copyright page of many commercially published books may have a string of numbers (e.g., "1 2 3 4 5 6 7 8 9 10" or numbers in reverse order); the lowest number showing usually indicates the printing. So the listing 4 5 6 7 8 9 10 would indicate that the volume in hand is the fourth printing of that edition. Not all publishers use this method of printing delineation, and often there is no way to know the impression of a book. For popular books that get many printings, the numbers might go 99 98 97 96 95 94 93, and so on. Again, the lowest number indicates the impression.

AS EARLY AS the sixteenth century, before copyright was firmly established, but still in times that had some protections for stolen texts, a world of piracy among printers existed. A *piracy* (or *pirated edition*) is one that has been printed without the permission of the author, and usually without any payment to him. Especially during the times of the "pamphlet wars," when one author after another attacked his "enemies" by issuing a pamphlet espousing a side of a controversial issue, only to have the enemy respond with his own pamphlet, printers could easily set into type and print, practically overnight, a new pamphlet, or a copy of a particularly popular one. If printer A was selling many copies of one of these pamphlets, printer B could get a copy, set into type an "identical" version of it, and sell it on the street or in his shop for a good profit (part of which came from the fact that he did not have to pay the author any royalties). Piracy is mentioned here because a pirated pamphlet could carry some indication that it is a "25th printing," indicating its popularity, which was intended to pique the interests of the reading public. It may actually have been a first printing of that particular publisher, who stole the text to make money.

Issues

All copies released to the public at one time are said to be "issued" on that date. They constitute the issue of the publisher of that title. A publisher could print twenty thousand copies of a book and issue half of them in April, five thousand in June, and the rest in September. This would constitute three issues of the volume. So a scholar could deduce that "this copy is the first edition, second issue." Usually, if the volume is indeed the same edition and the same printing, it is impossible to figure out what issue it is. Sometimes, however, the issue can be determined because the difference in issues is chronological. That is, one issue will precede the other, so changes could have been made between the issue dates. For instance, a first issue might be released in one kind of binding and the second issue in another. It may be possible to deduce the order of the issues: "In the red binding of the first issue" as opposed to "In the green binding of the second issue." The cover art could have

changed between issues. A publisher announcing the first issue of an edition might have an advertising piece that states, "In a lovely gold-stamped, ribbed, maroon cloth." If the scholar finds the ad, and then sees a copy of the book in a binding of another color, she might deduce that the volume in the other color is a later issue. (This is not necessarily the case, of course, but it is food for thought.)

In the nineteenth century it was common for publishers to place advertisements into new books. These ads could be on a single leaf or a whole printed pamphlet, bound into the covers (usually at the back of the volume). By observing what books are listed in the ads, and by examining their dates, the librarian may be able to see that the book in hand was issued much later than the date on its title page. That is, a book listed in the ads may have come out in 1877, but the title page of the book containing the ads says that the book in hand is dated 1875. If this situation arises, the 1875 book is either a later issue (but with an earlier date on its title page) or a later impression that retains the title-page date of the earlier impression. In other words, variations in typography, binding, or advertising matter may help the bibliographer distinguish one issue from another. But even the recognition of different issues may not allow the scholar to determine which issue came first. Hence, a bibliographer might say, "First issue with red cloth; second issue in blue cloth; third issue in wrappers. Chronological order of issues not determinable" (or "Order of issues is arbitrary but used to distinguish different issues").

IF A PUBLISHER prints, say, ten thousand copies of a book, binds them all, and then sells only half of them, it has paid for the binding of the second five thousand copies that may have to be pulped or sold at a loss. It is something of a gamble to bind all ten thousand copies, not knowing if they will all sell. It would be more economical not to bind half the edition, see if the sales exceed five thousand copies, and then bind up as many more as are needed to keep the sales going. The first five thousand copies would be issued at one time, and the rest would be later issues.

State

It was common in the handpress period for a printer to stop the press, make a change (usually a correction of a typographical error that he had spotted during the printing), and go on with the pressrun. (See chapter 4 for "stop-press corrections.") This operation created what is called a *state variant*, an alternate reading at one point in the text from how the text reads in another copy. So if the printer, after running off, say, two hundred copies of a pressrun, noted the typo "hapy," he would stop the press, correct this to "happy," and continue to print the last copies of the book. The result was a text in two states, one with the error, one with the correction. Often it is easy to spot such a correction and to determine which is the "first state" and which is the "second state," for it would not make any sense for a printer to stop printing if the text read "happy" and change the type to read "hapy." The bibliographer could say, "The text exists in two states," and then delineate what they are, how they differ, and what order they came in.

But if the printer changed the typo of "back porch" to the correct reading "black porch," it might be difficult to determine which state is the first and which the second. Further, it is possible that in stopping the press, the printer might have taken out several lines of type to reset them to correct a mistake, and then introduced other typos while resetting. So if a line that is perfectly good (that is, it contains a state variant with a correct reading) matches up with the equivalent line in another copy of the book that has a typo, it is possible that the typo is the later state, not the earlier one. Determining priority of state can be a tricky business.

As the sidebar on *Innocents Abroad* shows, ten copies of "identical" volumes of the same edition, same printing, same issue could exist in ten states if that many stop-press corrections had been made. A bibliography (or a dealer's catalog) may state: "This is the first edition, third printing, second issue, fourth state (priority of state not clear)." And there is yet another phenomenon to consider: the state of a volume is not necessarily tied to its printed text; it could also refer to the binding. The cover, as noted earlier, could be a green cloth for one copy of the edition and a brown cloth for another. Or the binding could have the frog in the lower left corner of the front cover, or in the center of the front cover. These are state variants of the binding. In a bibliographical description is a category called Notes (see the section "Descriptive Bibliography" later in this chap-

IN DOING THE collations for Mark Twain's *Innocents Abroad* (Hartford: American Publishing Company, 1869), my collating group discovered the following: Twain, on his pilgrimage to the Holy Land, stops into a European cathedral, and in its catacombs he says that he sees the distant monks walking by in the dark underground with "flickering candles." In doing the collations, we picked up an alternative reading, "flittering candles." That is, one copy of the first edition had "flickering" and another had "flittering." The two volumes looked exactly alike, with the same title page, same binding, same text, same pagination, and so forth. The difference was in these two words. That is, the text existed in at least these two states. (Because we collated six copies of this first edition, we found at least six states, because variations in all these six volumes existed. That is, no two copies of the six we checked of this edition were identical.) An editor had to decide on the better of the two readings, the one most "authorial." (See the section "Textual Bibliography" later in this chapter.) When I bring this up in a bibliography class, my students uniformly opt for the reading "flickering," because it is the word most familiar to them. But a check of a dictionary of Twain's day shows that both words were current, and Twain could have chosen either because they were both present in the vocabulary of the day. To assign a priority to these two state variants would be pure guesswork. Perhaps a check of Twain's vocabulary in all his other writings might militate for one reading over the other, but even that would be guesswork because he might have carefully chosen the less-used word for this sentence. Here we have a state variant with no determinable priority.

ter), and state variants should be mentioned in this data field.

Also, state variants can exist in matter accompanying the printed volume, like dust jackets or advertising pieces. And the term also applies to illustrations that are bound or tipped into a volume (including frontispieces and any image printed by any means). Copperplate engravings will lose their fine definition after a relatively short pressrun. After perhaps twenty or twenty-five prints are made from a plate, the image will lose some of its fine lines and sharpness. So a copperplate engraving can be an "early state" or a "later state," the latter having lost some of its sharpness. Also, artists may alter plates for one reason or another, so a changed image, an added or repositioned signature, or a blurring out of part of the original image could be intentional by the artist, and any of these would constitute a different state of the plate.

And finally, the state of a text can be related to its completeness. For any reason, a publisher or an author may wish to remove an illustration, a page, even a chapter from a volume—or add something to the text in like manner. This, too, creates a different state from the one in which the book is complete. So a first edition, first state could lack three illustrations, while the second state has them tipped in where the publisher put them (and maybe where the author demanded they be put). These additions or subtractions may take place between the first and the second *issue* of a book, so it might be accurate to describe the book as "first edition, second issue, second state." In this instance the issue and the state are linked, but that is not always the case. Carter adds,

> It is, of course, perfectly possible for different issues and different states to co-exist within an edition. For instance, some corrections may have been made to the text during printing (producing variant *states* of the leaves involved). Then one fearful howler, pilloried by a reviewer, has to be dealt with by substituting a corrected leaf (or cancel) in the copies still undistributed, which will thereafter constitute a *second issue*. Yet copies both of the first and second issue are likely to show an indiscrimi-

nate mixture of variations of state, none of which (it must be repeated) has any bearing on the question of priority of issue. (*ABC*, p. 134)

This terminology can become confusing and bewildering, but a mastery of it is crucial if one is to be conversant with the language (and the concepts behind it) of the rare book world. One other key term must be discussed.

Points

When there is a crux in two texts—that is, a point at which the two versions of the same text vary—that crux is called a *point*. Carter puts it this way:

> A point is any peculiarity in a book whose presence in or absence from a particular copy serves to distinguish it from other copies not so marked. It is most often used of those bibliographical peculiarities that provide the evidence (or alleged evidence) for priority of issue, binding variants, misprints, variant advertisements, cancels, textual changes, etc. (*ABC*, p. 170)

The term is a simple bibliographical word with a fairly clear meaning, but Carter and others poke fun at those who make too much of points, seeking them out (even the minutest variants like the loss of a serif on a letter in one copy of a book), and parading them as if they were treasures unearthed from a pharaoh's tomb. Carter says,

> Some collectors hate, and a few despise, points. Others love them, as do most booksellers' cataloguers. For, as Richard Curle once said, 'Books without points are like women without beauty—they pass unnoticed in a crowd. But books with points excite immediate interest . . . therefore there is an instinctive tendency to dwell on points, to exaggerate their significance [see point-maniacs], and even to discover points that are not really points at all [see issue-mongers].' (p. 171)

And indeed, Carter does have an entry called "Point-maniacs," in which he pillories those who take points to an extreme. It is too long to quote here, but those in special collections and rare books should read his brief exposition on those who "love [points] to excess" (p. 171). The key to points for the present text is that they are variations in two (or more) texts, and they can sometimes tell scholars about the way texts were composed and transmitted, information that can be useful if an author's work is studied for the way it was conceived, brought to life, and then transmitted to the world.

At this point I wish to turn to the other three branches of bibliography: Descriptive, Historical, and Textual. But first it is worth pointing out that other scholars, using various terminology, divide the larger concept of bibliography in different ways. Robert B. Harmon, in his *Elements of Bibliography* (cited in note 2), sees the field bifurcated into (1) Enumerative Bibliography and (2) Analytical and Critical Bibliography. This latter branch he then subdivides into (a) Descriptive, (b) Textual, and (c) Historical. Roy Stokes, in his *Bibliographical Companion* (Metuchen, NJ, and London: Scarecrow Press, 1989), lists the divisions of bibliography as (1) Enumerative or Systematic, (2) Analytical or Critical, (3) Descriptive, (4) Historical, and (5) Textual (see pp. 18–21 for his seriously inadequate discussions of these).

Another "branch" of bibliography that falls under Enumerative is National Bibliography, which, of course, means the study of the great books (and the standard references) that focus on the works of one nation. See, for example, Roger C. Green, "National Bibliography," in Robert B. Downs and Frances B. Jenkins, eds., *Bibliography: Current State and Future Trends* (Urbana, Chicago, and London: University of Illinois Press, 1967), pp. 14–41.

The four-part scheme adopted in this volume is specific enough to present the overall field sufficiently to satisfy the needs of rare book and special collections practitioners and is general enough not to drown readers in the minutiae of these fields.

Descriptive Bibliography

With all this information about formats and cancels, editions and printings and issues, and so forth, along with the information imparted in chapter 4 about the book as a physical object, we are now ready to look at the second branch of bibliography, **descriptive bibliography.** The topic is practically endless because books have had endless manifestations over the centuries, and it is impossible for a scholar to make broad generalizations that will give "comprehensive" advice without having seen millions of books, with all their idiosyncrasies. The best this text can do is provide an overview of the subject with some basic guidance on how to create an honest, reliable book description.

I must add that such descriptions will appear in scholarly bibliographies and even in booksellers' catalogs, especially for volumes coming from the handpress period. Many enumerative bibliographers and well-schooled dealers are familiar with this kind of description, and for a librarian to see the information such descriptions impart and not to understand it is tantamount to discussing books with a defective vocabulary.

AN EXAMPLE OF the need to understand book descriptions appears in the volume by Patricia Lockhart Fleming, *Upper Canadian Imprints, 1801–1841: A Bibliography* (Toronto: Toronto University Press, 1988). For each entry, Fleming includes a data field called Collation, and she uses the formulaic presentation of signatures that will be described later in this chapter. The beginning of one of her Collation entries looks like this: $2^0 \ldots$, $\pi A^2 B$-C^2, A-I^2 K-2B$^2 \ldots$ (p. 277). A simplified version and full explanation of such a "collational formula" will be presented later. Anyone working in rare books should be able to read this description with full understanding.

The grandfather of all descriptive bibliographers is Fredson Bowers, a name that should be familiar to all in the rare book world—especially to those who wish to describe the volumes they are observing. His landmark study, *Principles of Bibliographical Description* (Princeton, NJ: Princeton University Press, 1949), offered for the first time a wide-ranging, standardized system that attempted to describe all books, but especially those of the handpress period. His goal was to achieve consistency among scholars and booksellers, librarians (particularly, but certainly not limited to, those in rare books and cataloging), and anyone else who wanted to tell someone what the book he was describing looked like—how it was made up. If the librarian in Tuscaloosa used the Bowers method of description on a volume she was holding, the scholar in Cape Town would know what that volume looked like and how it matched, and was different from, the one he was looking at. Bowers's 505-page volume tried to be comprehensive. That is, he tried to prepare bibliographers for every printing peculiarity they might encounter in describing handmade books. It was, of course, impossible to achieve comprehensiveness because the variations were seemingly endless, and Bowers could not anticipate *every* such peculiarity in the makeup of books. His work, however, raised the awareness of those in the rare book world of the need to create some standard of description that would be understandable from one bibliographer to another, no matter where in the world each was working, and, for the most part, no matter what language each was using (especially for the collational formula, described later in this chapter).

Those working in the rare book world must share a vocabulary so that there will be no obfuscation or misunderstandings among them. And they must employ a practice of book description that leaves nothing to the imagination, that is truthful, straightforward, and comprehensive enough to describe a volume with no chance that someone will misinterpret what is being described. There is probably no such thing as a "complete" bibliographical description; that would entail telling the reader what every leaf and letter looked like. But a thorough description should have certain features that leave little of importance unsaid. The bibliographer begins with general information about the book under scrutiny and narrows down, in his description, to the copy at hand.

The "ideal" bibliographical description contains the following data fields (if all this information is available):

- Bibliographical Data
- Statement of Format

- Collation (also called the Collational Formula)
- Notes

BIBLIOGRAPHICAL DATA

The Bibliographical Data field contains the basic cataloging information: Author, Title, and Publication Data (this last broken down into City: Publisher, Date). It may also contain other data—the kind described earlier in an enumerative bibliography: number of pages, dimensions of the page, contents, and so forth. For a modern book, it may also give the ISBN and the book's stated price. But the kind of bibliographical description examined here is primarily for books from the handpress period (say, before 1801). Using words, numbers, and symbols, in the typical bibliographical description, the cataloger or scholar states what the volume in hand looks like and why the copy in hand is possibly unique.[22]

Title-Page Transcriptions

Because there are many ways for printers to set the text of title pages, the bibliographer has three ways to show what that page contains. The first is simply to give all the pertinent data the page contains, as follows:

> Thomas Watson. *An Ecclesiastical History of England, Scotland and Wales: With Illustrations of the Principle Cathedrals in these Realms.* London and Edinburgh: Printed by R. Coles for Jonathan Bell, Bookseller; Edward Carlisle and Sons; and Cambridge University Press, 1788

This is simply a transcription of the information on the title page. It does not tell the reader anything about the typography of the original, nor whether there are any decorative elements on the page (anything printed in a second-color ink, engravings, woodcuts, printer's flowers, or decorative rule), or anything else worth mentioning. It was common in early printing to have a quotation on the page, possibly in Latin and sometimes accompanied by an illustration. The sample transcription above does not show any of this.

The second way to show what the title page contains is called a *quasi-facsimile* transcription. Using typography, the bibliographer can show all kinds of things that are printed on the title page.

> THOMAS WATSON / *An Ecclesiastical History of / England, Scotland and Wales / With Illustrations of the Principle Cathedrals in these Realms.* / [engraving of cathedral; in blue] / London and Edinburgh / [tapered rule] / Printed by R. Coles for Jonathan Bell, Bookseller; / Edward Carlisle and Sons; and Cambridge University Press. / 1788

The author's name, on the original title page, is the first line on the page, it is printed with regular and then small capitals, and it sits on a line by itself. (The slash indicates the end of a line.) The next three lines contain the title in italics. This is followed by an engraving, printed in blue ink, and the cities of publication are next. A tapered rule (sometimes called a *bulged rule*—depending on which part of the rule is being described) is beneath the cities, and so forth. In the past, before computers, and therefore appearing in some printed volumes, italics were designated by a single underline; small caps were denoted by a double underline; full caps were shown with a triple underline (symbols still used in editing). The quasi-facsimile does not indicate the size or the font of the type (though it does show italics; and if the bibliographer desires, he can show "[in Fraktur type]" or other faces); but it gives a better picture of the page than does the simple title transcription. And a quotation on the page can also be indicated in brackets, either with the words "[3-line quotation]" or by actually giving the full quotation.[23]

Another type of "transcription" is not really a transcription: it is an actual facsimile of the original title page. The reproduction of the page is usually accompanied by a verbal and typographic transcription, so that the reader can see, in the same typeface as the rest of the printed bibliography, what the facsimile shows. The bibliography of *Benjamin Franklin's Philadelphia Printing* uses this method, and it shows why such a method does not always work.[24] As the reproduction of page 321 shows, this bibliography, in its practice of giving a full-page facsimile of the first page of each work that Franklin printed, gives a picture of a large newspaper; this reproduction is almost useless because the original image had

to be reduced to a tiny fraction of its original size, yielding about 2-point (and, hence, practically illegible) type. The good thing about this method is that, for most items, the reader can see what the original actually looked like and can also see all the typography (though not the colors) of the original without having to decipher a formulaic, quasi-facsimile rendering of it. (See figure 9.2.)

STATEMENT OF FORMAT

Once the full data of the title page are rendered, the descriptive bibliographer moves into the data field for showing how the book is made up—that is, how all the signatures of the book are formed and gathered. This field begins with the book's format.

The Statement of Format is simple: using the full word or one of the standard abbreviations (see p. 259 above), the bibliographer simply delineates the book's format. The format is determinable by the methods explained earlier—by observing the number of leaves in a signature, the direction of the chainlines if the paper is laid, the position of the watermarks if there are any, the deckles on the book's edges (if they have not been trimmed off), the proportions of the book, and so forth. Texts may have been printed in more than one format, and which one is in hand could yield vast differences in price and significant differences in authoritativeness.

COLLATION OR COLLATIONAL FORMULA

The next part of a bibliographical description is the Collation (or the Collational Formula), a listing of the gatherings in the volume, using the signatures at the foot of the pages, along with other symbols and numbers to designate other things within signatures. Here is a simple, typical collational formula:

$$8^o: \pi\text{-}\pi^2 \text{ a-d}^8 \text{ A-I}^8 \text{ K-S}^8 \text{ T-T}^6 \text{ (*4) } (\pm\text{G}^7)^{25}$$

The 8° indicates that the volume in hand is an octavo. In that place there could as well have been the word "octavo," or "8vo." This shows that the book depicted in this formula has 8 leaves to a signature and that its pages have vertical chainlines. The colon separates the statement of format from the collational formula. Usually signatures are signed, but when they are not, as is common for some of the first

64 Fox 1737

distributed (Minutes of YM I, 394, 400). In an undated account book entry Franklin charged Pem-
berton and Morris the sum of £80 "For 2000 Geo.
Fox Spelling Books" (Ledger A & B, p. 142). The
first edition of this school book composed by Fox
and Ellis Hookes was printed in London in 1673
(Wing F 1859), eventually enlarged, and frequently
reprinted in England and the Colonies, Reynier Jan-
sen, William Bradford's successor, printed the first
Philadelphia edition in 1702. Evans found a titleless
copy of the Boston (Rogers and Fowle), 1743 edition
at NN and for some reason entered it in his bibliography under entry 4138 as a 1737 Newport-James
Franklin imprint. Alden, *Rhode Island Imprints*, No.
40, corrected the error, and the editors of *STE* have
reassigned the Evans number to BF's Philadelphia
printing.

COPIES: PP. PU.

133 [FRANKLIN, Benjamin (1706–1790)]. Poor
Richard Almanack for the Year 1738. [First and
Second Impressions].   [1737]

COLLATION: Foolscap 8° in fours *A–C⁴*. Pp. *1* title, *2*
preface, *3* anatomy of man's body, symbols, notes,
4 planets' motions; verses, *5* chronology, *6* explanation; observations, *7–18* January to December, *19*
eclipses, *19–21* court days in Middle Colonies, *21*
general meetings; fairs, *22* catalogue of European
rulers, *23* BF adv.; J. Wilkinson adv., *24* roads
northeastward and southwestward, T. Grew adv.

ORNAMENT: *3* No. 10.

TYPE: [within single-rule frame] BF long primer,
black letter.

PAPER: American, unmarked.

LEAF: 6.8 x 3.9 in.

REFERENCES: Evans 4141, Hildeburn 561, Campbell
110, Drake 9604.

NOTES: Advertised as just published in *Pa. Gaz.*, Nov
3, 1737. In Nov., 1737, BF sent "1000 Almanacks
of 1738" to Sister Ann in Newport (Ledger A & B,
p. 246), and evidently the usual 400–500 copies to
Fleet in Boston (*Boston Evening Post* adv., Dec. 12,
1737) and Timothy in Charleston (*S. C. Gaz.* adv.,
Jan. 5, 1737–38). The use of traceable series of distinctive frame rules in the formes of this almanac
makes it possible to distinguish two complete ma-
chinings. The only example of the one impression is
the CSmH copy, which because it exhibits one un-
proofed page (August) is considered the earlier; the
other nine extant copies are of another and presum-

ably later impression (see Miller, *Almanacs*, pp.
100–101 and plate 3).

COPIES: PU. CSmH, CtY, DeWin, MB, MH, NN,
PHi, PPAK, PPL, PPRF; NBLiHi.

Poor Richard, 1738.

A N

Almanack

For the Year of Christ

1 7 3 8,

Being the Second after L E A P Y E A R.

And makes since the Creation	Years
By the Account of the Eastern *Greeks*	7246
By the Latin Church, when ☉ ent. ♈	6937
By the Computation of *W. W.*	5747
By the *Roman* Chronology	5687
By the *Jewish* Rabbies	5499

Wherein is contained,

The Lunations, Eclipses, Judgment of
the Weather, Spring Tides, Planets Motions &
mutual Aspects, Sun and Moon's Rising and Setting, Length of Days, Time of High Water,
Fairs, Courts, and observable Days
Fitted to the Latitude of Forty Degrees,
and a Meridian of Five Hours West from *London*,
but may without sensible Error, serve all the adjacent Places, even from *Newfoundland* to *South-
Carolina*.

By *RICHARD SAUNDERS*, Philom.

PHILADELPHIA:
Printed and sold by *B. FRANKLIN*, at the New
Printing-Office near the Market.

[133]

LAY, Benjamin (1677–1760). All Slave-Keepers   134
that keep the Innocent in Bondage, Apostates.
Printed for the Author.   1737 [1738]

COLLATION: Foolscap 8° in fours *A–2M⁴* (B2, C2,
2M2 unsigned; 2G2, 2K2 signed G2, K2). Pp. *1*
title, *3–5* preface, signed Benjamin Lay, Abington,
Nov. 17, 1736, 6–269 text, 270–271 excerpts from
Paradise Lost, Book XII, *272 blank*, *273–277* contents, *278* errata, *279–280 blank*.

FIG. 9.2A Page 64 from C. William Miller, *Benjamin Franklin's Philadelphia Printing*: 1728–1766 (Philadelphia: American Philosophical Society, 1974). This is an example of a bibliographical entry that uses a facsimile "transcription." That is, rather than simply
giving the title and other bibliographical information in words, this entry includes an actual facsimile of the title page containing
all the pertinent information. Note also the extensive data offered in this volume for each entry: a collation of the volume; mention
of any ornaments; information on typeface(s); a description of the paper (with notes about watermarks, if any); leaf dimensions;
notes of various kinds; and a list of known copies. Few bibliographies are this thorough. Used by permission of the American
Philosophical Society.

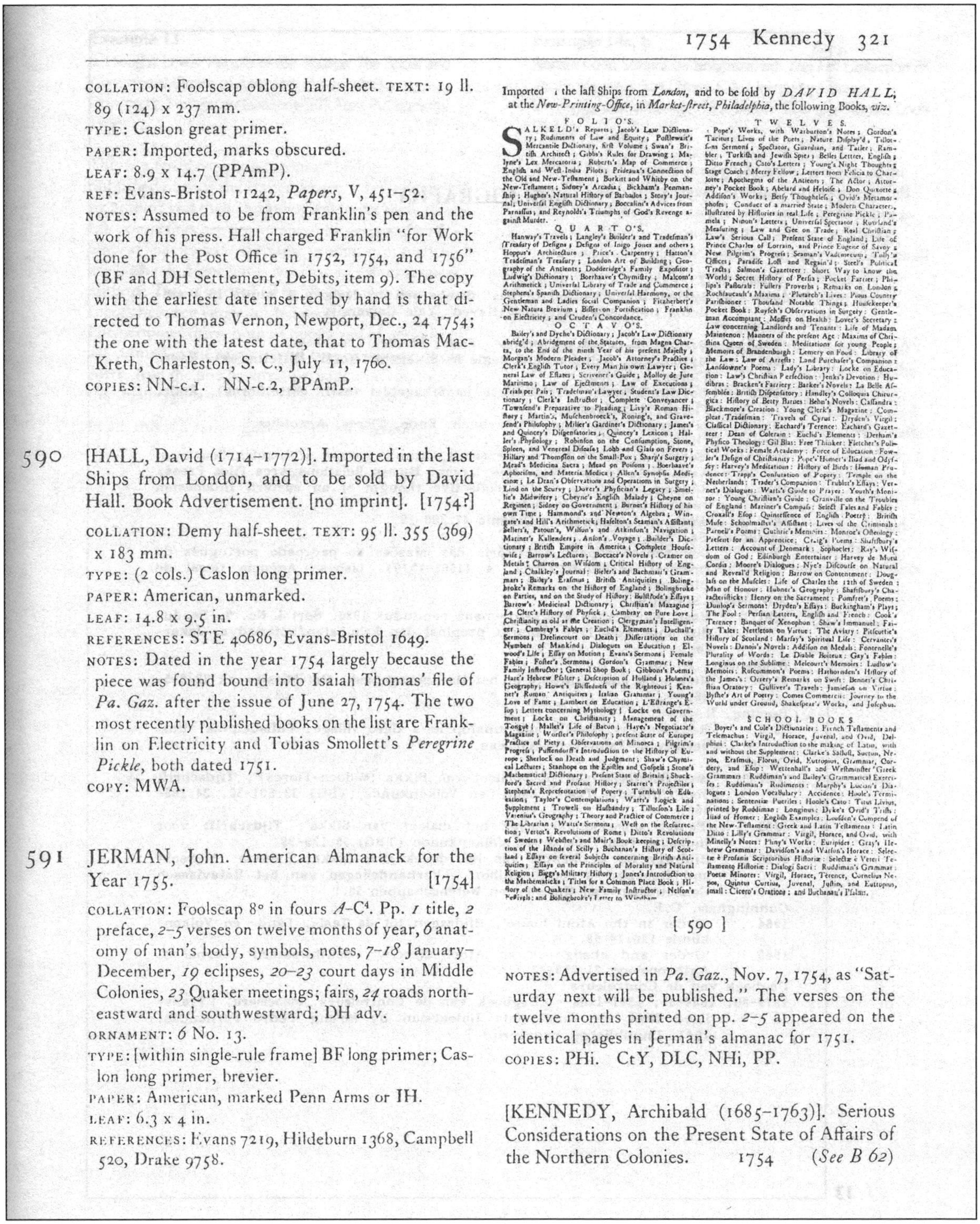

1754 Kennedy 321

COLLATION: Foolscap oblong half-sheet. TEXT: 19 ll. 89 (124) x 237 mm.

TYPE: Caslon great primer.

PAPER: Imported, marks obscured.

LEAF: 8.9 x 14.7 (PPAmP).

REF: Evans-Bristol 11242, *Papers*, V, 451–52.

NOTES: Assumed to be from Franklin's pen and the work of his press. Hall charged Franklin "for Work done for the Post Office in 1752, 1754, and 1756" (BF and DH Settlement, Debits, item 9). The copy with the earliest date inserted by hand is that directed to Thomas Vernon, Newport, Dec., 24 1754; the one with the latest date, that to Thomas MacKreth, Charleston, S. C., July 11, 1760.

COPIES: NN-c.1.   NN-c.2, PPAmP.

590   [HALL, David (1714–1772)]. Imported in the last Ships from London, and to be sold by David Hall. Book Advertisement. [no imprint].   [1754?]

COLLATION: Demy half-sheet. TEXT: 95 ll. 355 (369) x 183 mm.

TYPE: (2 cols.) Caslon long primer.

PAPER: American, unmarked.

LEAF: 14.8 x 9.5 in.

REFERENCES: STE 40686, Evans-Bristol 1649.

NOTES: Dated in the year 1754 largely because the piece was found bound into Isaiah Thomas' file of *Pa. Gaz.* after the issue of June 27, 1754. The two most recently published books on the list are Franklin on Electricity and Tobias Smollett's *Peregrine Pickle*, both dated 1751.

COPY: MWA.

591   JERMAN, John. American Almanack for the Year 1755.   [1754]

COLLATION: Foolscap 8° in fours *A*–C⁴. Pp. *1* title, *2* preface, *2–5* verses on twelve months of year, *6* anatomy of man's body, symbols, notes, *7–18* January–December, *19* eclipses, *20–23* court days in Middle Colonies, *23* Quaker meetings; fairs, *24* roads northeastward and southwestward; DH adv.

ORNAMENT: *6* No. 13.

TYPE: [within single-rule frame] BF long primer; Caslon long primer, brevier.

PAPER: American, marked Penn Arms or IH.

LEAF: 6.3 x 4 in.

REFERENCES: Evans 7219, Hildeburn 1368, Campbell 520, Drake 9758.

Imported ı the laſt Ships from *London*, and to be ſold by *DAVID HALL*, at the *New-Printing-Office*, in *Market-ſtreet, Philadelphia*, the following Books, viz.

[590]

NOTES: Advertised in *Pa. Gaz.*, Nov. 7, 1754, as "Saturday next will be published." The verses on the twelve months printed on pp. *2–5* appeared on the identical pages in Jerman's almanac for 1751.

COPIES: PHi.   CtY, DLC, NHi, PP.

[KENNEDY, Archibald (1685–1763)]. Serious Considerations on the Present State of Affairs of the Northern Colonies.   1754   (*See B 62*)

FIG. 9.2B Page 321 from *Benjamin Franklin's Philadelphia Printing*. Compare with figure 9.2A. In this example, the facsimile is less successful. The original page was a newspaper, and to reproduce the whole image meant reducing the original to practically illegible size. Used by permission of the American Philosophical Society.

leaves in a printed book, bibliographers traditionally use the Greek letter *pi* (π) to show an unsigned gathering. In this case, there are only 2 leaves in this unsigned signature (possibly a half title and a title page). We can see this because the second π has a 2 after it, indicating that it is the second such leaf.

This information is immediately followed by some lowercase letters, indicating that there are four gatherings of preliminaries ("prelims")—signed "a" through "d," each of which is an octavo signature, which we know because the number 8 after the "d" indicates 8 leaves in each gathering. The main text of the book begins with the uppercase *A*. "A-I^8" indicates 9 signatures, each a perfect octavo. "K-S^8" indicates 9 more such signatures. The bibliographer could have written "A-S^8," which is a fairly common way to show these gatherings. The reader would simply assume that a J signature does not exist, especially because the letter *J* did not exist until about the end of the eighteenth century. This bibliographer chose to make the lack of a J gathering explicit by showing all the letters in sequence that are in the book.

The S fascicle is the last of the regular octavos. It is followed by a gathering with only 6 leaves: "T-T^6." Because the book is printed "in 8s" (as printers and bibliographers would say), the pressman would have had 8 pages of type in the bed of the press for each pressrun. The π signature has only two leaves, and no printer would have had a separate pressrun for only those 2 leaves (4 pages). Nor would the printer have had a pressrun with only 6 leaves, as we see are in the T signature. It is certain that the π signature was printed at the same time as the T signature—as a regular octavo signature would have been.

Following the alphabetical part of the collational formula is a parenthetical "*4," showing that the first four leaves in each signature are signed (that is, all the leaves of the book that precede the fold in each gathering have signatures at the bottom of the rectos). This is followed by "(±G7)," indicating that the seventh leaf of the G signature is a cancel. The minus sign shows that the original leaf was removed; the plus sign shows that it has been replaced by another leaf.[26]

THERE IS SIMPLY no way to predict what unusual makeup of a volume might come along, and hence what unusual collational formulas are waiting to be found. Printers did what they did, not following the practices of the printers around them, and sometimes producing peculiarly composed books, as is the case with the Thatcher book on demonology mentioned in a previous sidebar. Another book in our personal library is a tall, thin folio dated 1744, with the following collational formula:

$$F: π-π^2 \ A-I^2 \ K-T^2 \ U-U^2 \ X-Z^2 \ Aa-Ff^2 \ (*2)$$

This means that the book is composed of simple (2-leaf) folio signatures, and that *every leaf is signed* other than the two at the beginning. Also, M^2 is unsigned for some reason, and U^2 is clearly signed "B^2."

The book is *Kurtze doch Gründliche Abfertigung Deren In Sachen Decisi Mandati Nunc Executionis Ihro Hochfürstlichen Gnaden zu Fulda Wieder Des Herrn Hertzogs zu Sachsen-Weymar und Eisenach Fürstl. Durchlaucht . . . Durchgehends enthaltenen Ungründen, häuffigen Falsch- und Unwahrheiten auch besonders erkünstelten Rechts-Verdrehungen: Mit angefügter standhafften Demonstration* (Fulda 1744).

Typos in the signing are not uncommon. But having every leaf (except a couple) signed *is* unusual, to say the least.

The sample collational formula given here is straightforward and simple. As Bowers shows, the printing practices during the handpress period were so varied that thousands of possible shapes and features of collational formulas are possible. No system can depict all of the possibilities comprehensively.

NOTES

The last data field for a bibliographical description is Notes. Because a primary aim of the description is to present a verbal picture of the item in hand, this field should have a good deal of copy-specific information—details that are likely to be specific to the copy being described. Hence, the bibliographer looks for things that possibly vary from one copy to another. For instance, typographical peculiarities like printing errors that could have been caught during a pressrun and been corrected are worth not-ing. This does not mean the bibliographer must read through the entire volume looking for typographical errors and instances of broken type. It does mean, however, that she should look for areas of typogra-phy that stand out in which an error might equally stand out: half titles, title pages, section headings, chapter titles, running heads, page numbers, signa-tures (the signatures at the bottom of rectos and the order of the bound signatures in the book), catch-words (the words, or partial words, printed in the outer bottom margins that signal the first word on the next page), captions to illustrations, or any-thing else typographic that might have been changed during the printing of the page.

The Notes field should also describe the actual volume in hand: the binding,[27] missing or torn pages, the endpapers, the presence of signatures or inscriptions of former owners, library markings, bookplates, foxing (the orangey or blackish spots caused by mildew), tidelines (places on the leaves where water has left a stain in a line across the pages), binders' tickets, booksellers' tickets, chil-dren's scrawlings, former readers' marginal notes and underlinings, booksellers' codes or prices, or anything else that may make the copy in hand dis-tinct from all other copies.

This Notes section may also have the kind of information that appears in colophons (number of copies done; names of printers, binders, or typefaces; the kind of paper the book was printed on; and so forth). The bibliographer may also add the presence or absence of plates,[28] a description of the frontis-piece if there is one, whether the book has a dust jacket or not, and the presence of blanks (flyleaves, for example). But these kinds of things are likely to be the same for all other copies. Nonetheless, per-haps to distinguish the volume from forgeries, this kind of information should be in the notes, too.

Dust jackets present their own problems, though they would not be part of a bibliographical descrip-tion for books from the handpress period (because they were not used then). If a book was issued sev-eral times over a period of years, or if it came out in more than one manifestation (regular version,

deluxe version, book-club version), the dust jackets might vary significantly.

Anyone working in rare books should know the protocols of bibliographical description and should, at the very least, not be intimidated by such descrip-tions in scholarly bibliographies or booksellers' or auction catalogs.

Descriptive bibliography, then, is like a science in which "experiments" should be replicable. That is, two scholars working independently, maybe in dif-ferent parts of the globe, describing "identical" cop-ies of a book from, say, 1650, should come up with practically identical descriptions. If the two copies differ, their descriptions should show how, so that a third party in another part of the globe will know what the two volumes look like and how they vary. Unfortunately, however, descriptive bibliography is not a science, so these two bibliographical descrip-tions will probably not be identical, no matter how much the books look alike. But the scholar relying on these descriptions will have a good chance of pic-turing the books if the bibliographers have used the same system of transcription and description.[29]

Historical Bibliography

Books are historic objects, influencing all kinds of people, movements, ideas, and creations, and, them-selves, influenced by and related to the vast world around them. Bibliography, as the word's etymology suggests, is writing about books. And historical bib-liography is writing about books in history and ema-nates from all the things that influenced their creation, reading, manufacture, movement, buying and selling, collecting, theft, censorship, illustration, and anything else that aids in the understanding of the Book.

Clearly, this branch of bibliography is exception-ally broad, for there are practically no areas of schol-arly inquiry that are outside its purview. That is, there is a practically infinite number of questions to be asked about books in general and about specific ones and an equally infinite universe of information "out there" to help researchers answer those ques-tions. Roy Stokes says,

In its broadest sense [historical bibliography] comprises the whole history of the book from its beginnings to the present day. . . . No detailed examination of a book can be done without regard to the social, cultural, economic, artistic background against which it was produced. Each book was produced by a particular society to serve clearly defined purposes[,] and methods at every stage of production depended upon these circumstances. Historical bibliography, therefore, includes the history of printing, illustration methods, binding, paper making, typography, authorship, bookselling, publishing, reading tastes, government control and legislation, etc.[30]

Robert B. Harmon has a similar take on the subject:

Broadly speaking, historical bibliography involves the history of books and of the people, institutions, and machines producing them. As a study, historical bibliography ranges from technological history to the history of art in its concern with the evidence books provide about culture and society. In this sense historical bibliography becomes archaeological in nature, with a never-ending amount of dated physical evidence.[31]

These two authors are on the right track, but they do not go far enough in suggesting the range of disciplines that historical bibliography entails.

For instance, a researcher working in an area of bookbinding may wish to examine the cultivation of goats, sheep, cows, or pigs; the development of butchering techniques and flaying methods; the evolution of the creation and use of chemicals; artistic movements over the ages that influenced decoration; the use of gold and the manufacture of gold leaf; the history of cord making; the employment of varnishes; the manufacture of tools, paper, cloth, and adhesives; printing techniques; the relationship between binding and book sales; the transition from the roll to the codex; environmental conditions and controls that affect the longevity of binding materials; the depiction of books in art; the biographies of great bookbinders and those who influenced them (and those they influenced); the world of collectors and booksellers; the history, manufacture, compo-

sition, and longevity of dyes; the causes of deterioration in books; natural disasters that might have changed the course of binding practices; the many materials that have been used over the centuries to bind books; and much more. Many of these topics can be subdivided by country, city, or date. If the researcher is curious about the colors used in bindings, she might want to turn to an entomologist to enlighten her about the cochineal, a lapidary expert to learn about lapis lazuli or cinnabar, a chemist to learn about the manufacture of blue-green dyes emanating from copperas (iron sulfate), an expert in agriculture to research various oils, a climatological scientist to learn about the history and physical properties of airborne pollutants, a historian to find out about events that may have affected the availability of certain raw materials, an economist to see how commodity prices may have affected the costs of labor or materials (which would affect the choices of materials binders used in their work), a textile expert to learn about the manufacture and availability of different cloths, a scholar of literature to see how bindings played a role in the writings of great authors or to learn how these authors' books were bound and decorated before they were released to the public, and so forth. If honey was ever used in a particular geographical location in gilding (which it was in many places), the scholar may want to consult an apiculturist for any number of things: sources of honey, kinds, uses, properties, ways of manipulating (e.g., straining, cooking, storing) it, and so on.

The possible sources of information for this bookbinding scholar can be much wider than this listing indicates. There is a world of information about the world in which bindings were designed and created, applied and decorated, bought and sold. There are many specialty binders who do nothing but "decorator bindings," and an equally broad world of binding collectors (personal and institutional), all of whom can be researched and written about. Then there is the huge realm of bookbinding bibliography: lists of books about bindings, binders, collections, and collectors.

Other examples of historical bibliography are evident in the work of Richard Schwab and others, who turned to nuclear scientists and cyclotrons for help in analyzing the inks Gutenberg used in his printing;[32] Sandra Sider, who did extensive genealogical work to uncover the identity of a book's former female owner;[33] and the scholar of medieval manuscripts who looked at the clothing style of a woman in a manuscript's illumination to figure out the volume's date.[34] A researcher trying to figure out the date and country of origin of a medieval manuscript may turn to the world of equestrian history, in which an expert in saddles, stirrups, or bridles could elucidate such things.

To explain why or how a particular author had certain details of architecture, topography, garb, meteorology, or cuisine in his work may take an examination of his reading or his travels, the people he knew, the education he got, or the vividness of his imagination based on his childhood experiences. This investigation could necessitate research in family papers, correspondence, diaries, transportation methods available in the author's day, and much more.

As suggested earlier, books—especially those of the distant past—can pose many "problems," or generate many questions. "Where did this detail in this author's text come from?" "When was this book rebound and by whom?" "Who owned this volume?" "Was this book popular in its day?" "Where did this book's information come from and is it reliable?" "Where did the decorations in these endpapers come from?" "Is this book a forgery or a fake?" "Who printed this broadside?" "What techniques of restoration were used on this pamphlet and are they reversible?" "Who made these distinctive clasps for this folio manuscript's binding? If this is determinable, the date and place of origin of the book may be determinable." "How many copies of this book were printed?"[35] "Why is the ink in this book fading? And is it damaging the paper?" "Why is there only one copy of this book in WorldCat?" "Is the varnish on this nineteenth-century marbled paper anything like the varnish used on violins?"[36] "What were the extant laws regarding (copyright) (printing) (bookselling) (moneylending) (censorship) (taxes on paper or cloth or leather) when this book was written or made that influenced its text, its distribution, or its manufacture?"

There is no end of challenges. To solve endless problems and answer endless questions about books, historical bibliographers can turn to endless sources of information. The keen researcher can identify the problem areas (like those in the preceding questions), and can then figure out whom to turn to—what areas of inquiry must be approached—for answers. Worlds of knowledge can be opened through historical bibliography. People working with special collections and rare books, because of the materials they work with, and because of the very nature of their professions, must be historical bibliographers.

As purveyors of knowledge, librarians owe it to their patrons to offer as much information as they can about individual volumes and manuscripts in their collections and about the broad subject areas in these collections. As purveyors of books, dealers will want to uncover as much information as they can about the materials they want to sell. Historical research helps librarians and scholars, and it could help them line their purses—especially if they uncover important information that makes a title or a particular copy extremely important.[37] But beyond the monetary value of such research, its intellectual, cultural-historical value can be inestimable, and many booksellers are supremely proficient, insightful historical bibliographers.[38]

Historical bibliography can uncover provenance information that can reveal a book's historical influences, the habits of former owners, a text's popularity, its uniqueness, and on and on. The benefit to social historians from this kind of bibliography can be inestimable. Booksellers and scholars like to know that "this is the first book to _____," whatever that may be: the first book printed on paper made from straw or esparto grass; the first to be printed in Hawaii or Jamaica; the first ever to mention the body of land now called "North America"; the first to recognize Uranus as a planet; the first to deal with nuclear fission; the first to contain a volvelle;[39] the first to reveal a scientific discovery or invention; the first in the West to be printed from moveable type; the first to be illustrated with chromolithography or collotypes or photographs; and so forth. "Firsts" are grounded in history, so they help historians in specific disciplines; they are grounded in technology, so they help scholars working in the history of those technologies.

People want to know these things; scholars need to know these things; historical bibliographers do the research to uncover these things. Librarians, scholars, rare book dealers, and others are the beneficiaries of historical bibliographical research. This branch of bibliography covers the globe.

Textual Bibliography

At the risk of sounding like a broken record, the field of textual bibliography is huge;[40] it has generated an extensive literature that encompasses or is reflected in the other three branches delineated here. It is not in the purview of the present volume to expatiate on the wide-ranging, minute, and complex practical and theoretical issues in this important field.

The aim of this volume is to present the information that people working with special collections and rare books need to know. So the presentation here about textual bibliography will necessarily be brief. The bibliography at the end of this chapter will lead readers to further texts that delve more deeply into the field than is appropriate here. On the other hand, a good deal of detail is necessary to present the key concepts and terms that rare book people must know. Also, because one of the responsibilities of rare book specialists is to direct their clientele

to reliable, authoritative texts, they should know of the issues dealt with (and some of the conclusions arrived at) by textual bibliographers and know the key vocabulary of this field, because it is a jargon used throughout the rare book world.

Another phrase designating this field is *textual editing*, but this is more a designation of the activity (editing), while *textual bibliography* implies the application of scientific method, an understanding of technical issues and practices along with writing and publishing, and a knowledge of the basic "solutions" and "theoretical approaches" to establishing *reliable texts*. The textual bibliographer cannot merely get a graduate degree in some discipline and then become a responsible editor of works in that field. She first needs a grounding in bibliographical theory, in the history of this discipline,[41] in the related fields of bibliography (especially descriptive and historical), and in paleography, printing history, the history of the manufacture of paper and ink, the history and practices of bookbinding, and much more—including a thorough analysis of the biography of the person whose work she is editing and the history and condition of the world in which that author lived.

As noted, as a discipline, textual bibliography has generated its own jargon, many terms of which those in rare books should be familiar with. (Once again, key terms are printed here in boldface.) Already mentioned is **reliable texts.** The goal of textual bibliography is to produce texts that scholars can rely

---

A FAVORITE STORY of academics in the field of textual bibliography recounts the work of F. O. Matthiessen, the great scholar of American literature and author of the heralded scholarly study, *American Renaissance: Art and Expression in the Age of Emerson and Whitman* (London and New York: Oxford University Press, 1941). In writing about Herman Melville's novel *White Jacket*, Matthiessen sees the phrase "soiled fish of the sea," and he builds an argument

that Melville was influenced by the Metaphysical poets of the seventeenth century, who used startling imagery to convey their ideas. Of the phrase "soiled fish of the sea," Matthiessen says, "The *discordia concors*, the unexpected linking of the medium of cleanliness with filth, could only have sprung from an imagination that had apprehended the terrors of the deep, of the immortal deep as well as the physical" (p. 392). Although Matthiessen's interpretation was

ingenious and grandly stated, it was, embarrassingly, based on a typographical error, for Melville had written "coiled fish," and Matthiessen had relied on an inferior edition with the typo. The lesson is that scholars must be able to distinguish a good, well-edited text from a cheap, careless one and should check their sources and quote from reliable editions. In textual bibliography, the editor aims to produce a text with no such "soiled fish."

on, that are as close as possible to the **author's final intentions,** as nearly as these intentions can be determined. The reliable text, therefore, contains readings that its author would probably approve of (hence the term **authorial texts**). The bibliographer must look circumspectly at all the extant versions of a given text done during the author's life,[42] compare them, list the variants among them, and try to determine—following basic bibliographic theory and a large body of historical information—which readings are **authorial** and which are not; which the author wrote last;[43] which the author himself would have approved of; and so forth.

Naturally this kind of work relies heavily on the editor's immersion in the text, the author's writing practices, the world around the author (hence, historical bibliography), and a good deal of speculation—though this speculation is based on a deep understanding of the author's practices and on the world in which the work being edited was produced. The more the editor knows about the author, his practices, and the world in which he lived, and the more schooled the editor is in textual bibliography, the less speculative are her decisions about what goes into the final text.

The aim, then, is to produce an edition of a work that scholars can rely on for their scholarship—a version that removes any nonauthorial readings that could have been introduced by an egocentric or inconsiderate editor, an incompetent typesetter, or anyone else who had access to the text before it went to press.

A bit of history, sketchy as it will be here, will show how the field of textual bibliography developed.

German scholars in the nineteenth century, working on manuscript texts, wanted to produce what we now call **definitive editions** of classical works. The term implies that the versions they strove to produce would "define" the work as the best possible text achievable, with the fewest errors and nonauthorial readings. They came up with "scientific" methods[44] that emanated from the work of Aldus Manutius, one of the great fifteenth-century scholar-printers, who carefully compared versions of a work and tried to publish books with no errors and with authoritative texts. Aldus created **scholarly editions** by gathering all the manuscripts he could get for a single text, comparing them, listing all the places in which they differed (called **cruxes**),[45] and then selecting the reading at each crux that seemed to be the "best" one. (This notion of "best" will be dealt with later in this chapter.) The aim was to produce a text that scholars could rely on as accurately reflecting what the author actually wrote and intended.

Manuscript editing reached a pinnacle of scientific development in the nineteenth century. The editor of, say, a work by Cicero gathered all the manuscripts of that work, **collated** them (that is, compared them against one another minutely), found every point of variation among them, and then built a "genealogical chart" showing the relationships among them all. Because the original, right from the author's hand, was gone, editors looked for the earliest one as being

WHEN I WAS working on Mark Twain's *Pudd'nhead Wilson* and *Those Extraordinary Twins*, I needed to follow the author's movements from the United States to Europe to know what his spelling predilections were; to know about his wife's ailment (syncope, a fainting disease akin to epilepsy); to be familiar with some vocabulary that his audiences would have understood but that current readers would have trouble with; to know how copyright worked in England and America and why he wanted to publish the novel in both countries simultaneously; to know about the recent publication by Francis Galton on fingerprints* and that Twain had read that book; and so on. Essential also was a familiarity with his handwriting and his use of abbreviations and other writing symbols (like the caret for inserting words or the paragraph sign). It took many years of work, more than a decade, to be ready to edit his novels. So while there may be some speculation in deciding on what readings to choose for the edited text, such speculation is at a bare minimum, and knowledge of many things usually leads an editor to select reliable readings for the final edited version.

*Francis Galton, *Finger Prints* (London: Macmillan, 1892).

EARLY MANUSCRIPTS WERE written out on vellum—animal skin—which was expensive. Authors would almost certainly not have done their first, rough drafts on this surface. Instead, they used wax tablets, which could hold quite long texts. These tablets were flat boards with raised edges that held wax on their surfaces, front and back, and they could be hinged together to create many "pages" of text. Rather than "writing," the authors incised their words into the wax with a stylus. A blunt end opposite the point of the stylus allowed for "erasures"—that is, allowed the author to rub out the text so that a correction could be incised in. The full text, in wax, would be given to a scribe, who would transfer it to the permanent surface of parchment. It is extremely unlikely that extant manuscripts are written in the hands of the original authors, though we can never know. The point here is that the so-called ur (i.e., original) text—the first one produced by the author—is unlikely to exist, and editors have to work with the earliest scribal version they can find.

A problem, then, with all manuscript versions of a text is that each was filtered through the minds and hands of the scribes, which, naturally, means that variants were introduced into the texts from the first "permanent" versions on. No scribe can copy verbatim and *ad literatim* (i.e., word for word and letter for letter) without introducing some change, partly because of human error and partly because the notion of the sanctity of the author's original did not exist. Because the scribe's aim was to get the author's ideas across, he was not bound by modern notions that we must not deviate in any way from the author's original.

as close, chronologically, to the author's composition, and therefore presumably as close to his original intentions, as possible.

A genealogical relationship, then, existed among manuscripts of a single text. Such a structure may be depicted as shown in table 9.2.

This abbreviated chart shows twelve manuscripts: A_1, A_2, A_3, B_1, B_2, C_1, C_2, C_3, B_{2a}, B_{2b}, C_{2a}, and C_{2b}.[46]

In the manuscript-editing world, this chart is called a **stemma,** and the branch of endeavors that create these charts is called **stemmatics,** in which we can see the genealogical relationship of all the manuscripts. In this stemma the manuscripts are divided into three branches. All manuscripts in the whole tradition of this text have one of three readings at the first crux: "man," "guy," or "fellow." In the A branch, at one particular crux, all manuscripts have the word "man." At that very crux, in the B branch, all the manuscripts have the word "guy." Also at that crux, all the manuscripts in the C branch of the stemma have the word "fellow."

Back to the A branch, at another crux, the manuscripts with the word "man" at the first crux vary in three ways: "happy," "glad," and "joyous." That is, A_1 has the word "man" at the first crux, but "happy" at the second crux. A_2 has "man" at the first crux, but "glad" at the second one. And so on. A full stemma will have as many entries on it as there are manuscripts, and it will show which items cluster with which others in each branch. Sometimes, by carefully placing individual manuscripts into the stemma, an editor can determine where it came from, its priority with respect to others on its branch, its age, and therefore its level of authority.

TABLE 9.2

[Ur manuscript]*

A version ("man")			B version ("guy")			C version ("fellow")		
A_1 ("happy")	A_2 ("glad")	A_3 ("joyous")	B_1 ("old")	B_2 ("aged")		C_1 ("fat")	C_2 ("thin")	C_3 ("huge")
				B_{2a} ("odd")	B_{2b} ("peculiar")		C_{2a} ("cold")	C_{2b} ("icy")

*Printed in brackets because it is not extant.

ON MY WORK on Layamon's *Brut,* an Early Middle English manuscript in 33,000 half lines of alliterative, rhyming verse, I found that the scribe accidentally copied out nearly 90 lines a second time, inadvertently skipping backward in his copying and repeating those lines. Fascinatingly and revealingly, the two "identical" passages do not agree with one another. They vary in many places—changed words, dropped lines, variant spellings, rearranged words, and so forth—proving that scribes were not constrained to follow their models slavishly, but had the latitude to change the texts they were copying.

Stemmatics and the editing of classical and medieval manuscripts are the forerunners of twentieth-century textual bibliography. In the twentieth century such great bibliographers as R. B. McKerrow, W. W. Greg, Philip Gaskell, G. Thomas Tanselle, O M Brack Jr., Warner Barnes, Vincent Dearing, Fredson Bowers, William B. Todd, and others led the scholarship in the field from superb formulations of theory and practice to minute analyses of all the subtopics that textual editors needed to consider to produce reliable editions. As Tanselle sums it up,

> If the third quarter of the twentieth century can be considered—as it often is—an age of editing, one of the principal reasons is the existence and influence of two American organizations: the National Historical Publications Commission (NHPC), renamed in late 1974 the National Historical Publications and Records Commission (NHPRC); and the Center for Editions of American Authors (CEAA), succeeded in 1976 by the Center for Scholarly Editions (CSE). The NHPC (NHPRC) has since 1950 given encouragement and assistance to a large number of multi-volume editions (more than four dozen) of the papers of American statesmen, especially those of the late eighteenth and nineteenth centuries; the CEAA, from 1963 through 1976, gave its official approval to volumes in fourteen editions, predominantly of the works of nineteenth-century American literary figures. As a result, massive scholarly editions have been produced in an unprecedented quantity during these years; hundreds of scholars have been connected with these projects, and widespread discussion and awareness of the prob-

lems and aims of editing have been engendered. The presence of these editions has dramatically altered the scholarly landscape in American history and literature within a generation.[47]

The aim of the editors is to get into print **definitive, reliable, authoritative** texts of great or important writers.[48] The Committee on Scholarly Editions, like the Center for Editions of American Authors before it, has, for their editors, many requirements that look like those used for editing manuscripts. Of course, the editor must gather all appropriate texts for comparison (collation) that the author might have had a hand in producing. Certainly, the author's manuscript(s), if extant, would be key to evaluate, along with all editions printed during the author's life—and even posthumously published editions if it can be established that they were based on (or included) materials that the author had a hand in. If the author died in 1915, an edition published in, say, 1917 would probably not be worth examining, unless it can be shown that that edition was printed from copy the author himself had supervised the printing of or read the proofs for.

Collations of all versions of the text (manuscript and printed) needed to be done and checked, and checked again. In fact, if versions of the text had to be reproduced, many collations may need to be done, and proofreading at least a half dozen times at each stage of the work was mandatory for the volume to receive the CEAA seal of approval.

Key to the thoroughness and success of the CEAA editions was a complete listing of variants. The editors would assemble a team for the collations, as already mentioned, making a chart of every crux they found. This so-called **collation table** had to be proofread against the original texts that were collated to make sure that each variant found among the several collated versions was recorded—and recorded accurately. The collation table had columns, one for each source collated, with a listing of the variant and the page and line number where it occurred in that version of the text.

Two categories of variants were identified for (and therefore were entered into) the collation tables: **substantives** and **accidentals.** The former were significant variants in meaningful units: changes,

FOR SIX YEARS (1965–1971) I was involved in the pre-editing activities of many volumes for the Center for Editions of American Authors (CEAA) when I was at the University of Iowa, in its Center for Bibliographic Studies. And through 1980, I worked assiduously on a CEAA edition (Mark Twain's *Pudd'nhead Wilson* and *Those Extraordinary Twins*—both of which eventually were published by W. W. Norton in its Norton Critical Edition series). The extensive methods of work the Bibliographic Center employed are beyond the scope of the present text, but one practice is worth mentioning because it had long-term implications for the larger project and because it led to the changeover from the CEAA to the Committee on Scholarly Editions (CSE).

To create the collation tables (see text), one person in a group read the text aloud while others around the table checked their own versions of the text. If we were collating, say, a base text against a manuscript, a serialized version, and two printed versions, there would be five people at the table (or ten: five principle readers and five backups to make the collation more accurate than with only five of us). If the text were fascinating, as was the case with most of Mark Twain's writings, the readers would get caught up in the content of the book and miss many variants. For instance, when we were collating *Huckleberry Finn* and *Tom Sawyer,* we checked the collation tables after a reading session and found that the auditors had missed many variants. The editors (who included O M Brack and Warner Barnes) devised a method for reading that improved the group's accuracy somewhat: the reader read backward, enunciating all words, punctuation, paragraphing, italics, and other typographic peculiarities, variant spellings, and so forth. It was practically impossible to get caught up in the content because the text was invisible.

The original looks like this:

"Well," I says, "s'pose we got some genies to help us—can't we lick the other crowd then?"

"How you going to get them?"

"I don't know. How do they get them?"

When the reader of the group read it aloud, backward, it sounded like this:

(quotes) / question mark / them get they do (cap) how. (period) know don't [with the apostrophe noted verbally] I (quotes) / paragraph / (quotes) / question mark / them get to going you (cap) how (quotes) / paragraph / (quotes) / question mark / then crowd other the lick we can't (dash) us help to genies some got we s (apostrophe) pose (quotes) comma says I (quotes) comma (cap) well (quotes) / paragraph / [This passage is from chapter 3 of *Huckleberry Finn.*]

It is clear that backward this passage is practically impossible to follow, and the concentration of the collators was not distracted by content; hence, accuracy in finding the variants improved. The method worked, but we eventually decided not to do this backward reading, instead reading the text forward several times, slowly and in monotone, to catch the variants, because the backward reading was difficult to follow.

The critic Edmund Wilson learned of the efforts of this collation group (supported by a grant from the Modern Language Association [MLA]), and he pilloried them in his now famous essay "The Fruits of the MLA," in which he says,

It seems that eighteen of these Mark Twain workers are reading *Tom Sawyer,* word by word, backward, in order to ascertain, by this drudgery by attention to the story or the style, how many times "Aunt Polly" is printed as "aunt Polly," and how many times ssst! is printed as sssst!*

Though Wilson did not at all understand the backward reading, which we in the end abandoned, he embarrassed the MLA and its editors, and they eventually suspended the funding of the editorial projects until the CEAA reemerged as the CSE, with a different funding structure.

This exposition is part of the lore of the world of textual bibliography and should be part of the knowledge of those working with rare books, especially those charged with their selection for library collections.

*This passage is quoted by John E. McIntyre in "The Likes of Edmund Wilson May Never Be Seen Again," *Baltimore Sun,* July 28, 2002, http://articles.baltimoresun.com/2002-07-28/entertainment/0207280338_1_kipling-edmund-wilson-patriotic-gore.

deletions, or additions of words (e.g., "man" in one version and "guy" in another), the addition or loss of a sentence or paragraph, name changes, and so forth. And accidentals were such things as variations in spelling (color/colour), punctuation ("he was here, she was not" / "he was here; she was not"), paragraphing, italicization,[49] underlining, or boldface. A substantive change instantly changes the meaning of the text; an accidental variant usually does not change the meaning, although there are such accidentals as "Let's eat, Grandma" in which the loss of a comma significantly changes the text's meaning. This is an **accidental with the weight of a substantive.**

The CEAA and CSE editors, then, did minute collations of all the texts the author could have had a hand in producing, compiled a collation table of all substantive and accidental variants, and used this table as a guide in selecting readings at every point where there was a crux (a variant) for the final edited text. The editor had to do her homework—in selecting versions of the text, making collation tables, doing a great deal of background work, studying the theories and practices of textual bibliography, learning the handwriting (or keyboarding) practices of the author, and so forth. This kind of preparation gave her a sound basis for making editorial decisions at each crux. The "best" reading—that is, the best decision at each crux—was usually based on all this preparation, with a strong influence from the application of textual bibliographical theories. The editor needed to be able to justify every editorial decision, and in some cases she needed to explain a decision in a note at the back of the text.

For instance, for *Pudd'nhead Wilson*, every printed edition of the novel, from its first appearance in serial form in the *Century Magazine* in 1893–1894, had two sentences in a particular order. I examined the manuscript carefully and found that Twain had, almost unseen, inserted (with a caret) the first of these sentences' text at the end of the second sentence. That is, one sentence was written margin to margin—one full line long—into the text above the second sentence, but it actually had been inserted with a caret that was placed *after* the other sentence. They were always printed in reverse order until my

Norton Critical Edition fixed this error. This change required an explanatory note in the Norton edition.[50]

The notion, then, of the "best" readings was based more on theory than on personal taste. The editor needed to justify a reading at a crux with respect to bibliographical theory, authorial practices, the idiosyncratic methods of composition of the author for this particular text, or some other reason consistent with textual bibliography. She should never decide on a reading at a crux based on what she conceives is a more aesthetic, more euphonious, more meaningful, or more pleasing reading.[51]

A base text has to be chosen as the point of comparison for all other versions to be collated against. This base text is known as the **copy-text,** and its choice has engendered a substantial literature.[52] When doing the actual editing, the textual bibliographer looks at a crux, at which there are at least two readings, possibly more, and either leaves the copy-text as it is, not accepting any of the variants, or incorporates one of the variants into the text being edited. Every change the editor makes in the copy-text is recorded in a table called **Emendations of the Copy-Text,** letting the reader know exactly what the copy-text reading was and showing all the possible changes that could have been made for each crux. If there is a crux (showing a point of variation) at which the editor could change the copy-text, but does not do so, this is recorded in another table called **Rejected Variants.** The idea is to give the reader the whole picture: all the places where there are cruxes, all those used to emend the text, and all those that were passed over and not used. The reader can then say, "I would have changed the text at this point where the editor did not." But if the editor has explained all his editorial decisions in an introduction or in notes, the reader should theoretically agree with the editor's decisions for every crux.

Table 9.3 shows what an editor might have to work with. The editor has determined that the author read proofs for the 1913 edition and made substantive changes throughout this later version. Hence this 1913 edition has great authority, and substantive readings therein should be incorporated into the final, newly edited version. One common thought in

TABLE 9.3 Textual Editing: The Original Text and a Collection of Variants

A. Original Text

When Melanie called out she was hurt John responded with a cry of his own.

B. Collation Table, showing readings from four editions

Copy-text	1888 edition	1901 edition	1913 edition
(1.5) Melanie called	(1.5) Melanie cried	(1.4) Melanie called	(1.4) Melanie called*
(1.5) hurt	(1.6) ~,	(1.5) ~,	(1.4) ~,†
(1.5) responded	(1.6) replied	(1.5) answered	(1.5) responded
(1.6) cry	(1.6) ~	(1.5) ~	(1.5) yelp
(1.6) own.	(1.7) ~.	(1.5) ~!	(1.5) ~!

*The numbers in parentheses indicate page and line number of the reading.

† When the variant is an accidental and the substantive reading (in this case, a word) stays the same, the collation table shows the word in the first column and uses the squiggle to indicate that the word doesn't change in the other texts, but the punctuation does.

textual editing is that an author is likely to make substantive changes to a text, but he would not bother with accidentals, which are often created by editors or compositors. That is, substantives have a greater chance of being authorial than do accidentals. For an isolated accidental, then, an editor is justified if he ignores it if it does not change the meaning of the text. However, when the author's hand is visible in a passage in which he is making a number of substantive changes, it is more than just likely that he is also changing accidentals. So an editor may feel justified in accepting as authorial those accidental variations (see table 9.4).

The edited text, with all the changes made and the possible emendations not used for the copy-text, is the textual bibliographer's version of what he thinks are the author's final intentions, what the author would have approved of with respect to all the decisions made to bring the text to its "final" edited form. The tables "Emendations of the Copy-Text" and "Rejected Variants" show the reader all the cruxes—all the places where there were variants, any of which could have been (or were) incorporated into the edited text. These give readers the opportunity to see where the text was edited and where it might have been edited, and thus also allows the

TABLE 9.4 Textual Editing: The Edited Version and Textual Apparatus

C. The Edited Version (i.e., the copy-text readings incorporating the editor's changes)

When Melanie called out she was hurt, John responded with a yelp of his own!

D. Table Emendations of the Copy-Text

(1.5) hurt, 1888, 1901, 1913 ~, CT ~ ^ *

(1.6) yelp 1913†

(1.6) own! 1888 ~. 1901, 1913 ~! CT ~.

*This shows that the copy-text lacked the comma and that the other three editions had it. The squiggle shows that the word "hurt" stays the same; the caret shows that where a piece of punctuation could be, there is none.

†This shows that the variation that was used to emend the copy-text comes from the 1913 edition, implying that the other two editions agreed with the copy-text reading.

E. Rejected Variants

(1.5) Melanie called 1888 ~ cried

(1.5) responded 1888 replied 1901 answered

reader to disagree with the editor's choices for emendation.

To preempt such disagreement, and to explain all the editorial choices, the editor must have a thorough introduction (1) delineating all the texts collated and explaining why they were chosen (and why others were not), (2) giving a full background and description of the texts collated (and showing why they could contain authorial readings), the author's compositional practices, the movement of the author through the world at the time the text was composed (if this movement has any bearing on the editorial process), the reasons for the decisions made in selecting from among variants, and (3) explaining anything else that the reader needs to know that justifies why the editor has come up with this final version. If the editor had problems in making decisions at any of the cruxes, these should be explained. At times, faced with two perfectly good, equally justifiable readings, both with the same level of authority, the editor may just have to flip a coin to decide which to choose. Usually this is not the case: most decisions should be made on the basis of sound bibliographical theory or other criteria that guide the editor to a decision.

ONE FEATURE OF a good scholarly edition will help researchers in quoting from the final edited text. If the new edition has the word "steamboat" or "wash-tub" hyphenated at the end of a line, there is no way for the scholar to know if it is a single word or a hyphenated word. One standard feature of the CEAA/CSE volumes is a chart titled "End-of-Line Hyphens in the Present Volume." In the cases of "steam-/boat" and "wash-/tub," this chart would say "steamboat" or "wash-tub" to show how the word is or is not hyphenated. The scholar will thus know how to style the word if she is quoting the sentence in which it appears.

With all the apparatus beyond the final edited text—a listing and description of all versions of a text, a thorough introduction, tables showing Emendations of the Copy-Text, Rejected Variants, End-of-Line Hyphenation, Notes, and whatever else the editor needs to reveal that led to constructing the final text—with all this, the reader should have a full understanding of how this text was established and the ability to see and evaluate the editor's decisions at every crux.

There are four ways to present the final edited text. The first is called a **clear text,** with nothing on the printed pages other than the text of the work. There will be no footnotes of any kind, no signals anywhere in the typography to show the reader where emendations were made (or could have been made) or where notes exist to elucidate the text, and nothing else to impede a smooth reading of the text. This method allows the publisher to print a scholarly edition with no apparatus at all, offering a scholarly, reliable text in an inexpensive format.

The second method of printing the text contains all the scholarly apparatus, before and after the text (which is still a clear text). The third method is to put indications of editorial activity into the text to alert readers to the cruxes (where the editor had to decide between or among variants) and to the explanatory notes. This kind of presentation will impede smooth reading, but it saves the time of scholars who are interested in the history of the composition and publication of the text and who want to examine how the final text was arrived at.

A fourth method of presentation is actually a nineteenth-century practice, the **variorum edition,** in which all textual variants and notes are printed onto the pages of the edited text. The reader need not flip back and forth, from text to editorial apparatus, to see all the cruxes or to see the notes. This method of printing can yield pages that seem heavily lopsided, with perhaps a few lines of text at the top of the page and the rest of the page showing cruxes and notes.

These kinds of presentations will not affect the quality of the final text. Anyone working in rare books should know from the information presented in such scholarly editions that she is dealing with reliable versions of the text—reliable enough to be selected for a library and to be recommended to readers for their trustworthiness as authorial editions. Also, those in special collections should know the terms *CEAA, CSE, collations, definitive edition, authorial,* and all the other words printed in boldface in this discussion of textual bibliography. Scholars and booksellers will often use these terms, and librarians must know the words and the phenomena they refer to.

Bibliography in all its manifestations and ramifications is central to special collections. Those dealing with rare books must be fully conversant with books and other media that purvey information, and the terminology and concepts revealed in a thorough study of bibliography is essential for understanding the creation, search for, dissemination, and preservation of information, and for communicating with others in the field.

A Note on Paleography

Anyone working in the rare book world should be able to read various handwritings. Of course, if the volumes in a collection are in classical or medieval Latin, the reader should be able to read that language, if not with some fluency, at least with an ability to transcribe a text accurately—the idea being that an accurate reading will lead the reader to bibliographic sources that could be useful in identifying the date and place of the manuscript and possibly offer other information.

Paleography, then, is the science of deciphering old handwritings and, if possible, the ability to read (and understand) old texts. Because alphabets have evolved, and because for many centuries scribes have been using abbreviations, the paleographer must be able to figure out what a text says by deciphering the handwriting and expanding the abbreviations. The present text is not a handbook on paleography, so this topic is presented only cursorily here. It is a reminder, however, that a person working with rare books may need a workshop or two in paleography—a workshop focusing specially on the handwriting of that scholar's needs. A class in seventeenth-century Greek script will not be much use to a bookseller who has just acquired a library of classical Latin texts.

Many texts have been published on this discipline, and many of these do indeed focus on particular handwritings of specific times. Scholars / librarians

I WORKED FOR about seven months on an early thirteenth-century English manuscript. When I first encountered it, the handwriting was seemingly impenetrable, but after a half hour I was working my way slowly through the text, and within an hour I was making good progress. I made a chart of the common abbreviations this scribe used and some of the peculiar ways he made a few of his letters, and, because I was fairly familiar with his dialect of early Middle English, within a few days I was reading the text with good fluency. It took time and perseverance, and it was really fun being able to read from the vellum original (instead of the terrible copy-flow that I had been supplied, which was so badly done that it was truly useless).

/ booksellers / collectors need to be familiar with the basic tool of the texts they are handling, and that "basic tool" is language. And because manuscripts are, by their very nature, unique, every manuscript scribe may present his or her own idiosyncrasy in handwriting. For this reason, while a particular reference book or a few might be good starting points for paleographers, they may find themselves making their own charts of the idiosyncratic writing practices of the scribes they are dealing with.

■ ■ ■

As noted at the outset of this chapter, Bibliography as a formal academic discipline has practically disappeared from the curricula of colleges and universities. An occasional course or two might be offered in English or History Departments or in a library school, but the extensive and deep training of bibliographers through focused classes is practically gone from academia. However, the kind of training offered by this discipline in its branches is essential for much rare book and special collections librarianship. At the very least, anyone working in rare books must know the vocabulary and the concepts behind the words in the field. It is the standard jargon of the trade.

The importance of good bibliographies (and how to recognize and compile them) is essential. Being able to do a solid, reliable bibliographical description

Bibliography on Bibliography

PERHAPS THE MOST prolific, wide-ranging, and insightful of all bibliographers, G. Thomas Tanselle taught classes in bibliography for more than forty years, starting at the University of Wisconsin, and then in Rare Book School (RBS) at Columbia University and the University of Virginia. For the course, he developed, over the years, a massive bibliography listing texts in many areas of inquiry. The most recent version in print (that is, on paper) is from 2002, and it runs 370 pages! The URL to access the online version is www.rarebookschool.org/tanselle.

Tanselle also teaches the Introduction to Scholarly Editing course at RBS, and for that class he has put together another syllabus of 257 pages, also available online at www.rarebookschool.org/tanselle/syl-E-complete.090302 .pdf. Between them, these syllabi constitute the most extensive listing of the best sources on the subjects that are covered in the present chapter.

should be second nature to anyone working with rare books—especially old ones. It practically goes without saying that knowing the words of the trade without knowing their precise meaning is essentially useless. Being comfortable with going beyond your immediate rare book realm into historical research to elucidate things about your immediate rare book realm can have exceptionally rewarding consequences, revealing worlds of information that scholars can profit from. Knowing how authoritative editions are derived can be valuable. Bibliography is an extraordinarily rich and exciting field, complementing and underpinning the world of rare books.

Chapter 10 will look at related subjects: collecting and handling books and manuscripts, with examinations of sources of materials, markets for books, and much more. Enumerative bibliography teaches us how to capture and disseminate information about information sources. Chapter 10 concentrates on the practical end of acquiring the tools that contain the information. Descriptive bibliography shows us how to show others what items we have in front of us. Chapter 10 shows us how to acquire and evaluate those items. And again, all people dealing with special collections materials will need to know the vocabulary and the practices of collecting and handling books.

Readings in Bibliography

As I mentioned earlier, the Tanselle syllabi are excellent sources of information about the broad field of bibliography. (They are *Introduction to Bibliography* [Charlottesville, VA: Book Arts Press, 2002 and other dates] and *Introduction to Scholarly Editing* [Charlottesville, VA: Book Arts Press, 2002 and other dates].) They are, however, overwhelming in their comprehensiveness and also in that they list publications chronologically, not an easy configuration for someone looking for the work of particular scholars. This listing could contain thousands of items. Here is a brief bibliography of informative works in the field.

Baender, Paul. "The Meaning of Copy-Text." *Studies in Bibliography* 22 (1969): 311–18.

Baker, William, and Kenneth Womack. *Twentieth-Century Bibliography and Textual Criticism: An Annotated Bibliography*. Westport, CT, and London: Greenwood Press, 2000.

Bates, Marcia J. "Rigorous Systematic Bibliography." *RQ* 16.1 (Fall 1976): 7–26.

Berger, Sidney. *The Design of Bibliographies: Observations, References and Examples*. London: Mansell; Westport, CT: Greenwood, 1991.

Besterman, Theodore. *The Beginnings of Systematic Bibliography*. London: Oxford University Press, 1936 (and later reprints).

———. *A World Bibliography of Bibliographies and of Bibliographical Catalogues, Calendars, Abstracts, Digests, Indexes, and the Like*. Geneva: Societas Bibliographica, 1955 (and many other editions).

Blum, Rudolf. *Bibliographia: An Inquiry into Its Definition and Designations*. Trans. by Mathilde V. Rovelstad. Chicago: American Library Association, 1980.

Bowers, Fredson. *Bibliography and Textual Criticism*. Oxford: Clarendon Press, 1964.

———. "Certain Basic Problems in Descriptive Bibliography." *Papers of the Bibliographical Society of America* 42 (1948): 211–28.

———. "Current Theories of Copy-Text, with an Illustration from Dryden." In Brack and Barnes, *Bibliography and Textual Criticism*, pp. 59–72.

———. *Essays in Bibliography, Text and Editing*. Charlottesville: University Press of Virginia, 1985.

———. *Essays in Bibliography, Texts, and Editing*. Charlottesville: University Press of Virginia, 1975.

———. "The Function of Bibliography." *Library Trends* 7.4 (1959): 497–510.

———. *Principles of Bibliographical Description*. Princeton, NJ: Princeton University Press, 1949 (and later editions).

———. *Textual and Literary Criticism*. Cambridge: Cambridge University Press, 1966.

———. "Textual Criticism." In *The Aims and Methods of Scholarship in Modern Languages and Literatures*, ed. by James Thorpe. 2nd ed. New York: Modern Language Association, 1970, pp. 29–54.

Brack, O M, and Warner Barnes, eds. *Bibliography and Textual Criticism: English and American Literature, 1700 to the Present*. Chicago: University of Chicago Press, 1969. An exceptional volume of critical essays in the field. A few of these are listed separately in this bibliography.

Breslauer, Bernhard H., and Roland Folter. *Bibliography: Its History and Development*. New York: Grolier Club, 1984.

Bruccoli, Matthew J. "Getting it Right: The Publishing Process and the Correction of Factual Errors—With Reference to 'The Great Gatsby.'" In *Essays in Honor of William B. Todd*, comp. by Warner Barnes and Larry Carver; ed. by Dave Oliphant. Austin, TX: Harry Ransom Humanities Research Center, University of Texas at Austin, 1991, pp. 40–59.

Campbell, Frank. *The Theory of National and International Bibliography*. London: Library Bureau, 1896.

Cohen, Philip, ed. *Texts and Textuality: Textual Instability, Theory, and Interpretation*. New York: Garland, 1997.

Colaianne, A. J. "The Aims and Methods of Annotated Bibliography." *Scholarly Publishing* 11.4 (July 1980): 321–31.

Dearing, Vinton. "Methods of Textual Editing." *William Andrews Clark Memorial Library Seminar Papers*, 1962, pp. 1–34; rpt. in Brack and Barnes, *Bibliography and Textual Criticism*, pp. 73–101.

Delfino, Erik. "Book History and Library Education in the Twenty-first Century." In Hawkins, *Teaching Bibliography*, pp. 81–87.

Downs, Robert B., and Frances B. Jenkins. *Bibliography: Current State and Future Trends*. Urbana, Chicago, and London: University of Illinois Press, 1967.

Esdaile, Arundell. See Stokes below.

Foot, Mirjam. "Historical Bibliography for Rare-Book Librarians." In Hawkins, *Teaching Bibliography*, pp. 25–31.

Ford, Margaret Lane. "Deconstruction and Reconstruction: Detecting and Interpreting Sophisticated Copies." In *Early Printed Books as Material Objects: Proceedings of the Conference Organized by the IFLA Rare Books and Manuscripts Section, Munich, 19–21 August 2009*, ed. by Bettina Wagner and Marcia Reed. Berlin and New York: De Gruyter Saur, 2010, pp. 291–303.

Gallup, Donald. *On Contemporary Bibliography: With Particular Reference to Ezra Pound*. Austin, TX: Humanities Research Center, University of Texas at Austin, 1970.

Gaskell, Philip. *A New Introduction to Bibliography*. London: Oxford University Press, 1972 (and later editions).

Gottesman, Ronald, and Scott Bennett, eds. *Art and Error: Modern Textual Editing*. Bloomington: Indiana University Press, 1970.

Greethan, D[avid] C., ed. *Scholarly Editing: A Guide to Research*. New York: Modern Language Association, 1995.

———. *Textual Scholarship: An Introduction*. New York and London: Garland, 1994.

———. *Theories of the Text*. Oxford: Clarendon Press, 1999.

Greg, W. W. "The Rationale of Copy-Text." In Brack and Barnes, *Bibliography and Textual Criticism*, pp. 41–58. Greg (1875–1959) is one of the fathers of modern bibliography.

———. *Sir Walter Wilson Greg: A Collection of His Writings*, ed. by Joseph Rosenblum. Metuchen, NJ: Scarecrow, 1998. This collection includes eleven of Greg's essays.

———. "What Is Bibliography?" *Bibliographical Society Transactions* 12.1 (1911–1912): 10–12.

Harmon, Robert B. *Elements of Bibliography: A Simplified Approach*. Metuchen, NJ, and London: Scarecrow, 1981.

Harner, James L. *On Compiling an Annotated Bibliography*. New York: Modern Language Association, 1991.

Hawkins, Ann R., ed. *Teaching Bibliography, Textual Criticism, and Book History*. London: Pickering & Chatto, 2006.

Hellinga, Lotte. "Editing Texts in the First Fifteen Years of Printing." In *New Directions in Textual Studies*, ed. by David Oliphant and Robin Bradford. Austin, TX:

Harry Ransom Humanities Research Center, University of Texas at Austin, 1990, pp. 126–49.

Howard-Hill, T. H. "Enumerative and Descriptive Bibliography." In *The Book Encompassed*, ed. by Peter Davison. Cambridge: Cambridge University Press, 1992, pp. 122–29.

Krummel, D. W. *Bibliographies: Their Aims and Methods*. London and New York: Mansell, 1984.

Lang, Susan. "Converging (or Colliding) Traditions: Integrating Hypertext into Literary Studies." In Cohen, *Texts and Textuality,* pp. 291–312.

Mallaber, Kenneth A. *A Primer of Bibliography*. London: Association of Assistant Librarians, 1954.

McGann, Jerome J. *A Critique of Modern Textual Criticism*. Chicago and London: University of Chicago Press, 1983.

McKenzie, D. F. *Bibliography and the Sociology of Texts*. London: The British Library, 1986.

———. "Printers of the Mind: Some Notes on Bibliographical Theories and Printing-House Practices." *Studies in Bibliography* 22 (1969): 1–75.

McKerrow, Ronald B. *An Introduction to Bibliography for Literary Students*. London: Oxford University Press, 1928 (and later editions).

———. *Prolegomena for the Oxford Shakespeare: A Study in Editorial Method*. Oxford: Clarendon Press, 1939; rpt. 1969.

McLaverty, James. "The Concept of Authorial Intention in Textual Criticism." *The Library*, Sixth Series 6 (June 1984): 121–38.

Moorman, Charles. *Editing the Middle English Manuscript*. Jackson: University Press of Mississippi, 1975.

Needham, Paul. "Copy-specifics in the Printing Shop." In *Early Printed Books as Material Objects: Proceedings of the Conference Organized by the IFLA Rare Books and Manuscripts Section, Munich, 19–21 August 2009*, ed. by Bettina Wagner and Marcia Reed. Berlin and New York: De Gruyter Saur, 2010, pp. 9–20.

Papers of the Bibliographical Society of America. New York: Bibliographical Society of America. One of the premiere periodicals in the field since its first issue in 1906.

Pearson, David. "The Importance of the Copy Census and a Methodology in Book History." In *Early Printed Books as Material Objects: Proceedings of the Conference Organized by the IFLA Rare Books and Manuscripts Section, Munich, 19–21 August 2009*, ed. by Bettina Wagner and Marcia Reed. Berlin and New York: De Gruyter Saur, 2010, pp. 321–28.

Pollard, Alfred William. *Alfred William Pollard: A Selection of His Essays*. Comp. by Fred W. Roper. Metuchen, NJ: Scarecrow, 1976. This volume contains nine bibliographical essays by Pollard, including "Practical Bibliography" (pp. 86–97); "The Objects and Methods of Bibliographical Collations and Descriptions" (pp. 98–115); "Some Points in Bibliographical Descriptions" (pp. 116–29); "The Arrangement of Bibliographies" (pp. 130–43); and "New Fields in Bibliography" (pp. 184–90).

Proof: Yearbook of American Bibliographical and Textual Studies. Columbia, SC. Now defunct, this was an important periodical in the field from 1971 to 1977.

Robinson, A. M. Lewin. *Systematic Bibliography: A Practical Guide to the Work of Compilation*. Cape Town: University of Cape Town, School of Librarianship, 1963 (and later editions).

Rollins, Carl Purington. "The Printing of Bibliographies." *Papers of the Bibliographical Society of America* 16 (1922): 107–17.

Scheibe, Michaela. "The 'Biography of Copies': Provenance Description in Online Catalogues." In *Early Printed Books as Material Objects: Proceedings of the Conference Organized by the IFLA Rare Books and Manuscripts Section, Munich, 19–21 August 2009*, ed. by Bettina Wagner and Marcia Reed. Berlin and New York: De Gruyter Saur, 2010, pp. 269–78.

Schneider, Georg. *Theory and History of Bibliography*. Trans. by Ralph Robert Shaw. New York: Columbia University Press, 1934; New York: Scarecrow, 1961.

Shillingsburg, Peter L. *Scholarly Editing in the Computer Age: Theory and Practice*. Athens: University of Georgia Press, 1986.

Stam, Deirdre. "Preparing Library School Graduate Students for Rare Book and Special Collections Jobs: Assignments and Exercises That Work." In Hawkins, *Teaching Bibliography*, pp. 72–80.

Stokes, Roy, ed. *Esdaile's Manual of Bibliography*. London: George Allen & Unwin, 1967. (This is Stokes's edition of the bibliographical manual of Arundell Esdaile.)

———. *The Functions of Bibliography*. London: André Deutsch, 1969.

Studies in Bibliography. Charlottesville: University of Virginia, University Press of Virginia. This has been the primary publication in the field of bibliography since its first volume (1948/1949) till today. It has had only two editors in its history, Fredson Bowers and David VanderMeulen. The journal's website calls the publication "the pre-eminent journal of analytical bibliography, textual criticism, manuscript study, and the history of printing and publishing" (www.bsuva.org).

Tanselle, G. Thomas. "The Concept of Format." *Studies in Bibliography* 53 (2000): 67–116.

———. "The Editorial Problem of Final Authorial Intention." *Studies in Bibliography* 29 (1976): 167–211. Tanselle has been the most authoritative, productive, and eloquent writer on bibliography for more than half a century. Only a few of his publications are listed here; all could be read with profit.

———. "Greg's Theory of Copy-Text and the Editing of American Literature." *Studies in Bibliography* 28 (1975): 167–229.

———. "Issues in Bibliographical Studies since 1942." In Peter Davison, ed., *The Book Encompassed.* Cambridge: Cambridge University Press, 1992, pp. 24–36.

———. *A Rationale of Textual Criticism.* Philadelphia: University of Pennsylvania Press, 1989.

———. *Selected Studies in Bibliography.* Charlottesville: University of Virginia Press, 1979.

———. "Textual Criticism and Deconstruction." *Studies in Bibliography* 43 (1990): 1–33.

———. *Textual Criticism and Scholarly Editing.* Charlottesville and London: Bibliographical Society of the University of Virginia, University Press of Virginia, 1990. A collection of some of Tanselle's essays.

———. *Textual Criticism since Greg: A Chronicle, 1950–1985.* Charlottesville: University Press of Virginia, 1988 (and later editions).

Thorpe, James. "The Aesthetics of Textual Criticism." In Brack and Barnes, *Bibliography and Textual Criticism,* pp. 102–38.

———. *Principles of Textual Criticism.* San Marino, CA: Huntington Library, 1972.

Van Hoesen, Henry Bartlett, and Frank Keller Walter. *Bibliography: Practical, Enumerative, Historical: An Introductory Manual.* New York and London: Charles Scribner's Sons, 1928.

Williams, William Proctor, and Craig S. Abbott. *An Introduction to Bibliographical and Textual Studies.* 2nd ed. New York: Modern Language Association, 1989.

Willison, Ian. "Editorial Theory and Practice and the History of the Book." In *New Directions in Textual Studies,* ed. by David Oliphant and Robin Bradford. Austin, TX: Harry Ransom Humanities Research Center, University of Texas at Austin, 1990, pp. 111–25.

NOTES

1. Sharon Tabachnick, "Reviewing Printed Subject Bibliographies: A Worksheet," *Journal of Academic Librarianship* 15.5 (November 1989): 279–84; this statement is on p. 280.

2. This branch of bibliography is sometimes also called Systematic Bibliography; see Robert B. Harmon, *Elements of Bibliography: A Simplified Approach,* rev. ed. (Metuchen, NJ, and London: Scarecrow Press, 1989), pp. 47–79.

3. Some bibliographical styles do not require full names or page numbers. I have always found this idiosyncratic and gratuitously unhelpful to the researcher. It is no problem for the scholar to record this information while doing the scholarship, while the source material is in hand. Why not make the reader's job easy by citing these things?!

4. See Sidney E. Berger, *The Design of Bibliographies: Observations, References and Examples* (London: Mansell; New York: Greenwood, 1991).

5. *MLA Style Manual and Guide to Scholarly Publishing,* 3rd ed. (New York: Modern Language Association of America, 2008); *Chicago Manual of Style,* 16th ed. (Chicago: University of Chicago Press, 2010); *Publication Manual of the American Psychological Association,* 6th ed. (Washington, DC: American Psychological Association, 2009). Editors using one of these styles may tell a prospective author, "Use MLA," or "Use Chicago," or "Use APA." The style manuals listed here have some overlapping characteristics, but they differ in many ways—especially the APA style, which has many idiosyncratic features. A host of publications will lead authors to the correct use of each of these. The details of these styles are beyond the scope of the present text. The main point is that those in the rare book world need to know them and to know when to use each of them.

6. Before computers, typographic coding was restricted to what typewriters and printers had at their disposal. Especially in the world of manual typewriters, italics were not possible, so they were traditionally indicated with underlining. Boldface could be achieved by backspacing and overtyping. Small caps were impossible, as were printers' flowers. Though typographic and spatial coding have been in use for centuries, these design elements were written about extensively by Herbert Spencer, Linda Reynolds, and Brian Coe in a few volumes and in a series of articles, published in the periodicals of different disciplines. These articles, recycling the same infor-

mation, delineated six spatial and three typographic coding systems, which, used in combination, could create eighteen styles. A summary view of these styles is in Berger, *Design of Bibliographies*, pp. 108–11; *Journal of Documentation* 31.2 (June 1975): 59–70; and other articles with the same or similar text and slightly varying titles, published in various journals.

7. For an abbreviated version of the following discussion, see Sidney E. Berger, "Book Format, Part One: Broadsides, Folios, and Quartos," *Biblio* 2.5 (May 1997): 45–49; and Sidney E. Berger, "Book Format, Part Two: Octavo, Duodecimo, and Sextodecimo," *Biblio* 2.6 (June 1997): 50–53.

8. Dealers are likely to label a modern novel-shaped book as a "quarto" or an "octavo," though the terms scarcely apply if the book has been printed on today's high-speed presses, which use huge sheets of paper that are folded and cut and assembled in the machine. A John Steinbeck, Stephen King, or John Le Carré novel will appeal to buyers on the basis of edition, points, and associations, not on the basis of format. For books produced on huge presses, the traditional terms designating format are essentially useless.

9. This sentence is printed in boldface to make this point: size is not the issue; the number of folds in the original printed sheet is the key issue. Too many book "experts" look at a book, consider its size, and proclaim what its format is. This is not the way to figure out the format.

10. To confuse matters further, the word *folio* is also used to designate a leaf in a book. The tenth leaf is sometimes referred to as the "tenth folio." Hence, when a book's pages are numbered, the book is said to be "paginated"; but when each leaf is numbered, the book is said to be "foliated."

11. There should usually be no confusion in the use of the word *signature*, because the word designates all the leaves sewn into the book in a single sewing operation and the letter at the bottom of the page. A third use of this word should also not confuse anyone: it means a person's autograph somewhere in a book. It is thus possible to say, "The G signature in the book has the author's signature above the signature on G2" (G2 being the second leaf of the G signature).

12. The terminology can be overwhelming to a newcomer to these concepts, but rare book librarians, booksellers, experienced book collectors, and scholars must be conversant with these words. The more you use them (correctly), the easier it gets to understand them. It should also be added here that a volume that is, say, a folio in 10s may have some of its gatherings in 8s or 4s, especially common when these anomalous signatures are at the beginning or end of the volume. The predominating construction (e.g., "almost all signatures in this book are folios in 8s") for the whole volume will give the book its format designation, not the anomalous signatures.

13. The term *large-paper edition* is common in the rare book world, but it is not accurate. Because the version of the text printed on a smaller sheet would have been printed from the same setting of type as the large-paper version, both versions would be of the same edition.

14. C1 is conjugate with C2 with the bolt (fold) at the top of the signature; C1 is conjugate with C4 with the bolt at the spine. C3 is conjugate with C2 through the fold at the spine; C3 is conjugate with C4 through the fold at the top.

15. In the early print shops, in the fifteenth century, printers were publishers, and they usually created their own types, so if they needed some oddball sort (a *sort* is a piece of type), they could design and create one themselves; such sorts would not look like anything else in any font.

16. From the duodecimo ("12mo," or "twelvemo") on, almost all formats are designated by their Italian names. The Italians being the great printers in the incunabula period, scholars have adopted their terminology for assigning the names of formats. Hence, the sextodecimo is simply called the "16mo," pronounced "sixteenmo." Even smaller books, whose names do not contain the Italian suffix *-mo*, use the "mo" pronunciation. For instance, trigesimo-secundo (that is, three 10s plus a 2) is called "32mo" or "thirty-twomo."

17. Sidney E. Berger, "Stop the Presses! A Primer on Cancels," *Biblio* 2.9 (September 1997): pp. 56–57. See also R. W. Chapman, *Cancels: With Eleven Facsimiles in Collotype* (London: Constable; and New York: R. R. Smith, 1930).

18. Stereotyping was such a perfected craft that pages printed from stereos looked identical to those printed from the original type. It is practically impossible for even the most experienced typographer, scholar, or bibliographer to look at a printed page and determine whether it was printed from type or plates.

19. John Carter, *ABC for Book Collectors*, 8th ed. (New Castle, DE: Oak Knoll Press; London: The British Library, 2004), p. 87.

20. Those involved in rare books should also be aware of the term *editio princeps*. Carter says, "Latin for *first edition*. Purists restrict the use of the term to the first printed edition of a work which was in circulation in manuscript before printing was invented. It is common usage for any first edition of a classical author. There is old and respectable precedent for its use in a wider sense, simply as a synonym for first edition; but this is apt to sound a trifle affected today" (*ABC*, p. 87). Some booksellers, not knowing this fine point, simply use the term to mean an early first edition. It sounds expensive.

21. The phrase "follow the flag" is sometimes also used to help scholars decide which of two editions of a text, published in the same year but in different countries, is the "true first" edition. If no documented priority of issue to the public is determinable, the one published in the author's country is assumed to be the first edition, though, of course, this is subjective and could be pure guesswork. One fascinating case involves Mark Twain's *Pudd'nhead Wilson* (Hartford: American Publishing Company, 1894; London: Chatto & Windus, 1894). The book was published in both countries in the same year, and booksellers trying to sell the English edition like to say, "This edition was published a few weeks before the American edition, and so is the true first." This is based purely on greed, for there is no documentary evidence of this fabrication. The only reason booksellers make this claim is to be able to charge a premium price for the "true first." In fact, both books were published simultaneously, on November 28, 1894, so that Twain could get copyright in both countries at the same time. See Mark Twain, *Pudd'nhead Wilson and Those Extraordinary Twins*, ed. by Sidney E. Berger (New York: Norton, 1980), p. 176. To "follow the flag" in this instance, scholars would call the American Publishing Company edition the true first, but both editions are equally firsts. Or to be really fastidious, a scholar might say that the sun rose on England before it did on America, so the British edition was released to the public before the American edition. Hence the Chatto & Windus edition is the true first by about five hours. This kind of ludicrousness has gone into the thinking about first editions for nearly two centuries. The "truth" is sometimes asserted by covetous booksellers and overly proud collectors. For other than affecting price and bragging rights, it really makes little difference which one is a true first.

22. For a concise treatment of this topic, see Sidney E. Berger, "The $A^8B^8C^8$s of Bibliographical Description," *Biblio* 2.11 (November 1997): 58–59.

23. Bowers has a long discussion about title-page transcriptions (pp. 137–41). He says that there are different levels of "minuteness" in the details the bibliographer chooses to give.

> From the point of view of the scholar, minuteness down to the last detail is, of course, the most desirable in order that the maximum amount of evidence may be available for reference. On the other hand, the writer [i.e., the bibliographer] is somewhat forced to draw a line beyond which the recording of detail would make for confusion in an impossible attempt to equal a photograph by descriptive means. (p. 138)

The key point here is that the aim of the transcription is to give the reader of the bibliography as much information as possible without inundating him with data. Bowers calls the two methods delineated here the "quasi-facsimile" and the "simplified" methods. As with much of Bowers's minutely detailed text, the discussion is enlightening but dense with observation. Bowers opts for the quasi-facsimile method.

> Quasi-facsimile remains the only accurate method of transcription yet devised by which a title-page can be compared for variation in setting with reasonable prospects of success. The readability of simplified description does not make up for the fact that it is completely useless for serious bibliographical investigation and so has no place in a work which purports to be a bibliography and not a catalogue. (p. 139)

This is the point made at the beginning of this section on descriptive bibliography. When a scholar has looked at a million books for all the variations they contain, he will find yet another variant in 1,000,001. Bowers adds, "It may readily be admitted that no rules for maximum completeness [in a title-page transcription] can be drawn up to apply without exception to every bibliography" (p. 139). He has sections in these pages on how to describe borders and "rule-frames" on title pages, line endings, swash *S*'s, ornaments, double *VV*, ligatures, misprints, broken sorts, letters in wrong fonts, engraved title pages, and much more. The level of his own minuteness is awe-inspiring and deadly. This note dwells at length on what, in the larger picture of this volume, is a small issue. But such dwelling is important in that it shows the kind of thinking that has gone on in the world of rare books, and also that anyone working in this field must be able to produce careful transcriptions of title pages and must be conversant with them so that she can understand them in the scholarly bibliographies she must use and in the catalogs of learned booksellers.

24. C. William Miller, comp., *Benjamin Franklin's Philadelphia Printing, 1728–1766* (Philadelphia: American Philosophical Society, 1974).

25. Sometimes the numbers are printed not as superscripts: A-I4 K-T4 U2. Bowers himself shows both methods. On p. 130, his collation reads: 8°: A-R⁸ S². Below on the same page, he shows A3ᵇ-B1ᵃ. Here, because he must show the recto ("a") and verso ("b") of the leaf, he needs to indicate these with the superscript. So he does not raise the numbers above the line. Bowers tried to do the impossible in this book: show the reader how to do a collational formula for every possible printing and binding variation. Because there were no standards among printers, each was free to do things any way he wished. The number of variations that have to be accounted for in a collation is seemingly endless.

26. If the parentheses had only "−G⁷," the reader would know that the seventh leaf of that signature was removed and not replaced. This could be discernible if the stub of G⁷ were visible. But even in a tight binding, where the stub were not exposed, a 7-leaf signature would indicate the loss of a leaf.

27. A good description of the binding may be revealing as well as useful. As mentioned in the section "State," bindings can be first, second, or later states, information that could be tremendously important to bibliographers, collectors, librarians, or booksellers.

28. Engraved plates, printed on an engraving (or rolling) press, are not part of the printing of the text of the book, even when the plates are printed right onto the pages that are printed from type. If the plates do come from another press and are tipped or bound into the volume, this is not visible in the collational formula, but it should be shown in the Notes section.

29. If Bowers overwhelms with his massive volume on *Bibliographical Description*, Philip Gaskell offers a much more humane presentation of the topic in his superb volume, *A New Introduction to Bibliography* (New York and London: Oxford University Press, 1972). His chapter on this topic (pp. 321–35) is a good introduction to the subject. Much of the information in the Gaskell volume is excellent reading for those working in rare books and special collections, and it is highly recommended. It is so well received in the world of bibliography that it has reached a point at which people will say, "Look into Gaskell." The volume replaced the equally excellent (for its era) book by Ronald B. McKerrow, *An Introduction to Bibliography for Literary Students*

(Oxford, at the Clarendon Press: 1927, and later printings).

30. Roy Stokes, *A Bibliographical Companion* (Metuchen, NJ, and London: Scarecrow Press, 1989), p. 20.

31. Robert B. Harmon, *Elements of Bibliography: A Simplified Approach* (Metuchen, NJ, and London: Scarecrow Press, 1989), p. 86.

32. See Thomas A. Cahill, Bruce H. Kusko, and Richard N. Schwab, "Analyses of Inks and Papers in Historical Documents through External Beam PIXE Techniques," *Nuclear Instruments & Methods* 181 (1981): 205–8.

33. Sandra Sider, "Bibliographical Note: Searching for Mary Anne," *RBML* 10.1 (Spring 1995): 40–41.

34. Sidney Berger, "The Dating of Medieval Manuscripts," unpublished study.

35. This question is commonly asked about the Gutenberg Bible. Of course, scarcity affects value, so if the answer is "only ten copies," a bookseller might jack up a price considerably. This question leads a researcher into the realm of publishing history, printing, book distribution, reading habits, availability of a particular text, references to that text in the works of other authors, the history of paper manufacture, and many other areas of inquiry—all the province of historical bibliography.

36. This question is engendered by the Rosamond Loring pamphlet at the Houghton Library at Harvard University in which a Mr. [Charles] V. Saflund explains to Loring how to coat marbled papers. A newspaper clipping shows Saflund to be an amateur violin maker, and his description of the varnish he uses for his marbled papers could have come from his work on violins. See Sidney Berger, "Introduction," *Marbled and Paste Papers: Rosamond Loring's Recipe Book: A Facsimile of Her Manuscript Notebook* (Cambridge, MA: Houghton Library, 2007). The introduction is on pp. 11–29; the discussion of the beeswax and "pure white soap" mixture that was used as a varnish is on pp. 24–25.

37. In January 2012 I received in the mail a catalog from a bookseller in which he offered "The first Japanese book on chess" and "The first book on a foreign language published in Japan." This kind of historical research enabled the dealer to ask appropriately high prices for these volumes. Collectors love "firsts." See Rulon-Miller Books, List 116, items 16 (p. 3) and 26 (p. 5), on the Web at www.rulon.com/Catpages/list116/list116.html.

38. See appendix 3 for a discussion of booksellers' catalogs. The Rulon-Miller catalog cited in note 37 is a good example of a catalog carefully researched.

39. Volvelles are disks (often attached to pages of a book) that turn. The "text" on the volvelle lines up with a "text" on the page such that calculations can be done, something in the nature of a circular slide rule. "A volvelle or wheel chart is a type of slide chart, a paper construction with rotating parts. It is considered an early example of a paper analog computer" (see "Volvelle," Wikipedia, http://en.wikipedia.org/wiki/Volvelle. Wikipedia cites Nick Kanas, "VOLVELLES! Early Paper Astronomical Computers," www.astrosociety.org/pubs/mercury/34_02/computers.html).

40. An overview of the field of textual bibliography can be found at "Textual Criticism," Wikipedia, http://en.wikipedia.org/wiki/Textual_criticism. A seminal collection of essays, edited by O M Brack Jr. and Warner Barnes, is highly recommended reading: *Bibliography and Textual Criticism: English and American Literature, 1700 to the Present* (Chicago and London: University of Chicago Press, 1969).

41. Textual bibliography is a discipline of its own. At the University of Iowa in the 1960s, the English Department oversaw a unit called the Center for Bibliographical Studies in which a wide range of activities took place to prepare texts for editing by scholars extensively trained in all aspects of bibliography. Courses in bibliography were taught at many universities then, though they began falling off with the coming of "New Criticism" in the 1970s and '80s. Today there are still textual (and other) bibliographers, but bibliography as a broad discipline in the academic community as a whole is much diminished.

42. It is possible that editions of a text published after the author's death could contain much authority, especially if the readings in it were drawn from a version of the text that the author worked on, and if it can be proved that the reading represented the author's final intentions.

43. Last writings by the author presumably show an author's final intentions. On the other hand, it can happen that a publisher or editor can inveigle a writer to make changes in his text for a second or subsequent edition. According to Wikipedia ("Textual Criticism," http://en.wikipedia.org/wiki/Textual_criticism),

> [Fredson] Bowers and [G. Thomas] Tanselle argue for rejecting textual variants that an author inserted at the suggestion of others. . . . Tanselle discusses the example of Herman Melville's *Typee*. After the novel's initial publication, Melville's publisher asked him to soften the novel's criticisms of missionaries in the South

Seas. Although Melville pronounced the changes an improvement, Tanselle rejected them in his edition, concluding that "there is no evidence, internal or external, to suggest that they are the kinds of changes Melville would have made without pressure from someone else" [Tanselle, "The Editorial Problem of Final Authorial Intention," *Studies in Bibliography* 29 (1976), pp. 167–211; the passage quoted is on p. 194].

44. The word *scientific* here implies that the work of the editors would be replicable by other editors using the same textual bibliographical methods.

45. As the text indicates, the word *crux* means a place in a text at which two or more versions of that text vary. One text may have a word in singular, another in plural; one text may have a comma where the other has a semicolon; one text might have a sentence or a paragraph lacking in another version of the text. In textual bibliography, these cruxes are sometimes simply called **variants.**

46. A small but excellent book on stemmatics is that by Paul Maas, *Textual Criticism* (Oxford: Oxford University Press, 1958), which spells out all the operations of editing from manuscripts and shows how the stemma is formed.

47. G. Thomas Tanselle, "The Editing of Historical Documents," *Studies in Bibliography* 31 (1978), pp. 1–56; this statement is on p. 1. In his first footnote, Tanselle points out, "But history and literature are not the only fields that would mutually profit from a more encompassing discussion of textual problems; many editorial projects are now under way in philosophy and the sciences, and the fundamental questions which editors must ask are the same in those fields also" (p. 56). Note that the Center for Scholarly Editions is now known as the Committee on Scholarly Editions. See www.iupui.edu/~peirce/writings/cse.htm.

48. Tanselle points out that the CEAA concentrated its efforts on American writers, but its successor, the CSE, had a wider charge: to edit the works of any important author. He says that the CSE was interested in supporting editorial work of "any kind of material from any time and place" (Tanselle, "Editing," p. 3).

49. It is true that to italicize a word changes its emphasis and could completely change its meaning, but this is still an instance of an accidental.

50. See Mark Twain, *Pudd'nhead Wilson and Those Extraordinary Twins*, ed. by Sidney E. Berger, 2nd ed. (New York and London: W. W. Norton, 2005), p. 222, note for 66.3–4.

51. Sometimes editors take the role of god in their decision making. As the Wikipedia article on "Textual Criticism" says,

> Bowers confronted a similar problem in his edition of *Maggie*. Crane originally printed the novel privately in 1893. To secure commercial publication in 1896, Crane agreed to remove profanity, but he also made stylistic revisions. Bowers's approach was to preserve the stylistic and literary changes of 1896, but to revert to the 1893 readings where he believed that Crane was fulfilling the publisher's intention rather than his own. There were, however, intermediate cases that could reasonably have been attributed to either intention, and some of Bowers's choices came under fire—both as to his judgment and as to the wisdom of conflating readings from the two different versions of *Maggie*. (http://en.wikipedia.org/wiki/Textual_criticism)

In other words, Bowers judged some of the readings from one earlier edition as "better," and some from the other edition as "better." He looked at two perfectly "authorial" versions of the text and, for his own final edition, incorporated readings from both of them, thereby creating a text that never existed before. His judgment seems to have been based on aesthetics, not bibliographical theory, so his critics were probably justified in complaining.

52. The Wikipedia article on "Textual criticism" says, "The bibliographer Ronald B. McKerrow introduced the term *copy-text* in his 1904 edition of Thomas Nashe, defining it as 'the text used in each particular case as the basis of mine'" (http://en.wikipedia.org/wiki/Textual_criticism).

CHAPTER 10

BOOK COLLECTING
AND HANDLING

*Collectors of all kinds of objects have occasion to consult the books written about
their fields; but because books are themselves the objects that the book collector is
interested in, it is not surprising that the urge to put bookish information into books
has been particularly strong and that a vast literature of book collecting exists.*
—*G. Thomas Tanselle*[1]

OST LIBRARIES ARE LIVING ENTITIES, EXPANDING AND CONtracting in staff and holdings, and greeting scholars and other patrons regularly. The expansion of the collection is the subject of the present chapter, under the general rubric Book Collecting. The term, of course, could be expanded to Collection Building, for special collections departments, as frequently shown here, add many genres of materials besides books. As the opening sentence reminds us, libraries contract now and then, so this chapter will also consider weeding as a natural and essential rare book department activity.

As chapter 2 explained, collecting is one of the essential activities in a rare book department. Departments generally build to their strengths (their level 4 and 5 collections), add to their collections with good restraint at level 3, and treat the other two levels appropriately. This is not done haphazardly. In fact, *nothing* is done haphazardly in modern libraries. Over centuries of analysis and practice, libraries have developed "best practice" policies, procedures, and strategies that evolve with the times. The American Library Association, for example, is now carefully built up with many focused divisions, each with its own policies and practices, codified and revisited regularly to stay up to date with emerging technologies, changing laws, new ways of thinking about old operations, and a careful consideration of how librarians can continue to help their patrons retrieve and use information.

Librarianship is, after all, a service profession, and our clients (anyone who seeks any kind of information) deserve the best service the library can give them. A point made many times here is that the bottom line for libraries is being able to connect patrons with information. And that is what this chapter is about, for building collections is one way to continue to add information to the arsenal. The logical place to start, then, is at the collection development department.

Collection Development

Every library that adds to its holdings has a collection development program, even if this program is not spelled out formally. The librarian acquires items; this is collection development. Most libraries are more organized than just "There's an important book for our patrons; I'll get it." It starts in a collection development department (hereafter Collections), with its skilled and focused staffing, its collection policy, and its ties to others in the institution. As this text has shown already, so it is not necessary to reiterate in any detail, a rare book department should have a five-level plan for collecting, or something equivalent that distinguishes among "must haves," "pretty darn important," "nice to have," "maybe we will keep," and "don't need." This might seem like something of an oversimplification, but this is pretty much all a department needs when it is deciding whether to order or to keep an item.

> **FOR MANY YEARS** I have been teaching classes in library schools. One of the things that has surprised me time and again is that my students— at all levels in the program—are fairly innocent about how collections grow. Only those who have taken a course in collection development have a notion, and even they cannot know fully what it is about until they have experienced it in a real-life setting. Classroom instruction may give them a textbook approach to the subject, but on-the-job learning will immerse them in the activities of a collections department and will teach them *one way* to do it. No two departments are the same, and no two departments operate in the same way.

THE LITERATURE OF THE FIELD

As the quotation at the opening of this chapter indicates, a tremendous literature exists about books and book collecting. It is important that special collections librarians be familiar with the standard reference books in the areas of their collections, along with the related scholarly publications. Such familiarity will make them better librarians, more knowledgeable about their holdings, and more able to help their clients. This point has been made elsewhere in the present volume, but it should be reiterated in the context of collecting because part of the librarian's responsibility is to bring into the department as much secondary literature about the collection's strengths as the library can afford and has space for. The librarian, then, like a collector, must be a subject specialist in whatever areas the department is strong in.

G. Thomas Tanselle says that no book in any field is flawless. So

> the best way for readers to become less uninformed is to read widely enough that they begin to recognize discrepancies between books and relative strengths and weaknesses in them. The education of collectors—or of anyone else—cannot consist of the reading of one or two prescribed books; it must involve the building up of a body of facts and attitudes.[2]

And just as booksellers as subject specialists sometimes publish in their fields, so should librarians consider doing so. Doing the work to get an article or book published will make them better scholar-librarians, and publications may help them in moving up the ranks of their institutions.

THE COLLECTIONS "DEPARTMENT"

In the larger library there will be a collection development department. In special collections someone will be responsible for collections. In small rare book departments perhaps all the personnel will do some kind of work that eventuates in the acquisition of materials. This includes items solicited as gifts as well as those purchased. Because rare book departments vary widely in their personnel and in the ways they operate, it is difficult to make generalizations on how books are selected and acquired. The final decisions are made by one or two people in the department, the selection possibly by many. It is useful to look briefly at the structure of a general Collections department, for some of its components can be translated to special collections operations.[3]

Selection for the library is done in Collections. Those identifying items to acquire, called "bibliographers," are assigned to areas of their expertise: East Asian, Literature, Native American, Renaissance, Physics, Mathematics, Foreign Languages, and so forth. This is their primary responsibility in the library. They are joined by selectors, who have primary jobs of their own (catalogers; professors; administrators who are experts in specific fields; staff who, likewise, are knowledgeable about one or two areas of collecting; and others). Add to this scholars who may work for long periods at the library and who may be tapped to help in selection, faculty at all levels throughout the institution, and anyone else who can contribute suggestions of things to acquire.

The rare book department will generally be small enough not to be able to have its own bibliographers, though it is possible that the department has an endowed position or two to cover a particular collection, thanks to a donor. If the department's holdings are broadly based, covering a wide range of subject areas, no single librarian is likely to be expert enough to do selection in all of them. So she needs a network of people to help her locate things for the collection.

MY OWN LIBRARY is in a museum, so I have a built-in team of selectors: the curators of the museum's collection. Over the centuries the museum has built its library to support all the museum's activities, and today most of the institution's areas of collecting for the museum have specialists who need research materials to help them put on exhibitions. These are highly intelligent specialists who know the bibliography of their areas, and I have an arrangement with them to contact me and my staff if they need particular books or if they see specific manuscripts or other materials on the market that they would like to have, for research or exhibition.

The suppliers of information (that is, those who can help the rare book department in its collection building), as already pointed out, will be the others who are affiliated with the institution in some capacity, usually faculty with their own specialties,

but also administrators, advanced graduate students who may be able to locate items important for their own research,[4] support staff with their own areas of expertise, and visiting scholars who use the collection for their research.

The rare book staff, of course, should also be fully inculcated into the needs of the department and should always be on the lookout for good material. And they should all be plugged into the academic community around them, for with the right kind of outreach (see more on this in chapter 11), they can encourage faculty from across the curriculum to engage their students in the activities and collections of the rare book department. The presence of many people in the department is good for many reasons, including the fact that they can be educated about the importance of the rare book department and its holdings, and they can also be encouraged to keep their own antennas up for things the department may wish to acquire. So even a small special collections department can have many selectors working for it.

ACQUISITION BY GIFT

A good deal has already been said about the need for rare books personnel to work with those in development and about the legal document that brings in materials from donors, the Deed of Gift. A few generic observations are in order, however.

There are always more things to buy for the collection than there is money. All personnel in rare books should always be on the alert for ways to bring in resources to buy books or to bring in the books themselves from donors. Under the rubric of Public Relations, which will be covered in chapter 11, some strategies will be offered for engaging people to get them interested in and supportive of the department. Collectors can be found in many venues (book fairs, lectures on bookish subjects, specialized workshops, bookstores, book-collector clubs, the special collections department itself), and these are the kinds of places that rare book librarians are likely to go, so for the librarian to meet a collector could be only a kind word away.

As already mentioned, some of the great special collections in the world's libraries were built by maniacal, brilliant, focused collectors. The fact that many of these collections wound up in libraries is a tribute to the skills and perseverance of librarians and the generosity and kindness of the collectors. Good librarians can bring out this kindness and can make it obvious to the potential donor that the *only* logical place his books should be is in the library. Gifts are the best way to bring books into the collection.

ACQUISITION BY PURCHASE— FROM BOOKSELLERS

By far the most common way that the collection grows is through purchase, and from the many sources the librarian has available, the most common is the world of booksellers. This book has already established that dealers are the librarians' best friends when it comes to building a collection. Booksellers have their eyes open all the time for ways to increase their own bottom lines, and through their friendships with librarians, they can be excellent suppliers to rare book collections.

Booksellers list their holdings on the Web, through their own websites and through the agglomerating sites such as AbeBooks, BookFinder, Amazon, Add-ALL, and many others. There are dozens of such sites, for all countries, offering hundreds of millions of books. In fact, in the last fifteen years, the Web has changed the world of bookselling more than any other phenomenon in history—perhaps even more than printing did. Before online listings, to get their books into appropriate hands, dealers had to rely on catalogs, auctions, open shops, and word of mouth, along with their own knowledge of special collections departments to which they could quote perti-

nent items. Today a huge percentage of the books for sale in the world is in digital form, and the information on what is available is as close as the nearest computer with a connection to the Internet. So rare book librarians can find millions upon millions of items for their collections at their fingertips. Today there are still hundreds of booksellers who issue catalogs, mailed to their select customers. If a librarian is on good terms with a bookseller, and if she purchases occasionally from that dealer, the dealer may send advance copies of his catalogs, so it pays to be a good customer.

With this immense availability of things to buy, the librarian should always be on the lookout for titles to seek, authors whom she had not heard of before, topic areas to purchase in, and so forth. The more the librarian immerses herself into the collection she oversees, the more she will know the bibliography in the fields of her level 4 and 5 collections. This awareness should lead to the creation of Want Lists. The librarian can interpret every item on the want list as a gap in the collection. So a periodic check of the major search services on the Web may help the librarian to fill in those gaps.

Want Lists

An experienced rare book librarian, who becomes an expert (or a near-expert) in a field collected by his library, will know what is there and what is not. He will keep his eyes out for the things he wants that will fill the gaps in the collection. And he will make a want list of items the collection needs. These lists are not just for the librarian's own benefit; they are to be sent out to booksellers far and wide, with a note that says, "These are items we are looking for. If

I WARNED YOU that I would go back again and again to the idea that the prime mission of the librarian is to link his patrons with the information they need. The want list is an attempt to do this. It is a way of adding information to the collection; the beneficiaries of this information (contained in the books the librarian has acquired from the list) are the readers. UC Riverside had a fairly strong Book Arts collection, so I was eager to keep as full a collection of the key periodicals in this field as I could. On my want list was *Matrix 3*, the third volume of the excellent publication *Matrix* from the Whittington Press. I must have asked a hundred dealers if they had that volume, the only one the library lacked. When I left UCR, I had not been able to acquire this book. So it stayed on my want list, and to this day I scour booksellers' shelves and catalogs and online search outlets for this elusive volume. It is almost like a Mission for me to find that book and fill the gap in the collection—and get that darn thing off my mental want list.

you have any of them, please send us a quote. If you do not have any, please keep an eye out for them and quote them if you find any."

Completism in Collecting

Keeping want lists leads to the notion of "completism," the aim of every collector to put together a "complete" gathering of whatever he collects. If he goes for Doves Press books, he himself will feel incomplete until he has one of every title that came off the press. The problem for most collectors is that, even if they do get "one of each" of what they seek, the collector's gene in them sees other, related things that "belong" in the collection, and the process continues until another level of "completeness" is reached.

I HAVE A friend who collected hotel shampoos. When she had masses of them, she branched out into conditioners. My friend who started with the Kelmscott Press got all those books and then branched out into other contemporary presses, along with William Morris manuscripts, furniture, household objects, and more and more until his house was a turn-of-the-century museum of all things surrounding the world of William Morris. Even the Folger Shakespeare Library has untold numbers of things from Shakespeare's world that do not directly relate to Shakespeare. Is it possible for a collection to be "complete"? Yes. If the collector wants a copy of every book written by Edgar Rice Burroughs, and then, following the standard bibliography, acquires one of each, that collection is by definition complete. But, can any collector ever feel his collection is complete? Once he has all the books, he then might want every edition, or every variant printing, or every variant dust jacket, or every advertising piece for these books, or some autograph materials of the author or the author's friends or family, or relevant scholarship, or a lock of the author's hair, or . . .

For a rare book librarian, the notion of completism can be a guiding principle in collecting, or a millstone that drags her into despair. It is difficult enough to reach a sense of being "complete" in one small, private collection. Rare book collections are usually broad in their holdings, making it essentially impossible to "complete." For some, the lack of completeness is like a spur, an incentive, and a thrill—the thrill of the chase. Librarians who collect have their own want lists, and they will often have them for the collections they oversee. Because of the diversity in the world, the fecundity of writers and artists, the efforts of printers and binders, illustrators and scribes, booksellers and bookbinders, there is no telling what is right around the corner for your collection.

AS A SERIOUS collector of decorated papers and books on the subject, I think I know the bibliography of the field well, and I have my own want lists to "fill in the gaps." Today I learned of a Swedish marbler I had never heard of before, and I was offered a large collection of books showing his marbles—completely new to me. This is part of the "thrill of the chase." Rare book librarians get such opportunities for they have a host of booksellers, and maybe even some private parties, out there looking. There is never a shortage of great things to add to the collection, and often items come in—or come across the librarian's path—that are startling and wonderful.

So, armed with want lists and the Web, with a strong completist urge, and, with any luck, a decent budget for acquisitions, the special collections librarian can hunt down stray bits and pieces, volumes and manuscripts, and so forth, and can go on for years "filling in the gaps" for others. This is one of the things that make rare book librarianship such a joy. And from the bookseller's perspective, it makes his life exciting, knowing that particular clients want certain items and then finding these things. Many booksellers get a rush from being able to find a rare or unusual item and placing it perfectly in the right library, private or public. Yes, bookselling has its fiscal rewards, but for some, this other function—supplier—is a reward too. Even many a completist librarian is never fully satisfied because a fully purchased want list does not guarantee that new items are not just around the corner. That is why for many rare book librarians there is an excitement in the field. Any phone call, e-mail, or envelope could reveal something new for the collection.

IN THE EARLY 1970s I worked for several years for Herb Caplan of Argus Books in Sacramento. I recall numerous occasions when an item came into his shop that he was thrilled to be able to acquire and to place exactly where it should have gone. He told me once, on the acquisition, at considerable expense, of one particularly choice manuscript, "This is going to _____," and he named the institution. I said, "They don't even know about it" (he had just acquired it), "and they probably can't afford it." He said that they would take it—it was perfect for them. And he would donate it. "I know they can't afford it. So I'll give it to them. They need this." He told me of the tremendous pleasure he had in getting the item into the right hands. The pleasure of adding important things to a strong collection is in the hand of more than the librarian.

ACQUISITION FROM BOOKSELLERS' CATALOGS

An old way for dealers to sell books is through printed catalogs that they hand out at their shops and at book fairs and that they mail to customers around the country and around the globe. This method has been in place for centuries.[5] In the past, hundreds, if not thousands, of booksellers mailed these catalogs out regularly. Since the coming of the Internet, the number of paper-based catalogs has dropped off significantly, for a dealer can now have an audience far beyond what his mailing list contained (perhaps only hundreds of recipients), while the Internet offers millions of potential customers. Any book, listed by author, title, subject, or keyword, can be offered to countless patrons in an instant, worldwide.

Nevertheless, the custom of sending out catalogs survives, and many great ones—and many perfunctory ones—are mailed out each week. Possibly with the influence of Tom Congalton and Dan Gregory of Between the Covers Books, and with computer technology and the falling prices of color printing, one important trend in booksellers' catalogs has been the inclusion of color images of every book listed in a catalog.[6] Other booksellers had used color pictures in the past, but now whole catalogs are filled with them.

Acquiring books by catalog is sometimes problematic. To begin with, if a librarian knows that a particular dealer has books the library is interested in, she should go through the catalog the moment it gets into her hands, for choice items often disappear quickly. If she spots a book or manuscript she wants, she should call the bookseller instantly, rather than waiting to finish reading the listing, because all it takes is one call to snag the piece, and someone else out there might be looking at the catalog at the same time. Some dealers on one coast may mail out catalogs to the opposite coast a day earlier than they mail them to local addresses, to give all purchasers an equal chance to buy. On a phone call the librarian can have the bookseller hold the item she wants until she has a chance to read through the rest of the list.

ONE BOOKSELLER IN the South offers items that I collect assiduously. I sometimes call him out of the blue to ask if he will have anything in his next catalog that I may want to get. He knows me well, and a few times over the years he has let me buy things before the catalog goes out. If I get him early enough, he does not have to list that item in his catalog, and there is room for him to list another book. The moment I get one of his listings, I go to it eagerly—even if I get it when I am hungry and it is late when I arrive home to find his offerings. I read the list before I make my dinner. On several occasions I call him in a moment, and I am too late. This has happened to me, also, in my professional position. It is frustrating to miss a good item for myself or for my institution, but it is a fact of life in the rare book world.

Another possible problem with some dealers' catalogs is that the descriptions they give may not be perfectly accurate. When an item arrives that the librarian has ordered and he sees that the book is not as described, the dilemma is whether to keep it or return it. Most booksellers have a reasonable return policy, so if the decision is to return it, the librarian should call the dealer immediately and explain why the item is not satisfactory. It could be that it is a wrong edition, it has some defects, or it is not the book ordered.

Booksellers' catalogs are often filled with erudite and extensive scholarship of many kinds: biographies of authors, extensive bibliographical information about the book (number of copies, the paper it was printed on, the edition, impression, issue, or state, points showing places of variation in copies, information about illustrators or binders), the place of the book in its discipline or in the history of printing, and much more. Some booksellers have excellent reference libraries of their own to draw upon, which is logical because they are specialists in their own areas, and it is natural for them to have acquired the best tools of their trade. So their catalogs can be small theses on the important books they are purveying. Some catalogs are like scholarly essays on the bibliography of particular topics, and some catalogs become collectors' items themselves. And they are good tools for librarians to learn from, especially about the importance of particular fields or subject areas and what the current prices are for particular items and for the popularity of certain subjects. (Appendix 3 of the present volume is a small dissertation on dealers' catalogs.)

ACQUISITION FROM BOOKSELLERS' QUOTES

If the librarian has a good relationship with a particular bookseller, he might ask the dealer to phone or mail a quote to give the library the right of first refusal for an item. This yields a good relationship between the two parties, and it helps the library's collection to grow. So it might be a good idea for a special collections person to ask the dealer if she is willing to do this now and then. Of course, this means being on good terms with the booksellers, which should not be a problem, for the dealers want to be friends with the librarians who can buy their wares. But beyond this, the merchant and the librarian are, in some respects, kindred spirits in that they both should enjoy what they do, they should meet on the common ground of the products they deal with and the subjects they are interested in, and they should have much to talk about, as friends do. Innumerable stories circulate through the world of rare books and manuscripts—tales and gossip about the books and the booksellers, the buyers, sleepers, overpriced and underpriced books, big collectors and their collections, "things I have seen," "things I sold and would love to have back again," donors, "things I'd love to find," and on and on. With a friendship begun in business but extended beyond the commercial

A NUMBER OF years ago I ordered a book from a dealer's catalog that was described as being in good condition: no bumps or scrapes, no discoloration, no underlining or other writing in the book, no labels or bookplates pasted in, and so forth. When I opened the package I reeled back from its smell. It must have been stored in the dank cellar of an old building for decades. There was no visible mold, but the stink was enough for me to want to seal it into a plastic bag and get it out of the house. I called the bookseller and told him that his description in his catalog was deceptive, for it neglected to mention the volume's redolence. He offered to send my money back to me and told me to keep the book anyway. He knew there was a problem, but he did not mention it in his catalog. (I told him to send half my money back, for I still wanted the book and I didn't want him to lose any money on it. I was able to get out most of the stench with some extensive treatment.) Most booksellers would not have been caught in this situation, and the ABAA dealers—from the Antiquarian Booksellers' Association of America—are fairly scrupulous in their descriptions.

It is difficult to know exactly what you are getting if you order out of dealers' catalogs, though their write-ups of each item will tell you much. There is nothing wrong with asking the dealer to send the item on approval, with no guarantee that you will buy it but a strong suggestion that you will. You should not ask for items on approval that you are not serious about. If the dealer has an on-approval policy, you should decide whether you want to buy the item or not as quickly as possible. Every day the book is out of the dealer's hands is another day he cannot sell (or even offer) that book.

world, it is not unusual for dealers to be happy to offer quotes to librarians, giving them first rights of purchase. Hence, quotes will come in the mail, by e-mail, or by phone, and librarians must act on them just as quickly as they should act on items sent on approval, for quotes are of books the dealer wants to sell but cannot until the librarians getting the quotes decide whether they want the items or not.

Getting a quote from a bookseller, of course, does not obligate the librarian to buy, but the pressure is sometimes there: a librarian who is given an exclusive opportunity does not want to pass it up. But this implies that the opportunity to buy a piece involves an item that the librarian really wants, and this is not always the case. There should be no hard feelings if the librarian declines for any reason.

NEGOTIATING WITH BOOKSELLERS

The heading here is "Negotiating with Booksellers." The advice: Don't. Most of the time when a dealer offers the library an item, a good deal of care has gone into its pricing. Also in the price is how much the seller spent for it, her gas or petrol in acquiring it, perhaps the hotel room she had to stay in and the edibles and potables she consumed when she was on the buying trip on which she acquired the item, her overhead (heat, electricity, water and sewer, mortgage or rent, storage space, employees, shelving, and much more), how much effort she went through to clean up the book and make it a presentable copy, how much research she had to do to price it right, and a host of other considerations that will be dealt with later in this chapter—things that affect the price of a book.

Booksellers use different strategies for settling on a selling price. One is, "I bought this book for $__, so if I double or triple my money, that gives me enough profit to make the transaction worthwhile. I know it is worth more than I will ask, but at a good price the book will sell more quickly than if it is priced much higher, and I would like to get my money out of this soon rather than tying up my cash in the volume." Another strategy is, "I would like to maximize my profits. I will do all kinds of research to see what features of this item make it special, what might enhance its desirability to a potential buyer. I will have it repaired by a conservator or bookbinder. By laying out a certain amount of money to make the item more presentable, I can more than recoup the costs of fixing it up. I will squeeze every penny I can out of this book."

Regardless of the way booksellers come about pricing their goods, they are nonetheless professionals who should be shown the respect of their expertise. They have profits to make, lives to live, and books to sell. If they come up with a particular price, you either pay it or you do not. If you do, then the price was right for you. If you do not buy the item because of its price, then maybe someone else will at the price you thought was too high. If that is the case, then, again, the bookseller has priced the book appropriately. Someone bought it at whatever price the dealer had on it, so the book was priced right. Sometimes the price the dealer asks is too high, and he may look at that volume on his shelf for years.

And if the dealer did indeed pay a lot for it, he may not want to sell it at a loss, so the price stays high.

Professional booksellers should be given credit for the expertise they have acquired over the years at their own expense. Remember, when someone needs an appraisal for a collection, she should turn to an experienced bookseller who knows the prices in his field. Because of all these things, the librarian can assume that the price the dealer is asking is justifiable and should not complain or ask for a "deal" when the price seems too high. The buyer does not know how much the seller paid for the item, how much effort and expenditure of time and resources went into acquiring it, how much time the bookseller spent on research and cleaning and writing up the volume, and so on. One good practice is to assume that the dealer has a good reason for the price he is asking, and then say yes or no to the purchase. Do not ask for "accommodations."

If the price is high and you don't have the money in your budget, but you really want the piece, you may ask the seller for "terms," but this does not mean coming down in price; it means, "May the library pay for this over a period of time?" An example is the B. Traven purchase that UC Riverside made that was paid for over several years. The sellers got 100 percent of the price they originally asked, but they did not get it all at once. Some dealers need to make their profits quickly and cannot make such arrangements, but many dealers will be happy to accommodate the library. They will eventually get their asking price, they may not have to pay taxes on the profits all in one year, they will have the satisfaction of seeing an important sale made to just the right library, and they will be able to maintain their friendship with the librarian with no tensions between them. And the librarian will make an important acquisition on affordable terms. So the only kind of "negotiation" the librarian should make is on the length of time over which the payment should be made, not on the price.[7]

ACQUISITION FROM BOOK SCOUTS

One character in the book trade with a long and checkered past is the book scout. This person is like a middleman, always on the lookout for books he can buy cheaply and make a quick profit on, even if the profit is small. Some scouts are bottom feeders, looking in thrift shops, at garage sales, at library book sales, at flea markets. Some feed higher on the food chain: looking in secondhand shops and upscale resale stores, and also at estate sales in good neighborhoods.

The chief characteristic of their profession is that they buy at rock-bottom prices, and they can turn over their purchases quickly. They soon learn what books the dealers are willing to pay well for, and they become savvy about a wide range of books (or subject areas) that will sell. They may become experts in a broad variety of fields, not on the content or the importance of the books they handle, but on the salability and general values of these items. Scouts know that if they consistently get good books, certain dealers will pay well for them. They also know that the dealers sell the books to collectors and to libraries. So some of the scouts rise in the food chain to become booksellers, but operating without a shingle, so to speak. They do not necessarily have a formal business, a premises where people can look at their offerings, or even a business name (though some I have known have graduated to real booksellers). But somewhere in their evolution they learn that they can cut out the middleman (the dealer) by going straight to the purchaser (the librarian).

The point of this is that many a fine book that winds up in special collections could come from a scout. There is a general picture of scouts as "dumpster divers" (and certainly some of them are) whose books are shabby and forlorn. But that is not necessarily the case. There are many people who collect in their own areas and know a good book (outside their area) when they see it. So librarians should not automatically turn away phone calls or e-mail messages from people who begin, "I just got this book . . . ."[8]

A last word about scouts: Sometimes the scout does this as an avocation. The person could be a teacher or a postal worker, an attorney or a physician, who happens to love books and book sales in all their manifestations. They can spot sleepers, and they know what booksellers would be interested in them. Special collections librarians themselves can

be scouts. And they should welcome scouts into their departments because important and affordable items can be acquired from them.

> **AS A YOUTH** I was not a formal scout, but on a number of occasions I spotted what I knew was a valuable book for which the seller was asking a pittance. I knew which bookseller would want it, and I bought it and made a small but satisfying profit from it. Though I was not really a scout, in these instances I was scouting. Many people fall into this gray area of "semi-scout" or "ersatz scout." And they keep good books circulating through bookshops and libraries.

ACQUISITION FROM THE WEB

Most of the rare books that a librarian will buy will come from booksellers at fairs, in quotes, and through their catalogs, and from auctions and book fairs. But increasingly, rare books are showing up on the Web and are winding up in special collections. When books first became web commodities, about twenty years ago, booksellers loved it. Until then their stores were filled with books and with a tiny number of patrons compared to all the book buyers in the world. The off-the-street traffic who entered the bookshops could not possibly browse shelves comprehensively, and that number was small compared to the number of potential book buyers worldwide. Through search services such as those offered by many book dealers, who essentially used *AB/Bookman's Weekly*, the dealers could reach a wider, but still restricted, audience.

Today, all kinds of books are available on the Web, from volumes costing 1 cent (the sellers make their profits from the postage and handling fees) to books going for dozens of thousands of dollars. Rare book sales, which were once the province of antiquarian book stores (and their catalogs) and high-end auctions, are becoming increasingly common over the Internet. The main caution for the buyer is that such purchases take place without the buyer's being able to handle the volume or manuscript, and only through direct contact can the buyer feel comfortable that the item is as described. If an item comes in to the buyer that does not match up satisfactorily with the seller's description—or for any other reason is not to the buyer's liking—the buyer has a right to return it. Dealers do not want to get books back in the mail, so the more experienced sellers are fastidious about how carefully they describe items they sell online. Less experienced sellers may not give an accurate verbal picture of the item for sale, so the librarian (or other buyer) should carefully assess who the seller is and may wish to call before placing the order. A strategic phone call can reveal things to the buyer that the bookseller's description was not explicit about.

Most online sellers have a return policy, and the rare book librarian should know what it is for every purchase made online. One standard feature of the return policy is, "books may be returned within __ days of purchase" (usually a few days or a week), but the seller may require a phone call or e-mail message notifying him that the item is on its way back. Sellers may also require the returning party to pay for the postage in both directions. And, of course, for valuable books, the person returning the item must package it with at least the same care as was given by the seller and should pay for the appropriate insurance for the returned package.

AB/BOOKMAN'S WEEKLY AND THE COMING OF ONLINE BOOK SALES

AB/Bookman's Weekly deserves a section to itself. This publication contained a compendium of books for sale and books sought, and for many years it was one of the most eagerly read periodicals in the book world. It was a major source of buying for libraries, dealers, and collectors, along with others looking for special titles. It is mentioned here because it is a

bygone means of collecting for librarians and others, and some people still miss it dearly. (The periodical will henceforth be called "*AB*.")

When *AB* was flourishing, it had no rivals. If anyone went into a bookshop and asked the dealer to find a book, if it was not on the bookseller's shelves, she would say, "I have a search service; give me your name and contact points and I will try to find a copy of the book for you." This "search service" was almost certainly *AB/Bookman's Weekly*. Eric Holzenberg says, "[A] single issue of *AB Bookman's Weekly* in its heyday might have contained seven thousand titles for sale."[9] The magazine had several parts. First were preliminaries like information about coming book fairs or other bookish events. The second part contained a scholarly article or two about the book trade. This was followed by "Books Received," a listing of books that were sent for review (they were not reviewed in *AB*, only listed), then obituaries, when appropriate, and then a section of "Trade Reviews," reviewing books that had something to do with books. Every issue also had a feature titled "Describing Condition," calling for a regularized vocabulary to describe what a book looked like (see appendix 3 on dealers' catalogs), immediately followed by the section that was the reason thousands of avid collectors, booksellers, and librarians subscribed to *AB* in the first place: listings of "Books Wanted" by the thousands. It was aimed at the trade, though many private parties and, of course, many libraries, subscribed to it. Anyone could purchase a little box along one of the edges of a page notifying readers: "If you want to sell ____ [a specific book, or an item in a particular collecting field], please contact me because I am looking for it." If you were a bookseller with many customers asking for particular titles, you

THE PAGES OF *AB/Bookman's Weekly* were truly bare bones. There were no illustrations, no fancy typography, no color, no nothing but line after line of listings, in three unimaginative columns. Someone outside the fraternity and sorority of the book world, watching a collector or bookseller scrutinize the pages, might assume the person to be mad, for there was clearly no text to read, nothing to rivet one's attention. Quite the contrary: this was a place of discovery and a place to make money. Obscure books could lie fallow on shelves for decades with no eyes falling on them—or with potential buyers in a seriously limited supply looking at them. But *AB* opened up these books to a wide world of potential buyers by the hundreds of thousands, through the eyes of the "Search Services" dealers.

could buy a whole page or two or more and list endless numbers of titles. The listings were brief, usually just author and title (sometimes, but almost never, with a date: "Horne, R. H. Ballad Romances. 1846.")[10] No italics, no boldface, no typographical niceties. That was all—just the bare bones of a description, along with the name of the "Wanter" somewhere on the page (usually at the top) and his contact points (usually just an address). The author names and titles were printed in three columns, yielding about 240 entries per page. Dealers (and some private collectors) would pore over these listings and perhaps come upon a title they owned and were willing to sell.

The last section of the magazine (much smaller than the "Books Wanted" section) was "Books for Sale," also listing thousands of titles, with brief bibliographical descriptions, briefer condition statements (usually a letter or two), and prices asked. A typical entry looked like this: "Lawrence, T. E. Seven Pillars of Wisdom. Lon: Jonathan Cape 1935. 8vo. 672pp. 1st trade ed. Sl wear t/b of sp. Sl loose at top. Unobtr sig o/w VG+. $105." (Octavo. First trade edition. Slight wear to back of spine. Slightly loose at top. Unobtrusive signature, otherwise very good plus.)[11]

Generally, booksellers would read all the ads, those wanted and those for sale. Collectors and librarians tended to look first at those for sale, though many read through the whole issue. The scholarly articles were generally by experts whose experience was valuable, and the reader could pick up collecting and selling trends, prices, and other useful information.

I ASKED THE people in Receiving in my library to get every issue of *AB/Bookman's Weekly* to me the minute it came in so I might have a good chance of getting anything I saw that I wanted for the department. Often I spotted a volume for the department, and I immediately contacted the bookseller, if I could get her number from Directory Assistance (phone numbers did not accompany the "Books for Sale" lists, and there were no computers, hence no online phone books), but often I was too late.

Little by little, with the coming of the computer, books got listed on the Internet, and *AB* lost its base because customers could now search online by author, title, or subject—sometimes two or all three of these, and greatly faster than they could from the printed page. And rather than having a few thousand books in a bookshop to look through, or a similar number in each issue of *AB*, customers started having dozens of thousands, then hundreds of thousands, then millions to pick from. "The rise in popularity of online book sales parallels the decline of the revered *AB*" (Holzenberg, p. 39). As the magazine faded into the sunset, the number of books sold online increased tremendously.

> Unwilling or unable to compete with the online sites, the magazine shrank steadily in volume throughout the 1990s; and by December, 1999, issues were running at 32 pages each, with only six pages of "Books Wanted" and ten pages of "Books for Sale." The demise of *AB Bookman's Weekly* was announced on Exlibris shortly thereafter, on January 25, 2000. (Holzenberg, pp. 39–40)

With increased online sales, at first, booksellers were thrilled: thousands upon thousands of books that had languished on their shelves for ages now found customers across the United States and around the globe. A book on roadside verse that had sat on a bookshelf since 1970 in California now found a customer in Wichita.

For a couple of years, booksellers cleared out thousands of books from their stock that would never have found a local customer. But with the proliferation of sites selling books, and with a proliferation of copies now coming to light and being offered for sale worldwide, competition set in royally. Rather than finding one or two copies of a book, book buyers were finding dozens or scores of them. Competition drove the prices down, and the booksellers no longer had anything approaching a monopoly.

Today rare book librarians with want lists can search online, and, even for scarce books, can often find what they are looking for. For librarians seeking obscure items, the chances go up every day that the things they want will become available with a

THE BOOK REFERRED to in the text, *Verse by the Side of the Road* by Frank Rowsome Jr. (Brattleboro, VT: Stephen Greene Press, 1965), was difficult to find when I began looking for a copy in 1990. On March 9, 2012, a search for this title on AbeBooks turned up 394 hits, a host of which were selling for only $1.00. Online selling has killed off publications like *AB*, and it continues to grow daily. BookFinder alone (a rival of AbeBooks) has over 150 million books listed.

quick online search. If they are searching for particular titles, and do not find them, they can assume that these items are scarce and possibly worth what a bookseller wants to charge. One bookseller searches the Web to help him price books he wants to offer, and if he cannot find an online copy, his catalog reads "Not net," indicating the item's scarcity. You can be sure this rarity adds to the price of almost everything that is in the same "not net" category.

A drawback to the online sale of books is that it has become so easy, now people who were not booksellers, but who found interesting books at thrift shops and flea markets and garage sales, are offering these finds on the Web under a "bookshop" name: "Pine Street Books," "Volumes from the Hills," and other made-up names that make them sound like legitimate booksellers. (The Web has made them "legitimate" booksellers, but not always schooled ones.) Many of these people have little or no understanding of the book world, let alone the bookselling world, and they do not know how to describe the books they are selling; they get titles, dates, and authors' names wrong; they claim that a book is a first edition when it is not; they do not understand how to describe condition; they do not know how to read publishers' codes to indicate what edition or printing (impression) the book is; they do not know the common jargon of the rare- and used-book world, so they make up their own words which are so idiosyncratic that others cannot tell what they mean; and so on. Buying books from the Web is now more a gamble than ever before.

So special collections librarians, looking for particular titles, and finding them on the Internet, are not assured that what they want is actually what the dealer is offering. Perhaps it is best to restrict their purchases to legitimate dealers with good track records for knowing the bibliography in the field. That means knowing the kind of things just mentioned: what is a true first edition, how to describe foxing or a slightly shabby dust jacket, or where the "points" are on a volume to distinguish its state (see chapter 9 on bibliography).

Buying from the Web has become a reflex action for most people collecting books. If they want a copy of an item, they turn immediately to one of the standard book-search sites. The prevailing sentiment is becoming, "If it isn't there, it must not be available." Millions of books, however, are available somewhere, just not on the main search sites. And those titles that are on these sites are not necessarily ones the librarian is seeking.

ACQUISITION AT BOOK FAIRS AND EPHEMERA SHOWS

As this text has already shown, book fairs are great places for rare book personnel to visit, for several reasons, not the least of which is that they are great venues for finding great books. There are different levels of book fairs, from the highest (ABA and ABAA) to the middle (the local chapters of the parent organizations and the localized bookselling organizations, delineated earlier) to the paper and ephemera fairs. They are all worth going to. And each librarian can create her own strategy for attendance.

One way to "work" the fair is to move methodically, starting in aisle 1 and going up and down the aisles sequentially. Another is to take the fair brochure listing all the dealers, mark the ones most suited to your buying (those who carry your level 4 and 5 books), and head straight to them. As with getting a dealer's catalog in the mail, the librarian should act quickly or choice items might get plucked up by another customer.

No librarian can memorize everything in her collection, and it will happen that she finds a great book for her library but cannot remember whether a

ONE CASE IN point to show how little many booksellers know about the things they are selling: Harry Duncan and Kim Merker (of the Cummington Press and the Stone Wall Press, respectively) printed a book in 105 copies, *Golden Child* (Kansas City, MO: Hallmark, 1960), for Joyce Hall, the owner of the Hallmark company. The text was the libretto of a *Hallmark Hall of Fame* opera by Paul Engle. It was printed on special paper; was bound in orange, brown, tan, and cream-colored gingham cloth with paper labels pasted to the front cover and spine; and contained original photographs of the opera, tipped in. It was issued in a slipcase with no dust jacket. A copy of this version of the book was once offered on the Web at about $150. Hallmark also issued a facsimile edition, also in a hard cover, but the gingham cloth with its labels was photographed and printed onto paper for the cover of this cheap edition. Hence there was no cloth, no paper labels, no slipcase, and no original photographs tipped in. The cheap version had a dust jacket, however, which is lacking on some copies.

Some booksellers call this the "First Printing," when it is really the first facsimile; the first printing was done by hand, on a handpress, on beautiful paper, and was numbered and signed by the librettist and the composer, Philip Bezanson.* When a host of ignorant booksellers see the facsimile edition, they assume it is the rare version in a slipcase. Because at one time a price of the limited edition was listed at about $150, over the years I have seen copies of this cheap version offered for $150, $200, and up, with the sellers often boasting that it has a lovely, perfect dust jacket (as if this added to the price). The fact that it has the jacket marks it as the facsimile version. One bookseller, knowing the difference, described the cheaper one in his ad by explaining that the copy he was selling was the later facsimile edition, not the one limited to 105 copies.† But this notice did not deter the silly dealers, who could have read that description, which was on the Web for more than a decade. One bookseller, with no idea what he has in hand, says of the copy for sale: "Original patterned cloth with paper label on spine, fine. In good dust jacket with pieces missing from rear cover." I have seen this mistake over and over for more than twenty years: if it has a dust jacket, then the cover is the paper version, and the labels the dealer sees are printed on the paper cover. With the object right in his hands, this dealer cannot discern the difference between cloth and paper for the cover and a separate printed-and-pasted-on label rather than a title that is not even a label.‡ Rare book librarians should take the descriptions they find on the Web with much caution.

*To compound the confusion, E. P. Dutton came up with another edition illustrated by Leonard Everett Fisher (New York: Dutton, 1962), and several booksellers, in their greater ignorance, call this the "First Edition." And this in the face of dozens of copies of this text on the Web by another publisher, published two years earlier. What are these people thinking? In a case like this, it is not only ignorance (which possibly can be excused), but also foolishness.

†John and Mary Laurie, knowledgeable booksellers, say in their description, "This is the trade offset edition of the handprinted edition"; see their description on the AbeBooks website, www.abebooks.com/servlet/Search Results?an=paul+engle&bsi=30 &tn=golden+child&x=66&y=15 &prevpage=1. Despite the fact that this information has been available on AbeBooks for many years, other booksellers either don't read this or choose to ignore it, and price their book as if it is the rare limited edition. One bookseller says, "Paper-covered boards with applied labels." Not right! If the boards are covered in paper, then the labels are not applied, they are printed onto the paper.

‡This copy observed March 11, 2012; but this error (mistaking the paper, dust-jacketed version for the cloth slipcased one) has been on the Web for more than fifteen years.

copy is already there or not. Using a mobile device, a librarian may be able to search the library's catalog (or to telephone someone in the department if it has weekend hours, because most of these fairs take place Friday evenings and on the weekend) to see if the item is already in the collection. If this cannot be determined, there are two strategies the librarian can take. The standard practice is to ask the dealer to hold the volume until she has a chance to search the library's catalog. It is not fair to ask the bookseller to take the item off the shelves just for one librarian who may wish to buy it. One good practice is to say to the dealer, "Sell this at the fair; but if it does not sell here, please quote it to me on Monday." This approach gives the seller the chance to make the sale at the fair, but if he does not, he might have a sale for the piece through the quote he sends out. For unique items (special copies of books, manuscripts, original materials of other kinds), it is obvious that the piece is not in the library's collection. The librarian should either commit to the purchase or leave it be. This choice entails knowing the collection well and also knowing the department's budget—whether there is enough money in the coffers to afford the book or manuscript. If the coffers are short, can the librarian be certain that she has a donor in the wings to help the library pay for the piece? Some librarians will go out on a limb and overcommit the budget so that an important piece will not get away. Know your collections, your budgets, your limits, and your donors. Book fairs do not allow the librarian the luxury of a week or even a day to decide what to get.

MY OWN EXPERIENCES at book fairs could fill a large volume. On the point about unpredictability, I have a host of tales. One bookseller specializes in books and manuscripts—and often artifacts—concerning medicine. But I always visit his booth because he is one of the friendliest of the dealers and I enjoy his company, and also because, every now and then, he brings to the fair something for me—having to do with paper. The things he brings for me are completely out of his specialty, but he finds them in his search for stock, and he knows just the kinds of things I will buy. Other dealers with specialties outside those of my library may come across something worth showing at a fair, despite not being in their own bailiwicks, so I go to just about every booth at a book fair and ask the proprietors for the kinds of things I am looking for. I have often made purchases for my library in the most unlikely booths. And this way I get to know the booksellers.

The ephemera fairs are especially exciting for at them librarians will encounter items beyond books and manuscripts that may be perfect for their collections. Special collections are special in more ways than one. They hold books and manuscripts on well-focused collection areas, but they also are repositories for scholars working in those areas who are there to learn everything they can from the library's holdings, so it is often part of the librarians' mandate to offer information in all formats and genres. Ephemera exist in innumerable forms: tickets, labels, advertising pieces, political buttons, photographs, drawings, and on and on. There are hundreds of categories of things that fall under the rubric of "ephemera," and librarians should be on the lookout for such things, for they never know what kind of materials their patrons could profit from. Also, bibliographic utilities may have highly developed catalogs for books and great online finding aids for manuscripts, but ephemera are usually not too well cataloged—despite being rich sources of information. This is an area of collecting that librarians must pursue to add unusual, informative materials to their holdings.

The ephemera dealers, like their book and manuscript counterparts, are experts in their fields, and they can guide librarians to wonderful resources. One dealer might specialize in maritime trade cards, another in plumbing and lighting, another in sports, and so on. Some postcard dealers show at these fairs, bringing thousands upon thousands of cards with them, usually organized geographically or by subject. They have thus done a good portion of the librarian's searching. These fairs are definitely not at the ABAA or ABA level, because ephemera are often acquired in mass and presented to the attendees of these fairs in cardboard or wooden boxes. Great bargains are to be had at these shows, though some dealers overprice their goods. But this is a venue more conducive to haggling and negotiating about price (though some dealers quote firm prices), and part of the fun is in locating remarkable things you have never seen the likes of before and getting them at reasonable prices.

Book and ephemera fairs are tremendously educational. Librarians will learn about what is hot on the market, specific books and their values, booksellers and their stock, and much more. For some people, it is like going to a museum of great objects and being able to touch all of them. Some shows are for a single day. Some are for Saturday and Sunday. The great ABAA fairs run the better part of three days, beginning on a Friday evening (which costs a premium price for admission) and ending on Sunday afternoon. For serious collectors (and this includes many rare book librarians), it will take most of that time to do the fair thoroughly. These are some of the prime sources for collecting, and they are highly recommended for anyone working in a rare book department, if for no other reason than they are an excellent way to learn of the value of books.

BUYING AT AUCTIONS

Because of the very nature of rare book departments, it is likely that they will look to auctions for some of their acquisitions. For many librarians, the auction world holds as much of a thrill as does a top-flight antiquarian book fair. The higher-end auction houses—Christie's, Sotheby's, Bonhams & Butterfields, Swann—will offer one treasure after another, and the excitement of the bidding raises people's pulses, expectations, and hopes. The plus side also includes the possibility of getting an item at a great price. The minus side is becoming mesmerized by the tingle of the bidding and winding up paying far more for an item than it is worth.

Auctions yield opportunities, but there are pitfalls as well, and the auction houses play by well-established rules that bidders should be aware of. Anyone working in rare books should understand all the rules and operations and how auctions work.

To begin with, the basic unit for sale at an auction is a "lot," which could be a single item or many. When auction houses, after looking carefully at a library, decide that it is worth their while to take it on for sale, they will break it into lots, consisting of one volume or many. High-priced items will wind up as single-item lots; lower-priced volumes may be in lots of dozens of pieces. Some of the smaller, regional auction companies do not print catalogs for their sales. They may have large tables filling rooms, and anyone in the room can bid on what is "lotted." For instance, at New England Book Auctions, a buyer might see a single lot of three hundred cookbooks. The lots are usually comprised of items that go together, so that if someone is buying in a particular subject area, she will not be forced to buy a lot with only one or two things that are of interest to her. Lots with single items are what they are: one piece to be bid on for the lot. Most auctions have catalogs listing all lots, with a suggested range of prices given for each lot—usually with some level of precision because the auction houses will have experienced "appraisers" working with pricing guides, booksellers' catalogs, reference works in the auction house collection, and much knowledge. But lots with many items in them, which also must be appraised (for the catalog must give a range of values that the expert in the house thinks the books will sell for), can hide treasures. This is where the excitement of the auction could lie, because large lots may have special volumes, inserts in the volumes, variant dust wrappers, and so forth that add significantly to the value of a piece, but which the person compiling the catalog for the auction did not have time to discover.[12]

The auction house gathers—from a single collection or from many sources—a host of items to put up for sale.[13] A single collector may have a huge library. She may go to an auction house to offer the entire collection for a single sale. Other auctions offer lots from many consignors. Some exceptionally famous sales have dispersed the collections of Jerome Kern, Estelle Doheny (sold by Christie's for the Roman Catholic Diocese of Los Angeles, to whom she had willed the collection), Robert Hoe, H. Bradley Martin, Thomas Winthrop Streeter, John Quinn, and many others. (The catalogs of these sales have, themselves, become collectible, partly because of the importance of the books they list, and partly because they are compendia of fine scholarship and useful to librarians, collectors, booksellers, and scholars.) An auction house might put out an advertisement announcing, "Now taking consignments for auction: books and manuscripts on natural history." When the house has enough items for a full sale, it can schedule the sale. "Enough" items could mean a hundred or two hundred, or it could mean five hundred or more.

Most major houses publish—in paper form and online—catalogs of their sales, usually weeks before the sale date. These catalogs are sold to prospective bidders, but sometimes a potential buyer can call a house and, to encourage sales, it will send a free copy in the mail. Auction houses will also offer a full run of their catalogs in a year for a set price—like subscribing to a magazine. If the house is so big that it has auctions on all kinds of goods (photographs, export porcelain, jewelry, wines, cars, books, carpets, and so forth), the subscriber can order only the catalogs in his collecting area. And if the auction house has many catalogs under the rubric of "books, manuscripts, autographs," or some other book-related topic, the collector (librarian) may wish to buy individual catalogs that offer books only in the areas of the library's collection.

The catalogs have the typical information: introductions about the items for sale, a section explaining the conditions for the sale, advice to prospective bidders, warranties of the house for the goods to be sold, and then a list of all the lots, often with photographs of each lot, good descriptions of everything in the lots, often bibliographic references, and then estimated prices. Most auction houses give a range of prices: "$750–$1,000." These values are arrived at by the experts who work in the houses and are often fairly good indicators of value. But these figures can be grossly inaccurate, depending on several variables. If an item that has not been on the market for decades (or is unique, as with manuscripts) comes onto the auction block, all it takes is two avid (and well-heeled) collectors to drive the price far beyond the high estimate. Supply and demand are at the root of all prices, and if the demand is strong and the item scarce or unique, there is no way to predict what the final hammer price will be. So even the experts in the auction house, who specialize in the areas of the books being sold in a given auction, can be significantly off in their estimates of value. Sometimes hammer prices are twice or three times the catalog's high estimate.

On the other end of the spectrum is the item that is overvalued by the auction house, such that the low estimate is still too high for the bidders. Or even if the range of prices is "correct," at any given auction there just may not be anyone in the audience (local or remote) interested in that item. It will go unsold and be "bought in" (the term for a book that does not sell at the auction). Further, many consignors will put a reserve on the things they offer for sale. This means that they are unwilling to let an item sell for too little; they would rather keep it than have it sell for too little. The reserve may be 20 or 25 percent under the low estimate listed in the auc-

tion catalog. For instance, if the catalog lists a lot at "$5,000–$7,000," the reserve might be $4,000. The auctioneer will start the bidding at, say, $3,000. If the highest bid he can generate is $3,500, the lot is bought in—unsold—and returned to the consignor. (The consignor still must pay a fee to the auction house for all the work done to get the book to the block in the first place.) Reserves are not published figures. Bidders must not know how little the owner is willing to take for an item. Some sales announce, "There are no reserves in this auction," indicating that there are some great bargains to be had. All lots will sell (if there is even one bid on them), no matter how low the bids.[14]

In the past, the catalogs often gave short shrift to descriptions of condition of the items for sale, but in recent years this has been rectified. For instance, Robert Wilson complains,

> very little space is given in a catalogue entry to physical description of an item. This includes an indication of the presence or absence of a dust jacket, of missing plates or illustrations, or of other such important factors of condition. It cannot be assumed that a book is perfect or in fine condition just because there is no statement to the contrary in the catalogue. ("Buying at Auction," p. 42)

This statement was made in 1977. More recently, auction companies have been more responsible in their descriptions. In the long run, it was in their interests to do so, for they did not want purchasers to be returning defective items. A typical entry of today looks like this: "Upper hinge cracked, small withdrawal sticker on lower pastedown; spine panel folds expertly reinforced, light wear to spine panel ends and a tiny chip from lower flap fold."[15]

Auction houses must do their diligence with respect to the things they sell. They do not want to be caught up in scandal or in illegal activities. Hence, it is in their best interests to verify the legal ownership by the consignors of anything that they will be putting up onto the block. They do not want to sell stolen goods or items smuggled illegally out of countries. Hence, the "Conditions of Sale" section of their catalogs usually spells out their responsibilities and how they have fulfilled those. The Swann Auction

Galleries catalogs say, in all capital letters:

> THE AUTHENTICITY OF THE PROPERTY LISTED IN THIS CATALOGUE IS WARRANTED TO THE EXTENT STATED IN THE "LIMITED WARRANTY." EXCEPT AS PROVIDED THEREIN, ALL PROPERTY IS SOLD "AS IS" AND NEITHER SWANN NOR THE CONSIGNOR MAKES ANY WARRANTIES OR REPRESENTATIONS OF ANY KIND OR NATURE WITH RESPECT TO THE PROPERTY OR ITS VALUE, AND IN NO EVENT SHALL THEY BE RESPONSIBLE FOR CORRECTNESS OF DESCRIPTION, GENUINENESS, ATTRIBUTION, PROVENANCE, AUTHENTICITY, AUTHORSHIP, COMPLETENESS, CONDITION OF THE PROPERTY OR ESTIMATE OF VALUE. NO STATEMENT (ORAL OR WRITTEN) IN THE CATALOGUE, AT THE SALE, OR ELSEWHERE SHALL BE DEEMED SUCH A WARRANTY OR REPRESENTATION, OR ANY ASSUMPTION OF RESPONSIBILITY. (This statement comes from Swann catalogue 2276, Part II, April 17, 2012; it is also on their website at catalogue.swanngalleries.com/pdf/OnlineTerms _Conditions2010.pdf.)

The "Limited Warranty" section explains what Swann means by its "warranty." The preceding one in caps seems to contradict the warranties in the "Limited" section. For instance,

> Unless otherwise indicated in the respective catalogue descriptions (which are subject to amendment by oral or written notices or announcements made by Swann prior to sale), we warrant for a period of three (3) years from the date of sale the authenticity of each lot /catalogued herein. (p. [4])

Similar statements pertain to authenticity, condition, the applicability of the warranties to the original buyer and not to anyone else, and so forth.

The point of all this is to warn all buyers that sometimes auction houses, doing their best, make mistakes and that there are often remedies for their errors. Buying at auction, as already noted, is a gamble, and these warranties underscore the risks. But all the statements about guaranteeing authenticity, condition, provenance, and so on are seriously undercut when the auction house itself knowingly sells materials that are suspect. In fact, greed sometimes leads an auction house to obtain for sale items it knows are contraband or pieces with murky provenance.

As noted, all items come from consignors—the people who own the pieces and who hope the bidding goes wild on the auction floor. Sometimes the consignor is a bookseller, possibly one who has acquired an item out of her own realm of expertise and who would rather sell the book at auction than

---

THE QUESTIONABLE ACTIVITIES of some auction houses have been in the news for decades. One of the most egregious cases involves Sotheby's and its sale of antiquities, thoroughly examined in Peter Watson's *Sotheby's: The Inside Story* (New York: Random House, 1997).* Though this case is beyond the scope of the present volume, it does raise the issue of the legality of all auction houses' activities. Watson shows that Sotheby's was involved in the robbing of graves of their antiquities (in Italy), arranging for their being smuggled out of Italy to other countries, and bringing them to auction in New York and elsewhere. The auction house also rigged bids, created false "authentication" papers, and falsified records to hide its crimes.†

*This volume is a second edition of Watson's *Sotheby's: Inside Story* (lacking "The" from the title; London: Bloomsbury, 1997). The Random House version updates by a few months the information given in the Bloomsbury version.

†The Watson book, along with the *60 Minutes* television segment documenting these activities, raises a red flag about the whole world of auctions, especially the legitimacy of the actions of some auction houses. In my own experience, one auction house sold items that were clearly taken (almost certainly stolen) from a particular library. One of the items even had a bookplate of the library still attached, with no evidence that the volume had been legally deaccessioned. It was fairly clearly a stolen book, but the auction house ignored this and put the piece on the block anyway, without contacting the library. Even auction houses with the best intentions can get sidetracked.

> **AT ONE AUCTION** at a European house, I made offers on a number of lots and got two-thirds of the ones I bid on. When the sales results were posted, I noticed that other lots that I was interested in (but did not bid on) did not sell. I contacted the auction house and asked about them. The proprietor told me that they did not sell. I asked the auction house if they were still available, and I was told that the consignor was willing to take the lower of the estimated prices less 20 percent. So I was able to acquire other lots after the sale.

do the proper homework to find out why the book in hand might be valuable, and then find the right customer for it. If the consignor is well known or important, either as a collector or as a public figure, the auction catalog will usually identify that person. If the owner is obscure and of no great importance (no one whose name would add value to the item[s]), or if the consignor wishes for any reason not to be known, the auction catalog may say something like "Property of a Gentleman" or "Property of an Important Collector," or will simply not mention the consignor at all.

The consignors will usually have their collections appraised, sometimes by the auction house. The auction house will usually charge a fee for the appraisal, which is to be expected. The potential consignor is paying for a professional service. It might be possible for the seller to negotiate a "free" appraisal if she decides to use that auction house to sell the collection (or item). The house, however, might be tempted to offer high appraisals to lure the seller. But there is no guarantee that any price will actually be realized on the auction floor. In fact, there is not even a guarantee that any particular item will sell at the auction. Many times the bidding starts out too high, or there is a lull in the excitement of the auction, or for any number of reasons, some lots receive no bids and are pulled in. That is, they are not sold, and they eventually go back to the consignor.

Consignors share the proceeds of each lot with the auction house. That is, when an item sells, the consignor takes most of the selling price, but the auction house gets what is called the *seller's premium*—anywhere from a small to a fairly large percentage (maybe up to 25 percent). If the sales promise to yield substantial returns, the consignors may be able to negotiate good terms with the auction house. For an item that might sell for, say, $500,000 or more, the consignor may negotiate paying the auction house only, say, a 10 percent seller's premium. Sometimes the owners may go from one auction house to another to get the most favorable terms—that is, the firm whose sale will yield the greatest prices, and the firm that will take a smaller fee for its services than does its competitors.

Great prices do not guarantee the best return for consignors, for if the auction house has high premiums for the sellers, the prices realized in the sale will be divided between the consignor and the house, and the house will take a good percentage of the selling price. Hence, if the seller's premium is 25 percent of the hammer price (the final, winning bid on the auction floor), the consignor will get only $750 for a book that went for $1,000. Similarly, there is a *buyer's premium*, often the same as the seller's premium. So the book that sold for $1,000 will cost the buyer $1,250. The auction house premiums have netted the house 50 percent of the sale price of the book. It is true that the auction house does have its expenses to cover and must make a profit, but premiums as high as 25 percent add substantially to the cost of any item, and 25 percent deducts substantially from the seller's take.

Buyers' premiums are listed in the catalogs for each sale. Sellers' premiums are usually not listed because, as just mentioned, the consignor may be able to negotiate for the premium. For instance, if one item is estimated at a high price—say $500,000—the consignor would have to give up $100,000 to the auction house if the premium were 20 percent. For a single lot, the seller might negotiate for a 15 percent (or lower) premium; the auction house will still be making a good deal of money on the lot, and may consider doing this so that the consignor will not go to another house.

The consignor must weigh the possibilities: pay a smaller premium at a smaller house, which draws a particular clientele, or pay the higher premium for the premiere house and hope that *its* more affluent clientele will be able and willing to pay more for the item on the block. It is a gamble all around, for even the finest items could be seriously underbid for any number of reasons: lack of just the right bidders, time of day, competing events that drew away some potential bidders, and so on.

BUYERS' AND SELLERS' premiums were once about 10 to 12 percent, but over the decades they have climbed to more than twice that at some houses. Because consignors could play one auction house against another for the lowest seller's premium to be paid, the two most prestigious houses, Sotheby's and Christie's, colluded to fix their premiums. It was, of course, illegal, and they were caught and fined. The Wikipedia article on the scandal explains:

> In 2000, allegations surfaced of a price-fixing arrangement between Christie's and Sotheby's, another major auction house. Executives from Christie's subsequently alerted the Department of Justice of their suspicions of commission-fixing collusion.
>
> Christie's gained immunity from prosecution in the United States as a longtime employee of Christie's confessed and cooperated with the U.S. Federal Bureau of Investigation. Numerous members of Sotheby's senior management were fired soon thereafter, and A. Alfred Taubman, the largest shareholder of Sotheby's at the time, took most of the blame; he and Dede Brooks (the CEO) were given jail sentences, and Christie's, Sotheby's and their owners also paid a civil lawsuit settlement of $512 million.*

Today these houses still retain perhaps the highest premiums in the business—usually 25 percent—while some of their competitors maintain lower ones. A recent Swann catalog says its buyer's premium is 20 percent.†

*See http://en.wikipedia.org/wiki/Christie%27s#Price-fixing_scandal.

†See the Swann catalog for Sale 2276, Part II, for the auction on April 17, 2012. It says, "[T]he purchase price paid by a purchaser shall be the sum of the final bid and a buyer's premium of 20 percent of the final bid on each lot, plus all applicable sales tax" (p. [3]).

The bidding, however, does not necessarily all take place on the auction house floor. Potential buyers can submit a bid in advance and need never be in the house. They can bid by phone—in real time—during the auction. Today there is also bidding by fax, the post, and e-mail. A good practice for librarians to follow is not to bid by themselves, but to have a bookseller do their bidding. Because the books or manuscripts the library wants are valuable and will thus be expensive, it is important to look at each item to check it for completeness, condition, points (see chapter 9, "Bibliography"), and so forth. If the items a librarian wants are at an auction in a remote city, it might not be possible to see the desired lots in person. It might be useful for the librarian to contact booksellers she often deals with to see if they will be at the auction. If so, the librarian could ask a dealer to inspect the items and execute the bids. Even if dealers charge a fee for this service, the librarian might be able to secure some lots at good prices.[16] It is a kind of insurance for the library against getting a defective item and against paying too much.[17] Further, booksellers are some of the most knowledgeable book people in the world, and they can advise the librarian on such matters as condition, the likelihood that the book will sell for the estimated price, who the competition might be for the lot, the existence of a better (or cheaper) copy, whether the copy on the block is worth getting, and so forth. This is what the bookseller does for a living day in and day out, and having such an expert on the librarian's side can be economical and practical. It is likely that the dealer knows more about many items in the sale than do the compilers of the auction catalog.

Two other things militate for the use of a bookseller as bidder for the library. First, because the librarian turns to an expert in the field, it is probably the field of the dealer's own business. Hiring the seller to bid for the library may be a way of eliminating him as competition for the lots the librarian wants. Second, unscrupulous auction houses may take a mail-in bid from the library and start the bidding at that point, rather than at a much lower point, as it might have done without the library's bid. For instance, a manuscript may have an estimate of $1,000–$1,250 and a reserve of $800. The auction house would probably normally open the bidding at about $600. If the library tenders a mail-in bid for $1,000, the auction house may open the bidding at $1,000, knowing that it can sell the manuscript for at least that much because it has a firm bid in hand at that level (from the library). However, if the library does not send in a bid at all, but has the bookseller do the bidding, the lot may open at $600 and sell for $800. That is, having a dealer on site at the auction can save the library money. Adjusting opening bids like this is unethical, and it may be illegal, but there is nothing to stop an auction house from doing it.

The librarian would do best with a bookseller who knows the librarian and the library, its collections, its budgets, and its abilities to exceed its high bids. Sometimes a dealer can go one or two bids beyond what the library has said is its highest offer and get the lot. Even if it has to pay a bit more than it originally intended, the library will acquire important items for its collection, and in the long run will not be disgruntled at the extra bids (especially because, over the long haul, the bookseller will be saving the library on other bids).

And finally, with respect to having dealers bid for the library, it is good to have the bidding done at the point of the auction, where the dealer can assess the tenor of the bidding, the excitement and buzz of the action, and can back off when things are getting out of hand. This dynamic cannot be gauged with a mail-in or telephone bid. And, as already noted, by hiring the bookseller to bid for the library, the librarian is eliminating one competitor: the bookseller herself.

As I explained earlier, parties (librarians, private collectors, booksellers) can be active participants in an auction without being there. They can submit what is called a "commission bid," a bid sent in in advance of the sale. If an item is estimated to sell for $10,000–$15,000, if the reserve on the item is $7,500, if the commission bid sent in is $8,500, if the bidding begins at $6,000, and if there are no other bids for the lot, the person who has sent in the commission bid should get the lot for $7,500—the lowest price acceptable to the consignor. But there is no guarantee that the auction house will honor the $7,500 reserve, especially because it knows there is a

buyer out there willing to pay $8,500. The more the item sells for, the more the auction house makes—from the buyer and the seller, thanks to their premiums. The customers (and the consignor) must trust the honesty of the auction house. And for the most part, these houses are trustworthy. But Watson has documented an instance when Sotheby's personnel—one who knew the reserves and another who knew the commission bids—colluded to raise the reserve so that the item would sell for more than the original reserve that the consignor placed on the lot.[18]

Two other practices make auctions suspect as fair purveyors of books. The first is called the *ring*. "A ring is an agreement by a group of bidders, usually dealers, to refrain from bidding on certain items in return for advantages later."[19] One excellent book on the topic, analyzing the happenings of a well-known auction of 1919, is Arthur Freeman and Janet Ing Freeman's *Anatomy of an Auction*. Chapter 1 begins with a quotation from the *Oxford English Dictionary*:

> "A 'knock-out' is a combination of persons to prevent competition between themselves at an auction by an arrangement that only one of their number shall bid, and that anything obtained by him shall be afterwards disposed of privately among themselves." . . . Terminology varies, but "knock-out" . . . has come to mean both the entire arrangement or "combination" itself, and the private meeting of the participants to "knock out" or redistribute the purchases and share the incremental money as "dividends." The private auction is also called the "settlement," and this name is given as well to the handing-over of cash after the secondary transactions. "Ring" is the name for the society of participants in the original arrangement; a sale is said to be "ringed" if substantially affected by such a group.[20]

In the case of a ring, the auction house is not culpable. The house either does not know about it (because it is a booksellers' ploy to keep bidding prices low) or cannot do anything about it. The practice is illegal (and has been since 1928; see Freeman and Freeman, p. 29), but there is no guarantee that it is not still done today.

The second practice is *chandelier bidding* (also called *rafter bidding*),

[a] practice, especially by high-end art auctioneers, of raising false bids at crucial times in the bidding process in order to create the appearance of greater demand or to extend bidding momentum for a work on offer. To call out these nonexistent bids, auctioneers might fix their gaze at a point in the auction room that is difficult for the audience to pin down.[21]

Telephone bidding could be a form of chandelier bidding, and it behooves all librarians and others at auction to bid sanely, keeping within the budgets they have set for each lot.

> **SEVERAL YEARS AGO,** from the East Coast, I bid on a number of lots at a California auction. I got several of them, and every one was at my very top bid. There was no way for me to know, for instance, whether there was really an under-bidder for every lot I got at my top bid. That is, if I sent in a bid for $500, but the bidding in the auction house stopped at $150, the auction house may have charged me the $500—the maximum that I was willing to go to buy the item. If I got one or two lots at my top bid, that may be legitimate; to have gotten all my bids at top bid was suspicious, but I could not prove that these prices were illegitimate. Today, auction houses may keep a record of the bidding, and the buyer may ask for that record. But even this evidence can be fabricated. This kind of practice can lead potential buyers at auctions to steer clear of them.

One possible drawback of auctions is that the catalogs do not always give precise, accurate descriptions of condition, and "condition is all" with respect to the value of a book. Further, the catalog is prepared weeks before the sale and is mailed out to prospective buyers. Between the writing of the description of the items in the catalog and the actual sale, the lots are open for inspection to anyone who can go to the auction house to see them. So the handling of the items might change the condition for the worse before the sale, and the auction house cannot change the catalog copy. When a book is purchased at auction, it is bought "as is," so it is important, if possible, for the bidder to make a final examina-

tion of each lot he wants to bid on just before the sale. This is one good reason for librarians to rely on booksellers who will be at the auction to do the bidding in person. Some auction houses keep the books on view for several days before the sale, but not the day immediately before the sale, so it may mean that the librarian or his representative must be at the sale site two days before the auction. This might be possible for dealers who live locally to the auction house, but not for those commuting for the event.

Because viewing exposes the books and manuscripts to wear, some auction houses allow potential buyers limited access and under the scrutiny of employees who watch for mishandling. These employees also are trained to observe if anything laid into a book is removed, for sometimes the insertions are worth more than the book.

As the section on book evaluation later in this chapter indicates, many booksellers buy for stock at auctions, so prices realized and listed in such volumes as *Book Auction Records* and *American Book Prices Current* (see the section "Appraisal Tools—Paper-Based Guides" later in this chapter), though actual hammer prices (excluding buyer's premiums), often reflect the items purchased by booksellers at what they themselves consider wholesale rates. So any party (not a bookseller) at an auction may outbid a dealer and still get a lot at a good price.

The behemoth of auctions today is eBay, probably the most populated auction site in history. The number of books available on this giant engine is incalculable. The variety and quality of books here varies from top to bottom, and the egalitarian nature of the site makes it a goldmine for searching and a dangerous pit for serious but not-too-well-informed buyers. Because anyone can sell on eBay, the buyer must be ready to encounter totally inexperienced sellers trying to make a quick dollar or pound or euro.

Auctions can yield great bargains or they can suck in a bidder who winds up paying far more than he should for a lot. They can be fun, frustrating, fascinating, and infuriating. Special collections librarians should be plugged into the auction world with subscriptions to the catalogs of the major auction houses. Even if the library does not participate in auctions, the catalogs are often treasure houses of information about particular volumes and about book prices, authors, historical movements, important books in history, and much more. The catalogs are worth reading as part of the rare book librarian's education. And the auctions can yield treasures that the librarian will never see the likes of again.

THE LIBRARIAN'S "EVALUATION EDUCATION"

Earlier I recommended that the librarian should trust the bookseller with respect to the price she puts on the things she is selling. However, sometimes booksellers, for whatever reason, come up with prices that are unjustifiably high. Trained, experienced rare book librarians will know values also. It is part of their job. And they should be able to tell if the price is high from the moment they see what the dealer is asking or after a check of the key reference tools (see later in this chapter). The longer the librarian is in the field of rare books, the more he should know about book prices, particularly in the fields in which his library collects. In chapter 2, I said that one of the first things a rare book librarian should do when he is new in his position is to get to know the collection under his aegis. This, of course, means getting to know what is on the shelves, what collections are strong and which are not, who the key authors are, what subject areas the collection contains, and on and on, with respect to the actual library holdings. It also implies that getting to know the collection means learning the values of the things on the shelves and getting a handle on what other items that might be brought into the collection might cost.

If your library collects architecture books and you are not familiar with that field, you should start looking at books and manuscripts and photographs in the area so that when a dealer offers you an unusual item, you can say, "This is fairly priced" (or not). Such an education comes from many sources.

When a library is known for its collections in certain subject fields, it is likely that the librarian will get quotes from dealers who know of these collections. (How dealers get to know what your collection holds will be revealed in chapter 11, "Outreach.") The dealers' quotes will contain prices. It is impossible to memorize specific prices for thousands

---

THE AMATEURISHNESS OF book selling "at auction" on eBay is exemplified by an offer of Dard Hunter's *The Literature of Papermaking, 1390–1800* published by Last Word Press. The eBay entry says, "Originally published in New York in the 1920s by Burt Franklin." Clearly the seller does not know that Burt Franklin is a reprint house and that the original was published by Dard Hunter himself (Chillicothe, OH: Mountain House Press, 1925). A massive amount of misinformation exists on the Web, and it is nowhere better exhibited than in the eBay offerings of uninformed, amateur booksellers. Here, for instance, is the description of another eBay offering (James Allen's *As a Man Thinketh*):

> James Allen's classic bestseller. As you read the words of this book you will without doubt understand the reason why its contents have stood the test of time and been the foundation of countless other works buy [sic] some the greatest authors of the last 100 years. Picture is of actual book [no punctuation] This book does have wear, tanning of pages and discoloration on the cover. But it is a very clean readable book!!!! Has all of its pages. Writing in pencil on the inside of cover, looks to be motivational words (looks to be almost all erased). Writting [sic] in pencil also on the next page takes up about half the page. Will leave it up to the buyer to remove if they wish. Name written in pen on the inside reads marjie [sic] Millar about inch and a half long. Other wise [sic] Book [sic] is in Wonderful condition for the age!! Thank You!

Would you buy a book from someone with this level of expression? Incidentally, the purveyor names the publisher (Grosset & Dunlap) but neglects to give a date. And the starting bid is $199.99. In April 2012, a copy of this book published by Grosset & Dunlap (dated 1941) was offered on AbeBooks for $3.97, with free postage.

---

of items. But the librarian will begin to get a sense of ranges of values for various kinds of books and might be able to remember the values for specific titles. Similarly, booksellers' catalogs are compendia of prices, often with pictures showing what particular titles look like. The more the special collections librarian peruses these catalogs, the more she will see what titles are available and what they are selling for. And "peruse" is the right word: the librarian should spend much time with catalogs that offer many books in the fields of her library's level 4 and 5 holdings. Reading the entries carefully, looking at the pictures if there are any, remembering certain subareas of collecting that might be germane to the collection, learning the authors whose names continue to recur, and *looking at the prices* are strategies for learning the values of the books the librarian will want to acquire.

Another strategy for learning book prices is to visit the bookstores that specialize in the kind of things the library collects. This exposes librarians to the appropriate booksellers (those who are possibly destined to be their friends), and it exposes them to the books and manuscripts that they need to know about. Browsing the shelves is crucial.

> **I BROWSE THE** shelves in dozens of bookstores each year. I will pick off the shelf books I already own, ones that I am thoroughly familiar with, and often I will do so only to check the dealer's price. It may look odd to see a customer pull a volume off the shelf, open it slightly to the front endpaper, then return it to the shelf without looking further into the book. But this is what many experienced bookmen do. "I own a copy of this book. I am curious to know how this bookseller has priced his copy." It is like a game: Guess the price. In the areas of collecting that I am most familiar with, I often do just this: I take down a book and think, "$25." This comes not from wanting to know what the book is worth, but from *knowing* its value and wanting to know if the dealer knows as well as I do. I can judge the quality of the bookseller's knowledge about the areas of books he is selling by seeing how well he knows the prices he has on certain books.

There is hardly a better education on current book values than that available at a book fair. But before this topic is expatiated on, there must be a diversion into the antiquarian book trade.

The Antiquarian Book Trade

Much about the antiquarian book trade has already been revealed in these pages. But more needs to be said. At the highest level is the ABAA (The Antiquarian Booksellers' Association of America) and, in England, the ABA (the Antiquarian Booksellers' Association), composed of the so-called highest order of bookmen.[22] These organizations are governed by a board of peers, with codified documents on best practices and ethical conduct, qualifications for membership, lists of members, and so forth. There are dues to be paid, and some booksellers who refuse to become members think that they would get insufficient return for their dues to make it worth their while to join. But the ABAA is a highly organized, professional group with much support for its members. (The organization's website contains much information and is well worth looking at. At www.abaa.org, select "About Us.") Also, the cachet of being an ABA or an ABAA member carries a good deal of weight in the rare book world, and some of the benefits of membership are incalculable.

The organizations hold large, important, and extremely high-end book fairs a few times throughout the year, usually in prominent cities (the ABAA fairs are yearly in New York and Boston and are every other year in Los Angeles or San Francisco [alternating from the north to the south], and sometimes in Chicago; the ABA fair is held in London). As already pointed out, these are excellent venues for finding great books for the library's collections. But they are also good opportunities to chat with booksellers you are familiar with, meet others you should know (and who should know you and your collections), and to meet colleagues—all of which can redound positively on your library's holdings in various ways.

Further, to be an ABAA or an ABA dealer confers upon the bookseller a sense of authority and reliability, which goes a long way in establishing relationships between dealer and client and in opening doors to collection building for rare book libraries. Some dealers of the same caliber as those in the ABAA may have turned down membership, for any of several reasons, and the savvy librarian should get to know who these sellers are and should patronize them too. Being an ABAA member does not confer the status of deity on any of these people.

BEING AN ABAA member is a sign of long-standing expertise and honor in the profession, but every now and then an apple turns sour. One bookseller was ejected from the organization for being a breaker: one who takes beautiful, important books and breaks them up because he can make more money selling the parts than he can by selling the volumes intact. Another, a California specialist in modern fiction, was brought in to appraise a collection and wound up making an embarrassingly (and unethically) low offer for the books to a widow who did not know their worth and who was mourning the death of her collector husband. It is a serious conflict of interest and breach of ethics to be paid to appraise a collection and then buy items from that collection. This dealer took thousands of valuable books from the widow and gave her a pittance. On top of that, the whole collection had been willed to a university, and when the dealer finished his depredations, the university got fewer than 20 percent of the books it was supposed to get. The dealer was (and still is) an ABAA member. There are scoundrels everywhere. Word gets around in professions. Rare book librarians should be in on the "gossip" of their trade and should avoid doing business with these villains.

Hence, not all antiquarian books are sold through ABAA or ABA members. There is a huge trade in books beyond these bastions of propriety and highspots. Local bookseller organizations throughout the country are composed of dealers from the highest to the middle range of selling. MARIAB (the Massachusetts and Rhode Island Antiquarian Booksellers), the Booksellers Association of Southern Nevada, Portland [Oregon] Area Used Booksellers Association (PAUBA), the New Hampshire Antiquarian Booksellers Association (NHABA), the San Diego Booksellers Association (SDBA), the Vermont Antiquarian Booksellers Association (VABA), and many others

have goals similar to those of the ABAA, with rules of operation, entrance requirements, codified standards, and so forth. Not all the booksellers in these consortia strictly focus on "used and rare" books, but many of them do, and many of their members are significant suppliers of important items to local collections. It stands to reason that pickers (the term often used in the trade for local booksellers who comb through all kinds of book sources—including the holdings of other booksellers) are on the lookout locally for materials that would appeal to local collections.

Although it is a thrill to go to a great ABAA fair and see booths full of treasures, some of the best and most exciting fairs are those held by the members of the local organizations. One main reason is that the specialized materials they sell in their booths may fit perfectly into the libraries of local rare book facilities, and the prices will be generally lower than they would be at the ABAA fairs. ABAA dealers, in going to the "big" fairs, spend a great deal of money on transportation for themselves and for the books they will be exhibiting, housing, food, local transportation, booth rental (which can be quite high), rental of vitrines and shelves, compensation for the helpers who unload and reload their vehicles, postage and insurance for the treasures they ship or take to the fair, and so forth. The cost of doing the fairs for more local organizations' members is a fraction of the costs at ABAA fairs. So books, much more modest in their intrinsic value to begin with, will be affordably priced at most of the members' booths. And though most of these local organizations' members are not in the ABAA, this does not mean that they do not find treasures as well. At most of these local book fairs, the rare book librarian is likely to find hundreds, if not thousands, of truly remarkable books.

There is also the International League of Antiquarian Booksellers (ILAB), many of whose members are from the United States, and many of those U.S. members are also ABAA members. ILAB book fairs are also worth attending. And, because the organization *is* international, its fairs are all over the world. In the last two years ILAB fairs have been held in Los Angeles, London, New York, Paris, Tokyo,

Barcelona, Bologna, Amsterdam, Oslo, Toronto, Chelsea, Boston, Melbourne, Stuttgart, San Francisco, and Copenhagen. Attending these fairs, if budgets permit, exposes librarians to the best books for sale from the best booksellers all over the world and gives them a chance to learn about the local book scene in all these venues. Not all rare book librarians will be able to afford to go to all these exotic places, but the ILAB fairs occur often enough in the United States to make it possible for some of them to attend.

There would be no antiquarian book market if there were no antiquarian books—but the term *antiquarian* is used loosely in the rare book world. Strictly speaking, an antique is a hundred years old. But not all books sold by "antiquarian book dealers" are that old. They also purvey expensive books from recent years. A book produced in the last year and released to the public yesterday, in an edition of five copies, on handmade paper, and with beautiful signed etchings and a tooled leather binding might wind up in an antiquarian bookseller's catalog, two months after its publication, at a premium price. The book is not, strictly speaking, "antiquarian," but it is valuable and expensive. Several characteristics of books qualify them to be in the category of "antiquarian," which, in the wider context, means "valuable," or "rare," or "expensive," so that is what winds up in the "antiquarian book trade."

The subject matter; the hand-done, special binding; the author; special illustrations (especially engravings or hand-colored images); other elements of decoration; the book's provenance; a signature of an important person; a variant printing of a sought-after volume; a book retaining its scarce dust jacket—these are some of the things that add to the value of a piece and qualify it to be listed under the rubric of "antiquarian." Booksellers seek out such items; collectors do, too; and the two ends of this partnership work together to keep valuable books moving through the world.

From the perspective of the rare book librarian, rare and valuable items are of interest not so much for their monetary value, but more for their research value, a point made throughout this book. So dealers should (and do) seek out things for special collections libraries that add to the intellectual offerings of the department. For the library, the price is secondary to the volume's usability for scholars. But the valuable books with good research potential belong in the secure confines of a rare book department.

It must be emphasized that the age of a book usually has little to do with its value on the antiquarian market, though, of course, incunabula (books printed in the West before 1501) will always have premium values because they are constantly and eagerly sought after). But passing time does diminish the availability of books, for they get permanently removed from circulation by being put into academic libraries, they succumb to the ravages of time, or they succumb to the ravages of human beings. So the stock of "antiquarian" (that is, sought-after, valuable) books seems to be holding steady, even in the digital age. As some books become permanently unobtainable, others join the ranks of "about to be unobtainable," while still others go from "common" to "uncommon" to "scarce and desirable," and thus ready to be taken into special collections.

AS WILL BE reiterated in chapter 13, "Special Collections Departments Today," there are so many books in the world now, and so many more being produced, that special collections departments will never want for more and yet more things to add to their collections. The number of book catalogs I get in the mail each week from high-end dealers, and the number of items offered at one auction of rare books after another, along with all the quotes I get from booksellers—all prove that the rare book trade has a rosy future and that special collections departments will always have temptations floated before them. As for the alarmist predictions about the demise of the book in a digital world, I am confident that books have a secure future and that rare book departments will never have a paucity of items they could acquire.

As noted in the section on evaluating books, items in the "antiquarian book market" that are in pristine condition are eagerly sought out; but the market also has a place for ragged copies of particularly valuable, passionately fought-for volumes. A shabby copy of Poe's *Tamerlane* will probably be evaluated in six figures. Even a single leaf of the Gutenberg Bible will probably be priced in six figures as well. One of the powers that enable items to fall under the loose rubric of "antiquarian" is the old market force of supply and demand. And antiquarian books will fall on the "short supply, high demand" side of the equation. Rare book librarians intent on filling gaps in their collections, eager to add to their storehouses of research materials for their patrons, will seek out such materials in the antiquarian trade, so they must be familiar with how this trade works, with the dealers and their wares, and with the protocols of buying and selling in the rarefied rare book market.

Hence, for rare book librarians (and, really, for anyone dealing in rare books and manuscripts), two key things are at play: the availability of "just the right" materials and the ability to afford them. Special collections librarians must work in both realms, seeking out items they want for their collections and seeing to it, if possible, that their coffers are full enough to acquire the items they locate for their departments. That is why, earlier in this book, there is a chapter on fund-raising. And because many acquisitions that rare book librarians will make come from this trade, they must be almost as conversant with the trade's practices as are the dealers themselves.

One area in which an understanding of the antiquarian trade is important is in the decision making necessary in selecting a purchase, especially if the librarian thinks a bookseller's price is too high. This requires of the librarian a good grasp of evaluation. Another area of the book trade the librarian needs to know is which dealers can supply the items the library is looking for. How should the book be acquired: by direct purchase from a bookseller or at auction? If one dealer has a copy of an item the library needs, can the item be located at a more reasonable price from another dealer? The trade poses dozens of such questions. The more the librarian is inculcated into the rare book fraternity and sorority, the more of these questions she will be able to answer. The rare book world is not a mysterious realm, with secret handshakes and encoded passwords. It is a complex realm with a finite, carefully honed vocabulary, filled with eccentric and (usually) wonderful people, well-defined practices, its own etiquette, accepted procedures, an old code of behavior that most within the circle follow, and its challenges and rewards. The more the rare book librarian is enmeshed in this world, the more comfortable she will be with her dealings, the more she will learn, and the more fun she will have. And the better off will be the collection she oversees.

Appraisal and Book Evaluation

A key skill shared by the rare book librarian, the rare book dealer, and the rare book collector is the ability to figure out what a book is worth monetarily. In chapter 7, in the section "Marking Books for Security," the dual notion of monetary and research value was discussed. Here the focus is on monetary value, one of the attributes of all the objects that people collect, and an absolutely essential attribute to understand, mostly because the value of the objects in librarians' care comes into play in acquisition, deaccession, insurance assessments, the reception of gifts, and many other activities. Value is based on many criteria.

The most important reason that librarians need to know how to evaluate books is that one of their prime responsibilities is acquisition, and they are likely to be offered many older items, no longer in print, for which a current value must be assessed so that they are not paying too much for them. As already explained, evaluations of gifts may be necessary for institutional statistics. If an item from the collection is being deaccessioned, its value may determine whether it winds up in a dumpster, in the hands of a dealer, or on the auction block. A volume being shipped out to another institution for exhibition or to a conservator for treatment needs to be insured. So the librarian needs to be able to place a value on any item coming in or going out. And the figure arrived at should be the item's fair market value.

FAIR MARKET VALUE / REPLACEMENT VALUE

Although the notion of what fair market value (FMV) is should be fairly obvious, there is much latitude in the final estimate. As Wikipedia says,

> Fair market value (FMV) is an estimate of the market value of a property, based on what a knowledgeable, willing, and unpressured buyer would probably pay to a knowledgeable, willing, and unpressured seller in the market. An estimate of fair market value may be founded either on precedent or extrapolation. Fair market value differs from the intrinsic value that an individual may place on the same asset based on their own preferences and circumstances. (http://en.wikipedia.org/wiki/Fair_market_value)

The simple formula is this: If Buyer A is willing to pay $100 for an item, it is worth that much to him. But if Buyer B would not pay over $50 for the same item, it is worth *that* much to *her*. This is not a quadratical equation; it is simple business sense. Wikipedia adds,

> An estimate of Fair Market Value is usually subjective due to the circumstances of place, time, the existence of comparable precedents, and the evaluation principles of each involved person. Opinions on value are always based upon subjective interpretation of available information at the time of assessment. This is in contrast to an imposed value, in which a legal authority (law, tax regulation, court, etc.) sets an absolute value upon a product or a service.

Because the value of an item is tied to personal knowledge and experience, and to when and where the item is being appraised, the best an appraiser can do is to come up with a range of values, based on many criteria.

Also, the idea of "replacement value" is nebulous. The ostensible meaning is how much it would cost to replace a book if it is lost or irreparably damaged. But in the rare book world, many books cannot be replaced. A librarian or collector could search for decades for an item, only to find one (or not) after such a protracted search. Also, many copies' values lie in their uniqueness: a copy signed by an author or prominent owner, one in a special binding, one with a sterling provenance. These are clearly copies that cannot be replaced.

APPRAISAL CRITERIA

The two most important criteria affecting the value of a book are (1) supply and demand and (2) condition. As with all commodities and services, if the supply is short and the demand is strong, prices will rise, and vice versa. Both conditions must apply. A manuscript, which by its very nature is unique, for which there is no demand is essentially worthless. A book printed in a million copies for which there are a million and a half customers could have significant value. And in the rare book world there is a saying: "Condition is all." A book can be a rare first edition, signed by its author, with a decent dust jacket and all the points for a first issue, but if it has a defect (bumped corners, foxing, loose joints, scuffed binding, underlining, marginal notes), the condition is

---

THE *GUILD OF* Book Workers Newsletter [GBWN] reported on one famous binding:

> In their February [1996] issue, the magazine [*Art & Antiques*] noted, in their section on Market, a book priced at $55,000 being shown at the 29th California International Antiquarian Book Fair in Los Angeles. The book was *King Solomon's Mines*, London 1885, signed and inscribed by the author, H. Rider Haggard. It was a presentation copy studded with 100 diamonds, emeralds, rubies, and sapphires, each in a gold setting, in what they said was the first application of modern design to jeweled bindings. They neglected to mention the binder but Peter Verheyen wrote to inform them that Don Glaister had bound this copy. (*GBWN* 105 [April 1996]; see www.guildofbookworkers.org/resources/newsletters/gbw105gbw105 08.html.)

Whatever the original book was worth, this copy was a true collector's version.

compromised, and the value will fall. Collectors want their books in the best condition possible—as they were when they first left the publisher's hands. Librarians, too, would like books in pristine condition, but for the sake of research, and in the absence of perfect copies, it may be necessary to acquire a volume that has seen better days. A shabby copy is better than no copy at all for a researcher.

Many features of books can affect their value. Certain collecting areas are always strong: books on war, cookbooks (though these are often produced in large quantities, so few of them soar to exceptional values), books about books (printing; papermaking; collecting; fakes, forgeries, and facsimiles; calligraphy; ink; type and typography; type specimen books; bibliography; binding; and many other subtopics), children's books, pop-ups and other movables, and so on. Certain authors are highly collectible (Mark Twain, Ernest Hemingway, Joseph Conrad, Stephen King, J. K. Rowling, and dozens of others). Illustrated books can be valuable, especially if the artist is famous or if the images are in color (hand-colored illustrations usually command high prices). Books that are "firsts" can be valuable: first editions, first printing with a particular characteristic (illustrations, maps, a dust jacket), first book printed on a particular kind of paper, first book printed in _____ (any city or country), first book to mention _____ (a country, a planet or constellation, a disease, an invention, a new species, and so on).[23]

Common books that are bound by famous binders, or are in spectacular bindings, are highly collectible. So are volumes with sterling provenances: a book from Thomas Jefferson's or John F. Kennedy's library, a book that was on the *Titanic*, a book that was on a space mission, or the like. It may be difficult to prove the provenance, and librarians should be alert for books with a famous person's bookplate or coat of arms. Even papers of authentication to prove the provenance can be faked.

One particular kind of provenance can add significantly to a book's value, but it too should be looked at with great care: signed copies. In booksellers' catalogs, one is likely to see the words *signed* or *inscribed* printed in all capital letters or in italics (or, sometimes, both). This is an important feature of a book, for a signature or inscription could add significant value to it. A signature is just the author's name in his handwriting. An inscription is a message from the author to someone: "For James Smith, Thank you for buying my book." "To my good friend So-and-so, on the occasion of our mutual debauch." An enterprising bookseller might be able to identify the person to whom the book is inscribed, and if that

---

ONE POPULAR TERM in the bookseller's vocabulary is "First thus." Be wary of this one. It means that the book being described is *not* a first edition. If it were, the word *thus* would not be used. The term means that something in the makeup of the book at hand never appeared in other editions. For instance, the book could be the first of this title to have illustrations; or it could be in a special binding; or it could be the first book printed in the South during the Civil War or the first printed on a field press or on board a ship, or anything else. Whatever the feature is that has never before appeared in any other manifestation of this title, it qualifies as a "first thus" book, regardless of how unimportant and even silly the variation is. And because the phrase "First Edition" carries powerful cachet, and adds significantly to the price of most books, the dealer may enjoy using the word *first* as an enticement—and perhaps also as a justification for raising the price of the book. Sometimes, however, the "firstness" really has nothing to do with the preciousness of a title. "First thus" could refer to the fact that the book is the first one printed on really cheap, acidic paper and perfect bound.

A second term popular with booksellers that has always amused me is "First and only edition." The bookseller wants the prestige of the notion of "first" (because this generally allows her to raise the price), but the fact that this is the "only" edition may also make the item seem scarcer and more desirable, so the dealer combines the two words into an absurdity. If it is the "only" edition, then by definition it is automatically the "first."

person is important, the price could go even higher. A Woody Allen book, inscribed to Sidney Miller, would usually not be more valuable than any copy signed by Allen. But an enterprising bookseller may learn that Sidney Miller was one of the actors in Allen's movie *Everything You Always Wanted to Know about Sex*, and would then make a point of this in his description.

> **AN APOCRYPHAL STORY** about Robert Frost is part of the rare-book-world lore. Frost was notorious for signing anything put in front of him, so a great number of his books are signed. He even copied out lines from his poems or whole poems onto the flyleaves of many of his books. A bookseller, wanting to capitalize on an ordinary copy, wrote into his catalog: "This is a rare unsigned copy."

Sometimes things laid into (or tipped into) a volume make it more valuable than a copy lacking these things. A book with its original advertising piece (not originally issued with the book) will be worth more than a copy lacking the ad. A book of poems might have a flyer laid in announcing a poetry reading of that volume's author. Already mentioned (see chapter 4) is the extra-illustrated book: one that has been disbound and then rebound with blank leaves onto which all kinds of things have been pasted, usually related to the volume itself. Typical things to tip in are engravings (usually taken from other books), variant printed leaves, drawings, newspaper clippings, and the like. Some volumes are "extra-illustrated" to the tune of added volumes.[24]

One other phenomenon will add to the value of a book: In the nineteenth century the craze for collecting all manifestations of a book prompted publishers to issue titles in more than one form. There might be a regular edition issued in a cloth binding, a deluxe edition bound in leather, a super deluxe in leather with an extra set of prints in a portfolio, or with the illustrations hand colored, and so forth.[25] Sometimes the text would be printed on a larger sheet of paper and bound in a larger size. It would be called the "Large-Paper Edition," and it would have been created to appeal to collectors who want all the versions of the things they collect.

Some collectors of the works of certain authors like to have contact with the writers whose works they collect, when they can. This could lead to a correspondence that will become part of the collector's holdings. A collection with such ancillary materials could have tremendous value, especially if the author's letters contain substantive, research information. Collections rich in this kind of extra intelligence are excellent for scholars, and librarians should seek them out with the same assiduity as the collectors displayed in gathering the materials in the first place.

The things that could escalate the value of a book or manuscript are legion. It depends on the research skills and the imagination of the person doing the appraisal. Librarians and collectors should understand why booksellers price their stock the way they do. Appraisal is a key operation of the special collections staff.

> **SOME CONTEMPORARY PUBLISHERS** employ a modern equivalent of the nineteenth-century practice of issuing titles in more than one form. I once went into a large brick-and-mortar bookstore and encountered, near the entrance, a cardboard rack of Stephen King's newest novel. There were five vertical rows of copies of this paperback, each with a different color cover. That is, the cover art and text for all five versions were the same, but the background color of the paper cover differed. One was blue, one red, one green, and so forth. A true collector, a completist (see the section "Completism in Collecting" earlier in this chapter) would need to get one of each manifestation to have a complete collection. The publisher knew that this person would need to buy seven copies of the book: one in each color, a hardbound version, and a reading copy. This last would allow the collector to keep the others in mint, "unused, unopened" condition.

APPRAISAL TOOLS

Already noted is the fact that online tools exist for helping the librarian (and anyone else) to evaluate books. Before the Web, people in the book world relied on some major reference tools, some of which are still available now in digital form.[26]

Paper-Based Guides

Before computers, *American Book Prices Current* (*ABPC*) and *Book Auction Records* (*BAR*) for the United States and Great Britain, respectively, were essential tools.[27] They listed the prices of all items that sold at auction for the preceding year at the major (and some of the lesser) auction houses. The information was published in a large, fat volume once a year, and libraries had shelves of these important pricing tools. These were mentioned in chapter 2 in the discussion of books to keep in the rare book department, despite the fact that many people from the public wanted to have access to the volumes whenever the library was open. Today, these tools are published digitally. The website for *ABPC* says,

> American Book Prices Current is an annual record of books, manuscripts, autographs, maps and broadsides sold at auction. Regions covered include North America and the UK, with sales from such other countries as Switzerland, Germany, Monaco, the Netherlands, Australia and France.
>
> ABPC is not just a transcribed record of titles and prices, copied unquestioningly from the season's auction catalogues. ABPC is the standard tool used by dealers, appraisers, auction houses, scholars and tax authorities. It is, moreover, the only work in English in which each listing of printed material has been checked as to title, format, date of publication, edition, and limitation. Sales of autographs and manuscripts are reported in a separate database. For these reasons, ABPC is an essential tool for buying, selling and evaluating books, serials, autographs, manuscripts, broadsides, maps and documents, based on actual figures realized at auction.[28]

The database is available on DVD and is mailed out once a year. It is a fairly unappealingly designed database, with no frills. In fact, it does not look designed at all. But it is loaded with information, as the preceding blurb indicates.

Book Auction Records began in 1903, published in book form, and the series survived, a volume a year, until 1996. One bookseller has for sale Volume 93 (1995 [published in 1997]).[29] As with *ABPC*, the *BAR* volumes had their drawbacks. Of course, no pricing guide can be complete, and these volumes merely listed items that came up for auction, not the millions of titles that did not. So a search in *ABPC* and *BAR* might yield no mention of a volume that a librarian wanted to know the value of. Further, and a serious drawback, was that even if a librarian found the title she was looking for, there was no way to see the book that was at auction, so whether the item she was holding was the same as the one listed in the volume was impossible to determine. And even if they were the same, there was no way to compare condition, bindings, or other copy-specific features because the *ABPC* and *BAR* texts did not always give enough information to describe the copy auctioned. They even skimped on a description of condition, which, as noted, is an important part of the value of a book. Further, it was not always clear from the price realized at auction whether the price listed included the buyer's premium or not. (See "Buying at Auctions" earlier in this chapter.) The digital version explains that all prices given are hammer prices (that is, the final bid price), not showing the buyer's premium. If that premium was low or high (12 percent or 25 percent), the actual price paid was significantly different from the hammer price. So the listing in these volumes was approximate at best and quite misleading at worst. *ABPC* and *BAR*, it must be remembered, were not published as price guides, per se. They were simply notices of prices realized at auctions. But they were always one of the first things librarians, booksellers, and collectors would consult for prices. Booksellers liked to say something like, "This is a scarce book; no copies have been on the auction block in the last twenty-five years." Of course, not being offered at auction was not necessarily a mark of rarity.

Yet another consideration is that the guides did not reveal the identities of the purchasers. Many dealers replenish their stock by buying at auction. If the buyer is a dealer, the price paid is more on the wholesale than on the retail end. So prices—even those clearly known from the auction records—could be retail or wholesale, and the user of the guide will not be able to find out which they are. Additionally, the prices realized in an auction room (the hammer prices) could be grossly inflated if there were two aggressive adversaries competing for the same item. If their purses were large enough, and if price were no object, they could bid any item to a level far beyond the item's intrinsic worth.

Another price guide has been around since 1964: *Bookman's Price Index (BPI)*. It is now published digitally, though its early incarnations in book form were as eagerly consulted as were *ABPC* and *BAR*. It lists books from the United States, Canada, and the British Isles. Its website says,

> The number of titles listed in each volume is approximately 15,000; in the course of a year some 50–60,000 books are described.
>
> Volumes do not supersede previous volumes. Each volume covers catalogs from the previous 4 to 6 months.
>
> Entries Include: Title and author, edition, year published, physical description (size, binding, illustrations); detailed description of the book's condition including flaws, amount of wear, comment on scarcity; price as listed in catalog; catalog source and number.[30]

These volumes are filled with information of prices asked, as opposed to the prices actually realized at auctions. Hence there is no way to know whether the books listed in *BPI* actually sold. And the prices asked could have been so high as to discourage buyers, and the unsold volumes could be sitting on the dealers' shelves still. Further, once a volume of *BPI* is a few years old (and older), the prices listed in them lose some of their meaning. A dealer wanting to price a volume in his hands may look back through fifteen or twenty volumes or more before he finds the last one that came onto the market *in a dealer's catalog*. The twenty-year-old price may be difficult to translate into a current evaluation. And the subject matter, author, or whatever was the selling point of the book may have gone out of fashion in the intervening twenty years. Also, the description of condition is subjective: there is no way to look at the volumes listed in *BPI*, so the reader must rely on the accuracy of the person who described the book's condition. As pointed out in appendix 3 on booksellers' catalogs, there is no standard vocabulary for describing condition, so one person's "pristine" might be another's "very good"; one person's "good +" may be another's "fine −."

THERE ARE INNUMERABLE examples of unbridled bidding at auctions. An acquaintance of mine, Richard Manney, was a brilliant collector. Among the treasures in his library was Edgar Allan Poe's *Tamerlane*, a storied book known in only about a dozen copies. He bought it at a Sotheby's auction on June 7, 1988, for an astronomical price ($198,000), being forced to go much higher than the auction house's high estimate by about 100 percent. There was one other insistent bidder, and they fought it out, with Manney taking the prize. (This copy is now in the Susan Jaffe Tane Collection.)* The lesson is that the prices listed in the auction price guides are not always good indicators of the actual dollar value of a book at any given time and place.

*See Jeanne Schinto, "Poe, Dickens, George Washington, and an Olivetti Typewriter" *(Maine Antique Digest* 38.4 [April 2010], www.maineantiquedigest.com/stories/index.html?id=1826). Schinto says of the Manney volume, when he sold it at another Sotheby's auction, "On October 11, 1991, it sold again at Sotheby's, to Baltimore book dealer Stephan Loewentheil, for $143,000. It is now in the Susan Jaffe Tane collection." Also see "Nevermore: The Edgar Allan Poe Collection of Susan Jaffe Tane," an exhibition catalog from Cornell University (www.library.cornell.edu/communications/TanePoeCollection/taneintroduction.html). Manney lost almost $60,000 on the book, thanks to the fever of the auction room.

William Baker cites another important pricing guide:

Since 1988 an alternative has appeared on the market and is now available on CD-ROM. Michael Cole's *Annual Register of Book Values* (*ARBV*), published by the Clique Ltd., York, England, is divided into six subject-based volumes: *Modern First Editions, Literature, The Arts & Architecture, Early Printed Books, Science & Medicine,* and *Voyages, Travel and Exploration.* In *ARBV*, prices are given in sterling and in dollars, and there are more British book dealers cited than American ones. Descriptions are those from catalogs and, on the whole, there is far less detail given than in *BPI.* More books at the lower end of the price range are included. Cole writes: "Emphasis is placed throughout on books falling within the lower to middle range of the pricing scale (£10–£250; $20–$500) rather than restricting selections to the unusually fine or expensive. In so doing [*ARBV*] provides a realistic overview of the norm, rather than the exception, within the book trade" (p. vii). More than 94,000 entries are recorded in the eighteen volumes published in 1992, 1993, and 1994. Association copies, fine bindings, and fore-edge paintings are all separately listed. A wider range of booksellers than in *BPI* is present in *ARBV.* The individual volumes rest easily in the hand and are far less bulky than the hardly portable *BPI.* ("Price Guides," pp. 15–16)

This British guide was paralleled in the United States by a series of volumes produced from 1993 to 1999 by Edward N. Zempel and Linda A. Verkler, who, using the model of *BPI,* listed thousands of books from booksellers' catalogs. The title for their 1993 volume was *Book Prices: Used and Rare, 1993* (Peoria, IL: Spoon River Press). They quoted prices in U.S. dollars and British pounds, and they concentrated on fairly common volumes, valued between about $20 and $300. There was also a series called *Huxford's Old Book Value Guide*[31] that came out in about a dozen volumes beginning around 1989, each listing about 25,000 books, but the principle of selection was not clear nor were there too many high-end dealers listed. So for high-priced, more valuable books this guide was not greatly useful. An earlier effort was a series of volumes compiled by Mildred S. Mandeville, *The Used Book Price Guide,* starting in 1972. The so-called 5 Year Edition of that year was "compiled from many hundreds of catalogs received from United States and Canadian used book dealers between May, 1967 and May, 1972. Prices were taken from the latest catalogs."[32] About 74,000 entries were listed in this two-volume set. For the most part, these older reference tools are not too valuable to any librarian or other book buyer today. They may be looked at today only as a guide to what kinds of books were available and of interest (enough interest to list) back when they were published.

The point is that these standard, "reliable" volumes may have been relied on because that was all there was before computers, but even then, the prices they listed had to be extrapolated, re-visioned, analyzed carefully, and modified, while being compared to the specific copy being held by the person who was consulting the price guides in the first place. Most experienced book people located what they were looking for in *ABPC, BAR,* or *BPI* (the most-consulted of these guides), checked the prices listed, and then, using their own experience, judgment, intuition, and knowledge of their customers, came up with a price that seemed reasonable to them.

If the items they were trying to evaluate did not appear in any of these guides, most of them would automatically call the book "scarce," put a high price on it, and hope it sold at that price. Of course, a parallel tactic was to try to find a comparable book and see if *that* had come onto the market at some point. If so, it might be possible to use the prices for comparable items to help them price the one in hand. This, of course, was necessary for manuscript materials, because the chances were fairly slim that a particular manuscript had a published record of its sale (though that did happen sometimes—but usually with records that were old). For manuscripts, the best the dealers could do was find comparable items in the price guides.

Patricia and Allen Ahearn, of Quill & Brush Books, are experts in the prices of books by American fiction writers. They have published extensively on this topic, including their well-known volumes on book collecting and their series of author price guides.[33] They say about these lists,

> The AUTHOR PRICE GUIDES (APGs) include a facsimile of the author's signature; a brief biographical sketch; an up-to-date list of the author's first editions (American and British) with entries for limited and trade editions; number of copies printed (if available); how to identify the first edition; and estimated value. (www.qbbooks.com/author_price_guides.php)

There are 219 such guides, giving prices for books from Edward Albee to Richard Wright. These are about as authoritative as such guides get, but, again, they become dated quickly, and the prices fluctuate. That is one of the reasons the Ahearns have been doing these guides over and over through the years. And as will be clear in the discussion of digital price guides (see the following section), it takes many years of practice to know what values listed in these guides are reliable and which ones are not. The fact that these lists are compiled by experts with decades of experience gives them a patina of authority, and they are generally quite reliable. But as the price guides age, authors go in and out of currency and demand, new caches of books are found (raising the number of "treasures" available on the market and driving prices down), and a host of other things occur that can affect the prices listed in the guides. They are good starting points for evaluation, but they must be used with caution, and in conjunction with other sources of information (especially the online ones).

Digital Pricing Tools

All the guides that have survived (that is, all mentioned thus far except *BAR*) have been reincarnated in digital form. But the "new" phenomenon of online bookselling has created what has become perhaps the most used "go-to" price guide in history. Rather than heading straight to *ABPC* or *BPI*, most book people now head to one of the many bookselling venues on the Internet. For many the two most commonly used are AbeBooks (www.abebooks.com) and BookFinder (www.bookfinder.com), listing close to 200 million books (not that many titles—but that many volumes). There are also AddALL (www.addall.com), which, like the others, is an aggregating site, pulling in information from many smaller bookselling sites, Amazon (www.amazon.com), and Alibris (www.alibris.com). Amazon also owns Bibliofind, which apparently no longer exists by that name, eBay has its own Half.com (www.half.ebay.com), and Powell's Books has its own site as well (www.powells.com).

One site, AcqWeb (www.acqweb.org/pubr/rare.html), lists scores of sites for booksellers worldwide. This is a tremendously useful site for finding booksellers throughout the globe. And, of course, focused on our purposes for the present volume, the ABAA (Antiquarian Booksellers' Association of America) has a site that lists all its members, with a book search on its home page and with links to their online offerings.[34]

It must be understood that these are not, per se, pricing sites. They are bookselling sites, and the items listed in them may not be any more accurately described than are those in *BPI*. That is, these lists, coming from people from all walks of life—amateurs working out of their closets and ABAA and ILAB dealers with dozens of years of expertise—are as variable in their accuracy as are the levels of experience and knowledge of the people who are listing the books. If the librarian or collector knows the bookseller, and knows that that dealer is a reliable, experienced, knowledgeable expert, then the listing is likely to be authoritative and trustworthy. But the Web is filled with hundreds—maybe thousands—of "off brand" sellers who find books at garage sales and thrift shops and try to make some money by selling them on the Web, not knowing too much about the things they are trying to sell.

As noted in the section on appraisal, prices for a particular item could be all over the map, mostly because Bookseller A has a true first edition and knows it; Bookseller B has one and does not know it, and offers it for far under its market value; Bookseller C has a reprint edition and does not know that it is not a true first edition, and offers it for the price of a true first; Bookseller D has a remaindered copy with a black mark along the edge of the pages at the foot of the book, which he does not notice, and offers the item as a first edition; Bookseller E has a completely different edition, does not know that it is not a first edition, and asks a high price for what is worth a twentieth of what he is asking; and so forth. Trying to figure out what these unschooled booksellers have is like trying to decipher a code in the dark. Respected and known booksellers—especially those in the ABAA and many in the other regional booksellers' associations—will usually be educated enough to know what an item is worth, but even they get things wrong sometimes, putting a grossly high (or a surprisingly low) price on an item. All these prices are on view on these bookselling sites, and potential buyers must decipher with care the descriptions (often terribly inadequate and inaccurate) of the items they are considering acquiring.

So while using the bookselling sites just listed can be useful, and in some cases extremely accurate as to the value of a book, it takes experience (trial and error), a sixth sense, and lots of careful analysis of various kinds to know whether the prices asked are reliable. For some of the Tarzan books, for instance, it is important to know that some were published by McClurg, some by Grossett & Dunlap, and some by Edgar Rice Burroughs himself. Some are individual editions, some are reprints. Some published in the red cloth may have great value, while others that look alike, right down to the dust jacket, but released in a green or blue cloth, could be worth a twentieth what those in the red bindings are worth. And so forth.

That is, the librarians specializing in the collections in their own libraries must know the bibliography of their fields so that they can know how to read between the digital lines of these online bookselling sites. They must be able to distinguish among first editions, later editions, reprints, facsimiles, variant issues and states, book club versions, and so forth.

This kind of information comes from years of on-the-job training, reading copiously in the bibliographies of the trade, networking strategically with booksellers, other librarians, and expert collectors, handling thousands of books, poring over booksellers' catalogs, doing bibliographical research into subject and author texts, learning what the key reference books in the field are and how to use them, and so forth. A book like the present one cannot teach these things; but it can make you aware of the kinds of things you must do to become proficient in the rare book world.

Pricing books is no mystery. It is not like cracking a code or being a lucky guesser. It takes a good knowledge of the tools available, much skepticism with respect to "published" information, excellent networking, years of immersion in the book world, and the sixth sense that that kind of immersion imparts.

YOUR OLD BOOKS

One of the joys of working in a rare book facility is the variety of fascinating, unusual, scarce, or beautiful items that come across the collector's, librarian's, or bookseller's desk. The source for any one of these parties could be any other one of these parties. That is, a collector, librarian, or dealer might go to one of the others with a treasure he has just acquired or he wishes to sell or donate. Similarly, rare book librarians will frequently get phone calls, from people outside the bookish network, asking if the librarian can help the caller identify or appraise an item: "We found it in the attic"; "It was my great-grandfather's"; "I got it at a local auction."

Already noted in chapter 2 but worth mentioning again here is Peter Van Wingen's pamphlet *Your Old Books* (see www.rbms.info/yob.shtml). It is not strictly a collecting tool, but it will help the librarian deal with collectors (or potential donors) in evaluating the things they must think are treasures. (Why else would they contact a rare book librarian for help with appraisal?!) Evaluation *is* a part of collecting, and this pamphlet will be a good starting place for people to help them evaluate their books (and learn about the collecting world).

Weeding and Deaccessioning

We have already looked at weeding in chapters 2 and 8 (with a focus in chapter 8 on legal issues). But now it is important to discuss the whys and hows of weeding—the process of selection and disposition.[35] As the earlier chapters explained, for many reasons books (individual ones and whole categories of them) may become ripe for removal from the collection. Although the elimination of books from the library may not seem like a topic that falls under the rubric of Collecting and Handling, what is germane is the overall collection policy of the library, and under the notion of building and shaping the collection is the concomitant notion of removing things to make the collection better focused and more relevant to the library's mission and its users.

Further, space is finite, and living libraries continue to grow. They all will someday get full. Shelves will little by little fill up, so libraries will need strategies to make room for new acquisitions. If they are lucky, well endowed, supported by good fund-raisers and generous donors, and so forth, new space can sometimes be found. But one standard solution to tight shelves is weeding—one of the necessary evils of the rare book world.

Special collections librarians are usually reluctant to take things out of the collection. If an item wound up in that department, there must have been a good reason to have put it there in the first place. The rare book department, after all, is not like the public library, which acquires multiple copies of popular books to satisfy a general, lay public who want to read the latest best-sellers. When these become better-sellers, then good-sellers, then not-so-good-sellers, then deadwood on the shelves, they no longer meet the demands of the public library's patrons, and it is not a difficult decision to get rid of the duplicate copies (maybe even all copies for books that have been around for years with no use). But special collections are usually built of carefully selected titles that fit into the department's mission, one primary characteristic of which is that it is to serve scholars. The holdings of rare book libraries are usually carefully built up and sacrosanct.

However, the older the department gets, and the longer it exists in its institution, the more likely that the mission of the department will evolve, the level 5 areas may sink to a level 4 or 3 (or lower), and books once thought essential for scholars are no longer being sought out, are taking up valuable space, and are ready for consideration for removal.

RBMS, as chapter 2 showed, has created a code of ethical behavior for rare book librarians. It is now in its third edition (2003), a streamlined version of the second edition of 1992. The latter is titled *Standards for Ethical Conduct for Rare Book, Manuscript, and Special Collections Librarians, with Guidelines for Institutional Practice in Support of the Standards*, and it contains a section titled "Deaccession of Materials from the Collections."[36] That section's opening paragraph reads,

> In the deaccession of rare books and manuscripts, the special collections library must weigh carefully the interests of the public for which it holds the collections in trust, the interests of the scholarly and cultural community, and the institution's own mission. The institution must consider any legal restrictions, the necessity for possession of valid title, and the donor's intent in the broadest sense.

Naturally the department would not weed out books or other materials that are of interest to any potential patron, nor will it knowingly break any laws by deaccessioning any item. Donor Deed of Gift documents may contain such strings as, "No volume of this donated library may be disposed of by the donee for any reason," or some other such restriction. (This is why it is strongly in the library's interest to guide the donor in filling out the Deed of Gift, and why the librarian should discourage strings of any kind.)

The RBMS document then says that the removal of items must be done with the same kind of meticulous care as went into their acquisition, the public interest and needs of the library's users must be considered, and it must be done with full transparency. It adds,

> Responsibility to the needs and reputation of the library requires that, in preparing for and accomplishing any deaccession, the special collections

library must take care to define and publicly state the purpose of the deaccession and the intended use of monetary or other proceeds of the deaccession, to avoid any procedure which may detract from the library's reputation for honesty and responsible conduct, and to carry out the entire process in a way which will not detract from public perception of its responsible stewardship.

As the rest of the code of ethics emphasizes throughout, there should never be the hint of a conflict of interest, the appearance of any hasty and foolish decision making, or any activity that would reflect badly on the institution. Apart from illegal and careless weeding, the institution's reputation is at stake and should be guarded in all activities. One thing that could hurt the institution is if someone in the public hears about the deaccessioning after the deed is done. The public, who, with their taxes, are supporters of many institutions (especially state or local colleges and universities), are in effect part owners of the materials being deaccessed, and any community is likely to have outspoken, outraged citizens who think the weeding was done in secrecy and against their wishes. No institution can afford to have irritated citizens bringing suit, going to the press, and raising a stink. Transparency, with full disclosure accompanied by full explanations, is essential in deaccessioning. And RBMS cautions, "The library must not allow materials from its collections to be acquired privately by any library employee, officer, or volunteer, unless they are sold publicly and with complete disclosure of their history."

Items (or whole collections) may be sold, given away, traded to other institutions, or thrown away. The San Francisco Public Library raised a furor in about 1996 when it weeded (the less incendiary term is "de-selected") dozens of thousands of books and put them into dumpsters. What the library did was perfectly legal and even responsible since it had a mandate to weed and it carefully analyzed its collection to select appropriate books for removal from the collection. But the library did not notify the public properly (or at all), and when word got out, there was heck to pay.[37] Some communities do not permit sale of any community property. The San Francisco

Public Library experience is instructive in what was done and what was *not* done. It was not legal to sell state property, and no library wanted the thousands of books that SFPL needed to weed from its collection. The only way to do the weeding was to put the books into dumpsters. The library was acting purely legally, but the public saw it as a betrayal of their trust, and the civic outcry got the library director fired.

Little more need be said here. Deaccessioning is often necessary. It must be done with caution, careful and circumspect analysis, openness, and logic. No patron of the unit that is weeding should be hurt by it. There should never be the slightest hint of a conflict of interest in the operation. And much as most rare book librarians abhor the idea of disposing of their charges, sometimes there is no alternative.

Holdings in Different Media

This brief section is here to remind you of a question brought up in chapter 1: "What belongs in a rare book and special collections library?" A challenge for the librarian, as noted in the earlier section on completism in collecting, is to gather everything that may be of use to the library users. A look at a Civil War collection is instructive.

Naturally there are books and manuscripts (especially correspondence from soldiers) that are essential holdings for such a collection. But a glance at the catalogs of Raynor's Historical Collectible Auctions (www.hcaauctions.com) will reveal a wide world of other things that scholars could benefit from and that a special collections department focusing on the Civil War should consider adding to the holdings. In almost every one of its catalogs, Raynor's lists bullets, silk ribbons, various weapons, pieces of clothing, soldiers' tools (powder horns, match holders, bandanas, and much more), broadsides on paper and cloth and wallpaper, photographs of various kinds, hats, jewelry, prints on the back of glass plates, glasses, medical devices, decks of cards, smoking pipes and bags of tobacco, boxes, toys, mourning badges, medals, and a host of other things. The company even has an icon to click on at its website that is titled "Civil War Artifacts" (see www.hca auctions.com/catalog.aspx?category=7). Where do special collections librarians draw the line? Is anything here worth acquiring for their patrons? What kind of research are their patrons doing? What could they benefit from? Most of these items, clearly, belong in a museum rather than in a library, but the rare book department is already a repository of various oddball things. (Like the polo mallets and ox yokes mentioned in chapter 1.) And librarians may be sensitive to the needs of particular patrons as well as the potential needs of future ones. It is possible that they will want to acquire some of these things.

IN THE EXHIBITION of library treasures that I curated for the Peabody Essex Museum, a ship's diary was included, wherein the writer, in a delightful passage, mentions visiting an ostrich farm. The diary was accompanied by an ostrich egg on which was painted a picture of the diarist's ship and a note saying that the egg was a gift from Cape Town, where the egg was acquired. The institution does not have too many eggs, but this one was a natural for us to acquire because its original acquisition was recorded in the accompanying diary that we bought. It is housed with the museum objects, not in the library. But libraries not affiliated with museums may wish to acquire the diary and would then be responsible for taking care of a painted egg as well, because they came as a package. UC Riverside had a metal Buck Rogers lunch pail that came with a collection of science fiction materials. The point is that rare book departments must be ready to acquire unusual items in nontraditional forms, sometimes because they come with larger collections of more germane materials, sometimes because they add significantly to the research potential of the department.

Storage and handling will, of course, be a consideration for such nontraditional materials, as will the public relations fallout if someone who learns about such acquisitions complains that the library should be using its resources for more traditional things. So any such acquisition (by purchase or donation) must be justifiable to all constituents. Some things may be so exciting that they deserve to be announced to (or shared with) the public.

One implication of having nontraditional materials and forms in the library's collection is that the librarian must become something of an expert in housing and handling these odd pieces. That is, each thing deserves the same level of security, appropriate housing, and proper environmental storage as does every book, manuscript, and photograph in the collection. Most objects will do well in a "standard" library environment, but certain fabrics (and their colors) would not do well exposed to the light that would be fine for books. Bringing in unusual research materials may make it necessary for the librarian to consult a museum or a preservation or conservation expert on the housing and handling of these materials. But these things, if carefully chosen, can enhance a collection immeasurably and could help scholars in unpredictable ways.

Handling

In chapter 12 much will be explained about handling the collection. Here it will suffice to say in a general approach that anything the collector (e.g., the rare book department) collects must be handled in such a manner that the longevity of the item and the full access to the information the item contains should be maintained for as long as possible. As noted in the discussion about marking books for security (see chapter 7), the librarian does not wish to cover up any bit of information the researcher might need. In handling and processing special collections materials, the librarian should honor this aim. It is part of collecting, as well as part of security and preservation.

Hence, the librarian must be scrupulous about how the items in her care are processed, stored, and handled, and about maintaining the proper shelving and environment for everything in the collection. Improper handling will lead to damage, and damage often results in the loss of some kind of information from the injured item. The librarian must also consider, before an item is acquired, whether the department is an appropriate venue for handling it. If a donor has given the library a substantial collection of a famous nineteenth-century writer, with the mandate (and the funds) to acquire artifacts relating to that author, does the librarian then acquire an outfit that the writer was wearing on the occasion of a famous speech? or a death mask made from soft plaster or wax?

■ ■ ■

A massive literature exists on book collecting. For the special collections librarian—and for anyone else working in the field of rare books—a knowledge of the subjects this chapter has discussed is imperative. There is seemingly no end to the collectibles that could wind up in academic or personal collections. Hundreds of millions of books and manuscripts are now "out there," and as people die or decide to divest themselves of their holdings, their collections get recycled, through commercial or philanthropic channels. At the same time, more and more books are being produced today than ever before in history, and many of these will wind up in rare book departments. Librarians, booksellers, and collectors (serious, focused ones or casual accumulators) need to understand how this cycling and recycling of rare materials works.

This chapter raises the issues and discusses the processes, problems, and, in some cases, the solutions. But, although much will remain the same in the world of collecting, this world is also evolving, for all parties involved in it. Part of the collector's education lies in the experiences she has in all the realms discussed here. Being active accumulators immerses people into the world of collecting, the best way to learn how to do it, and what not to do.

One means of adding to collections is through contact with people outside the library—all kinds of people. This contact is accomplished through outreach, the subject of the next chapter.

NOTES

1. G. Thomas Tanselle, "The Literature of Book Collecting," in *Book Collecting: A Modern Guide*, ed. by Jean Peters (New York and London: R. R. Bowker, 1977), pp. 209–71; this statement is on p. 209. Tanselle has also written a thorough examination on collecting itself, not with a focus on books. It is a thoughtful and penetrating article. See "A Rationale of Collecting," *Studies in Bibliography* 51 (1998): 1–25.

2. Tanselle, "The Literature of Book Collecting," p. 271.

3. The structure of the collection development department has already been discussed in chapters 1 and 2, but it must be repeated succinctly here under the topic of "building the collection."

4. Presumably doctoral candidates are working at the institution in an area covered by the faculty, so their requests for research materials in their areas will mesh with the needs of the faculty in those areas. These students should be encouraged to approach the library for help in acquiring the materials they need—whether those items are for the open stacks or for special collections.

5. There are also lists or actual catalogs that publishers would print up and bind into copies of their publications. It cost them little for this kind of advertising, but they were able to present their wares only to those who bought the books that contained the catalogs or listings, and there was no guarantee that these readers would look at the lists of books available from that publisher. (See appendix 3 on booksellers' catalogs.)

6. The Between the Covers catalogs are also enhanced with cartoons and good descriptions, and the company's website is a model of attractiveness and wit. The key issue for this text is that the standard set by Congalton and Gregory—using photographs of every book, showing all defects when there are any (like the ragged edges of a dust jacket)—has made buyers more confident that they are not buying a pig in a poke, but that they are actually seeing what they are considering acquiring. The owners of Between the Covers may not have been the first to illustrate in color every book they list in their catalogs, but they have certainly popularized the practice.

7. I am sure there are librarians who have special relationships with certain dealers in which negotiations over price are acceptable. The stance presented here is my own, and I have tried to live by this rule throughout my career. On one occasion, however, my library was offered a large number of items, as individual purchases. The price was fairly high, in total and for each item. I asked the bookseller if he would give the library a special price if we took all the items he was offering. He was delighted, having expected us to take only a few, and he was glad to have all the pieces off his shelves. So the price he came up with was satisfactory to both of us.

8. In a category similar to scouts are estate liquidators who buy out "everything left" in an estate after a formal sale of its furniture and appliances. Often books wind up in the mix, but out of the sales, and the liquidators can find themselves possessing some excellent volumes or collections. They often know little about book values, and they may think grandly and offer books at vastly higher prices than the books are worth. On the other hand, when they buy in large lots, as is the case with estates, they probably have quite small amounts of money tied up in the books, and they can be guided to the proper pricing tools. A librarian who gets to know someone in the profession may benefit from this acquaintance.

9. Eric Holzenberg, "Second-Hand and Antiquarian Books on the Internet," *RBM* 2.1 (March 2001): 35–44; this statement is on p. 38 (http://rbm.acrl .org/content/2/1/35.full.pdf + html).

10. More than 99 percent of these entries did not have a date. They looked like this: "Preston, Richard. Men at Arms." Nothing more. This entry is from the bookseller Camelot Books, listed in *AB* 86.21 (Nov. 19, 1990), p. 2018, column 2.

11. This entry is from the bookseller Great Epic Books, listed in *AB* 86.21 (Nov. 19, 1990), p. 2069, column 3.

12. As Robert A. Wilson observes about large auctions— with multivolume lots: "It is simply not possible [for the cataloger] to leaf through every book looking for items inserted by collectors." See Wilson, "Buying at Auction," in *Book Collecting: A Modern Guide*, ed. by Jean Peters (New York and London, 1977), pp. 38–57; this statement is on p. 41.

13. Of course, auctions sell all kinds of goods. The focus here is, naturally, on books and manuscripts and on anything else that might wind up in a special collections department. As chapter 1 showed, this could be almost anything: a famous writer's desk or lock of hair, a pen, clothing, tools of various kinds, or anything related to the history of an institution whose papers are in the library.

14. Even if the auction catalog announces that there are no reserves, there might still be reserves, and the auction house can see to it that a volume is bought in if the bidding is too low.

15. This is the description of condition for F. Scott Fitzgerald's *All the Sad Young Men* (New York: Charles Scribner's Sons, 1926), listed in the catalog of Bonhams, Auction No. 1793, *Fine Books and Manuscripts*, p. 99, for the auction to take place April 15, 2012, lot number 5368. In the same

catalog, Alvin Jewett Johnson's *Johnson's New Illustrated (Steel Plate) Family Atlas* (New York: Johnson and Ward, 1863)—lot number 5183—gives the following description of condition: "rebacked with corners renewed, original spine laid down. Some scattered spotting and occasional light dust-soiling but overall contents clean, a few plates starting from stubs, a few chips to endpapers, hinges reinforced with cloth tape, light soiling to cloth." *Starting*, it will be remembered, means that the leaf (or the hinge of the binding) is beginning to split, but it is still attached.

16. According to John Carter and Nicolas Barker,

> The normal commission charged by booksellers for executing bids at auction is ten per cent, which may seem expensive for a well-known and bibliographically uncomplicated book of high but stable market value—one, that is, which does not involve much expert examination or much expert estimation of price. But over a series of transactions "on commission" the bookseller will probably engage a great deal more professional skill and spend a great deal more time in his customer's interest than is adequately repaid by his ten per cent. This of course is payable only on successful bids; yet for the lots on which he is outbid he will have provided equally full service—in advice as to the probable price, in collation and appraisal of the material, in attendance (often with wearisome waiting between lots) at the sale and in the highly skilled business of the actual bidding. (*ABC for Book Collectors*, 8th ed. [New Castle, DE: Oak Knoll Press; London: The British Library, 2004], p. 30)

The importance of a knowledge of auctions to the rare book librarian is attested to by the fact that the entry on this subject in the *ABC* is the longest one in this invaluable book, comprising pages 28–32.

17. Because dealers are often at auctions on behalf of their customers, it is possible that Collector A will ask the bookseller to represent him at a sale, and the dealer will have to say that he is already engaged to buy for another client the very items that Collector A wants the seller to bid on. This has happened to me more than once.

18. See Peter Watson, *Sotheby's: The Inside Story* (New York: Random House, 1997), pp. 211–14.

19. Watson, *Sotheby's: The Inside Story*, p. 215.

20. Arthur Freeman and Janet Ing Freeman, *Anatomy of an Auction: Rare Books at Ruxley Lodge, 1919* (London: The Book Collector, 1990), p. 29. Chapter 2 in this volume, "'The Ring,' Theory and Practice: A Digression" (pp. 29–57), is instructive on how

rings work, some famous rings, and why people bidding at auction (or buying from booksellers who have acquired books at auction) should be cautious. In the infamous Ruxley Lodge sale, there was not a single ring, but at least four of them, held by the booksellers who had "ringed" the original public auction.

21. See "Auction—Chandelier or rafter bidding," Wikipedia, http://en.wikipedia.org/wiki/Auction #Chandelier_or_Rafter_Bidding. In his exposé, Peter Watson speaks of the "routine deceptions of the auction process" (*Sotheby's: The Inside Story*, p. 218), including fake bids made by representatives of the auction house who pretend to be taking bids on the phone. In the auction house there will be a bank of phones, staffed by house employees. They are all seated until the bidding on a particular lot begins, at which time they stand up, each holding a paddle showing the number of the actual bidder, whom they are presumably speaking to on the phone while the bidding is going on. As the price rises, one by one the employees sit down, as the person they are speaking to drops out of the bidding. The hammer descends at the last bid (after "Going once, going twice, sold to ___"), and the last bidder is either someone in the auction house (either a customer or an auction house employee representing a bid made before the sale) or someone on the phone. But Watson documents a Sotheby's practice of having false bids made at the telephone by house employees who have no one on the line. See Watson, *Sotheby's: The Inside Story*, p. 220. He says, "[T]hree members of the Zurich staff were on the telephones to London during the sale, pretending to make bids on, . . . in all, seventy-one lots." Watson adds that when he questioned a Sotheby's employee about the practice, the employee "said that there was nothing wrong in what Sotheby's had done in this instance. We asked the company in London if it was regular practice for fake telephone bids to be employed in its auctions. It refused to comment" (pp. 220–21). Watson concludes, "It is impossible to know how often this technique is being used, or has been used in the past," but it is clear "that fake telephone bids have puffed up Sotheby's auctions" (p. 221). It is necessary to point out that the aim here is not to single out Sotheby's. Presumably with all the negative publicity it has gotten over the years, it has now cleaned up its act. Christie's was also implicated in various activities that got it censured and fined. The aim here is to point out the flaws in the auction system that should make anyone in the rare book world proceed with caution when buying at auction.

22. The ABA website explains:

> Founded in 1906 and the oldest organisation of its kind in the world, the Antiquarian Booksellers' Association is the senior trade body for dealers in antiquarian and rare books, manuscripts and allied materials in the British Isles. Its membership also extends to many of the leading booksellers overseas. Members are elected solely on the basis of proven experience, expertise and integrity. They are expected to observe the highest professional and ethical standards and to foster the mutual trust and respect that exists between the trade and the public. (www.aba.org.uk/about-the-aba)

The ABAA has an equivalent statement: "The Antiquarian Booksellers' Association of America was founded in 1949 to promote interest in rare books and foster collegial relations. We maintain the highest standards in the trade" (www.abaa.org).

23. This propensity to look for "firsts" is a great hobby of some booksellers. Sometimes they do extensive research to find out what a particular volume is the first of, and then highlight this feature prominently in their catalogs or quotes.

24. Extra-illustration is also called *Grangerizing*, "after James Granger, an eighteenth century English biographer. Granger's *Biographical History of England* (1769) included areas for readers to illustrate the pages" (see "grangerize," Wiktionary, http://en .wiktionary.org/wiki/grangerize). One copy of Washington Irving's biography of George Washington (*The Life of George Washington* [New York: G. P. Putnam, 1855–1859]), offered for sale by bookseller James Cummins, was described in the bookseller's catalog as follows:

> A lavishly extra-illustrated set of the first edition of Irving's popular biography of his namesake, expanded from 5 volumes to 10. The final volume has a manuscript memorandum of the added plates tallying 885 engravings, 333 woodcuts (some eighteenth-century), 41 maps and 8 letters (including an autograph letter from publisher George Putnam and a clipped signature from Josiah Quincy) for a total of 1267. The memorandum notes that the set was finished on November 4, 1885. (www.jamescumminsbookseller.com/ pages/books/245882/extra-illustrated-washington -irving/life-of-george-washington)

This kind of excessive extra-illustration might create a magnificent set of books, but it is often created at the expense of dozens or hundreds of other books that have been turned into cripples.

25. Note that the word *edition* is not accurately used here because all the copies would have been printed from the same setting of type and would thus be of

the same edition. These were variant versions or manifestations or presentations—not variant editions.

26. A good treatment of appraisal tools, though now a bit dated, is that by William Baker, "Price Guides: An Assessment," in *Rare Books & Manuscripts Librarianship* 11.1 (Spring 1996): 9–20. All articles from *RBML* are now available online at http://rbm .acrl.org. The Baker article is at http://rbm.acrl.org/ content/rbml/11/1/9.full.pdf+html.

27. The appraisal tools discussed in this section are called *paper-based,* but that is only because they were once originally on paper. Some of them have made the transition into the digital world.

28. See www.bookpricescurrent.com. Another paragraph from this website explains "shortcomings" of *ABPC*:

> In keeping with previous editorial policy, auction lots consisting of groupings of miscellaneous volumes are not listed, for the prices realized by such lots can give no accurate indication of the value of individual items. Similarly, listings of badly broken runs or seriously incomplete sets of printed books do not appear. Listings of books in non-Western languages realizing less than $100 have been selectively excluded, as have peripheral works such as panoramas. Items which are sold by auction houses as "a collection of plates" or which are deemed to be bound prints rather than books, are excluded from these pages. *Listings of books after 1900 frequently appear without format or binding information.* In such instances it may be assumed that these books are octavo or duodecimo and bound in cloth or boards. (italics added)

Because a great number of twentieth-century books are listed, a good portion of this database is fairly light on information. The editors themselves recognize their imperfections:

> As to effort and diligence, we try like mad to get it all correct, but as we are human beings and imperfect, we do not accept legal responsibility for the information in our databases. Having said that for the benefit of our lawyers, let us reiterate that we want to do as excellent a job as we possibly can.

29. See www.stylophile.btinternet.co.uk. This site says, "The last available volume was published in 1996 and the new team will soon be releasing details of new multimedia developments." To date, I have not been able to discover a replacement.

30. The publication also contains appendices of fore-edge paintings, along with inscribed copies and fine bindings. The older volumes are available in digital form for $625 each (as of March 2012), purchasable at the website www.gale.cengage.com/servlet/ BrowseSeriesServlet?region=9&imprint=000&title Code=BPI&edition=.

31. *Huxford's Old Book Value Guide* was published by Collector Books, part of Schroeder Publishing Company in Paducah, Kentucky. The earlier volumes were compiled by Bob or Sharon Huxford, or both, but the later ones, after 1998, had no attribution.

32. Mildred S. Mandeville, *The Used Book Price Guide* (Kenmore, WA: Price Guide Publishers, 1972), p. 7.

33. Some of Patricia and Allen Ahearn's books are *Book Collecting: A Comprehensive Guide (1989 Edition)* (New York: G. P. Putnam's Sons, 1989); *Book Collecting: A Comprehensive Guide, 1995 Edition* (New York: G. P. Putnam's Sons, 1995); *Book Collecting 2000: A Comprehensive Guide* (New York: G. P. Putnam's Sons, 2000); and *Collected Books: The Guide to Values* (New York: G. P. Putnam's Sons, 1991, and an edition in 1998). See the Ahearns' website for their series of author price guides: www.qbbooks.com/author_price_guides .php. Each guide is a listing of the works of a single author, mostly the first editions. There is also a guide for the Limited Editions Club. The Ahearns also published an article on the subject: "Pricing Scarce and Rare Books and Manuscripts," *Rare Books & Manuscripts Librarianship* 9.1 (1994): 31–38.

34. The ABAA site is at www.abaa.org. One feature of this website is its series of interviews of rare-book sellers of the ABAA. These biographical pieces are revealing and entertaining, informative, and worth the time to listen to, for they give viewers a good insight into what goes into the making of a rare-book person. These should be part of the education of people working in the antiquarian book world.

35. The Texas State Library and Archives Commission published *CREW: A Weeding Manual for Modern Libraries* (Austin: Texas State Library and Archives Commission, 2008), revised and updated by Jeanette Larson. The full text is available online at http://issuu.com/tslac-library_development/docs/ crewmethod08. It was originally written for public libraries, but it has some good information that may be useful to special collections librarians.

36. *Standards for Ethical Conduct for Rare Book, Manuscript, and Special Collections Librarians, with Guidelines for Institutional Practice in Support of the Standards,* 2nd ed. (Chicago: American Library

Association, 1993; published as a separate pamphlet in 1994). It is available online at www.ala.org/ Template.cfm?Section = speccollections&template = /ContentManagement/ContentDisplay.cfm& ContentID = 8969. I quote from the ethical standards, second edition, because all the text about deaccessioning was removed from the third edition. Presumably, the topic is so well established and accepted as a necessary evil in the rare book community that it is not even part of an ethical-standards discussion.

37. See Michael J. Ybarra, "Talk about Throwing the Book at the San Francisco Library," *Los Angeles Times*, September 3, 1966, http://articles.latimes .com/1996-09-03/news/ls-40094_1_san-francisco -public-library. This reporter quotes an angered San Francisco resident, who claims that "the library indiscriminately accelerated the pruning of its collection, rushing dump truck after dump truck of carelessly selected old books to landfill sites, especially after it became clear that design changes had reduced the new building's capacity." The selection for weeding was not "indiscriminate." And, as I said, it was perfectly legal. The library has a weeding policy, and it was prohibited from selling state property. No other libraries wanted the SFPL discards, they could not be given away to anyone, so disposing of them was the only option. In *Boston College Magazine*, Winter 2003, http://bcm.bc.edu/issues/winter_2003/letters.html, Michael Abramov writes about weeding, "This is an accepted practice, and it is taught at library and information schools throughout the United States. Books are deaccessioned because of their condition or outdated information; because there are duplicate copies in the library; or because a particular book simply does not leave the shelf and has little or no enduring value." De-selection is necessary in most libraries.

CHAPTER 11

OUTREACH

HE PRECEDING CHAPTER DEALT WITH BUILDING COLLECTIONS. The aim, of course, is to be able to offer patrons the maximum amount of research materials that the library can afford, store, and make available. But the best-built collection must be advertised so that it will draw the patrons the library serves. If the collection is hidden, no one will know about it, and no one will come to use it. With little or no use, the department cannot justify its existence. The special collections department, therefore, must reach out to all potential users and donors and to the administration.

In the past there was a view that rare book departments are exclusive clubs open only to those qualified to use them, forbidding and unfriendly places that the unwashed must stay away from. This view may have been justified for many libraries, but it was a formula for bad publicity for the department and its parent organization, and it worked counter to what most librarians believed: that they were keepers of information and that their mission was to share that information with those who needed it. In the last fifteen or twenty years, most rare book departments (and the profession of special collections librarianship itself) have tried to change the perception and the actual practice. That is, they were once interpreted as units in the library that collected, cataloged, and preserved materials, and not much more than that; but they are now reaching out as units of service to their constituents. By promoting themselves as welcoming and not exclusionary, eager to help researchers and not isolated and closed off to users, the departments are fulfilling more than ever before their role as service units aiming to foster scholarship and goodwill.

One thing that created the perception of the library as a snobbish and almost hostile place is that special collections departments have closed stacks. For patrons who are accustomed to working in an open-stack environment, where they can browse and handle any volume they wish to examine, a closed-stack unit implies, "You are not trustworthy to have direct access to our treasures"; "We do not trust you to know what to do with our materials or how to handle them." Despite the superior access to collection information that we now have with online systems (which allow virtual browsing), the lack of direct access to books and manuscripts is still off-putting for many patrons. Another thing that made people think they were not wanted in rare book departments was the attitude of many of the librarians who oversaw these departments. Some rare book librarians do take the stance that the department contains "better" books than are in the rest of the library and that it draws "better" clients—that it should allow in only those who qualify for entrance into this elevated realm.

SNOBBISHNESS ON THE part of special collections librarians is not just a stereotype. I have experienced this attitude—almost an arrogance—in more than one special collections department. Early in my career I visited one such department and was made to feel unwelcome because I did not have a "reputation" in the scholarly world at the time. I felt that I was being allowed to use the materials I needed almost against the better judgment of the librarian. This was definitely promoting the wrong image for the department, and, though it is not common today, I am sure it still exists. The special collections librarians I know now are friendly, welcoming, and professionally oriented to helping their users. This is as it should be. The negative impression about rare book departments that I have heard people speak of has come from faculty, staff, and—especially—students, and also from visiting scholars.

The transition from "closed" to "open," from exclusive to welcoming, is an ongoing process, and it takes librarians good at outreach to accomplish. An overriding tenet of this book, reiterated from one chapter to another, is that the special collections librarian has a mandate to share the department's materials with anyone who needs them. Outreach is a tool for this sharing. It may seem reductionist to say that more outreach yields more use, more use yields better statistics to justify the department's

existence, and better statistics yield greater support from above. But for the most part, libraries do work this way—especially when the resources are available to shift support to rare books.

Further, good outreach is a way of advertising the department to the world, which could bring donations of books or money, or both, to the library and other kinds of support to the institution. As Dan Traister says,

> promotion involves imperatives other than publicizing new acquisitions, attracting new donations, and giving an attractive airing now and again to old holdings through exhibitions. Readers must feel invited and welcome to, and comfortable in, the rare book department.[1]

And "readers" means all kinds of users: faculty, graduate and undergraduate students, administrators, outside scholars, genealogists and others from the public looking for old photographs or records of their local homes, school groups from primary school on up, private parties wanting information about books they found in their basements or maps from their attics, and anyone else who might need help. A strong effort has been under way for the last, say, twenty years in most special collections to open rare book departments to all.

Outreach now means creating an environment completely congenial to patrons, anticipating their needs, and letting them know, before they get to the library, that they are welcome and can avail themselves of the amenities the department has supplied for them. Traister says,

> Retrofitting reading rooms to provide outlets for laptops or a wireless environment; functional workstations as well as reading facilities; scanning as well as reprographic facilities; speedy turnaround for all forms of copying; onsite meeting and classroom space; provision of materials and technology for instructional and student use in those non-reading room spaces—including rare books and manuscripts as well as online capabilities; quiet and pleasant surroundings: these are no longer "amenities" but necessities of doing business in a customer service-oriented environment.

And he adds,

> Rare book librarians must also perform services such as ordering materials—again, including rare books and manuscripts where they are available and affordable—for the use of specific classes and readers, a species of tailored reader services applied to a part of the library where such service has rarely been traditional.

Special collections departments may be asked to acquire for faculty or even students particular volumes, possibly more efficiently than can be done through the regular collection development process, and to keep them in the department for classes to use.

Exhibitions and Department Tours

Outreach can take many forms. One obvious form is exhibitions. These usually are a themed display of some of the department's holdings. Most special collections departments have display cases, inside the department or out. Those inside can show some of the more valuable items from the collection; those outside will exhibit less valuable pieces. It is important that the librarian check the cases for their security and environment. (More about this in chapter 12 on preservation and conservation.)

To reach as wide an audience as possible, the exhibits should be attractive, with visually striking items on show, and with captions that explain why each piece was chosen for display. In museums this is down to a science, with competing theories of what kinds of things should be shown and how much information the labels should have. Also, the labels should be large enough to be read easily and positioned such that patrons do not have to stand at a particular angle or bend awkwardly to read them. And the exhibits should be advertised in some way to let the public (as well as all others in the immediate institution) know of their existence. A good press release, an article in the school and local newspapers, an interview for the campus or local radio or TV station, flyers placed prominently in local libraries, Tweets or e-mails or blogs or Facebook notices,

or any other kind of outreach is desirable. The rare book librarian may wish to announce personally guided tours for interested groups, if time allows. If possible, the attendance for the exhibit should be monitored. This is easy to do if the cases are in the department, in sight of a reception desk or reference librarian who is positioned regularly in sight of the vitrines. The more viewers the better.

For this reason, no exhibit should be up for too long—perhaps three to four months at the most. The more shows there are, the more visits the library will get, especially if these displays create a buzz. These shows do not have to take a great deal of the librarians' time, though elaborate displays may do just that. In a museum, more likely than not, there will be a full chain of command through which such displays must go for approval. In academic libraries, the head of the special collections department should be able to do the decision making about the topic and the individual inclusions for the display, with the help of one or two staff who are appointed for just this task. That is, if staff and resources allow, the department should have two or three people charged with working on exhibits. The time and resources expended are well worth the investment if the buzz about these shows brings in visitors and good comments that go to the administration. (Hence, it may be useful to have a Comments Book on hand at the exhibit, asking viewers to write about their reactions to the shows.)

A concomitant element of outreach with exhibitions is a catalog or, at least, a checklist of the display. These do not need to be elaborate, but with the cost of printing considerably less than it was before computers, a catalog does not have to be an expensive or time-consuming project. In the digital world, we can design our labels for the cases and then arrange the information on these labels into a page layout.

The computer has simplified the production of exhibit publicity materials tremendously, and now it is possible to create checklists and catalogs with ease. Because captions for the items in the show must be written, and because many of these are long and explanatory, and because the show needs an

MODERN TECHNOLOGY IS certainly helpful for producing outreach materials, but even without the use of a computer—with only a two-color Xerox machine—twenty years ago I was able to produce a decent-looking catalog printed on attractive paper, with illustrations, for next to no cost. By literally cutting and pasting illustrations, by writing good, thorough captions for the items on display, and by pulling them all together with an introduction and some notes at each new section of the listing of everything in the exhibit, I was able to create an informative and attractive catalog for the show.

introduction and introductions to each section of the display, these have to be produced anyway just to get the exhibit into the vitrines. It is trivial to bring them together with the computer to create a checklist or brochure or a fully conceived catalog. Libraries in museums, however, probably will not be given the go-ahead for such publications because the museum is really in the business of creating full-volume catalogs for their museum shows, and it is unlikely that they would approve of anything less than splendidly produced catalogs. The museum, after all, has a brand to maintain, and an inexpensive checklist for an exhibition of its library holdings would not be up to par for the brand.

The importance of exhibitions is underscored by the fact that RBMS encourages them by giving awards for exhibition catalogs.

> The awards, funded by an endowment established by Katharine Kyes Leab and Daniel J. Leab, editors of "American Book Prices Current," recognize outstanding exhibition catalogs issued by American or Canadian institutions in conjunction with library exhibitions, as well as electronic exhibition catalogs of outstanding merit issued within the digital/web environment.[2]

Five awards are given, for expensive, moderately priced, and inexpensive catalogs, brochures, and digital presentations. Even merely submitting a catalog, whether it is a winner or not, is a kind of outreach, because each year a list is published of all the submissions, and they are all shown at the RBMS Pre-

conference (before the ALA Annual Conference) and then again at the ALA Annual Conference each year.

The central purpose of the exhibitions can be purely educational, as Lucy S. Caswell says:

> The traditional reasons for exhibits in college and university libraries are often taken for granted. . . . Within the academic library certainly education should be the primary aim. Exhibits may be related directly to classroom projects . . . or to continuing education programs. . . . [E]xhibit planners should always be able to relate their show to the academic enterprise.[3]

Of course, "increasing circulation by calling attention to exhibited materials has long been accepted as an appropriate rationale for exhibition."[4] "Increasing circulation," for rare books, means bringing more and more people into special collections. Keeping up the number of visitors to the department is desirable, for the more patrons who come in, the more the department can justify its existence, and the more resources it can request.

One of the by-products of these exhibits is the ability of the rare book department to "show off"—that is, to reveal to visitors what the department's holdings are. Another offshoot is internal: the efforts to produce a good show teach the librarians about their own collections and get them closer to becoming subject specialists in the areas of the display than they were before. A third benefit could be, as noted, the production of a catalog, which, if properly done, can be a significant (or even a modest, but worthwhile) contribution to scholarship. Exhibitions are ways to disseminate information, so they are, as well, a means for the librarians to fulfill their mandates.

If the exhibition is not merely a display of some of the department's holdings, but is truly a contribution to scholarship—as a good exhibit should strive to be—its curator may wish to go beyond the library to acquire items from other institutions. This is obliquely a form of outreach, notifying other institutions of the public events of your library. Whether the request to borrow is honored or not, other librarians will learn of your activities and collections.

"Reaching out" can be accomplished by "bringing in." Giving department tours allows the librarians to show off the collection's treasures, expose the department's resources and services to visitors, and generate goodwill. The tours should be for all: K–12 students, undergraduate and graduate courses, local groups of all kinds (religious, civic, social, philanthropic, and so forth), administrators wanting to show off the institution and its treasures, scholars from inside and outside the institution, potential donors, friends groups, book-collecting groups, and anyone else who could profit from the experience. This is part of the open-door policy I have spoken of.

Naturally the "tour" cannot be a full exposure to the department's facility. Security is important, and one element of security is not revealing to those outside the department where all the treasures are. A tour is more a reception at which the librarian welcomes guests; shows them the department's public spaces; discusses the collection's history, holdings, strengths, treasures, research offerings, and connections with its clientele; and perhaps has a show-and-tell segment displaying some of the collection's highlights.

As I just mentioned, anyone, from kindergarten on up, should be allowed in and given a tour. It is good to expose children to the materials, possibly impressing on them the importance of first-hand knowledge and use of primary materials. Try to shape the tour to the audience, of course. The youngsters who see the materials in my department are fully engaged when I show them the ship's diary that mentions a trip to a South Africa ostrich farm, and I display the painted ostrich egg acquired on that trip. They are riveted when I show them the Civil War vest Bible with a bullet in it; the Bible, carried in the soldier's vest pocket, saved his life. And they are also agog when I show them the Bible sent by the president to the soldier to replace the one with the bullet in it—the replacement signed by Abraham Lincoln. These students could be your scholars or donors of the future.

This kind of outreach should include the highest levels of the administration. Offering the chancellor or president a tour keeps the department in her ken. And you can tell her if she wants to impress dignitaries or donors, she can bring them to the department. With only a short lead time you can pull out treasures for the visitors. Department tours can serve many functions.

Publications

Though the main kind of publication a department can do is an exhibition catalog, other kinds are possible. Today, publications can be analog or digital, and special collections librarians may wish to do them both for a single text. For instance, the department may produce small pamphlets, each highlighting a single collection. These can be handed to anyone who arrives at the library to do work in particular collections. The pamphlet for one collection will be handed to the patron, and it can also be mailed out—one form of outreach. But nowadays, the text can also be put onto the department's website for the benefit of distant researchers.

PUBLICATIONS NEED NOT be limited to exhibition catalogs. The National Archives in Kew Gardens, London, has hundreds of pamphlets about the archives, most of them bi- or trifold sheets highlighting individual collections. Available on racks throughout the reading rooms, they are wonderful guides to this massive archive.

Naturally, the department will "publish" other kinds of documents, like the information sheets that are given to patrons: statements of department policies and procedures, price lists for chargeable services, statements about copyright and the patrons' responsibilities, and so forth. If a scholar writes in advance about coming to visit to do research, it is useful to send her a packet of these publications, partly to prepare her for her work at the department, and partly to show how responsible and thorough the department is in dealing with its users. This kind of outreach stamps the department as being run in a professional manner. Sending such paper-based materials has a different impact from telling the patron, "Look for our policy statements on the Web." There is nothing wrong with that tactic, but the paper documents are impressive and definitive in their corporeality. Either way, the information is published and is a form of outreach.

Some special collections departments publish a newsletter or fact sheet detailing what the unit is up to: new acquisitions, progress in cataloging or processing, discoveries in the stacks, articles about particular collections, upcoming events or publications, honors or awards or other activities of the staff, introductions of the staff (especially new employees), and so forth. The newsletter might also be used for development purposes: a delineation of what friends group is available for readers to join, calls for assistance in conserving volumes, a list of "wants" that the readers may be able to help the library acquire, the announcement of an endowed fund for some commemorative purpose (the fund to be used for acquisitions or some other activity), or anything else that the department conjures up as a development opportunity.

Another form of outreach, generated by anything noteworthy that happens to (or in) the department, is the issuing of news releases. One way to keep people aware of the department is to announce through the press anything positive that might make the news. One aim of a good press release is to get free publicity for the body that issues the release. If the document is written well enough, it might catch the eye of an enterprising reporter and generate a phone call or a story. It might simply be an announcement of an important milestone or acquisition ("Rare Book Department Acquires 200,000th Volume," "New Department Head Named," "Special Collections Celebrates 35th Anniversary," "John Smith Library Receives Extraordinary Gift," "Spectacular Set of Books Purchased by Library"). This kind of publicity could generate various kinds of interest from the public, including gifts of like materials from people who, until they read the story that the press release generated, did not know that you collected in the area of the item written about.

Though of much lesser impact, other kinds of "publishing" include the creation of bookmarks, pencils or pens, or other kinds of handouts for patrons.

SEVERAL YEARS AGO, when I was head of special collections at UC Riverside, the Antiquarian Booksellers' Association of America (ABAA) had a major fair in the Los Angeles Convention Center. I offered the organizers of the fair a large exhibition of treasures from the J. Lloyd Eaton Collection of science fiction, fantasy, horror, and Utopian literature. They loved the idea, so when the fair opened, the department filled eighteen display cases with attractive, important, historical books and periodicals. About two weeks before the fair a press release was sent out notifying the public that the science fiction books would be on display. This generated a couple of brief newspaper stories and reports on TV. A few hours before the materials were about to leave the library for the Convention Center, I phoned several area newspapers and TV stations that some of the great science fiction treasures of all times were being delivered to the loading dock at the building at such and such a time. I hired a Brinks truck for the delivery. When the truck pulled up to the dock, reporters were there. I had a box of especially attractive volumes ready at the door of the truck, and when the photographers and reporters gathered at the back of the truck, I pulled out a beautiful Jules Verne first edition with a lovely gold-stamped red cover. The photographers posed us with me standing at the truck holding the bright red book, with the name Brinks showing on the truck, and with a Brinks guard, his gun prominently in the picture, standing beside me. This photograph made it to several newspapers that evening and the next morning, along with statements about the wonderful exhibition and the fact that Ray Bradbury was scheduled to be there to sign posters that we had printed up announcing the existence of the Eaton Collection. The picture, the story, and the sensation brought out hordes of science fiction fans. The publicity that UC Riverside generated with the exhibition of science fiction books brought in one gift after another from people who did not know until the exhibition was announced in the press that the school collected in that area. The whole idea of outreach is to make the public and others aware of the department and its holdings. This event had extraordinary, long-term benefits.

Anything that lets the public know about the library is a form of outreach. They can be generic products with the department's name on them or with more information (phone numbers, e-mail addresses, hours of operation, statements of particular holdings), or they can be for specific events or commemorations that the department celebrates. Handouts are a fairly inexpensive form of advertising.

Faculty Engagement

One excellent way to do outreach is to engage the faculty, either in helping with the exhibitions or in bringing their classes into the department for lectures or seminars where they can feature original materials. In helping with exhibits, the faculty bring in their own expertise and make the displays more authoritative than most librarians can make them. To have a professorial expert working on the selection and commentary for the exhibit lends an air of authority, and it actually reduces the librarian's work in that he does not have to do extensive research to make the show educational; the faculty member brings that proficiency to the project.

Having the faculty bring their students into the rare book department—even bringing in undergraduates—reinforces to those students the importance and value of original and rare materials and eventually makes them better scholars than they would be without such an understanding. The experience is also building up a clientele for the future. For this reason, it may be advantageous, also, to solicit such visits from high school classes.

Faculty are always looking for materials they can use for their own research. But not all of them know what the rare book department holds. Letting them know what your department has in their fields, with a phone call or e-mail message, might prompt (or tempt) them to go to the department. It could also affect their teaching in that they may assign to their students projects that require the use of the department's original materials. The essays the students write could be guides for the faculty.

Engaging the faculty often runs hand in hand with engaging the students. The librarian should offer

NO ONE CAN predict what effect a visit to a special collections library might have on young people. Recently, I mounted an exhibition at the Peabody Essex Museum showing some of the treasures of the library. I have given several tours to potential donors, to friends groups, and to parties "off the street," as part of a goodwill effort to bring in new museum members. By far the most enthusiastic, inquisitive, and excited group I gave a tour to was a class of junior high students and their teacher. The one-hour visit turned into nearly two hours, and it could have gone on longer, owing to the questions and comments of the students. They were more than inquisitive, they were animatedly engaged with the items in the vitrines, and they asked about a host of things that the adults who had seen the exhibit had not questioned. Bringing students to the library may engender in some of them a long-standing appreciation for books; bringing them to special collections may inculcate in them an understanding that there is much more to the library than just the books they can browse on the shelves. Through their wonder and awe, they may someday remember that, when they have research to do, there is a special place in the library for them to do it.

professors sessions in the department reading room where the students can be exposed to original materials. They may see the power that these things have. Make it clear that, for the most part, original materials have not yet been digitized and are not available anywhere other than in the department. And even items that have been scanned and are available on the Web might not have "all the information" presented in digital form. Seeing and handling the originals is a much more visceral experience than is seeing a picture of the original. The students could be the scholars of the future—or the donors of the future. This kind of outreach could have long-term benefits of various kinds.

Another by-product of faculty engagement, beyond educating the professors on what the department holds, is that they can become unofficial bibliographers and selectors for the department. It is important to let the faculty know that if they spot an item that would be ideal for the library to own (espe-

> **IN MY LIBRARY** at the museum, I have a good working relationship with all the curators, and they all know that if they see an item that would enhance their scholarship on the exhibitions they are working on, they can contact me and I will try to acquire whatever they want and need. Recently, however, one curator asked me to get an item at an auction, the estimated selling price of which was $1,000,000–$1,250,000. Sadly I had to tell him it was just beyond my budget.

cially for the rare book department), they should contact the department quickly to see if the library needs and can afford to acquire it. They should be instructed about how to distinguish the rare from the common item; for the former they should contact special collections; for the latter they should notify Collection Development.

One way of encouraging the faculty (or curators) to contact you is to contact them when items they might be interested in come along. A phone call or e-mail message telling them of a rare piece they may be able to use in their research lets them know that the department is there to serve them and that they should be as vigilant in their areas as the librarian is.

Equally important is the outreach the librarian does for the leaders of the institution. As I mentioned earlier, it is not enough merely to be responsive to administrators' needs; these needs should be anticipated. Those in special collections should have a finger on the pulse of the institution and should always be alert to ways the library can serve everyone in the hierarchy—especially those above the library. It helps the leaders to lead, it engenders goodwill, and it shows that the librarian understands the importance of the teamwork that makes the organization effective and successful.

Outreach to Students

Already noted is the engagement of the students through the faculty. But it is possible for the department to reach out to students directly. With an ability to send messages to every student, special collections personnel can notify all students that research materials are available for their use in the rare book department and that reference services are offered there, too. At some institutions the emphasis may be on faculty, external scholars, and graduate students working toward advanced degrees, but there are great benefits to reaching out to all students, including undergraduates, and even to high school classes from local schools.

Because the rare book department holds books of a special nature, it is generally able to support extensive instruction in courses on the history of the book, medieval codicology (if the department has volumes of—or even leaves from—medieval manuscripts), the history of art, and many other subject specialties. Certainly the department will have collections directly related to the disciplines covered by the faculty in their classes; so the librarian can engage the faculty to require that students do research from primary materials for their term papers. This kind of outreach guarantees that students will use the department—to the benefit of all involved.

A number of writers have commented that it is important to bring students into the special collections department.[5]

Digital Outreach

In doing research, modern scholars will turn first to the Web before entering a library.[6] And with sophisticated search engines and online databases by the thousands available to them, this is a logical avenue of operation. With respect to outreach, the rare book library should try to get as prominent a position as it can on the institution's home page. Many university home pages have a direct link to the library—a single click or two and the researcher is into the institution's collection.

In this sense—the positioning of the library icon on the institution's home page—outreach simply means easy accessibility to researchers. If the library is not easy to locate, the possible interpretation is that the institution does not value it enough to make it prominent. Rare book librarians cannot expect that their departments will be front and center, but the

IN A RANDOM search of university home pages, I found the following: The University of Wisconsin, Madison, and Vassar College have home-page links to "Research"; the cursor placed on it opens a drop-down menu with "Libraries." UC San Diego has a link to "Libraries" on the home page, as do Grinnell College, Tufts University, Mills College (though hard to find, requiring a scroll down), University of Washington, University of Idaho (scroll down), Macalester College (scroll down), University of North Dakota (scroll down), Carlton College, Cooper Union, Stanford University, University of Oklahoma, and many others. Some schools require some extra clicking, like Reed College, Louisiana State University, University of Florida (Gainesville), Texas Christian University, Middlebury College, and others. Brigham Young University's home page requires the searcher to go to Lee Library, at which there is a tab for Special Collections. This is an improvement over their old system, where clicking on "Library" yielded "Server Not Found." But the special collections page is poorly designed and does not entice a reader in at all. DePauw University takes you from the home page to "Site Map." Look over this large, dense page, scroll down, and you will see under "Academic Resources" a bullet for "Libraries." Some of these are quite user-unfriendly forms of outreach. It is clear from the prominence of other activities on campus that athletics trumps libraries in almost every instance.

parent library should be, and the special collections should be easily accessed from the library's page. This might require some lobbying, for many administrators see the nuisance factor of having to rethink and redo the website, but in fact this should be an easy fix that the rare book librarian should press for (without being too obnoxious in the process).

Outreach through Social Networking

With younger generations (and even older ones) fully embracing social networking, the special collections department must embrace this technology if it wants

its presence known to as wide an audience as possible. Kate Duttro, on the website Job-hunt.org, says,

Unsurprisingly, the use of social media has doubled since 2007, but I am surprised that Nielsen Online shows older population segments increasing fastest. For example, FaceBook began with 18-to-34-year-old university students, but by now, nearly a third of users are 35–49 and a quarter are 50 or older. LinkedIn gains about two million users every two weeks.[7]

The site adds, "If we consider the number of Internet users accessing 'member communities' (think Twitter, FaceBook and LinkedIn) as a measure of social networking, then its use exceeded use of e-mail (66.8% vs. 65.1%) in 2008. Internationally, the demographics of social networking is twice as large as in the US, and it continues to grow faster than here." And she points out that "academics who refuse to use social media are effectively barricading themselves in the ivory tower."

The numbers relating to social networking are staggering. Jeff Bullas, on his site Jeffbullas.com, lists "20 Stunning Social Media Statistics,"[8] including such statistics as these:

1. One in every nine people on Earth is on Facebook (This number is calculated by dividing the planet's 6.94 billion people by Facebook's 750 million users)
2. People spend 700 billion minutes per month on Facebook
3. Each Facebook user spends on average 15 hours and 33 minutes a month on the site
4. More than 250 million people access Facebook through their mobile devices
5. More than 2.5 million websites have integrated with Facebook
6. 30 billion pieces of content are shared on Facebook each month
7. 300,000 users helped translate Facebook into 70 languages
8. People on Facebook install 20 million "Apps" every day
9. YouTube has 490 million unique users who visit every month (as of February 2011)

10. YouTube generates 92 billion page views per month (These YouTube stats don't include videos viewed on phones and embedded in websites)

11. Users on YouTube spend a total of 2.9 billion hours per month (326,294 years)

. . .

16. 190 million average Tweets per day occur on Twitter (May 2011)

17. Twitter is handling 1.6 billion queries per day

These statistics were compiled in 2011; these numbers have gone up appreciably since.

Anecdotally, those socially networking are doing so more than they use their phones. That is, people are more likely to send a text message than they are to call someone. As early as April 20, 2010,

> [f]or teenagers, texting on mobile phones has dethroned actual voice calls when it comes to connecting with their friends, according to a new report released today by the Pew Research Center.
>
> The report also shows that when teenagers do bother with an old-school phone call, it's more often to contact their parents than their peers. This trend reflects a digital divide between generations of mobile phone users but also some psychological strategizing on the part of teens.[9]

There is no doubt that the greatest information dissemination media in history are in play right now, and libraries must use them if they want to connect with the widest audience they can reach.

In chapter 1, I warned that rare book departments should not position themselves as exclusive, above the "rabble," separate and better. This is the "ivory tower" that Duttro speaks of. It is essential that all departments in the library—especially special collections—reach out to the widest constituency possible, and with the growth of social media sites like LinkedIn, Twitter, and Facebook, such outreach is easy. As with the advice given earlier on using press releases to get information out to the world, the use of social media to spread the word about the rare book department allows for a viral spread of infor-

mation. Departments should use these media sites, create blogs, and be creative in the use of digital means to broadcast information about department holdings, acquisitions, happenings (lectures, exhibitions, availability of tours), hours, location, means of getting to the library, staff, and anything else to create a buzz about the department. The department should encourage users to blog to others about the (presumably good) experiences they had working in the collection and the treasures they found there. The library should encourage dialogue and commentary, testimonials and narratives about users' impressions and praise. Considering the way information spreads today (and the word *viral* is appropriate), librarians must embrace social media perhaps more than they employ any other kind of outreach.

Public Programs

Already mentioned, but worth commenting further on, is the use of public programs. The rare book librarian should always be on the lookout for opportunities to bring in speakers, to engage the public with programs of interest to the community (the general populace or the scholarly "public"). This tactic shows the department to be a center of intellectual ferment, willing to reach out to various constituencies, to reveal its holdings as part of an active program encouraging use, and to engage audiences onsite to discuss issues of importance with them.

The programs can be unpretentious lectures open to the public, scholarly symposia, workshops on various skills (book appraisal, book collecting, simple conservation techniques for collectors, cataloging rare books, or making decorative papers), or talks by authors, for example. They can be major conferences with speakers from across the nation and beyond. They can be focused on a niche audience (a gathering of scholars who study a single author or a narrow topic).

Public outreach in the form of programs—whether to the public or to targeted audiences of scholars or collectors in particular fields—is a crucial means of raising awareness and use of the rare book depart-

PUBLIC PROGRAMS CAN have far-reaching and valuable effects. Two cases in point: At the University of California, Riverside, after Stephen Blumberg's arrest and while the stolen books were being cataloged for their return to their victim libraries, I hosted a symposium on library theft. Speakers included William Moffitt (a well-known librarian who, at Oberlin College, held a meeting on theft), Susan Allen (librarian at one of the Claremont Colleges, which lost a vast number of books to Blumberg, and who became an expert in library security), and J. Steven Huntsberry (the police officer at Washington State University who finally arrested Blumberg and recognized him as the same thief who had been hitting libraries all over the country). We had planned for about one hundred people to attend the meeting, but nearly twice that many showed up, and my department got excellent press for its responsibly addressing a crucial issue in the rare book world.

More recently, I spearheaded an Art Museum Libraries Symposium—two conferences at the Peabody Essex Museum (September 2010 and September 2012). About 165 registrants at the first and about 150 at the second heard two dozen speakers discuss data unity, access to information, archives, and so forth. The buzz from those meetings is still heard. We were able to get substantial funding for these meetings, and through evaluation forms and much follow-up activities we have learned of the efficacy of the meetings: many people have told me that the symposia guided them in the ways they operate in their libraries and they ways they interact with others. My Phillips Library and the Peabody Essex Museum in which the library resides are now looked to as hubs for intellectual activity and groundbreaking in the museum library world.

ment. It engages the staff in preparation for these events, and in such preparation they become more experienced librarians. This kind of outreach takes time and effort, but in the long run, it is worth it. But it also takes resources, and sometimes the institution cannot afford to put on such programs. There are travel expenses and honoraria for the speakers, lodgings if the speakers come from afar, food, printing and mailing costs for save-the-date cards and programs, and much more. Much of this can be done inexpensively online, but a card in the hand will likely get more attention than will an e-mail message among the hundreds that people delete daily. Funds may be available from IMLS (the Institute of Museum and Library Services), NEH (the National Endowment for the Humanities), NEA (the National Endowment for the Arts), or any of hundreds of private foundations or commercial companies with philanthropic arms. The rare book librarian must, of course, get the buy-in of the institution's administration, and with that, some institutional funds may be freed up. One stance the librarian can take is that such outreach makes the organization (and therefore its administration) look enlightened and on the cutting edge of progress.

Outreach to Underserved Populations

An important component of a successful outreach program is targeting underserved populations. In the library world, this usually means making public libraries open resources to all people, regardless of their economic status, their religious affiliations, their race or ethnicity, or anything else that might be used as a misguided rationale for excluding someone from access to a library.[10] But the notion of outreach to underserved people should also encompass the idea that all materials should be open to all. It is politically correct and morally right to welcome into the rare book department all those with legitimate research needs.

After all, special collections departments often hold rich genealogical and historical materials that would appeal to wide classes of users. Many rare book holdings include historical photographs of neighborhoods, families, businesses, houses, events, and trades—the kinds of information that anyone might be interested in using. The American Library Association has a document titled "Six Steps to Creating a Library Outreach Program,"[11] in which they say that the librarian should, among other things, "Identify the underserved areas of your community,

. . . Locate social service agencies and/or community groups currently working in underserved areas, . . . [and] Contact potential partners." This is an egalitarian approach to running a rare book department, and it is socially responsible. Anyone using the department's holdings should be subject to the same kind of scrutiny and receive the same services as anyone else. The librarians should judge the appropriateness of the research the patron wants to do and make the department's holdings open to all who qualify for use.

Outreach to Potential Donors

Chapter 6 has already looked at ways to raise money for the institution and the department. It should be reiterated here that one specific target audience for outreach must be those who can help the organization with their largesse. Friends groups, others who have shown an interest in the library, modest donors with capacities for support greater than their recent donations, and others whom the development department personnel have identified as capable of supporting the library or the larger institution may be offered special tours or lectures, may be invited to tea or cocktails, may be allowed into a book sale before the public is, or may be brought in for a talk on the library's progress and a private showing of library treasures or recent acquisitions.

Some outreach is specifically to get the world to know of the library's special collections; some is to increase use. But the outreach to potential donors aims at raising resources (in the form of cash or gifts in kind) for the library. Programs like "Adopt a Book," "Conserve a Book," "Buy a Book," "Endow a Position," or "Name That Reading Room" can have excellent results.

■ ■ ■

In a nutshell, the rare book librarian is not working in an ivory tower, in seclusion, in an exclusive club—pick your metaphor; she works in the world of information and is responsible for getting that information out to the world, and for bringing the world into the department to get more of it. No matter the means or the audience, outreach is good for all concerned.

The basic commodity, information, is there for the taking, but only if it is kept alive and accessible. The aim of the next chapter is to show how "keeping it alive" can be accomplished.

NOTES

1. Daniel Traister, "Public Services and Outreach in Rare Book, Manuscript, and Special Collections Libraries," *Library Trends* 52.1 (Summer 2003): 87–108, http://findarticles.com/p/articles/mi_m1387/is_1_52/ai_111853140/?tag=content;col1.

2. See www.ala.org/news/pr?id=9541. This site links to the "Katharine Kyes Leab and Daniel J. Leab American Book Prices Current Exhibition Catalogue Awards" site at www.ala.org/acrl/awards/publication awards/leabawards, which gives information about eligibility and submissions and lists winners for the last ten years.

3. Lucy S. Caswell, "Building a Strategy for Academic Library Exhibits," *College & Research Libraries News* 46.4 (April 1985): 165–66, 168; this statement is on p. 165.

4. Caswell, "Building a Strategy," p. 165.

5. To cite just two, see Susan M. Allen, "Rare Books and the College Library: Current Practices in Marrying Undergraduates to Special Collections," *Rare Books & Manuscripts Librarianship* 13.2 (Spring 1999): 110–19 (http://rbm.acrl.org/content/rbml/13/2/110.full.pdf+html); and Pablo Alvarez, "Introducing Rare Books into the Undergraduate Curriculum," *RBM (Rare Books and Manuscripts)* 7.2 (Fall 2006): 94–103 (http://rbm.acrl.org/content/7/2/94.full.pdf+html).

6. For a fuller treatment of digital outreach, see chapter 13, "Special Collections Departments Today."

7. The date of this posting is uncertain—either 2009 or 2012. It can be seen at www.job-hunt.org/job-search-for-academics/social-media-academics.shtml.

8. See www.jeffbullas.com/2011/09/02/20-stunning-social-media-statistics.

9. The source of this is Adam Hadhazy, "Teens Prefer Texting vs. Calling . . . Except to Parents," in TechNewsDaily, www.technewsdaily.com/359-teens-prefer-texting-vs-calling-except-to-parents.html.

10. Most of the extensive literature on outreach to underserved populations focuses on public libraries, but there is no reason that the notion of such outreach cannot also apply to the holdings and services of rare book facilities.

11. See www.ala.org/ala//aboutala/offices/olos/ outreachresource/docs/six_outreachsteps.pdf.

CHAPTER 12

PRESERVATION, CONSERVATION, RESTORATION, AND DISASTER PLANNING

T O GET TO INFORMATION, THERE MUST BE INFORMATION TO GET to. The cliché that nothing lasts forever may be true ("forever" is a really long time), but in the rare book (and archives and museum) world, some things have been around for thousands of years and seem to be going strong. What it takes is a means of keeping things going—preserving them. And not just one means, but many.

Three core concepts are Preservation, Conservation, and Restoration, in that order of importance for the library world. Though in some circles these words may have overlapping meanings, for librarians they are quite distinct. Preservation is the global treatment of library collections; Conservation is the treatment of individual items; and Restoration is the treatment of individual items in such a way that they are brought back to as near pristine condition as is possible.

Restoration

In fact, for special collections librarians and many others in the rare book world, the term *restoration* is hardly used except in possibly nefarious situations, because such treatment that leads to the hiding of defects can be deceptive. Restoration of an item allows its owner to pass it off as "like new" or "in excellent condition," when in fact its defects have been hidden by the restorative treatment. Hence, the concept of "restoration" is usually frowned upon in the rare book world.

On the other hand, if you are a bookseller and you live from your profits, and if you can maximize your profits by "getting rid of" imperfections in something you want to sell and thus being able to raise your price considerably, having an item restored may be quite lucrative. It is not illegal to repair a binding, clean up smudges, erase underlinings, or replace a missing leaf with a facsimile that cannot be detected. But it may be illegal to pass off as pristine and original something that

355

was not so fine before its treatment.[1] Hence, the concept of restoration is usually looked down upon by ethical people in the rare books world.

This is not so for museums. Pots and dishes, silver and gold, statues and paintings, carpets and costumes are routinely sent to the restorer to fix them up and make them as pristine as possible for display. Not all museums want to hide the defects or the repairs, but many of them do, and there seems to be no prohibition on doing this.

In a restored object, the repair adds to its monetary value, but in a museum setting that is not the issue. The beauty and aesthetic pleasure the item offers, and its ability to teach its viewers about the world in which it was made, are more to the point—just as was the intellectual value of books that are rubber stamped for security purposes (as chapter 7 showed). So in museums the notion of restoration is not objectionable. For people in the book world it may be objectionable because—before an item enters a library collection—its monetary value can be a powerful incentive for restoration, but that treatment can be a form of deception.

If a dealer has a fine press book with a few pages lightly underlined in pencil and with a former owner's bookplate on the pastedown, both of which would reduce the monetary value of the volume, is he justified in carefully erasing the underlining and removing the plate? If these treatments remove all trace of the "damage," the dealer might be able to sell the volume at its highest retail value—as a perfect, unblemished copy. Whether this is moral or ethical or not remains to be seen. However, if the joints between the pastedown and the free endpaper are torn, the bookseller might be able to have a conservator replace them with a perfect sheet with no split, and then pass the book off as in mint condition. That is, where does a simple "clean-up" end and actual restoration begin? A copy with split joints might be worth $100; a perfect copy might be worth $750. The cost of replacing the endsheets might be low enough to justify this restoration—for the bookseller. But caveat emptor: let the buyer beware. If the dealer does not reveal the restoration, the buyer thinks she is getting a perfect copy of something. Does she need to know that the volume has been fixed?

In the book world the word *sophistication* is used. The term means taking an imperfect copy and making it whole. John Carter says of *sophisticated*,

> This adjective, as applied to a book, is simply a polite synonym for doctored or faked-up. It would be equally appropriate to a second edition in which a first edition title-leaf had been inserted, to another from which the words second edition had

---

SEVERAL YEARS AGO I bought a piece of porcelain that was from a paper company whose works I collect. It broke at one point and I called a museum restorer for his advice. He told me that he could do a superior gluing so that it would be as solid as it was before being broken but that the mend would be visible. He also said he could restore the piece to hide the cracks completely. This would have increased the value of the piece because no one could tell that it was ever broken. One of the most famous restorations ever done was performed on the incomparable Portland Vase, a glass vessel of exquisite beauty and perfection, dating to about AD 5–25. It was smashed in a drunken fit in 1845, and after a couple of unsatisfactory restorations, it was finally restored to near perfection between June 1, 1988, and October 1, 1989, by Nigel Williams and Sandra Smith.* A museum does not wish to have a treasure on display with its defects showing glaringly. In the case of the Portland Vase and thousands of other important pieces, restoration is justified.

*The full story is told in the Wikipedia article "Portland Vase," in which we learn that "[l]ittle sign of the original damage is visible"; see http:// en.wikipedia.org/wiki/Portland _Vase. The first two restorations got pieces of the vase back together, but with thirty-seven small fragments left over that the restorers did not know what to do with. The journey of those pieces and the eventual replacement of them back into the smashed vase is a tale of restoration at its best.

been carefully erased, to a first edition re-cased in second edition covers, to a copy whose half-title had been supplied from another copy (made-up) or another edition or was in facsimile.

It is therefore naturally a term very rarely found in a catalogue description except in its negative form, unsophisticated; e.g. "a somewhat shaken but entirely unsophisticated copy of this rare book." First noted use, 1790.[2]

It is clear from Carter's entry that "made-up" or "sophisticated" (that is, "restored") copies are considered damaged goods in the rare book world.

From the librarian's perspective, however, a sophisticated copy is better than no copy at all. That is, if a collection has a gap in it of an important book, and if the librarian has been looking for some time for this volume, a damaged or sophisticated copy might be better than the gap. The problem is that buying such mended books encourages their production. It is a balancing act for a librarian to want to acquire something to enhance the collection and to want to reject it because it was sophisticated. If there are users who could profit from this text, the librarian might be willing to overlook the copy's sophistication. If the item appears on the rare book market with some regularity, the librarian may wish to wait for a more "honest" copy. It is not at all immoral or unethical for the librarian cognizantly to acquire the made-up volume, but it is incumbent on her to make sure this sophistication is in the cataloging record and perhaps also mentioned on the copy itself.

Another consideration is whether the item will be used for a library exhibition. The institution does not want the viewers to see that books or manuscripts in its possession are in poor condition. It could be a bad reflection on the library: this vitrine contains a book that the librarians themselves may have allowed to get into bad condition. This could be the conclusion of a casual viewer of the display. The label of the piece could dispel this notion. It might say, "This item is extraordinarily scarce in any condition. The volume here is one of only a few known to exist, most of which are in compromised condition." Perhaps before putting a damaged item into a show, the librarian should look for another piece instead or should do some minimal conservation work to make the piece look less damaged. As will be noted later in the section on conservation, any repair work done to a piece should have formal records of its treatment; these records should be kept on file and be immediately accessible, and the fact that work has been done should be prominently noted—with the treatment records available to anyone who wishes to see them.

In general, the whole idea of restoration should be only an extremely small part of the librarian's operation. Although various levels of repair may take place, only the minimal repairs required to keep the items in usable condition should be done. Full restoration is costly and is usually beyond a reasonable range of activities for rare book materials.

Preservation

As stated at the beginning of this chapter, preservation is a global activity—or, really, a series of global activities.[3] That is, caretakers of the library doing preservation work are protecting the collection as a whole by taking a number of steps, all of which, working together, will maintain and protect the holdings over a long period. As with conservation, the aim is to keep everything in usable condition. Use is the key here. If an item is preserved in a condition in which it cannot be used, it might as well not exist.

> **I ONCE HEARD** someone say that the best form of preservation for most library materials is to put them into deep freeze. Then the acids in the papers and leathers would not cause the things to deteriorate. Of course, this may work as a preservation activity, but any item so treated could not be used. This is not really practicable, for, as noted, use is the central issue. But see later in this chapter in the section "Disaster Recovery," where freezing wet books is an acceptable treatment.

All libraries (indeed, all those possessing rare books) need to do things to preserve their holdings, but special collections departments stand to lose a great deal more from neglect in preservation than does the rest of the library—primarily because of the value and irreplaceability of the items in their care. Also, special collections are more likely to have cheap paperbacks or old cloth-bound books from the nineteenth century (and books bound in leather) than is the rest of the library; and these volumes need more preservation oversight than do those that can be found on the open stacks of the regular collection. Thus, while preservation is important for the whole operation, it is especially important for the rare book department.

THE PRESERVATION LIBRARIAN/OFFICER

Preservation is such an important and complex series of undertakings that a fully trained preservation officer is a desideratum. But unfortunately, many administrators do not see the need for such a position. (Most member libraries of the Association of Research Libraries do have preservation departments. An issue now is that those departments are being downsized because of the decrease in library binding activity and the increase in digital curation activities.) Part of the problem is that deterioration takes place so slowly over such a long time that it is not immediately detectable. Also, a full-time position is expensive: having someone in that position will require the institution to do a job search and pay for relocation expenses, salary, benefits, perquisites, an office, and so forth. The attitude of "we have done well without a preservation officer for all these years (or decades), why do we need one now?" pervades libraries and other cultural heritage institutions. That "we-have-done-without" argument, however, does not really hold water when you examine the long-term effects of whatever was done without.

Responsible rare book librarians will know that preservation is a core activity and that a trained professional should be doing it. In the absence of a preservation expert, the librarian should have a basic knowledge of the issues. But even with a good understanding of what must be done at the preservation level for the collection, the librarian may not have the time (and may not be given the resources) to do preservation work. Strong advocacy for a preservation person to be on staff, if only part time, must

IF A LIBRARY does not hire a sufficient number of qualified catalogers, its backlog can grow to gargantuan levels. One good librarian might be with the collection for dozens of years and know how to find what is there, but when he leaves, the lack of proper cataloging will be obvious, and patrons will be at sea trying to find the resources they know are there but which are now unobtainable. In such a situation, the administration's "we have done without trained catalogers for a quarter of a century, why do we need one now?" is easy to answer. With preservation, the damage is not so visible; it does not have the same immediate impact on library operations as does inadequate cataloging. So the question, "We have done without a preservationist for fifty years; why do we need one now?" is harder to answer.

be the librarian's responsibility. The librarian may work with development to try to locate donors to endow this position, if possible. It can be an uphill and frustrating challenge, but preservation is an essential activity, and the effort to get a permanent person doing it is worthwhile.

Preservation Training

Preservation requires specialized training, and courses in the field are available throughout the country, mostly in library schools, but also at conservation organizations like the Northeast Document Conservation Center (NEDCC, www.nedcc.org/home.php) and the Conservation Center for Art and Historic Artifacts (CCAHA, www.ccaha.org). The AIC (American Institute for Conservation of Historic and Artistic Works, www.conservation-us.org) also offers workshops. And there is a vast literature available for self-study in the field. Also, the Internet holds extensive resources for anyone working in library preservation. A few excellent sites are the one for the AIC, CoOL (Conservation OnLine), and the Conservation DistList (Cons DistList), the latter now subsumed under the former.[4] Also, the American Library Association, the Society of American Archivists, and ALCTS (Association for Library Collections and Technical Services) along with several state library associations and other city and state organizations offer workshops.[5]

The preservationist should get as much training as possible and should hold workshops in the library for all staff, focusing on the basic activities that all librarians should know to preserve the collection. Also, resources are available from several organizations to pay for preservation training. The National Endowment for the Humanities (NEH) is the grandfather of all organizations for extensive help with preservation education. Its preservation office was started in the 1980s (Division of Preservation and Access, www.neh.gov/divisions/preservation). The NEH offers many public programs and gives a host of grants for all kinds of activities in preservation, including for training. The Institute for Museum and Library Services (www.imls.gov; the institute has a Conservation Assessment Program) and some private foundations have resources to support preservation activities.

Further, it is essential that each person on the staff be enlightened on basic preservation activities: how to handle books and manuscripts, how to use special cradles or foam pads to hold books while they are being used, how to train the patrons to do the same, how to use snakes or other devices to hold pages open in tightly bound books (rather than holding them open with your hands), how to turn pages, the necessity for washing hands before using department materials, how to recognize problems of all kinds, how to monitor and regulate the environment, what kinds of things patrons may take into the reading room and what is forbidden, and so forth. The most immediate threat to the longevity of any library material is handling, so the staff and patrons must be schooled in the proper treatment of all things from the collection.

KEY ACTIVITIES

As Susan Soy explains, there are three basic activities in preservation—Advocacy for Preservation of the Entire Collection, Stabilizing Environmental Controls and Storage Conditions, and Implementation of Preservation Activities by Knowledgeable and Trained Staff.[6] The first of these, as noted earlier, is essential, for too often preservation flies beneath the radar of many administrators who do not see the need for (or the fruits of) it. Also important are the last two words of this activity: *entire collection*. In a way, this inclusivity presents a complication that can make preservation seem like a hopeless (or tremendously expensive) case. All kinds of materials must be preserved: paper, leather, vellum, wood, metals, films and photographs of various kinds, digital "materials," glass and plastics, threads and cloth, hair (people's and animals'), stones and gems, and a host of other things that might wind up in a special collections department. Each has its own optimum preservation-storage conditions, and it is impossible to create an environment that caters to all these optimum conditions at once. A compromise must be reached that works best for most of these, and possibly a separate room with its own isolated conditions can be created for, say, photographs or some other material with more exacting standards (e.g., storage at low temperatures) than are needed for those of the rest of the collection. Preservation is a global activity, so the librarians in charge of it must think broadly about all the holdings when they decide what to do to extend the collection's life.

Monitoring the Environment and the Collection

Because deterioration—while it is occurring—is invisible, the librarian must monitor the environment constantly for the things that make materials deteriorate.

TEMPERATURE AND HUMIDITY In the past, librarians could use drum-type *hygrothermographs* that measure temperature and humidity and have a paper chart that rotates while two pens leave lines on the chart recording current readings. These machines, also called *thermo-hygrographs*, are still in use in many libraries and museums. The charts should become permanent records in the department's archive.

In recent years new digital hygrothermographs have become available. They are small and portable, they can record large amounts of data, and the information they store can be downloaded to a computer, from which pie charts, bar charts, and other kinds of readouts can be generated. The Image Permanence

Institute offers the PEM2 (the Preservation Environment Monitor), that

> calculates and displays, in real time, values that reflect the decay rate of organic materials stored in a given location. These values, known as preservation index (PI) and time-weighted preservation index (TWPI) show how temperature and humidity combine to influence the rate of decay processes such as paper discoloration, dye fading, deterioration of plastics, and textile embrittlement. PI and TWPI values alternate on the PEM display with temperature and RH on a 15-second cycle. Thus, it is possible to determine on sight the overall quality of storage conditions with respect to the "natural aging" rate of all types of organic objects in collections. The display can be turned off, if desired, without interrupting data collection. . . . Stored data can be uploaded from the PEM to a computer via a memory card that is inserted into a slot on the side of the PEM. All data in the PEM can be copied to the memory card in less than 20 seconds. Each card can hold data from as many as 16 PEMs. The card can be read by most Windows® laptop computers or by a desktop computer that is equipped with a card-reader accessory. (see www.imagepermanence institute.org/environmental/pem2-datalogger)

Also, "The PEM2 will run for approximately 10 years on one set of 4 AA batteries and will retain all 10 years of data for upload at any time."[7] This kind of monitoring is ideal for rare book departments or for any area in which rare books are kept, but it must be accompanied by the ability to adjust the environment once the monitor has detected a problem. The department must work closely with the physical plant, which is in charge of all the mechanicals at the institution.

LIGHT LEVELS A library cannot run without light. But light is damaging, so the rare book librarian must mitigate the damage as well as he can. Beth Lindblom Patkus, author of the NEDCC Preservation Pamphlet on "Protection from Light Damage,"[8] says,

> Light is a common cause of damage to library and archival collections. Paper, bindings, and media

(inks, photographic emulsions, dyes, and pigments, and many other materials used to create words and images) are particularly sensitive to light. Light damage manifests itself in many ways. Light can cause paper to bleach, yellow, or darken, and it can weaken and embrittle the cellulose fibers that make up paper. It can cause media and dyes used in documents, photographs, and art works to fade or change color. Most of us recognize fading as a form of light damage, but this is only a superficial indication of deterioration that extends to the physical and chemical structure of collections. Light provides energy to fuel the chemical reactions that produce deterioration. While most people know that ultraviolet (UV) light is destructive, it is important to remember that all light causes damage. Light damage is cumulative and irreversible.

Innumerable bindings—especially the cloth publishers' bindings of the nineteenth century—manifest this damage in the fading that is apparent on the spines of the volumes. It seems that green-dyed cloth was particularly susceptible to fading, as was purple (popular in the nineteenth century—a dye that faded to brown), but cloth of most other colors has faded as well because of light exposure. Further, papers made after about 1875 were generally weak and acidic, and light can accelerate their deterioration. Witness today's newspaper left in the driveway in the morning. By the time it is picked up in the evening, having been exposed to perhaps only eight hours of sunlight, it is already turning yellow. (Newspapers, printed on the lowest-quality paper, are an extreme case, but even better papers begin to deteriorate slowly when exposed to light.) Libraries must bare their holdings to light; there is no way to use the collection without being able to see it. It is important, then, to monitor the levels and kinds of light that the materials are exposed to.

A website called Preservation 101 offers this information:

> A light meter is used to measure visible light in units of lux or footcandles. A separate UV meter is required to measure UV energy in microwatts per lumen. Some UV meters can also measure visible light by changing detectors within the device. A

35mm camera with a manual light meter can also be used to measure visible light levels. . . . [A]rtificial light does not change significantly, but monitoring natural light can be problematic because it differs according to the time of day, the weather, and the season. Readings should be taken at times when the light is brightest to be sure that the highest light levels are being recorded.[9]

AIR QUALITY A good HVAC system will filter the air in the library, keeping pollutants at a minimum. There is a sizable literature—much of it on the Internet—on the gaseous and particulate pollutants in the air, with many companies offering monitors to check on these things. Chris Muller and Richard Corel claim that "[t]he 'cause-and-effect' relationship between levels of gaseous pollutants and the damage caused to materials and artifacts remains elusive. There is no real agreement on what actually constitutes an acceptable environment with respect to airborne gaseous pollutants."[10] Nonetheless, air-quality monitoring is recommended because there is no doubt that polluted air is damaging to library materials, and it could be toxic to people as well. Many kinds of air-monitoring devices are available on the market, or the institution can bring in an air-quality expert to do the examination.

One of the problems with air quality, as already noted, is pollutants, which can get through even the best HVAC filters if these get dirty when they are not regularly cleaned or changed. So they need to be changed or cleaned regularly. Again, a good relationship with the physical plant personnel is necessary for them to be willing to take care of the filters, not an easy task if these are large, in a roof unit, or in some other difficult-to-get-to place. The librarian should meet with the physical plant personnel early on in her tenure to explain that poor environmental conditions can damage our cultural heritage and that they are crucial players in preventing this damage.

A point already made, but worth repeating, is that all this monitoring merely identifies the problems; it does not solve them. Once problems are recognized, the librarian must work with the proper people to rectify the conditions.

Visual Monitoring

All this scientific equipment is useful for monitoring things that the naked eye cannot see. But visual monitoring is important as well. Some obvious things to look for are dust (which can harbor dust mites), clutter (which can be combustible), stacks of books or boxes that can fall, blocked doors that can inhibit movement (especially in an emergency when the building must be evacuated), and overused electrical outlets that can cause fires. Also, pests of many kinds can damage collections. Sometimes they can be seen scurrying here or there, or the damage they cause can be detected: covers chewed, holes in volumes, webs visible, frass (the tiny pellets that are the insects' bodily waste—it looks like fine sawdust), and other signs.

Insects and rodents can get into a building in a number of ways, so the visual monitoring should include an examination of ducts and fixtures that come from outside the department, plants and trees and grass that are close to the building, doors that are adjacent to spaces where people might eat or drink, cracks in the building's walls, floors, or ceilings, and even the clothing, bags, books, and papers that people bring in. A thorough visual examination will include a careful monitoring of the perimeter of the exterior of the building as well. (See the section "Integrated Pest Management" later in this chapter.)

THE RARE BOOK department of a major university recently found insects in the entryway of the department. Staff now have a special vacuum cleaner that they use on books and papers that patrons bring into the department. There is no way to use this vacuum on people's clothing, but anyone coming in from outside the building could have larvae or their more mature insect forms on them from having walked under trees, sat on the grass or an outdoor bench, or deposited waste into a trash bin.

A tool for visual monitoring is the sticky insect trap, a device that can take many forms depending on the brand used. Some are box-shaped, some are flat. One common type is a little triangular tube containing pheromones and an adhesive. The pheromones attract the insects in the area, which enter the tube, and the adhesive traps them in the tube. The traps can be placed unobtrusively in any area of the department, under or on top of shelves, in corners, in stacks or staff work areas, in closets, or anywhere else that the librarians wish to monitor. If the traps draw insects, they not only reduce the number of pests that are roaming in the collection, they also do not damage the bugs. That is, the traps leave the creatures in good enough shape that they can be identified, and if any insect needs to be handled in a particular way, a specific treatment can be devised to eradicate it. (The point is that generally these creatures are not alone; if you see one, you know others are probably there, too.) When the trap is placed, it should be dated, and it should be inspected at regular intervals.

> THE AIM OF sticky insect traps is not to eradicate the bugs, though the insects caught in them are no longer chewing on library materials. Their aim is to identify the problem in the first place. Any facility that houses rare books and special collections materials (including bookstores and private residences) could profit from the use of these traps.

Other Monitoring Tools

There are many kinds of tools for monitoring. The NEDCC Preservation Leaflet 2.2, "Monitoring Temperature and Relative Humidity," by Beth Lindblom Patkus, mentions many of them: thermometers, "Simple dial-type hygrometers," "Humidity indicator strips or color cards," "Sling psychrometers," "Battery-operated (motor-blower) psychrometers," "An electronic temperature/humidity meter," "Min/max digital thermohygrometers," "A recording hygrothermograph," and "Dataloggers."[11] This comprehensive pamphlet is important reading for rare book personnel. The author stresses the importance of collecting information during regular monitoring and recommends that someone in the department should be assigned to do it regularly, using a care-

fully thought out checklist so as not to forget to monitor everything that has been identified as necessary to observe. She adds,

> Records of weather conditions and special events (exhibit openings, for example, where unusual numbers of visitors alter temperature and RH in a space, or a failure of the boiler or air-conditioning system) should be maintained so that changes recorded by the instruments can be interpreted usefully. Regional weather records are available from the National Oceanic and Atmospheric Administration (NOAA), Washington, DC. They may also be available from a local or college weather station or local airport.

This information is also available on the Internet. One site to look at is that of the National Climate Data Center (www.ncdc.noaa.gov/oa/ncdc.html); another is a site called Weathersource (at http://weathersource.com, select Past Weather Reports). The department should employ as many forms of monitoring as are practicable and affordable. In the long run, the damage that is averted by the actions taken based on the information that the monitoring provides will save the library a great deal of resources. Conservation is expensive, and items that need conservation often suffer a loss of some information when they are treated. Monitoring allows the librarian to head off further damage.

A STABLE ENVIRONMENT

Stabilizing the environment is also essential.

Temperature and Humidity

Because variations in temperature and humidity cause many library materials to expand and contract, and because high humidity levels can cause mold to grow and low humidity can cause some materials to become brittle, having a stable environment is extremely important. If the optimum temperature is 68° ($\pm 2°$) and if the optimum humidity is 50 percent (± 2 percent), these levels should be maintained as consistently as possible. But it is better to have the collection at consistent temperature and humidity levels than it is to have it fluctuate radically around the optimum levels. Sherelyn Ogden's NEDCC Pamphlet 2.1, "Temperature, Relative Humidity, Light, and Air Quality: Basic Guidelines for Preservation," says,

> Fluctuations in temperature and relative humidity are also damaging. Library and archival materials are hygroscopic, readily absorbing and releasing moisture. They respond to diurnal and seasonal changes in temperature and relative humidity by expanding and contracting. Dimensional changes accelerate deterioration and lead to such visible damage as cockling paper, flaking ink, warped covers on books, and cracked emulsion on photographs.[12]

Recently research has shown that those levels (68° [±2°] and 50 percent humidity) were too stringent for most repositories and that wider ranges were acceptable (though consistency is still stressed). Ogden says,

> Authorities disagree on the ideal temperature and relative humidity for library and archival materials. A frequent recommendation is a stable temperature no higher than 70° F and a stable relative humidity between a minimum of 30 percent and a maximum of 50 percent. Research indicates that relative humidities at the lower end of this range are preferable since deterioration then progresses at a slower rate. In general, the lower the temperature the better. The temperature recommendations for areas used exclusively for storage are much lower than those for combination user and storage areas. Cold storage with controlled humidity is sometimes advisable for remote storage or little-used materials. When materials are taken out of cold storage, however, the radical, rapid temperature changes they experience may cause condensation on them. In such cases, gradual acclimatization may be required.

Some libraries have an intermediary room that allows cold materials to warm up gradually before they are brought to a reading room, avoiding condensation on the cold materials.

Literature is increasing on the wider topic of sustainability, and in the next few years we will see thinking evolve about optimum storage conditions, types of hardware to employ, the sustainability of a collection as opposed to its mere maintenance, and so forth. In the European Union there is a new focus on the "20-20-20 targets," a way of looking at elements of the environment that cause deterioration. The European Union "Climate Action" website explains,

> EU Heads of State and Government set a series of demanding climate and energy targets to be met by 2020, known as the "20-20-20" targets. These are:
>
> * A reduction in EU greenhouse gas emissions of at least 20 percent below 1990 levels
> * 20 percent of EU energy consumption to come from renewable resources
> * A 20 percent reduction in primary energy use compared with projected levels, to be achieved by improving energy efficiency. (http://ec.europa.eu/clima/policies/package/index_en.htm)

Although preservation is not the main focus of this initiative, it is a by-product of it. Reduced emissions will reduce the production of gases that are deleterious to library materials. In the meantime, a good HVAC (Heating, Ventilation, and Air Conditioning) system is essential, and is expensive. In the long run, however, the expense of acquiring, installing, and maintaining such a system is worth what is put into it; it is like a form of insurance. The system must constantly monitor the environment, particularly for temperature and humidity, and it should be kept running at all times. As Ogden says, "Additional costs incurred by keeping the system in constant operation will be far less than the cost of future conservation treatment to repair damage caused by poor climate." And the system should be monitored at regular, frequent intervals to make sure it is working.

Recent literature showing that there is a great evolution in thinking about sustainability and preservation is appearing on the Internet. For instance, the practice of keeping temperature and humidity levels stable at a fairly narrow range is being rethought. At the United Kingdom's National Museum Directors' Conference (NMDC), a document was released titled "NMDC Guiding Principles for Reducing Museums' Carbon Footprint."[13] A key statement in this piece says, "There is a recognition that museums need to

WHEN I GOT to UC Riverside, my staff and I monitored the environment every minute of every day using an old drum-and-chart hygrothermograph. We saw that on the weekends there was a spike in temperature and humidity in the summer. I called the physical plant on campus and was told that because the department was closed on the weekends, personnel turned off the HVAC system. I explained why this was a terrible practice, and the enlightened engineers agreed to have the system run constantly throughout the year. Without the monitoring, we would not have known about this practice.

approach long-term collections care in a way that does not require excessive use of energy, whilst recognizing their duty of care to collections." The issue concerns preservation directly: HVAC systems consume large amounts of energy, mostly because they have to work hard to maintain narrow levels of control of the environment (particularly temperature and humidity). By easing the restrictions—that is, by widening the acceptable range of these conditions—a museum can save money by using less energy, which saving comes in the form of reduced use of fuels. The next sentence in this document says,

> There is general agreement that it is time to shift museums' policies for environmental control, loan conditions and the guidance given to architects and engineers from the prescription of close control of ambient conditions throughout buildings and exhibition galleries to a more mutual understanding of the real conservation needs of different categories of object, which have widely different requirements and may have been exposed to very different environmental conditions in the past.

The guidelines the NMDC promulgates, delineated in the document's appendix 1, say, "For the majority of objects containing hygroscopic material (such as canvas paintings, textiles, ethnographic objects or animal glue) a stable relative humidity (RH) is required in the range of 40–60 percent and a stable temperature in the range 16–25°C [60.8–77°

F]." These ranges are much wider than those traditionally quoted as ideal for library materials. But research seems to indicate that collections can be "sustained" (i.e., preserved) with this wider range of conditions.[14]

How environmental monitoring and control will be done in the coming years will depend on the ongoing research into the preservation needs of particular media, new thinking about sustainability as a larger picture in the operations of the entire facility, and the kinds of resources that libraries, archives, and museums will have at their disposal—this last directly influenced by economic conditions in the world around them.

Light

With light, the issue is not really stability; it is the fact that the light is there. The department cannot operate in the dark, so some light is necessary, and for the reading room and office spaces, good levels of light must be maintained for the comfort and efficiency of the staff and patrons. But as Ogden says,

> Light accelerates deterioration of library and archival materials. It leads to weakening and embrittlement of cellulose fibers and can cause paper to bleach, yellow, or darken. It also causes media and dyes to fade or change color, altering the legibility and/or appearance of documents, photographs, art works, and bindings. Any exposure to light, even for a brief time, is damaging, and the damage is cumulative and irreversible. (www.nedcc.org/resources/leaflets/2The_Environment/01Basic Guidelines.php)

For these reasons, everything to mitigate light damage should be done. Fluorescent lights give off UV rays that are particularly damaging. Bulbs and fixtures can be fitted with UV-filtering sleeves. Windows can be covered with UV-filtering film or curtains of various kinds. Lights can be turned off in areas where no one is working.

Some libraries have lighting systems that are activated by movement, so that lights are off until someone enters the area. Some libraries have lights on timers. The stacks are in the dark until someone turns the dial on the timer, giving him a set amount of time for the lights to stay on, after which they automatically go off. This saves electricity and keeps light away from the collection when no one needs to have it on. Newer bulbs are available with lower UV emissions, but they still should be filtered if possible. One rule of thumb is that any library material that is being used should be well lit for the user, but at all other times it should be sheltered from the light. Books should be shelved in the dark unless someone needs to get to them. Manuscripts, photographs, and other light-sensitive materials should be sleeved or boxed or otherwise kept away from light until they are used. Special collections departments sometimes have cases in which some of the department's holdings are on display. These displays should be temporary. Millions of nineteenth-century publishers' bindings are in cloth with fugitive dyes. If the cloth has not yet faded on particular volumes, these should be put into phase boxes to keep them from the light.

THE BRITISH MUSEUM had cases for exhibiting treasures of its collection. The cases were covered with heavy velvet cloths, and a patron had to raise the cloths to see inside the vitrines. This guaranteed that the items on display were protected when no one was there to view them.

VENTILATION

As invisible as the slow deterioration of library materials and the fading of pigments that are exposed to light is the deterioration of objects because of the air around them. Tombstones lasted for centuries until the Industrial Revolution started pouring pollutants into the environment. Anyone who has observed the old tombstones in New England cemeteries will know how damaging polluted air can be. The cut stone lasted for centuries with no loss of text; but in the last 150 years, the surfaces of the stones have worn away merely from exposure to the polluted air.

This is visible proof of how damaging the environment can be.

The *V* in HVAC stands for ventilation, an important component of indoor air quality. The air should be filtered at all times, and the filters must be cleaned or replaced regularly. When I first got to UC Riverside, a fine black dust was settling on everything in its Special Collections Department—so fine it could hardly be seen. But it was detectable when we cleaned the display cases with white rags. It turned out that the black dust came from filters in the HVAC system that had not been cleaned or replaced in over a year. The dust was harmful to the books, but it was also being breathed in by the staff and patrons. As Ogden explains,

Pollutants contribute heavily to the deterioration of library and archival materials. The two major types of pollutants are gases and particulates. Gaseous contaminants—especially sulfur dioxide, nitrogen oxides, peroxides, and ozone—catalyze harmful chemical reactions that lead to the formation of acid in materials. This is a serious problem for paper and leather, which are particularly vulnerable to damage caused by acid. Paper becomes discolored and brittle, and leather becomes weak and powdery. Particulates—especially soot—abrade, soil, and disfigure materials.

As with the other kinds of deterioration, that from air is slow acting and fairly invisible. But it is a constant threat and should be continuously monitored. Ogden says that the air intake vents should not be located where polluted air from outside the building is likely to be sucked in. Sometimes the air intake is located on the outside of the building where vehicles pass.

Automobiles and industry, major sources of pollution, will probably be beyond control. Other sources, however, may be reduced. These include cigarettes, photocopying machines, certain types of construction materials, paints, sealants, wooden storage/display materials, cleaning compounds, furniture, and carpets. (www.nedcc.org/resources/leaflets/2The_Environment/01BasicGuidelines.php)

AT UC RIVERSIDE, one major air intake unit was at the loading dock behind the library. When a truck was making a delivery and had its engine running, the smell of its exhaust was noticeable in several parts of the building, including in special collections. I often had to call the Receiving Department to have them instruct the drivers to turn their engines off. The exhaust was bad for the collection and the people.

INTEGRATED PEST MANAGEMENT

Pests can be tremendously damaging to the collection, and monitoring for these creatures is extremely important. But the best way to handle them is to create an environment that anticipates how they might become a problem before they actually do, and act accordingly. No single method will work. Because the pests can enter the collection in various ways, the librarians—with the physical plant's assistance, and possibly also the help of professional entomologists and preservation personnel—can devise a plan specific to the institution. The old method of managing pests was with pesticides, some of which could stain library materials and be toxic to human beings. In recent years a method for keeping pests at bay using a variety of techniques in tandem has been developed: Integrated Pest Management (IPM).

Beth Lindblom Patkus, in her NEDCC Preservation Leaflet 3.10 titled "Integrated Pest Management," says:

> Pesticides often do not prevent infestation, however, and application of pesticides after the fact cannot correct the damage already done. Pesticides have also become less attractive because of a growing awareness that the chemicals in pesticides can pose health hazards to staff and damage paper-based collections. Newer extermination methods such as controlled freezing and oxygen deprivation have shown promise as alternatives for treatment of existing infestations, but like pesticides, they do not prevent infestation. Prevention can be achieved only through strict housekeeping and monitoring procedures. (www.nedcc.org/resources/leaflets/3Emergency _Management/10PestManagement.php)

One of the clichés of library management is "No Food or Drink in the Library." These consumables bring pests. If there is food or liquid in the environment, pests smell it out and come for a meal. Even mere water can draw insects. But most libraries know that it is nearly impossible to keep food outside. Staff must eat. So do patrons, and if the institution is a college or university, students spending long hours in libraries get hungry and thirsty. How can library officials be expected to enforce the no-food/no-drink rule? Students can even be militant about this. "We pay a lot for our tuition, and we work hard to get good grades. Some of that work *must* be done in the library. We cannot waste time packing up our books and papers just to go outside to eat." In most institutions the no-food/no-drink policy has been jettisoned. Some have even installed vending machines in the library. This means that the institution must be especially careful about protecting the library collections with assiduous monitoring and a strong antipest program. IPM is such a tool.

The "integration" in "Integrated Pest Management" refers to employing several activities, all of which, in concert, discourage pests from entering the building. Keeping food and drink out of the library is part of IPM, but as just noted, this prohibition is practically unenforceable. For the special collections department, this prohibition is enforceable in the department, but the department is usually in the larger building—and it is in the larger space that IPM must begin. In fact, IPM should begin outside the edifice. Plants and shrubs and trees should be trimmed back to keep them off the building envelope. Ivy is particularly insidious, because its tentacles cling to the building, often holding on by creating tiny fissures in the façade where its nanoparticles allow the plant to affix itself to the stones or bricks. The *New Scientist* article "Ivy Uses Nanoparticles to Cling to Walls" explains: "Ivy stems grow disc-shaped rootlets which secrete a yellowish substance. . . . [A] gel containing globules about 70 nanometres across . . . seems to supply the sticking power."[15] The ivy houses all kinds of pests, and the tiny fissures it makes in the building's surface will allow moisture to penetrate. In cold climes, the moisture in the cracks will

IN ONE LIBRARY where I was working, at about 6:30 p.m., a pizza delivery man showed up at the circulation desk with freshly baked pizzas and asked, "Where is Study Room B?" Students, working on a project together in that room, had ordered out. The circulation desk personnel told him to take his pizzas back to his vehicle. There was a no-food/no-drink policy in that library, and the students knew it. This shows that students ignore the rules when they are hungry and that the library must monitor the patrons' activities. At that school, also, students often were caught smuggling in tacos and candy, soft drinks and small packages of food that would fit into their purses or backpacks. A team of library staff would sweep through the library unannounced on an irregular schedule and grab any food they saw, drop it into a large garbage bag, and leave a sheet of paper on the desk in front of the startled students—the sheet reading something like, "We have a no-food/no-drink environment. Please obey." During the two years or so that these monitors worked, the incidence of infestation in the library dropped to record lows. (Interestingly, there was practically no negative reaction from the students—no complaints that their food and drink had been confiscated. The "No Food and Drink" signs that were posted prominently throughout the library, even on its front doors, made the students aware that their violation of this policy was wrong, and for the most part they simply accepted the loss of their edibles and potables.)

freeze, expand, and cause the surface to crumble. Little by little, over time, the fissures expand, and moisture and even living creatures can get through the walls. Any plant matter that touches the building can be damaging, by bringing insects or water to the building's surface.

Patkus in her IPM leaflet says,

Some insect species that threaten collections thrive in small, dark, undisturbed spaces, in other words, in conditions that are common to storage areas. Insects will set up housekeeping inside dark, tight spaces (such as corrugated boxes), and are attracted to piles of boxes or other materials that are left undisturbed for long periods. Insects also live in

quiet spaces like corners, the undersides of bookcases, and behind furniture. Dust and dirt help to provide a hospitable atmosphere for pests. Dead insects or insect debris can attract other insects. Dirt and clutter also make it difficult to see pests, so a problem may go unnoticed for some time.

Clearly, some simple actions under IPM are to do away with clutter, keep corrugated boxes out of the department, or, if this is not possible, at least monitor them closely and frequently for infestation. Keep dust away with a regular cleaning schedule. Try to check under bookcases and behind furniture. The department must be kept as dirt-, dust-, and clutter-free as possible. Frequent monitoring is one of the keys to IPM.

Patkus warns that routes of entry for insects should be under careful scrutiny. She says,

Windows and doors should be tightly sealed; weatherstripping may be necessary. Doors should not be propped open regularly. Openings around pipes should be sealed, as should cracks in the walls or foundation. Vents should be screened to keep out birds and rodents. A planting-free zone of about 12 inches should be maintained around buildings to discourage insects from entering. Plantings should be properly cared for and not over watered. The area around foundations should be graveled and graded away from a building to avoid basement flooding.

One possible source of contamination is incoming materials. Any books, manuscripts, newspapers, boxes of any kinds of collections, and so forth can contain various bugs (along with mold spores and rodents). The rare book department—and the library in general—should have a holding area somewhere for certain types of incoming items, especially newspapers, magazines, or anything else that might have been stored in an attic or a basement, particularly the latter, where moisture and darkness are congenial homes for pests. When any container is delivered to the department, it should be opened in an area isolated from the rest of the collection and then scrutinized carefully for signs of infestation. Perhaps the department can use some kind of insulated

AT RIVERSIDE THE special collections department moved to a temporary facility while seismic renovations were being done on the main library building. On the first morning that we were in the temporary building, which was on the ground floor of an old library, we had an infestation of roly-poly bugs (also called "pill bugs") right at the front entrance of the building. They had crawled under the door and a few dozen of them were on the floor about ten feet into the library. I called the campus entomologist who assured me that they were harmless. He said that they ate dead plant matter and that they posed no threat to the collection or to the human inhabitants. Most were dead or moving slowly and near death. We swept them out and called the physical plant personnel to put some kind of rubber attachment on the bottom of the doors to keep the bugs out, which they did that day. The following day the bugs were there again, inside the door. I showed up especially early the next day and found that the flower beds, about ten feet away from the front door, were filled with water. The automatic sprinklers filled the flower beds, and the little creatures were washed out of their habitats, from under the bushes. I again called the physical plant and asked why it was necessary to flood the flower beds. Couldn't the plants just get a slight watering? The campus personnel, the following day, reduced the amount of water they used, and the bugs never showed up again. The message: the librarian can work well with other campus personnel (in this case the botanists, entomologists, and the physical plant) as part of the Integrated Pest Management plan.

container to hold the acquisition for twenty-four hours, with one of the insect-detecting traps in the container. This may not be necessary for most books or manuscripts, but the chamber should be available if the librarian has even a slight suspicion that the item(s) might be contaminated. Patkus, in her IPM leaflet, says,

> Examine incoming material immediately to see if there is evidence of infestation. Work over a clean surface covered with [a] blotter or other light paper. Remove all objects from storage or shipping enclosures and look at the binding, pages, and hollow (if any) in books. Examine frame backings and mats, wrappings, and other accompanying materials. Look for live creatures, insect droppings, larvae, or bodies.

This kind of scrutiny may seem like overkill, but it is better to be sure that incoming items are pest free than it is to find out later that there is an infestation in the stacks that could have been avoided.

If insects do get into the department, the monitoring traps spoken of earlier, if properly placed, will reveal the problem. They should be placed in the department in the areas most likely to have insects: near doors and windows, where incoming materials are unpacked and stored, near sources of water (like staff rooms or water fountains), at sources of heat, in cloth-covered furniture, and so forth. Patkus says,

Documentation is essential; monitoring will be useless without it. The number of insects, the types of insects, and their stage of growth should all be recorded for each trap. Dates and locations of trap replacements should be noted. Detailed records should also be kept of any other evidence of activity, such as live or dead insects or their droppings.

She discusses chemical and nonchemical treatments of the environment and what to do when bugs are spotted, and she warns that the librarians should not take the treatment into their own hands; they should consult a professional exterminator or a conservator with expertise in eradication before any action is taken to get rid of the pests. Obviously, the actions should be taken quickly, for bugs can spread rapidly if they are not contained and done away with efficiently.[16]

Integrated Pest Management is only one of several issues dealing with preservation of collections. In some respects it is preemptory, and in some it is reactive. But a comprehensive IPM plan, carried out assiduously, will go a long way to protecting the collections.

CLEANING THE COLLECTION

All the activities concerned with monitoring and controlling the physical environment in the library are preservation activities. They protect the collection and the people who work in it. One means of preserving the collection is keeping it clean. Michèle V. Cloonan's "Cleaning the Newberry's Collection"[17] delineates a project that she designed and oversaw. She says that "[t]here is no doubt that such cleanings discourage insects and rodents, uncover leaks in plumbing and heating systems and expose adverse stack conditions." She adds that there are other benefits of the cleaning project, one of which is to allow the staff to identify items that need conservation treatment.

Cloonan says that there are two basic methods of cleaning: (1) vacuuming in conjunction with hand cleaning and (2) air blowing "used with dust collectors." She describes the full method of cleaning using the slower and more expensive (but gentler and more protective) process of vacuuming. This need not be done with highly trained, expensive professionals; she was able to hire students to do the work, and after careful training and with her oversight, they were able to do a first-rate job on their own.

The Newberry's cleaning was done immediately before the collection was moved. She says, "[C]leaning, tying and wrapping before the move assured minimal fragment losses during the move and prevented further damage to already brittle or deteriorated materials." She adds that dusty books will clog filtration systems in the library. And she emphasizes that "[u]nfortunately, very few libraries can afford the luxury of full-time stack maintenance personnel," so cleaning is often put off, sometimes for decades. As with other kinds of threat to a collection, dirt and dust buildup is slow and "invisible." If the library can afford it, a cleaning should be done about every ten years, naturally depending on how efficient the HVAC system is in keeping the air free of particulates. Heads of special collections departments should keep this in mind and be sure to figure it into an upcoming year's budget.

WORKING WITH THE PHYSICAL PLANT

As noted already, it is important for the rare book personnel to have a good relationship with the institution's physical plant, those who take care of all the facilities in the organization. For some librar-

ies, this means the building in which the department is housed, but, of course, it also means more than the edifice. Outside the building are all kinds of threats—including flora, insects, dust, spores, air pollution, rodents, and water—that can get into the building in various ways. Physical plant personnel are trained to protect the contents and the envelopes of the buildings (and the people in them), and the librarian must be on good terms with these people.

As with getting to know the police and fire department personnel, meeting the physical plant staff can be a great boon to the special collections librarian, who may wish to bring in a physical plant person to give the department a careful analysis of the preservation-related issues the librarian should be aware of. The librarian may be schooled in the problems, too, and together, they can come up with a workable plan to protect the department's holdings. This kind of liaison is a valuable opportunity for the librarian not only to enlist the services of the physical plant people, but also to explain to them why their help will be invaluable in protecting our cultural heritage by protecting the building and its contents. By making the physical plant "part of the rare book family," the librarian is forging a relationship that will pay off when the library needs a quick response for any kind of preservation problem the librarian recognizes.

EXHIBITIONS

Though already mentioned, it is worth reiterating that exhibiting the department's holdings is a good form of outreach and that the displays should be done in vitrines that have been vetted for their preservation characteristics. Mary Todd Glaser, author of the NEDCC Preservation Leaflet 2.5, "Protecting Paper and Book Collections during Exhibition," says, "Although exhibition can complicate or even compromise preservation efforts, measures can be taken to minimize risk or damage."[18]

Glaser has five basic principles for exhibition. One standard practice, if it is practicable, is to mount in the exhibits facsimiles of the items the librarian wishes to display (Glaser). If the copy is good enough, it gives the viewers an adequate representation of what the curator of the exhibit wishes the viewer to see without loss of information or experience. And, of course, it saves wear and tear (and fading) of the original. (Whether libraries follow this dictum depends on whether they agree that patrons will be content to see facsimiles rather than originals.) Second, Glaser says that nothing—especially valuable material—should be exhibited long term. Further, she says the light levels should be kept as low as possible, the items on display should be exposed to the least amount of ultraviolet light as possible, and that "cases and frames [should be] enclosed, sealed, and made of materials that will not damage their contents."[19]

Display cases vary in quality and in the features they offer. Some can be hermetically sealed and air conditioned. The lighting systems in them vary, with some using fiber optics, which do not create any heat in the cases. All vitrines should be high security. There are also alarmed exhibition cases, which is a good idea for those that are in, or abut, public spaces. Cases can be freestanding or wall mounted. Freestanding ones should be bolted to the floor, if this can be done without being unsightly, and, ideally, the cases should be within sight of library personnel at all times. Clearly, security is one aspect of preservation.

Among many other suggestions, Glaser says that silica gel may be used in cases, especially during seasons when the humidity is high, to keep the contents of the vitrines dry; but controlling the humidity and heat in the rooms where the display is mounted is the best way to protect the items on show. Also, anything that comes near or into contact with the items in the exhibition should be carefully chosen: mats for pictures, shelving, wood in the vitrines, lining cloths for the cases, barrier materials, "Sealants and Paints," and "Cloth, Gaskets, and Adhesives in Cases." Any of these can give off gases or contain acids, and some cloths can bleed, their colors staining the items that touch them.

The items on display should not be shown in a position that puts strain on them in any way or will cause any kind of distortion. The proper kind of cradles and supports, frames, mats, and lighting should be used to minimize damage. And Glaser's last advice is that the exhibition should be mounted with the assistance of the conservators, whose expertise in caring for rare materials should be tapped. The Rare Books and Manuscripts Section of ACRL has the standing Curators and Conservators Discussion Group that

> [a]dds to the body of information on Curator/Conservator relations and encourages the education of curators and conservators about their respective professions; provides a forum for discussion about topics of mutual interest; identifies, recommends, and facilitates creation of continuing education seminars through the Education and Professional Development Committee; publicizes issues concerning curators and conservators by encouraging the publication of relevant articles in appropriate journals. (See ALA Connect at http://connect.ala.org/node/65373.)

The premise of this group is that conservators have a great deal of information on best practices in conservation, but they may not understand all the ways library materials contain and "release" information; while curators (the rare book librarians) understand all the ways these materials can be used, but they may lack the technical expertise of what can be done to extend the useful life of the damaged or fragile items in their care. These two groups, together, can work out standards for best practices for all library materials and can also decide between themselves the best ways to mount various items in exhibitions— using the best cases, the best lighting, and so forth.[20]

For further information on the exhibition of rare materials, another text is useful. The National Information Standards Organization (NISO), in 2002, approved of a document titled "Environmental Conditions for Exhibiting Library and Archival Materials," which establishes

> criteria to minimize the effect of environmental factors on deterioration of library and archival materials on exhibit. Specific parameters are recommended for exposure to light, relative humidity, temperature, gaseous and particulate contaminants, display techniques, and case and support material

components. The standard is intended as a guide for librarians, archivists, exhibition designers, and others involved in preparing library and archival materials for exhibition.[21]

Those working in rare books should familiarize themselves with this important report.

OTHER PRESERVATION ISSUES

Some of the recommendations in this section overlap with the field of conservation, but because I am talking about treatment and handling of mass amounts of materials, I have put them under "preservation," which is the global handling of the collection. Similarly, another preservation issue concerns moving collections with minimal damage. This topic has been covered in chapter 2 and is revisited later in this section.

Shelving for Books

Library holdings must be shelved. Certainly, they should not be left on the floor—or in cartons of unprocessed or recently acquired materials. If these are in boxes, the cartons should be archival and should be on shelving, off the floor. Flooding is always a possibility, from broken pipes, leaky toilets or water fountains, heavy storms, faulty roofs, or other sources. As the Library Preservation and Conservation website says, for books,

> Adjustable metal shelving, with powder or baked enamel coatings or anodized aluminum, is ideal for most books and manuscripts. The shelves must be wider than the objects, and the uprights regularly placed and firmly secured. Wood shelves are not recommended, since they may emit harmful gases. If no alternative exists, wood shelves should be coated with barriers such as wood sealants, which are applied directly to the shelving. Metal shelving should not be installed against an outside wall or beneath liquid-bearing pipes. (www.library .cornell.edu/preservation/librarypreservation/ mee/management/shelving.html)

Of course, the shelves should be deep enough to accommodate the largest books. That is, no books should be so large that they are sticking off the shelves. They are likely to be bumped when someone walks by or wheels past a book truck. Libraries naturally have oversize volumes, which should be shelved apart from the regular volumes. In fact, there are shelves for oversize, super-oversize, and enormous books, all of which should be shelved such that they are not protruding from the shelves. Large volumes (often called *folios*)[22] should not be shelved standing up; it could hurt the bindings or, for loosely packed shelves, cause the books to bend or skew in their boards. They should be stored lying down, maybe two or three to a shelf. For the mere convenience of the staff, it is easier to pull out a large volume if it is on the bottom of a stack of three books than it is to extract one from underneath seven or ten volumes. Also, if possible, the aisles in which these folios are stored should be wider than those for smaller books. Although this may seem obvious, it needs to be articulated because there are libraries with narrow aisles housing quite large volumes. It is hard on the shoulders and backs of those who want to page those books, and it could lead to their damage if the books have to be taken down at awkward angles.

One tenet of libraries is that books should not be stored on top or bottom shelves. The ones on top are hard to reach, especially for short people, and they are vulnerable to dripping water. The ones on the bottom are vulnerable to the water from floods and mops, and they, too, are difficult to take from the shelves because it requires a bit of contortion to see their call numbers. This is especially true for folios lying flat. But few libraries have the luxury of not needing to use those shelves. Libraries grow, and when shelves get full, it is easier to employ an empty neighboring shelf (e.g., a top or bottom one) than it is to shift lots of books to create space.[23] A similar tenet is that shelves should not be packed tightly. Getting a book off a tightly packed shelf subjects it to having its headcap (the top part of the spine) pulled loose, and millions of books show this damage. But again, as collections grow, they take up more and more space, and it is easier to pack a shelf tightly than it is to shift the collection to keep the shelves loose.

Shelves on which there is plenty of space for books should have bookends of some kind, the free-standing ones or the ones that are attached to the undersides of shelves and that can be slid back and forth to hold up the books on the shelves beneath. Bookends should not have any abrasive qualities (no scratchy surfaces, no projecting ends on any of their parts) that will damage the books they hold up. For areas in the country subject to earthquakes, some kind of system should be in place to keep books from falling off shelves in a temblor.

One system to hold books on their shelves employs a long, thin metal bar that is affixed to the underside of shelves. When there is any movement of the building, the bar swings down in front of all the books on the shelf beneath. This mechanism will prevent those books from falling, but it will not keep them from being pushed backward on the shelf from the wave motion of the quake. In the Northridge quake mentioned in the sidebars here and in chapter 2, UC Riverside's Special Collections Department had more than 4,500 books fall to the floor, mostly from the top three shelves. The books on the lower shelves were jolted into a wave pattern on their shelves, some books hanging over the front of the shelves ready to fall, and some on the same shelf pushed to the back. The damage to the ones that fell was devastating: large quartos and folios, and even thousands of octavos, with smashed bindings, covers broken loose from textblocks, crushed corners to volumes whose covers did not detach, and piles and piles of books strewn in the aisleways, some quite far from the shelves they fell from.[24]

The Preservation Officer, Sheryl Davis, devised a system of bungee cords stretched across the top three or four shelves throughout the department. They were inexpensive, easy to install, and easy to use. All the librarian had to do to get a book from the shelf was push the bungee cord up and grab a volume, which could be done with one hand. Also, the bungee cords were easier on the books than were the metal bars because the cords were flexible and soft.

Housing and Shelving for Papers

Papers should be stored flat in acid-free, archival boxes, preferably in folders or sleeves inside the

ALL OF THE Los Angeles basin is subject to earthquakes fairly frequently, though most of them are practically undetectable. But some are cataclysmic, and libraries have been seriously damaged because of them.

The Delmar T. Oviatt Library at California State University, Northridge was damaged in the January 17, 1994 Northridge Earthquake, as were most other buildings on the campus. The epicenter of the 6.7 magnitude quake was about a mile from the California State University, Northridge campus.

The Oviatt Library has three structural parts: the original reinforced concrete core building built in the early 1970's and two wings that opened in 1991. The Oviatt core suffered repairable structural damage in the Northridge Earthquake and reopened in August 1994. The east and west wings were built as steel frame structures to be more earthquake resistant. However, the earthquake instead gave engineers an education about the performance of steel frame buildings in quakes. Severe structural damage to the wings during the earthquake eventually led to demolition and rebuilding of the wings. Four-inch thick steel base plates cracked where the four-story high vertical steel structural columns came into the foundations of the wings.*

Though rigid steel is solid, there was no give in the structure, and the building cracked in places. That is why wood structures do better in quakes than do brick buildings.

*See the California State University, Northridge website at http://library.csun.edu/About/Quake). This site has an Earthquake Photo Gallery that shows the damage the library suffered.

boxes to keep them from shifting. If the archival boxes are full, the sleeved documents may be put into folders and stored upright—just so that they do not sag down in the boxes if they are stored upright. Putting documents into Mylar or paper enclosures is expensive and time-consuming, and it adds bulk to the collection, taking up more space than did the papers by themselves. But the best practice dictates protecting fragile paper documents by stabilizing them, especially if they are to be moved. Movement from the shelves to a reading room is one thing; moving them around in a shelf reconfiguration of the library or in a temporary movement out of the department as for a renovation of the space will subject the papers to a good deal of stress. Documents that should be kept flat could be turned upright by movers. This could cause the papers to "fall down" inside the boxes and get bent or crushed. Hence, boxes should be fairly full and the documents inside them should be as carefully stored as time, space, and resources will allow.

As just explained, boxes should ideally be full enough that the folders stand upright and not curl down, which could damage the papers. Photographs on paper (and other media, like glass slides, film-based slides, tintypes, and so on) should not rub up against one another, so they should be individually housed, also in archival, acid-free sleeves. Thin pamphlets may also warrant being individually sleeved. Maps and charts, and other large-format flat papers like broadsides and prints, will need special care in moves.

Large map cases with, say, four or five drawers in each unit stack up to a convenient height for librarians to access the contents. If the library needs more drawers, stacking the units higher is possible, but it increases the difficulty for the staff of getting to the contents of the drawers, and this awkwardness could lead to damage of the items when they are taken from the drawers. Such a stacking up should be avoided if possible. Also, some of the flat files are quite large, so adequate room in the aisles should be available for the staff to open the drawers fully so that they can take things out without having to torque their bodies or the items.

As already mentioned, rare book departments will contain items made from a wide variety of materials, and the preservation conditions, materials, and treatments of all these things will not be uniform. The best the library can do for rare (and even open-stacks) materials is to come up with a strategy (and with a physical environment) that is congenial to as many of the library's holdings as possible, and then try to modify conditions and the physical space to accommodate special materials.

Work Spaces in the Stacks

When a librarian pages items for a patron, it may be necessary to have some worktables near the storage shelves for the pager to look at books or papers before bringing them to the reading room. It is greatly counterproductive for a librarian to have to take something from the shelves and walk a good distance with it to lay it down to examine it to see if it is appropriate for the patron. The stacks should contain good work spaces in the aisles close to the collections, for the convenience of the staff and the safety of the items being consulted. Hence, in an area with large flat files, the library should have sizable worktables, big enough to accommodate large maps, charts, and volumes.

This, of course, means that the library must have adequate space for such work areas, which is not always the case. Libraries that have grown from housing small collections to taking up large areas usually did not have the luxury of foresight into the space needs of those working where collections now fill every inch. But if a special collections department is purpose built, there is time to plan for such needs.

WITH RESPECT TO shelving, the librarian must decide how items in flat files will be "shelved" during a move. One moving company promises that the large flat files and map cases in which these single-sheet pieces are housed will be appropriately filled so that every drawer is packed tightly, allowing the movers to lift the drawers out of their cabinets and carry them vertically with all their contents protected. No "falling down" or bending of the documents can take place if the drawers are properly filled. The company guarantees that it will use only smooth, non-abrasive archival materials to fill the drawers. This solution is much better than is the time-consuming (and hence expensive) alternative of taking all materials out of their drawers and packing them separately for the move—and then trying to return them to their original drawers after the move. Also, if drawers of flat items are stuffed full so that nothing can shift around during a move, it is possible for the movers to take the entire flat file, drawers and all.

Reformatting

One intermediate step in conservation may simply be reformatting.[25] That is, some items may be in such bad condition that they cannot be adequately conserved. Or the conservation may entail expenses far beyond the item's worth. If a surrogate can be made from the original—a digital copy, a microfilm, a paper photocopy—the replacement piece may be the best the library can offer to researchers, who can at least get much of the original information the item contained. A photocopy is better than no copy. Also, reformatting for the most part reduces the handling of the original substantially, so even though the piece does not go to a conservator (unless, of course, the conservator is the one who makes the surrogate), its life is extended by the reduced handling it will receive when a surrogate is available. Sometimes an item is in such disrepair that it is too fragile to be copied, so it might have to go to a conservator to stabilize it before it is reformatted. Until recently, reformatting was usually not used in special collections except for older materials (from the nineteenth century and before) when replacement copies could not be had or were far more expensive than the reformatting was. Nowadays, many special collections departments are digitizing substantial and important collections so that a wide audience has access to them and so that the originals can be handled much less often.

The Association for Library Collections and Technical Services of the ALA has a section called PARS, Preservation and Reformatting Section (see www .ala.org/alcts/mgrps/pars). Its missions, as the website simply states, are "preservation and reformatting of library materials in all types of institutions; applying new technologies to assure continued access to library collections." They are an active group, with publications, workshops, committees, interest groups, and working groups.

Perhaps the oldest and most used form of reformatting, going back to the 1920s,[26] is microfilm, not originally seen as a preservation medium. The standards for preservation microfilming were not set until the 1970s. Today microfilming is rivaled by attempts at achieving true preservation with digitization. According to Michèle V. Cloonan, "c. 1928, libraries, including the Library of Congress, Harvard

AT UC RIVERSIDE, one particular volume from our science fiction collection was required reading in a course at the university. It was the only cataloged copy in the country at the time, and our copy, in excellent condition at the beginning of the first class in which the book became required, started showing wear after only three uses. The class had about fifteen students, and it was going to be taught regularly by the professor. The volume dated to the early twentieth century and was probably out of copyright; and under the guise of fair use (see chapter 8 on legal issues), we photocopied the full text, then made about a half dozen copies from the first copy. Now the text could be read by at least six students at a time, and the reformatting saved the original from further deterioration. So even in special collections reformatting can be useful.

University Library, and the New York Public Library, begin microfilming projects that are not aimed specifically at preservation but pave the way for preservation microfilming."[27] Untold numbers of microfilms exist, holding images of every imaginable analog piece of library material. Massive newspaper microfilming projects have been under way for decades, and huge collections of manuscripts (and individual ones as well, not part of larger collections) have been microfilmed, along with pictures of a vast range of ephemeral items. Microfilming is considered a preservation medium because the black-and-white films have a longevity of about 500 years, and those in color will be usable for about 250 years. The website *Library Preservation and Conservation Tutorial* says,

> If microfilm has a quality polyester film base, is exposed and processed to international standards, is housed in stable protective enclosures, and is stored under the appropriate conditions, it will last for a minimum of 500 years. The longevity issue is vitally important, as it delineates the main difference between microfilm and other reformatting technologies such as digital imaging.[28]

It is clear that microfilming, "ancient technology" as it seems (the process is over one hundred years old), is still being used as a preservation medium until something else guaranteed to work comes along. This kind of reformatting is a fairly inexpensive, perfected technology: all you need is a camera, film, a way to develop the film, and a fairly simple machine that can project a light through the film. Today's microfilm readers offer good images on a screen (depending, of course, on the quality of the original film and photography), and the ability to make paper and digital copies. Although many administrators eschew microfilm for newer and more glitzy digital technology, they might be better served by the older and more proven method of reformatting. (See later in this chapter for a discussion of digital preservation.) One of the principle differences between microfilm and digital "preservation" is that in the former, once the original format is created (a reel of microfilm), it can be stored for centuries with essentially no monitoring, while the latter (a digital image) requires constant monitoring and updating, being migrated to newer platforms. In the long run, the film costs a fraction of what the digital format costs, and it will last far longer.

Another method of reformatting is simply to make paper-based copies using Xerox (dry) copying techniques. This uses a good deal of paper and fills a lot of space, but it is a proven, reliable preservation method and must be considered in any preservation program. If for no other reason, photocopying is far less expensive than is digitization, what with the latter's need for expensive hardware and software, constant monitoring, perpetual reformatting, and the costs of electricity to keep the originals "alive" and accessible.

The White-Glove Controversy

The Library Preservation and Conservation website says,

> When staff or users consult the text of a rare or unique item, they should use white cotton gloves, which help to prevent the transfer of the skin's natural oils onto the vulnerable leaves. Users should also use cotton gloves to handle nonpaper [sic] materials, such as microfilm, photographic prints, and negatives, touching only areas away from the images.

(www.library.cornell.edu/preservation/library preservation/mee/index.html)

Cathleen A. Baker and Randy Silverman, two noted conservators and preservation experts, in their article "Misperceptions about White Gloves," say,

> Institutional insistence that patrons and special collections staff don white cotton gloves when handling rare books and documents to prevent dirt and skin oils from damaging paper-based collections is inherently flawed; gloves are as easily soiled as bare hands. Cotton gloves are extremely absorbent, both from within and without.[29]

They add,

> Cotton gloves may not even help keep the reader's hands clean. In addition to accumulating dirt on the outer surface of the glove, warmth resulting from insulating the hand stimulates eccrine sweat gland production (Hurley 2001), causing hand dampness that is subsequently wicked through the porous fabric, increasing the likelihood the glove will attract, absorb, and distribute surface grime to the paper being handled. (p. 4)

Baker and Silverman also say that there is no scientific evidence that handling library materials (except for some kinds of photographs) without gloves damages them. They claim, "Wearing gloves actually increases the potential for physically damaging fragile material through mishandling, and this is especially true for ultra thin or brittle papers that become far more difficult to handle with the sense of touch dulled" (p. 5). Their conclusion is,

> White cotton gloves provide no guarantee of protecting books and paper from perspiration and dirt, yet they increase the likelihood of people inflicting physical damage to collection material. Implementing a universally observed, hand-cleaning policy is a reasonable and effective alternative to glove-use. (p. 8)

The most recent view on white gloves and rare materials is this: do not use the gloves, except for certain kinds of photographs or for artists' books bound in metals that may be damaged by fingerprints. My advice is, keep clean, soft, white gloves on hand in the reading room and in the stacks in case they are needed. But for the most part, they are not needed for almost all library materials.

Deacidification

From about 1875 on, hundreds of millions of books and documents were produced on acidic paper. The acid comes from lignin, a component of the wood pulp from which the paper was made. It also comes from the papermaking process: beating the cotton pulp to macerate it to separate the fibers did not challenge the machinery; wood pulp, however, tougher than cotton or linen fibers, required more beating, so chemicals were used to break down the fibers. (In chapter 4 the difference between mechanical pulp and chemical pulp is explained.) To make the paper white, manufacturers used various kinds of bleaches, which, themselves, were acidic, and if the bleach were not properly washed out of the paper, it would remain as an inherent vice to weaken the fibers over time.

Acids could also be introduced in inks, alum rosin sizing, or sheets of paper or other materials (leaves or flowers or silk ribbons) pressed or bound into a book. As noted earlier, sometimes illustrations had tissue guards (also called offset sheets) laid or bound in to keep the pigment of an image from bleeding onto the facing leaf; but the tissue guards themselves were made of acidic paper, and the acid migrated to the leaves touching the guards. One common source of acid burn is the adhesives used to glue down the endsheets or the turn-ins on the binding; another is the acid that exists in the pigments used to dye leather covers.

At first the acidity—the inherent vice in the material—was not noticeable, but over a short time the pages started to yellow and become brittle.[30] Today billions of items in libraries are quietly eroding, albeit at a slow rate. The acids do their worst on the fibers during the first, say, fifteen or twenty years. From then their damage slows down, and anything that is fifty or seventy-five years old has already seen the worst period of its degradation, unless it is stored in poor environmental conditions.

Nonetheless, untreated items are still degrading, and something can be done to slow down or stop the damage. There are two kinds of deacidification:[31] treatment on a single item or mass treatments, of large numbers of items at once. Mass processes must be done off site, while the treatment of single volumes or documents can be done at the library—even in the special collections department. In fact, because of the nature of rare book collections, mass deacidification is almost never an option for their holdings, mostly because in such treatment bindings can be harmed and the process alters the original.

Although the actions of the conservator are really a form of conservation, when they are done en masse, they are a form of collections maintenance, and thus fall under the rubric "Preservation." An alkaline buffer can be introduced into the paper (and cloths) of books that will arrest the acids and act as a buffer against future deterioration. Such buffers will not make the paper stronger. The LISWiki website says,

> Deacidification processes are either aqueous (using water) or non-aqueous (not using water). Most deacidification processes use some type of alkaline earth metal to neutralize acidity. This ingredient is carried and placed into the fibers of the acidic material through a gas or liquid carrier (Zachary 2002, 7). Documents can either be treated individually or in groups (mass deacidification).
>
> Aqueous processes cannot be used on documents that are sensitive to water, or that contain water-soluble inks or dyes. Aqueous processes can only be used on single items, and cannot be used on bound documents and books, unless the books are taken apart, treated, and rebound.
>
> Non-Aqueous deacidification processes use solvents or gases to carry the alkaline buffering agent. They are well-suited to treating books and other bound materials because the gas or solvent is able to penetrate deep into the crevices and close spaces of books and treat the material evenly.[32]

Historically there have been several processes purveyed by about a half dozen companies. Most of them are now history, with only the Bookkeeper process, operated by Preservation Technologies, now in use in the United States for mass treatment.[33] In Europe methods derived from Wei T'o are still in use. For a discussion of the Wei T'o product, used in non-aqueous deacidification, see www.weito.com/Weito%20non aqueous%20deacidification%20system.htm.

Although it is good for the special collections librarian to know about deacidification and mass deacidification, the latter has little place in rare book librarianship. The objects in her care, if they need to be deacidified, will be treated one at a time by a trained conservator or, possibly, by the librarian herself. Cans of deacidifying sprays are available on the market; they need little training to be used, and if the spray is used on properly selected documents or volumes, there is little danger that the item treated will be harmed. Collectors or booksellers, wishing to deacidify books or documents, can use this method with no training, especially the Wei T'o spray cans that are available at many conservation supply houses.

Deacidification is a boon to libraries and their patrons, for in its mass application it can extend the useful life of millions of books and other paper-based materials. It must be used with care, however, for some processes can discolor the items treated (it might change the color of illustrations or binding materials); aqueous methods can cause metal staples hidden in some bindings to rust; it may cause some volumes to cockle; if treatments are done en masse, large numbers of items must be shipped to the company doing the work, and such shipping—especially of rare and valuable items—could be damaging and costly. Joachim Liers, in his study "Mass Deacidification: The Efficacy of the Papersave Process," says,

> In extreme cases, e.g., very brittle paper, the introduction of too high an alkaline reserve can neutralise the benefits of the deacidification by reducing the paper's flexibility. Therefore, the requirements concerning the results of the deacidification treatment should not be established generally but depending on the material to be treated.[34]

Deacidification requires much work on the part of the rare book librarian. Selection of a process is important, as is selection of particular items for the treatment. It will not do to take large numbers of items, or small groups of things, and send them off for treatment without a careful analysis of what can withstand the treatment and what cannot, what is worth deacidifying and what is not. Decisions must be made with an item-by-item evaluation. The use of mass deacidification is probably not called for with special collections materials. But this does not mean that rare book librarians should not use deacidification at all. It is appropriate for individual items that are acidic, and it should be considered for the treatment of single items. Some volumes or documents may need to be spot tested for colorfastness or other characteristics. There is a risk of cockling or some other kind of physical change in the process. A careful plan must be delineated in the decision making.

Rare book departments need to consider this method of preservation because the items they house are of particular importance to scholarship. That is one of the reasons the things are in the department in the first place. And with special collections, which may contain large numbers of items that are not necessarily monetarily valuable, there is likely to be a good number of pieces printed in the last 125 years—which means many things on acidic paper.

Tools and Equipment

Rare book departments should have available to their readers various tools and equipment that are designed to reduce wear on the materials the patrons will be using. The aim is to make the readers' experience as rich as it can be while minimizing the stress they put on books and other items.

A standard prohibition in special collections is the use of pens. The library should have a supply of pencils (with no. 2 leads) available. The softer leads are erasable, so if a patron marks a library item, the marking should be easy to remove. Other items prohibited in the reading room are the patrons' backpacks or briefcases, their own folders or books, bulky outer clothes, or any other item in which library materials can be sequestered. That includes the patrons' notepads. So the department should have sheets of notepaper available for users. Before the scholars leave the department, library staff should go through these sheets to make sure nothing has been hidden between them. Lockers should be provided for backpacks and other carrying bags, and coatracks should be available. These are, of course, security measures, but security is a form of preservation.

Books often do not lie open at 180-degree angles, so cradles should be available—made from foam or other soft, nonabrasive, archival materials, and snakes and other weights should be provided. As has already been explained, snakes are cloth tubes filled with some heavy substance (buckshot or sand, for example) that can be draped over the edges of a book's leaves to hold the volume open. That way, the patron does not have to hold the book open with his hands. The cloth they are made from (and the cloth covering other kinds of weights) must naturally be colorfast, soft, and smooth so that they will not abrade the library materials. Many rare book departments also have bookmarks printed for their patrons, sometimes with information about the library or some other advertisement about the department. They should be printed on acid-free, archival paper, and patrons can use them in the materials they are consulting in the reading room. These bookmarks protect the materials by keeping the patrons from using their pencils or their own, possibly acidic, markers.

Opening a book too much—beyond the angle it opens comfortably by itself—can break the spine or, for perfect-bound volumes, can crack the spine and cause leaves to break loose from the binding. Bookrests should be provided, and the department should have them in many sizes and adjustable to different angles. Really tightly bound volumes may need to be restricted to 90-degree opening angles, so snakes and bookrests will certainly be useful to keep the user's hands off them.

In recent years special collections departments have eased up on their restrictions on the use of cameras in the reading room. Patrons may now photograph certain materials with the department's approval. To make the picture taking easy on the books, some departments are supplying good tables with special lighting apparatuses. The Rare Book and Manuscript Library at the University of Illinois at Urbana-Champaign has a written policy, "The Rare Book & Manuscript Library Personal Photographing Form," that states,

> Permission of a librarian is required for the use of personal digital cameras. Items to be photographed must be evaluated for condition and handled as directed by Reading Room staff. Material designated as restricted or fragile may not be photographed. Final permission to take pictures is granted conditional on the full and accurate completion of this form.[35]

Certainly, restrictions must be clearly stated and assiduously reinforced. The longevity of the library's holdings is at stake.

Some rare book departments have two other tools. One is a lighted magnifier for examining manuscripts, illustrations, or anything else that needs to be enlarged. The other is a light sheet for revealing watermarks in paper. The first of these is easy to obtain: any store that sells equipment for people who have eyesight problems will have a variety of magnifying glasses with lights. They come in various sizes and shapes, and they are fairly inexpensive. To look at watermarks, patrons can use the Fibre Optic Light Sheet, manufactured by Preservation Equipment Ltd in England.[36] The device consists of a plastic sheet, rigid but quite thin, attached to a thick tube, containing fiber optic filaments that light up the entire sheet. This can be slipped into a book under a leaf to illuminate it from behind. It is so thin that the book can be closed without putting any stress onto the binding. The light will reveal the watermarks as well as can be done by holding up a loose sheet of paper to a strong light source behind it. Using the light sheet makes it possible to reveal the watermarks without holding the book up to a light at an awkward angle. The device gives off no heat and is not damaging to paper.

Scholars may need measuring devices for illustrations, bindings, or other phenomena, so the library should have a good ruler or tape measure on hand. These should not have any sharp or abrasive parts, and there should be ones long enough to measure large folios.

Of course, the department must have the standard photocopying and scanning equipment, but whether patrons are allowed to do their own copying is a local decision. For fragile and rare materials, there should be a restriction. And the patrons should not be allowed to copy anything until they have been given permission. All copying or scanning equipment should have a book-minder-type bed onto which volumes can be laid without having to open them 180 degrees. This means that only one page at a time can be copied, and though patrons will want to save money and time by doing two facing pages at once, this must be forbidden. Some departments have a copying limit of a certain number of pages from a single volume or a particular percentage of the whole text. A department may not allow patrons to do any copying, so the copying machines are kept out of the clients' sight. Restrictions for the copying of manuscripts should also be in place, and the department's policies should be spelled out carefully in a document that the librarians can hand to researchers. A paper document (or one fixed in digital form on the library's website) carries more authority than does an oral statement.

Lamination and Encapsulation

An old method of preservation/conservation of paper documents was lamination, sealing an item between two sheets of a plastic film, usually using some form of adhesive, and creating a sealed, waterproof container. In September 1963 a UNESCO document described the process as "a satisfactory method of preservation of books and documents in their original form."[37] The document, now a half century old, presented lamination as a method of preservation, state of the art in its day, but now wholly discredited because lamination is irreversible. Lamination creates a microenvironment, inside of which condensation can form if the item is exposed to a warm environment, and, if the laminated item is not properly deacidified before treatment, its inherent vice continues to do its damage inside the capsule.[38]

Encapsulation is today preferred to lamination. In encapsulation, the document is placed between layers of archival transparent film, and the upper and lower layers are attached to one another with double-stick tape, sonic welding, or some other means, but with the corners left open so that no microenvironment can form and so that the film can easily be removed and the document taken out with no damage. The sonic machines are elaborate and expensive, but they do beautiful work, their seams practically invisible. But anyone with a little training can become proficient at encapsulation by hand using the double-stick tape. Melinex or Mylar films are nonacidic and can be used safely to encapsulate all paper materials. Deacidifying papers (if possible) before they are encapsulated will prolong their life, and the process, completely reversible, allows them to be removed from the capsule for treatment or other handling.

Book Enclosures and Shrink-Wrapping

Some volumes are in shaky or "compromised" condition and should not be left on the shelf without some kind of protection. Some of them may have red rot and will stain neighboring volumes. Chapter 2 has shown the benefits of shrink-wrapping. As explained in chapter 2 of this volume, shrink-wrapping is an excellent technique for moving weak, damaged, fragile items. The process, one of two that librarians have brilliantly adapted from the food industry (the other, freeze-drying, will be considered later in this chapter), is inexpensive, and anyone can be trained to do it. Other enclosures are useful but can be expensive, and they take up more space. For many decades librarians have been constructing phase boxes, so called because they were thought of as one phase of a book's handling, intermediate between being on a shelf uncovered and being fully conserved. These boxes can be constructed from archival board. NEDCC's Preservation Pamphlet 4.5, "Protecting Books with Custom-Fitted Boxes," shows clamshell and phase boxes, explains their use, and shows how to construct them.[39]

Because of the fiscal realities of libraries—especially rare book departments—the "phase" boxes usually become the permanent enclosures for the books. There is nothing wrong with this because they do protect the volumes they hold, but they are not airtight, they are not rigid and strong, and they do not stop deterioration (as with powdering leather). They will, however, protect their books and their neighbors on the shelves, and they will prevent loose parts (like detached covers or loose backstrips) from being separated from the books. Librarians, booksellers, or collectors can buy commercial boxes or can make them. Box-making machines are available if the library needs a large quantity of them.

Other kinds of enclosures include Solander boxes and slipcases. The Solander box (also called the "fall-down-back box") is named after Swedish botanist Daniel Solander (1733–1782). Wikipedia says,

> The case is usually constructed of hardcover or wood, and has a hinged lid connected to its base. Both lid and bottom sections of the box have three fixed side sections or "lips"; the lid is slightly larger so that the side pieces "nest" when the case is closed. The fourth "spine" side has flexible joints where it joins the main top and bottom pieces and so goes flat onto the surface where the box is opened. The front-edge of the case often contains a clasp for closure. The exterior is covered with heavy paper, fabric or leather, and its interior may be lined with padded paper or felt, especially if made for a book. All materials should be acid-free for conservation.[40]

The great benefits of the Solander box are that it opens completely, so that items inside can be taken out and replaced without damaging them; the box, if properly made, can be nearly airtight and will protect the enclosed items from dust and light; and it can be acquired in quantity in standard sizes or can be made to order. The drawbacks are that they are costly to make—much more expensive than phase boxes—and they take up a good deal of space. For a few volumes that need protection, they are relatively compact. But large quantities will add significantly to shelf space. A shelf that is tightly packed may be able to accommodate one or two such boxes, but the shelf will get even tighter with the boxes.[41]

Slipcases pose the threat of having whatever is slipped inside them damaged if the case is too tight or the items inserted catch on the sides of the case.

Also, with a slipcase, the spine of a book can be exposed, leaving the item exposed to light and air (unless the slipcase is a double case, with one shell that slips into the other). In their favor is that they are inexpensive to make, and they do allow a damaged item to be moved with a reduced chance of being damaged further.

Many companies offer other kinds of enclosures, including various kinds of boxes, encapsulation, and envelopes. In the special collections department these can be quite useful in protecting fragile, valuable materials. The librarian, bookseller, or collector just needs to know that the materials these enclosures are made of are not abrasive and that they are acid free and archival.

> **OVER THE YEARS** booksellers have used various kinds of plastic bags and sleeves when they ship books. Just because something is plastic and is from a bookseller does not guarantee that it is archival. I bought some beautiful, heavy-gauge plastic bags from a company that specialized in these bags, and I stored some of my prized and more delicate books in them. After about fifteen years some of the bags began to crack and fall apart; some of them turned yellow. Some cockled or dried out and shrank in odd ways. As soon as I saw this deterioration, I got my books out of the bags. Better to leave the items on the shelves unprotected than to leave them touching these deteriorating plastic bags.
>
> Also, some fine presses or booksellers will ship books in cardboard boxes that are made of cheap brown paper. If the books inside are wrapped in paper, the acids in the brown paper of the box could migrate right through the "protective" paper of the boxes. Although the boxes might shield the books from light and from jarring damage if they are dropped, they could be working their insidious evil silently and invisibly inside.

Copy Machines and Scanners

Someone once said that photocopying is the greatest substitution for reading ever invented. It is true that since the invention of the Xerox machine, scholars have asked librarians to "make me a copy of that (essay) (article) (chapter)." It makes sense because the patron has a finite time in a library reading room and can maximize her time by taking text home to read at leisure when the library is closed. Trillions of pages of text have been photocopied since the technology has made that possible. According to Kitty Nicholson, "In 1960, an estimated 70 million copies were made [by the Xerox process]. Twenty-five years later an estimated 500 billion copies were made."[42]

Nicholson explains the differences between electrostatic and non-electrostatic copying, saying, "Conservators should be aware that there are preservation problems associated with some types of photocopies, though generally non-electrostatic copies present far more problems than electrostatic copies." She cites William Hawken, who "compiled a detailed survey on the large number of copying systems that were known in the 1960's (11). Stability problems are of three types: unstable images, unstable supports, and poor adhesion between image and support."[43] Unstable copying essentially means that if rare book departments rely on electrostatic and nonelectrostatic copies, they could be losing access to the materials they own, especially if they make a copy and get rid of the original, as was a practice in some libraries.

This scholarship was cutting edge when it was published. But we have come a long way. When the medium was fairly new—in the 1960s and '70s, the light sources used in the machines gave off UV rays. Nicholson says,

> Ultraviolet exposure does remain a concern. In the early days of photocopiers, the sensitizing light source was filtered green to match the optimal sensitivity of the photoconductive surface. This filtering conveniently removed all ultraviolet (17). Today a variety of light sources may be used. As glass transmits ultraviolet rays between 325 and 400 nanometers, copiers with ultraviolet-producing lights such as fluorescent, tungsten halogen or xenon flash will expose documents to some ultraviolet. (18)[44]

And she mentions the possible preservation problems caused by the ozone and nitrous oxide gas, by-products of photocopying, that could damage paper or images (especially color images) on paper. Her conclusion about electrostatic copiers and color photocopiers is that "[t]hey are potential sources of pollutant gases and may be hazardous both to people and to art and artifacts." This was the state of the art in the 1980s when Nicholson was writing.

However, today's copiers are more sophisticated, with advanced technology that requires less damaging light sources. Anne Jordan's article "Archives: Reference Photocopying"[45] says that the amount of light the documents being copied are exposed to is extremely small and will do little damage to the items. But if they are copied many times, they might see some damage. Her recommendation is that a master copy for future copying be made, and subsequent copies should be made from that master, not from the original. She says, "Making a single photocopy of a document or photograph constitutes only a small exposure to the damaging effects of light and heat, effects that are multiplied in repeated copying" (p. 3).

By 2000, the literature was showing the same concerns. The (British) National Preservation Office published *Photocopying of Library and Archive Materials*,[46] which says, "Inexpert handling and the heat and light generated by machines are the primary causes of damage" (p. 1). Their conclusion, however, is the same as Jordan's:

> The amount of UV radiation emitted will vary between machines but according to research undertaken so far it is thought unlikely that the short exposure during the making of a single copy will cause any measurable damage. Concern should be raised, however, when an item is subjected to multiple or frequent copying. (p. 2)

The document also says that handling could cause more damage than would exposure to light. So they have several recommendations of what *not* to bring to the photocopying machine—what they call "Materials Most at Risk," including

- books which weigh 10 lb or more or which are more than 2″ thick. These are difficult to handle and strain is put on the binding in trying to obtain a copy.

- books which are larger than the photocopier platen [this, of course, includes newspapers]
- vellum bindings, which can be brittle and prone to damage under pressure and/or heat
- books with historically important or fine bindings
- books with fold-outs which are larger than their covers are extremely vulnerable to tearing
- books with torn or brittle pages will deteriorate further if subjected to the photocopying process
- parchment
- items with seals attached
- perfect bound books, which are glued rather than sewn, such as many paperbacks, cannot take the strain of being opened to 180° without the risk of breaking
- books stapled or stitched through the sides
- books with broken sewing or loose pages
- books with tight bindings
- books with torn, missing or deteriorating covers
- large sheet maps, plans and charts
- newspapers (pp. 3–4)

This list can be useful for a special collections department as part of a form that shows patrons what may not be copied from the collection. And it is a useful reminder for anyone wanting to make photocopies of what should not be subjected to the process.

Though the more common form of reformatting today is digitization, photocopying is still common enough for me to have spent so much time on it here. Both forms of copying subject books to stresses, and these recommendations are a practical part of a preservation program.

It is obvious that no one wants to damage an item, under any circumstances, especially in a special collections department. Damage is cumulative and may be quite subtle from one handling to another. Photocopying subjects all items to handling, so only the gentlest kind of handling should be employed in copying. Any treatment that puts stress on the material should be avoided.

Moving the Collection

This topic has been covered in chapter 2 of the present text. It is worth mentioning here that one of the key issues of moving is that the collection is subject to damage during the operation; a move could be a preservation nightmare. All things in a collection could suffer physically if they are mishandled. They will be moved from a stable to an unstable environment. They will be, for a time, out of the secure perimeter of the special collections department. They may be in the hands of outsiders—bonded or not— and are thus subject to theft or mutilation of one kind or another. All of these are preservation issues, and the special collections staff must be exceptionally vigilant during the move, at both ends and in between.

All this activity and planning falls under the rubric of preservation and conservation, because the careful intellectual and physical work being done for the move aims to get the collection from point A to point B with no damage or loss. Those in special collections must pay particular attention to this because they are in charge of some of the most valuable and important objects the institution has. A preservation officer should be part of the planning team.

THE PRESERVATION PLAN AND ADAPTIVE PRESERVATION

The rare book department may have a formal Preservation Plan, delineating all its policies and practices and including what kinds of actions should be done on what schedule: regular walkthroughs to look for evidence of mold, the presence of water or infestation, or clutter; regular cleaning; regular monitoring of the environment, with a scheduled reading of the recorded information gathered by the monitoring equipment; statements about standard practices for patrons; perhaps a yearly or semiyearly visit from the physical plant personnel for their inspection; guidelines for deacidification of the collection; and so forth. If there are any signs that anything is wrong—in or outside this plan—the department should take immediate action, adapting the actions to the needs, and perhaps adding to the preservation plan.

Further, the department must keep meticulous records pertaining to anything that reveals deterioration or the possibility of it. If there is a mold outbreak, the time of its discovery should be recorded, along with photodocumentation and a written report delineating what the problem was and what was done to take care of it—with an analysis of its cause and a record of the changes that were made to prevent it from recurring. If an individual item is identified with any kind of damage, this should be recorded somewhere in the online record so that future staff will know that a patron later on did not cause the problem. And, as will be discussed later in this chapter, any conservation treatment should be recorded as well. As already noted, the environment should be monitored constantly and the records of conditions stored for future use.

Every facility presents its own challenges, so the librarian must adapt her activities, records, policies and procedures, and report keeping to the situation at hand. A comprehensive preservation program takes good planning, institutional resources, a dedicated staff who are schooled in (and who buy into the importance of) the preservation activities, and an understanding administration willing and able to support the program. It takes good relations between the special collections personnel, the administration, the physical plant, and all others involved in the department.

PRESERVATION ASSESSMENT

Although the main library must do its own preservation assessment—that is, an evaluation of the collection and the building housing it to see what items are in the greatest need of preservation—the special collections department should have its own such assessment. It may also create a report for the department alone and then have that document embedded into the larger assessment of the library. This approach, however, may effectively hide the rare book needs in the larger document, so it will probably be better to have a separate assessment, embodied in a separate document, with the news of its existence broadcast to all library personnel, the local police and fire departments, the physical plant

of the institution, and anyone else deemed appropriate.

The reason is obvious: in a disaster of any kind, or in the preservation planning for the institution, those working on the assessment should understand the high level of priority that the special collections department should have because of the nature of the materials stored there. Any preservation planning should recognize the importance of rare materials and should recommend their immediate care in an emergency of any kind. The document that emerges from this preservation planning should recommend that special collections' needs be addressed before the needs of the objects outside the department. Of course, in a museum rare book department, objects from the institution's collection could be much more valuable than are the books, and a triage of what to save and what to let perish might be necessary.

An institution's archives may well be housed in the special collections department, and many documents in an archives are unique and irreplaceable and carry valuable information about the history of the institution and many other topics. This alone should convince administrators to give focused attention to—and support the creation of—a discrete preservation assessment project for a special collections department. Of course, the main holdings of the department, beyond the archives, can also be of inestimable value, so their preservation should figure high in the institution's preservation-planning priorities.

One element of the preservation assessment is the collection condition review. A professional consultant (or a consulting company specializing in such assessments; the Northeast Document Conservation Center in Andover, Massachusetts, for example, is one such agency) should be hired to do this assessment, though perhaps the institution may already have a preservation librarian capable of creating this report. The report can be quite long and detailed, with photographs, statistics, drawings, and a thorough explanation of what condition the building and the collection are in, where items are deteriorating, and where the building needs upgrading; and with many recommendations of what to do to bring the building and collection into a better, more stable state. The report may wish to offer minimal (i.e., easy- and inexpensive-to-implement) solutions; actions to take if there are good resources committed to the collections; and top-of-the-line actions if resources are no object.

Another element in such an assessment may be a list of personnel the assessor thinks would be desirable for the institution to have on hand to bring the collection to a safe level of preservation. A recommendation of adding personnel, of course, would fall under the last of the levels just described: expensive and top-of-the-line, because personnel, especially those with advanced training and experience in preservation, are not inexpensive.[47]

Conservation

Along with the preservation plan, which works at a comprehensive level in the department (and in the library as a whole), there must be a conservation program, if resources allow, to repair damage to individual items in the collection. Most rare book libraries do not have resident conservators available, so the department head should have some kind of plan to allow for repair.[48]

THE AIM OF CONSERVATION

The aim of conservation is not to make damaged items look better or merely to stop the damage (though these are by-products of conservation). The basic premise and guiding principle is that conservation should extend the useful life of an item without reducing its intellectual value. That is, whatever information the item has, the conservator must try to retain it all while allowing patrons to have access to the original piece for as long as the treatment will allow. As already explained, many conservators, especially those new in the profession, will not understand what the intellectual value of an item is, where it lies, and how it is ferreted out by scholars. And many curators, especially those new in the profession, will not be conversant with the most recent conservation treatments, materials, and practices available. So they must work closely with one another. The curators (the rare book librarians,

booksellers, or collectors) can explain why an original endpaper must be retained, why a mildewed leaf that looks terrible might have provenance information on it that must not be lost, or how a terribly stained inserted scrap of paper inside a binding might reveal something about the original binding of a book, the nature of its sale, its edition, or its provenance. The conservators can explain how a new kind of mending tissue from Germany is as good as, or better than, a Japanese tissue that they have been using for decades. Together the curator and the conservator can come up with a plan that satisfies the needs—and meets the recommendations—of both.[49]

THE TREATMENT PLAN

The message, of course, is that curators and conservators must work in tandem when a book is sent off for repair. Once a treatment plan is decided upon by these two parties, the conservator must create a document detailing the results of his conversations with the curator. The plan should include everything about this volume worth recording:

- What the problems are with it (i.e., why it was taken in for conservation)
- What the treatment proposal is, based on conversations with the curator
- What steps will be taken to fix the volume or document
- What the piece looks like (this accompanied with photographs) at the beginning of the project (eventually there will be photographs of what it looks like at various stages of treatment, and what it looks like when the treatment is completed)
- What the conservator finds as the treatment progresses
- What materials are removed from or added to the item during treatment

Sometimes during treatment the conservator uncovers something that was invisible at the start of the treatment, and he must consult with the curator to decide if the original plan must be stuck to or if a new direction must be taken.

THE CONSERVATION TREATMENT REPORT

Emanating from the plan just delineated, the conservator must create a full report, which should include the following information:

- The call number of the item (or whatever information is used to retrieve it)
- Standard bibliographic information (author, title, city of publication, publisher, and date for books, and equivalent information for manuscripts); for early books there may also be a collation included in the record, along with a record of the number of pages, the illustrations and their type and placement in the volume, and the presence of tissue guards, bound-in bookmarks, or anything else worth mentioning
- A name of a librarian or curator who is responsible for bringing the work to the conservator
- The conservator's name
- The date of the transfer to the conservator
- The date the item was inspected (by the conservator in tandem with the curator)
- The date the item was returned to the curator before the actual conservation treatment begins (if it is returned)
- A full description of the item, including its genre (e.g., book, manuscript, letter, photograph, newspaper, glass plate negative, etc.), textblock, paper, and binding
- A description of the item's component parts (e.g., book printed in black ink on white paper, bound with blue cloth over boards, etc.)
- The item's measurements (perhaps for the closed book including the dimensions of the cover and also the dimensions of the textblock); this may be complemented by the dimensions of the item after treatment, if the size differs
- The item's condition and structural integrity
- Whether the item has any foreign substances (powder, frass, dirt or dust, etc.), tip-ins, or items laid in

- The item's overall condition, with a listing of any damage present
- The treatment objective
- The proposed treatment decided upon by the curator and conservator (at this point the document should be signed and dated by the conservator and curator); sometimes more than one treatment can be proposed, figuring in costs, time, and extensiveness of the work to be done, and describing various results; hence, this proposed treatment may include a budget
- An estimated time of completion of the conservation work
- A detailed description of the actual treatment, accompanied by before, during, and after photographs, and including a full listing of the materials used (and possibly the company that made the materials)
- A date on which the conservation work was completed and the book returned to the curator
- A signature line for the curator and the conservator corroborating the return
- A statement about whether the item was additionally given its own housing (e.g., a slipcase or protective box)

There may also be a line in the form for "Change in Plans," for it might be that the conservator, in the middle of his work, learns something about the item that would make the original plan not as good as originally suggested. The record should contain information on the time the whole operation took, the materials used, the costs involved, and whatever other information the librarian or the conservator needs. The report may also contain a section called "notes," in which are recorded anything the conservator may wish to state about the item treated, the treatment, the materials used, the success at achieving the objective of the treatment, or anything else that may be useful to future users of the conserved piece.

This information should be retained in a file—on paper or online—and the fact that the book has been conserved should be put into the cataloging record along with a note that the file delineating the treatment is available for inspection. That information may also be placed on or in the treated item so that patrons using it will be informed of the conservation work. If any part of the original item had to be removed (fragments of paper or binding, the original cover, a dust jacket, laid-in pieces, endpapers, or anything else), these should be housed in Mylar sleeves or some other kind of enclosure and retained with the report.

THE PRINCIPLE OF REVERSIBILITY

One of the tenets of conservation, as already noted, is that whatever treatment is done, the conservator should try to maintain all the information the item contains. Another tenet is that, as much as possible, no treatment should be irreversible. In the nineteenth century a conservation practice for leaves in a book was to put a covering of thin silk over the leaf—called *silking*. The fine adhesive would dry invisibly, and the silk was so thin that the text on the page was completely legible; the silking was essentially indiscernible. Within a few decades, if the book was not properly housed (and even if it was, in many cases), the adhesive dried out, turned white and powdery, and began to obscure the text, and the silk began to pull off the sheet. Silking was usually reversible if it was done over a sheet that contained no fugitive colors or pigments and if the adhesive was soluble. Newer methods of repair using Japanese mending tissue (made from kozo fibers) have become the norm in rare book conservation, and these repairs are, themselves, reversible.

Another method of conservation already discussed earlier, lamination of leaves of paper, was once popular. As Grace Dobush says,

> in the early 20th century, lamination was a celebrated new tool in the conservator's arsenal. Among its proponents: the National Archives and Records Administration (NARA) and the Library of Congress. From the late 1930s until the 1980s, NARA laminated what may total thousands of documents—including the Emancipation Proclamation and Louisiana Purchase paperwork. Now modern conservationists are trying to make the best of it.[50]

And as *Guidelines for the Care of Works on Paper with Cellulose Acetate Lamination* says,

> First introduced in the 1930s, lamination quickly became the primary choice for repairing and strengthening papers on a large scale. Now, however, conservators recognize that the materials used in lamination may degrade, damaging the very objects the process was intended to preserve. . . . The lamination process involved deacidifying a document, layering it between tissue and thin sheets of plastic, and fusing them together in a heated press. (http://anthropology.si.edu/conservation/lamination)

This paper shows why lamination is damaging. And the damage is irreversible because the lamination cannot be undone.

The conservation community has since proclaimed that no treatment should be irreversible, and every attempt has been made to come up with methods of treatment that can be redone if a better one comes along. However, as Paul Banks has said, "No [conservation] treatment is reversible."[51] No matter what work has been done, the item treated can never be returned 100 percent to the condition it was in before that treatment. So the rare book librarian, working with the conservator, must understand where in an item information lies, must know the physical materials of the item (what it is made of, if it has inherent vice, how it is put together, and so on), must settle on a treatment that is as reversible as possible and that removes the least information possible, and must record all actions taken on the item in its treatment.

The present text is not a manual on conservation. The aim here is to present some general principles and to let conservators and curators, booksellers, collectors, and other readers know what is possible and what cautions are in place. For specific information about treatments and places to go for them, consult the CoOL sites cited in note 4. A world of assistance is available from some of the best conservators in the world.

CONSERVATION TRAINING

As with preservation, librarians should have some basic training in conservation. This, of course, does not mean that they will be doing the conservation treatments themselves, though there is nothing to stop a librarian from doing them. The knowledge the librarian (or the bookseller or collector—or anyone else handling rare books, manuscripts, and ephemera) has is useful in the conversation she will have with a conservator brought in to work on damaged items. That knowledge, also, will help her develop preservation standards and practices for her collection. But the knowledge need not translate to action. As Beth Doyle says,

> Not everyone has the skills to be a conservator[;] it is extremely complex work requiring fine motor skills, a working knowledge of organic chemistry, an understanding of materials dating back millennia, a basic understanding of preservation and conservation theory, and the ability to translate all of that into practice. To be successful you need extensive training, internships and mentors that allow you to practice your skills while learning new ones.[52]

All librarians will profit from a knowledge of conservation, but those in special collections will surely want to know as much as possible about the kinds of materials and treatments available for the rare materials in their care. At worst, they should learn the vocabulary of conservation so that they can communicate intelligently and intelligibly with conservators.

There is no shortage of opportunities for those in the rare book field to get training in conservation. Because the library world is closely aligned with archives and museums, and because there are training programs in these fields as well, the prospects for education are extensive. At one website alone, the Smithsonian Museum Conservation Institute, are listed dozens of programs (www.si.edu/mci/English/learn_more/taking_care/conservation_training.html). Because this site focuses primarily on art conservation, not all of these programs focus on books and manuscripts, but inasmuch as special collections departments are likely to have a wide variety of objects beyond paper-based materials, many of these programs could be useful to those in rare books. The Wikipedia article on the same subject (art conservation) has another listing of institutions that may be useful to librarians, booksellers, and collectors (http://en.wikipedia.org/wiki/Conservation_and_restoration_training).

The CoOL website, referred to a number of times in this book, has a link to "Educational Opportunities in museum, library, and archives conservation/preservation" (http://cool.conservation-us.org/bytopic/education/). The site has general information, resources for conservation educators, and an extensive list of training programs worldwide. Anyone wishing to get information/training in conservation for library materials should begin by consulting the CoOL website.

BASIC SKILLS

The amount of education available, and the breadth of topics that this education could cover, is extensive. As noted, the rare book person will not necessarily be doing the work himself, but being conversant with all that can be done is important for responsible stewardship of a collection. Some of the areas of knowledge are essential; others are useful. In fact, much of what has been covered in chapter 4 of the present volume—information about the physical makeup of the materials in the collection—is important to know. With respect to actual treatments, the following topics should be in the rare book person's arsenal. This list is not meant to be definitive; it covers only some basic areas of concern.

- What kinds of things the librarians can do in-house and what must go to a conservator
- Decision making based on type of collection and its use
- Whether parts of an original item that will be reformatted will be saved or not (and how it all will be recorded)
- Basic information about the materials the items in the collection are composed of (papyrus, parchment, paper [coated and uncoated; waterleaf and sized; white and colored; etc.], plastics, metals, cloths [starch-filled; acrylic-, pryoxylin-, or vinyl-impregnated; plastic-coated], grains in paper and cloths, leathers and other animal-skin covers, strings and cords, Plexiglas, etc.) and recommended environmental conditions for their storage

- Identifying and treating red rot
- Materials and techniques for repairing paper (mending tissues, adhesives, deacidification techniques and options, removing creases, leaf casters,[53] washing and bleaching, etc.)
- Tools (threads, needles, adhesives, bone folders, knives, awls, spatulas, brushes, cutting mats, calipers, scissors, tweezers, straight edges, hole-punching jigs [for creating holes for binding], weights, moisture barriers, blotting papers, etc.)
- Book structures (how to identify and describe various kinds of bindings and parts of books, and knowing how to fix damaged parts [e.g., splitting hinges, torn headcaps, or starting joints])
- Book enclosures (slipcases, drop-leaf boxes, phase boxes, envelopes, etc.)
- Identification of infestation types
- Cleaning pages and bindings
- Different kinds of damage and repair options for each kind
- How to work with conservators (those on staff or independent)

This listing is suggestive in that every library will engender its own specific problems that need their own treatments.

A key point to make is that special collections librarians usually do not have broad specialized training in conservation (they may have taken a bookbinding workshop or one on the handling and care of photographs), so they should not feel competent to do all kinds of repairs and treatments. It is always best to rely on a professional conservator if one is available and if there are resources to cover the cost. Many items in a rare book department are valuable and a careless treatment on a damaged piece can make matters worse.

OTHER CONSERVATION ISSUES

As with a knowledge about preservation, the curator of rare books must understand where *information* exists in all items with respect to the conservation of these items. The information is not just in the texts; it is also in the physical elements of the item—its paper, binding, type, margins, or edges. So curators must know how to direct a conservator to do conservation treatment that extends the useful life of the object without taking information away. And, for simple treatments, curators must know the bulleted points in the preceding section. They must also be sensitive to the balance between the costs of repair, the value and replaceability of damaged objects, and the options available for dealing with these objects.

Rebacking, Rehinging, Rebinding

In some cases a book with a damaged cover may cost a good deal to replace or rebind, but only a small amount to put into a phase box. If the librarian feels safe that the book will seldom be used, a box is probably the best option. However, if the cover of a book is severely damaged, three binding options exist: rebacking, rehinging, and rebinding. In the first of these, the backstrip may be torn away from the book. If it can be reused, or if it must be replaced, the conservator will **reback** the volume. In *Bookbinding and the Conservation of Books: A Dictionary of Descriptive Terminology*, Matt Roberts and Don Etherington say,

> The term is used primarily with reference to books covered in leather, as this type of repair is seldom feasible in the case of paper-covered books, or a publisher's cloth (edition) binding, unless the book is rare or has a binding of unusual attractiveness, e.g., a Victorian illustrated cover. Used in a strict sense, however, it refers to the renewal of the original spine covering. The term may also be applied to the reattachment of the original spine material, usually after repair or restoration. Unless a substantial portion of the original spine can be restored and reattached, it is usually replaced in its entirety. In either case, it is customary to lay a new strip of leather over the spine of the text block, over which the original spine is glued. The leather beneath is extended under the leather on the sides, thus effectively creating new joints. (http://cool.conservation-us.org/don/dt/dt2787.html)

The process costs considerably less than does rebinding the volume, and a patron can use a well-rebacked book without fearing that its backstrip will fall off or that the book will fall apart.

If the hinges of the book are weak or broken, the conservator can lift the back off the volume, put a strip of cloth or leather around the textblock in such a way that it covers part of the front and rear boards, and then replace the backstrip. This process gives the book new hinges. **Rehinging** yields a perfectly sound volume and can add years of use to it.

Sometimes the original binding is in such bad shape that it needs to be replaced. As with rehinging, **rebinding** will extend the useful life of the volume, but by replacing the original binding, the conservator is removing some of the important information that book had. It may be important for a scholar to know what the original binding looked like, what it was made of, what artwork it had, what typeface it was stamped with, what materials it was made from, or what color it was. Hence, a full record of the treatment of the book should be kept, and information about the rebinding should be noted in the volume's cataloging record, as explained earlier. If possible, the original binding could be kept in a file or in a box with the rebound book. (If the rebinding simply puts a new case on the book, it is said to be **recased**.)

These methods of treatment aim to allow the materials to be used for extended periods. In poor condition, they might not be usable at all, but with proper intervention, the texts are preserved with minimal loss of information.

Packing and Shipping Rare Books

Books and other library materials move through the world, among publishers and printers, casual readers, collectors, scholars, booksellers, libraries (for research and for exhibition), museums, archives, thrift shops, and others. An item in need of specialized conservation might need to be shipped to an appropriate conservator if there are no such practitioners at hand. A preservation issue is, how are these materials packaged for shipping? If the packaging is done correctly, the item in the container will arrive in good condition, the shipping not having injured it at all. If it is packed poorly, it could be ruined.

As Steven Smith and Beth Russell point out, museums have decades of experience in shipping their objects to other museums for display, so some industry standards have developed to protect the objects.[54] They add that the packages for museum shipping

> must be . . . durable, for at a minimum, a good shipping container is designed to be used twice—first on the trip to the borrower and again on the trip back to the home institution. If an object is part of a traveling exhibit, however, its container must be able to withstand repeated disassembly and reassembly as it travels from venue to venue. (p. 87)

Chapter 2 of the present text considered the interlibrary loan of special collections materials. The emphasis in the present chapter on preservation is directly on the actual packaging of the transferred materials.

There is not much literature on the packaging of rare books for shipping, but Smith and Russell cite Paul Banks's "Preservation" article in the *Encyclopedia of Library and Information Science*,[55] in which Banks mentions the importance of proper packaging, and he advocates for the use of pressure-sensitive, double-sided tapes, which make his packing useful for only one-way shipping. Smith and Russell's article describes a method that works for multiple shippings.

I ONCE RECEIVED a very expensive fine press book in a package with tire tracks over it. The book had been dropped by the United States Postal Service and had been run over by one of its trucks. The binding was cracked and ugly. Certainly the printer could not have anticipated such maltreatment, but with another layer or two of bubble wrap or cushioning, the book might have survived unscathed. Another costly book was shipped to my home, and the carrier, substituting for our regular postman, left the book on our front step rather than on our enclosed porch where our mail was usually delivered. Naturally, it rained that day, and by the time I got home from work the box was soaked—and so was the book. Putting the book into a plastic bag inside the box would have averted this disaster—and preserved a copy of this wonderful and scarce book.

The essential elements of proper packing for rare books are materials and methods that guard against puncturing, being dropped, and being exposed to poor environmental conditions. The package should be watertight (or, at least, its contents should be watertight) and rigid enough to withstand exceptionally poor handling. Labels should be affixed in such a way that they cannot be loosened and removed during shipping. A shipping label (or an invoice or bill showing the name and address of the sender and recipient) should be put inside the box. And valuable items should be sent insured, with the sender and addressee able to track the package's progress.

Wet Materials and Freeze-Drying

In a disaster involving water, the librarian has a few options. As with the use of shrink-wrapping, freeze-drying is a librarian's and conservator's adaptation of a food-industry practice.

When library materials get wet, they can begin to mildew quickly, especially in warm, moist ambient conditions. A book that has been wet can possibly be saved from mildew if it is stood up, fanned out, and placed in a dry room with good air circulation (fans running). Any materials with coated papers should be treated quickly because the clay in the coating can fuse, forming a solid block of papers into a thick slab of cardboard. No amount of conservation work can resuscitate such a volume. So coated leaves should be carefully pulled apart and interleaved with dry towling or waxed paper. This could leave the book misshapen, but it will save it so that its contents will still be accessible.

If many volumes are soaked, there may not be time or personnel enough to do this kind of individual treatment. A quick fix for really waterlogged books and for large numbers of items is to freeze the wet materials as soon as possible. This means having some local freezer available. The emergency plan should include an arrangement with a business or a campus unit that has a freezer available. Eventually the materials can be freeze-dried. The items may come out cockled or discolored, not fitting perfectly flatly into their bindings, but they should still be usable.

Digital Preservation

Chapter 13 of this book will talk about rare books and special collections in a digital environment. But this is an appropriate place to talk about "digital preservation." The phrase is in quotation marks here because of the controversy over the notion that

---

AT A CONFERENCE in Beijing I gave a talk on preservation, focusing mostly on paper-based and other special collections objects. An oblique, single, passing remark about the problems with digital preservation elicited a most heated response from someone in the audience who was adamant that digital *was* preservation, that the technology was perfected, that the Internet Archive Wayback Machine was the answer,* and that only a fool and a luddite could believe that digital preservation had not yet been achieved. The virulence of his pronouncements, accompanied by his abso-

lute refusal to believe otherwise, was typical of an attitude I have encountered several times from people convinced that "digital is the answer" to our preservation problems. Despite this, untold numbers of books and articles are still being published discussing how such preservation can be secured. The phrase "can be secured" means that it has not yet been achieved.

*For the Wayback Machine see http://archive.org/web/web.php. This site says, "Browse through over 150 billion web pages archived from 1996 to a few months ago." This is

impressive, but how many Web pages have not been recorded? Who has selected these 150 billion? On the basis of what? What has been missed? The amount of information generated in a few weeks today may add up to 150 billion Web pages. No site or hardware can capture it all. This site was the brainchild of Brewster Kahle and Bruce Gilliat who, in 1996, "developed software to crawl and download all publicly accessible World Wide Web pages, the Gopher hierarchy, the Netnews bulletin board system, and downloadable software." See the Wikipedia article "Wayback Machine" at http://en.wikipedia.org/wiki/Wayback_Machine.

IN SOME OF the special collections classes I teach, I require the students to have for their term papers at least three paper-based sources. More and more the students do not hear this (or see it, because it is written down on the paper-based documents I give them when I discuss their assignments). Recent classes have produced one essay after another with only online sources. Often a student will draw only from the Web for his source materials for a written assignment, when I know of books that would have been better resources for him to have drawn from than the digital ones he used. He never located the better source on the Web; he relied on a flawed, poorly researched, and too brief Wikipedia article. In the seven years I have been at my present position as the director of a rare book library, I have heard more than a hundred times, "Are your holdings on the Web?" This short-sighted question, coming from an ignorance about all the implications of digitization, is becoming the norm. People expect to have instant gratification when they do their research. The digital world offers this, they think, but it cannot deliver all the time. And the broad publicity about the Google Books project, in which millions of books are being captured digitally in full text, has spread to the population the notion that *all* books are now becoming available on the Web, so people simply believe that if they go to their computers, they will be able to find any book they want.*

*For the Google Books project see www.google.com/google books/library; this page has links to other pages that will explain what the project is all about and how it works. Because this project has had major legal challenges, mostly with respect to copyright and authors' rights, it has been headline news, so information about it has been broadcast to a wide audience. It is worth repeating that many people simply expect that library holdings—in full text—are available and accessible if they can be guided to them. I have even heard a library director say to a crowd, "Our library's holdings are being digitized," when he meant to say that the library's catalog was being digitized.

"digital" is a form of "preservation." In a nutshell, many people think that digitization is *not* preservation. Others think that the problem of impermanence of library materials has been solved by digital technology. One common notion is that digitally stored information is excellent for quick access, far more easily accessed than any data stored in analog formats. But to date there is no technology that guarantees long-term preservation in electronic form.

The term *digital preservation* has two meanings: (1) the use of digital technology to preserve things that were originally created in analog form, and (2) the attempt to preserve information that was created in digital form (the current term is texts *born digital*). For both meanings, the key issue is to try to maintain access to information in a medium that has, to date, no secure, proven-long-term preservation tactics, though we seem to be getting closer with digital repositories.

A vast and rapidly growing literature on this topic exists—for good reason. The evolution of digital technology is faster than the evolution of practically any other technology in history. It is impossible for anyone to keep up with the changes. And there are so many changes that the literature on them comes pouring forth in articles, books, lectures, and symposia. With shifts from one platform to another, with changes in whole methods of creating and saving information, and with the steady evolution of software and hardware, the digital world itself has a built-in obsolescence factor that makes "preservation" seemingly evanescent.[56]

Ross Harvey quotes Natalia Bergau:

Making the digitized material available and visible online is only one of the challenges faced. . . . Another lies in assuring long-term access to them. Digitised materials—like other digital data—are also fragile items and need special measures and arrangements in order to be accessible despite technological change. While the preservation of paper documents is well understood and is supported by a well-established infrastructure and a profession of librarians and other experts, the preservation of digital objects in general and digitized material in particular is a relatively new task for libraries and poses great challenges in terms of the expertise and resources required.[57]

As noted earlier, the technology is evolving too quickly for anyone to promise that digital methods are guaranteed to preserve information to perpetuity—or even for a decade. The 5¼-inch floppy disks gave way to 3½-inch ones, which gave way to CDs and DVDs and thumb drives and hard drives and clouds. What the next incarnation of information "preservation" will be is anyone's guess.

For special collections and rare books, the whole topic resonates. A frequent question from visitors to rare book libraries is, "Are your holdings digitized?" The public, students at all levels, and even advanced scholars no longer turn to the library as their first recourse in their research. They turn on their computers, go to Google or some other search engine, and hope (even expect) to find the information they need. Too often people (even those who should know better) hear that we are digitizing our catalog and assume that this means we are digitizing our holdings—full text. Librarians must explain that digitizing the catalog means getting the finding aids online—putting our cataloging records into digital form and posting them on OCLC WorldCat. Once we do this, anyone worldwide who has access to a computer and an Internet connection can learn what we have in our collection. But what people learn is the titles, authors, and subjects of the monographs and the existence of manuscripts containing key names and topics; they cannot automatically see the full text of these holdings. Perhaps it is wishful thinking, but access to full texts is what the patrons want and expect. So the rare book librarian's task is to educate her clientele about what *digital* means with respect to the department's holdings.

The problem, then, is in dealing with ways to make digital information "permanent"—figuring out how to extend access to digital data for at least as long as we have access to analog materials. Deborah Woodyard-Robinson says,

> The preservation of digital resources is about finding ways to maintain our digital heritage, whether it exists in the form of e-journals, database records,

Web sites, emails, digital images, audio-visual materials, interactive programs, or any other kind of binary data. Libraries frequently engage with a wide variety of these resources and understand how quickly and easily we lose use of them when computers change or links break.[58]

She says that many solutions for the problem of digital preservation have been proposed and that "many opinions have been voiced about whether these solutions will work. While it is often perceived that these opinions contradict or argue with each other, the real answer is in finding the balance of what works in a particular situation" (p. 1). The claim of this issue of *Library Trends* is that there is no single answer; each individual collection poses its own unique problems and requires its own solution. The contexts in which each collection resides will help a librarian determine what solution to adopt. Woodyard-Robinson says,

> [T]he context in which digital preservation challenges apply is a highly important factor in making the right choice of a solution. For example, the context of the data can change its meaning and use. The context of the resource can change its relevance and integrity. The context of a collection in an organization can impact its value, and the context of a collecting organization can affect legal rights and obligations for digital preservation. (p. 1)

This is promising rhetoric, for it implies that once an organization figures out its "context," it will come up with a way to create preservation digitally. Woodyard-Robinson even says, "The articles in this issue [of *Library Trends*] illustrate a variety of solutions in a range of contexts, from the implementation of large systems to issue-specific solutions that are still in development" (pp. 1–2). But the "variety of solutions"—again implying that these solutions have been perfected—is a problem in itself, because not one of these can offer preservation to perpetuity, and the very variety shows that there is no single silver bullet, which people in the preservation field are still looking for. She acknowledges at the end of this quoted passage that these "solutions . . . are still in development." This says it all.

Part of the problem has to do with "[t]he heterogeneity of digital materials being collected [which] increases complexity in systems and solutions" (Woodyard-Robinson, p. 2). This heterogeneity leads one author (MacKenzie Smith) to recognize "that complex systems benefit from an incremental building approach such as spiral development."[59] A desideratum in the rare book world (and in the world of information as a whole) is to come up with some universal solution that works on all kinds of information in all media for all kinds of institutions. But this is presently a chimera. Too many institutions are working independently on the problem, and the world of technology is changing too rapidly for a universal solution to be formulated. If "universal digital preservation" can become a reality, it will take worldwide cooperation. The prospect is not yet on the horizon.[60]

Robert P. Spindler is the author of the NEDCC Preservation Leaflet 6.5, "Digital Preservation" (www .nedcc.org/resources/leaflets/6Reformatting/05 DigitalPreservation.php). His long opening section, "Corruption and Loss of Digital Information," is a sobering discussion of the many ways that digital texts are not permanent. The storage media can degrade or become obsolete. Migration is probably not a solution yet (though it may be in the future). Spindler says,

> Migration is the process by which files created in one software program are moved to a more recent version of the same program, moved to a completely different program, or moved to a data format standard that may be read by several programs. Total migration failure, or the inability to read a file originally produced in a different program, is becoming less frequent with textual/ numeric data, but it is a more common problem with digital audio and video information.
>
> As software developers strive to enable more efficient, flexible, and creative data processing, they create new products that may not correctly render a file created in another, similar software program, or even an older version or release of the same program. In the early days of personal computing it was not uncommon for a word processing

file to be completely unreadable by different word processing software.

His statement that migration failure "is becoming less frequent" reveals that it is still a problem. He adds,

> Now many software programs are compatible in being able at least to display information produced in different software, but often the rendering is not completely accurate—in word processing it is common for errors to be introduced in a file opened with a different program than the one used to create it. Formatting errors and incorrect replacement of certain characters are common results of migrations of text files from one software environment to another.

And about another technique, emulation, he says,

> Another approach to preservation of software-dependent content is emulation. Emulation involves writing software and/or building hardware that allows a computer to imitate the appearance and functionality of obsolete software. This approach has been commonly employed for several decades (especially for hardware like obsolete computer keyboards), but recent research suggests that emulation has not achieved completely accurate reproduction of the original appearance and functionality of simple video games. Further research and testing of emulation solutions is in progress.

Woodyard-Robinson talks about other things in the *Library Trends* issue. "Steve Knight . . . explains for us the origins of preservation metadata and the perceived need for its creation."[61] As Woodyard-Robinson points out, "Another important aspect of preservation metadata work internationally is the need for consensus among digital archiving communities on what metadata is required in a system for long-term preservation" (p. 3). She adds, "Technical metadata is proving particularly challenging to create and manage" (p. 4). The search for a solution is like that for a cure to cancer: we know what the problems are; we know that there are many kinds of problems; we can attempt to create ad hoc treatments at a local level, some of which work to one degree or another, some of which are stop-gap "solutions" to use until something more reliable comes along. We can almost see the light at the end of the passageway, but that light keeps receding as we think we are getting closer to it. What we would like is a solution that works for all kinds of problems, but the kinds of problems multiply as technology changes, and there are too many kinds of problems.

A problem that runs parallel to (or beneath) all the attempts to create digital preservation is hinted at by MacKenzie Smith when she mentions the "daunting task" that relies on technology, "core staff competencies, and cost models" ("Exploring Variety in Digital Collections," p. 6). There is a cost to all this, and that cost—in coin of the realm—as noted earlier, is long term. Even if true digital preservation can be achieved, can institutions afford it? What long-term activities must be undertaken to make it work? Will there be a need for a preservation team (or even a single person) who can check on all materials being stored digitally to make sure they are not deteriorating? Will that team or person need to be in charge of migrating the data to newer and newer platforms? Who will be designing these platforms? At what cost? Who will pay for it? Will migrations be developed that do not cause a loss of any data? Will there be a time at which no further transfer/migration will be necessary?[62]

The implication for all libraries is that we are still a long way off from true "digital preservation." But that does not mean that special collections departments—or anyone in the rare book world who wants to preserve information—should give up on preservation. What it means is that there should be a continued concerted effort to save library and archival materials the way that they have been handled for decades: with well-thought-out preservation programs, with continuing development of conservation materials and practices, and with a reliance on the methods that have proven themselves as true preservation media: use of microfilm and acid-free, permanent-durable, archival papers.

Relatively common items are being digitized through the Google Books project and others like it. Rare materials that can be accessed in only one venue should be on the list for such treatment because

"MICROFILM? WHAT AN ancient technology! Why would anyone want to film anything these days?! We have digital means of capture." This is a likely response to any suggestion to continue to film. But microfilm is at least a simple, proven, reliable means of preservation, while digitization is not. And the short- and long-term costs of filming are much lower than are the costs of digitization. At the American Antiquarian Society, for instance, a microfilming project for American newspapers—a project that has been ongoing for decades—continues. I am not necessarily advocating that our special collections libraries should not digitize (it is, after all, a wonderful medium for access to information), nor that they should all go back to filming. I think it is important to recognize the value of that older technology and to consider it in the larger picture of what preservation activities the department should adopt.

these are the hardest to do research from unless one is on-site where they are. Digitization should be part of a forward-looking special collections department program, but it should be undertaken with the understanding that access is the impetus for the digitization, not preservation. Of course, a digital surrogate can reduce the handling of the original, so in the short run it serves a preservation function.

One of the points that Ross Harvey makes is that, though archivists and librarians are generally looked to as the preservers of research materials, for recently created digital items (and also, by implication, unique items like manuscripts, personal notes, and early and working versions of texts in any medium), the creators should be involved in their preservation (Harvey, *Preserving Digital Materials*, pp. 29–32). He says, "Not only are new kinds of stakeholders claiming an interest or claiming control, but higher levels of collaboration among stakeholders are also commonly understood to be necessary for digital preservation to be effective" (p. 29). Citing Hodge and Frangakis, he lists other stakeholders: "commercial services, government agencies, individuals, rights holders, beneficiaries, funding agencies, and users."[63] And, citing a UNESCO report, he mentions other stakeholders: "Hardware and software developers, publishers, producers, and distributors of digital materials as well as other private sector partners."[64]

It is clear that there are many stakeholders, but prime among them for the purposes of this text are rare book librarians around the world who are custodians and gatekeepers of millions upon millions of unique documents in their holdings. Their mandate is to get information out to potential users. One means of achieving this is through cataloging to let the world know what they have, and another means is to digitize their collections to make that access to the texts themselves possible.[65] Some librarians still do not trust digital surrogates for preservation, so they download important texts onto paper (and reformat analog materials to other analog formats). Although digital texts take up negligible space in a department, and analog materials can take up vast spaces, the sense of security that the physical objects impart and the one-time cost (as opposed to the long-term costs of digitization with its migrations and emulations) can be strong incentives not to digitize. To achieve wide use *and* worldwide access, they may reformat to paper and digitize, but this maximizes the cost of "preservation and access"; many institutions cannot afford to do both.

Another thing to consider is that many administrators want their libraries to be seen in the most progressive light, and they do not understand the issues of the temporality of digital preservation. They want to be seen as running state-of-the-art institutions, so they discourage analog methods of preservation as "old fashioned" and expensive. Convincing these administrators of the unpredictability of the preservation of materials when digital preservation is the method chosen can be a full-time—and futile—endeavor. What the administrators may not understand—beyond the oxymoronic nature of the phrase "digital preservation"—is the long-term costs of the operation. Harvey says,

> A sustainable environment that supports digital preservation over time [is] essential, and this is related to ongoing funding. To be sustainable, digital preservation activities [have] to be built into "normal operating activity" and a good understanding of the context [is] required.[66]

Rare book librarians can make a good case for the need for digitization because their departments hold great numbers of unique pieces, and the widest access to these documents is afforded digitally. But they must also not lose sight of the ephemerality of digitized materials (at least for the present) and must make a case for a hybrid approach to reformatting for preservation. Harvey points out that too often "digital preservation programs are funded only for a few years" (p. 113). "This is an impediment to planning programmes that aim to preserve material for long periods of time, perhaps to perpetuity" (p. 113). In all literature on "digital preservation," the sense that such preservation is time-bound hovers. The urgency to see the activity in long views and to plan for what will happen when the materials "preserved digitally" will need some kind of renewing is always in the conversation. The hybrid approach—creating digital surrogates for immediate and worldwide access, but also making analog copies—may be the best way to go, if resources permit.

Spindler concludes his "Digital Preservation" leaflet (see www.nedcc.org) with this sobering paragraph:

> Effective digital preservation requires an enduring commitment to active management, access to trustworthy infrastructure, and continuing investments in technical staff, software, and hardware. Long-term digital preservation is usually a cumulative endeavor; thus as more content and more diverse formats are acquired, the resources needed to assure the survival of digital information grow over time. In addition, continuing changes in technology will require research into and development of migration and storage solutions that will work with the technologies of the future.

At the root of this is a recognition of the ongoing and increasing cost of this kind of preservation—costs in human power, hardware, and software. Many in the library world understand this and therefore opt for such primitive methods as microfilming and photocopying, which take up more space but which cost, in the long run, a fraction of what digital practices cost, and which are more reliable (at least for now).

A great deal more on digital preservation can be said. As noted earlier, the literature is enormous and burgeoning. In the rare book and manuscripts world, librarians and others who are in a position to digitize must be aware of the issues, the problems, the proposed solutions, and the great dilemma of achieving true preservation in digital form. They must balance—and possibly employ—several techniques, with the understanding that their efforts will yield access more than they will yield long-term preservation. They must carefully select objects for digitization, considering audiences, staffing, methods of preparation and digitizing, costs, legal issues, importance and uniqueness of materials, and much more. Many monographs in special collections departments, and especially manuscripts, photographs, and ephemera, are unlikely to make it to such initiatives as the Google Books project, so it is incumbent on those in the rare book world to think seriously of making their holdings available digitally to the widest audience possible.[67]

Disaster Planning

One of the most important preservation activities is planning for disasters. Poor planning can lead to the loss of vast numbers of volumes and manuscripts, while good planning can mitigate the effects of a disaster and save most or all of the affected collection. As with many topics considered in the present volume, there is a large literature on this subject. One excellent place to begin is with the Northeast Document Conservation Center (NEDCC) leaflet by Beth Lindblom Patkus and Karen Motylewski, "Disaster Planning."[68] Much of this part of the chapter will be drawn from this excellent document (cited here as "Patkus").

As the NEDCC Guidelines say:

> Disaster planning is complex; the written plan is the result of a wide range of preliminary activities. The entire process is most efficient if it is formally assigned to one person who acts as the disaster planner for the institution and is perhaps assisted by a planning team or committee. The institution's director may play this primary role or may delegate the responsibility, but it is important to remember that the process must be supported at the highest

level of the organization if it is to be effective. The planner should establish a timetable for the project and should define the scope and goals of the plan, which will depend largely on the risks faced by the institution. (Patkus)

KINDS OF DISASTERS

The most common forms of disaster are related to fire, water, and pest infestation. Some come from nature (floods, typhoons, hurricanes, wildfires, lightning strikes, insect or rodent invasions), and some are the result of human actions (arson; leaky pipes; clutter- and dust-caused fires; improperly cared for roofs, gutters, downspouts, and windows; careless maintenance of environmental controls; inadequate security). The preventive measures the librarian, bookseller, or collector must take to mitigate each of these kinds of disaster will depend on the individual circumstances in which the collection is kept. Hence, each disaster plan must be written with respect to the specifics of the collection for which the plan is written.

IDENTIFYING THE RISKS OF YOUR OWN INSTITUTION

Every academic or personal library or bookstore has its own layout, with differences in building materials and structures; placement of windows, doors, and pipes; organization of holdings; geographical challenges; and so on. In southern California, disaster planning must include contingencies for earthquakes; in Seattle, for extensive rains; on the Gulf Coast, for hurricanes and high humidity levels; for the Midwest, tornadoes; in some parts of the country, for extensive and intensive cold spells that could cause pipes to freeze and burst; and for almost everywhere, torrential rains, which can cause drains to fill and back up, water to pour in from windows, roofs to leak, and mildew to form. So each disaster plan must be tailored to the particular library or bookstore that prepares it.

Patkus warns,

> Consider man-made disasters such as power outages, sprinkler discharges, fuel or water supply failures, chemical spills, arson, bomb threats, or

other such problems. Take note of the environmental risks that surround your institution. Chemical industries, shipping routes for hazardous materials, and adjacent construction projects all expose your institution to damage. While all institutions are not vulnerable to all disasters, any event that is a real possibility should be covered under your emergency plan.

The plan should consider the nature of the architecture of the building holding the collection (the location of pipes, water fountains, toilets, stairways, elevators or escalators, drains of various kinds, windows, power sources, skylights; the envelope, including bricks and mortar, stonework, windows; the kind of roof the building has and whether it is flat or sloped; and other structural elements); the site on which the building sits (where the building is with respect to the local water table, nearby features of the landscape like streams or rivers or other sources of water; slopes, volcanoes, or faults); where power lines are, local flora or fauna, highways or roads, the aridity of the region and its climate; the presence of shrubs or trees; and so on.

Patkus asks, "Do gutters and drains work properly? Are they cleaned regularly? Are windows and skylights well sealed? Is there a history of leaks or other building and structural problems?" She then mentions "fire protection systems, electrical systems, plumbing, and environmental systems . . . fire extinguishers . . . fire alarms and a fire-suppression system"; and she asks,

> Are they well maintained? Are they monitored twenty-four hours a day? Are fire exits blocked? How old is the wiring? Is it overloaded? Are electrical appliances unplugged at night? Is auxiliary power available if needed? Are water pipes in good shape? Are there water detectors, and do they work? Are there any problems with the climate-control system?

She then discusses the materials that objects in the collection are composed of, the shelving, the nature of the storage areas in the building, whether the collection has items stored on or off the floors, housekeeping procedures, whether the collection is inven-

toried and insured, and so on. She asks, "Have collection priorities been set? In other words, do you know which collections should be salvaged first in the event of fire, water, or other emergency? Do you have a backup priority list if you cannot reach the highest-priority objects due to building damage or the nature of the disaster?"

BY STUDYING THE literature on disaster planning and trying to anticipate the kinds of calamities that might befall your institution, you might be able to ward off serious consequences of various kinds of catastrophes. Sometimes, however, a disaster strikes from which you learn what you never anticipated. As described earlier in this chapter, at UC Riverside, during the massive Northridge earthquake, we had thousands upon thousands of books thrown to the floor, mostly from the top three shelves. The volumes that did not fall were on shelves in a wave pattern, some near the front of the shelves ready to fall off, others next to them near the back of the shelves. Looked at from above, the books on such shelves sat there like the letter *S*. We learned that the mitigation—the planning—was best done for the top shelves, and the solution that we came up with (bungee cords) was tailored to our particular experience based on geographical location and the way our building moved during the temblor.

All these things will affect what goes into the collection's disaster plan. The plan, as Patkus shows, should consider the risks that the library faces, the kinds of collaboration it takes to make the preparation as thorough as possible, and the resources that should be lined up in case of emergencies. Such resources include emergency kits or cabinets (with plastic sheeting, plastic milk crates, extension cords, bullhorns, tape, flashlights, rags and napkins and other absorbent materials, trash bags, brooms and mops, safety glasses, rubber boots, waxed paper or freezer paper or both, sponges, rubber gloves, drop cloths, notepaper and pens, a first aid kit, and other materials, along with a dehumidifier, a wet vac, an electric fan, and some emergency cash), liaisons with police and fire personnel, information about insurance and ambulance services and about water and power companies, arrangements with a local vendor of some kind who has a freezer (to hold books and other materials that are wet), and so forth. There should be a list of the things that must be kept in the emergency cabinets, along with fresh batteries, and someone should periodically check the cabinets for completeness.[69] Patkus says that

> many disaster-planning guides have published lists of supplies and companies that provide disaster services as well as sources of technical assistance. Research these services thoroughly—it is an essential part of the planning process. If possible, invite local service providers to visit your institution to become familiar with your site plan and collections in advance of an emergency. It is also a good idea to plan for back-up companies to provide critical supplies and services in case there is a community-wide or regional disaster. Consider coordinating with other local institutions.

In case the disaster might be covered by FEMA (the Federal Emergency Management Agency), it is good to have the agency's contact information on hand. (FEMA was responsive to UC Riverside's needs in the Northridge quake, and its assistance helped the library repair thousands of books.)[70]

The NEDCC leaflet also mentions setting priorities, which begin with human safety and then move on to records about the collection's holdings and then the areas in the collection that should receive the highest priority for salvage. "Objects or collections of great importance to the institution must be identified ahead of time. If this is not done, valuable time may be wasted salvaging materials of little value or spent arguing about what should be saved first" (Patkus).

THE WRITTEN DISASTER POLICY

Though each disaster policy should be tailored to each entity that writes it, every one should contain certain elements:

1. Introduction—stating the lines of authority and the possible events covered by the plan

2. Actions to be taken if advance warning is available
3. First response procedures, including who should be contacted first in each type of emergency, what immediate steps should be taken, and how staff or teams will be notified
4. Emergency procedures with sections devoted to each emergency event covered by the plan. This will include what is to be done during the event, and the appropriate salvage procedures to be followed once the first excitement is over. Include floor plans.
5. Rehabilitation plans for getting the institution back to normal
6. Appendices, which may include evacuation/ floor plans; listing of emergency services; listing of emergency response team members and responsibilities; telephone tree; location of keys; fire/intrusion alarm procedures; listing of collection priorities; arrangements for relocation of the collections; listing of in-house supplies; listing of outside suppliers and services; insurance information; listing of volunteers; prevention checklist; record-keeping forms for objects moved in salvage efforts; detailed salvage procedures (Patkus)

This Patkus/Motylewski text is twenty years old (see note 68), but it is still as up-to-date a guide as is available for the general construction of a disaster plan. To make it even easier than following the suggestions of this leaflet, another instrument is available.

THE dPLAN™

To help anyone needing a disaster planning tool, NEDCC and the Massachusetts Board of Library Commissioners collaborated to create the dPlan.[71] The dPlan website says that

> dPlan is a free online tool that simplifies the process of writing a disaster plan for your collections. dPlan provides a comprehensive fill-in-the-blank template into which you enter information about your institution. Data entered by the user is stored on a secure server and output in a standard format, resulting in a customized disaster plan that can be regularly updated. (www.dplan.org)

In other words, the user needs only to enter information about her institution and its collection(s) into the dPlan template, and the instrument creates a written plan that the user can then modify in any way (and update), depending on local circumstances. But many local circumstances are already figured into the plan, depending on how specific and extensive is the information that is entered into the template. I especially encourage you to look at the "Frequently Asked Questions" page to get an idea of what the plan is all about, how to use it, how the full version of it differs from the dPlan Lite version, and so forth (www.dplan.org/faq.asp#enterdata).

This plan is available free to all nonprofit institutions. It considers more things than almost any preservation person could have thought of on her own, and once all the raw data are entered into the template, it does the work of creating the plan. The librarian's job is to assemble all the raw data, which can be a challenge when it comes to technical information about architecture and geography. But the effort taken to get the data is well worth the final product.

THE PRESERVATION OFFICER—
TRAINING THE STAFF

This disaster policy will do no good, no matter how comprehensive it is, if no one on staff is aware of it. And being merely aware of its existence is not enough; the staff must be familiar with the details: Who does what? in what order? What actions must be taken with what kinds of disasters? What tools, supplies, and equipment are available—where is it, and how is it accessible—to help with the emergency? Who should be notified and in what order? What vendors must be contacted for what kinds of emergencies? Each staff person—and that includes personnel in special collections and as many others in the institution as can be instructed—should be given particular tasks and responsibilities.

As noted earlier in this chapter, if the institution has the resources (and many do not), it should have a permanent full- or part-time preservation officer whose job is to run a full preservation program. The program would naturally be tailored to the institution, and it would include, among many other tasks,

> **TO DEAL WITH** emergencies, all staff should be assigned specific responsibilities. At UC Riverside one person—with a backup in that person's absence—was in charge of clearing the building; another person was charged with going from room to room and area to area in the stacks to alert patrons that they had to evacuate the building; another was instructed to contact people on the telephone tree to notify them of the incident.

creating a preservation policy, part of which would be a disaster planning document. This officer should create the disaster plan and then should hold workshops for all staff, answering the questions posed in the preceding paragraph. Every staff person should be able to answer the question, "In an emergency, what am I supposed to do?"

Disaster planning is exceptionally important. It can take vast amounts of time and human power. But in the long run, it can save the institution untold grief and resources. It is a form of insurance, and institutions are encouraged to invest in a preservation officer position. For the rare book and special collections department, which has the most to lose, disaster planning is crucial. The department head or her appointed staff person should work closely with the preservation officer, especially in the area of prioritization of the collection for preservative action. It should be noted, too, that everyone working with rare books—dealers, private collectors, scholars—should have their own plans of action, for when disaster strikes, trying to figure out what to do can take time, and time lost could be books and manuscripts lost.

Too often the rare book department is understaffed, so the many things that need to be done in a disaster may not be accomplishable by the few people who work there. Working with administrative and other personnel in the institution, and the police and fire departments, the head of the rare book department can recruit several people who can be made to understand that special collections should be high in the priorities assessment when a disaster strikes. Departmental records (shelflists, acquisition records, finding aids, and the like) are important to save, if possible, along with items from the most significant parts of the collection: exceptionally valuable items, unique pieces, level 5 materials if possible, crucial documents having to do with the history of the institution, and any collections that are frequently used and important and that contain manuscript materials that are obviously unique.

The point of this preceding paragraph is not really to help you decide what to prioritize; it is to point out the practically futile effort of prioritization, especially for large collections with hundreds of thousands of items that fall into the categories just delineated. Get a dozen employees of a large rare book department to prioritize what they would save, in what order, and you might wind up with fifteen lists, no two alike. Once the obvious top items are delineated (departmental records,[72] institutional charters, Gutenberg Bibles, the Eliot Indian Bible), one guide may be the collection development policy, which lists the department's holdings by levels of collecting.

However, a rich library with many level 5 collections might have them spread all over the department's stacks, and gathering them hastily in the face of a catastrophe can take more time than the staff has. On top of this is the sense of urgency—maybe even panic—at the time of the disaster, which may well hamper staff efficiency. And there may not be enough time to act at all if the disaster is already at hand. The disaster plan should have the prioritization clearly laid out, with maps to the key shelves, rooms, and vaults to guide the rescuers.

At the forefront of the effort, however, and clearly stated in the disaster plan, is the number one edict: human beings come before collections. In the face of a cataclysm, if the saving of a single piece of the library collection (no matter how valuable and irreplaceable that piece is) puts anyone in jeopardy, the piece should be left where it is, and the staff person should be headed for safety.

The disaster plan must, indeed, be tailored to the institution, but it should also be tailored to the overall safety of the people who interact with the collection. It is a key document that all staff should be familiar with. And it should be reviewed and updated regularly.

Disaster Recovery

Disasters can strike everywhere, so the extensive literature on recovery deals with recovering in all kinds of settings. Libraries pose particular problems, of course, in that they contain thousands or millions of individual objects made from many materials, all with their own preservation needs. And rare book departments, as the discussion of prioritization of things to list in the disaster plan shows, pose particular problems for creating a recovery plan.

With any luck, good planning, and good execution, the disaster plan has kept the losses of the department to a minimum. Nonetheless, if there has been a disaster and the special collections department has suffered, recovery is the next step in the cycle back to "normal" operations. And, as with everything else in the world of library operations, there should be a plan.

Damage is caused mostly by fire, water, smoke, and mildew, but infestation of various kinds can also be devastating, especially if it has gone on for a long time, undetected. The damage that the disaster preparedness plan did not prevent must be handled in a professional, carefully thought-out manner. A number of documents are available on the Internet. The present text will look at that of Cornell University as one that can be used as a model. Developed by the Cornell Department of Preservation and Collection Maintenance, it is titled "Disaster Response Plan" (see the Cornell document, referred to in note 68). As the introduction to this document explains,

> The Disaster Plan is organized to move from first response (see Phone Tree, page 2) through the steps involved in recovering from a minor disaster, usually involving fewer than 500 volumes, followed by steps to be taken in the event of a major disaster. The last section of the manual contains appendixes which explicate the text and include a list of additional supplies and services available locally and regionally. (p. i)

When a disaster hits, those on the scene—or those who learn about it first, no matter where they are—obviously cannot handle by themselves the work the damage creates. Extensive damage requires extensive

AT UC RIVERSIDE a burst pipe was spewing water onto stacks full of books in the library basement. The staff got to the emergency supplies quickly and covered the shelves with plastic sheets, pulled the wet books from the shelves, and took them to a room with many tables on which the books could be air dried or interleaved with blotting papers. The whole operation took about an hour. They later learned that the water came from a sewage pipe, and they all had to get tetanus shots because they exposed themselves to the possibly tainted water.

Another water problem occurred in about 1989 at the American Antiquarian Society. A torrential downpour late on a Friday afternoon, before a three-day Labor Day weekend, caused the building's dome to leak onto a collection of glass slides. Fortunately, the librarians who were still in the building (many had departed for the holiday) spotted the leak and were able to take innumerable wet glass plates and lay them onto the floor, flat, where they dried over the weekend. No images were lost, mostly because the trained librarians and the conservator knew how to handle the plates.

action, with the help of many people and organizations. That is why it is essential to have a telephone tree available, posted prominently in more than one place in the department. In fact, at some institutions, a credit-card-sized telephone tree has been made for all employees to carry in their wallets or purses. This document lists, in priority order, the people who must be called. The Cornell model mentions the unit head (the librarian in charge of the department), what it calls "Customer Services (maintenance)," the "Unit Emergency Coordinator," the director of preservation/conservation, and the "UNIT DISASTER ACTION TEAM" (p. 2). This last entry is left blank in the Cornell document, to be populated by whoever is on that team. Add to these the police and fire departments, for obvious reasons. When a disaster strikes, the library (especially the rare book department) is at its most vulnerable. "Strangers" will be running into the building, a sense of chaos could be operative, and security becomes lax when there are seemingly more pressing things to attend to (fires, water incursion, smoke, and so forth). The police can direct activities and be on hand to protect the collection. This is one of the things the special collections librarian should have guided the police to do in an initial meeting with them. The telephone tree should be updated at least once a year.

The Cornell document distinguishes minor from major disasters. If there is a fire, the librarians should call the fire department, evacuate the library, and call emergency services. For water problems, contact the physical plant personnel, cover bookshelves with plastic sheeting if the water is coming from above,

and get books off bottom shelves if it is coming from below. But make sure that the water is not tainted.

Wet books can be air dried by propping them open standing up, in a room with good ventilation, circulating air (a couple of fans will do), and good temperature and humidity controls. This is why it is important to have a good HVAC (heating, ventilation, air conditioning) system in working order. Some books may be so wet that they need to be frozen, so it is important for the library to have an arrangement with a local organization that has a freezer (on the institution's site or nearby, say, at a butcher shop or a supermarket). The disaster preparedness plan should have a list of possible places to contact, with names and phone numbers. Because this list would be prepared far in advance, the librarians should ask the parties whose assistance they seek to give them emergency (after-hours) numbers. As the Cornell document says, books or serials with coated (shiny) paper should be interleaved as soon as they can be handled because the clay or other filler that gets burnished to make the paper shiny can fuse, merging neighboring slick papers into a single block that cannot be salvaged. (The Cornell document, pp. 7–9, has more information about drying paper materials.)

THE DISASTER ACTION TEAM

If a disaster strikes at a small institution, there may be only a few people involved in the mitigation: a library director, a cataloger, and a reference person, for instance, along with whatever administrative positions exist and the fire and police departments. At a larger institution, there may be a large staff on hand, each of whom should be given his own specific duties. One element of the disaster recovery operation is having meetings with the whole crew, training them in the operation, and assigning specific tasks.

The Cornell document recommends that the library have a number of positions. (This document is tailored to that institution; it might not be possible for other institutions to match the ones Cornell designates.) The document recommends (1) a Disaster Response Administrator; (2) a Disaster Recovery Director; (3) an Emergency Coordinator; (4) a Library Specialist; (5) a Building Representative; (6) a Recorder; (7) a Communications Director (see the section "External Communications / Public Relations" later in this chapter); (8) a Central Disaster Action Team (the full staff, with specific assignments); and (9) a Regional Emergency Mutual Response Team (people beyond the library and, in many instances, beyond the institution itself; pp. 15–18). Although this is a fairly extensive list of people, it has a few features that all institutions should have on their own teams: a leader, a library representative, a building expert (like someone from the physical plant), a broad array of kinds of assistance, and people from within and beyond the institution.

As I said earlier, the telephone tree should list all the people who need to be contacted, in the order of contact. More than one employee should be authorized to hire outside vendors to do flood and fire mitigation as soon after the disaster as possible. It should not be necessary to wait for someone to return from vacation, for example, to authorize the use of a freezing company or the purchase of needed supplies.

For rare book departments, the sense of urgency to save their holdings is especially great. Compared to the volumes in the general library, materials in special collections are more valuable, harder to replace, unique, and, in general, more precious in more ways than one. In the opening chapters of this volume, I spoke of the importance of the connections the rare book librarian makes with all other library and institutional personnel. When there is a disaster, those connections can come in handy, for the others will understand the importance of the materials in the special collections department and should eschew their own areas to help with the rare books and manuscripts.

A good leader for the department will be on hand to guide others in what they can do to mitigate the losses. She will know how to direct the actions of others in what areas of the collection to save in what order, how to handle fragile materials, where to put them, what simple conservation steps should be taken for each thing or genre of items, and so forth. Cornell's "Disaster Response Plan" (p. 10) gives a helpful prioritization listing—delineating the things that place items high on the "save-me-first" listing. It mentions monetary and research values, fragility, vulnerability, replaceability (and its attendant costs), "Why is preservation of this material critical?," and other issues. It also mentions that there are other things besides collection holdings that ought to be considered at the top of the priority list, including shelflists and computers. Each collection should create its own priorities list and have it available for all staff to use, along with a map showing the location of each entry on the list.

As the Cornell document says,

> In the event of a major disaster, it may become necessary to coordinate a large number of people and activities and commit significant amounts of money. Success of the recovery effort depends on action that is quick but organized and deliberate. Clear definitions of duties and chain of command are necessary to avoid confusion and to insure the safety of the people working at the recovery site. (p. 13)

The number one thing to remember—to reiterate what was said earlier—is that human life is at the top of the priority list for saving. In a major disaster, notification of others who can help is at the top of the list of things to do. For the school's own plan, the following steps are delineated, and they constitute a good list of actions that are the basis of any disaster recovery plan.

$ Alert appropriate staff members (see Disaster Phone Tree); name a meeting point.

$ The Emergency Coordinator should contact Major Disaster Action Team leaders.

$ Contact the University Office of Risk Management and Insurance. . . . Public Safety can contact representatives from this office after hours, if necessary.

$ Coordinate with emergency services (Public Safety, Fire Department) to determine when and where it is safe to enter building.

$ Take action to contain damage, e.g., spread plastic sheeting over shelves.

$ Reduce relative humidity and ensure good air circulation to control mold growth; do not turn off heat needed to keep pipes from freezing; keep air conditioning on if possible; use fans, open windows, etc. to keep air circulating. Large commercial dehumidifiers may be brought into the facility if needed. Monitor temperature and relative humidity throughout the recovery process.

$ Assess nature and extent of damage; take detailed notes and photographs for record purposes.

$ Identify a disaster command post, with necessary telephones, desks, and supplies for directing the recovery effort.

$ Make recovery plans; do not start removing material until a general plan of action is made.

$ Decisions must be made and action taken quickly; mold can start growing on wet material within 48 hours. (Cornell document, pp. 13–14)

The Cornell document author(s) chose to use dollar signs rather than bullets for this list of actions. Whether or not this was a recognition of the fiscal nature of a disaster cannot be determined, but it is clear that the better the plan and the more efficiently it is carried out, the lower the fiscal impact the disaster will have on the institution. The third dollar sign entry guides the reader to the document's appendix 6, which is titled "Insurance." Coming back from a disaster can cost millions, and if the disaster recovery team can save thousands of books (especially valuable ones from a rare book department) rather than having to replace them, the monetary savings can be significant.

SPECIFIC TREATMENTS

Underlying all the activities that the disaster response team must take is the urgency for timely action. Mold can begin to appear within forty-eight hours after materials have been wet; some library materials can be saved if fast action takes place, but might be lost if too much time passes between the disaster and the response. The Web contains a few tools to guide the responders in their actions, prioritizing their treatments and identifying the correct measures to take. One useful such tool is that published by the Western Association for Art Conservation (WAAC). The association's excellent chart titled "Salvage at a Glance" shows what to do with many kinds of media (paper documents and manuscripts, maps and plans, books, parchment and vellum manuscripts, works of art on paper, paintings, computer media, compact disks and CD-ROMs, sound and video recordings, black-and-white prints, color photographs, cased photographs, negatives, transparencies, color transparencies, motion pictures, and microforms), how soon they must be treated, handling precautions, packing methods, and drying methods.[73]

As has been stressed here, prioritization is important because the team working on materials after a disaster does not want to spend a great deal of time on, for instance, modern magazines (e.g., *Life, Look, Cosmopolitan, U.S. News and World Report*, and others like these) because these exist in great quantities in many libraries and are also available on microfilm and, in some instances, digitally. It is true that works printed on coated (i.e., shiny) stock will be ruined if they are not quickly interleaved to prevent the leaves from sticking permanently together, but that should be an operative and driving force for volumes like art books, which could have great intrinsic value, not for magazines that are close to worthless. So the WAAC chart, valuable as it is, should be used with an understanding of the level of prioritization of the items damaged based on their value and replaceability, not on the medium they are printed on.

For the most part, however, all personnel working on the actual salvage should be guided by a trained conservator. The Cornell document discusses methods for washing items dirtied with mud, for instance

(p. 20), and for packing wet library materials (p. 21),[74] but this should be done only under the tutelage of an expert trained in conservation treatments. For digital materials, only an information technology expert should be consulted.

The main kinds of treatments performed during a disaster-recovery operation deal with water, fire, and smoke problems, but in some parts of the country—mainly on the West coast of the United States—earthquakes can cause extensive damage. As mentioned earlier, books on top shelves are sometimes flung off in a wave pattern. This leads to a particular kind of damage, especially for leather-bound volumes or those in weak cloth: books will fall in such a way that their boards can be smashed off their textblocks, with the blocks flying in one direction and the covers going in another. And front and back covers are not likely to go in the same direction. To salvage piles of books (sometimes in piles up to the knees), the staff should lift each item carefully vertically, smoothing out bent leaves or clusters of leaves,

and lay it flat on its side, perhaps stacking items on top of one another to let the top volumes press flat the leaves of the volumes beneath. At the same time, and in the same general area, the staff should gather loose covers and try to keep them with the stacked books. This will help later on in the subsequent joining of textblocks with their proper covers. As with all other kinds of disasters, earthquake damage should be documented with photographs and extensive text, describing the damage and the disposition of the books after the temblor.

INSURANCE

If the aim of preservation and conservation is to extend the useful life of items, making the information they contain accessible for as long as possible, then with the loss of an item, one form of "preservation" is finding a replacement for it. If an item is damaged, another form of "preservation" is repairing it. But replacement and repair are costly, and most institutions cannot afford to take these measures if the losses are the result of a disaster that affects hundreds or thousands of items. With good insurance, this problem may be solved.[75]

Many institutions are "self-insured." This could mean different things from one institution to another. For items to be insured, they must be evaluated. For special collections, insurance can be, ironically, a nonissue, for it is impossible to put accurate, current values on an extensive collection of books, manuscripts, ephemera, photographs, and all the other things that wind up in the department. For private parties, and also possibly for rare book dealers, it is one thing to get a policy that covers a collection (or a dealer's stock) as a whole, and another thing to get insurance on an itemized collection. The holdings can be itemized and appraised individually (which costs a fortune because it is extremely time-consuming for large collections and requires the services of trained experts), or a policy can be written to cover the collection as a whole. But would an insurance company pay out on such a blanket figure?

For rare books, insurance companies will want itemized appraisals. They may even employ someone to verify the appraised value of an item that is lost in a fire or flood or to theft. Their own appraisers could

AFTER THE NORTHRIDGE quake, UC Riverside library staff took extensive photos of the damage. As the photographs showed, books in some aisles of the stacks were piled high on top of one another, pitched helter-skelter, with covers in one place, texts in other. The photos also showed books hanging over the edges of shelves, ready to fall. Almost all disaster photos are startling and dispiriting, and they have, for many people, an emotional impact. This was certainly the case with the earthquake photos at UC Riverside. The careful documentation we made went into the FEMA report, and the school received substantial FEMA support for repairs. One additional note: When we were finally able to stack up and try to organize on tables the books that had fallen, we found covers (usually those in leather) not only fully detached from the textblocks but also so far removed from them that the covers could not be matched with their proper texts. Months later, when we were arranging for the damaged volumes to be shipped to a conservator, we had to send along boxes of books and separate boxes of covers; most of the latter had to be discarded and new covers used. It was quite shocking to see the damage the earthquake caused.

> **AN ACQUAINTANCE OF** mine had a large, valuable collection of books. He consulted his insurance company, which insisted that he have every item evaluated individually. It cost him a fortune to get the coverage. But he soon learned that values put on the books he owned were not always perfectly accurate, though he had an expert do the appraisal. Copies of the books he owned appeared at auction now and then, and the hammer price could have been double—or half—what his copy was appraised at. Did the auction price affect the price of his own books? This is only one of many circumstances that could affect the appraised values of a collection.

come up with figures that differ significantly from those of the collector's or bookseller's appraiser. In a rare book department, as books age, some of them increase in value (though age often has little to do with the value of an item). Hitherto unknown copies of a book could come on the market, reducing the rarity of the title. And auction prices could be quite different from one another for the same title depending on the condition of the book and its provenance, on the dynamics of the auction, or for a host of other reasons. The owner must revisit appraisals periodically to see if they are current.

Having insurance for books—especially for those in special collections—is important, but what that insurance looks like, how the items are valued, and how a department collects on losses if the institution is "self-insured" will be determined by each librarian depending on the circumstances of his own institution. There is, of course, also insurance for people, because people can be injured in a variety of ways in a disaster. Besides direct injuries, a catastrophe can cause various ailments—for example, infection caused by contaminants at a disaster site, long-term anxiety problems, or pulmonary difficulties arising from contaminated air. The institution should have clearly written policies showing who is covered (full-time employees? part-timers? temporary staff? interns? volunteers?) and what the coverage is. This kind of coverage is usually in the employee's benefits package.

Part of the disaster recovery experience has to do with the paperwork that must be kept with respect to all the problems caused by the disaster. Problems concerning people, books and manuscripts, building damage, conditions of pipes and windows, and whatever else is affected by the disaster should be recorded. Thorough documentation should be kept, delineating all damage, with as many photographs as it is possible to take. The cabinet containing

> **INSURANCE VALUES FOR** special collections holdings were kept "current" at the University of California, Riverside. Every year I got a note from the office overseeing insurance asking me to update the values of the items in the department. I thought of this as farcical for many reasons, not the least of which was that I had no clue as to the value of the collection as a whole, and I obviously did not have time to evaluate hundreds of thousands of items just to "keep the valuations up to date." I was able to satisfy the office asking for the information by maintaining a file folder in which I kept several kinds
>
> of documents: (1) Letters from booksellers quoting certain items to the department; the quotes obviously had prices. If we had the item, we now had a recent price for it; if we bought the item, we could say what its value (to us) was because the price we paid was what its current value was. (2) Booksellers' catalogs listing some items that I checked to see if we had copies of (if we did not, I would have bought them). If we had copies, I would mark the items and their prices. (3) Handwritten notes I had made when I saw a volume in a bookstore or at an antiquarian book fair. The notes gave authors, titles, publica-
>
> tion data, and prices. When I got back to the library, I looked up the item in our catalog and if we had it, the notes would go into the file.
>
> By the end of the year I had a fat folder of values (albeit not a good appraisal of our own specific copies), and I sent the batch to the insurance-information-seeking office. I did not hear from them again until their next annual request for "current valuations" from the department. I never knew how the information was used or stored, but it seemed that what I sent was sufficient for them to record the information they needed.

mitigation supplies should thus hold some disposable cameras.

EXTERNAL COMMUNICATIONS / PUBLIC RELATIONS

Devastating as a disaster can be, it can sometimes be slightly mitigated with good public relations. This is an opportunity for a library to get itself into the public eye, to let the community (local and beyond) know what benefits the library offers to its patrons and scholars everywhere by the services it provides. The disaster allows the library to bare its losses, and it gives it a chance to appeal to the community for assistance.

During the disaster-recovery period, publicity should be contained to a single voice. That is, one person should be designated to be the speaker for the institution so that a single, accurate message is offered to the public. Every employee or anyone else working on the mitigation of the disaster should be instructed to refer reporters (or anyone else asking about the disaster) to that one speaker.

■ ■ ■

Preservation and conservation are such large issues—in terms of the amount of information available about them and also in terms of their importance in dealing with rare books—that this chapter has been extensive, but not definitive. There is clearly much more to say, and with the fields evolving the way they are, with new theories, new technologies, and new practitioners looking at the disciplines from fresh perspectives, the literature will continue to grow.

Anyone working with rare books—librarians, booksellers, archivists, collectors, and others—must be alert to the issues raised here. If preservation and conservation are not practiced, items will be lost, information will be lost, and we may never be able to recover that material.

NOTES

1. In the world of antiques, it is unethical to take any object that has been damaged, fix it up so that its flaws are fully removed or hidden, and pass it off as in original condition.

2. John Carter and Nicolas Barker, *ABC for Book Collectors*, 8th ed. (New Castle, DE: Oak Knoll Press; London: The British Library, 2004), p. 207. In the quotation, I believe the phrase "to a first edition re-cased in second edition covers" should be reversed: "a second edition re-cased in first edition covers." The terms *sophisticated* and *made-up* can also be used for volumes from a multivolume set in perfectly good condition, but that were brought together from different sets. That is, a *three-decker* (also called a *triple decker*—a set of books issued in three volumes) may be composed of volumes from different sets. If all volumes are identically bound and are truly of the same edition, impression, and issue, there may be no way to know that these books were not part of a single set. Sometimes something on the copyright page, in the binding, or in the printing could show that the set was made-up. It is possible also that the paper in one volume of a multivolume set does not match that in the other volumes. That the volumes were pulled together from various sources to make up a full set, if this is evident, will have a negative impact on the set's value. Carter's distaste for the practice can be seen, also, in his entry for "Made-up; Made-up copy":

   A made-up copy is one whose imperfections—the lack of a single leaf or more—have been made good from another copy of the same edition. The term is seldom met with in booksellers' catalogues, since making-up is often either unrecognised or unavowed. But a scrupulous cataloguer describing such a copy, especially of a book so rare or important that shortcomings may be pardoned, will specify it as having, e.g. "pages 63–66 from another and shorter (or equally clean) copy." Making-up with leaves from a copy of a different (usually later) edition—i.e. faking-up—is a bibliographical felony and valid grounds for divorce between buyer and seller. (p. 147)

3. Susan K. Soy's "Defining Preservation" is a good introduction to the key terms and activities of the field. See www.ischool.utexas.edu/~ssoy/pubs/dfngprsv.htm.

4. CoOL's website is http://cool.conservation-us.org; the Cons DistList archives are available at http://cool.conservation-us.org/byform/mailing-lists/cdl. The CoOL list is a huge site with an enormous amount of information. Cons DistList is still going strong, and it accepts queries from anywhere in the world pertaining to conservation issues. It is read by experts, and they will respond with the latest

information available. Although these are properly *conservation* sites, anyone working in preservation should know about them, because the latter is the parent of the former, and preservation officers need to know conservation treatments and activities. CoOL has another site called "Conservation/Preservation Information for the General Public" (http://cool.conservation-us.org/bytopic/genpub) that also contains links to a huge number of resources. CoOL has a whole subsite called "Educational Opportunities in Museum, Library, and Archives Conservation/Preservation" at http://cool.conservation-us.org/bytopic/education. An excellent summary of the state of preservation education by Karen F. Gracy and Jean Ann Croft is "Quo Vadis, Preservation Education? A Study of Current Trends and Future Needs" (N.p.: n.p., n.d., but c. 2006); this can be found at www.sis.pitt.edu/~kgracy/Quo_Vadis_pt1.pdf.

5. See websites as follows: American Library Association (www.ala.org/alcts/confevents/preswk); Society of American Archivists' Continuing Education Calendar (www2.archivists.org, select Education and Events—Continuing Education—Calendar); Association for Library Collections and Technical Services (see www.ala.org/alcts/ano/v15/n1/ano15n1_evts_preservation and www.ala.org/alcts/confevents/past/workshop/preservation); LAPNET (the Los Angeles Preservation Network—http://lapreservation.wordpress.com); the California State Historical Society (http://californiahistoricalsociety.blogspot.com/2011/02/imls-funds-free-preservation-workshops.html); Workshops and Continuing Education for librarians sponsored by the Massachusetts Board of Library Commissioners (http://mblc.state.ma.us/advisory/workshops/index.php); the New York State Program for the Conservation and Preservation of Library Research Materials (www.nysl.nysed.gov/libdev/cp/); and many others.

6. See Soy, "Defining Preservation."

7. These PEM dataloggers, at the point of this writing (2012), cost $349 each if the institution purchases up to nine of them; they are $299 each if the order is ten or more.

8. See www.nedcc.org/resources/leaflets/2The_Environment/04ProtectionFromLight.php. This is an excellent source of information about light, the damage it causes, methods of monitoring it, and what to do about the deterioration it causes. For more on light, see p. 364 of the present text.

9. See http://unfacilitated.preservation101.org/session4/prac_environ-light.asp. The subtitle of this site is "Preservation Basics for Paper and Media Collections." It is hosted by the Northeast Document Conservation Center (NEDCC).

10. "Air Quality Monitoring in European Museums: 2000 to Present," a paper presented at the 7th Indoor Air Quality Meeting 2006 (Braunschweig, Germany, November 15–17, 2006); see www.iaq.dk/iap/iaq2006/Muller_IAQ2006.pdf.

11. See www.nedcc.org/resources/leaflets/2The_Environment/02TemperatureAndHumidity.php. The text contains an excellent annotated bibliography of mostly online (and a few paper-based) resources.

12. The NEDCC leaflets, brought together in a single volume in print and on the organization's website, are a treasure trove of information about preservation. As individual, online publications, they can be easily updated when newer versions are issued of each pamphlet. Some of the information in this chapter comes from these (as cited). Sherelyn Ogden's pamphlet 2.1, "Temperature, Relative Humidity, Light, and Air Quality: Basic Guidelines for Preservation," is at www.nedcc.org/free-resources/preservation-leaflets/2.-the-environment/2.1-temperature,-relative-humidity,-light,-and-air-quality-basic-guidelines-for-preservation. Each of the pamphlets has suggestions for further reading, and they should be consulted as part of the rare book librarian's preservation education. The Lyrasis Preservation Services Leaflet "Environmental Specifications for the Storage of Library & Archival Materials" (look for it at the Lyrasis site, www.lyrasis.org/us-and-Services/) is also useful.

13. Available on the Web at www.nationalmuseums.org.uk/media/documents/what_we_do_documents/guiding_principles_reducing_carbon_footprint.pdf. The Image Permanence Institute at the Rochester Institute of Technology has been working on sustainability for years. The institute's director, James M. Reilly, has written on the subject, and his lecture titled "Sustainable Stewardship: The New Thinking on Preservation Environments and Building Operations" is available at www.youtube.com/watch?v=InAU191z9Uk. Another source to look at, on funding for sustainability, is Abby Smith Rumsey's *Sustainable Economics for a Digital Planet: Ensuring Long-Term Access to Digital Information*, produced by the Blue Ribbon Task Force on Sustainable Digital Preservation and Access (N.p.: San Diego Supercomputer Center [?], February 2010). This 110-page report is available in full at http://brtf.sdsc.edu/biblio/BRTF_Final_Report.pdf.

Another important report is that done by the National Digital Information Infrastructure and Preservation Program (NDIIPP), released by the Library of Congress in 2010. It is titled "Preserving Our Digital Heritage: The National Digital Information Infrastructure and Preservation Program 2010 Report." Jane Hedberg, in her "Preservation News" column in *College & Research Library News* (June 2011), says,

> The 141-page report reviews the program's progress on four major goals: developing a growing national preservation network, creating a content collection plan that will seed a national collection, building a shared technical platform for networked preservation, and fostering public policy that is conducive to digital preservation. The next phase for NDIIPP includes expanding the National Digital Stewardship Alliance (begun in 2010) to all 50 states, developing cutting-edge tools and services for the Alliance, and encouraging public support for preserving digital content as the public good. (p. 364)

The report is available on the Internet at www .digitalpreservation.gov/multimedia/documents/ NDIIPP2010Report_Post.pdf. (The version linked to this URL has 135 pages.) The report spells out the problem: "The digital era presents clear challenges for such an undertaking: the escalating scale of data creation, the globalization of information exchange, and the immaturity of standards and best practices, among many" (p. 1). (This statement ends just this way: ". . . among many.")

14. An article, tentatively titled "Sustainability and Preservation: A Literature Review," by Rebecca Meyer, Shannon Struble, and Phyllis Catsikis, is forthcoming in Michèle V. Cloonan, ed., *Preserving Our Heritage: Perspectives from Antiquity to the Digital Age* (Chicago: American Library Association, forthcoming). It contains much bibliographical information on the topics of the present discussion. The Image Permanence Institute has published *IPI's Guide to Sustainable Preservation Practices for Managing Storage Environments* (Rochester, NY: IPI, 2011[?]). IPI is an important organization for special collections librarians to know about because its main focus is preservation of all kinds of rare materials. Its website explains,

> IPI is a nonprofit, university-based laboratory devoted to preservation research. It is the world's largest independent laboratory with this specific scope. IPI was founded in 1985 through the combined efforts and sponsorship of the Rochester Institute of Technology and the Society for Imaging Science and Technology. Funding for

IPI's preservation research and outreach efforts has come primarily from the National Endowment for the Humanities, the Institute of Museum and Library Services, and the Andrew W. Mellon Foundation. IPI provides information, consulting services, practical tools and preservation technology to libraries, archives, and museums worldwide. The imaging and consumer preservation industries also use IPI's consulting, testing and educational services. (www.imagepermanence institute.org/about/about-ipi).

IPI's publications are useful for learning about preservation issues pertaining to the kinds of materials housed in special collections departments. See www.imagepermanenceinstitute.org/resources/ publications.

15. See www.newscientist.com/article/mg19826 575.700-ivy-uses-nanoparticles-to-cling-to-walls .html. The article is dated May 21, 2008, and the magazine issue is no. 2657.

16. One excellent source to consult for information on IPM is the UNESCO document prepared by Thomas A. Parker, *Study on Integrated Pest Management for Libraries and Archives* (Paris: UNESCO, 1988). The full text is on the Internet at www.unesco.org/ webworld/ramp/html/r8820e/r8820e00.htm. A more recent treatment, from the University of Illinois, Urbana-Champaign, is available at www.library.illinois.edu/prescons/services/ipm/.

17. Michèle V. Cloonan, "Cleaning the Newberry's Collection," *Abbey Newsletter* 6.4 (August 1982), http://cool.conservation-us.org/byorg/abbey/an/ an06/an06-4/an06-410.html. Another document on cleaning stacks is "Stacks Cleaning Procedures," from the University Libraries of the University of Washington (see www.lib.washington.edu/preservation/ libraries/clean. The document says that there are three reasons to clean the collection: (1) "Reduce dust and dirt which can sustain or attract mold, insects, and other pests in the collections"; (2) "Keep dust and dirt out of the interior of books, photos, tapes, and CDs where it can be abrasive and cause damage over time"; and (3) "Create a pleasant working environment for both staff and patrons which also promotes respect and care for our collections and facilities." This site gives excellent, thorough information on the cleaning process. An equally thorough treatment is on the Harvard site, "Cleaning Library Materials" (http://library.harvard .edu/preservation/care-and-handling), which has a link to "Specifications for Cleaning Rare Books and Manuscript Boxes" (http://library.harvard.edu/ sites/default/files/cleaningrarebooks2010.pdf).

Its section titled "Procedure for Especially Fragile or Damaged Books" is quite useful.

18. See Mary Todd Glaser, www.nedcc.org/free -resources/preservation-leaflets/2.-the-environment/ 2.5-protecting-paper-and-book-collections-during -exhibition. Some of the information in this section is taken from Glaser's excellent text (and is cited as "Glaser").

19. Glaser expatiates at length on these recommendations. The gist of the leaflet is that the curator of the exhibit must be as cautious as possible in mounting the display and should always select the most conservative option (when there are choices) in deciding how to (and how long to) display materials.

20. Cathy Henderson's useful article on the relationship between curator and conservator, "Curator or Conservator: Who Decides on What Treatment?," can be seen in *Rare Books & Manuscripts Librarianship* 2.2 (Fall 1987):103–107, http://rbm.acrl.org/ content/rbml/2/2/103.full.pdf+html.

21. "Environmental Conditions for Exhibiting Library and Archival Materials" (Bethesda, MD: NISO Press, 2001). This set of standards, with its thorough text and appendices, runs to twenty-seven pages of excellent information, and should be consulted by anyone mounting an exhibit. See www.niso.org/apps/group _public/download.php/6482/Environmental%20 Conditions%20for%20Exhibiting%20Library%20 and%20Archival%20Materials.pdf. This document is designated ANSI/NISO Z39.79-2001 (ISSN: 1041-5653).

22. You will hear librarians say, "Those books are in the folio section." This means the area in which really large books are stored. The bibliographical meaning of the word *folio* was explained in chapter 9, "Bibliography."

23. A corollary to not using bottom shelves because of their inaccessibility is that these shelves should be well lighted. In some libraries, the lighting is not properly configured, and it could be difficult to see call numbers or spine titles on the lower shelves.

24. The collection at the time was on the third floor of the Rivera Library, and we noticed that books on the upper floors were more likely to fall than were volumes on the first two floors. Soon after the quake, FEMA (the Federal Emergency Management Agency) funded a massive seismic upgrading for the building, but the horses were already out of the barn.

25. The Northeast Document Conservation Center (NEDCC) Preservation Leaflets publication (already cited a number of times here) contains nine pamphlets on reformatting and eight on conservation procedures. They are valuable resources of information for anyone working with rare books. See www .nedcc.org/free-resources/preservation-leaflets/ overview.

26. See "Microform," Wikipedia, http://en.wikipedia .org/wiki/Microform.

27. Michèle V. Cloonan, "Preservation Timeline," in *Preserving Our Heritage* (Chicago: American Library Association, forthcoming).

28. See www.library.cornell.edu/preservation/library preservation/mee/preservation/microform.html. This site has a good deal of information about microform reformatting, looking at such subjects as various kinds of film (silver-gelatin, diazo, and vesicular), standards, film generations, camera negatives, print master negatives, and a great deal more. Much of this information seems to have been taken from the NEDCC Preservation Leaflet 6.1, "Microfilm and Microfiche," written by Steve Dalton (www.nedcc.org/free-resources/preservation -leaflets/6.-reformatting/6.1-microfilm-and -microfiche). Dalton says that though there are no guaranteed preservation-level color microfilm processes,

> one (positive) color transparency film, Ilfochrome, . . . is considered quite promising for preservation. Unlike other color microfilms, which generate their dye image during processing, this film has color layers built directly into its emulsion. Testing at the Image Permanence Institute (Rochester, NY) suggests that the life expectancy of the dyes is excellent—possibly 300 to 500 years—when the film is not exposed to light. The research also suggests, however, that the film's polyester base may be less resistant to deterioration than some other polyester bases. Even so, the life expectancy of the base may be as much as 200 years or more.

This leaflet is copyrighted 2007. A commercial company, Genus—The Microfilm Shop (www.microfilm .com/pdf/colour_micro_flyer-1.pdf), guarantees that their films, using Ilford Colour Micrographic Film, will last five hundred years. The company says,

> Using the very latest RGB laser technology colour TIFF images can be written to colour microfilm at up to 160 line pairs/mm. An innovative colour management system takes care of exact colour fidelity. Specific Metadata can be added next to the pictures for indexing[,] and nesting options

allow different numbers of images to be grouped together to optimize capacity.

So by combining digital and analog technology, Genus promises perfect color reproduction and longevity far beyond what is currently considered "preservation level."

29. Cathleen A. Baker and Randy Silverman, "Misperceptions about White Gloves," *International Preservation News* 37 (December 2005): 4–9, http://archive.ifla.org/VI/4/news/ipnn37.pdf; this quotation is on p. 4.

30. Conservators like to use the word *embrittled*: "The paper became embrittled within a decade"; "The document suffered from embrittling (or embrittlement)." Microsoft Word's "Smell Check" does not recognize this as a word, though the online *Merriam-Webster Collegiate Dictionary* says that the word's first recorded use was in 1902 (www.merriam-webster.com/dictionary/embrittled). For the present text I will avoid the use of this jargon word, but anyone working in the rare book world should know it because it is common among conservators who work on rare materials. Maybe someday "Shell Check," imperfect as it is, will recognize the term.

31. There is a large literature on deacidification. See Jeannette Adams, "Mass Deacidification Annotated Bibliography 1990–2010" ([Washington, DC]: Library of Congress Preservation Directorate, January 2011), www.loc.gov/preservation/resources/deacid/deacid_bib2011.pdf. This supersedes the work by Carole Zimmerman, "Bibliography on Mass Deacidification" (Washington, DC: Library of Congress Preservation Office, 1991), http://cool.conservation-us.org/byauth/zimmerman/massdeac.html.

32. See http://liswiki.org/wiki/Deacidification. The reference to Zachary is to Shannon Zachary, *Mass Deacidification in 2002 and the University of Michigan Experience*, ARL 224 (October 2002): 6–9. Zachary builds on the useful study done by Michèle V. Cloonan, "Mass Deacidification in the 1990s," *Rare Books & Manuscripts Librarianship* 5.2 (Fall 1990): 95–103, which contains a good discussion of the history and types of deacidification and a survey of all then-current methods of mass treatment. Matt Roberts and Don Etherington's entry on "non-aqueous deacidification" says that in this method, "alcohol, or some other non-aqueous solvent, [is used] for the deacidifying chemical. Aqueous methods cannot be used to treat archival materials in cases in which the ink is susceptible to the action of water" (p. 176). For this reason,

in selecting items for treatment, the librarian must carefully test inks and other pigments (in illustrations and bindings, for instance) to see if they will run when they are treated with water.

33. The Preservation Technologies website says,

The patented Bookkeeper treatment process has set a new standard for safety and effectiveness in removing harmful acids from paper. Developed to meet the standards of the United States Library of Congress, Bookkeeper is the only mass deacidification process that meets current and projected OSHA, FTC, and EPA consumer and environmental requirements. (www.ptlp.com/about.html).

The site also states,

The Bookkeeper Spray System is virtually odor free and dries in minutes. Bookkeeper will not damage inks, adhesives, or binding materials. It is non-clogging, non-toxic, non-hazardous, non-flammable, and contains no CFC's and is completely safe for the environment. (www.ptlp.com/system.html).

34. Joachim Liers, "Mass Deacidification: The Efficacy of the Papersave Process," http://iada-home.org//pr01jb_i.pdf. The abstract states, "Introducing a high amount of alkaline reserve into already damaged paper can reduce its flexibility, rendering general minimal requirements for an alkaline reserve pointless from a conservator's point of view."

35. "The Rare Book and Manuscript Library Personal Photographing Form," www.library.illinois.edu/rbx/pdf/Personal_photographing_form.pdf.

36. Preservation Equipment Ltd's website is www.preservationequipment.com.

37. "Preservation of Books and Documents by Lamination," UNESCO (September 1963), http://unesdoc.unesco.org/images/0014/001477/147710eb.pdf.

38. Roberts and Etherington add that the lamination material itself—the cellulose acetate—could cause damage, for it "may be more vulnerable to the action of the atmospheric gases such as sulfur dioxide, particularly if the acetate contains metallic impurities" (p. 150). As late as 1982, when the Roberts/Etherington volume was published, lamination was an accepted method of preservation. They say that it is a,

method of protecting and preserving embrittled or otherwise weak papers, maps, etc., by placing them between sheets of thin, thermoplastic material, which, when subjected to heat and pressure, with or without an adhesive, seals the paper in and protects it by making it more or less impervious to atmospheric conditions. (p. 150)

The term *encapsulation* is absent from this volume. The inferiority of lamination to encapsulation cannot be overstated. In fact, lamination is now seen as a positively damaging treatment.

39. See "Protecting Books with Custom-Fitted Boxes" at www.nedcc.org/free-resources/preservation -leaflets/4.-storage-and-handling/4.5-protecting -books-with-custom-fitted-boxes. The National Park Service's *Conserve O Gram* Number 19/23 (July 2001), titled "A Phase Box for the Protection of Books," is a useful publication, showing tools and diagrams and giving directions on their making. The piece was written by Per Cullhed and "was adapted from 'The 5-Minute Phase Box,' *Abbey Newsletter*, Vol. 24, No. 2, 2000." (See www.nps.gov/museum/ publications/conserveogram/19-23.pdf).

40. See "Solander box," Wikipedia, http://en.wikipedia .org/wiki/Solander_box. For many excellent images, enter "solander box" in Google's image search tool (www.google.com/imghp); see p. 128 of the present text.

41. NEDCC Preservation Leaflet 4.6 is Richard Horton's "Card Stock Enclosures for Small Books" (www .nedcc.org/free-resources/preservation-leaflets/ 4.-storage-and-handling/4.6-card-stock-enclosures -for-small-books). Pamphlet 4.7 by Christopher Clarkson is on "The Book Shoe," a four-sided open enclosure that leaves the book exposed at the top and fore-edge (www.nedcc.org/free-resources/ preservation-leaflets/4.-storage-and-handling/ 4.7-the-book-shoe-description-and-uses). These pamphlets have been updated for the NEDCC publication. And Pamphlet 4.8 is "Polyester Film Book Jacket" by Richard Horton (www.nedcc.org/ free-resources/preservation-leaflets/4.-storage -and-handling/4.8-polyester-film-book-jacket).

42. See Kitty Nicholson, "Photocopier Hazards and a Conservation Case Study," *Book and Paper Group Annual* 8 (1989), http://cool.conservation-us.org/ coolaic/sg/bpg/annual/v08/bp08-05.html.

43. Nicholson cites William R. Hawken, *Copying Methods Manual* (Chicago: American Library Association, 1966).

44. Nicholson's note 17 cites W. E. Virchow, "Exposure to Xerox Copier Safer Than 10 Seconds of Sunlight," *Bulletin of the American Group-IIC* 7.2 (1967), p. 21. Her note 18 refers to Garry Thomson, *The Museum Environment* (Boston: Butterworths, 1981), p. 157, and to P. M. Cassiers, "A Review of Architecture and Process Configurations for Electrophotography," *Journal of Photographic Science* 25 (1977), p. 133.

45. Anne Jordan, "Archives: Reference Photocopying," National Park Service *Conserve O Gram* Number 19/7 (July 1993), www.nps.gov/museum/ publications/conserveogram/19-07.pdf.

46. *Photocopying of Library and Archive Materials* (Reading, Berkshire, England: National Preservation Office, February 2000).

47. A case study from the University of Tennessee is a useful place to start looking into collection assessments. See Mary Ellen Starmer, Sara Hyder McGough, and Aimée Leverette, "Rare Condition: Preservation Assessment for Rare Book Collections," *RBM* 6.2 (Fall 2005): 91–106, http://rbm.acrl.org/content/ 6/2/91.full.pdf+html.

48. Because conservation can be quite expensive, and because most rare book libraries do not have funds dedicated to it, and because most institutions cannot justify the cost of a conservation laboratory and people to staff it, the activities may need ad hoc funding, so working with the development department is a good strategy. Adopt-a-book/Save-a-book events will call attention to the department's needs and may generate support from friends groups or others sympathetic to the collection's needs.

49. It cannot be overemphasized that the curator and the conservator must work together closely in deciding on treatments for each item under scrutiny. For a good discussion of this interchange, see Roberta Pilette and Carolyn Harris, "It Takes Two to Tango: A Conservator's View of Curator/Conservator Relations," *Rare Books & Manuscripts Librarianship* 4.2 (Fall 1989): 103–111, http://rbm.acrl.org/ content/rbml/4/2/103.full.pdf+html. Ideally, the two will settle on a treatment plan that is congenial to both. But as Pilette and Harris conclude,

> There will always be occasions when the conservator feels the request for a particular treatment is not in the best interest of the item(s). The curator may feel caught between conservation demands and outside demands. How curator and conservator resolve such a problem will depend on the working relationship they have established, the degree of respect and trust each has for the other's knowledge and abilities, and the willingness to work together to arrive at the best possible conservation decision. (p. 110)

Jan Paris has written the NEDCC Leaflet 7.7, "Choosing and Working with a Conservator" (www .nedcc.org/free-resources/preservation-leaflets/ 7.-conservation-procedures/7.7-choosing-and -working-with-a-conservator). The assumption in this leaflet is that the curator does not have a conservator on staff; but either way, the information here is quite good.

50. See Grace Dobush, "NARA's Secret History of Lamination," *Family Tree* (December 29, 2010), www.familytreemagazine.com/article/nara -lamination-history.

51. Paul N. Banks (1934–2000) was one of the founders of the modern school of conservation. Among his influences has been what have come to be called his *Ten Laws of Conservation.* Cloonan says of Banks's laws, "The *Laws* have never been published, but they have been disseminated for decades by Banks' former students." The one quoted here is his Tenth Law. See Michèle V. Cloonan, *Preserving Our Heritage: Perspectives from Antiquity to the Digital Age* (Chicago: American Library Association, forthcoming); this statement is in her introduction to chapter 4, "Conservation." Chapter 4 of the Cloonan text publishes these laws. They are important enough to reproduce here:

  1. No one can have access to a document that no longer exists.
  2. Multiplication and dispersal increase chances of survival of information.
  3. Books and documents deteriorate all the time.
  4. Use causes wear.
  5. Deterioration is irreversible.
  6. The physical medium of the book or document contains information.
  7. No reproduction can contain all the information contained in the original.
  8. Authenticity cannot be restored.
  9. Conservation treatment is interpretation.
  10. No treatment is irreversible. (from a proof copy of Cloonan's book, cited above)

  Wikipedia's brief biography of Banks is at http://en.wikipedia.org/wiki/Paul_N._Banks.

52. See Beth Doyle, "The Importance of Library and Archives Conservation (and Why We Should Continue Training Library and Archives Conservators)," http://prescan.wordpress.com/2009/08/18/the-importance-of-library-and-archives-conservation-and-why-we-should-continue-training-library-and-archives-conservators/.

53. A leaf caster is a machine that can fill holes in sheets of paper. It is sometimes referred to as a "paper in-fill machine." For the application of one, see the Eclipse Paper Conservation site at www.eclipsepaper.com/leaf%20casting.htm.

54. Steven E. Smith and Beth M. Russell, "Special Delivery: Packing Rare Books for Shipping," *Rare Books & Manuscripts Librarianship* 12.2 (Fall 1997): 87–96, http://rbm.acrl.org/content/rbml/12/2/87.full.pdf+html.

55. Paul Banks, "Preservation," *Encyclopedia of Library and Information Science* 23 (New York: Dekker, 1968): 97–99. Smith and Russell also cite John Franklin Mowery's "Packing Books for Travel," *Guild of Bookworkers Journal* 23.1–2 (1984–1985): 58–68, in which Mowery describes heavy-duty crates for packaging heavy or extremely valuable items.

56. No attempt at comprehensiveness in bibliographical references is in order here. One recent, extensive bibliography on the subject of digital preservation is in Ross Harvey's *Preserving Digital Materials*, 2nd ed. (Berlin and Boston: de Gruyter / Saur, 2012), pp. 222–40. This excellent volume covers the broad topic circumspectly. The chapter headings are a guide to scholars wishing to see current issues and how they are being thought about: chapter 1, "What is Preservation in the Digital Age? Changing Preservation Paradigms"; 2, "Why Do We Preserve? Who Should Do It?"; 3, "Why There's a Problem: Digital Artifacts and Digital Objects"; 4, "Selection for Preservation—The Critical Decision"; 5, "What Attributes of Digital Materials Do We Preserve?"; 6, "Overview of Digital Preservation Strategies"; 7, "'Preserve Technology' Approaches: Tried and Tested Methods"; 8, "'Preserve Objects' Approaches: New Frontiers?"; 9, "Digital Preservation Initiatives and Collaborations"; 10, "Challenges for the Future of Digital Preservation."

57. Natalia Bergau, *Report on Digital Preservation Practice and Plans amongst LIBER Members with Recommendations for Practical Action*, Europeana *Travel* (www.europeanatravel.eu/downloads/D1.3._ET_report_final_23092010.pdf); cited by Harvey, *Preserving Digital Materials*, p. 22.

58. Deborah Woodyard-Robinson, "Introduction," in *Digital Preservation: Finding Balance*, spec. issue of *Library Trends* 54.1 (Summer 2005): 1–5; this statement is on p. 1. In this passage she mentions the change in computers and the breaking of links, but we lose use of the resources for other reasons as well. Software becomes obsolete, the disks or drives we store information on deteriorate, sites get hacked, information can be affected by copyright issues, data will be lost in its transfer to later platforms (reformatting will always result in an altered text), and so forth. One patently obvious example is the transfer of an analog text (in a book) to a digital one: information about the paper and binding will not transfer. This is true of information reformat-

ted from digital to digital storage. Reinforcing the notion of the fragility of digital records, Margaret Hedstrom wrote "Digital Preservation: A Time Bomb for Digital Libraries," *Computers and the Humanities* 31 (1998): 189–202, http://deepblue.lib.umich .edu/bitstream/2027.42/42573/1/10579_2004 _Article_153071.pdf. The following year (1999), Abby Smith wrote a report for the Council on Library and Information Resources (CLIR), published as a pamphlet titled *Why Digitize?* (Washington, DC: CLIR, 1999), www.clir.org/pubs/reports/pub80 -smith/pub80.html. One section of her report is titled "Digitization Is Not Preservation—At Least Not Yet." She says,

> Though digitization is sometimes loosely referred to as preservation, it is clear that, so far, digital resources are at their best when facilitating access to information and weakest when assigned the traditional library responsibility of preservation. Regrettably, because digitization is a type of reformatting, like microfilming, it is often confused with preservation microfilming and seen as a superior, if as yet more expensive, form of preservation reformatting. Digital imaging is not preservation, however. Much is gained by digitizing, but permanence and authenticity, at this juncture of technological development, are not among those gains.

More than a decade later (at the present writing), many people still take this stance.

59. The MacKenzie Smith article is "Exploring Variety in Digital Collections and the Implications for Digital Preservation," in the *Library Trends* issue cited in note 58, pp. 6–32. The opening sentence of the Smith abstract says,

> The amount of digital content produced at academic research institutions is large, and libraries and archives at these institutions have a responsibility to bring this digital material under curatorial control in order to manage and preserve it over time. But this is a daunting task with few proven models, requiring new technology, policies, procedures, core staff competencies, and cost models. (p. 6)

She adds that with their efforts with the institution and outside assistance, "we are beginning to see ways of managing arbitrary digital content that might make digital preservation an achievable goal." Her phrase "few proven models" is deceptive in that it implies that there are a "few proven models." She really means "no proven models." And her last phrase, "might make digital preservation an achievable goal" actually explains the current situation. They are not there yet.

60. Ross Harvey says, "Narrowly focused localized solutions are not considered likely to be the most effective" means of preservation. See his *Preserving Digital Materials*, 2nd ed., p. 30.

61. Deborah Woodyard-Robinson, "Introduction," p. 3. She is referring to Steve Knight, "Preservation Metadata: National Library of New Zealand Experience," *Library Trends* (see note 58), pp. 91–110. Knight's abstract says,

> Development of approaches to preservation metadata has been an integral component of international efforts in the field of digital preservation. The focus of the community engaged in this work is currently shifting, and there is, as yet, no formal agreement around a conceptual framework and identification of required data elements. At the same time attention is now turning to the more complex task of building sustainable technical, infrastructure, and policy frameworks that will enable organizations to implement preservation metadata strategies practically at a local level. (p. 91)

The model of creating preservation strategies at a local level is appealing—for individual institutions. But it does not yield a uniform, universal strategy that can be promulgated as a form of "digital preservation" for all. And, of course, at the writing of Knight's piece (in 2005) the model had not yet been created. It has not yet been perfected at the present writing.

62. A parallel question might be, how many technologies (of any kind, in any field) have been developed that have reached "state-of-the-art" and that never need to be revisited for improvement?

63. Gail Hodge and Evelyn Frangakis, "Digital Preservation and Permanent Access to Scientific Information: The State of the Practice: A Report Sponsored by the International Council for Scientific and Technical Information (ICSTI) and CENDI" (2004), cendi.dtic .mil/publications/04-3dig_preserv.html; cited by Harvey, *Preserving Digital Materials*, p. 229.

64. The UNESCO text is *Charter on the Preservation of the Digital Heritage* (Paris: UNESCO, 2004), portal .unesco.org/ci/en/file_download.php/4cc126a26 92a22c7c7dcc5ef2e2878c7Charter_en.pdf; cited by Harvey, *Preserving Digital Materials*, p. 239. Although Harvey's text is on the preservation of *digital* materials, many of his observations apply as well to analog objects.

65. Of course, the dissemination of information may be restrained by some of the issues raised earlier in this book, having to do with legal (contractual

or copyright) restrictions on holdings or the desire to control the release of materials that could undercut the institution's profitable use of the texts.

66. Harvey, *Preserving Digital Materials*, p. 105. He adds that the librarians must know precisely what they are preserving—that is, they must prioritize clearly in selecting items for digitization. The costs are so great for this that most institutions just cannot save everything. So a careful prioritization must be done. Other features of an effective preservation plan are that it should be figured into the regular budget of the institution and not funded ad hoc as a one-time endeavor; the plan should be far-reaching, considering not merely one or two generations of digital technology or one or two generations of librarians and archivists, but many generations; "[i]t should be based on clear definitions of what it is that we are trying to preserve—the 'essence' of a record"; "[i]t should be based on stable, widely used, and clearly defined standards, including a limited number of standard data formats where possible"; there should be good management-information and preservation metadata; "[i]t should recognize that digital preservation is an active process"; and "[i]t should not be based on proprietary data formats or systems" (p. 106). The text was published in 2012, and Harvey says that many institutions now have some preservation policy planned or in place, which indicates that these organizations have some budget set aside for the activity. He says, "the high percentage of organizations with policies, budgets, and solutions in place augurs well" (p. 106). In this sentence he probably does not mean "solutions," for to date no true solutions have been found. He offers the ERPANET (Electronic Resource Preservation and Access Network) tool for helping librarians and others select digital preservation technologies (see pp. 109–10). The chart has a telltale sentence, under the rubric of "Preservation period":

> As digital systems only have a lifespan of about five to 10 years at the highest and digital objects must be preserved for much longer periods, it is important that the system is able to efficiently export objects and their context data in standard formats in order to migrate them into a new system. (p. 109)

He cites ERPANET, *Selecting Technologies Tool* (2003), www.erpanet.org/guidance/docs/ ERPANETSelect_Techno.pdf.

67. Even booksellers should consider such sharing, though, of course, the availability of a digital text might impact the sale of the analog original. On the other hand, such digital exposure could be an advertisement for the original and could foster its sale.

68. Beth Lindblom Patkus and Karen Motylewski, "Disaster Planning." This is Leaflet 3.3 in the NEDCC Preservation Leaflet Series (www.nedcc.org/free -resources/preservation-leaflets/3.-emergency -management/3.3-disaster-planning). NEDCC acknowledges that the text was "Reprinted with permission from 'Disaster Planning for Cultural Institutions,' by Beth Lindblom and Karen Moty- lewski, published originally as Technical Leaflet #183 by the American Association for State and Local History (Nashville, TN, 1993)." Although this leaflet was written many years ago, it is still the latest version in the NEDCC volume of preservation publications because it is comprehensive and circumspect and fully applicable today. Other online publications are worth looking at. See, for example, NEDCC's "dPlan The Online Disaster-Planning Tool for Cultural and Civic Institutions" at www.dplan .org. See also "Disaster Planning and Preparedness Guidelines" and its accompanying "Library Disaster Plan Template" (http://calpreservation.org/wp -content/uploads/2013/05/CPTF_disaster_plan _2003.pdf), created by CalPreservation.org (the California Preservation Program; http://calpreservation .org/about). There is also Sally A. Buchanan and Toby Murray's *Disaster Planning: Preparedness and Recovery for Libraries and Archives: A RAMP Study with Guidelines*, 1988 (http://eric.ed.gov/?id= ED297769). Another important and thorough text is that published by Cornell University, "Disaster Response Plan." This forty-five-page document is at www.library.cornell.edu/preservation/disaster. It is referred to in the present text as the "Cornell document." Although it was written specifically for Cornell University, it contains a wealth of information adaptable to other institutions—not merely academic libraries.

69. The Cornell document (see note 68) also lists items that should be kept in a freezer, if one is available to store wet materials, as well as folding plastic crates, plastic pallets, plastic 5-gallon buckets with lids, hard hats, blotting paper, polyester film, safety goggles, protective aprons, and a walkie-talkie, among other things. (See the Cornell document, appendix 2, p. 31.)

70. Along with lists of the supplies the library needs is a list of the vendors that may need to be consulted in an emergency. The Cornell document (cited in note 68) has such a list for that school in its appendix 5, titled "Local and Regional Services and Supplies." It includes contact information for many

kinds of vendors, and it deals with the following: Chemicals; Containers; Cleaning Supplies; Cold Storage; Compression, Air; Data Recovery; Dehumidifiers; Dehumidification On-Site; Electrical, Emergency Repair; Extension Cords, Fans, Portable; Film/Photographic Recovery; Flashlights; Freeze-Drying; Generators; Heaters; Janitorial, Emergency Service; Ladders; Leaks, Repair; Lighting, Emergency; Maintenance Assistance; Polyester Film; Pallets; Plastic Sheeting; Plumbing, Emergency Service; Pumps; Respirators; Salvage & Recovery (Cleaning, Drying, Odor-Removal, etc.); Tapes (Various); Trucks (Refrigerated); Trucks (General); Wet/Dry Vacuums (Cornell document, pp. 38–40.) Naturally each library should have a similar document with local vendors listed.

71. dPlan is available at www.dplan.org. With the publication of its pamphlets for more than a quarter century, NEDCC has been in the forefront of preservation education in this country, and its leaflets are used worldwide, accessible free on its website. They are updated as needed, so they are goldmines of state-of-the-art information on a wide range of preservation issues. Anyone working with rare books and special collections should know of them. dPlan was funded by the Institute of Museum and Library Services and by the National Center for Preservation Technology and Training (NCPTT). See http://ri.dplan.org/contactus.asp.

72. Before computers were on the scene, one of the basic tenets of disaster recovery was that high on the list of things to save was the shelflist, the record of all the department's holdings. Today, in most libraries, that information is online. So saving computer records may take top spot in the prioritization of things to save. It is important to have backups for all cataloging records for the department.

73. "Salvage at a Glance," created by Betty Walsh, is at http://cool.conservation-us.org/waac/wn/wn19/wn19-2/wn19-207.html. This useful tool was originally "[p]ublished as an insert to the *WAAC Newsletter*, Vol. 19, No. 2 (May 1997)." The website explains, "This chart was written as a ready reference to the BCIMS [British Columbia Information Management Services] disaster plan. Originally, the chart was modeled on a table of recovery priorities written by Julia Niebuhr Eulenberg, in *Handbook for the Recovery of Water Damaged Business Records* (Prairie Village, Kansas: ARMA, 1986), 47–48."

74. The Cornell document also has brief guidelines on how to salvage paper, books, paintings, floppy disks, sound and video recordings, photographic materials (prints, negatives, and transparencies), motion pictures, microforms, and parchment and vellum (pp. 21–25).

75. Of course, *replacement* implies that there are copies available, but for rare books this is not always the case. And *repair* implies that a damaged item can be fixed, also not always the case. Sometimes the damage is so extensive that there is no way to undo it or to bring back all the information the item held before it was damaged.

SPECIAL COLLECTIONS DEPARTMENTS TODAY

HE UNIVERSITY OF CALIFORNIA'S CALIFORNIA DIGITAL LIBRARY (CDL) has a page called "Digital Special Collections" on which is the following:

> The Digital Special Collections Program (DSC) supports collaboration between libraries, archives, and museums throughout the State of California to provide access to a world class digital collection that serves an array of end users, from researchers and scholars to K–12 students. (www.cdlib.org/services/dsc)

The Harry Ransom Humanities Research Center at the University of Texas at Austin has a Web page called "Culture Unbound: An Investment in Discovery." Its opening paragraph says,

> The digital revolution has influenced virtually every aspect of library and museum services, from the automation of internal record-keeping systems to the digitization of physical collections, from the acquisition of new "born-digital" works to the use of technology to present traditional collections and engage audiences. Digital technology enables the full range of holdings—audio and video recordings, print materials, photographs, artworks, artifacts, and other resources—to be cataloged, organized, combined in new ways, and made accessible to audiences in a variety of formats. (www.hrc.utexas.edu/contribute/capital/digital/)

Chicago's Newberry Library says on one of its Web pages, "The Newberry supports research and learning through a number of digital collections based on its holdings, as well as through online exhibitions, publications, reference materials, and other digital resources" ("Publications and Digital Resources," www.newberry.org/publications-and-digital-resources). And the U.S. National Archives (NARA—National Archives and Records Administration) has a vast digital presence in its Archives Library Information Center. The center's website explains,

The Archives Library Information Center (ALIC) is more than a traditional library. Recognizing that our customers no longer expect to work within the walls of a library, these pages are designed to provide NARA staff and researchers nationwide with convenient access to content beyond the physical holdings of our two traditional libraries. ALIC provides access to information on American history and government, archival administration, information management, and government documents to NARA staff, archives and records management professionals, and the general public. (www.archives. gov/research/alic)

What these sites and quotations have in common is that they address the present and future realities of libraries, archives, and museums. We are now in the Information Age when users want everything.[1]

Although special collections distinguish themselves by the rare, beautiful objects they hold, they are nonetheless in the middle of a technological revolution that affects every one of their users, their holdings, their ability to serve their clientele, and almost every aspect of their operations. If a curator finds a book with red rot and wants to fix it, she may turn immediately to the Web for advice. If a patron wants a piece of information and asks a reference librarian for assistance, the chances are the librarian will go to his computer to seek bibliographical information or cataloging records. A preservation officer wanting to know what the temperature and relative humidity of a room in the library have been for the last month will turn to a digital Datalogger and may send that information to her computer or to another librarian instantly by e-mail. And, directly to the point of the present volume, if a researcher in Malta needs to see the text of a unique copy of a pamphlet held in a library in Quito, Ecuador, he may locate that copy on OCLC WorldCat, send a text message to the Ecuadorean library, and receive a digitized copy of the pamphlet within a day.

Earlier in this book the subject of universal bibliographical control (UBC) appeared. This is the unattainable ideal of librarianship: the ability to offer to anyone in the world (with a computer and Internet access) any piece of information from anywhere else on earth. One reason that it is unattainable is that there is too much information. Another reason tradi-

tionally given for the impossibility of achieving UBC is that there was no storage, retrieval, and delivery system around to make it possible. Today we are on the cusp of eliminating that objection: an expanding network of computers, with increasing memory capacities, linked with electronic methods of capturing information (including scanning and reformatting of analog into digital text), and supported by vastly growing numbers of computers and users combine to get us closer and closer to UBC. As the earlier chapter claimed, this is an asymptotic endeavor: we will never achieve 100 percent bibliographic control. But the amount of information being created and made accessible in digital form grows by endless gigabytes and terabytes.

One case in point, on a large (though in the global sense quite small) scale, is the Online Archive of California (OAC). The OAC "provides free public access to detailed descriptions of primary resource collections maintained by more than 200 contributing institutions including libraries, special collections, archives, historical societies, and museums throughout California and collections maintained by the 10 University of California (UC) campuses."[2] The site hosts "more than 20,000 online collection guides," and it grows almost daily. Of course, in theory, the aim of the OAC is to host every bit of information about every collection in the state. But this is clearly impossible. Further, the site gives only the collections' finding aids, not full content of these collections.

There is no mystery to this. Nor does the information we can access in tremendous quantities leave us starry-eyed. Computers have been with us for enough generations that we automatically turn to them for most of our information needs. The use of computers to scan for keywords in a huge text (or on the Internet), to enlarge images of digitized pages, and to organize information is becoming so common that people no longer wonder at it the way they did when they first saw the technology in operation. "Look it up" used to mean, "Search for it in a book." Now it means going to a computer and hitting some keys. There is usually no sense of surprise when we turn to the Internet for data; in fact, we sometimes may be surprised when we *cannot* find what we are looking for. And when we are looking into the holdings of almost any research library, we expect to see a phrase at a live link that says, "Search Our Online Catalog."

In 1996, Henry Raine and Laura Stalker wrote "Rare Book Records in Online Systems,"[3] in which they observe, with the coming of computers to aid in the storage and dissemination of cataloging records, "we now have powerful tools for describing and providing access to the book as a cultural artifact and object of beauty and value, as well as to the text it contains" (p. 103). They were, of course, talking about the expanding capabilities of catalogers to get endless information to a worldwide audience, and their aim was to create a template that would guide all catalogers to use the same vocabulary and styling of cataloging records, among other things. The point here is that back in 1996 the power of modern technology was guiding one of the operations of special collections departments—cataloging rare materials.

In departments filled with *objects* (some of great rarity and value) and into which scholars and readers come to handle physical things, we are now seeing a transformation that began when computers were being adopted for library work in the 1960s. Patrons, on-site and remote, can do much work through electronic means. Today, it is inconceivable that a special collections department could function without Internet access, e-mail, computer systems holding billions of cataloging records, digitization of some collections, perhaps online exhibitions of collection holdings, digital reference and publication, and much more that the computer makes possible. That is, the physical objects are now no longer the only things that researchers turn to special collections departments for. They come for the parallel information that they can access digitally, in the form of databases, electronic image files, and packages of information leased or purchased from offsite vendors. (When a special collections department leases such a package, the patron often cannot access it from a remote computer; the license agreement usually limits use to the terminal[s] in the special collections department.) Also, if a scholar needs to see, for instance, a particular photograph in a library collection, she may be able to use a local digital finding aid to locate a record of it, or even a digitized image.

When handheld calculators were invented and became commercially available in the 1970s, the entire industry of slide rules practically disappeared overnight. But when commercial television arrived on the scene after World War II, radio did not disappear. Some technologies drive out others; some force others to adapt for their survival, as radio has done.

The point here is that no technology will ever replace the need for the special collections department, will ever make the use of rare books and manuscripts and other rare materials obsolete. Technology will enhance operations, not eliminate them. What all this means for special collections is limited only by the imaginations of those working in these departments (and also by the resources those departments have). What we see today is rare book departments still visited by thousands upon thousands of users, partly because the research materials they want are not (yet) digitized, and partly because there is still a desire to handle physical objects. Viewing them online may be convenient, but holding the originals imparts a sense of authenticity and humanness to the work.

For some kinds of research, digital surrogates[4] simply will not be sufficient. There is a broad interest, for instance, in bookbinding history and technique, and—with an eye on bibliographical description—in the materiality of books and manuscripts. Looking at binding structures, leathers and cloths, cover and text papers, decorated papers on bindings, and other physical characteristics of books offers a scholar information that is generally not visible in a digital representation of the item. And the number of manuscript items that have not been digitized far exceeds the number of those that have. For at least another generation, scholars will need to work in the departments' reading rooms, handling original materials. So some kinds of research must always be done with original materials.

Further, as Clifford Lynch says,

special collections are a nexus where technology and content are meeting to advance scholarship in extraordinary new ways. We can see existing special collections are being supplemented and expanded by digital representations of the physical materials; tomorrow's special collections will include a growing proportion of material that has always and only been digital. Information technology is reshaping both stewardship and use of these collections. (p. 4)

Lynch points out—as is one of the main themes of the present volume—that linking researchers with the information they need (what he calls "stewardship") has become easier with digital technology, and it remains "an *obligation* of good and responsible stewardship" (p. 4; italics in the original). He says that if we have analog originals *and* digital representations, we are more likely to be able to retain the research materials for a long time than if we had only one of these. And he adds that in the future, an increasing amount of holdings in special collections will be digital.

Another point Lynch makes is that digital materials

> are in most regards and for most purposes at least as good as the physical originals. . . . Indeed, practically speaking, digital representations often offer a better engagement opportunity than the original in museums, archives, or special collections, even in person, and extend that opportunity worldwide through the Internet. (pp. 4–5)[5]

It is true that those needing to look at the physical objects (books, documents of various kinds, photographs, maps, and so forth) should have access to them. But for most researchers, the information contained in these objects is central to their scholarship, and being able to access this information in any form (especially digitally from a remote site) is perfectly sufficient for their purposes. The savings of time and money (for travel, housing, and local arrangements, for instance) in getting to the place where the original materials are held will grow once the information scholars need is available digitally. It is essential, then, that those in special collections work to acquire the resources to digitize, and then carefully choose what they digitize, and do it well.

In prioritizing for digitization, librarians may well put aside millions of manuscripts as low-priority choices because the likelihood is that remote users would not want to use the pieces in question. Maybe someday we will have a system worked out in some libraries of DOD—not "Print on Demand" but "Dig-

itize on Demand." In the past, many libraries had a policy that allowed a patron to request the microfilming of all or parts of a collection. The patron would pay for the filming, plus a service fee and even postage, and would then be loaned a copy of the film, for use for a specified length of time (e.g., six months), after which the films would be returned to the library.[6] It is not so easy to keep control of digitally "loaned" texts, and libraries that make electronic copies today put them onto their websites and make them available, usually for free, so libraries can assume they will have no control over such copies henceforth.[7]

As Lynch says, with digital imaging scholars can look closely at texts: pages, words, individual letters and pieces of punctuation, and even strokes of the quill or pen. He cites the miraculous work done on the Archimedes palimpsest, a document that was in such poor condition that practically nothing by Archimedes was visible. But with enhanced digital technology and much more, scientists and scholars were treated to the texts of the great mathematician that had not been seen in hundreds of years, and two of which were hitherto unknown.[8]

One common theme for special collections librarians is that they must recruit the researchers of the future. Today, as in the last few decades, librarians are encouraging faculty to create lectures and assignments that bring students in to see and use the rare books. Exposure to original research materials can inspire students to become scholars, and it certainly enriches the learning experience for anyone. Susan Allen says, "We all know that if students can be lured into special collections and exposed to the rare books, manuscripts, photographs, and other materials in our care, a certain kind of seduction will often take place."[9]

Although the use of special collections today is just as much an issue as it has been for decades, so are the challenges. Sidney Huttner says,

> The more successfully one advertises one's jewels, the greater grows the concern for their security; the more one stimulates and encourages use, the more one increases the preservation challenge. The more time one takes to understand and inter-

pret collections, the less time one has to evaluate potential acquisitions, encourage potential donors, participate in collegial and professional activities, or anticipate the impact of changing research strategies and new technologies. And as the size and variety of the collections and operations grow, so too do the managerial challenges of selecting and training an appropriate staff and supervising its activities, assuring adequate supplies and equipment, and planning the use of space and facilities.[10]

The challenges of raising resources; maintaining full operations with inadequate staffs; finding qualified catalogers and other staff; justifying the department's existence in a tight economy (what economy is not tight?!); doing enough of, and the right kind of, outreach to bring in users; and much more—all of these have not changed much over the years.

So special collections libraries today, in many respects, are the same as they have been for decades. Michèle V. Cloonan and I say about rare book librarianship,

The world has changed in many ways since then,[11] yielding new issues, yet some of the issues of those days have always been—and will always be—of deep concern. There will always be a focus on the basics of librarianship (not just for special collections): acquisitions, cataloging, funding, security, access, scholarship, preservation and conservation, space, and so on. Added to these are the higher-tech issues of digitization, new methods for conservation, innovative approaches to bibliographic scholarship, the creation of online finding aids, expanding approaches to cataloging that include the description and preservation of digital and other new formats, legal issues concerned with electronic information, scanning materials for remote access and preservation, new expanded audiences, the education of the information specialists of the future, and so on.[12]

We also talk about the strengthening of the field of archives:

We are only beginning to develop the conceptual framework for the new archive/museum/library

world, but the frequency with which we now use the terms "cultural heritage" and "cultural heritage information" demonstrates the beginning of a shift in our thinking.

What we are suggesting is that the present (and future) state of our profession will necessarily be an amalgam of multiple worlds: the world of books as artifacts and historical documents, housed in museums, libraries, archives, preservation societies, and other institutions, and the world of cyber-information (which may not be viewed as institution specific). We cannot ignore either or we will be doing a major disservice to the profession. (Cloonan and Berger, p. 90)

These words are as operable today as they were in 1999 when this was written. In fact, the convergence of libraries, archives, and museums has spawned its own acronym, LAMs, and a burgeoning literature discusses the mutual challenges, problems, and solutions these kinds of institutions have.

WITH THE RECOGNITION of the overlap in operations of libraries, archives, and museums, Diane M. Zorich, Günter Waibel, and Ricky Erway wrote an influential report, "Beyond the Silos of the LAMs: Collaboration among Libraries, Archives and Museums" (Dublin, OH: OCLC Research, 2008, www.oclc.org/resources/research/publications/library/2008/2008-05.pdf), looking at various kinds of collaboration and the catalysts that spur collaborative projects. One of the points they make is that collaboration can be within an institution, between institutions (two or many), and among all kinds of stakeholders beyond the LAMs. For the present text, I can envision booksellers collaborating with librarians in the building of collections and also in the production of reference tools in subject areas common to the two. Opportunities for collaboration are endless and can be productive, for those involved and for others who can share the fruits of their efforts.

So in some respects, today's special collections department is no different from its counterpart of previous times. Cloonan and I reveal only a few of the concerns of libraries in the past that are still ongoing:

> Books are still being produced in record numbers. Libraries get bigger every year. Predictions that the library of the future will be solely a virtual world are unfounded and short-sighted—even embarrassing. Libraries will continue to add books and manuscripts to their collections for generations to come. Hence, the traditional concerns will remain: How will they be able to afford these? Where will these be stored? How will they be conserved? How will the cataloging of the future differ from that of today? How will libraries encourage donors to give books, manuscripts, and money? Will we be able to keep security systems ahead of increasingly sophisticated thieves? How will collection development continue to tie its efforts to researcher and other user needs? What are the legal issues concerning acquisition of gifts, literary and republishing rights, copying, reformatting, access, and so forth? (Not to mention the cyber-law issues.) How will the world of the bookseller/vendor continue to affect our lives? Should items be loaned out? What is the safest and best way to put on exhibitions? Should we weed from the collection? How shall we educate future librarians/information specialists? and should they be considered faculty? staff? or something else? (Cloonan and Berger, p. 91)

Nothing is new here. Only the date has changed, as has some of the language (e.g., "cyber"), and it is clear that these are the same questions that librarians will be asking in the future.

This continuity of traditional operations, linked with the new world of online scholarship, was recognized as far back as 2008 when the Research Libraries Group (RLG) in Philadelphia held a symposium about digitization and the humanities. Merrilee Proffitt and Jennifer Schaffner, program officers at OCLC Programs and Research, wrote "The Impact of Digitizing Special Collections on Teaching and Scholarship: Reflections on a Symposium about Digitization and the Humanities."[13] They speak about walking down the two roads of scholarship, analog and digital, and they say that "we'll be travelling both the wide smooth road through the screen and the narrow difficult road of books and archives for a long time to come" (p. 4).

The scholars at this symposium "emphasized the critical roles rare books, archives and other materials play in . . . teaching and research" (p. 4). Proffitt and Schaffner say,

> The primary users of primary resources [the professors] presented clear imperatives for collections and custodians: work with faculty to understand current research methods and materials; go outside the library or archive to build collections and work with faculty; and continue to build digital and material collections for both teaching and research. (p. 4)

These suggestions have been operable in the rare book world now for many years. The first of these, however, is being stressed less and less today because the professors themselves understand the new technologies and research methods and materials, and thus have become valuable resources to the librarians. The idea of going outside the library is repeated in the recommendations of Richard Salonen and others in later meetings (see later in this chapter and note 14). Librarians have finite resources and may well be able to rely on researchers outside their institutions for help in building research packages for their patrons. Scholars "unanimously called for expanded collection and digitization of primary sources" (Proffitt and Schaffner, p. 5). A strategy that Proffitt and Schaffner suggest is for special collections librarians to get to know which scholars are producing banks of digital images for their own research, and then to have these banks uploaded, with the proper introductions and metadata, into the library's database holdings, "along with the scholarly results"; they say, "We must ensure custodianship of their discoveries and we must ensure that these important scholarly results will be included in collections" (p. 5).

If there is a drawback to all the information available online, it might be that there is too much of it, as Proffitt and Schaffner say (p. 6). Anyone doing research on Google or other search engines will get hundreds of thousands or millions of hits for most queries. Fortunately, these engines have built into them a prioritizing feature, which tries to agglomerate the most pertinent, important sites at the top of the display. The librarians' aim has always been to have their patrons—especially students at all levels—use primary materials. Now, if those materials have been digitized and made available in an online environment, the students can use them without having to go to the library. This is not, however, really the same as using the materials firsthand, and in a sense, digitization is contradictory to the move to have students handle original books and manuscripts. Perhaps the digitized versions will arouse the users' curiosity and inveigle them into the special collections department to see the originals. If so, the librarian should not say, "I am sorry; this is now available on the Web. To preserve the original, please use the online version." (Unless, of course, the original is too fragile to be handled.) Having lured the patron into the department, the librarian should happily bring out the original materials.

AT UC RIVERSIDE I got to know many professors, and I was happy to arrange special showings of rare materials in the rare book reading room to classes. I even made it possible for professors, under strict supervision, to bring materials into the classrooms. This engendered much goodwill from the faculty and enthusiasm among the students.

Some important issues rise to the surface of this broad topic—ongoing concerns for today and the future.

Access versus Preservation; the Reading Experience

Chapter 12 discussed the evanescent nature of digital records and attempts to make digitization a true preservation medium. Whether this permanence is achieved or not, special collections departments owe it to their patrons to give them the greatest amount of information the departments can provide. Massive (and increasing) amounts of information are available in digital form, much of it complementary to department holdings. Some of this is available simply through web searches that can be done from any computer with Internet access. But, as just mentioned, much is available only from vendors whose online products are available only through libraries, if these libraries can afford to purchase the databases.

VENDORS LIKE ADAM Matthew Digital (along with dozens of others) create packages of research materials by digitizing the holdings of special collections departments all over the world and selling these packages to institutions. Additionally, a vendor might create a reference database and sell access to it to a special collections department. My own department, for instance, subscribes to ShipIndex.org. This site lists by name thousands of ships and gives bibliographic sources in which a researcher can find information about the vessels. A watered-down version of this site is available on the Web, and a library can subscribe to the much-expanded version with vastly more information for each entry. All the information is available digitally from the vendor. The number of such online products is growing daily.

Any scholar could go to a university to use a particular collection, but that can be expensive, what with travel, lodging, and food costs. If the institution has digitized the collection the scholar needs and has put that data on the Web, perhaps the scholar can access it from the computer. But the cost of scanning and mounting a collection could be prohibitive, and the institution may simply not be able to afford such a project. This is so for perhaps 99 percent of the collections in rare book departments. Digitally available information is a boon to scholars, but it is expensive to produce and maintain, and it is probably no exaggeration to say, today, that less than 1 percent of the information in most repositories is available online. And as chapter 12 indicated, digital resources are excellent when they exist in accessible ways, but they are not yet to be seen as "preserved." Digitization is an access medium, not a preservation one.

Anecdotally, also, there is the view that people prefer to read text from paper and not from a computer screen. Reading from a screen is fine for seeking information, for answering reference questions, and for short periods, but it is tiresome and less comfortable than doing so from the pages of a book or magazine, especially because the paper-based texts are portable and can be manipulated to adjust to the reader's posture. This argument has been brought into doubt recently with the increase in the use of e-readers (Kindles and Nooks, for instance). Manufacturers of these and other hand-held devices, and makers of laptops, tablets (including iPads, a word that has reached generic status for these small, handheld computers), and their e-reading cousins, tout the readability of their products.

Younger generations brought up in the digital era are completely comfortable with reading from screens, even long, extended texts. So special collections departments, when they are rationalizing why they do not digitize their holdings, no longer can use the excuse that their patrons prefer paper-based texts. Despite the fact that digitization is not preservation—it is access—rare book libraries owe it to their clientele to scan as much of their holdings as they can so that remote users can have access to information that exists in only one place or a few places.

One of the objections to converting text into digital form was that it is expensive, and that is true. But some of the expense had to do with the time it took to scan analog texts. Today's scanners are far faster than are those of the past. Microfilmed texts can be converted into digital ones automatically and economically in special readers. All library opera-

tions take time and therefore cost money. Digitization is now not so expensive as it once was, and the expense is often justifiable in the increased access it affords. And as noted several times already, special collections departments are repositories of texts and images that are rare and not widely available. They must think of ways of opening their holdings to the widest possible readership, and digitization is one means to do so.

The word *access* has appeared many times throughout the present text—no wonder because one basic theme of this book (as with all librarianship) is that offering access to library holdings is the primary responsibility for librarians. Today, as has been commented on, digital technology has increased access to information thousands of times over. Several of the speakers at the ARL conference "An Age of Discovery: Distinctive Collections in the Digital Age" (cited in note 1) discussed the nature of digital information: that it can exist in cyberspace and be accessed from anywhere that there is Internet access. Because the information any database holds is no longer constrained by its physical origin, databases from two or dozens of institutions can be combined instantly and retrieved from anywhere. Digitization has thus led to cooperation among special collections. In fact, one session at the ARL meeting was called "Collaboration to Build Cross-Institutional Collections."[14] Today's special collections librarians should be looking in this direction if they wish to meet their prime directive on access to information. The technology is here. The scholars are waiting.

MY BROTHER WRITES a wine newsletter which he sends out by e-mail. In the past, I would open the document on my screen, print it, and then read the paper version. Little by little, I began reading it while it was printing out, and when the printing was done, I would grab the paper document and then finish reading it on paper. Over the years, however, I would hit Print and begin reading the text on the screen, only to continue to read it on the screen, scrolling from one page to another until I was finished with the entire newsletter. The typeface and layout of the text were legible and congenial, and other than having to hold my head in one position while I was reading, my comfort level while I read the text was about the same as it was for reading from the paper document. Even for most older readers—and especially for Gen Xers, Gen Yers, and Millennials—reading from a computer monitor or a handheld device is becoming the "natural" way of taking in information. The implications for special collections are far-reaching. There is no reason now to refuse to digitize reference materials of all kinds because the department's clientele are comfortable with accessing information from a variety of digital devices.

Open Access; Collaboration

The question arises, however, whether the institutions contemplating such partnerships—or merely considering putting their own collections online—should hold back and instead work with a commercial vendor (as already explained) so that the access is restricted to those who can pay for it. This approach may give the institution some income, a strong incentive for many libraries.

Peter Suber explains, "Open-access (OA) literature is digital, online, free of charge, and free of most copyright and licensing restrictions" (www.earlham.edu/~peters/fos/overview.htm). He adds, "OA removes price barriers (subscriptions, licensing fees, pay-per-view fees) and permission barriers (most copyright and licensing restrictions)." Such restrictions may be rooted in legal issues, such as the privacy of the originators of the information or constraints placed on certain materials by donors or other former owners. But for information that is basically in the public domain, an institution can still require permission for use and may even charge fees for use whether it holds the rights to the materials or not. Today's special collections librarians may have a choice between charging for use (by themselves or by going through a commercial vendor) or allowing free use to anyone who needs the information. As just pointed out, it is a balancing act between wanting to help all patrons/scholars and perhaps being able to raise some resources for the department. The rare book librarian should work this out in close collaboration with the library director(s) and anyone else in charge.

Anne R. Kenney gave a talk on this topic at the conference "An Age of Discovery: Distinctive Collections in the Digital Age, October 2009" (cited in note 1). Her presentation was "What Changes with Digital Content? Three Key Issues." One of her slides showed what her audience thought of the notion of using a commercial vendor to disseminate department content as opposed to offering that content through Open Access. She posed this proposition to her audience: "I am willing to commit my institution to forgo one-on-one arrangements with commercial entities around digitization of special collections materials in favor of collective arrangements involving multiple research libraries" (Kenney, slide 7). Responses by clicker directly from the audience revealed that 56 percent agreed strongly, 37 percent agreed, 11 percent disagreed, and 1 percent disagreed strongly. Clearly there is a strong movement among rare book librarians toward the free dissemination of information. Nonetheless, commercial companies are still convincing special collections libraries to allow them to digitize great numbers of collections and offer them for sale (or lease). This makes sense for many libraries because the companies pay for the scanning and indexing, and they market the products worldwide, offering royalties to contributing libraries. This is too tempting for most departments to ignore. (One additional consideration is that the digitized package is controlled by the vendor for only a set period—say, five years—and then the institution owning the originals is free to market the materials in any way it wishes, for a fee or by Open Access.)

If the department does not want to go commercial, it can mount its own digitized collections on its website (at its own cost), or it can collaborate with other institutions to create composite collections available in a single search. Collaboration of this kind is now an ongoing model, as Anne R. Kenney explains in her follow-up piece on the conference;[15] at this meeting, titled "The Collaborative Imperative: Special Collections in the Digital Age," Clifford Lynch and many others called for collaboration on an expanding scale. Kenney says,

> It was not lost on most attendees that the kinds of issues being discussed would not have been seriously considered by many even five years ago. Much has changed, but one thing is clear: as special collections face a new renaissance in the Digital Age, research libraries are challenged to reconsider institutional practice, and especially the collaborative imperative that connects institutions, digital communities, and the users we serve.[16]

She points out that recent emphasis on digitization of library materials focuses more on the holdings of special collections departments than on the holdings of the larger library. For obvious reasons, it makes more sense to share unique or hard-to-find texts than it does to scan texts that are available in many repositories.

With respect to whether a special collections department should opt for going with a commercial entity or sharing special materials collaboratively in an Open Access arena, she asks, "[C]an we resist the temptation to enter into special deals for special collections digitization that may offer short-term gains but ultimately be of disservice to our institutions and our users?" (p. 21). At the May 2009 ARL Membership Meeting, most of the attendees said they would go for the collaborative path. The mood in the profession is more toward sharing information than it is making a profit from it. Kenney and a group of fellow ARL members came up with a list of nine principles to guide special collections libraries in collaborative digitization projects.

Principles to Guide Large-Scale Digitization of Special Collections

Principle 1: Distinct collections demand extra vigilance in digitization.

Principle 2: Libraries must respect any donor-imposed restrictions on the digitization and use of materials.

Principle 3: Libraries should seek the broadest possible user access to digitized content. This includes patrons of other libraries and unaffiliated researchers.

Principle 4: Libraries should receive copies of all digital files generated from their collections, with the option for complete local access to the files (to the extent that copyright law allows).

Principle 5: Any enhancements or improvements to the digitized content should be shared on a regular basis with the supplying library.

Principle 6: Restrictions on external access to copies of works digitized from a library's holding should be of limited duration.

Principle 7: Libraries should refrain from signing nondisclosure agreements (NDAs) as part of digitization negotiations.

Principle 8: Libraries should ensure that the confidentiality of users is protected in the vendor's products.

Principle 9: Libraries should refrain from charging fees or royalties for access to or noncommercial use of public domain materials held in their collections. (p. 21)[17]

One point that Kenney makes is that social networking has changed our way of disseminating information, and large-scale digitization projects should incorporate social networks into their operations (p. 25). She cites efforts by the Church of Jesus Christ of Latter Day Saints to build a massive genealogical database by enlisting the input of people outside the project, and also the efforts of devotees of the Grateful Dead, invited by the University of California, Santa Cruz, to enter as much data as they have on this group to enhance the analog collection that UCSC has in its special collections. Kenney says the "ability to connect content and community is a key theme in the digital domain" (p. 26). Each database that is compiled collaboratively, among institutions and between institutions and individual contributors, represents a separate community, devoted to a single topic (or a few related topics). Kenney adds, "[I]t will be critical for librarians and archivists to engage sensitively with the community to help preserve and protect its work" (p. 27). She also states that such projects open the world of information to everyone, not just to scholars and researchers, professors and their students, but to anyone with an interest in the topics of the digitized materials. And making the information available to a broad general audience costs practically nothing more than does making it available to the institution's immediate clientele (p. 28). The digitization projects will benefit from the input of the widest possible world of contributors. Finally, Kenney concludes, "Our success may well depend on our ability to seize the collaborative imperative that links institutions to a participatory information environment" (p. 28).

Another issue related to the spread of information gathered from many sources is that new media offer new ways to bring about such a spread. In the past, libraries could put links onto their websites so that anyone coming to those sites might search by keyword for certain kinds of research materials or for materials on particular subjects. It was also the practice to create sites that would be searchable by Web browsers like Google and Yahoo!. Today, librarians can "advertise" their holdings on many social media "channels," like YouTube, Flickr, Twitter, MySpace, Facebook, LinkedIn, and scores of others. Many departments have blogs that feed information to a growing audience—information about recent acquisitions, the completion of a finding aid, the discovery of an important volume or manuscript in the collection, upcoming events, and whatever else scholars may want to know about the holdings, personnel, or activities of a department.

Today's special collections departments must look to today's technology for many reasons, not the least of which is that, as this discussion has emphasized, many people beyond the traditional team of librarians and scholars are able to contribute to the storehouse of knowledge that librarians wish to gather and make accessible.[18] Collaboration can be with anyone. The one proviso is that the librarian have the final say of what goes into the storehouse. As the Wikipedia experience has taught, not all contributors are well informed, nor are they all impartial. The information librarians provide must be vetted before it is made "public."

Cataloging

It is clear that despite all the excitement of new technology and its myriad applications in the library world, some things will not change. Most special collections departments have backlogs, sometimes huge accumulations of uncataloged monographs and unprocessed archives and manuscript collections. No amount of modernity, symbolized in state-of-the-art technology, will rid us of these backlogs. Cataloging and processing must still go on. As institutions age, there is no cessation of the production of more archival material to be processed. And as active collections get added to, with new and antiquarian books and all kinds of special collections items, the cataloging backlog may not diminish much, if at all.[19]

Growing databases like OCLC WorldCat may help catalogers copy already-created online records, which may speed up some processing. But if special collections departments catalog to rare-book standards, such a shortcut may not save too much time. Thanks to relatively inexpensive photographic equipment and techniques, it may be possible for catalogers to attach color images to their records, especially useful for descriptions of visually important materials like illustrations, tipped-in samples, bindings, or dust jackets, for instance. Modern technology may increase our cataloging options and capabilities, but it has not diminished the need to continue to catalog.

Data Unity

At the 2010 Art Museum Libraries Symposium,[20] three presentations discussed data unity, the merger of cataloging systems of the library and the museum that would allow a researcher to see the institution's holdings in both systems (the library's and the museum's) with a single search. Not all special collections are in a museum that has its own database for searching museum objects. But many rare book departments are linked with other departments, perhaps in local or statewide consortia. The consortia may have historical societies or athenaeums, museums, or other kinds of local groups in them, each with its own collection. These collections could contain books and manuscripts and the other things common to special collections, but they may also contain all kinds of "museum objects," including prints, drawings, maps, charts, posters and other kinds of broadsides, many types of ephemera, furniture, china, silver, kites, clothing and various kinds of textiles, sculpture, and so on. Data unity would be a great boon to scholars doing research in *any* field, on *any* genre of material, saving them time and opening up worlds of information that they did not know existed.

Rose Sherman of the Minnesota Historical Society gave a presentation at the PEM symposium[21] in which she explained how her organization "implemented a single search engine that queries several online collections at once, bringing it ever closer to the vision of central access—or data unity"; she pointed out that "MARC-based library catalogs supported some of the back-office library functions such as circulation and serials control, [but] they didn't support museum collections tracking functions such as acquisitions, loans, conservation, location management, patron use, or digital asset management" (PEM symposium, pp. 23, 24). And she explained how several data-mining programs were purchased and combined to allow patrons, doing a single search, to do a global search of the organization's holdings in all genres and a search of the holdings of the other institutions in the consortium. There are naturally financial and technical issues involved in such an undertaking, but the result is earth-shaking for the users: tremendous savings in time in doing research, and a level of comprehensiveness in research never before imagined by the user. Of course, the librarians and museum curators were additional beneficiaries, as were all in the consortium, whether they were patrons or employees.

The relatively small size of the Minnesota Historical Society possibly was one of the factors that made this level of data unity possible—it did not have millions of books and more millions of museum-type objects to catalog. The important thing to get from the society's experience is that such a search system is practicable, especially with the growing sophistication of technology.

At the same symposium, Elizabeth O'Keefe spoke of what she calls "Cross-Collection Searching of Library and Museum Collection Information" (PEM symposium, pp. 26–32). She described the Morgan Library's project of data unity, and she said that the data unity within an institution can be enhanced if the internal search can be linked to an external one:

> Object records often contain bibliographic references to material about the object. Enabling easy navigation from the object record references to records for these resources in the library catalog, in external catalogs such as WorldCat, or in abstracting and indexing databases, would take advantage of curatorial research and leverage the relationship between the two databases. (PEM symposium, p. 30)

Among other things, O'Keefe mentioned the need for the various databases that are to be unified to match up in vocabularies (p. 30), but, she said, "inconsistencies can be resolved by behind-the-scenes mapping of museum object types to library subject terms for object type, and/or support for retrieval of variant terms using word-stemming and the like" (p. 30).

One of the main impediments to achieving data unity is that library cataloging systems and those for museums differ radically. As O'Keefe explained,

> At the moment, the cataloging practices of the two communities are different. Library catalogers adhere to data format and data content standards developed for the types of materials libraries own; conforming to these standards enables libraries to take advantage of shared cataloging and to make information on their holdings accessible in wide contexts, such as consortial and union catalogs. Library systems are built to process this data. There is no comparable industry-wide standard for museum collection information. Every museum system has a proprietary data format, and records are created using a mixture of local and industry practice.

In other words, the unification of various catalogs in a single institution, in a consortium, or in the wider world is desirable[22] and, now, possibly achievable, though, in practical terms, it is impossible beyond the consortium level because the world of information is so large. And a great deal of hands-on work needs to be done to make incompatible systems compatible. Where we will be ten or twenty-five or fifty years from now is anyone's guess.

The Evolving Audience

The audience of a library is related, of course, to the kind of institution the library is in (or whether it is, itself, a freestanding institution not connected to a larger entity). A local library with a special collection focused on, say, the architecture of the community will have photographs of buildings and streets, residents and events, and civic records of building permits, architects, blueprints, drawings and other renderings of houses and commercial buildings, and so forth. The library's users will be homeowners,

IN MY OWN experience, a few of my writings have become available all over the world on the Internet, and I have fielded questions (and in some cases invited people to our home) from Australia, England, Germany, Spain, France, and elsewhere. The explosion of information availability connects people as they have never before been joined. Similarly, people are using the Internet more and more as their first resort for research, and with an increasing amount of information being put onto the Web every day, scholars worldwide are becoming the equivalent of local scholars, interested in connecting with any organization that has data they can use, no matter how remote the originals are.

Further, the new technology has made it simpler than ever before to copy (that is, digitize) the originals and send images instantly to anyone, anywhere. We speak of a "global economy." We can also speak of the "global library," with branches at every Internet-connected computer keyboard in the world.

There is a rule of thumb about library collections: the more items in their collections that are cataloged, the more use the libraries will have. Corollary to this is, the more items from a single library that are locatable in online databases, the more queries this library is likely to have. Further, most special collections, with their inevitable and ongoing backlogs, are adding new records to their catalogs regularly. So despite the increasing availability of full texts of books and articles on the Web, special collections departments will continue to get research requests, especially because much of their holdings are unique and will not be picked up by Google Books or other such digitization projects.

architects, historians, possibly artists, students, city planners, attorneys, genealogists, and others.

Because special collections departments hold such special materials, often of local interest, they are likely to get many local users. Special collections at larger institutions will have more broadly based holdings and will thus see users from a much greater geographical diversity accessing their collections. And today, with technology expanding the availability of materials worldwide, the audience for rare book department holdings may come from anywhere in the world.

As explained in chapter 10, the book trade was changed radically with online bookselling. A dealer with a walk-in trade into her shop of seventy-five people a day had seventy-five pairs of eyes browsing her shelves. When she put records of her stock online, she had, overnight, millions of viewers looking at what her shelves held. The result was a speed-up in trade, with increased sales, which necessitated an increase in acquisition of books to accommodate the wants of an expanding audience. Book sales (of new and used items) continue to increase, despite the availability of digitally available texts. People still want books and manuscripts and the other things a special collections department has.[23] And with the immense spread of information made possible through digitization, audiences have expanded and burgeoned to global proportions. Rare book departments are now seeing reference questions coming in from distant scholars, on other continents. There may be a diminution of use of some things that are now available on the Web, but there should continue to be a steady stream of local and distant users of the rare items in special collections departments that are not being digitized: photographs, manuscript materials, ephemera, exceptionally rare books of which only a few copies exist, and so forth.

Reference

Today's special collections departments, as just mentioned, are continuing to get on-site use, and patrons continue to pose queries online, in letters, and on the phone. It almost does not matter whether texts exist in digitized form on the Web; researchers still want information gathered firsthand. If they cannot be at the library to do it themselves, they will continue to rely on department personnel to help them.

However, special collections departments are turning to an increasing number of online databases

EVEN WITH A burgeoning number of texts being digitized and made available online, reference librarians in special collections are no less burdened by the requests of patrons. My own library is a case in point. Every week I get letters and phone calls, and my staff get e-mails sent to our reference line, from distant scholars. Older researchers who have gotten used to such personal service still ask for it. Younger ones often try the Web first, and then turn to the staff for help when they cannot find what they are looking for. Also, libraries with large manuscript holdings will continue to be approached for reference assistance because most of those materials are not available in any way other than on-site.

Librarians themselves are evolving with the technology and are turning increasingly to the Web as a first source of information for their patrons. But older librarians, ones who have worked in a department for a long time and who know the analog collection well, will still turn to paper-based sources to help their patrons. One of my librarians has been with the institution for over forty years, and she is a goldmine of information about the library's holdings. She is adept, as well, with online searching, but her first instinct is not always to go to the computer, as is the case with many younger librarians.

offered by commercial vendors (see "Leased Databases" later in this chapter). At the same time, librarians are doing what they can to learn of and acquire new publications (in analog form) that support the research in their departments. And they still rely on booksellers—who send catalogs or who offer quotes of individual items—to fill in gaps in the rare book holdings and to add manuscripts or photographs or other ephemeral materials in the department's areas of strength.

Space

Even if greater and greater portions of department budgets are being spent on digital texts and databases, most special collections will continue to grow in the realm of analog materials. Eventually, most of them will run out of space. The department will have to find additional space in the institution, look to off-site storage, build more shelves for its holdings, seek new accommodations, or weed the collection.

Libraries in general in the last few decades have been using off-site storage for the materials that they wish to keep, but for which the demand is low. This is true for special collections as well. The librarian must, of course, make sure that environmental conditions in off-site housing are appropriate for rare materials of all kinds and that security is just as strict as it is at the main collection.

All the concerns that librarians have had for centuries with respect to space (Is there enough? Is the space configured properly? Is it environmentally safe? Is it safe from thieves and other predators? Is there sufficient room for growth? Can the space we have accommodate all the department's needs?) are still on their minds, and it is still part of their responsibilities to strive to answer yes to them. Regardless of the increasing use of digital technology, these questions will remain current.

Digitizing Texts

Earlier in this chapter I said that I was an advocate for digitizing special collections department holdings. Most special collections have materials worth digitizing. The so-called wave of the future—making texts available in electronic form and mounting them on the Web—is actually the wave of the present. After all, this activity *is* one way librarians can accomplish their prime directive of making their holdings accessible, and the cost of the technology is now within the budgets of most libraries.

PRIORITIZING FOR DIGITIZATION

The librarian needs a strategy to decide what to convert to electronic form. Several characteristics of department holdings will influence whether they are high or low on the priority list. For instance, if

THE UNIVERSITY OF California, with its ten campuses, has two massive off-site storage facilities, SRLF and NRLF (Southern/Northern Regional Library Facility), each with enough shelving to hold millions of books. Each off-site facility also has a special floor for rare books—spaces with extensive security and their own HVAC systems. The facilities also have their own staffs, and for the rare-materials area, they have a reading room to allow on-site research. Visiting scholars can usually get to these facilities as easily as they can get to the campuses that hold the original materials, and by allowing on-site use, the facilities save the books from travel back and forth from the facility to the owning library. Such accommodation for a plethora of books is expensive to create, but for some institutions this way of handling the space problem is cheaper than would be building onto the old structure or creating a new one altogether. Some libraries solve the problem of space by collaborating with other local institutions. The Five Colleges in western Massachusetts (UMass Amherst, Smith, Mt. Holyoke, Hampshire, and Amherst College) have formed a consortium. In effect they share libraries in that they have a cooperative collecting program, making it unnecessary for every campus to acquire every book it wants for its students. The space and fiscal resources this arrangement saves can be a model for other schools in proximity to peer institutions.

an item is unique, the information it holds can be viewed in only one place. If that information is in an area of research of deep interest to scholars, the item would be near or at the top of the priorities list for digitization. Level 5 collections achieve that designation because they may contain unique or extremely scarce items, so the special collections librarian might cull from such holdings items to scan. The Historical Voices website[24] poses the following questions as guides for conversion to electronic form:

- Is the source of sufficient cultural interest to warrant the level of access made possible by digitizing?
- Will digitization enhance this interest, or are the original materials sufficient for this purpose?

- Are visitors now using the proposed source materials?
- Are materials being used as much as they might be?
- Is current access to the materials so limited that digitization will create a new audience?
- Would digitization create an opportunity to show interrelated materials in context?
- What type of hardware and software will your visitors be using and will they be able to access the type of formats and file-sizes your project would necessitate?
- Are you intending to create a printed publication, an online exhibit, an image, text or audio database, and/or embark on a digital preservation project?
- Will the digitized object serve as a surrogate for a deteriorating original, or will it be used for online presentation?

Clearly, cultural and use issues drive the selection. The more important the item is as a record of the culture, the more it deserves to be scanned. And the more use the item will get, and thus the more in demand it will be, the higher it will be in the prioritization.

Usually the prioritization is done with one eye toward the client: who will use the materials, in what way, and for how long? What materials are likely to get the most use? What digitizing formats are the optimum to use? Because the mandate of the profession (often repeated in this book) is to get information into the hands of the patrons, one strategy is to allow the patrons themselves to select (or suggest) what to scan. Paper forms in the reading room and online forms on the department's website should be available to the department's clientele, allowing them to request the digitization of certain materials. These requests, of course, are not binding; they are only suggestions, because whether digitization is done or not depends on many factors, including whether there are resources enough to do the work and what the librarians know about patron use statistics. One person could passionately request the copying of something he is working on, but the librarians know that he is the only one in fifty years to have used these things,

AT THE ROBERT W. Woodruff Library at Emory University, the library has created a special form for faculty to request the digitization of materials. The form says,

> The Digitization Selection Committee welcomes proposals for new digitization projects. The form below is used to recommend groups of materials for digitization, to be evaluated by the Digitization Selection Committee. Proposals recommended for digitization as well as the schedule for digitization will be posted on this web guide under Current Activity. The proposal consists of three different parts. Parts 1 and 2 [outline] the content of the proposed collections, non-duplication, rights issues/permissions, and intellectual value. Part 3 is a form for the selection committee to complete. Faculty are asked to contact their respective subject liaison or other library staff to submit proposals on their behalf.*

The library is clearly committed to digitization, for it has created its own Digitization Selection Committee. The form does not indicate that the committee is free to reject the professors' requests, but that is probably implied by the fact that a committee will decide on what to scan.

*The Emory site is at http://guides.main.library .emory.edu/content.php?pid=245572&sid=2028551.

and no one is ever likely to want to see them again. The final decision must be in the librarians' hands.

CONTROL OF RIGHTS OF SCANNED MATERIALS—DIGITAL RIGHTS MANAGEMENT

As suggested earlier, if a special collections department mounts digitized texts on the Web, it is difficult to patrol for their misuse. A fairly new field of operation has sprung up that affects libraries that scan and mount their holdings: Digital Rights Management (DRM). The Wikipedia article on DRM says,

> Digital rights management (DRM) is a class of access control technologies that are used by hardware manufacturers, publishers, copyright holders and individuals with the intent to limit the use of digital content and devices after sale. DRM is any technology that inhibits uses of digital content that are not desired or intended by the content provider. DRM also includes specific instances of digital works or devices. Companies such as Amazon, AT&T, AOL, Apple Inc., BBC, Microsoft, Electronic Arts and Sony use digital rights management. In 1998 the Digital Millennium Copyright Act (DMCA) was passed in the United States to impose criminal penalties on those who make available technologies whose primary purpose and function is to circumvent content protection technologies.[1]

> The use of digital rights management is controversial. Content providers claim that DRM is necessary to fight copyright infringement online and that it can help the copyright holder maintain artistic control[2] or ensure continued revenue streams.[3] Those opposed to DRM contend there is no evidence that DRM helps prevent copyright infringement, arguing instead that it serves only to inconvenience legitimate customers, and that DRM helps big business stifle innovation and competition.[4] Further, works can become permanently inaccessible if the DRM scheme changes or if the service is discontinued.[5] Proponents argue that digital locks should be considered necessary to prevent "intellectual property" from being copied freely, just as physical locks are needed to prevent personal property from being stolen.[6] ("Digital Rights Management," Wikipedia, http://en.wikipedia.org/wiki/Digital_rights_management)[25]

Although DRM is usually seen as a tool for content creators (in the film or music industries, for example), librarians, particularly those in special collections, should be aware of it and possibly avail themselves of it if they are considering mounting onto the Web, from their collections, digital images or written texts that might allow them to raise revenue for the library. This issue was discussed in chapter 8 of the present text. There is no prohibition against a department raising money through the sale of access to the content of its holdings. A rare book department that owns the property rights to an unpublished novel may contract with a publisher or filmmaker for commercial use of the piece, with a one-time payment or extended royalties going to the library. A department that owns the only copy of a text that is, say, from the sixteenth century may likewise profit from its publication. By mounting a copy of the text onto the Web, the library may lose some control over it and may see it get used without the library's permission. Today's special collections librarians should work with their institutions' IT department along with the organizations' counsel to determine the best (and most profitable) use of their departments' holdings. Not all libraries wish to go to this length and may wish to make all their materials available for free. Either way, the librarians should be aware of the issues.

Digital Photography; Scanning

In the past, patrons wanting images from a special collection either were given permission, for some items, to make photocopies themselves or have them made (usually for a small fee or to cover the cost of the copies) by the librarians. But with the coming of digital cameras, many rare book departments have begun allowing the patrons to take their own pictures with little or no fee. The Houghton Library at Harvard University has a form for such photography:

Digital Camera Use Policy

The following policy is designed to assist readers with note-taking by permitting limited use of digital cameras. Its continuance depends on Readers abiding by the rules and not disrupting the quiet work of fellow Readers.

Photographs are for study purposes only and cannot be reproduced, transferred, published, or posted on the internet. Images for publication or distribution must be ordered through the library.

Use of digital cameras is subject, but not limited, to the following conditions:

- All candidates for photography must be flagged and examined by the desk attendant for physical condition, copyright issues, and donor restrictions before approval will be given.
- No tripods, camera flashes, or special lighting. Audible features on the camera must be turned off.
- No pictures may be taken of the room itself, other readers, or the staff.

- Staff will designate the work location for patrons using cameras. Patrons may not stand on chairs nor rearrange furniture to get a better image.
- Materials must be handled properly and with great care. Staff will assist with setting up materials properly: 1. Bound volumes must be supported in a book cradle; no pressure can be applied to the bindings. 2. Loose manuscript material must remain in its folder and kept in order at all times. Documents must be kept flat on the table. If leaves are fastened together, please see desk attendant before proceeding.
- No more than 50 pages or 20 percent of any manuscript or book (whichever is smaller) can be photographed.
- A Houghton Library or Harvard Theatre Collection flag must be photographed with each item.
- It is the responsibility of each reader to keep complete and accurate citations (complete call number, including item numbers and/or page numbers) for all items photographed. Requests for permission to quote, or subsequent orders for high-resolution or photographic images, will not be processed without this information.
- The library reserves the right to deny requests or revoke permission for any reason.

The Copyright law of the United States (Title 17, United States Code) governs the making of photocopies or other reproductions of copyrighted material. Under certain conditions specified in the law, libraries and archives are authorized to furnish a photocopy or other reproduction. One of these specified conditions is that the reproduction is not to be "used for any purpose other than private study, scholarship, or research." If a user makes a request for, or later uses, a photocopy or reproduction for purposes in excess of "fair use," that user may be liable for copyright infringement. The user agrees to defend, indemnify, and hold harmless the Houghton Library, the Harvard College Library, and the President and Fellows of Harvard College against all claims, demands, costs and expenses incurred by copyright infringement or any other legal or regulatory cause of action arising from the use of the Library's materials.[26]

Many rare book libraries saw charging for photocopying as a way of raising a small amount of revenue and discouraging people from asking for the service. But such a policy is counter to the librarian's responsibility of connecting people with information. Also, getting photocopies and being able to read them at leisure out of the library maximizes the researcher's time in the reading room. Today, many special collections departments have no restrictions on using a digital camera in the department.

Computers in the Reading Room

Similarly, librarians recognize that keyboarding a text is far faster than is taking notes by hand, and it creates text that is manipulable, as for cutting and pasting into a document. So the old restriction that patrons can take only a pencil and some sheets of paper into a reading room is being relaxed with the permission to bring in laptops as well. For this reason, special collections departments are now making power connections available to users, along with Internet access through Wi-Fi or Ethernet. The point here is that the department should be as welcoming as security and physical conditions allow because the librarian's aim should be to increase use and patron satisfaction.

The use of a computer can entail hardware and software issues that can complicate connections. The New York Public Library, to protect itself from patrons unable to use their laptops in the NYPL reading rooms, has the following information on its website:

Limitations and Disclaimers
- Laptop owners may use the connections during all hours the Library is open.
- Operating systems and software packages other than Microsoft Windows may be used, but no assistance in configuration or troubleshooting will be provided.
- Due to insurance limitations and warranties, Library staff cannot install Ethernet network interface cards on users' laptops.
- If you would like to purchase an Ethernet card

to connect through the Library's network, local computer stores sell and install these products.
- The Library does not download, provide, or install any software for laptop users.
- No guarantee is provided that a laptop will be able to make a successful connection, even if the above software configurations are installed, since many factors (including other software packages on the laptop) may interfere with a connection.
- The Library assumes no responsibility for any alterations or interference with a laptop's configuration, operation, or data files resulting from connection to the Library's network.
- The Library assumes no responsibility for damage, theft, or loss of any kind to a user's equipment, software, data files, or other personal property brought into or used at the Library's facilities.[27]

Computers and technology can be unpredictable and temperamental. In a litigious world, in which library patrons sometimes demand services beyond what is reasonable, having a published statement of this kind could preempt an unpleasant discussion between the librarian and a user.

The restrictive attitudes of the past have evolved with technology, and today more and more special collections departments are allowing the use of computers in reading rooms.

Security

As chapter 7 showed, security in special collections can be complicated, but the need for it is ongoing and will always exist. Along with the tools mentioned earlier (e.g., motion, sound, and movement detectors), rare book departments are using sophisticated modern technology for protection. Some libraries have fingerprint readers for access to rare book stacks. Retinal scans are now available to identify people.

Though not digital, one modern technology in use in many libraries is RFID—Radio-Frequency Identification, the use of a wireless non-contact system that uses radio-frequency electromagnetic fields to transfer data from a tag attached to an object, for the purposes of automatic identification and tracking. Some tags require no battery and are powered by the electromagnetic fields used to read them. Others use a local power source and emit radio waves (electromagnetic radiation at radio frequencies). The tag contains electronically stored information which can be read from up to several meters (yards) away. Unlike a bar code, the tag does not need to be within line of sight of the reader and may be embedded in the tracked object. ("Radio-Frequency Identification," Wikipedia, http://en.wikipedia.org/wiki/Radio-frequency_identification)

Items in special collections departments generally do not circulate, so RFID technology will not be used for this library function. But the RFID tags can be used for inventorying, a security measure, among other things. The department may have an alarm system that detects whether an item containing a tag is being taken beyond the secure perimeter of the library. If an item is stolen, the tag can be used to identify it if it is located. Some tags require a power source, but others do not. Hence, the life expectancy of some tags makes them too costly to use.[28] "Even though some of these devices are built to have up to a 10 year life span, they have limited life spans. Passive RFID tags, however, do not require batteries, and can be much smaller and have a virtually unlimited life span." (www.technovelgy.com/ct/technology-article.asp?artnum=2)

Forensics

Rare book departments deal with valuable objects. As in the world of art, forgeries and fakes in the book world are always lurking. For generations scientific equipment has been employed to detect spurious items. Today we can use computers and modern detection devices in this effort. High-powered microscopes can analyze the components of the materials that make up books and documents. Not specifically related to books, but an example of ultramodern

technology, is the work of Weimin Wei, whose article "Estimation of Image Rotation Angle Using Interpolation-Related Spectral Signatures with Application to Blind Detection of Image Forgery" explains a method for detecting anything that has been added to an image (e.g., a print, a painting, a drawing—which could also mean an image in an artist's book, for instance) after the original image was created.[29]

A similar use of technology is explained in B. L. Shivakumar and S. Santhosh Baboo's "Detecting Copy-Move Forgery in Digital Images: A Survey and Analysis of Current Methods," in which the authors explain that

> [t]he availability of low-cost hardware and software tools makes it easy to create, alter, and manipulate digital images with no obvious traces of having been subjected to any of these operations. As result we are rapidly reaching a situation where one can no longer take the integrity and authenticity of digital images for granted.
>
> . . . Copy-Move forgery is performed with the intention to make an object "disappear" from the image by covering it with a small block copied from another part of the same image. Since the copied segments come from the same image, the color palette, noise components, dynamic range and the other properties will be compatible with the rest of the image, thus it is very difficult for a human eye to detect.[30]

As mentioned, some books that come into special collections departments have artwork in them—especially artists' books of the twentieth century. Or prints are offered, presumably of well-known artists. Images produced from digital originals could be forged, and this technology will help the librarian or bookseller to determine if they are genuine or not.

One feature that can enhance the value of a book is whether it is signed by its author or illustrator, editor or publisher, or a famous former owner. Madasu Hanmandlu and colleagues published "Off-line Signature Verification and Forgery Detection Using Fuzzy Modeling,"[31] a method to verify the authenticity of signatures. The literature on computer forensics applicable to the book world is extensive and growing. This is not a field of study that is likely to come across the desk of scholars, purveyors, and librarians dealing in special collections materials, but they should know of its existence, and when a suspicious document or other item appears, they should avail themselves of this technology when practicable.

We have already seen the use of a cyclotron in the analysis of Gutenberg's inks.[32] Those in the book world are eager to adapt cutting-edge technological advancements to their own purposes.

Collection Development

One obvious arena in which modern technology is used in rare book librarianship is collection development. In the past—before the Internet was on the scene—anyone searching for a book or manuscript, either a specific title or an item for a subject collection, had to rely on bookstores, booksellers, or serendipity. As I said earlier, today hundreds of millions of books are available on the Internet on sites like AbeBooks, BookFinder, Alibris, viaLibri, Powell's, Barnes & Noble, AddALL, BookSearch, and oth-

ONE LIBRARIAN I know was offered a text in Japanese, thought it was overpriced, and searched on the standard sites for another copy. No luck. So she went to an international site that specialized in East Asian books and found an equivalent copy for about one-fifth the price. Librarians who seek non-English-language texts should become familiar with the online sites of booksellers in other countries.

ers. Some of these sites search the holdings of several sites. The AddALL site (www.addall.com) says, "Search and Compare among 40+ sites, 20,000 sellers, millions of books!" And BookFinder (www.bookfinder.com) says, "Search engine that finds the best buys from among 150 million new, used, rare, and out-of-print books for sale. Includes textbooks and international titles."

This chapter is titled "Special Collections Departments Today," and though online searching is not at all new (it has been going on for nearly twenty years), the Internet and the modern technology that makes it possible are still two of the most important tools we have to build our collections—and to save

UNTIL ONLINE SEARCHES for books first became possible—around 1995 with Michael Selzer's Bibliofind*—nearly all library acquisition and personal buying were done through vendors, bookstores, individual dealers, and other kinds of sales, but with the purchaser not being able to do broad searching. At first, being able to list their stock online was a great boon to booksellers because rather than having a walk-in trade of a few dozen people a day to see their shelves, they could display their wares to literally millions of potential customers. Books that had sat on shelves for years, even decades, were now looked at

by a vast clientele, and sales of long-held volumes skyrocketed for a few years. But as more and more books were advertised as available on the Internet, with an increasing number of people becoming "book dealers" (anybody could go to garage sales, flea markets, library book sales, Salvation Army–type thrift shops, and the like, pick up salable books cheaply, and sell them on the Web), competition equally skyrocketed. Now instead of searching fruitlessly for a book that has eluded a buyer for decades, she might find one or two or thirty copies. If it were one or two, the price might be high. If it were thirty, the

buyer could compare the copies on offer and pick the cheapest one. Those selling their books online would price their copies just under what others already listed were going for. Selling on the Web fairly quickly went from a seller's market to a buyer's market, thanks to the extensive competition. What might have been perceived as a rare book, seldom seen, might suddenly be available in a dozen or more copies, having emerged from hiding on the shelves of booksellers (amateur and professional) all over the country—even all over the world.

*See www.linkedin.com/pub/michael-selzer/20/85a/4a7.

money. Whenever a dealer offers a book to a special collections department, the librarian can easily search for other copies on the Web, from domestic and international databases, to see if less expensive copies are available.

Computer Databases of Users

For many years now, special collections departments have been able to store user information in their online databases. This is especially important when something seems to be missing, for the librarian can see who the last user of it was. Before computers were used for such information storage, this kind of information was stored on paper or microfilm, and while it was possible to trace this data, it required extensive, time-consuming searching. This storage of information is useful for security and for department statistics: How many users has the department had? Where do they come from? What are their contact points? What kinds of materials are being used? What specific items have been used? Is there a trend in the subject matter of paged items over time?

THE PHILLIPS LIBRARY at the Peabody Essex Museum has, among thousands of other things, a particularly wonderful manuscript—a log book of two important ships—the log kept by Nathaniel Hathorne (father of Nathaniel Hawthorne, who put the *w* into his name to distinguish himself from his father). Patrons often pointed out that sixteen pages were missing from the numbered leaves, but our paper catalog card had a handwritten note dated 1954 explaining that at that time the pages were known to be missing. All subsequent users, then, were not suspected of having taken them. If a new librarian in 2005 was alerted to the missing leaves, she might seek the records of those who had used the manuscript. If the database of users was linked to the missing-leaves information in the cataloging record, she would know that users after 1954 were not to be suspected of having taken them. (Parenthetically, those missing leaves were rejoined to their original manuscript when they were acquired in a large lot in an auction in 2010.)

Also, item condition information can be linked with cataloging records: Was this item damaged in any way before it was given to a patron? How many documents were in a particular file folder? Did the correspondence in this folder contain the original accompanying envelopes? And are those envelopes still there? This kind of information can be linked to the electronic data kept on particular patrons' use of the department's specific holdings.

Further, if theft is suspected or mutilations are present, information can quickly be disseminated to other libraries and requests for information about the suspect(s) can be sent out efficiently. Networking on such an issue can help librarians catch thieves.

Leased Databases

One of the most extensive (and growing) areas of rare books and special collections activities today is the availability of databases that are obtainable, usually leased, from commercial entities. Already mentioned, for instance, is the Ship Index (at Shipindex.org), a vast databank on ships "[w]ith 142,804 entries in the free database and 2,784,640 entries available with premium access" (www.shipindex .org/about). The Internet is growing so fast that it is impossible for anyone, or any institution, to keep up with the amount of information available on it. Tennessee, for one small example, has its TEL: "The Tennessee Electronic Library (TEL) is a collection of 40 + databases that provide access to over 400,000 magazine, journal, and newspaper articles, essays, podcasts, videos, e-books, primary source materials, and more." (TEL is available to Tennessee residents; see http://tntel.tnsos.org.) This one small conglomerate of databases is typical of what is available from states, colleges and universities, law offices, hospital libraries, and many other entities that need information. A major university may have a hundred times that number of portals accessible. As increasing numbers of them are available on the Web, many for free, organizations are mounting them onto their own sites for access to their own constituents. Leased databases, created usually by commercial companies, are available in increasing numbers. Any party—academic, commercial, or nonprofit—can purchase access to them.

If booksellers or collectors, rare book departments or archives have a strong collection on a given subject and if a commercial database is available that has extensive information about that subject area (and if a library's patrons frequently use the holdings in that area), it makes sense for them to look for databases that would be useful to them. Commercial companies have been filling the niches of scholarship for decades by making copies of particular sources and selling access to these to whoever wanted them. They originally used microfilm, but the limitations of that medium were obvious: only those with copies of the films could access the data.

Today digital access to specialized packages is the norm. One key issue, of course, is that these packages are frequently expensive, and they are ongoing because they are often rented by the year. In a way, this arrangement makes sense, for if the database is added to or corrected, the purchaser will be getting the improved version each new year of the subscription. So there are annual access fees. As more and more of these become available, the amount of money that has to be expended to have them accessible grows. Special collections departments do not have endless resources. That is, their acquisitions budgets are usually insufficient for the analog materials they want to acquire. The added expenditures for digital materials may force the department to curtail its acquisition of books and manuscripts. It is a delicate balance, with the benefit of the department's patrons in mind: Will they prefer access to vast amounts of information in digital form, available only from the institution, or will they want the department to acquire books and manuscripts and other research materials for them? Even the wealthiest institutions cannot afford all the analog pieces they would like to get, let alone all the available digital resources.

This point should be reiterated in light of the content of chapter 12, which discussed the preservation of digital materials. The long-term costs of digital holdings could far exceed the costs of refor-matting into another proven-more-stable medium, like microfilm or paper. Even items born digital and maintained in electronic form will probably cost far more in the long run to store "indefinitely" than will a paper copy of the same text. So although rare book libraries today are embracing (read "purchasing") an increasing number of online resources, this practice comes at a short- and long-term cost that is inestimable. The practice takes resources away from other kinds of acquisitions, primarily those of the traditional special collections department.

Linked Open Data

In the last few years, a new use of technology has emerged thanks to advancements in the power of computers. This is Linked Data or Linked Open Data, the ability of computers to scan the Internet for sites that are linked by subject matter. The system uses the computer's ability to agglomerate sites that share subjects based on vocabulary. As early as 2007, Tim Berners-Lee was writing about the ability of computers to use controlled vocabularies and web-searching capabilities to make data interconnected. He says,

> Like the web of hypertext, the web of data is constructed with documents on the web. However, unlike the web of hypertext, where links are relationships anchors in hypertext documents written in HTML, for data they [link] between arbitrary things described by RDF. (www.w3.org/DesignIssues/LinkedData.html)

Wikipedia explains that RDF is

> Resource Description Framework (RDF) . . . , a family of World Wide Web Consortium (W3C) specifications [1][33] originally designed as a metadata data model. It has come to be used as a general method for conceptual description or modeling of information that is implemented in Web resources, using a variety of syntax formats.[34]

What all this means is that methods of doing research have been (and continue to be) expanded to include vast hordes of materials now residing (and to come) on the Internet, locatable in a single search through the miraculous linking of websites with overlapping vocabularies.

The sites that are in the so-called Linked Data Community are scannable by sophisticated browsers that retrieve data from all open sites and also are contributed to by site masters who wish to enter their data into the LOD (Linked Open Data) cloud. (See figure 13.1 for a diagram showing the contributing sites as of September 2011.)[35] What this means is that all the linked sites are automatically searchable by a browser, and links to searched key terms can be identified when a scholar enters the term(s) into a search box that is linked to the LOD site. Where we are headed, of course, is to a place similar to where we go when we search through Google, Yahoo!, Ask, Dogpile, or any other Web browser: we are led to so much information that we could be forever moving from one link to another. As an example, a Google search on the word *bookbinding* brought up 4,900,000

hits in less than a third of a second. The amount of information available to researchers is daunting—and steadily increasing—and, to complicate things further, the information locatable on the Web is not always reliable, even when it comes from seemingly reputable sources. For many years the following sentences have been available on the Internet:

> The book was invented 500 years ago by Aldo Manuzio in Venice, Italy. The so-called octavo format was a departure from previous manuscripts because it was handy, portable, and pocket-size. Manuzio even pioneered page numbering. Odd how Gutenberg gets credit while Manuzio is known to only a few.[36]

The ludicrousness of these assertions need not be commented on here. What was said earlier in this book must be repeated here, in a different context: special collections librarians today, like everyone else, can refer their patrons to the Web for vast

FIG. 13.1
Linking Open Data cloud

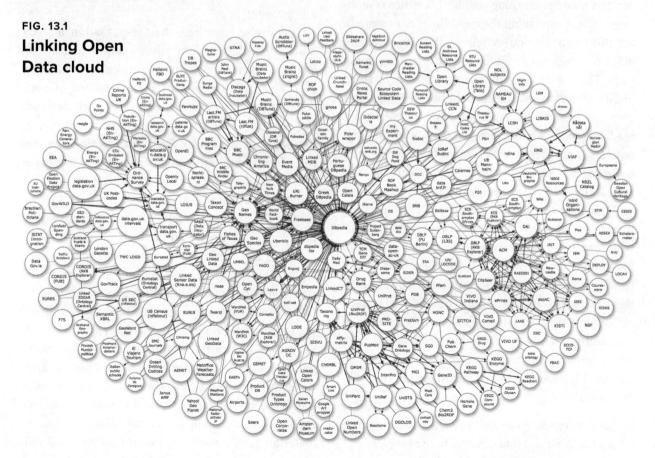

The Linking Open Data cloud diagram (by Richard Cyganiak and Anja Jentzsch, http://lod-cloud.net). Available under a CC BY-SA license (http://creativecommons.org/licenses/by-sa/3.0).

amounts of research materials, but there is no way to guarantee the authenticity and accuracy of everything the Web contains, and there is practically no way to get through *all* the information available. Readers must rely on the power of the search engines to locate the most reliable sources—so, as noted earlier, they must trust that the best ones are at the top of the list, rather than ones that paid in some way to make it to the top. And things will only get more complicated as an increasing amount of information is mounted on the Web. One of the promises of Linked Open Data may be one of its curses: the links could go on seemingly forever, swamping a researcher in so much data that it is impossible to ingest even a small fraction of it.

One point here is that today's special collections librarians are themselves relying increasingly on digital resources and directing their patrons to do so, while the accuracy and authenticity of those resources are difficult to monitor. Modern technology has made some things easier, but it has complicated (while expanding the capabilities of) research. For this reason, serious scholars will want more and more to check source information in analog materials. There may be a diminution of use of some library materials, but in the field of rare books, this does not seem to be happening. Special collections reading rooms are still being visited by traditional scholars, and special collections librarians are still acquiring analog materials to serve their clientele with an increasing storehouse of information.

A possible by-product of LOD and an expanding Internet, as already noted, is that researchers worldwide can have access to materials held at remote institutions, but now they can become part of the cloud group that comments on them, showing how they have meaning for groups beyond the materials' original primary audience. Knowledge about the availability of previously hidden collections and, with scanning, "firsthand" access to the actual materials (full text) are becoming possible. Clifford Lynch puts it this way:

> These materials evoke and attract a global stream of annotation and commentary, much of it greatly enriching the primary special collections content (for example, by identifying people, places, artifacts, or events depicted in photographs); the volume of this commentary may be too large for the stewards of the collection to effectively even review, and assisting and adjudicating its accuracy may be entirely beyond the capabilities of the hosting institutions.

He also points out that the commentary need not come from other institutions; it could come from private parties, and it may also reveal similar materials in private hands—adding to the storehouse of information about research sources. He says, "[S]uch widespread attention may in fact give rise to offers of contributions of related or supplementary materials currently in private hands, or identify linkages to materials held by other cultural memory organizations." And he concludes that what is being created is not a host of individual, geographically discrete collections on a given subject, but a special collections "re-structure[d] and re-create[d] . . . along logical intellectual lines, and indeed . . . new 'virtual' special collections that facilitate new kinds of scholarly investigation."

Lynch also mentions the "re-patriation and re-unification of geographically dispersed special collections," combining "cultural diplomacy with new scholarship."[37] One well-known instance of such cooperation and reunification, as Lynch reminds the reader, is the bringing together, digitally, of the pages of the *Codex Sinaiticus* ("which includes the oldest complete New Testament"). Its leaves now reside in collections at the British Library, the National Library of Russia, St. Catherine's Monastery, and Leipzig University Library. They now also reside in a single place on the Web.[38]

Lynch also speaks of other kinds of initiatives now under way or on the near horizon in which digital representations of fragile holdings in scattered institutions may be (or are being) collected by a single organization (like the British Library), with a digital copy given to the institution holding the original. This kind of program helps the holding libraries or historical societies in preservation, and it helps the world of scholars in that these representations are being made available on the Web. The kind of materials thus treated are exactly what special collections departments contain. And such an endeavor need not be restricted to public institutions: private parties may wish to contribute their own holdings to the growing databases of research materials.

Another issue concerning the modern special collections department is that just because many technologies are available to help librarians serve their patrons does not mean that older traditional activities and responsibilities have changed. That is, all that librarians in this department have been doing for a century must still be done: search for and acquire new materials; catalog, process, and store them; mount cataloging records onto a database accessible to all potential users; serve local and distant scholars; conserve and preserve all holdings; and so forth. It may be that the number of works available in full text on Google Books and other online databases is growing; but there will always be a need and a desire for scholars to work with primary materials—*in hand*, not from a computer screen.

Interdisciplinarity

One of the consequences of increased access to information on a global scale is that scholars in various disciplines can now connect with each other in ways never before possible. Wikipedia says, "Interdisciplinarity involves researchers, students, and teachers in the goals of connecting and integrating several academic schools of thought, professions, or technologies—along with their specific perspectives—in the pursuit of a common task" ("Interdisciplinarity," http://en.wikipedia.org/wiki/Interdisciplinarity). And this article points out that there has been a steady rise in the numbers of interdisciplinary programs since 1998.[39]

The implications for the present volume are great. Traditional special collections have become fertile ground for nontraditional users. Scholars in disparate fields can now learn of materials they did not know existed—things that may have an impact on their own research—thanks to the MARC-level cataloging of special collections holdings, with keyword searches, extensive subject headings, cataloging records enhanced with vocabulary from the RBMS-supported thesauri, and finding aids for manuscript collections entered online with EAD infor-

mation.[40] The extensive technicalities of EAD, DTD (Document Type Definition; see http://en.wikipedia.org/wiki/Document_type_definition), rare book cataloging, and Dublin Core (see http://en.wikipedia.org/wiki/Dublin_Core) metadata terms, among other factors to consider when creating cataloging records for monographs and finding aids for manuscript collections are beyond the scope of the present volume.

The important point is that such tools add vast amounts of information to cataloging records, and these records are available online, expanding the searching capabilities of scholars exponentially, because many records are linked to other records, which, themselves, are linked outward. Scholars the world over will be contacting special collections departments for information they are learning of through this network of cataloged and linked data.

As Richard Wendorf predicted nearly two decades ago,

> This multidisciplinary impulse has, on the one hand, created new, broadly conceptualized fields (and academic departments): women's studies, African-American studies, cultural studies, critical theory, sexual and gender studies, post-colonial studies. The same impulse, on the other hand, has simultaneously led to the creation of smaller but vigorous subspecialties—the history of the book; inter-relations between literature and the visual arts—that are central to the scholarly life of rare books and manuscript libraries.[41]

Costs and Resource Allocation

Wendorf adds that the new technology will, in one way or another, "affect our collecting, education, teaching, publishing, cataloging, and exhibition programs" (p. 10). As one of many questions the new technology raises, the question Wendorf poses about selection for acquisition stands out. He asks, "Does one purchase a missing book, or invest in software that will instantly generate hundreds of missing books in electronic, printable form?" (p. 11). As I already noted, the balance is fine between the acquisitions of digital and analog materials. And this balance—

in a way, for the librarian, this dilemma—has been accentuated with the availability of innumerable packages of research materials (books and manuscripts and photographs, for instance) available in the last few years digitally through commercial vendors.

Libraries—especially special collections departments—can be like black holes, swallowing up all their resources and wanting more. Give most active rare book libraries $100 million for acquisitions and they could spend it all. Give them another like amount: same result. There is no diminution of available resources to add to the department's collection, in analog and digital form. There are always other purchases, a facilities upgrade, an additional "needed" staff position, more cataloging or archives processing, more supplies and equipment, and more expenses to publicize the library and its holdings. And with evolving technology, a well-heeled department will want to upgrade to the latest platforms and hardware. There are collections to digitize and items needing conservation treatment. Practically no librarian will ever say, "We have all the (space) (resources) (money) (staff) we need."

For most rare book departments this situation is permanent, as it should be, because, as living entities, with, presumably, a growing clientele, they will continue to grow and expand. As already explained, the more cataloging records the department has online, the more patrons it will draw, who demand more resources, leading to more acquisitions, more cataloging, and more available information about the enlarged collection.

The Need for Self-Advocacy

Departments today must continue to promote themselves, to their users and to those who support the collections: library administrators, institution leaders, other internal users (students, faculty), and external parties of all kinds, including Friends groups, corporations and foundations, private researchers, distant scholars, and all others delineated in chapter 11. The head of the department should be the squeaky wheel.

Traditional budgets, over the last quarter century, have been stretched with the coming of the computer. Department budgets now have lines that once did not exist: computers, hardware and software upgrades, upgrades in the leased systems that hold cataloging records, digital databases holding worlds of information for our librarians and department patrons, IT personnel, staff development in learning new computer systems and databases, and so forth. If anything, it is more expensive now than ever before to run a special collections department, and budgets from the parent institution have not always kept pace. There is now, and there will always be, a pressure on the archivists and special collections librarians to work with development, as chapter 6 has shown.[42] The department must not lose its standard share of the institution's budget, and it should also be advocating for itself outside the institution, raising funds from foundations, corporations, friends groups, private donors, and wherever else it sees an opportunity. Librarians and archivists should continue to publicize the department's holdings through publications, exhibitions or simple displays, attendance at meetings, fund-raising activities, department tours, outreach to faculty and students, and in any other way appropriate and practicable.

Assessment

One of the newer areas of rare book librarianship is assessment. The activity has been in the library world for at least two decades, but the application of assessment to rare book librarianship is relatively recent.[43] Special collections libraries, as this volume indicates, are concerned with an exceptionally broad range of activities and theories in the world of books and manuscripts, and for them to be effective and prosperous, and successful in meeting their mandates, they must assess their activities and make adjustments to increase the number and quality of their successes. Christian Dupont, as the guest editor of an issue of *Rare Books and Manuscripts* (*RBM*), says,

> For the past several years, a national conversation has been building over how best to assess the qual-

ity and impact of higher education and the contributions that libraries make to research, teaching, and learning. . . . A growing body of literature and practice relating to assessment has been emerging on the library landscape, but it has tended to fragment over the usual organizational and disciplinary boundaries.[44]

He adds that "rare book departments and archives in general have not been well integrated into the strategic planning and core operations of academic libraries, and this marginalization has been particularly the case with regard to assessment" (second paragraph). The aim of this issue of *RBM* is to show that special collections librarians and archivists are now working on carrying out their own studies of "the effectiveness of their services and the efficiency of their operations." As Dupont explains, such assessment will give librarians and archivists a good picture of how successful they are at doing their jobs and can guide them to "best practices" in the field. Such assessment, additionally, gives these professionals the tools to inform their administrators about all the librarians' efforts, partly as a form of self-promotion, "and to promote awareness of the potential benefits and opportunities for integrating special collections and archives into larger institutional planning and assessment efforts."

Administrators will appreciate being informed of the work of the department, especially because they may be uninformed about what the department actually does and how the institution can benefit from the unit's treasures and talents. The political and even fiscal benefits that can accrue to special collections can be significant.

Dupont also points out that assessment in the rare book community is so important that RBMS[45] "formed a metrics and assessment task force that is currently examining needs for standardized definitions and metrics and best-practice guidelines for assessment activities in special collections." The existence of an extended issue of *RBM* devoted exclusively to assessment is testimony to the importance of this emerging field in the realm of special collections.[46] The efforts of assessment can be far-ranging because the activities of special collections depart-

ments are extremely broad. The Task Force minutes delineate the areas in which assessment may be carried out:

Accessioning, Acquisitions, Cataloging, Conservation/Preservation, Exhibits/Exhibit Loans, Instruction, Processing, Reference, Use/Circulation, Website Visits, Reading Room Visits/Visitors . . . Administrative Needs, Collection Development policies intersecting with users' needs (e.g. qualitative assessments toward the justification of why we have THESE expensive books HERE), Community Impact, Digitization/Digital Projects including metadata creation, Finding aid usage, ILL, and MPLP impact on public services, Outreach, including use of social media, Tools used to gather data in various areas (e.g., Desk Tracker, Knowledge Tracker, READ scale).

The task force will address these areas in the future, with the aim of publishing best practices for assessment in each of them.

The *RBM* essay by Lisa R. Carter, "Articulating Value: Building a Culture of Assessment in Special Collections," makes it clear that just claiming that special collections departments are important is not enough today when administrators want all employees and the units in which they work to demonstrate *how* they are important, and also *how important* they are. She says, "We can no longer simply assume value. Instead we must demonstrate impact" (her first paragraph), and she says that rare book departments must show not only how they are "special" but also how they are valuable. Certain measurable phenomena can be used to prove value. For instance, Carter mentions use statistics (the number of scholars who profit through the use of a department's holdings). These researchers' use of department materials that eventuates in presentations at conferences or in publications is certainly measurable. Also measurable is the educational use of the materials by teachers/professors and their students.

As suggested in chapter 6 on fund-raising, the department head should offer the head of the institution access to special collections as one of the stops on tours for prospective donors. If the institution eventually gets a donation, and if it can be shown that part of the donor's interest was in the library, the donation is a measurable result of the tour.

Another article in the same issue of *RBM*—by Martha O'Hara Conway and Merrilee Proffitt, "The Practice, Power, and Promise of Archival Collections Assessment"—makes it clear that assessment is as important in archives as it is in the rest of the library. They say that "research libraries must assess their existing special collections with the goal of reducing cataloging and processing backlogs, effectively disclosing existing collections, and strategically acquiring new ones." This is especially important in archives, which can hold vast quantities of unique and unpublished research materials. They advocate taking collection surveys that will help the archivists in "'appraisal, setting processing and other priorities, conservation decision making, and collection management.'"[47]

Over the last few decades librarians—especially in rare book departments—have been working to reveal "hidden collections." This issue will be taken up in the next chapter. It is sufficient in the present context to say that through good assessment, hidden collections can be identified.

As already noted, a good assessment—one that reveals collections—allows the staff to establish priorities for processing. As Conway and Proffitt say, the revelation of hidden collections leads to another form of assessment: establishing "research value" so that certain items will make it to the high-priority-for-processing list while others will be sent toward the bottom of the list. This evaluation of research value "can be used to guide important curatorial and collection management decisions and impel related and necessary activities, including the creation or revision of collecting policies and the preparation of a deaccessioning policy." And they also say that while the evaluation is ongoing, staff can easily check the collection for condition. A collection-condition survey is a desideratum in libraries, especially for special collections, and an assessment program allows for such an inspection.

One of the results of thorough assessments is an informed report, supported by measurable—thus demonstrable—criteria that the archivist or librarian can use to support a request for additional staff or other resources. Also, as Conway and Proffitt show, libraries undertaking assessment projects will do well to collaborate with other institutions in their region, even dozens or hundreds of them, thus reducing redundant work for them all. The result will be a consortium that produces finding aids and cataloging records that reveal many hidden collections. Pooling intellectual resources will eventuate in a host of benefits for the libraries' and archives' patrons, as well as for the departments themselves. In the assessments, the institutions will get a handle on what they own. Conway and Proffitt discuss the collaboration engendered by the Arizona Archives Summit, "an ongoing effort aimed at developing a collaborative, statewide model of 'best' collection management practices." The Summit is

> a multi-year project to develop a statewide collaborative model of collection management practices. The Summit brings together representatives from archives, historical societies, museums and libraries from around Arizona.
>
> Our goal is to preserve and make accessible Arizona's historical records by working together to: collect under-documented communities and subjects; decrease backlogs; move out-of-scope collections to more appropriate repositories; and reunite split collections.[48]

Conway and Proffitt say, "Not surprisingly, some of the toughest conversations for the Arizona planners were those that revolved around the transfer of split, out-of-scope, or unprocessed collections to a more appropriate institution." If institutions are willing to part with items that are not central to their core missions and are willing to transfer them to more appropriate collections, the result can be "that related materials are not scattered across repositories and that resources are not squandered on unnecessary competition for collections." They point out that such transfers are few, but at least the cooperative assessment activities bring to light for researchers the location of related materials at several institutions.

Assessment can be done in other areas of special collections librarianship. The *RBM* issue has an article by Joyce Chapman and Elizabeth Yakel on "Data-Driven Management and Interoperable Metrics for Special Collections and Archives User Services," showing how assessment can be used to improve the services the department offers its clientele; and another piece by Anne Bahde and Heather Smedberg on "Measuring the Magic: Assessment in the Special Collections and Archives Classroom," discussing how instructors in archives and rare books can assess the quality, and maximize the effectiveness, of their teaching. Bahde and Smedberg say that the instructors can claim they are being effective in the classroom, but "[m]ore and more we are being asked to back up informal observations of our own successes with formal assessment measures." The situation calls for measurable assessment, and they discuss the various kinds, starting with reaction assessments (questionnaires and surveys—these do not produce measurable data about how much the students have learned; they do measure satisfaction and, often, direct suggestions for improvement), in-class exercises, and take-home tests and essays, among other things.

The aim here is not to examine teaching/learning assessment in detail; it is more to show that today's special collections personnel, and those teaching in this field, must do various kinds of assessment to maximize the effectiveness of the department in its provision of services. Assessment is important in all areas of special collections librarianship. Rachael Hu's article on finding-aid and website design discusses the evaluation of the layout of online information and how such design affects the success or failure of researchers.[49] She says,

> For the special collections libraries and archives that deal in primary source collections and a variety of material formats, the online presentation of their materials gives rise to special challenges due to the complex nature of the descriptive records that provide access to the collections they manage.

She points out that the EAD (Encoded Archival Description) standards of the 1990s made fairly uniform the appearance of information for archival materials presented in digital form. And she says,

> The EAD standard also enabled archival collections to become systematically discoverable on the World Wide Web for the first time and encouraged the growth of websites dedicated to the aggregation of these descriptive records as well as providing environments to view digitally scanned facsimiles of objects from these collections.

The present text need not examine the fine point of assessing the design of online information. Librarians and archivists should, however, be aware of the importance of making the data they mount on the Web as user-friendly as possible. Hu says,

> As the creation and development of web content—both commercial and academic—grew, an important indicator of an archives' continued value became a user-friendly website displaying easy to find descriptions of its collections, whether published directly online or available at its physical location.

One crucial tenet, stressed throughout the present volume, is that the library's primary aim is to get information into the hands of its patrons. Poor design of data delivery is an impediment to this responsibility.[50]

In her afterword to the essays in this volume of *RBM*, Sarah M. Pritchard says that "[t]he key challenge in special collections . . . is getting the broader institution to care." She says, "Our assessment program has to demonstrate the value of special collections to advancing the mission of the entire library, and in turn the value of the library in contributing to the accomplishment of the university's goals."[51] Of course, assessment must go on with all practitioners in the rare book world. Booksellers must assess all aspects of their business, from acquisition to sales, and collectors must assess their collection limits (the scope of their collections and their ability to afford what they wish to add to their holdings).

One of Pritchard's suggestions is for librarians and archivists to look at the mission(s) of the parent organization and to form an assessment program that has its own mission statement that mimics the language of that of the institution. She says, "[I]t behooves us [librarians and archivists] to take the time to tease out those details [of the institution's mission] and emulate the phrasing we see in the university's own planning documents." In fact, the special col-

> **ONE OF MY** pet peeves is entering a website hoping, and even expecting, to find certain kinds of information and then having to search extensively for it. Sometimes it can be infuriating not to be able to find a person's name or contact points. One piece of information that some institutions—and many corporations and businesses—do not like to make prominent is employee phone numbers. It is obviously cheaper to have all information delivered by recorded messages. The time an organization has to allot for a human being to answer the phone and converse with a caller can be costly. Standard practice is to encourage a customer/client to look at a website or to hit the right (and the right number of) buttons on the phone to get the recording that satisfies the caller. Sometimes the inquirer cannot find a phone number at all; sometimes a number leads to a series of "press the button for more information" labyrinths. Sometimes the recorded messages do not lead to the kind of (or the specific) information the caller is phoning about. And often the caller will get a message like this one: "You have reached the customer service line. Our customer-service representatives are all busy taking care of other patrons. Your call is very important to us, so please stay on the line until the next operator is available. Your expected wait time is 45 minutes. This line is serviced Monday, Wednesday, and Friday from 11:00 a.m. to 11:15 a.m. Please hold for the next representative." There are few things worse for a special collections department than a disgruntled patron trying to get a human being on the phone or going to a website with a simple question and winding up spending ten minutes or a half hour looking for a way to contact *someone.* Assessing the availability of information on the department website or through other kinds of contact (e-mail, phone, postal mail) is essential. The patron comes first, so departments should do what they can to accommodate them and to get into their hands the information they need.

lections librarian might look carefully at the institution's mission statement and design an assessment program for her department around the important subjects emphasized in that statement. Issues could relate to local or regional, national or international contributions, undergraduate or graduate education, teaching in the professions, research and advancement for faculty, "clinical and extension services, or civic or community engagement" (Pritchard). There might be an emphasis on preserving cultural heritage, or on serving a nonacademic community, or on enhancing the prestige of the institution. The assessment program may focus on nontraditional communities, sustainability, keeping abreast of evolving technology, collaboration with other organizations (academic, governmental, social, professional), and so on.

Pritchard indicates that for an assessment program to be supported, it must appeal to those running the institution, who are usually more interested in things at the institution level than they are in things at the special collections level. Hence, administrators

> are not too interested in the library's internal operating stresses—rather, we have to show how our work can alleviate *their* stress! How can we help our institutions be more competitive and more financially efficient? What leadership are we contributing to the campus use of innovative technologies or to the articulation of new consortial models? We need to externalize the impact of our work. The desired outcomes go back to the articulations and emphases of institutional mission.

And she shows many ways for the special collections department to contribute to the advancement of the larger organization.

Today, perhaps more than ever before—and especially in times when nonprofits are struggling for support—special collections libraries must justify their existence in the larger institution. Assessment is an essential activity, and it can produce results in the form of reports and statistics that will demonstrate the worth of the department. Pritchard mentions just a few:

The value to the [institution's] mission can be demonstrated through assessing the ways that specific library services and resources help in recruiting faculty and graduate students, in securing research grants, in attracting philanthropy, and in producing scholarly publications and technical products such as software or devices. Special collections contribute to all of these dimensions but we have been disorganized in how we track and report those contributions.

Further, the assessment will guide the special collections staff to ways to improve their own operations.

Teaching

Special collections departments have for decades been part of the teaching function of their institutions. This will not change. Instructors will continue to impress upon students the importance of using original materials in their research. And special collections librarians should continue to welcome into the department all students with legitimate research needs. The librarians themselves may wish to be part of the teaching faculty of the institution, offering by themselves—or jointly teaching—courses on book history, bibliography, medieval codicology, archives, rare book librarianship (at a library school), or other topics that the librarian is an expert on. Departments will have special collections—that is, subject or author collections—and these may be the basis of courses in departments of history, English, science, or one of the social sciences.

Chapter 11 dealt with outreach. As noted there, one form of outreach is offering to faculty (and their classes) access to the library's holdings by permitting classes to meet in the special collections department, where original materials can be placed before the participants. It is desirable to have an employee of the special collections department sit in on these sessions to make sure the materials are handled properly, but this could be a good use of staff time because the information the department person learns from the session may be useful on the job. And teaching does not need to be limited to students: any patron who uses the department will benefit from the expertise of the staff, so all personnel in the department should be willing to help any patron. Even teaching patrons how to locate and use the department's databases is important, and with the increasing number of online resources that departments have today, such instruction is almost mandatory. One way or another—by word of mouth, by pamphlets in the department, in special fliers about the research a scholar can do in the department, or in other ways—the patrons should be informed about the resources available. More and more, special collections are thinking of themselves as teaching units, and this should continue as increasing amounts of information in analog and digital forms come into the departments.[52]

In tight economies—and even in times when resources are not tight—special collections departments must continue to show their relevance to the institution, and contributing to the teaching function of the organization is one key way to do this.

Exhibition

One form of outreach, as noted in chapter 11, is the mounting of exhibitions and, if they are affordable, the publication of catalogs of these shows. Exhibits are a good way to let the world know of strong or important collections and of reinforcing to the staff (and training them about) what materials the department owns.

From 1986 to today, the Rare Books and Manuscripts Section has given awards to institutions for the exhibition catalogs they have produced. The winning catalogs are selected by the Exhibition Awards Committee, whose charge is "[t]o recognize outstanding printed exhibition catalogs and guides, and electronic exhibitions, produced by United States and Canadian institutions."[53] It adds, "Although printed exhibition catalogs and guides must be associated with physical exhibitions, electronic exhibitions need not be." Awards are given at various catalog price levels (Expensive, Moderately

Expensive, Inexpensive, and Brochures [brochures were added as a separate category in 2001], and also for electronic catalogs [the committee has been giving awards for electronic catalogs since 2003].)[54] In 2012 there were thirty-six paper-based and seventeen electronic submissions.

These numbers show only exhibitions for which catalogs were created and submitted to the RBMS competition. An untold number of other exhibits are being presented at special collections departments throughout the country. And some institutions are not actually mounting the physical exhibits; they are putting up virtual ones on the Web. At the present writing, the Library of Congress has ninety-five such shows on the Internet.

As just mentioned, the value of such endeavors to a special collections department is inestimable, and a well-done exhibit could educate people all over the world, bring scholars to the library, and even help the development department in its fund-raising efforts. Today libraries are availing themselves of the most recent technology to create relatively inexpensive catalogs of their exhibitions and are mounting the information on the Web for worldwide distribution. With excellent means to reproduce color images inexpensively, librarians and booksellers have been able to disseminate vast amounts of high-quality, colorful, image-based or textual material.

IN ABOUT 1991, when I first had a computer at work, I was head of special collections and university archivist at the University of California, Riverside. I was busy from the minute I got to work early in the morning until I left in the evening. The administration told me what a time-saver the computer would be, and all librarians at the campus got one. As most of us learned, the computer saved us time in many of our duties, but the number of activities seemed to increase the more we got used to having this "time-saving" tool. About two years later we got a Gopher account so that we could communicate with our peers—inside and beyond our own institutions. The speed of communication was sometimes balanced by the frustration of using the Gopher system. If I was typing a message to someone and spotted a typographical error in my text, I could not correct it. The Gopher allowed the keyboarder forward movement, but did not permit going backward to correct mistakes.* I remember sending my first e-mail message to a colleague at the University of Wisconsin. She replied, "Welcome to the world of wasting two hours a day." These were prophetic words, but she was wrong: I wish it were only two hours a day!

Today e-mail has become the number one time-sink for almost all of us in libraries. The junk mail and the regular messages flow in— hundreds a day. Colleagues with offices a few feet apart may communicate electronically. And for some reason which I cannot understand, people insist on making appointments with one another using e-mail, sometimes sending a dozen messages before they agree on a time. One old-fashioned phone call could save many minutes of negotiations. Research no longer begins with a visit to a library; it begins with a Google search. The U.S. Postal Service is going broke because it has lost a vast number of customers to electronic messaging. Readers of this text will not need to be told what capabilities lie at their fingertips today. Rare book librarians, booksellers, collectors, archivists, and all others in academia are beneficiaries of the new technology, which has permanently and greatly changed their lives.

For the present text, the key issue here is that computers have made it simple and inexpensive to create modest exhibit catalogs and disseminate them worldwide—even ones with color illustrations and video graphics.

*The Wikipedia article on the Gopher protocol says:

> The Gopher protocol is a TCP/IP application layer protocol designed for distributing, searching, and retrieving documents over the Internet. Strongly oriented towards a menu-document design, the Gopher protocol presented an alternative to the World Wide Web in its early stages, but ultimately HTTP became the dominant protocol. The Gopher ecosystem is often regarded as the effective predecessor of the World Wide Web. (http://en.wikipedia.org/wiki/Gopher_%28protocol%29).

. . .

In 2000, Werner Gundersheimer, the director of the Folger Shakespeare Library in Washington, D.C., looked back a few years to his library's timing in getting into the digital game. That is, he did not want to be on the front line of bringing technology into the Folger, nor did he want to wait till it was too late to adopt the new digital technologies comfortably into the processing of his library's holdings. He says, "The transition from paper to OPAC and from old-fashioned rare book librarianship to integrated, state-of-the-art collections management has been rapid and practically seamless."[55] This may have been the feeling when Gundersheimer wrote those words. But one of the aims of the present volume has been to show that the "transition" from analog to digital is really only in a few narrow realms of rare book activities. Because of the nature of our collections—the hard materials we have gathered for decades and (for some libraries) for centuries—and because of the needs of our patrons, some aspects of *analog librarianship* will never be transitioned away from.

It is true that those dealing with rare books today have seen immense change in their worlds in some areas of action, while other areas remain fixed and seemingly immutable. One reason for this is that their basic missions, goals, and responsibilities have not changed, and many old methods of operation cannot be improved upon. This is as true for the special collections librarian as it is for the archivist, bookseller, researcher, teacher, and student. Another reason for this continuity in practice is that the basics of research are still the same: scholars need information and seek it in the traditional places. Knowing this, librarians and archivists make it available by employing all the tools at their disposal. Some of these tools are phenomena of a digital world. Booksellers need information to acquire stock and to learn about the things they sell, and they need a way of making that information available to others. Students need information to write essays and theses and dissertations. Faculty need access to research materials of many kinds for their own teaching and publications. Archivists need many kinds of information to help them process collections.

It all comes down to information acquisition and delivery, and today librarians, geniuses that they are at adopting and adapting technologies to their jobs, have reached a point at which they are using these technologies brilliantly to help their patrons. They are still dreaming of Universal Bibliographical Control. They know they will never have it, but they continue to strive for it by using every piece of hardware and software they have the resources to acquire, accessing every informational and image-based database they can get to, and networking with others to maximize the use of their holdings. Special collections librarians, like all others in their profession, are able today to deliver more information than ever before. As an increasing amount of data emerges into the world, rare book department staff can capture much of it for their patrons. If we consider where we were only fifteen years ago, we will be amazed at where we are now. But it will be even more amazing in the future.

NOTES

1. I have intentionally avoided using the now-trite phrase "in the digital age" in the title of this chapter. "Today" more accurately captures what this chapter is about. The "digital" phrase implies that modern libraries (particularly special collections departments) are fully digital, but one of the messages of this book is that older "technologies," policies, and practices, analog materials, and manual human efforts are still with us in rare book libraries. The Association of Research Libraries (ARL), on October 14–15, 2009, held a conference titled "An Age of Discovery: Distinctive Collections in the Digital Age." (The audio proceedings are available at www.arl.org/publications-resources/search-publications/term/summary/17?start = 40.) Because the scholarly world "went digital" in various ways in the 1960s, everything since has been "in the digital age," and unless some form of communication supplants this, we will be "in the digital age" henceforth. In this respect, the phrase has practically lost its meaning. The Clifford Lynch piece cited in note 4 was originally presented at this conference.

2. "The OAC is a core component of UC's California Digital Library (CDL) and is administered by the

Digital Special Collections program." See www.oac .cdlib.org/about.

3. Henry Raine and Laura Stalker, "Rare Book Records in Online Systems," *Rare Books & Manuscripts Librarianship* 11.2 (Fall 1996): 103–18, http://rbm.acrl .org/content/rbml/11/2/103.full.pdf.

4. Clifford A. Lynch takes issue with the word *surrogates*, saying that it implies an inferior substitute. He says,

> Until fairly recently, it has been near-universal practice to refer to these digital representations of physical objects as "digital surrogates," a faintly pejorative, sneering phrase that suggests their systematic and intrinsic inferiority to the source physical objects; this is often accompanied by rhetoric implying that real scholars always need to work with the originals. As I will argue, this is no longer true, at least in a universal and straightforward way, and I've preferred the more neutral term "digital representation" here.

See Lynch, "Special Collections at the Cusp of the Digital Age: A Credo," *Research Library Issues* 267 (December 2009): 3–9; this statement is on page 8, note 2 (http://publications.arl.org/rli267/4; www.arl.org/bm~doc/rli-267-lynch.pdf). The Lynch piece is also available along with the full audio proceedings of the conference (the ARL-CNI Fall Forum, "An Age of Discovery: Distinctive Collections in the Digital Age," held on October 15–16, 2009) at http://web.resourceshelf.com/go/ resourceblog/56702. ARL is the Association of Research Libraries; CNI is the Coalition for Networked Information.

5. Lynch refers the reader to an issue of *Digital Humanities Quarterly* 3.1 (Winter 2009), devoted to "collaborative research and documentation of imaged classical manuscript materials" (Lynch, "Special Collections at the Cusp," p. 9, note 6).

6. The library would get two copies of the film(s), one a master copy and the other for use. The films would be sent in boxes clearly marked with the library's ownership and a note saying that they were the property of the institution and must be returned. Additionally, the client using the films would be asked to sign an agreement prohibiting the commercial use of the films' contents without the written consent of the owning library. Thus, the library would have one of its collections filmed at no cost to the institution, it would get two copies, it would make a small profit (though mostly the fees charged just covered the library's costs), and it would be able to maintain some control over the texts or images that were filmed. The library could not,

of course, prevent the borrower from making his own copy of the film, but there was some protection over the unauthorized use of it.

7. Until extensive changes and additions are made to the copyright law relative to digital materials, the library must assume that a text made available digitally is no longer under the library's control. Just policing the world for unauthorized use of materials is daunting. Litigating for the same reason is practically futile, unless you are the Disney Corporation, which has a stranglehold over its copyrighted texts and images, characters and products.

8. See Reviel Netz and William Noel, *The Archimedes Codex: Revealing the Secrets of the World's Greatest Palimpsest* (London: Weidenfeld & Nicholson, 2007). Also see Reviel Netz, William Noel, Nigel Wilson, and Natalie Tchernetska, eds., *The Archimedes Palimpsest*, Vol. 1 (Cambridge: Cambridge University Press, 2011); and Vol. 2 (Cambridge: Cambridge University Press, 2011). The volume in question contains seven treatises by Archimedes, including two unique texts, *Method* and *Stomachion*, and the only known Greek version of *Floating Bodies*, along with other texts.

9. Susan M. Allen, "Rare Books and the College Library: Current Practices in Marrying Undergraduates to Special Collections," *Rare Books & Manuscripts Librarianship* 13.2 (Spring 1999): 110–19; this statement is on pp. 110–11 (http://rbm.acrl .org/content/rbml/13/2/110.full.pdf + html).

10. Sidney F. Huttner, "Waving Not Drowning: Rare Books in a Digital Age," *Rare Books & Manuscripts Librarianship* 13.2 (Spring 1999): 97–108; this statement is on pp. 100–101 (http://rbm.acrl.org/ content/rbml/13/2/97.full.pdf + html).

11. The word *then* refers to 1987, with the publication of my article "'What Is So Rare . . . : Issues in Rare Books and Special Collections," *Library Trends* 36.1 (Summer 1987): 9–22.

12. Michèle V. Cloonan and Sidney Berger, "Present and Future Issues for Special Collections," *Rare Books & Manuscripts Librarianship* 13.2 (Spring 1999): 89–94; this statement is on p. 89 (http://rbm.acrl.org/ content/rbml/13/2/89.full.pdf + html).

13. See Merrilee Proffitt and Jennifer Schaffner, "The Impact of Digitizing Special Collections on Teaching and Scholarship: Reflections on a Symposium about Digitization and the Humanities" (www.oclc.org/ resources/research/publications/library/2008/ 2008-04.pdf). This piece was published as an online essay; it is a publication of OCLC Programs and Research (Dublin, OH: OCLC, July 2008), and it is

paginated, which is reflected in the parenthetical citations in this text.

14. Three speakers presented case studies of how interinstitutional cooperation, through the sharing, building, and merging of databases, created exciting new resources for scholars. Richard Saloman's talk was on "Collaboration to Build Cross-Institutional Collections: Ancient Scrolls and Stone Tablets"; Katherine Skinner presented a talk on "MetaArchive Cooperative: A Collaborative Model for Digital Preservation"; and Will Noel spoke on "Lessons from Two Inter-Institutional Projects: The Islamic Digital Resources Project at the Walters Art Museum and the Archimedes Palimpsest Project" (see note 8 for citation).

15. See Anne R. Kenney, "The Collaborative Imperative: Special Collections in the Digital Age," *Research Library Issues: A Bimonthly Report from ARL, CNI, and SPARC* 267 (December 2009): 20–29, www.arl.org/publications-resources and www.arl.org/storage/documents/publications/mm09kenney-remarks.pdf. ARL is the Association of Research Libraries; CNI is the Coalition for Networked Information; SPARC is the Scholarly Publishing and Academic Resources Coalition.

16. Kenney is referring to the conference "An Age of Discovery: Distinctive Collections in the Digital Age," cited in note 1; this passage is on p. 20.

17. See the Kenney piece, referred to in note 15. The bulk of this article is a commentary on each of these nine principles, followed by a discussion of the implications of these large digitization projects.

18. A recent term for the pooling of many people's input into a final product is *crowdsourcing*, a term "coined by Jeff Howe in a June 2006 *Wired* magazine article [vol. 14, no. 6] 'The Rise of Crowdsourcing'" (qtd. from "Crowdsourcing," Wikipedia, http://en.wikipedia.org/wiki/Crowdsourcing#History). Wikipedia itself is a good example of the phenomenon. And as the history of Wikipedia has shown, materials drawn from many contributors must be carefully monitored and vetted for accuracy.

19. See the Raine and Stalker article cited in note 3. These scholars were writing about the need to maintain certain standards in the content and styling of cataloging records for rare books and special collections, across various cataloging systems. Such issues are much less on the minds of rare book catalogers today.

20. Art Museum Libraries Symposium, held at the Phillips Library, Peabody Essex Museum, September 23–24, 2010. Proceedings are online at www.pem.org/aux/pdf/library/AMLS2010.pdf. Hereafter referred to in the text as the "PEM symposium," and in parenthetical citations as "PEM." The online presentation of the proceedings shows the text in pages; hence citations to the online text give page numbers. The proceedings of the second Art Museum Libraries Symposium (September 21–22, 2012) are also at the PEM site.

21. Rose Sherman's talk, now online at the PEM symposium site (see note 20), is titled "Cultivating Wild Rice: How the Minnesota Historical Society Cultivates Data Unity" (pp. 23–26).

22. Elizabeth O'Keefe says, "Integration fosters serendipity and leads to more varied use of both collections, such as featuring library items in museum exhibitions or making museum items more accessible for hands-on study by researchers" (PEM symposium, p. 28). This piece contains much more about the possible impediments to data unity and some solutions.

23. This is not the place for a discussion of e-books (Amazon's Kindles, Nooks from Barnes & Noble, the Rocket eBook, the PRS-500 from Sony, Apple's iBooks, and others) and their place in rare book departments—if there is a place at all. The assumption here, as it is throughout the present text, is that traditional books and manuscripts and all the other things special collections departments hold will always be there, to be collected and used.

24. See "Digitization Projects: Key Issues for Archivists, Curators and Librarians," www.historicalvoices.org/papers/decide.pdf. Another site to consult is titled "Digitization," from Baylor University (www.baylor.edu/content/services/document.php/79806.pdf), which has a great deal of information and bibliographical references to informative online resources focusing on digitization of video and sound recordings. As this site reminds us, digitization is not just for "reading texts," it is also for audio and video files. Such materials often wind up in special collections departments.

25. The notes in the Wikipedia extract are to the following: 1: Digital Millennium Copyright Act, 112 Stat. 2863, 17 U.S. Code 1201-1205. 2: "Images and the Internet" (www.artistscope.com/protection.asp). 3: Christopher Levy (February 3, 2003), "Making Money with Streaming Media" (streamingmedia.com. Archived from the original on 2006-05-14. Retrieved 2006-08-28). 4: "DRM | Electronic Frontier Foundation" (https://www.eff.org/issues/drm, Eff.org. Retrieved 2012-01-07). 5a, b: "The DRM Graveyard: A Brief History of Digital Rights

Management in Music" (http://opensource.com/life/11/11/drm-graveyard-brief-history-digital-rights-management-music; at opensource.com. Retrieved 2012-01-07). 6a, b: "The Pros, Cons, and Future of DRM—Technology & Science—CBC News" (www.cbc.ca/news/technology/story/2009/08/06/tech-digital-locks-drm-tpm-rights-management-protection-measures-copyright-copy-protection.html. Cbc.ca. 2009-08-07. Retrieved 2012-01-07).

26. See "Digital Camera Use Policy," http://hcl.harvard.edu/libraries/houghton/digital_camera_policy.cfm. At the British Library (BL), no photography is allowed in its reading room, though some scanning is allowed. The library's reason is explained on a Q&A website:

> We are aware that there is a great deal of interest amongst our Readers in being able to use digital cameras in our Reading Rooms. However, this poses some significant issues for the Library in the areas of collection care and copyright. / Some material is difficult to photograph because of its size, format or condition and other items and media are very sensitive to damage from light or handling. While photography is generally considered to be preferable to photocopying, where an item is placed face-down, there are still risks to the collection if items are mis-handled. / Much of the National Archives' collection is unbound material and therefore different in terms of the copying issues presented. Also, a lot of their material is under crown copyright, making copying less restrictive. / We are, however, committed to finding a solution that is collection friendly, copyright compliant and what our readers want, so we have introduced self-help digital scanners in some Reading Rooms. We hope this will provide readers with the digital output required for research, whilst ensuring we meet collection care standards. The design of the scanners means we are able to open up more of the collection for copying and that some copyright issues will be addressed by the introduction of a faint BL water mark which appears on each scan. (www.bl.uk/aboutus/contact/previousfeedback.html)

This tactic shows that the BL understands the need for copying of its holdings, and this solution is a reasonable compromise.

27. This list comes from the New York Public Library Web page titled "Wireless Access and Laptop Docking at the Stephen A. Schwarzmann Building" (www.nypl.org/locations/tid/36/node/57920). The "Reading Room Rules" at the Rare Book & Manuscript Library at the University of Illinois, Urbana-Champaign include this statement: "Laptop computers are allowed in the Reading Room,

provided other users do not object to the noise they create" (www.library.illinois.edu/rbx/research_user_guide.html). This may be a wise addition to a special collections department's regulations.

28. RFID tags are excellent for inventory control in a commercial outlet in which items are sold; so the tag needs only a short life expectancy for it to be useful. Once the item is sold, the tag's function is gone. But for books, which will presumably be on the shelves indefinitely, an RFID tag with a short longevity (even up to forty years) will not be practical to use.

29. See Weimin Wei, "Estimation of Image Rotation Angle Using Interpolation-Related Spectral Signatures with Application to Blind Detection of Image Forgery," *Information Forensics and Security* 5.3 (September 2010): 507–17. To see an abstract for this article, enter "Weimin Wei" in IEEEXplore's search box (http://ieeexplore.ieee.org/Xplore/home.jsp).

30. B. L. Shivakumar and S. Santhosh Baboo, "Detecting Copy-Move Forgery in Digital Images: A Survey and Analysis of Current Methods," *Global Journal of Computer Science and Technology* 10.7 (Ver. 1.0, September 2010): 61–65; this statement is on p. 61 (651-644-1PB.pdf—Adobe Reader at computeresearch.org). The twenty-one references at the end of this essay lead to many more articles on the subject of forgery detection. The volume *Detecting Forgery: Forensic Investigation of Documents* by Joe Nickell (Lexington: University Press of Kentucky, 1996) may be useful to librarians, booksellers, and collectors dealing in documents. For serious scholars, the City University of New York's Fraud and Swindle Collection holds "2,200 books and original manuscripts chronicling frauds from the 6th century B.C. to the late 20th century." See Tatyana Gulko, "A Priceless Collection of Skulduggery" (www.cuny.edu/news/publications/salute-to-scholars/november09/skulduggery.html).

31. Madasu Hanmandlu et al., "Off-Line Signature Verification and Forgery Detection Using Fuzzy Modeling," *Pattern Recognition* 38.3 (March 2005): 341–56, www.sciencedirect.com/science/article/pii/S0031320304002717. The abstract to this article says,

> This paper proposes a novel approach to the problem of automatic off-line signature verification and forgery detection. The proposed approach is based on fuzzy modeling that employs the Takagi–Sugeno (TS) model. Signature verification and forgery detection are carried out using angle features extracted from a box approach. Each feature corresponds to a fuzzy

set. The features are fuzzified by an exponential membership function involved in the TS model, which is modified to include structural parameters. The structural parameters are devised to take account of possible variations due to handwriting styles and to reflect moods.

32. See Thomas A. Cahill, Bruce H. Kusko, and Richard N. Schwab, "Analyses of Inks and Papers in Historical Documents through External Beam PIXE Techniques," *Nuclear Instruments and Methods* 181 (1981): 205–8; and Richard N. Schwab, Thomas A. Cahill, Bruce H. Kusko, and Daniel L. Wick, "Cyclotron Analysis of the Ink in the 42-Line Bible," *The Papers of the Bibliographical Society of America* 77 (1983): 285–315.

33. The Wikipedia note is to "XML and Semantic Web W3C Standards Timeline" (2012-02-04), on the Web at www.dblab.ntua.gr/~bikakis/XMLSemanticWeb W3CTimeline.pdf.

34. "Resource Description Framework," Wikipedia, http://en.wikipedia.org/wiki/Resource_Description _Framework. The text of this article "was last modified on 10 July 2012."

35. See the Linking Open Data cloud diagram at http://lod-cloud.net.

36. This bizarre quotation comes from Nicholas Negroponte (http://web.media.mit.edu/~nicholas/Wired/WIRED4-02.html). The name he should have written is *Aldus Manutius*, the preferred form in serious writing. And when people refer to this printer, the standard way is to call him Aldus (and items from his press "Aldines"). I cannot imagine what that first sentence means or where the thought it expresses comes from. Negroponte was a professor at MIT and "co-founder and director of the MIT Media Laboratory" (see http://web.media.mit.edu/~nicholas).

37. Clifford Lynch refers the reader to his article "Repatriation, Reconstruction, and Cultural Diplomacy in the Digital World," *EDUCAUSE Review* 43.1 (January/February 2008): 70–71.

38. The *Codex Sinaiticus* website says,

> Codex Sinaiticus is one of the most important books in the world. Handwritten well over 1600 years ago, the manuscript contains the Christian Bible in Greek, including the oldest complete copy of the New Testament. Its heavily corrected text is of outstanding importance for the history of the Bible and the manuscript—the oldest substantial book to survive Antiquity—is of supreme importance for the history of the book. (http://codexsinaiticus.org/en)

The site explains,

> The Codex Sinaiticus Project is an international collaboration to reunite the entire manuscript in digital form and make it accessible to a global audience for the first time. Drawing on the expertise of leading scholars, conservators and curators, the Project gives everyone the opportunity to connect directly with this famous manuscript.

An excellent treatment of this codex is that on Wikipedia, at http://en.wikipedia.org/wiki/Codex _Sinaiticus. See the bibliography at the end of this article for many scholarly sources.

39. The Wikipedia article "Interdisciplinarity" says,

> Since 1998 there has been an ascendancy in the value of the concept and practice of interdisciplinary research and teaching and a growth in the number of bachelor's degrees awarded at U.S. universities classified as multi- or interdisciplinary studies. The number of interdisciplinary bachelor's degrees awarded annually rose from 7,000 in 1973 to 30,000 a year by 2005 according to data from the National Center of Educational Statistics. (http://en.wikipedia.org/wiki/Interdisciplinarity)

The "Further Reading" and "External Links" sections of this Wikipedia article show how interdisciplinarity is growing: the field now has journals and symposia devoted to it, academic programs and study centers have been developed focusing on it, and a growing number of articles are emerging about it.

40. EAD, Encoded Archival Description, is a method of cataloging nonbook materials equivalent to the MARC records used for bibliographic materials. The Wikipedia article on EAD states, "Such a standard enables archives, museums, libraries, and manuscript repositories to list and describe their holdings in a manner that would be machine-readable and therefore easy to search, maintain, exchange" (http://en.wikipedia.org/wiki/Encoded_Archival_Description).

41. Richard Wendorf, "Predictions and Provocations," in "Rare Book and Manuscript Libraries in the Twenty-First Century: An International Symposium," Part I, *Harvard Library Bulletin* 4.1 (Summer 1993): 9–13; this statement is on p. 9.

42. In the symposium referred to in the previous note, bookseller William S. Reese knew in 1993 what we still know now: "The costs of keeping the doors open, much less adding new material to library collections, have skyrocketed far beyond inflation." See Reese, "Fighting over the Scraps: Icon and Text in the Marketplace," in "Rare Book and Manuscript Libraries

in the Twenty-First Century: An International Symposium," Part II, *Harvard Library Bulletin* 4.2 (Summer 1993): 81–86; this statement is on p. 83.

43. The University Library at the University of Illinois, Urbana-Champaign, lists fifteen articles on assessment between 1990 and 2000 and another five between 2001 and 2010 (see www.library.illinois.edu/assessment/assessbib.html#bib90). It is telling that on the "Library Assessment @ Illinois" site there is a link to a page titled "Current Assessment Projects" (see www.library.illinois.edu/assessment/currentprojects.html#libwide), listing projects in the following areas: "Library-Wide Assessment," "Reference Services Assessment," and "Web Usability Studies," but nothing on special collections, though this library has a superb rare book department that carries out a host of important activities. Similarly, the University Libraries at the University of Washington (in St. Louis) lists its own assessment projects, in areas such as circulation and gate-count statistics, publications and presentations, the Teaching & Learning Program, User Experience, and Strategic Planning, but nothing in special collections (see http://lib.washington.edu/assessment). Typical of many libraries, Duke University Libraries has a full assessment program, with its own Assessment Core Team, but it, too, lists not a thing on the assessment of special collections departments.

44. Christian Dupont, "Guest Editor's Note," *RBM: Rare Books and Manuscripts* (Fall 2012). This statement comes from the opening paragraph of this "Note," drawn, here, from an advance set of proofs sent to me by Dupont. Pagination of the final published version was not available at the time of publication. All other articles in this issue will be cited hereafter as being from the *RBM* volume. I am grateful to Christian Dupont for making a copy of this issue available to me long before its publication.

45. The Rare Books and Manuscripts Section of ACRL (the Association of College and Research Libraries, a division of ALA). See the Metrics and Assessment Task Force at www.rbms.info/committees/task_force/metrics_assessment. The charge for this group says,

> The RBMS Task Force on Metrics and Assessment is charged with examining current practices for gathering and reporting information to demonstrate the value and impact of special collections and archives. The Task Force will conduct a survey of the literature and establish relationships with groups working on similar issues such as ARL, SAA, etc.; consider both what activities warrant assessment and how to undertake the assessment of those activities; and identify needs

for best practices and guidelines that will enable more meaningful assessment of the spectrum of what we provide to our various constituencies.

46. The minutes of the June 23, 2012, meeting of the RBMS Taskforce on Metrics & Assessment (see www.rbms.info/committees/minutes/2012/metrics minutes12a.pdf) point out that assessment can be part of an advocacy program, proving the worth of special collections to the institution and to the world of scholarship beyond. Assessment is also an opportunity "for demonstrating value, for advancing the profession, and for ensuring we get proper credit for the work we do."

47. For this quotation, Conway and Proffitt cite the OCLC report *Taking Stock and Making Hay: Archival Collections Assessment* (Dublin, OH: OCLC Research, July 2011), available on the Internet at www.oclc.org/content/dam/research/publications/library/2011/2011-07.pdf.

48. See the Summit website at www.azlibrary.gov/azsummit. The Arizona collaboration brings together more than six hundred institutions.

49. See, in the *RBM* issue, Rachael Hu, "Methods to Tame the Madness: A Practitioner's Guide to User Assessment Techniques for Online Finding Aid and Website Design" (http://rbm.acrl.org/content/13/2/175.extract).

50. The Hu article contains a useful overview of various kinds of assessment for delivering information online. Her conclusion is important:

> Given the rate that new technologies, devices, and applications are being built, we should expect that user behavior, preference, and expectation will likewise change over similarly brief intervals of time. Today's finding aid design or object display tool may not meet future needs. To stay on top of these sometimes small and sometimes dramatic shifts in user habits, a continual flow of small-scale assessment activities can be usefully maintained to monitor this progression and help archivists [and special collections librarians] ensure that the means of assessing their primary source materials remains relevant to their user communities.

51. See Sarah M. Pritchard, "Afterword: Special Collections and Assessing the Value of Academic Libraries" (see the citation to this issue of *RBM* in note 44).

52. In the library world—generally pertaining to the larger library—there is Bibliographic Instruction (BI), almost a discipline of its own. "Its goal is to teach users how to search, evaluate, and use information and how to use the library effectively

and independently" (see "Bibliographic Instruction," an ALA website at http://wikis.ala.org/professional tips/index.php?title = Bibliographic_Instruction). This site says of BI:

> All the activities involved in teaching users how to make the best possible use of library resources, services, and facilities, including formal and informal instruction delivered by a librarian or other staff member one-on-one or in a group. Also includes online tutorials, audiovisual materials, and printed guides and pathfinders.

A streamlined and focused form of BI should be available to all users of special collections departments, offered primarily by the reference staff but also by anyone else in the department who is an expert on particular collections or department holdings.

53. See www.rbms.info/rbms_manual/standing _committees.shtml#exhcat. The committee was originally organized under the title Exhibition Catalog Awards Committee, dropping the word "Catalog" in 2001. For a brief history of this committee, see www.rbms.info/committees/ exhibition_awards/first_ten_years/about-the -awards.html.

54. The original name of the committee spelled the word "Catalogue"; this was changed to the ALA-preferred version, "Catalog," in 2001.

55. Werner Gundersheimer, "Against the Grain," *RBM* 1.1 (March 2000): 14–26; this statement is on p. 16 (http://rbm.acrl.org/content/1/1/14 .full.pdf + html).

CHAPTER 14

OTHER ISSUES

HE WORLD OF RARE BOOKS AND SPECIAL COLLECTIONS IS highly complex, as all the chapters up to now have shown. Likewise, as the many sources cited thus far indicate, the literature of this world is extensive. A number of issues exist pertaining to special collections that have not hitherto been dealt with here. The present chapter takes up some of these.

Nonbook Collection Items

This book has made it clear from the opening chapter that books and manuscripts are not the only things in rare book departments. Two special categories of holdings merit separate discussion: ephemera and scrapbooks.

EPHEMERA, AND EPHEMERA FOUND IN BOOKS, MANUSCRIPTS, AND ARCHIVAL COLLECTIONS

There is a huge range of items that fall under the rubric "ephemera."[1] As the word indicates, ephemera are things created to last only a short time.[2] Under this rubric are hundreds of kinds of things that were expected by their makers to be discarded after use and that may wind up in special collections: labels, tickets of all kinds (e.g., for sports events, concerts, transportation, and circuses), matchbook covers, handbills, watch papers,[3] train schedules, greeting cards, postcards, newspapers, "Wanted" posters and other broadsides, packaging (e.g., for cigarettes, foods, household goods, and office supplies), blotters, trade cards, dance cards, baseball cards, napkins, paper placemats, certificates, and endless other items. Most of these carry words or images, or both, and they can be in unusual shapes and made from unusual materials.

As products of designers, commercial and non-commercial companies, artists, printers, and others, these items are part of the historical record of culture, and they have been serious targets of collectors since their appearance. They carry information of all kinds and are clearly appropriate additions to special collections; in fact, they embody the very phrase "special collection." Hence, endless ephemera collections reside in rare book departments everywhere. They can be excellent sources of information about products, transportation, people, politics, sociological or historical phenomena, printing, inks, graphic arts, hoaxes, and much more; but they can also be problematical. Many such collections are glued into acidic, crumbling scrapbooks. They are, themselves, often on deteriorating paper or have damaging adhesives on them. They can be voluminous, taking up a good deal of precious shelf space. They might require costly conservation treatments or time- and supplies-consuming rehousing. And to be accessible, they must be cataloged; creating cataloging records or finding aids for these collections can be costly. But they can also be quite attractive and be made the subject matter of exhibitions themselves or enhance displays of other materials.

Large caches of ephemera are often amassed by passionate collectors who understand their beauty, importance, and potential use. Most special collec-

---

I HAVE WORKED for decades in special collections, dealing with just about everything one could imagine. The obvious things, covered in the present volume, reveal the breadth of experience that rare book librarians should have—or that they acquire—in the day-to-day operations of the department. But the bizarre, the unusual, the unexpected occur, often things for which there is no precedent in anyone's experience, or at least in the literature of the field. Then the librarian must improvise, call a colleague for advice or discussion, perhaps consult the institution's counsel, or just come up with a path of action that seems best under the circumstances.

For instance, at one institution a librarian decades ago made a verbal agreement with a prominent scholar to take on deposit a collection of books and periodicals, manuscripts and field notes in a field that was once germane to that institution's interests. The institution, however, evolved and no longer collects in this area. The large collection (over 125 cartons) was stored in a basement of a house that the institution owns.

The dank conditions left all the cartons musty, and during a storm about twenty of them got soaked and were promptly moved to a freezer at the facility of a nearby vendor. The cost of storing the frozen boxes was being paid for from the library budget, even though the books and manuscripts were the property of the depositor. The scholar offered to give the collection in its entirety to the institution. Two scholars at the institution wanted to take the entire collection. This carried a good deal of weight in the librarian's decision making. The collection as a whole needed to be fumigated; twenty cartons needed to be freeze-dried; the whole collection needed to be cleaned; and then it all needed to be cataloged and processed. The donor had no money to help with any of these expensive procedures.

Perhaps others have encountered similar scenarios, but soliciting opinions about this would be useless. The circumstances were so idiosyncratic to the donor and the institution that it would be practically impossible to get advice from someone outside the institution. Some would say,

"Reject it all." But the two scholars eagerly wanted this collection, and the librarian understood their position and felt he must honor it. Some would say, "Take it all." But this does not address the ongoing costs of such a decision. Trying to raise money to cover some of the costs could take years, and there is no guarantee that enough could be raised to cover the substantial expenses of accepting, cleaning, and processing this collection. Every department will encounter its own peculiar situations, each of which will require its own unique handling.*

*In the present volume, in chapter 6, "Fund-raising," note 5 lists six reasons for not taking gifts. In the scenario painted in this sidebar, two criteria are germane: financial and space considerations make it unwise to take this collection. However, sometimes the circumstances warrant overriding these considerations. Strong support by the curators or the administration may make it necessary (and desirable) to take the collection. In some circumstances a donor could also be a wealthy patron of the institution, and taking the collection could be a good strategy in the long run.

tions holdings of ephemera were the brainchildren of individuals who gathered the pieces and created the collections in the first place, and then they (or their heirs) gave or sold the gathering to a special collections department. Their existence in the rare book world is important enough that *RBM* published a whole issue on this topic.[4] The article by Michael Twyman is an excellent justification for bringing ephemera into special collections departments.[5] His concluding paragraph has this statement:

> More significantly, if we want to catch the spirit of a period or flesh out the details of a particular occasion or situation, ephemera provide evidence of a kind not often found in other categories of documents. And if we seek to characterize the attitudes of a particular age and the nature of its language, it would be most unwise to exclude ephemera. What is more, our understanding of both graphic design and printing technology would be grossly incomplete if we took no account of the vast range of printed ephemera that has served society over the last few hundred years. (p. 57)

Clearly, ephemera have an important place in a special collections department.

Another issue is that many an ephemeris winds up in the pages of books, in family and other gatherings of papers, and in archival collections of various kinds.[6] Common are newspaper clippings, often containing information on a subject related to the materials they are found among. Other kinds of related things are book reviews, bookmarks, and pressed leaves (which can leave fairly intrusive acid stains on anything they touch—stains that can bleed through to other sheets as well). But not all ephemera in books are related to the books they are in.

Even if the piece has nothing at all to do with the book or papers, it is clearly a part of the book's or collection's history, and its presence may well be recorded in a cataloging entry, if the item could in any way shed light on the collection it was found in or the person or people who once owned the collection. An advertisement, clipped from an old newspaper, for a steamship excursion could say much about the book's former owner. A bookmark with an advertisement on it could reveal where a book

was acquired or where the book's owner had traveled. A photograph could show a relative of the book's owner and could lead to revealing research. Some ephemera may be immediately useful, like a prospectus or other kind of advertising piece for the book, a personal letter found in a manuscript of a literary text, or a receipt for travel of the book's former owner.

For the general collection, such ephemera will probably be discarded, partly because they could damage the book they are embedded in, partly because they often serve no purpose to the general reader, and partly because they would be too costly to preserve and catalog. They would be jettisoned in the same way as are dust jackets, which, themselves, have more of a claim to be retained than do ephemera found in books (see chapter 4 for a discussion of book jackets). And for rare book and special collections departments, it may make sense to toss out the ephemeris. But for the librarian, bookseller, collector, or archivist, ephemera could add significantly to the information the book contains, and great care should be exercised before the piece is thrown away. If the piece is retained, as just said, it should be part of the cataloging record, and it should be either kept with the book or kept apart in a place where it is as retrievable as is the book or manuscript. Either way, it should be housed in an enclosure that segregates it from its host, purely for preservation reasons. If it is removed to a different location, the cataloger may wish to put a note into the online record and possibly into the volume itself indicating that "an ephemeris has been removed from this volume and is available at ___."

Booksellers and collectors, likewise, may wish to keep the ephemera associated with the collections they have. Ephemera can reveal provenance information, which can be useful and actually increase the value of a book, fiscally and informationally. Also, many genres of ephemera can be beautiful (like postcards, advertising pieces, greeting cards, labels, and others), and they might make excellent additions to exhibitions.

The librarian should think of all the ways the ephemera may impart information and should save any piece that could be useful to someone. Even an ephemeris on a topic completely alien to the library's collection plan may be kept because of its design, shape, or printing, or because its illustration makes it a candidate for an exhibition. (There can even be a whole exhibition titled "Things Found in Books.")[7]

SCRAPBOOKS

Other nonbook collection items are actually in book form: scrapbooks. They deserve a separate discussion.

Special collections departments are likely to contain scrapbooks of many kinds. My own institution has them in abundance with the typical paste-ins: newspaper clippings, leaves and ferns, photographs, recipes, poems, trade cards, travel brochures, menus, correspondence, and so on. We also have scrapbooks containing cloth samples, coins, rocks, and other seriously three-dimensional objects.

Typically these items started out as generic blank books, produced in the millions in the nineteenth century when the craze for such collections was forming. The Wikipedia article "Scrapbooking" (en.wikipedia.org/wiki/Scrapbooking) traces the phenomenon to the compilation of commonplace books in the fifteenth century. There is also the *album amicorum* that was akin to our autograph albums. (See "Album Amicorum: Gems of Friendship in a Frightened World," www.palaceofthegovernors.org/album/articles.htm.)

The publishers of these blank albums (actually not "publishers" since there was no text) made them quite beautiful, often with artistic and elaborate bindings, but made from shoddy materials—as the existence of thousands of these that are crumbling will attest. Many scrapbooks contain treasures (including the ephemera just discussed), and in a way they themselves are "hidden collections," often with great research value. They are worth keeping, of course, but getting to the information they contain can be a challenge, and preserving and conserving them can be costly.

My aim here is not an expatiation on scrapbooks. It is more to present a few observations for people in the rare book world. Scrapbooks, like manuscript and archival collections, should be kept in the original order in which they were assembled, if possi-

ble, and if that order makes sense. But since many of them are falling apart, they should be conserved in the most practical way possible, which could mean the most economical way. This might mean disassembling the original and rehousing the pieces, in which case putting them in the most logical order is acceptable, just so long as there is a record of the original order of the contents of the album. The albums themselves, while once beautiful, could be in shambles. But they are a record of the artistry of the period they were made in, and perhaps, if space and resources allow, the covers should be saved.

The contents of the books should be assessed for the value they have for research, and finding aids should be created for them, with records indicating as extensively as possible what the albums contain.

Protocols

Although the running of a rare book / special collections department entails all kinds of policies and procedures, some often-unwritten practices must be observed, some of them quite obvious (the librarian does not leave patrons in the reading room unsupervised; junior—or even senior—staff should not reach out to potential donors without going through the proper chain of command and reporting structures of the institution). Some of the observations here are not strictly applicable only to special collections; they are commonsense advice for any department in the library, or even beyond it. But observation has shown that younger personnel may need this advice because common sense does not always play into the thinking of those new to the profession.

SENDING OUT DEEDS OF GIFT (OR DEEDS OF DEPOSIT)

A standard practice for a rare book department is to have a Deed of Gift signed by the donor(s) when an item is given. (See appendix 6, "Department Forms.") If the transaction is done by post (with the book[s] or manuscript[s] shipped into the department), the deed should be sent out to the donor in duplicate, with both copies unsigned. The donor should sign both and send them back to the department; then the department head (or whoever is designated to sign the deed) signs one copy and returns it to the donor. One employee, thinking he was saving a lot of time, sent two copies of the deed to the donors, and signed them both before they were sent. His thought was that there would be no need, then, to receive the donor-signed copy, sign it in-house, and send the fully endorsed contract back to the donor.

The donor needs a fully signed document for tax purposes. If he gets the two copies signed by the librarian, he now has all he needs for his taxes, and he has no incentive to send the two back for the final (librarian's) signature. The only way he can be forced to get a copy signed by the librarian is to send him, originally, unsigned ones. Some young staff members will not have thought this out, so they should be advised of the proper protocols for signing deeds.

ADMINISTRATIVE/FISCAL OVERSIGHT

Two basic documents, one mandatory, the other optional, are the responsibility of the head of special collections. The department is expensive to run. How much each library department is allotted depends on its demonstrated needs. The "demonstration" is shown in its budget. At the end of a fiscal year, the department has accomplishments. How (or whether) it records these accomplishments depends on several factors. These two activities—creating budgets and writing annual reports—are part of the department head's oversight responsibilities.

Budgets

The bottom line for all library activities is *resources*. The more you have of them, the more you can do, get, and share. And as mentioned in chapter 6 on fund-raising (and elsewhere in this book), a special collections department cannot have too much money. The budget should, of course, have all the standard lines: personnel, supplies and equipment, hospitality, dues and subscriptions, staff development, transportation, postage, and so on. But nowadays it should be incorporating new lines, as mentioned earlier in this text: digital initiatives, online databases, computer and other technology upgrades in hardware and software, possibly new positions in the department for IT personnel, web design, blog

and Facebook managers, and so forth. If they are not figured into the department's budget directly, the librarian should liaise with those in the institution who handle these things.

There are various kinds of budgets (lump-sum, line or line-item, formula, zero-based, and so forth). The librarian must be conversant with the one(s) used by her institution, and she must check where her expenditures are throughout the fiscal calendar. It is important for the librarian to know how much money is left in each line item of the budget as the fiscal year progresses.

Budgets submitted at the beginning of a fiscal year must be in line with the needs and goals of the institution and its ability to allocate. Reforecasts in midyear must take into account the likelihood of shortfalls or abundances. That is, if there is likely to be a shortfall in one line of the budget, the librarian must either shift to a lower gear in spending in that line, or try to work with the chief finance officer and other superiors to make up the difference. And if there is going to be money left over in one line, this should be dealt with carefully. It is probably better to return some money to the institution than to try to spend out the extra amount on things the department could well do without. (Some institutions may not let money from one budget line be used for another line of expenditure.)

The present text does not look too deeply into budgets because each department will have its own levels of funding, external and internal pressures, institutional policies and procedures, kinds of patrons with their various kinds of needs, and so on. But a few general statements may be useful. First, because the ultimate goal for the library is serving its patrons, linking them with the information they need, all budget decisions must be made with this in mind. Second, the department head must work out whether to advocate for more staff, more acquisition resources, more space, more technology and supplies, more staff development funds, more resources for conservation and preservation, or a combination of these. All of these cost money, and achieving a good balance of expenditures can be a challenge, especially in tight economic times (which seems to be always).

Some areas of library operations can be relatively invisible, especially those having to do with the infrastructure of the library building. Many a librarian goes about his business without doing a careful check of the collection and the building—as physical phenomena. Chapter 12 notes the importance of building and collection checks as part of a larger preservation program. It is easy to walk up the aisles and glance at the books, not taking much heed of the building itself. This is a form of benign neglect, for deterioration that a close scrutiny would reveal could be taking place. Deferred maintenance can lead to serious deterioration. Short-term maintenance could be done to stop cracks from becoming falling ceilings; early detection could stop a pest infestation or a dripping pipe from ruining shelves of books. Spotting crumbling mortar can lead to relatively inexpensive repointing of bricks rather than to a major refacing of a building. Early detection of defective caulking could prevent windows from falling out in a storm. All of this is a budgetary issue. The message here is that such building and collection surveys should be done regularly—maybe once every seven to ten years—and the librarian preparing a department budget must keep these things in mind. So budgeting is not only for the regular, ongoing expenses; it is also for the extraordinary activities that must be done to protect the collections. This kind of structural work—repairs in the building—usually is not figured into the special collections budget, but damage to the collection itself (caused by structural problems) must be figured into the department's expenditures, in its line for conservation.

The library world has seen innumerable instances of department cuts, especially in tight times. The special collections librarian may wish to negotiate where these cuts will take place. The first place administrators look for money-saving is in personnel, the most expensive part of running the department. But this is severely shortsighted because there is a paucity of truly qualified rare book librarians, and letting them go to save money in bad times can have disastrous long-term fiscal effects. If the position is not redundant—if the department really needs the slot and if its services will be negatively affected by the loss of the position, to the detriment of the patrons—

JUST TODAY I had a long meeting with museum leaders on how the library should be thinking about its budget. A key issue was that the museum has recently hired two curators, each in an area new to the museum's collecting; the library has to decide, with its limited budget, whether to begin building collections in these areas, and if so, how. Or if the institution should look into the other local libraries with research resources that the curators can tap. If the decision is to build an internal collection, should the library seek external support from donors who are interested in the areas of the two curators' work, or should it try to carve out of its own budget enough money to put together a reasonable research collection? The latter is out of the question, because the present budget is thin enough that it cannot sustain massive expenditures in two new areas—and it would indeed take large amounts of money because the two areas have vast numbers of books and manuscripts available. So the library, it seems, must start out slowly, working closely with the curators, to find out what essential works must be acquired. The curators and the librarian may wish to work closely with development to work up a fund-raising campaign for acquisitions in these two new areas. A related issue is that the curators themselves will have some restricted purchasing power for items in their respective areas. Should they be asked to use some of their own resources on their own research materials? This type of situation may well apply to new faculty, who could have faculty research funds to help them in their own work. Where should the money come from to build new collections? Is there money at all? Additionally, who is to decide what books and manuscripts to buy? Should librarians do the bibliographical work to identify items that would make a good core collection in the new areas? Or should the new employees create the want list? What is the librarian's or the curators' (or faculty's) responsibility in creating new collections? All this must be worked out in budgetary terms.

the cost of future replacement to restore services and reputation will often be great, if these things can be restored at all. Also, a personnel line once lost is extremely difficult to get reinstated. There is the persistent and always possible stance, "See? You have now gotten along without this position for a year (or more), so you probably didn't need it in the first place." This kind of thinking can be deadly, for the administrators who make such statements are usually not those who can understand fully the nature of the loss. This has been stressed before in this book, but it is so pervasive and lurking that it is important for it to be reiterated in a discussion of budgeting. The librarian should hold as firm as possible in creating the budget with respect to staffing.

Another, related, budgeting question is this: Can work now being done by full-time permanent staff be outsourced? This again will be an attack on personnel in the budget, for outsourcing may solve short-term problems, but it will generally yield loss of staff. If any of these cost-cutting measures truly makes sense—that is, if reduction of staff is doable—then the department head should not fight for a position that can justifiably be eliminated.

Annual Reports

Not all special collections departments do annual reports. They take some time; they are not always glowing, showing off the department in the best light; and the parent institution may not ask for one (possibly because the leaders already have so much to read that they do not want to be bogged down by more). But a fairly successful special collections department may wish to do such a report to highlight its successes and activities through the year.

Too often all the department's activities are performed over such a long stretch of time that no one can see the department's accomplishments in the aggregate, laid out in a clear, concise document. Success begets success, and it often reveals to those who were "looking the other way" (or preoccupied with their own activities) that the rare book department has been active and productive, touching the lives of many and bringing some good honor to the institu-

tion. The annual report will show that the organization is getting its money's worth in supporting this department.

The author of the report—presumably the department head or his designee—must lay out the important, impressive statistics (number of students/faculty/staff/outside scholars served; number of volumes/manuscripts paged and used; number of publications emanating from the department's work by its own staff and by its patrons; number of books, manuscripts, and serials acquired; number of cataloging records and finding aids produced; number of research questions answered; and so forth), and it may also highlight some of the department's most important events and acquisitions of the year. There should be a statement about how much better these numbers were for this year than were the numbers from the previous period. If the institution appreciates active employees, the report may list the talks given by the staff, conferences or workshops they attended, classes or workshops they taught or participated in, and any other professional activities that make the department stand out. And the report may show the amount of money spent in acquisitions and how that figure is responsibly within the department's budget.

All this can be done in a few well laid out pages, with charts or a clearly delineated spreadsheet, and with simple declarative prose. No boasting necessary. The numbers will speak for themselves. Administrators will think well of such progress, such success, and will be favorably inclined to support the department in the future.

Of course, this report puts pressure on the librarian to do another the following year showing yet more progress. But that is a good incentive for the staff to continue to strive to better the department's numbers and its services. A well-written, carefully crafted annual report can be a boon to the department and to the institution, which may wish to use some of its data and prose in various kinds of outreach. The rare book department, as chapter 1 said, is often the jewel in the crown of the institution. The report makes that jewel glow.

STAFFING AND HUMAN RELATIONS CONCERNS

Special collections department staff need specialized training, as this book shows. Some of that training comes on the job. Hiring just the right person takes careful selection, working with human resources, and observing appropriate protocols. New employees, also, should observe professional protocols.

Personnel Selection and Training

The training of a special collections librarian has already been covered in chapter 1. The selection of personnel is closely related. In some departments, which at many academic institutions are severely short-staffed, interns and volunteers are necessary for the department to function properly. Or if a department is allowed to add staff, the department head must naturally figure out exactly what services the department needs the most and create a position that suits those needs best. So writing a good job description is essential. Depending on the level of resources made available, and on the needs of the department, the new position can be anywhere from an entry to an advanced level. The higher on the hierarchy the position, the more training and expertise the job description must delineate. It must, of course, list the standard traits of "self-starter," "communicates clearly," "works well individually and on a team," and so on. And for many library positions (and even those for booksellers), there may be a requirement like, "Must be able to lift fifty-pound cartons." Although this might look discriminatory, and candidates who cannot meet this requisite may be dropped from the candidate pool, it is perfectly legal because the job absolutely requires the ability to work with lots of materials, often kept in cartons that can be quite heavy. As for the entry-level positions, the successful candidate should, if possible, have available for her use staff development funds.

Inasmuch as personnel selection and staff training are idiosyncratically linked to individual institutions, in terms of what each position requires and what each institution's personnel practices are, only a few other general observations are in order here. One phrase in the job description might be, "and other tasks as necessary," or something that allows the flexibility to require the worker to do things not clearly spelled out otherwise. Impartiality should be the governing attitude in hiring. Too often a known quantity (someone who has volunteered and has become friendly to the staff, for instance, or a close friend of an employee) gets the strong backing of that staff, when an outside candidate has better qualifications. Someone heading a special collections department presumably has more experience with staffing than do those working for her. She should

I HAVE OBSERVED, at one institution, two separate hiring situations, the first of which, bringing in an old friend of one of the senior staff, turned out to be disastrous, and the second of which, when the department head made a decision that countered the wishes of the staff, turned out to be tremendously beneficial to the department. In the first instance, when the two finalists came out even in the rankings of the department head, she went with the predilections of the staff. In the second, the head had her own ranking, and though the two candidates were close, one was slightly better than the other, and that turned out to be the right decision. Once the staff got over their own disappointment, they saw what a superior worker the new employee was and embraced that decision. And to reiterate what the text says, in another library a volunteer had worked tirelessly and well and was considered a shoe-in for a position that opened up. But when all outside candidates were evaluated, one of them was clearly better than the volunteer. The staff had gotten close to the volunteer and were greatly appreciative of his efforts, and they almost uniformly voted for him. But the department head chose the outside candidate, and that person proved to be invaluable. Again, such decisions cannot be made on the basis of personal feelings or a sense of gratitude; they should be made dispassionately, with a view to the job description and how each applicant's skills satisfy the position's requirements.

make it clear, if the situation permits it, that the head of the department has the final say in the hiring of new staff. And the department head must have the courage of her convictions and go with the candidate she feels is best, despite the possible discontent that this might create in the staff. It could be a difficult decision, but the welfare of the department, the collection, the library, and the institution could be at stake, and that should be the deciding factor.

A final observation about personnel: Good ones are hard to find. As this text indicates, it takes a great deal of training and knowledge to be a fully competent special collections employee. Tom Horrocks, director of special collections at the John Hay Library at Brown University, says, with respect to rare book library personnel,

> I can attest to the difficulty of finding qualified candidates. Archivists and manuscript librarians are relatively easy positions to fill, but not rare book catalogers or curators (subject specialists). Library programs are not turning them out. It's hard to find candidates who have subject expertise, language skills, and some special collections library experience in one package. (Personal communication to the author, January 18, 2013)

Graduate programs in library schools have so many required courses that students have little time to take classes beyond the core curriculum. When they do have time for an elective course, they are more likely to take a class in digital this or that than one in books as physical objects. Moreover, most schools do not offer any courses that might train a student in rare book librarianship. Those that do may have a course in the history of the book or rare book and special collections librarianship, but a mere two courses do not go far to prepare the student for the broad, specialized rare book world. (See more on this in chapter 1, on the training of the rare book / special collections librarian.)[8]

Hiring Staff

In the realm of adding personnel to a department, there is a standard practice that should be followed by everyone in the unit in which the hire is to be made. Although these practices may vary in some respects from institution to institution, some features of the entire process should be observed.

To begin with, the determination of whether to hire into the special collections department, though recognized by all who work in that unit, should be made ultimately by the director of that department. A lower-level employee should not be asking to be on a committee to draw up the job description (unless the job is in this person's area), nor should he be asking an administrator to add staff to the unit. Certain people should be charged with creating the job description. Others in the department may have opinions, but the proper people should be enlisted for this task. And the request should come from the department head, usually after some consultation with her superiors and usually in the form of a codified document created for adding personnel. Some employees want to be involved in everything, when it is often not their business.

During the screening of the applicants and the eventual interviewing, usually those in the area of the hire are involved, though, depending on the department's size and dynamics, all staff may be involved in interviews. Many variables here make this part of the process flexible, but unless they are specifically asked, staff outside the area of the hire may be excluded from the process and the decision. If they are, they may ask to be involved, but they should do so through the proper channels and not complain if they are still excluded.

Chains of Command

In all institutions there are chains of command. The standard protocol is that any employee needing advice or wanting to speak with an appropriate person about a situation should first approach her immediate supervisor before talking to someone else about the situation. Discussing the circumstances with anyone else is going outside the chain of command. There are, of course, instances when the employee has a complaint about the supervisor. If this is the case, the employee should consult with human resources. Again, this advice may seem so logical that it "goes without saying," but it needs to be said because many people do not know this.

Searching for and Moving to a New Job

Another bit of protocol that may seem obvious but is not for many inexperienced people is that if they are looking for new jobs, they should notify their supervisors. And if they get another job, they should give notice at least two weeks before they plan to leave—though an even longer notice is more professional. This is not a law or an absolute requirement, but it is a good practice. It takes time to refill a slot. Because the position needs to be filled, if the departing employee notifies a supervisor a day or two (or even as many as ten days) before departing for the new position, he leaves the library with a gap in the labor force that will take weeks to fill. For a number of reasons, the younger employee may wish his job seeking—and then his having been offered a new position—to be kept confidential. A supervisor must maintain that privacy. Further, the young job-seeker should notify his supervisor if he is offered another slot, before accepting the new offer.

DEVELOPMENT ACTIVITIES AND SOLICITING GIFTS

Some things, as just explained, may seem so obvious that they do not need to be written down and codified in a formal document. But because there is a good deal of innocence among people entering the profession, it may be well to delineate a few of the things that should be (or should not be) done in running the department. As mentioned earlier, the importance of protocol regarding potential donors must be stressed for all staff. The department can always use additional resources, so it may seem logical to a person new in the field to take every opportunity to raise money. One scenario, of innumerable ones possible, is that a new special collections librarian meets a wealthy scholar or potential patron in the library or a society person at a cocktail party. The person learns about the librarian's department and shows an interest in "helping out." The young librarian might initiate a relationship immediately and think

AN EMPLOYEE OF mine, about three years ago, silently sought other employment, never revealing her search to anyone in my library. She was offered a new position and told them that she would take it. She even signed a contract for the new job. Then she told her supervisor she was leaving at the end of the week. Her supervisor, who reported to me, came to my office, upset because she was losing a good employee, whose main complaint (that led her to look for another position) was that her salary was too low. We offered the young librarian an increase in her compensation, but it was too late. She was committed to the other position. (About eight months later we got a call from her asking if she could have her old job back. As I said, it was too late: we had already rehired into her position.) Her inexperience led to her unprofessional act, and it lost us the labor we would have gotten from one in her position while we went through all the gyrations of filling the slot. I explained to her in an exit interview (a phenomenon she was not expecting because she had never heard of such a thing) what she should have done. We learn from our mistakes; but our mistakes can have a bad impact on others. If she wants a recommendation later in her career, she will probably know not to ask us for one.

he is doing something praiseworthy if he soon solicits a gift for the department from this person. In reality, that potential donor may have already given to the parent organization, the library as a whole, or to the campus itself. It may be that the institution presently has an ask out to that donor (or is contemplating one, with a whole carefully thought out campaign), or possibly that person has made it known that she does not want to be solicited, for whatever reason. A solicitation from the junior special collections staff person could be exactly the wrong maneuver. Or it could be the right one, but ill timed. Or it could be the right one, well timed, but carelessly carried out.

The standard protocol for all such solicitations is that the institution's development department must be involved, from the beginning of the "campaign" to the end. And that department's experts are probably the ones to make the solicitation. The point here is that there are many well-intentioned employees who are naïve about proper channels of operation and who operate out of ignorance, not malice or stupidity, though the results of their actions sometimes look as if they were operating on the basis of these last two characteristics.

I COULD FILL this sidebar with dozens of "cases" in which young employees in special collections departments, thinking they were doing good, blundered in their actions, their timing, or their technique. A prominent author, who wrote in a field that my department collected avidly (it was one of our level 5 collections), left his papers to another university. One of my employees, as soon as the bequest was publicized, and without any consultation with anyone, wrote to the family of the deceased author and asked if they would reconsider and give the collection to us. This raised a kerfuffle, and my institution had to do some pretty agile two-steps to undo the mess. The junior staffer had never been counseled in the protocols of such situations, and he thought he was doing a great thing in trying to get the author's papers for our department. His motives were OK; his method was abominable.

Special Topics in Rare Books

This section looks at several issues not covered elsewhere in this book. These "orphan" topics are part of rare book librarianship, and those in (or coming into) the field should be aware of them.

MARKS IN BOOKS

Collectors, librarians, and booksellers want their books to be in the best condition possible. Among other things, this means that they do not want any former reader to have marked up the books in any way. For a bookseller, this could mean that a valuable book loses a good portion of its monetary worth. Likewise, collectors do not want defiled copies in their collections. And the special collections librarian might bring a relatively valuable book into the rare book stacks from the open collection, but might

not do so if that same book's value has been compromised because of marginal notes, underlining, signatures on endleaves, or any other kind of marks that diminish the item's value.

On the other hand, if the marks are remarkable in any way, they could enhance the fiscal and intellectual value of books. For instance, if the marks are made by a famous person, the provenance of the book (as having been in that person's hands or library) could add significantly to the book's worth. As just noted, the value that is enhanced might be monetary, but it may also be intellectual: Sir Isaac Newton's annotations in an early book on astronomy or one of the other sciences might contain valuable information.

COINCIDENTALLY, JUST TODAY one of my staff pulled a seventeenth-century book from our shelves that contained Cotton Mather's and John Winthrop's signatures on the front pastedown and John Hancock's signature on the rear pastedown. The volume is a religious text, probably not worth much on the open market. But the signatures enhance its value significantly.

Roger Stoddard of Harvard University curated an exhibit with the same title as this section, "Marks in Books." In his exhibition catalog (with the same title), he says that anyone can leave marks: "printers, binders, booksellers, librarians, and collectors," along with scholars and anyone else who handled the objects. Stoddard makes it clear that all kinds of marks are "historical evidence" (p. 2)—from manuscript to printing phenomena—and they can reveal much about a book, its manufacture, its use, its owners, and so forth. He says that special collections librarians and catalogers, conservators, and anyone else handling books should be sensitive to "the preservation of material evidence in order to make possible a better understanding of the circumstances in which books have been produced, circulated, received, and used" (p. 2).

The point here is that all kinds of marks (and this includes the more obvious ones: bookmarks, bookplates, binders' tickets, coats of arms on end-sheets or covers, and so on) can be useful to scholars, and special collections libraries should maintain them with care, and not succumb to the impulse to "clean up" a book by removing them.[9]

FINE PRESS BOOKS

In chapter 2, in a sidebar, the phenomenon of the fine press book was discussed with respect to the librarian's duty in protecting vulnerable books that are in open stacks. Rare book librarians must, of course, be familiar with the idea of the fine press (also sometimes called the *private press*) because books from these publishers often belong in the special collections department.

A fine press is generally the operation of a single party (or a small group of people), not working in the commercial world. Though a good deal of profit can be made from some fine press books, profit is not usually the motive for the operation. There is no corporate body directing what the press must publish. And usually the books it produces are created in small numbers (fewer than two hundred, say—though sometimes more), and they are done with high-quality production values: fine paper, elegant types, generous margins, quality bindings (often done by hand), good illustrations, and so forth. They are often numbered and signed, by the author, illustrator, binder, printer, or someone else responsible for the final volume.

Because of the small numbers and high cost of production, and because these books are often original editions from good authors, they usually are fairly expensive when they are new, though their cost could be underwritten by an institution, which would bring the prices down. For instance, several universities have had their own fine presses, and their support of the master printer meant that she or he did not have to live off the sale of the books. Two well-known such printers were Harry Duncan (University of Iowa and then the University of Nebraska, Omaha, publishing under the imprints Cummington Press and Abattoir Editions) and Kim Merker (University of Iowa, publishing for himself as the Stone Wall Press and for the university under the imprint Windhover Press). Their

books were lovely and important (they published the first and later works of many great writers), and they were issued at quite low prices.

The rare book librarian with particular areas of department strengths—especially author or press collections—should be alert to the productions of fine presses. The books do not wind up in the warehouses of the major distributors, and they often contain significant literary texts worth collecting for their scholarly value (not to mention the aesthetic value of the volumes). If the department holdings are of an author at a level 5 collection, and if a book by that author is issued from a fine press, the librarian should acquire it as soon as it comes out, if it is affordable, because private press books often go out of print quickly. If it must be bought later from the rare book market, the price is likely to be higher than it was at its release. Also, many private presses offer discounts for standing-order customers, so the library with a standing order will automatically get the books the press puts out and will save money at the same time.

> **THE SPECIAL COLLECTIONS** Department at UC Riverside had a good book arts collection, so when I got there I subscribed to the publications of the Bird & Bull Press, which specialized in volumes almost all of which fell under the book arts rubric. We got the discount, and we got the books, almost all of which are original scholarship, well designed, on fine paper, in beautiful bindings. Many of the B&B titles go out of print quickly, so the standing order insured that the department got all the press's offerings.

Although most fine press books will be in the rare book stacks, some, because of their original price, may wind up in the open stacks. But as with many trade editions of books, over time the value of many private press books climbs to a level that qualifies them to be under the protection of the special collections department. The responsible librarian will check the online catalog by press and will bring into the department all such valuable volumes.

ARTISTS' BOOKS AND ALTERED BOOKS

The Wikipedia article on artists' books says,

> Artists' books are works of art realized in the form of a book. They are often published in small editions, though sometimes they are produced as one-of-a-kind objects referred to as "uniques."
>
> Artists' books have employed a wide range of forms, including scrolls, fold-outs, concertinas or loose items contained in a box as well as bound printed sheet. Artists have been active in printing and book production for centuries, but the artist's book is primarily a late 20th century form. (http://en.wikipedia.org/wiki/Artist%27s_book)

Because artists' books are essentially works of art, because they are produced in small numbers (many of them are unique), and because they have been fairly popular as collectors' items, their prices have been high ever since they have been produced, for at least a century. So they often wind up in special collections departments—because of their monetary value and scarcity, and because they are sometimes quite fragile. They play a part in the academic world. In English and other literature departments, art departments, and even in library schools, they are a topic of conversation. Many of them contain poetry—a fairly simple and common genre to print. In art departments students are often encouraged or required to make their own such books. And in library schools they are discussed under the larger topics of acquisitions and collection development. Also, they often play a part in the teaching mission of the school, it being common for art students studying a particular artist, printer, or illustration technique, those taking hands-on lab courses in the making of artists' books, and those studying the history of the book to be taken to the special collections department to study these volumes. They are useful, too, for students studying particular artistic movements—Avant-Garde, Futurism, Modernism, Dada, Surrealism, Post-Modernism, Fluxus—because artists prominent in these schools worked in the medium of books.

The Wikipedia article says,

> In the early 1970s the artist's book began to be recognized as a distinct genre, and with this recognition came the beginnings of critical appreciation of and debate on the subject. Institutions devoted to the study and teaching of the form were founded (The Center for Book Arts in New York, for example); library and art museum collections began to create new rubrics with which to classify and catalog artists' books and also actively began to expand their fledgling collections; new collections were founded (such as Franklin Furnace in New York); and numerous group exhibitions of artist's books were organized in Europe and America (notably one at Moore College of Art in Philadelphia in 1973, the catalog of which, according to Stefan Klima's *Artists Books: A Critical Survey of the Literature*, is the first place the term "Artist's Book" was used). Bookstores specializing in artists' books were founded, usually by artists, including Ecart in 1968 (Geneva), Other Books and So in 1973 (Amsterdam), Art Metropole in 1974 (Toronto) and Printed Matter in New York (1976). All of these also had publishing programmes over the years, and the latter two are still active today.

Some schools have large collections of these, especially those with book-arts programs or departments that study or support the work of women artists, or do both, because many of the book artists are women. The books can be beautiful, imaginatively produced, colorful, cleverly designed, and entertaining, and they may have important texts of great literary or artistic value. Also, though not a perfect generalization, they usually are made of high-quality materials and with painstaking care. They may have innovative bindings and creative page layouts, and many hand-done touches (colored illustrations, calligraphy, moveable parts, and such). And they might employ several kinds of printing: letterpress (with hand-set type), *pochoir*, lithography, wood or copperplate engraving, or original art in each volume.

For the present text, it is important that rare book librarians know about these volumes, for they must decide what place artists' books have in their collections. They can be expensive, so a curator must decide whether an artist's book is worth the expenditure, especially if there are other books that could be added to the collection for the money that would be spent on the artist's book. Their value, of course, is tied to the missions of the department and the institution, and if these volumes would get good use, they should remain high in the rare book department's ranking of the five levels of collecting.

> **ANECDOTALLY, SOME SPECIAL** collections departments that have traditionally collected artists' books are cutting back on these for two main reasons: the books are often quite costly, and unless the department has a special fund just for these rarities, it cannot often justify the expenditure; also, there is a diminishing return on the acquisition of artists' books because fewer and fewer faculty and students are using them. Two other complaints that I have heard from a few special collections librarians are (1) that some of these books are made with inferior materials (acidic papers, cloths and colored papers with evanescent and fugitive dyes, imaginative but fragile bindings, adhesives that are not alkaline or that dry out and can discolor the pages), so these become conservation nightmares; and (2) that many of them are huge, oddly shaped, exceptionally fragile, or, in other ways, difficult to store on traditional library shelves. Hence they take up a good deal of space—definitely a bad characteristic in a department in which space is at a premium. Although I have seen no literature on these complaints, I have heard that some departments will no longer invest in these books. What impact this might have on the production of artists' books is anyone's guess.

A subgenre of artists' books is altered books: volumes that were published under one title and in one form and then were altered in some way, usually by artists, changing the original volume from a serious publication in itself into an object with a whole new vision. The artists who alter books "delight in transforming existing images and texts into something entirely new. . . . Inspired by [British artist Tom Phillips's] work, artists are continually finding new ways to cover, cut, and change books. They turn them into anything from shrines to colorful images that have little or nothing to do with the books they started out as."[10]

Some of the alterations are minimal, some are quite extensive. Large sections of leaves can be glued together; extensive groups of leaves may be cut to form hollows in books; text may be written or pasted over; the binding can be reconfigured in many ways, with concomitant reconfiguring in the volume's innards; the artists can use black markers to cover over (or highlighters to mark) texts. New materials can be introduced into the original volume: plastic or metal tabs, strings and ribbons, or pieces of credit cards; photographs, paintings, or other kinds of illustrations can be tipped in or done right over the original text pages, for instance. The only limits to the alterations are the limits of the artist's imagination.

As with artists' books, there may be a place in a special collections department for these imaginative volumes, but they pose the same questions as do the books done by artists: Are they affordable? Will they be used? by whom? What can people learn from them? Will they need special conservation or handling, special enclosures or shelving? And, finally, is there a place for these in the department's collection?

CANVASSING BOOKS (SALESMEN'S DUMMIES)

In the mélange of topics of this chapter on "Other Issues," there must be a note on *canvassing books*, also called *salesmen's dummies* or *salesmen's sample books*, volumes that often find their way to special collections departments. In the nineteenth century and through the early decades of the twentieth, one popular form of bookselling, especially in rural areas where bookstores were scarce or nonexistent, was the practice of selling door to door. The canvasser (book salesman) would have a sample volume—not a complete text—showing briefly what the final published book would look like, but revealing a few pages from here and there in the dummy: a title page, a table of contents, text pages, leaves with illustrations, and so forth. The prospective buyer would see also what the binding would look like on the final published version; and some books were offered in two, three, or more binding styles that the potential buyer could choose, each shown in various ways on the sample book. For instance, the dummy might be in a turquoise cloth, but pasted into the volume inside the covers might be strips of red, blue, or green cloth, or even deluxe binding styles in leather or with extra gold stamping. The buyer could choose which he wanted to order.

This was a complex world of design, printing, binding, sales, and salesmanship. The customer would subscribe to the volume; the salesperson would take the order and write it into the lined sheets bound in at the end of the canvassing book, entering the name and address of the buyer, the kind of binding ordered, and the price paid; and the book would be delivered when it was in print.

> **IN MY OWN** collection is a salesman's dummy with a spine and title page indicating the name of the publisher; the final, published volume not only carries a different publisher's name but also has a different decoration on the cover. My dummy, as is fairly common, has a leaflet laid in giving the salesperson advice on how to make the sale. Sometimes this advice is printed on the endsheets of the dummy.

The volume ordered might not look exactly like the one eventually delivered. For example, the dummy might contain illustrations that do not wind up in the final, published version. Or it might show the transfer of the text from one publisher to another before publication (or the preference of a publishing house to release the book under a different imprint from its own main one).

Salesmen's dummies are mentioned here because they are fairly numerous, but they are becoming more and more scarce as there is now a collecting trend that is taking them from the market. They are not the kinds of things that wind up in circulating collections because they contain only quite small parts of the full texts. So they wind up in special collections departments as part of the publishing history of the title and as examples of volumes from an important chapter in bookselling history. Special collections librarians should be able to spot them, understand what they are, and help their patrons understand them, too. Presumably many of them

were composed before the final published volume was ready for distribution, so they may contain useful early versions of texts, before authors' corrections or changes were entered. Hence, they can be useful for the textual bibliographer studying the evolution of a text.[11]

Current Trends / Future Directions

As I mentioned in chapter 13, special collections librarianship is evolving (as is the entire rare book trade). Though librarians in this realm must practice many traditional tasks, they must also be aware of and open to the new trends, technologies, and practices.

COLLECTING LITERARY MANUSCRIPTS

One field of traditional special collections activity is the study of literary manuscripts.[12] In the past— in the analog world—scholars were possibly able to compare drafts of a writer's text, perhaps seeing the text's growth from an idea to a finished product. With the increasing use of computers, this kind of scholarship is slipping away. So literary manuscripts now must be studied in a different way because they are only digital. The challenge for the special collections librarian is how to acquire, organize, and create access to such texts to help the literary scholar.

As early as 1984, Anthony Rota made a strong case for collecting twentieth-century literary manuscripts, an area that until then was done haphazardly and with not much foresight or circumspection.[13] Since then, the area of collecting literary manuscripts has burgeoned, and what at one time could be bought for little now may cost vast sums. Rota discusses these questions: What, exactly, is a literary manuscript (for instance, is a typescript considered a "manuscript," especially when the author composed on the typewriter and did not even have a holograph copy? [see Rota, p. 46]), and how desirable is it?

For the present text, a few main issues emerge on this subject. First, what manuscripts should the library acquire? Ones that support the department's monograph collection? Ones that complement the department's level 5 collections? Ones that support the research done at the library? Only ones the library can afford? Ones of local authors? Ones of established writers or those of young writers who show promise? Ones of writers whom no one else is collecting?

Second, should the department acquire only the most important manuscripts of an author or should it try to collect comprehensively? Naturally, either way, the department should understand that this decision is a commitment to extraordinary expenditures if the subject of the collection is in vogue—that is, commanding high prices because of stiff competition. Such manuscripts tend to be expensive and could thus take a disproportionate amount from a department's budget.

In one sense, it is logical to collect comprehensively because scholars working on an author want to do all their research in one place, if possible. It would actually impede the smooth flow of scholarship to have an author's literary manuscripts dispersed in several repositories. If the bulk of a writer's manuscripts are in one institution and a second repository is offered another manuscript, it could be a disservice to researchers for the second collection to acquire the piece and force scholars to visit two places. Unless there is an overriding reason to collect the item, perhaps the second institution should not acquire it.

AN AUTHOR MAY have written a dozen novels, the manuscripts of most of which are at Library A, but a text of a novel he wrote that focuses on bees comes on the market and is offered to Library B, which has a collection of materials on bees. The manuscript would be well placed at either institution.

The questions posed here should be addressed by each special collections department contemplating collecting literary manuscripts. They are a serious commitment of funds, but they are also extremely valuable intellectual resources for scholars.

THE SPECIAL COLLECTIONS DEPARTMENT AS A TRENDSETTER

Libbie Rifkin says,

> [C]ollecting decisions affect not only the reception of contemporary literature by scholars and students, but also the conditions under which it is produced. In both abstract and quite concrete ways, *curating is a form of cultural production.*[14] (italics in the original)

Although Rifkin focuses on poetry, the points she makes can be seen in a wider context. Her main point is that if institutions are strong customers of a particular literature (that is, if they continue to build their collections in a particular area), this encourages those writing in that area to continue to produce. She says, "The literary history of the latter half of the twentieth century won't be complete until we begin to understand the roles, both economic and aesthetic, that institutional collectors have played" (p. 124).

Two phenomena are brought to mind relative to rare book librarianship—and also relative to bookselling and collecting. First, if libraries are the main consumers of a genre of literature or of a kind of book, they themselves are keeping the producers of those books "in business." What would happen if libraries stopped collecting artists' books? The artists would lose a major population of buyers. And the private collectors, then the main purchasers of artists' books, would not have any institution into which to place their collections. The artists would have no outlet for their work, and the genre could dry up. Similarly, with poetry, the number of private parties who collect volumes of verse is relatively small. Libraries, in trying to keep up with the poetry "scene," are the main buyers of books of verse. Publishers who are interested in making profits (and there are some for whom profit is not a motive) may stop publishing books of poetry if the institutional market dries up. So institutional purchases could be important to "keep the poets going."

The second phenomenon linking departmental buying to the promulgation of culture (and more directly related to special collections) is that many libraries like to collect the papers of important people: writers, politicians, Hollywood personalities, people famous in their fields (physicians, inventors, technology innovators, sports figures). By purchasing the collections of certain people, the library legitimizes them as important and worth archiving, worth creating finding aids for, and worth presenting to a scholarly world as significant and valuable to study. In other words, the librarian who goes after the papers of, say, a minor writer who has published one modestly successful novel and a few short stories elevates that person to a status of academic approval and, in effect, sets that person above others whose papers are not in any institutional collection.

> **A LIBRARIAN IN** the Midwest decided to go after the papers of a number of science fiction writers. No one else had approached these authors, and she was able to get the archives of a number of them. In fact, the larger the collection became, the easier it was to convince writers to contribute *their* papers. Was it playing on the egos of the sf authors? Was it a relatively inexpensive way to build up a collection of sf writers' papers? Or was it truly building an archive of important materials? Perhaps only time will reveal whether the writers whose papers are now in this archive are worth studying.

Authors' papers, traditionally in *paper* form, though increasingly in digital form, wind up in special collections departments. The departments are building the canon. A writer who is championed by scholars—experts who read the author's works and find them of high literary merit and worthy of study—will possibly legitimately be elevated to the level of literary dignitary. But a writer who is elevated to "important" because a librarian has decided she wants the writer's papers may not be worth such honors as being in the company of the papers of more famous, truly superb writers. It is what Rifkin calls "authorization by association" (p. 129)—the fame accruing to a minor writer whose papers are in a collection alongside those of great writers.

It should be added, of course, that the reputation of the institution holding authors' papers will influence the esteem in which those authors are held.

Papers at Yale, Harvard, Syracuse, the Harry Ransom Center, the Bancroft Library at Berkeley, Yale, Princeton, and other top-ranked institutions will probably be those of more prominent authors than will be the papers held at smaller, less prestigious schools' libraries.

The point for the present volume is that it should be in the purview of special collections librarians to keep alert for the papers of writers whose corpus of work aligns with the department's collections. That is, if a department has an important special collection of a minor writer, it would be prudent for the librarian to try to have that writer (or his heirs) place his papers in the department. This approach is especially wise when the collection targets local writers. A small special collections department in a school or private institution may wish to locate the archives of important local authors. The principle is simple: anyone wishing to study a particular writer is likely to go to that writer's home territory.

Special collections librarians should be aware of the kinds of opportunities they have to influence scholarship and to preserve the works of writers who may be worth studying and who may find no other repository that thinks it appropriate to collect their papers. So one key task for the librarian is to get to know local writers and those who are not local but whose writings are in the library's level 4 and 5 collecting areas and whose papers would be a perfect fit for the special collections department.

Because literary papers could be quite fiscally valuable, the librarian should be a strong voice, with an author, about the historical, literary, and scholarly value of the papers and should appeal to the author's desire for immortality in being represented to perpetuity in an important archive. Many authors are happy to have their papers saved, and their reputations firmed up, in such a permanent way, with the promise that scholars worldwide will be able to find out, with an Internet search, where those authors' manuscripts are located. And many a writer will be happy to donate her archive to an appreciative, responsibly run institution that promises to preserve, conserve, catalog, and reveal to the world the author's writings. (The same kind of inducements may work on heirs of deceased writers.)

But authors may wish to sell their papers (and if we look at how much money most authors make with their writings, we can understand their wish for *some* significant income for their efforts). The institution may be able to negotiate a congenial deal, or the author may wish to go through a bookseller or manuscript dealer to place the collection in the institution. The intricacies of such arrangements are beyond the interests of the present text. But here is where the special collections librarian's friendships with members of "the trade" can come in handy. In chapter 2, a discussion about dealing with dealers looked at how the natural alliance between special collections librarians and rare book dealers was important. In the case at hand, such a relationship is essential. Similarly, if an author collection is in the hands of a private collector (not the author of the materials), the alliance between the librarian and the collector could bring fruitful results.

AS A SPECIAL collections librarian at the University of California, Riverside, I got to know the daughter of a prominent local writer. She was in her eighties when we met, and over several years I visited her many times and called her for long phone conversations. I took her to dinner when I traveled to see her, and in general had a delightful time getting to know her and listening to all her fascinating stories about her family. She was wonderful, funny, insightful, quirky, and delightful. More to the point here, she understood from my visits that the archives of her father and mother fit into UCR's level 5 collecting because her father was an important figure in the literary, scholarly, and social scene of the area in the first half of the twentieth century. This friendship eventuated in her selling all the family archives to UCR, which today has the best collection in the world of this writer's papers and art. She was delighted to place her family archives in such an appropriate and congenial setting (and to realize some income from the papers), and we were happy to add significantly to the collection.

The conclusion to draw in this discussion about libraries as trendsetters is that librarians can set the trends by buying judiciously (and making their purchases known through good cataloging and finding-aid creation—these records mounted on the Web), and they can stimulate the creation of literature and other kinds of writing by actively seeking out materials in areas that are often marginalized or ignored by most institutions. For instance, most academic institutions marginalized and essentially ignored almost all science fiction and fantasy literature, assuming they were not serious areas of scholarly inquiry. But a few special collections departments went after them assiduously and now have significant collections to be studied as part of literary or popular culture departments. Without the foresight of a few keen librarians, dozens of thousands of sf and fantasy texts would be unavailable for inspection.

COLLECTING DIGITAL MATERIALS

As noted in chapter 2, an increasing number of reference tools are being created in only digital form. This is true, as well, for journals, which are generally leased to a library. In the past, scholars could access only the hard copies of journals or reference works. Now access to these sources is tremendously more convenient: a scholar need merely sit at a computer and bring up whatever is available in digital form. And several or dozens of readers can use a single source at once, rather than having to wait for a volume to be returned by a single reader. Also, digital resources do not take up shelf space, do not need to be moved if a shelf-shift must be done, and do not need to be repaired because no damage can befall them. The benefits of digital resources are clear. But who owns them? What if the provider ceases to exist? What if the cost of leasing them skyrockets beyond the capacity of the library to acquire them? Where are the back issues? Who can access information when the electronic links to them cease to be? Rare book departments grapple with all these questions, and a forward-looking librarian must have a policy on how to handle acquisition of digital materials and their potential loss.

Closely related is the new world of digital books. Special collections departments with subject or author collections will wish to have available for their patrons the texts that fit into their level 4 and 5 collections. How can these texts be preserved and made available?

These two issues (reference and serial publication and book publication) are closely related to funding. Although recent years have seen a diminution of funding for libraries—and therefore for rare book departments—the librarian must balance acquisition between analog and digital sources. This is not merely a case of diminished funding, it is a case of divided funding, for some resources must be allocated to digital materials. Such considerations should be finely tuned in the department's budget.

RARE BOOK AND SPECIAL COLLECTIONS LIBRARIANS AND DIGITAL REALITIES; "DIGITAL PRESERVATION"; DIGITAL HUMANITIES

Though the relation between the special collections librarian and the digital world has been hinted at (and even expatiated on in places) earlier in the present text, a separate note is in order here. Clearly there is a need for special collections personnel to be on top of library automation. They need to know about cataloging; the creation of finding aids of all kinds and their mounting on the Web; the creation of various kinds of databases; digitization in all its uses; the difference in handling between items that have been digitized and those that were born digital; the impact that digital materials are having in the handling of personal papers, archives, and other digital texts; the need to assess the practicality of acquiring digital rather than analog books and journals when both are available (as examined in the previous section above); and much more.

One example of the kinds of things a special collections librarian needs to understand in the digital world is the relationship between computer technology and preservation. In their article "Mapping the Preservation Landscape for the Twenty-First Century," Ross Harvey and Martha Mahard discuss the similarities and differences in the preservation needs of analog and digital materials.[15] They begin, "Information technology has had a profound effect on the preservation landscape at the beginning of the twenty-first century, blurring the traditional boundaries separating cultural heritage institutions and demanding new skills and approaches to the management of cultural assets, whether digital or analog." Their article explains what these new skills and approaches are, including trying to come up with ways to generate principles that work for all kinds of materials.

Social networking is leading to new forms of writing and reading literature. If literature is being created in new forms, how will it impact collection building in special collections? What might the fiscal impact be, especially in a world in which many social networking sites are producing texts that may well be housed in a special collection? And how can such acquisition and maintenance be carried out by present personnel? What skills must be available in a special collections department to seek out and capture the worthwhile texts?

In a wider application, there is a whole new field of digital humanities, challenging the library to link with a huge array of disciplines. The Wikipedia article says,

> The digital humanities are an area of research, teaching, and creation concerned with the intersection of computing and the disciplines of the humanities. Developing from the field of humanities computing, digital humanities embraces a variety of topics ranging from curating online collections to data mining large cultural data sets. Digital humanities currently incorporates both digitized and born-digital materials and combines the methodologies from the traditional humanities disciplines (such as history, philosophy, linguistics, literature, art, archaeology, music, and cultural studies), as well as social sciences,[1] with tools provided by computing (such as data visualisation, information retrieval, data mining, statistics, computational analysis) and digital publishing.

> Digital humanities scholars use computational methods either to answer existing research questions or to challenge existing theoretical paradigms, generating new questions and pioneering new approaches. One goal is to systematically integrate computer technology into the activities

of humanities scholars,[2] such as the use of text-analytic techniques; GIS; commons-based peer collaboration; interactive games and multimedia in the traditional arts and humanities disciplines [as] it is done in contemporary empirical social sciences.[16]

Special collections librarians, always wishing to increase use and to serve the widest clientele possible, should closely ally themselves to those at their institutions who are conversant with digital technology and to those who work in fields that overlap with their own department's holdings. The benefits that can accrue are many, for the department and for the patrons—and, ultimately, for the institution.

THE WORLD OF digital humanities is burgeoning faster than anyone can keep up with. Today I found on the Web an announcement (from Hyper-Studio / Digital Humanities at MIT) for an "Annotation Studio Workshop," taught by Kurt Fendt. It offers a way to create annotations online to texts the reader encounters. "In this hands-on workshop you'll learn how to create, tag, link, and share annotations in web-based environments." The workshop is sponsored by the Comparative Media Studies program. There is also a link to the Digital Humanities Faculty Workshop event. This is a clear wave of the future in all humanities, and because the library is the central information resource, special collections librarians should learn about how to make their own holdings part of this new wave of information dissemination.

RDA (RESOURCE DESCRIPTION AND ACCESS)

Special collections librarians must try to keep current with developments in the library world, especially with respect to the activities that directly impact their departments. One of the newest developments, which will have a tremendous influence on rare book cataloging, is the implementation of RDA (Resource Description and Access), a new way of cataloging books that will make the use of AACR2 obsolete for many libraries. The RDA Toolkit website, under the headline "Day One for RDA Implementation Announced," says,

The Library of Congress (LC) announced today that they would move forward with full implementation of RDA: Resource Description and Access on March 31, 2013. LC cited the significant progress that has been made toward addressing the recommendations of the U.S. RDA Test Coordinating Committee report of June 2011, and the need for sufficient lead time to prepare staff for the switch to RDA cataloging as reasons for the timing of this decision. The U.S. National Agricultural Library and the National Library of Medicine, as well as the British Library, Library & Archives Canada, Deutsche Nationalbibliothek, and National Library of Australia, will also target Day One of their implementation of RDA in the first quarter of 2013.

With the backing of these key libraries, RDA is off to a good start, and—especially with the Library of Congress's switch to RDA—the new system looks as if it will be the cataloging tool of choice for the future.

So, while special collections librarians are not, themselves, necessarily catalogers, they must understand the new system so they can work with their catalogers—the same way and for the same reasons that they had to understand AACR2. As the Wikipedia article explains,

Resource Description and Access (RDA) is a standard for cataloguing that provides instructions and guidelines on formulating data for resource description and discovery. Intended for use by libraries and other cultural organizations such as museums and archives, RDA is the successor to the Anglo-American Cataloguing Rules, Second Edition (AACR2), the current cataloging standard set for English language libraries.

The Wikipedia article adds,

The primary distinction between RDA and AACR is structural. RDA is organised based on the Functional Requirements for Bibliographic Records (FRBR). These principles identify both the "user tasks" which a library catalog should make possible and a hierarchy of relationships in bibliographic data.[4] Descriptions produced using the instructions of RDA are intended to be compatible with any coding schema, including the data environments used for existing records created under the AACR2 rules.[4] [17]

The point here is not to discuss the mechanics or particulars of RDA. It is to make it clear that such changes in library operations will have an impact on the activities in the special collections department and that librarians need to be aware of this kind of change.

HIDDEN COLLECTIONS

In the preceding chapter I looked at assessment as a way to recognize hidden collections. For generations, librarians have been trying to identify important collections that have hitherto been unrecognized. The collections were there, but were not seen as unified subject collections, or were not seen at all. The aims of revealing these hidden materials are obvious: to let the scholarly world know what the library holds and to encourage use. Merely getting into the department's backlogs and pulling out hordes of uncataloged materials may have been effective in finding these hidden collections, but it was haphazard and serendipitous. As I noted in the preceding chapter, a careful assessment of the collection would reveal them, and then they could be placed at an appropriate level of the department's cataloging priorities.

In the United States, the Council on Library and Information Resources (CLIR) has a grant program for institutions to help them locate, process, and reveal to the world their hidden collections. The council's website says,

> Libraries, archives, and cultural institutions hold millions of items that have never been adequately described. This represents a staggering volume of items of potentially substantive intellectual value that are unknown and inaccessible to scholars. This program seeks to address this problem by awarding grants for supporting innovative, efficient description of large volumes of material of high value to scholars. (www.clir.org/hiddencollections)

CLIR also hosted a Hidden Collections Symposium in Washington, D.C., on March 29–30, 2010. (Symposium proceedings are available online at www.clir.org/hiddencollections/index.html/symposium20100329.html.)

For many years libraries have been facing the problem of exposing hidden collections. As Barbara Jones says at the beginning of her white paper on the subject, "From the beginning of the ARL Special Collections Task Force's work in 2001, it was clear that large unprocessed or under processed backlogs of rare book, manuscript, and archival materials were a major problem in research libraries around the country."[18] Despite having brief records of most of their manuscript holdings (and possibly no records at all of many others), most libraries have not been able to create full finding aids for these collections, and the information of what these collections contain is not online. This obviously translates into invisible collections—what the profession calls *hidden collections.* Winston Tabb says about the problem, "The magnitude and complexity of existing arrearages, the absence of appropriately workable standards to apply to them, and the limited funding available all compound this urgent problem."[19]

The solution is simple: catalog them, make finding aids for them, get the finding aids onto the Internet for universal accessibility. But the simple solution

MY LIBRARY WAS recently given a gift that will allow it to create an endowed line in the budget for personnel. My first decision in earmarking that money is for at least one cataloger/manuscript processor. My library is over two hundred years old, and it has the typical backlogs in manuscript processing. We have been successful at getting federal and private grants to allow us to process large numbers of manuscript collections, and those projects are now under way. But when they are done and all the money is spent, we will still have thousands of documents and collections that need processing. Backlogs are a way of life for most special collections departments. And, as an actively growing collection, ours will be adding to our holdings regularly. So even if we "catch up" (which practically no library ever does), the collections will continue to grow and necessitate more and more production of finding aids.

is made tremendously difficult because the preparation of such finding aids is expensive and time-consuming, and most departments do not have the staff or fiscal resources to do the processing. This has created vast backlogs in processing, and millions of collections remain hidden to researchers. As I have said over and over, the prime directive for librarians is to link their patrons with the information they need, and hidden collections work directly against that mandate.

The number of documents of importance in digital form—those worth cataloging and revealing to researchers—is growing at a pace that no library can keep up with. A single case in point may be a museum library that collects the research and publications of its curators. Or an academic library that wants to keep abreast of, and preserve, all the school's faculty research (not to mention the documents prepared by its administration and staff), much of which could have significant long-term use. Until all these documents are processed and cataloged (with meaningful, well-formed finding aids) and put onto the Internet (or into some retrievable form, somewhere), the institution will be accumulating growing hidden collections. One means of "saving everything" (that is, everything digital) is to have all activity on all institutional computers saved, backed up in some burgeoning database, until an archivist or manuscript processor can come along and appraise the whole kit and caboodle. When will that happen? Who will do it? Does the institution have the wherewithal to cover the costs of such a project?

On the surface of it, as these three questions imply, it is a losing battle. But it does not have to be, and many in the library world (especially those in special collections, in which departments much of the analog and many of the digital collections reside) are working on solutions.

Special collections librarians must be acutely aware of the problems of hidden collections and must work toward revealing them. This means looking for resources, dealing creatively with department holdings, possibly bringing in interns or qualified volunteers with training in cataloging and the creation of finding aids, the use of EAD (encoded archival description), and other technologies and data-

bases that will allow cataloged materials to make their way to open accessibility. A look at the ARL Task Force white paper shows in which areas work needs to be done. Here is the table of contents for that document:

I. "Hidden Collections" and the Challenge
   They Present
      A. The Extent of the Problem of Special
         Collections Backlogs
      B. Defining "Access"
      C. The Purpose of This Paper
II. Access: The Key to Excellent Service
      A. Increased Demand from Diverse Users
         for a Wider Variety of Services
      B. Measuring Patron Access Needs in This
         New Environment
III. How Much Access Is Enough Access? Factors
   to Consider
      A. Printed/Published Materials
      B. Unique/Archival Materials
      C. Recommendations
IV. Creating Access to Special Collections:
   A National Collaborative Project Approach
      A. A National Survey
      B. A Conference
      C. Seeking Funding
      D. Institutional Preparation for the Project

It is clearly not so simple as "just process the papers and get their finding aids online." Issues of demand, measuring patron needs and access, printed/published materials versus materials that are unpublished or in digital form, funding, and institutional buy-in are at work here—not to mention the availability of qualified personnel, physical space or online capacities, escalating amounts of materials to consider and handle, and so forth.

RBM (the RBMS journal) addressed an entire issue to this topic (*RBM* 5.2 [Fall 2004]). In that issue, Carol Mandel, in "Hidden Collections: The Elephant in the Closet," says that one of the key ingredients of tackling the hidden collections problem is teamwork (p. 107), not only in dealing with a single institution's collections themselves, but also in working on larger, profession-wide solutions. She makes it clear that there is no single solution ("there is no magic bullet" [p. 107]), and she says, "[A]mong the tools we must use is sustainable and searchable Web access at a variety of levels" (p. 107). And a key assumption for her is that "although the problem is national and international, the solution is going to be local" (p. 107). Each institution poses its own problems, has its own IT configuration, has its own personnel (each with varying levels of expertise—and sometimes too few to solve the problem), has only so much fiscal support available, and so on. She concludes, "It's just the beginning of a new era in making special collections accessible, and we have a lot of work to do" (p. 113). Another writer for this issue of *RBM*, Stanley N. Katz, in his essay "Scholars and Teachers: Hidden Partners for Hidden Collections," talks about enlisting the help of the patrons (scholars and teachers), who can advocate with the administration and with other funding sources on behalf of the library (*RBM* 5.2 [Fall 2004]; the Mandel essay is on pp. 106–13, and the Katz article is on pp. 115–22).

Although hidden collections have been on a front burner for special collections librarians for more than a decade, the problem has not been fully solved, nor will it go away. People dealing in information, with a responsibility to provide that information to their patrons, need to do whatever they can to tackle the backlogs, using every means at their disposal. It is at the root of their professional mandate. Whatever digital initiatives are in place at an institution, the librarian and the archivist must be involved, for ultimately they will be in on the preservation and presentation of the information that those initiatives generate.

The Survival of Special Collections Departments

This topic, on how rare book departments can survive in lean economic times, has been hinted at throughout the present volume. In chapter 1, the role of the department in the larger institution was discussed. In chapter 6, fund-raising, and in chapter 11, outreach, among other things, was stressed. The wider topic is making the special collections department relevant

and useful to many, and therefore indispensable. In all three places, there is a hint that without some serious fiscal and administrative support, the department could contract or be in danger of losing *all* support. The topic is not new. In 1993, *Rare Books & Manuscripts Librarianship* (*RBML* 8.2; http://rbm.acrl.org/content/rbml/8/2.toc) devoted a whole issue to how special collections can appeal to many outside its immediate clientele, making it a vital service for the institution and its constituents.

The issue's opening article, by William Goodrich Jones, points to the threat of loss or diminution of resources to all academic institutions if they cannot demonstrate productivity.[20] And if the institution loses resources, this loss is distributed to all its units, including the library. A special collections department that cannot demonstrate its value could be at the top of the library's budget-cutting agenda. Jones says,

> In libraries everywhere, flat (or even declining) budgets are apportioned between competing demands and constantly escalating materials prices, while library administrators attempt to respond to administrative calls for greater visibility and outreach to the publics they serve. (p. 81)

Though this was written two decades ago, some things do not change, and today's libraries are facing the same scrutiny and are under the same pressures to prove their worth or lose support.

Betty G. Bengston's article in this *RBML* issue is "an academic library director's view of special collections."[21] She says, "[I]n our special collections . . . the distinctiveness of our research libraries will be maintained. Research libraries have an obligation through our special collections to collect and preserve some part of our intellectual heritage" (p. 92). She warns,

> In our current environment, it is easy for special collections to become marginalized. A library director faces many critical choices about where to place resources. As resources shrink, most directors will choose to put them into programs essential to the library's primary clientele—usually defined as the university's faculty, students, and staff. (p. 92)

So Bengston says that special collections departments must constantly strive to be at the forefront of the library's activities and public view. The rest of her essay is on ways that special collections librarians can figure out in what direction the larger institution is going and can steer the department's course to match that of the parent organization. And her conclusion is as sound today as it was when she wrote it:

> Library directors are being forced to make difficult decisions about the collection and service programs in their libraries. Units that will do well are those that are forward-looking, user-centered, and adept in the use of technology. They must see the primary clientele, i.e., the group that pays the bills, as the group with first call on their services. (p. 96)

One of the problems that face special collections librarians is that often their superiors, not fully understanding the nature of rare book departments and their users, will justify withholding resources from the department on the basis of the widely disseminated news that Google and other entities are digitizing vast numbers of books and are making full texts of them (especially those in special collections) available on the Web. Their argument is that special collections do not need *more* resources (for staffing and acquisitions); they need fewer, because people can now access an increasing amount of information in digital form from the Internet. As David Zeidberg says, "[W]e must make our library leadership understand that digitized texts and images are only a new form of transmission. . . . Virtual libraries may provide [a] form of secondary access, but not a substitute for consulting the original firsthand."[22] And to reiterate what was presented in chapters 2 and 13 of the present text, Zeidberg reminds us that "[d]eveloping a virtual component of the library may work for new materials originally produced in an electronic rather than paper format, but though the technology exists to accomplish it, it is financially impossible to convert all retrospective collections to a universal virtual library" (p. 107). So the librarian's aim should be to educate those who make decisions about budgets that there will not be a diminution of needed resources with the coming of digital texts; there will be an increase of such a need.

■ ■ ■

Probably every special collections librarian reading this chapter will think of "other issues" that could have been raised here. Personal experiences, communications with colleagues, exposure to talks at conferences and conversations between sessions, and the general buzz of the profession will reveal topics that are not covered here. The aims of this chapter were to be provocative and suggestive, not definitive, and to pick up several topics that did not fit naturally into previous chapters.

What it comes down to is that the wide field of Rare Books and Special Collections continues to generate experiences, ideas, challenges, "situations," dialogue, and rewards. And it takes a good deal of knowledge, fortitude, and intuition, along with a strong sense of ethics, to be good at working in the field.

NOTES

1. The singular of *ephemera* is *ephemeris*, which will be used here. Two standard books on the subject are John Lewis, *Printed Ephemera: The Changing Use of Type and Letterforms in English and American Printing* (Ipswich, Suffolk, England: W. S. Cowell, 1962; an abbreviated paperback version was issued in London by Faber and Faber in 1969); and Maurice Rickards, Michael Twyman, Sally De Beaumont, and Amoret Tanner, *The Encyclopedia of Ephemera: A Guide to the Fragmentary Documents of Everyday Life for the Collector, Curator, and Historian* (London: The British Library; New York: Routledge, 2000). See also Rickards, *Collecting Printed Ephemera* (New York: Abbeville Press; London: Phaidon and Christie's, 1988).

2. The word *ephemera* is from the Greek prefix *epi*- and the root *hemera*, "(near to) (over) (after) a day."

3. Watch papers are small, round sheets of fine paper, inserted into pocket watches. The American Antiquarian Society has a collection of about 450 of them. The society's blog *Past Is Present* says, "Watch papers are round decorative papers placed between the inner and outer case of a pocket watch to protect its inner workings. They also served as advertisements for watchmakers as they often included names and addresses along with elaborate designs" (http://pastispresent.org/2011/good-sources/watch-papers-at-the-american-antiquarian-society).

4. See *RBM* 91 (Spring 2008) at http://rbm.acrl.org/content/9/1.toc. The papers were originally given at the 48th annual RBMS Preconference held in Baltimore in June 2007.

5. Michael Twyman, "The Long-Term Significance of Printed Ephemera," *RBM* (Spring 2008): 19–57; http://rbm.acrl.org/content/9/1/19.full.pdf + html.

6. For the sake of convenience, I will use the term *book* to indicate where the piece of ephemera was found, though the item could have been found among various kinds of nonbook materials.

7. For a light approach to this topic, see Richard Davies, "Found in Books," www.abebooks.com/docs/Community/Featured/found-in-books.shtml. This is one of many such sites.

8. For a further discussion of the hiring of special collections librarians, see Susan Stekel Rippley, "The Education and Hiring of Special Collections Librarians: Observations from a Recent Recruit," *RBM* 6.2 (Fall 2005): 82–90, http://rbm.acrl.org/content/6/2/82.full.pdf + html.

9. Naturally, not all marks are desirable. A child's crayon "adornments" to a scholarly book are obviously not desirable, nor are students' yellow highlighter marks, though the latter may tell a scholar what the student thought was worth highlighting. (See Roger Stoddard, *Marks in Books, Illustrated and Explained* (Cambridge, MA: Houghton Library, Harvard University, 1985.)

10. Gabe Cyr, *Mixed-Media Books: Dozens of Experiments in Altering Books* (New York and London: Lark Books, 2006), p. 6. This is a lovely volume, with excellent color illustrations of book objects and altered books.

11. On canvassing books, see Keith Arbour, *Canvassing Books, Sample Books, and Subscription Publishers' Ephemera,* 1833–1951 (Ardsley, NY: Haydn Foundation, 1996).

12. It would be, of course, possible to have scores of sections in this chapter under the rubric Collecting _____, with that blank filled in by many subheads: Children's Books, Medical History, Materials on the History of Computing (or the history of any discipline), and so on. But literary manuscripts have particular relevance to many special collections departments because such materials are tied not only to individual special collections but also to regions, cities, genres, and other areas of collecting likely to be in many rare book departments. That is why this subject has been singled out here.

13. Anthony Rota gave a talk on collecting literary manuscripts at the Rare Books and Manuscripts Section annual Preconference in 1984; it was published as "The Collecting of Twentieth-Century Literary Manuscripts" in *Rare Books & Manuscripts Librarianship* [hereafter *RBML*] 1.1 (Spring 1986): 39–53, http://rbm.acrl.org/content/rbml/1/1/39.full.pdf + html. This piece is worth scrutinizing for its observations on how to select and appraise such manuscripts. Two other articles from *RBML* are also worth reading: William Matheson, "Institutional Collecting of Twentieth-Century Literature," *RBML* 4.1 (Spring 1989): 7–41, http://rbm.acrl.org/content/rbml/4/1/7.full.pdf + html; and Thomas F. Staley, "Literary Canons, Literary Studies, and Library Collections: A Retrospective on Collecting Twentieth-Century Writers," *RBML* 5.1 (Spring 1990): 9–21, http://rbm.acrl.org/content/rbml/5/1/9.full.pdf + html. Also see Richard W. Oram's follow-up piece to Matheson's comments on the implications for special collections departments with respect to the shifting focus onto literary manuscripts: "The New Literary Scholarship, The Contextual Point of View, and the Use of Special Collections," *RBML* 8.1 (Spring 1993): 9–16, http://rbm.acrl.org/content/rbml/8/1/9.full.pdf + html.

14. See Libbie Rifkin, "Association/Value: Creative Collaborations in the Library," *RBM* 2.2 (September 2001): 123–37; this statement is on p. 123 (http://rbm.acrl.org/content/2/2/123.full.pdf + html).

15. Ross Harvey and Martha Mahard, "Mapping the Preservation Landscape for the Twenty-First Century," *Preservation, Digital Technology and Culture* 42.1 (March 2013): 5–16, doi:10.1515/pdtc-2013-0002.

16. "Digital humanities," Wikipedia, http://en.wikipedia.org/wiki/Digital_humanities. The two notes in the Wikipedia text are to 1: "Digital Humanities Network." University of Cambridge. Retrieved 27 December 2012; and 2: "Grant Opportunities." National Endowment for the Humanities, Office of Digital Humanities Grant Opportunities. Retrieved 25 January 2012. In the quoted passage, GIS refers to Geographic Information System (or Geographical Information Science, or Geospatial Information Studies). The Wikipedia article "Geographic information system" says, "A geographic information system (GIS) is a system designed to capture, store, manipulate, analyze, manage, and present all types of geographical data" (http://en.wikipedia.org/wiki/GIS).

17. The Wikipedia article is at http://en.wikipedia.org/wiki/Resource_Description_and_Access. Note 4 in the quoted passage is to Chris Oliver, *Introducing RDA: A Guide to the Basics* (Chicago: American Library Association, 2010), p. 128.

18. See Barbara Jones, "Hidden Collections, Scholarly Barriers: Creating Access to Unprocessed Special Collections Materials in America's Research Libraries," *RBM*, White Paper for the Association of Research Libraries Task Force on Special Collections, released on November 1, 2002; the quoted statement is on p. 88 (http://rbm.acrl.org/content/5/2/88.extract).

19. Winston Tabb, "'Wherefore Are These Things Hid?'[1] A Report of a Survey Undertaken by the ARL Special Collections Task Force," *RBM* 5.2 (Fall 2004): 123–26; this statement is on p. 123. Tabb's note 1 refers to the source of the first part of his article's title: Shakespeare's *Twelfth Night*.

20. See William Goodrich Jones, "Leaner and Meaner: Special Collections, Librarians, and Humanists at the End of the Century," *RBML* 8.2 (Fall 1993): 80–91; the explanation of the importance of productivity is on p. 81 (http://rbm.acrl.org/content/rbml/8/2/80.full.pdf+html).

21. See Betty G. Bengston, "Navigating the Mainstream: Key to Survival," *RBML* 8.2 (Fall 1993): 92–96, http://rbm.acrl.org/content/rbml/8/2/92.full.pdf+html.

22. See David S. Zeidberg, "Setting the Course: The Role of Special Collections in the Library," *RBML* 8.2 (Fall 1993): 106–11; this statement is on p. 107 (http://rbm.acrl.org/content/rbml/8/2/106.full.pdf+html).

AFTERWORD

HE AIMS OF THIS BOOK HAVE BEEN MANY, BUT THE BASIC ONE is this: If you are working with rare books and special collections, you need to know a lot of things. This book aims to tell you what you need to know, whether you are a librarian (the main audience for the text) or a bookseller, an archivist or collector, a historian, or anyone else who wants to know what there is to know that could be useful.

The scope here has been broad because the field of special collections is broad. And as historical bibliography has shown, there is really no end to what information might be useful to anyone working in the field of rare books. Hence, there is no "definitive" text for those working in rare books and special collections. Those in the rare book field cross paths with historians; with people in law, sociology, psychology, all areas of medicine, finance, preservation and conservation, architecture, science, technology; with professional and amateur writers, donors, scholars, students; and with adults and children. The users of the library's holdings might be local or remote, rich or poor, well educated or unschooled. The breadth of this field leads to its endless fascination.

As has been noted several times in this book, the world of information is expanding at a fast pace. Large quantities of information that might be useful to readers of this book have been produced since the writing of this text ceased and the book went into production. There isn't enough time in anyone's life to keep up with even a fraction of it. The present text has tried to look with some circumspection at the field, offering to those in this broad realm information about and advice on ways to approach special collections and rare books. A key point is that no two people/institutions/collections are alike; hence the general principles and specific information presented here will be useful only up to a point. Beyond that point, people will need to draw on their own experiences, follow the rules and regulations, policies and practices of their own institutions and states, and solve their own distinctive problems as they arise.

It behooves us all to stay current in our field, whether it be with new theories about access to information, changing laws, developing technologies, new ways of looking at customer service, evolving methods of information retrieval, cost-recovery issues, discoveries in book history, and anything else that might direct our thinking about the materials in our care and the people who use them.

Rare books and special collections are about *everything*. In a sense, the field is so broad that it encompasses everyone. Those who are the gatekeepers are in a position of responsibility and accountability, and we must strive to be as knowledgeable as we can so that we can be relied on by those who seek our advice and assistance. The present text offers an introduction to this knowledge.

The rare book world has its challenges and rewards, its fascinations and satisfactions. This text has aimed at opening this world to many readers. The more we know about the things we have in our lives—like books, manuscripts, photographs, archives, and the other things that make the book world a realm of endless fascination and responsibility—the richer we are.

RBMS THESAURI AND RARE BOOK CATALOGING

THE RARE BOOKS AND MANUSCRIPTS SECTION (RBMS) OF THE ASSOCIATION OF College and Research Libraries (ACRL), a division of ALA, recognized decades ago that standard cataloging for all acquisitions for the general collections would be inadequate for rare books because in the world of special collections, scholars need more information than is offered in a simple AACR2 (*Anglo-American Cataloguing Rules*, 2nd ed.) record. The RBMS Standards Committee (later called the Bibliographic Standards Committee) was charged with expanding the cataloging record for rare books to include information that could be useful to anyone working with these volumes.

A key concern was that catalogers needed a vocabulary to describe a number of features of rare books, and this vocabulary had to be used consistently across the profession. For instance, if a cataloger was describing a particular volume with marbled paper, she might describe this paper as Dutch Curl. That is one of the legitimate terms used for a marbled pattern. But French Snail is also an accepted term for the same pattern. It was important that all catalogers use the same terms for the same phenomena, and the thesauri addressed this need by listing the preferred terms for all rare book cataloging. As the RBMS website explains, "These thesauri provide standardized vocabulary for retrieving special collections materials by form, genre, or by various physical characteristics that are typically of interest to researchers and special collections librarians, and for relating materials to individuals or corporate bodies."[1]

The introduction to the Type Evidence thesaurus explains,

The Independent Research Libraries Association (IRLA)'s Proposals for Establishing Standards for the Cataloguing of Rare Books and Specialized Research Materials in Machine-readable Form (Worcester, Mass., 1979) called for a new field to be added to machine-readable cataloguing (MARC) formats for terms indicating the physical characteristics of materials catalogued (Proposal Five), including descriptions of the bindings. In the same proposal IRLA requested that the Standards Committee of the Rare Books and Manuscripts Section of ACRL work toward developing standard terminology for use in such a field. The RBMS Standards Committee undertook the development of a thesaurus of terms, and a field for such terms (755 "Physical Characteristics Access" [since merged with 655, December 2005]) was authorized for all MARC formats in January 1984.

In order to expedite publication of the thesaurus, the RBMS Standards Committee (now the RBMS Bibliographic Standards Committee) decided to divide it into several separate thesauri, each treating evidence of a different aspect of book production and history. The Printing and Publishing Evidence, Provenance Evidence, and Binding Terms thesauri for use in rare book and special collections cataloguing were published by the Committee in 1986, 1988, and 1988 respectively. (www.rbms.info/committees/biblio graphic_standards/controlled_vocabularies/intro ductions/TypeIntro.htm)

The Genre thesaurus came out in 1983. Others came out subsequently: Paper in 1990 and Type, also 1990.

The thesauri cover six areas of cataloging: Binding Terms, Genre Terms, Paper Terms, Printing & Publishing Evidence, Provenance Evidence, and Type Evidence. They are "living documents" in that anyone finding a term that should be in one of these lists but is lacking can submit that term to the Bibliographic Standards Committee, and it will be assessed for inclusion. This is easy to accomplish because the thesauri are now online and fairly simple to modify. The original versions, created before online capabilities, were published in paper pamphlets.

As is typical of a responsible, properly constructed thesaurus, each list had an alphabetical and a hierarchical listing. In the hierarchy each keyword (the preferred term) was given, showing what Broader Term was above it in the hierarchy and what Narrower Terms were below it (if there were any). There was often a Use For note, indicating that a Use For word was the preferred term and the others listed were essentially equivalent, but they were not preferred and were not to be used in the cataloging record. In the earlier example, for instance, if the preferred term was "French snail marbling," there would be a

note that said, "Use for Dutch curl marbling." Reciprocally, at "Dutch curl marbling" there would be a Use note: "Use French snail marbling," showing that "French snail marbling" was the preferred term that would wind up in the MARC record. Further, many entries had a Scope Note, giving a brief definition of the term. And there was also a listing for Related Terms—that is, words and phrases "used between related terms when it seems helpful to bring associated types of evidence to the attention."[2]

The great value of these lists is that they present a rich vocabulary, most of which should be in the word-hoard of people working in rare books. Special collections librarians, booksellers, and collectors, for instance, should know how to describe the many features of book bindings, should be able to use the right terminology for all kinds of features of paper (handmade, decorated, watermarked, sized, and so on), should be able to tell a Harlequinade (also called a Metamorphic pictures book) from a Mazarinade, and should be able to differentiate antique laid, modern laid, and wove papers. In fact, a mastery of the terms in these six thesauri would go a long way in the training of a rare book librarian. That is, the terms were developed for catalogers, but they should be familiar to all librarians working in rare books.

One problem was that there were hundreds of these specialized words, and it would take a good deal of time, special workshops, and a great deal of reading for a person to become conversant with all of them. So even highly trained rare book librarians (and specialist rare book catalogers) could not know all the words. But the thesauri were there as prompts. That is, a cataloger may look at an element in a binding and not know the word for it, but she would know that the term is in the thesaurus, and a careful scrutiny of the Scope Notes may reveal the proper term to enter into the appropriate MARC data field.

Hence, these thesauri not only were key documents for cataloging, they were (and still are) educational tools, guiding those working in rare books to a terminology they should try to master. The paper versions of these slender pamphlets were often propped close at hand to the special collections catalogers, but statistics over the years showed that they were not used to the extent that RBMS had hoped. The central problem was that there were so many terms to know, there were so many rare book catalogers who did not know the terms, and there were so many books to process that few catalogers wanted to take the time to look up every keyword, to check out the chain- and wirelines and watermarks, to figure out the typeface, or to look for signs of provenance. It was a balancing act: either take the time to fill the appropriate MARC data fields with all the keywords that the thesauri contain, or streamline the cataloging and triple or quadruple your output. Backlogs are annoying, to say the least, so most rare book catalogers worked on the backlogs, not on the data fields that the terms in the thesauri could have filled.

Increasingly capacious and sophisticated computers, employed in rare book cataloging, simplified the researchers' efforts because variant terms could easily be scanned and connected to preferred terms. No longer would someone need to page through the thesaurus to learn that French Snail was the preferred term and that Dutch Curl was to be eschewed in favor of its French colleague. Now the information is available at the cataloger's fingertips, and definitions of terms in the Scope Notes can be located with the same speedy use of the fingers.

NOTES

1. See www.rbms.info/committees/bibliographic _standards/controlled_vocabularies. This site, updated in September 2012, has links to all six thesauri. It also has a live link to Bibliographic Standards Committee members responsible for evaluating new submissions to the thesauri. That is, if anyone wants to change anything already in a thesaurus, or to add to any list, he may send suggestions to the committee from this link. There is a proposal form titled "Propose new terms or modifications to existing terms."

2. This quotation is from the introduction to the thesauri; see, for example, the introduction to the Paper thesaurus at www.rbms.info/committees/ bibliographic_standards/controlled_vocabularies/ introductions/PaperIntro.htm.

LEVELS OF COLLECTING AND THE RLG CONSPECTUS

YALE, COLUMBIA, AND HARVARD UNIVERSITIES IN 1974, AND SOON THEREAFTER (1978) Stanford University, believing that OCLC's cataloging system was not sufficient for the kind of records needed in rare book cataloging, formed the Research Library Group (RLG). In 1978 RLG adopted BALLOTS, the computerized processing system that Stanford created. This system was eventually called RLIN (the Research Libraries Information Network; www.oclc.org/research/partnership/history.htm).

The split from the OCLC database was occasioned by the need of research libraries to be able to catalog rare materials at a more sophisticated, granular level than OCLC cataloging permitted and to catalog materials not in Western alphabets, among other things.

RLG developed the concept of the Conspectus, "a formal structure and methodology for better defining and characterizing information resources within individual and 'collective collections'" (Mary C. Bushing, "The Evolution of Conspectus Practice in Libraries: The Beginnings and the Present Applications," http://klement .nkp.cz/Caslin/caslin01/sbornik/conspectus.html).

The OCLC website explains,

> At the beginning of the 1980s RLG and its members pioneered the Conspectus concept and infrastructure for research library collections. The RLG Conspectus was an inventory of research libraries' existing collection strengths and current collecting intensity. It was created through surveys using worksheets based on the Library of Congress's classification scheme.
>
> The RLG Conspectus became a widely recognized collection assessment tool that has found its way around the world. It provided a common language with which to describe collections and levels of collecting—a language lacking until RLG members created it. (www.oclc.org/research/partnership/history.htm)

Eventually, the Library of Congress (LC) adopted the Conspectus for its own assessment of acquisitions and cataloging practices. One main component of the Conspectus is its delineation of the five levels of collection that have since been used to guide librarians (including those in special collections) in their acquisitions. As the Library of Congress website explains, "The use of these collecting levels evolved from a tool for evaluation into a meaningful set of descriptors employed in library collection policy statements. These levels are used in the Library of Congress policy statements to define the extent of the Library's collections" (www .loc.gov/acq/devpol/cpc.html). The so-called five levels of collecting include a sixth, tier 0, which is a noncollecting level. The tiers listed here are from the LC website just cited:

0. Out-of-Scope: The Library does not collect in this area.
1. Minimal Level: A subject area in which few selections are made beyond very basic works. For foreign law collections, this includes statutes and codes.
2. Basic Information Level: A collection of up-to-date general materials that serve to introduce and define a subject and to indicate the varieties of information available elsewhere. It may include dictionaries, encyclopedias, selected editions of important works, historical surveys, bibliographies, handbooks, a few major periodicals, in the minimum number that will serve the purpose. A basic information collection is not sufficiently intensive to support any courses of independent study in the subject area involved. For law collections, this includes selected monographs and loose-leaf titles in American law and case reports and digests in foreign law.
3. Instructional Support Level: A collection that in a university is adequate to support undergraduate and most graduate instruction, or sustained independent study; that is, adequate to maintain knowledge of a subject required for limited or generalized purposes, of less than research intensity. It includes a wide range of basic monographs, complete collections of works of more important writers, selections from the works of secondary writers, a selection of representative journals. . . . In American law collections, this includes

comprehensive trade publications and loose-leaf materials, and for foreign law, periodicals and monographs.
4. Research Level: A collection that includes the major published source materials required for dissertations and independent research, including materials containing research reporting, new findings, scientific experimental results, and other information useful to researchers. It is intended to include all important reference works and a wide selection of specialized monographs, as well as a very extensive collection of journals and major indexing and abstracting services in the field. Older material is retained for historical research. Government documents are included in American and foreign law collections.
5. Comprehensive Level: A collection which, so far as is reasonably possible, includes all significant works of recorded knowledge (publications, manuscripts, and other forms), in all applicable languages, for a necessarily defined and limited field. This level of collecting intensity is one that maintains a "special collection." The aim, if not achievement, is exhaustiveness. Older material is retained for historical research. In law collections, this includes manuscripts, dissertations, and material on non-legal aspects.[1]

∎ ∎ ∎

In the rare book world, a knowledge of these levels is useful. This schema helps the librarian in selecting materials for purchase and for deaccession and in selecting items from the general collection that should be transferred to special collections. All individual collections in the department should be assigned a level number as a guide to present and future acquisitions. The listing of the collections by level should be in the department's collection development plan, or it should accompany the plan in a parallel document.

If the department wishes to create an approval plan with a vendor or wishes to establish strong relations with key dealers who supply items to the department, it will be useful to share this five-level collecting strategy with those vendors—especially with an approval-plan vendor, who will need it to select things to send to the library.

The collection development plan should be revisited regularly (perhaps once every year or two) to see if all the individual collections and collecting areas should remain at the level assigned to them.

NOTE

1. Level 5 includes what is referred to as *collections of record*, holdings that someone working in a field must consult because they contain key and possibly unique materials.

BOOKSELLERS' CATALOGS AND THE BUSINESS OF SELLING

DESPITE THE PROLIFERATION OF BOOKS AVAILABLE FOR SALE ON THE WEB, many booksellers have chosen to offer their wares in catalogs, a centuries-old practice.[1] Seeing an item presented in a catalog is not like seeing it in hand, but for many buyers it is better than looking at a description of it on a computer screen. Also, even books listed on the Internet follow certain practices that were born in the era of the paper catalog, so it is important for librarians (and anyone else acquiring books and manuscripts) to understand dealers' catalogs.

Because book descriptions and the catalogs they appear in are worked on by many people, with varying levels of knowledge about the things they are selling and with varying aesthetic sensitivities, the catalogs (and the descriptions of each item in them) will not be homogeneous in quality. The various ways that dealers list and describe books are enough to cause a sane person to consider taking up other pursuits than book collecting. But for rare book librarians, and for anyone else working with rare books, understanding catalogs is necessary.

Catalogs should not be mysterious. To understand them, the reader needs to know the extensive terminology that dealers use and to recognize inaccurate descriptions. This vocabulary, it is presumed, is the same as the one used by special collections librarians, but this is not always the case.

Dealers should also know the proper and more common terminology of book description, and many of them actually understand and employ the kind of bibliographical description presented here in chapter 9 on bibliography. But, of course, there is a great amount of inconsistency among the booksellers in their use of terms, arising because not all dealers are knowledgeable about the formal terminology of their trade, nor do all dealers want to (or are able to) have identical kinds of information in their catalogs given their vast differences in fiscal, research, and temporal resources. Of course, some variation is desirable, but it could lead to confusion, and the special collections librarian should be on the lookout for problems in book description.

In one respect, a discussion of dealers' catalogs may be germane to the work of special collections librarians: they may well find themselves creating exhibition catalogs or scholarly bibliographies based on their departments' collections, listing items from their holdings. These are much like dealers' catalogs in the kind of information they contain, which is bibliographical and descriptive, and often pictorial (only lacking a price for each entry).

Many librarians, book collectors, and booksellers with some experience may already know what will be presented in this appendix, but even the most experienced may profit in the long run if some of the recommendations presented here are adopted by the compilers, designers, and printers of catalogs and if greater consistency develops in this area of bookselling and book exhibition in libraries.

Many booksellers' practices deserve to be followed; some should be jettisoned. Some things in these catalogs are useful, helpful, and didactic; others are annoying, potentially deceptive, and sometimes downright preposterous.

When a potential buyer reads a dealer's catalog, he expects to find certain information. First, the author's name, the title, and the publishing information (city, publisher, date, edition) should be published accurately and with some consistency throughout the catalog. Second, it would be good to be able to see what is printed. Some catalogs have quite small type—page after page of it—maybe 5- or 6-point type. This is tiring and challenging, and is not conducive to a buyer's desire to acquire anything or a scholar's search for information. Third, a clear description of the item, with an accurate explanation of its condition, is key. As chapter 8 shows, the condition of a book has a central bearing on its monetary value. Librarians may not need to put condition into bibliographic records, but this information could be useful.

The catalog description should be thorough. The dealer should describe the look and, if germane, the odor of the item. Also, any peculiarity should be disclosed. Many years ago, a dealer showed me a good-looking copy of a sixteenth-century book that made a loud clicking sound when it was opened. Something hidden—maybe a piece of vellum inside the binding—was snapping against something else

as the cover was opened. Most likely the book would need to be disbound to silence it. Whether the sound would affect the price, the desirability, or the usability of the volume is not the point. A dealer should note a peculiarity like this in a catalog.

Describing Condition

In chapter 8 we saw the phrase "condition is all." Condition deserves its own discussion because it is a slippery notion and is an extremely important part of a book's description. A book in pristine condition will obviously be worth more than the same item in average condition. How much a special collections librarian is willing to pay for a book will be affected by the book's condition.

The words *pristine* and *average* are not necessarily standard terminology for the condition of books. But that is just the point: there are no standard terms. There is no Thesaurus of Book Condition Terminology as there are other RBMS thesauri. The publication *AB/Bookman's Weekly* once printed in each issue the following statement:

> A thriving antiquarian book trade is largely dependent on the effectiveness of catalogue and mail-order bookselling. Transactions by mail are possible as long as buyer and seller recognize the importance of accuracy in describing the condition of the books offered for sale.
>
> Terms used to describe condition of books are as varied and numerous as the creativity and imagination of bookmen can produce. When confusion reigns over descriptions by advertisers or quoters, dissatisfaction is the inevitable result. . . . A revised list of terms used in describing books is now published here in each weekly issue of *AB* to serve as a suggested guide and reference for bookmen.[2]

The text then denotes nine levels of condition: As New, Fine, Very Good, Good, Fair, Poor (Reading Copy), Ex-Library, Book Club, and Binding Copy. A short description is then offered for each. This is a helpful guide, and it would have been excellent if booksellers had uniformly adopted it across the profession.

But dealers are wont to use words like *pristine, perfect, bright, shiny new, unblemished, unsoiled, spotless,* or any number of other terms. Some erroneously use the word *unopened* to describe a tight new copy that is stiff when opened. But as chapter 4 shows, the word *unopened* describes a copy whose folds, usually at the top (and for smaller formats, at the fore-edge) of conjugate leaves, have not been cut. (*Uncut* denotes a copy that still has its deckled edges untrimmed. The words *unopened* and *uncut* are often used interchangeably by those who do not know any better.)

Even when *AB* was still being published, hundreds of dealers ignored its list and came up with their own words, and today, with *AB* a distant memory (driven out by online sales), practically no one in the book world uses its recommended vocabulary. This would not have been a real problem if what dealers invented yielded accurate and thorough descriptions. But too often, they use such obfuscations as "VG + ." What this means is anyone's guess. Is it equal to "Fine − "?[3] Some dealers even use a double plus ("Fair + + "), which muddles the picture even more. And if dealers choose to use their own definitions and vocabulary for describing condition, they should spell out what their words and symbols mean in a table at the beginning of the catalog.

Dealers should not be too elaborate or cute or innovative in their designations of condition. One catalog used the phrase "a very near fine copy." It is debatable whether this is distinguishable from "near fine," from the same catalog. Others terms in this listing are "overall, less than very good," "a much nicer than average copy," "otherwise about very good," "collectible condition" (a terribly muddy term because a horrible copy of an almost impossible-to-find book may be "collectible" to some), "wear to extremities, thus very good or a bit better," "a passable copy," "else a bright near fine copy," "a less than very good copy," "near fine," "very near fine," a "very good + or better copy," "only about a very good copy," and about another dozen variations on these terms. These are actual descriptions from one dealer's catalog.

Terminology for condition is likely to be imprecise because of the many gradations of condition that must be described. Reading dealers' catalogs can be a challenge (or a lark, depending on how the reader feels about the imaginative nature of the descriptions). What a reader hopes for is clarity, accuracy, and consistency, so she knows what the books look like.

Catalogs as Reference Tools

Dealers' catalogs can be superb fonts of information. Many booksellers, especially those dealing in expensive books, go to great lengths to research what they are selling. Some dealers' catalogs are magnificent reference tools, worth keeping at one's elbow. They can be valuable for the information they offer on authors, on printing and publishing history, and on historical and literary movements, and they can also be a general guide to book values and relative availability.

Unfortunately, other dealers can be careless or lackadaisical in their cataloging. Some are operating on tight budgets and cannot afford the cost of extensive research or the concomitant printing costs that lengthy descriptions necessitate. And some dealers work on a thin margin, charging low prices and making up in quantity what they do not earn in higher pricing.

Quasifacsimiles of title pages and collations for books from the handpress period would be useful in catalogs. The size of the volume, the number of pages, the number of volumes in a set, and comments about bindings distinguish one edition or printing from another. Dealers should describe the material of the binding accurately, distinguishing among calf, morocco, pigskin, vellum, and buckram. Also, no tool is so valuable in a catalog as an index, even if only of authors. A subject and title index would be a valuable bonus. There cannot be too much information in the catalog. But the more information that goes in, the more the catalog costs, in time of preparation and in paper. And many dealers cannot afford the extra expenses.

It is annoying (but understandable) that most dealers do not date their catalogs. Perhaps they want to suggest a timelessness to their efforts, but when a catalog is undated the reader cannot tell if the information is fresh or outdated, if the items might still be available or are likely to have been sold, or how current the prices are. Most dealers number their catalogs, but more important than the number is the date. One bookseller said that if someone finds one of his catalogs and sees an item in it he wants to buy, but then sees the catalog is two years old, the collector may not even try to find out if the book is still available. But because not every item in a catalog will sell, there is a chance, even a few years after the catalog was issued, that items in it are still obtainable. So this bookseller never dates his catalogs, because an old date can be a deterrent to sales.

Until the last, say, fifteen years, color illustrations in catalogs added considerably to the cost of printing. Today the additional expense is practically negligible, especially with digital cameras that can take pictures that can be downloaded into the catalog. There are no prints, no developing, and no intermediary to pay to create the picture. So many booksellers' catalogs today contain fine color images. And the better ones will contain tables of contents, indexes, transcriptions of title pages, collations of signatures for books from the handpress period, extensive descriptions of condition, clear and detailed descriptions of bindings, and notes on the item's provenance. Sometimes there are paragraphs about the author, the text, or the illustrations, and perhaps a paragraph positioning the book in the history of some movement or its relation to some major doctrine or moment in history. This could be followed by citations of sources and, perhaps, a citation of the standard bibliographies. This is all accompanied by the price.

An experienced bookseller can take what looks like a run-of-the-mill volume, do extensive research, and find out why it is a crucial book in the history of letters or science. Many a bookseller's research has revealed important, even monumental, volumes and thus enlarged the world of learning. Unfortunately, other dealers try to enhance the worth of their books by finding out "amazing and important" things about their goods and then highlighting these price-increasing details by printing them in boldface type in their catalogs. But some of their hype is unwarranted, and the buyer should try to see through the smoke and not be enticed into buying a book that is not as important as the dealer says it is.

Typographic Enhancement

Often dealers head the entries in their catalogs with what looks like a headline, printed in boldface or italic type. This is a signal that the item beneath this headline is really special in some way (and could be accompanied by a hefty price because of this specialness). The headline highlights some important feature of the book: "The Best Edition," "A Newly Discovered Edition," "Not in *NUC*," "This Artist's Finest Work."

Buyers who peruse catalogs generally are familiar with these terms and selling ploys and should be cautious. For example, "Not in *NUC*" refers to the fact that the item for sale is not in the 754-volume set of the pre-1956 imprints of the *National Union Catalog*.[4] Some dealers like to see if they have books that did not make it to this most imperfect reference tool.

NUC is an incomplete compilation of photocopied library catalog cards from selected libraries. Since that first publication, many supplemental volumes of *NUC* appeared in hardback bindings, and then series on microfiche cards were issued. It is imperfect in several ways, but for the present text, the key imperfections are that (1) *NUC* strove to be comprehensive but everyone knew it could never be, and untold vast numbers of titles are not listed there; (2) dealers look into the 754 volumes but they often do not look into the supplements, which may carry the title they seek; and (3) there were alphabetizing errors in the production of the volumes, so books sought at their proper alphabetical place might be in *NUC*, but not where they would normally be found. So when a dealer says "Not in *NUC*," the implication is that the item is scarce—if the Library of Congress and the other contributing libraries lack this title, it must be valuable.

One dealer even issued a whole catalog titled "Not in *NUC*." The implication of rarity presumably allowed the bookseller to justify higher prices than the items listed were really worth. Nowadays, few people consult *NUC*, because OCLC WorldCat is available. But *NUC* still lists many titles that have not made it into WorldCat.[5] And today many a dealer will enhance an entry in a catalog with the formerly magic phrase, "Not in *NUC*." Another thing about *NUC* is that the original cards often had handwritten annotations on them, which are perfectly legible in the bound volumes. But some of that manuscript information did not wind up in online records. So even today, a trip to the groaning shelves holding these massive volumes could be rewarding.

John Carter, in his *ABC for Book Collectors*,[6] makes fun of the "first" collectors, those libraries and private parties who must have first editions. The gloss and thrill of the *first* edition has a good deal of power in sales, and often booksellers want to highlight this word in a book's description. So the word *FIRST* will be printed in a catalog entry headline in boldface or all capital letters, to make it stand out as a great asset. Similar typographic enhancements are used on *signed*, *best*, *rare*, *scarce*, *hand-colored*, *unique*, and other such enticing words. This enhanced typography can be useful in calling attention to features that make certain items highly desirable.

Worse is the infernal phrase "first and only edition." If the item is the only edition, it is obviously the first. But dealers wanting to show the scarcity with the words *only edition* sometimes cannot avoid the temptation to add the magic word *first*. Hence, "first and only" has become a standard foolishness in many catalogs. Much better would be *sole edition*, suggested to me by Paul Dowling of Liber Antiquus of Chevy Chase, Maryland. Similarly, many catalogs highlight the words *first thus*, meaning that the volume described is the first in a certain format, such as the first illustrated version, the first in a torn paperback version with broken spine and severe tidelines caused by a flood from a broken bathroom pipe. "First thus" could mean nothing at all in terms of making the book better textually, more desirable to a collector or library, or more valuable in any way. But as just noted, dealers often just want to get that eye-catching word *first* into the entry description.

Collectors and librarians should have their antennae up for such unnecessary and possibly misleading practices.

Other words that are often highlighted are *original* (as in "original vellum"—not a true asset if the "original vellum" is torn or mildewed), *association copy* (not a big deal if the association is to someone unknown or unimportant), *unique, presentation copy* (not important if the presentation is from and to people no one knows anything about), *signed* (who signed it?), and *scarce*. These typographic bright lights may mislead one to think the volume is a bargain, or is at least worth the price the dealer puts on it. The terms must be used carefully by the catalog compiler and taken with a grain or a pound of salt by the buyer.[7]

One phrase that is amusing is "else fine." It means that the book has defects, usually enumerated, but "otherwise, this is in fine condition." This use of the word *else* in this construction (to replace *otherwise*) seems awkward, but it has taken hold in bookselling jargon and refuses to be displaced by more idiomatic phrasing.[8] Booksellers seem to embrace it, so when it appears, the potential buyer must look closely to see if all the defects are clearly delineated.

Translating Catalogs

Sometimes a catalog seems utterly mystifying because the dealer is using a vocabulary either unfamiliar to the reader or idiosyncratic enough that the rest of the world might not understand it at all. The better educated sellers and buyers become, and the more they employ the accepted terminology of books and the book trade, the more they will understand each other.

To save space (and therefore money), most dealers use abbreviations in their catalogs. Some of them are listed in the accompanying table. The problem is that not all dealers use these, and those who do, do not always use them in the same way or for the same phenomena. The abbreviations describing condition, for instance, are often subject to interpretation. And some of the abbreviations do not have exact definitions. Some dealers list abbreviations at the beginning of their catalog, some list them at the end, but most do not list them at all, and how they are to be expanded is not always clear.[9]

It would be useful if all booksellers got together and decided on which abbreviations to use and then used them consistently. Not a chance. The world is full of idiosyncratic people, our communication systems are insufficient to notify everyone of this desideratum, and they simply would not comply if they could, because of differences in personality, experience, learning, dialect, and inclination. But it would be good if dealers listed their abbreviations at the beginning of their catalogs and then used them consistently throughout the listings.

Librarians and collectors are not mind readers. Even those who are educated and experienced, and knowledgeable about the book world, need to be told explicitly what some whimsical abbreviations mean.

Abbreviations Culled from Dealers' Catalogs

The abbreviations listed here come from actual dealers' catalogs. The terms are not always the clearest or the ones traditionally used in the book world. They are listed here with periods, but many were printed without the periods in the catalogs they were taken from. Similarly, there are variations in the use of capital letters from one dealer to another. This list only suggests the range of abbrs. that dlrs. use. There are many others, idiosyncratically applied by idiosyncratic booksellers. Listed here are some of the more common ones (and a few not so common).

AB—*AB/Bookman's Weekly*
a.e.g.—all edges gilt
a.l.s.—autograph letter, signed
anony.—anonymous
assoc. cop.—association copy
BAL—*Bibliography of American Literature*
bds.—boards
bkpl.—bookplate
bkstrp—backstrip (i.e., the spine of the book)

bl.—blind (as in bl. st. = blind stamped)
BL—British Library
BLC—*British Library Catalogue*
BM—British Museum
BMC—*British Museum Catalogue*
BMSTC—*British Museum Short Title Catalogue*
BN—Bibliothèque nationale
bndg.—binding
bw, b/w—black-and-white (as in photographs)
c., ca—circa (about)
c.—copyright (as in "c. 1955"; possibly confusing because "c." could also mean "circa")
ch., chp., chpt., chptr—chapter
cl.—cloth
col.—colored
coll.—collected; collection
comp.—compiled (by); compiler
cond.—condition (as in "exc. cond.")
cont.—contemporary (as in "cont. bndg.")
cr.—crown (size of paper)
cvr(s)—cover(s)
DAB—*Dictionary of American Biography*
dec.—decorated (as in "dec. bds.")
disb.—disbound
d.j.—dust jacket
DNB—*Dictionary of National Biography*
d.w.—dust wrapper (same as "d.j.")
duodec.—duodecimo (= 12mo.; book format)
ed.—edited, edition, editor
edn.—edition
endpg.—endpage ("endpaper" is better)
endp(s).—endpaper(s)
engr(s).—engraving(s)
enl., enlg.—enlarged
e.p.—endpaper
ex.lib. (sometimes "exlib" or "ex-lib")—former library copy (something shows that the book was once owned by a library: a bookplate, edge stamps, call numbers on spine, library stamps, embossing, etc.)
ex(c).—excellent (condition; as in "ex. cond.")
exp.—expanded
extrms, extrems.—extremities (the outer edges of a book, especially the corners and edges of the binding; the catalog this was in said "Sl. wear to extrems.")
f.—fine
f, F, f°, F°—folio
f&g's—folded and gathered sheets (with respect to unbound books)
facs.—facsimile
fcp.—foolscap (size of paper)

ff.—leaves (i.e., folios; see "ll.")

ffep.—front free endpaper

fldg.—folding (as in "fldg. map")

fly—flyleaf (a blank leaf at the front or back)

fos—former owner's signature

fr.—front

fr. fly—front flyleaf

frnt.—front (but why abbreviate this?)

fxng., fxd.—foxing, foxed (foxing is the brown or rust-colored spots that appear on sheets or endpapers that have reacted to mildew or mold or are caused by some iron gall inks)

g., gd.—good (condition)

g.e.—gilt edges

hf.—half (as in "hf-bnd" [half bound]; "hf t" [half title])

ht.—height; half title

ill., illus.—illustrated, illustrations

IMO—International Money Order

imp.—imperial (size of paper)

inscrb. (or some variation of this)—inscribed (someone's signature)

inscrpt.—inscription (someone's handwritten note)

ISBN—International Standard Book Number

ISSN—International Standard Serial Number

ital., itals.—italic (type), italics

LC—Library of Congress

lg., lge.—large

lg. pap. copy—large paper copy (often noted in the item description in boldface type)

lib., libr.—library

ll.—leaves (as distinguished from pp. [pages]); also lines (as in poetry)

lt.—light (e.g., "lt. bkstrp. fading")

ltd.—limited

m.e.—marbled edges

med.—medium (size of paper)

mod.—moderately (somewhere between "sl." and "v")

mor.—morocco (leather)

ms, mss—manuscript(s)

n.d.—no date (of publication)

N.p.—no place (of publication)

n.p.—no publisher

nr.—near (as in "nr.f." [near fine])

NUC—*National Union Catalog* (usually refers to the 754-volume, Pre-1956 set)

OED—*Oxford English Dictionary*

obl.—oblong (usually denoting landscape format)

oct—octavo

or., Orig.—original

o/w, o.w.—otherwise (as in "spine removed, joints split, o.w. fine+")

p., pg(s), pp.—page(s)

p.c.—price clipped (as in "p.c. d.j.")

phots.—photographs

pict.—pictorial (as in "pict. cvr.")

pl(s).—plate(s)

port.—portrait (usually refers to portrait format, as opposed to landscape format)

prlms., prelims.—preliminary leaves/pages

prof.—profusely (as in "prof. ill.")

ptd.—printed

ptg.—printing

pts.—parts

pub.—published, publisher

pvt.—private(ly) (as in "pvt. ptd.")

qto., Q°—quarto

qtr.—quarter (as in "qtr. bnd.")

r.—recto (e.g., "B3r": the front of the third leaf in signature B)

r. fly—rear flyleaf

repr., rpt.—reprint(ed)

rev.—revised

roy.—royal (size of paper)

rpts.—reprints

rubd.—rubbed (binding worn, usually at the extremities of the boards and at the head and feet of the spine)

sig.—signature

sigd., sgd.—signed

sl.—slight(ly) (as in "sl. fxd.")

s.l.—sine locus (no place [of publication]; an archaic and unnecessary abbreviation; better is "N.p."—no place)

sm.—small

s.n.—sine nomine (without a name; archaic; better is "anony.")

sp.—spine (as in "sp. sl. torn off")

t.e.g.—top edge gilt

thk—thick

t.p., t-p—title page

trans.—translated (by). Translator

U.P., UP—University Press

usu.—usual(ly)

v.—very (e.g., "vg")

v.—verso (e.g., "B3v": the back of the third leaf of signature B)

v.d.—various dates (of course; what else did you think this could be?)

v.g., vg—very good (condition)

vig(s).—vignette(s)

v.p.—various places

v.y.—various years (of publication)

vol(s).—volume(s)

w.—width (used along with "ht")

w., w/—with

w.a.f.—with all faults (sold "as is," indicating that the item is defective)

wo., w/o—without

wraps, wrps.—wrappers (paper covers)

4to, 4°—quarto

8vo, 8°—octavo

12mo, 12°—duodecimo (also called "twelvemo")

16mo, 16°—sextodecimo (also called "sixteenmo")

32mo, 32°—trigesimo-secundo (also called "thirty-twomo")

Sizes of Books

In chapter 9 on bibliography is an explanation of book formats. Booksellers should, but often do not, understand how folios, quartos, octavos, duodecimos, and other formats are created. They should learn the terminology and what each term applies to. But they often refer to book sizes when they use these format terms, and librarians must understand that these words are usually being used incorrectly or with a bibliographical application different from that used in descriptive bibliography.

Denoting size in a dealer's catalog is important. In the United States, the preferable designation is in inches, although centimeters will work as well, and many American booksellers use the decimal system. Centimeters seem to be preferred for the rest of the world. (Some dealers give measurements in both systems.) The difference of a fraction of an inch or of a centimeter or three might indicate a different state or edition, a copy that has been trimmed (and hence possibly rebound), or something else crucial to the collector, librarian, or bibliographer.

Because many booksellers do not understand how books were originally put together, and thus are not clear on the origin and original meanings of the terms used for formats (folio, quarto, octavo, duodecimo, sextodecimo, and so forth—functions of the number of times the original sheets the books were printed on were folded), and because most of these terms have essentially lost their meanings in the modern world of printing where the "original sheet" concept is completely lost in monstrous high-speed presses, they might simply measure a book

and consult a chart to try to give a name to the format of that book. One such chart, listed in the sometimes valuable reference book *Glaister's Glossary of the Book*, gives the following terminology:

Name of format	Inches
Thirtysixmo	4 x 3⅓
Medium Thirtytwomo	4¾ x 3
Medium Twentyfourmo	5½ x 3⅝
Medium Eighteenmo	6¾ x 4
Medium Sixteenmo	6¾ x 4½
Cap Octavo	7 x 7¼
Duodecimo	7½ x 4½
Crown Octavo	7½ x 5
Post Octavo	7½ x 5½
Medium Duodecimo	7⅔ x 5⅛
Demy Octavo	8 x 5½
Small Quarto (usually less)	8½ x 7
Broad Quarto (varies up to 13 x 10)	8½ x 7
Medium Octavo	9½ x 6
Royal Octavo	10 x 6½
Super Royal Octavo	10½ x 7
Imperial Quarto	11 x 15
Imperial Octavo	11½ x 8¼

Source: Geoffrey Ashall Glaister, *Glaister's Glossary of the Book,* 2nd ed. (London, Boston, Sydney: George Allen & Unwin, 1979); p. 8. Glaister has a similar chart (on p. 71) on British Book Sizes.

All a dealer needs to do is measure a book in hand, find a dimension close to what this chart delineates, and he has a name for the "format." But, especially for modern books (that is, books after the handpress period), such terms are relatively meaningless. Are the measurements for the textblock or for the covers? Has the book been trimmed or rebound? Was it printed on sheets of paper or from one massive roll of paper in a giant press? So when a dealer uses a term like *folio* or *quarto* in a catalog, it is merely an approximation of what that dealer thinks is a standard size of a book of the dimensions of the volume he is holding. There is nothing scientific or historical or accurate about the term he uses.

Listing Sources

Most dealers are experts in the areas in which they sell. Their expertise comes from years of handling and learning about books in their field. They are familiar with general and specialized reference works, which allows them to speak learnedly or even definitively about their books. When they draw information from a source or refer to an item in a bibliography to elucidate the reader about the item for sale, they often cite their source or sources, partly to illustrate the importance of the item and partly to show they have a good grasp of their field.

Such references to sources are quite useful to the expert librarian or collector, and they instill a sense of confidence about the bookseller's expertise and the quality of the items listed in the catalog. But many a reader of the dealer's catalog will be in the dark about such references. To take two examples selected randomly: item 637 in General Catalogue 686 from Pickering & Chatto concludes with "Not in Becker"; and item 635 concludes with "Baudrier V 137; Houzenau & Lancaster I 13783." These are clearly references to sources that the dealer has consulted, and this catalog is filled with such references. But nowhere in the Pickering & Chatto catalog are those sources cited. Presumably the catalog editors assume their readers are experts enough to know the meaning of the references. This may be a fair assumption for most of the audience, who themselves are buying from a dealer who offers books in the collectors' and librarians' areas of interest. But the lack of a source list makes using the catalog difficult for the newer collector or the more generalist librarian. At best, the reference can send the potential buyer to the source to see what else it has to say about the topic at hand (the book being offered, the historical event the book deals with, the author, or whatever else is referred to in the dealer's catalog write-up). The citation of the source, moreover, marks the dealer as an expert who knows her books, and it gives her an air of responsibility and authority, so the customer feels that he is buying from a reliable source. At worst, the reader can simply ignore the citation.

Many dealers list sources in their catalogs or offer to give the reader additional information. In one Rulon-Miller catalog is the statement, "References will be furnished upon request." This offers sources without the need to print them in the catalog. If librarians or collectors see sources that they are unfamiliar with, they can contact the dealer directly. One warning is in order, however. The source the dealer lists could be a "decoy," especially the listing that begins with "Not in." This formula essentially says that a book would be expected to be found in a standard reference tool on the subject, but it is not there; hence the book is scarce (and therefore can command a high price). A dealer may say about a pamphlet printed in Newburyport in 1832, "Not in Evans" or "Not in AI." Evans and AI are the same source: Charles Evans, comp., *Early American Imprints, 1639–1800*.[10] Of course the Newburyport publication is not in Evans—as it should not be, because it was published in 1832 and Evans's listing went up to 1830. It was published too late. If the catalog says, "Not in Finklestein," the librarian or collector should try to find out who this Finklestein is and what he wrote.

Return Policies and Other Business Issues

Booksellers should have a note about their return policies in their catalogs. If an item comes into a library from a dealer and the book is not as it was described, the librarian may wish to return it. Merely changing one's mind ("I guess I just don't want this book. It's too expensive.") is not a good reason to return an item. But if the book was presented in the dealer's catalog as a first edition and it turns out to be a book club edition, the buyer has a reasonable cause to return it. Or if the dealer neglected to mention some defect in the volume (torn pages, water stains, foul odor, underlining, missing plates, bumped corners), this is justification to return it. Most dealers will allow returns even if the patron does not offer a reason. But the return should be made quickly.

Although hypothetical, the following return policy statement is typical: "All items are returnable within ___ days for any reason. The purchaser is responsible for the postage, the careful wrapping and handling, and all insurance on the returned items. We expect that items will be returned in the same condition that they were shipped out in." This is a reasonable policy and should not be abused. Some dealers have a "no return" policy; disappointed customers have no recourse. On the other hand, some patrons abuse the return privilege by sending back items for no particular reason; the dealer, in the meantime, has forgone the opportunity to make the item available to a legitimate purchaser. Many dealers require prior notification before an item is returned. This gives them time to begin marketing the item again and increases their chance of selling it. One dealer's catalog says, "Returns that were charged on credit cards will incur a 4 percent charge." And many catalogs add what is probably an unnecessary statement: "All items subject to prior sale." It does not take a genius to figure out that if a dealer has sold an item, it is no longer available.

Booksellers' catalogs should—and usually do—deal with other facets of the business as well. Dealers should list postage and handling charges (for single and for multiple volumes), and, if practicable, offer more than one shipping option. The catalog should specify appropriate taxes and identify what customers are affected. The catalog should explain billing and payment conditions (e.g., "Payment is due upon receipt" or "within ___ days after receipt"). Many dealers, understanding the fiscal labyrinths of most institutional libraries, allow them to be billed for their purchases and may even offer deferred payments. Many institutional libraries cannot pay for anything unless it is in hand. So the dealer will send the book with an invoice.

First-time customers with no credit rating with a dealer should expect to be asked for prepayment. The dealer, in exchange, should hold an item for several days to give the first-time purchaser a chance to send payment. Dealers should offer more lenient terms for proven customers with a good payment history. The dealer should note if credit cards are an acceptable forms of payment and which companies' cards they accept. All of this should be explained in the catalog.

Buyers should scrupulously adhere to a dealer's policies and accept them—especially when these policies are clearly spelled out in the catalog. They are logical and protect both parties. Dealers should never quote a book at one price and then—by any means—try to sell it at a higher price. Buyers should respect the expertise, overhead, and integrity of the dealer and refrain from bargaining for an item listed in a catalog. There are proper ways of dealing, on both sides, and a sensitivity to the other party's needs will result in mutual satisfaction. When the catalog spells out all conditions of the business transaction, both parties are playing with the same rules.

Librarians fit into this picture primarily as buyers. They may have special relationships with dealers, receiving early catalog mailings and a "library discount" for orders that exceed a certain amount. Librarians are also occasionally in a position to deaccession books, just as collectors are in a position to sell items. The dealer then becomes the buyer, and a similar sensitivity must operate.

Catalogs are an essential and sometimes formidable expense for many dealers. Costs can vary on their production, but catalogs with color illustrations, printed on fine paper, can be expensive. And there are expenses involved in their composition and research, printing, editing, binding, and handling and mailing. On top of this, the dealer has the expenses of acquiring, cleaning, arranging, pricing, and describing, not to mention all the other expenses of overhead in running the business in the first place.

Many mail-order buyers do not understand or always appreciate all the effort that goes into the bookselling business. If the buyer assumes that dealers are performing a service for him, he will usually not be dissatisfied with prices or the amount of time it takes to obtain the product. And buyers should remember that a dealer is doing well if half of the catalog offerings sell. This means that the dealer must keep a large stock of unsold books on hand, tying up resources, taking up space, and possibly even incurring expense in taxes, insurance, and storage costs. Collectors and libraries will have purchased a great part of their collection from dealers and their catalogs. They should be grateful that dealers' catalogs exist as an art form (albeit, in some cases, rather abstract art) as much as a medium of commerce.

For many buyers, reading dealers' catalogs is pleasurable. But they should not linger over them too long. They usually require a quick response. If the librarian finds an item she wants, chances are that there is someone out there who also wants it. If the price is good, chances of acquiring the item could be slim. One rule to follow is this: If you see something you want in a dealer's catalog, call immediately; don't even wait to finish reading the catalog. Have the dealer hold the item for you while you finish the reading. Many times librarians have heard, "Sorry, I *just* sold that to someone else. Only a couple of minutes ago." One tactic, at that point, is to ask the dealer to call back if the other buyer decides not to buy the book. Also, the librarian can say, "If you ever come across this title again, please call me first." Most dealers will be happy to work with you, especially knowing that they have a ready sale for some items.

If the librarians are good customers and enjoy a good relationship with the dealer, they may ask for a preview of his catalogs. Some U.S. dealers on the East Coast may send catalogs to the West Coast customers a day or two before shipping them locally. This gives all customers a chance of getting the catalog at about the same time. Another way to avoid missing out on good books is to send a want list to a dealer. If she can make a sale without having to put an item into a catalog, she frees up space in the catalog for another book and has a ready sale to boot.

Catalog Language and Its Uses

One dealer offers the following description in his catalog: "Bottom of spine lightly frayed, embossed stamp of previous owner, another label carefully removed, otherwise a fine copy." In a review of the seventh edition of John Carter's *ABC for Book Collec-*

tors, edited by Nicolas Barker (New Castle, DE: Oak Knoll Press, 1995), Michael Vinson points up Carter's impatience with dealers' catalogs that offer a list of a book's defects (like the one just mentioned and the one in note 8 in the present appendix) and then say, "Else fine." Vinson asks, "What else is there?"[11] The language of the book catalog can be deceptive.

One of the most amusing treatments of catalog language comes from David Magee's two little treatises, published as *A Course in Correct Cataloguing, or Notes to the Neophyte . . . The Two Parts Now First Collected & Reissued in the Author's Honor by His Colleagues in the NCC/ABAA, with a preface by James D. Hart* (San Francisco: n.p., 1977). Some of his observations are worth quoting here: "Every trade has its language. Plumbers, printers, and, for all I know, prostitutes have terms of reference by which they communicate with each other and their clients. The book trade is no exception" (p. [5]; the pages in this pamphlet are unnumbered). Magee says that the jargon is "perplexing perhaps to the uninitiated," and that there has been a recent "disturbing trend" among younger booksellers: They are "a group of youthful iconoclasts who have dared to tamper with the Holy Writ. They are not content with the innocent half-truths, evasions and exaggerations by which the bookseller in the past has extolled the virtues or cloaked the defects of his goods; they prefer to speak without trumpets and they know not when to tread delicately. The result is honest, insipid, and dangerously comprehensible" (p. [5]).

Magee then offers, in dictionary form, a list of the keywords (and their modifiers) in the description of books. "Rebacked" should always be modified with "'skillfully' or 'neatly' to prove that you don't send your books for repair to the local blacksmith," he says (pp. [12–13]). Never say that hinges are "weak"; call them "tender" (p. [20]). And if the hinges are a "trifle weak: it is not necessary to mention the rubber band that holds the covers on" (p. [18]). Magee is, of course, making fun of his own kind, but his admonitions warn dealers not to do what he instructs—that is, to obfuscate the truth. Clarity and honesty in catalog description are always preferable to obfuscation. And the use of proper terminology is necessary for all who use the catalog to understand what item the dealer is selling, what condition it is in, and what its defects are, if any. One of the aims of the present volume is to present that terminology.

NOTES

1. The text of this appendix is a modified version of a paper I published in *Biblio* 1.2 (September-October 1996): 42–46; and *Biblio* 1.3 (November-December 1996): 42–46.

2. This statement was presumably written by Jake Chernofsky, the long-time editor of *AB/Bookman's Weekly* and the editor when this was written. The entire section from the November 16, 1998, issue of *AB/Bookman's Weekly* is available at www .cattermole.com/page5.htm.

3. The examples of terms and symbols are not hypothetical. They come from actual catalogs that I have seen over the years.

4. The vast *National Union Catalog* enterprise, publishing millions of photocopied card catalog cards, was carried out by Mansell, the set's publisher, and at one time it was common to hear people refer to the set as "Mansell" ("I could not find it in Mansell").

5. The Wikipedia entry for *NUC* says,

> The NUC of Pre-1956 Imprints was an important resource for verifying bibliographic information and finding copies of books before the advent of large electronic bibliographic databases, such as WorldCat; the massive size and weight of the set make it less useful now. However, given that approximately 27% of the books listed in the NUC Pre-1956 Imprints were not listed in World-Cat as of 2005, it remains an extremely valuable tool for researchers. (http://en.wiki pedia.org/wiki/National_Union_Catalog)

6. John Carter, *ABC for Book Collectors*, 8th ed. (New Castle, DE: Oak Knoll Press; London: The British Library, 2004). This edition, updated by Nicolas Barker, is now fully available for free online as a link at the ILAB home page: www.ilab.org/eng/documentation/29-abc_for _book_collectors.html.

7. I once found a pile of Supreme Court Justice Earl Warren's bookplates in a bookseller's shop. He had acquired them in a large purchase from Warren's estate. I also found a couple of those bookplates affixed to the front pastedowns of several books in the dealer's shop. Were those books from Warren's library or were the plates affixed to books the dealer could not otherwise sell? And were these authentic bookplates in the first place? Were they really Earl Warren's? These are rhetorical questions, but they point out the potentially tenuous nature of some associations. What about the enticing association, "This copy was in a library in a state that ABRAHAM LINCOLN once wrote about"? Just how tenuous the association is can be key to the volume's value.

8. In the original publication of this piece on dealers' catalogs (see note 1), I had as a headpiece the following book description from a dealer's catalog:

> Ex. lib. Corners bumped. Green calf on spine and top half of front cover faded. Headcap torn, with loss of headband. Joints starting. Front free endpaper, flyleaf, and half-title wanting. Minor crayon writing on rear flyleaf. Sporadic underlining of text throughout. Two-inch tear in title page and first two leaves of Introduction, not affecting text. Three of six plates skillfully razored out. Some slight worming throughout. First and last dozen or so leaves lightly foxed. Else fine.

9. One bookseller who listed and expanded a group of abbreviations in a table at the beginning of his catalog used an abbreviation inside that was not listed in the table. It was "g.t. spine." I didn't know what it meant, so I called him. He took out his copy of the catalog, looked at the entry, and said, "Darned if I can remember what that means."

10. "AI" is American Imprints, the shorthand for Charles Evans's and Roger Bristol's work. Evans's original publication was titled *American Bibliography: A Chronological Dictionary of All Books, Pamphlets, and Periodical Publications Printed in the United States of America from the Genesis of Printing in 1639 Down to and Including the Year 1830, with Bibliographical and Biographical Notes* (Chicago: The Blakely Press for the Author, 1943–1955; in 13 volumes). Evans, of course, could not possibly get *every* imprint, and Roger P. Bristol's *Supplement to Evans' American Bibliography* (Charlottesville: University Press of Virginia, 1970) adds thousands of entries to the original volumes. Major libraries like the American Antiquarian Society and the Library Company of Philadelphia have identified thousands more. The Wikipedia entry on Evans is useful: http://en.wikipedia.org/wiki/Charles_Evans _(librarian).

11. Michael Vinson, review of *ABC for Book Collectors*, by John Carter, *Rare Books & Manuscripts Librarianship* 10.2 (Fall 1995): 102–04; this question is on p. 104 (http://rbm.acrl.org/content/rbml/10/2/100 .full.pdf + html).

PAPER SIZES

AS HAS BEEN MENTIONED NUMEROUS TIMES IN THIS VOLUME, ANYONE DEALING with rare books must know the terminology of the book. Chapter 4 presented a host of terms having to do with the book as physical object. Chapter 9 discussed the field of descriptive bibliography, in which more words were revealed, all of which are essential in the vocabulary of anyone who needs to describe the objects under his scrutiny. One of the difficult areas of such delineation is the terminology for paper sizes.

The problem is magnified for at least two reasons. First, handmade paper is made on molds, the sizes of which were never standardized. That is, papermakers (and paper-mold makers) made this tool to whatever size they needed, possibly for a particular printer who wanted a particular size, or possibly purely measured out at random. Second, over the centuries, paper was made in so many places that the terminology was never fixed—sheets of various sizes were given various names. One of the classic manuals on paper, E. J. Labarre's *Dictionary and Encyclopaedia of Paper and Paper-making, with Equivalents of the Technical Terms in French, German, Dutch, Italian, Spanish & Swedish*,[1] says this under the entry for "Sizes":

> A critical examination of the names of English paper sizes and their measurements in the following table reveals the entire nomenclature contains only 15 different names and not more than half-a-dozen basic sizes. These names are: Antiquarian, Atlas, Colombier, CROWN, DEMY, Eagle, Elephant, Emperor, FOOLSCAP, IMPERIAL, Hand, MEDIUM, POST, Pott, and ROYAL, of which only the seven sizes printed in capitals, and their derivatives, are in regular use. It may be said that only three of these, viz. Crown, Demy and Royal, and possibly Foolscap, are indispensable; all the other sizes vary from the one or the other of these that they could probably be abolished without causing inconvenience to the trade or the public.
>
> These fifteen names and barely a half-a-dozen different sets of measurements represent the framework on which the trade and custom have built up a bewildering number of combinations with the help of adjectives such as: Half and Single, Double and Quadruple, Large and Small, Broad and Long, Extra and Super, Reduced

and Pinched, Whole and Middle, or duplications of these such as: Double Quadruple, Extra Large, Small Double or Double Small, and even fractional additions like sheet-and-a-half or sheet-and-a-third. (p. 246)

Labarre adds that with all the combinations, there are at least one hundred names for paper sizes in English, and a single denotation of one size could represent "anything from 2 to 15 slight variations" in size (p. 247). He says, "The total number of different *names* of sizes in the table, including stationery and cards, exceeds 290" (p. 247), and that some papers, judged by their measurement, do not fall under any of the names, so a "printer would speak of a 'cut size'" (p. 247). His discussion goes on to explain the lack of uniformity of nomenclature, partly occasioned by manufacturers who give papers their own size designation, and partly because many papers are named for their uses: "Bag, Cap (Foolscap), Medium and Royal Copying, Chemists', Music and Writing Demy, Index-, Pasting-, Wedding- and Writing Royal, or even a combination of two sizes such as Imperial Cap, Medium Post and Royal Hand and, finally, a size-name preceded by a fancy name, e.g. Havon Cap and Kent Cap" (pp. 247–48).

Labarre's discussion goes on for pages. The points are (1) there is no standard terminology that is universally applicable to papers; and (2) there are no standard sizes that are fixed for any word that describes a size. This is a fascinating discussion, worth reading (the section is on pp. 246–52). And though his table titled "Ratio of Paper Sizes" is overwhelming (running from page 251 to page 267) and is supplemented by the "Table of Dimensions of Paper Sizes and Their Names" (pp. 268–72) that is even more useful, the overall effect is stultifying. The latter table, for instance, designates all the names of paper sizes to represent nine categories: Writing, Printing, Drawing, Wrapping, Boards, Cards, Envelopes, Notes, and Miscellaneous (with some papers used for as many as six of these categories).[2] The table lists papers as small as 3″ x 1½″ and as large as 72″ x 48″, and it designates papers that are over three hundred sizes.[3]

To simplify the matter, as Labarre shows, a "Standardization Agreement" was reached in England in 1925 "between the Federation of Master Printers and the National Association of Paper Merchants (then the National Association of Wholesale Stationers)" (p. 285), and they came up with "standard names and sizes for paper and boards" (p. 285). Papers were divided into "Writings" and "Printings." Labarre's table follows (see facing page).

Another frequently consulted guide to paper terminology, *The Dictionary of Paper*,[4] has a section on "Sizes of Paper" (pp. 400–402) that lists "some of the common sheet sizes" (p. 400), not all of them. And in general, these are listed by their use (and common sizes in the United States), not by arbitrary names. So there are Bible paper, Blotting paper, Bogus bristol, Book paper (coated and uncoated), Cover paper, Ledger paper, Railroad manila, and so on to Wrapping tissues and Writing paper. For each of these, several sizes are given, indicating that the lack of standardization in the United States matches that in Great Britain.

Almost all of this discussion has focused on the modern paper industry. It was much more chaotic and totally unstandardized in the handpress period, so designating papers by their size for sheets made from, say, 1800 and back is difficult. For those working with rare books, it is essential to know the kinds of things revealed in chapter 4, in the section "Paper." If a measurement of a full sheet of paper that is bound into the printed leaves of a book is needed, the scholar must determine the volume's format and try to "unfold" the leaf theoretically to reconstitute the full sheet. But unless the volume has deckles in two directions (vertically and horizontally), there is no way to know how much paper has been trimmed from the original sheet. And even horizontal and vertical deckles may not reveal the whole picture because a sheet could be trimmed from two sides and still have deckles showing on two sides of the volume. A folio or a quarto, with all four deckles intact, will show the original full sheet. It gets more difficult to "see" the full sheet with smaller formats.

If the sheets were watermarked (or even if not), it might be possible to reconstruct the original sheet,

Writings	Inches	Printings	Inches
Foolscap	13½ x 16½	Large Foolscap	13½ x 17
Small Post	14½ x 18½	Crown	15 x 20
Sheet and ⅓ Cap	13½ x 22	Large Post	16½ x 21
Sheet and ½ Cap	13¼ x 24¾	Demy	17½ x 22½
Small Demy	15½ x 20	Medium	18 x 23
Large Post	16½ x 21	Royal	20 x 25
Small Medium	17½ x 22	Large Royal	20 x 27
Medium	18 x 23	Imperial	22 x 30
Small Royal	19 x 24		
Super Royal	19 x 27		
Imperial	22 x 30		

Source: Labarre, p. 285.

especially if the book is disbound and the signatures can be unfolded and the original leaves reconstituted.

One other term that has been the subject of conversation and confusion over the years is *ream*. *The Dictionary of Paper* (3rd ed.) merely says that a ream contains "either 480 or 500 [sheets] according to grade" (p. 363). Labarre is more expansive, explaining the antiquity of the word, and says,

> The actual quantity of paper in a ream gradually became fixed through the centuries . . . probably in some relation to the amount of paper a vatman could make in a day, and has been in the neighborhood of 500 sheets for the last 3 or 4 centuries, though it may still contain, according to the class of paper, 472, 480, 504, or 516 sheets (also other quantities in various countries.) (Labarre, p. 222).

He points out that the "Standard Ream," the U.S. term, has 500 sheets, a "Printer's Ream" contains 516 (made up of 2½ quires [a quire is 20 sheets] of 24 good sheets), an "Inside Ream" has 480 sheets (or 20 inside quires), and so forth.

For the most part, those in the rare book world should keep 480 and 500 in mind as the most com-mon numbers of sheets in reams, and in the United States, it is almost always 500.

NOTES

1. E. J. Labarre, *Dictionary and Encyclopaedia of Paper and Paper-making, with Equivalents of the Technical Terms in French, German, Dutch, Italian, Spanish & Swedish*, 2nd ed., rev. and enl. (Amsterdam: Swets & Zeitlinger, 1952). This is one of the most comprehensive and referred-to guides to paper terminology.

2. The paper called "Double Foolscap" (also called "Chancery") measures 26½" x 16½" in a full sheet; it is used for all the categories except Cards (p. 270).

3. The smallest, 3" x 1½", is called "Gents' Card" or "Third or third Large"; the largest sheet, 72" x 48", is called "Emperor" (pp. 262, 272). The three hundred plus names show a good deal of imagination: "Prince of Wales," "Boudoir," "Intimation," "Albert," "Billet," "Czarina," "Viscount," "Copy" or "Tea Copy," "Small Half Royall," "Large Double Loaf," "Medium Lumber Hand," "Typewriter Double Cap," "Double Hambro," "Single Lump" and "Double Lump," "Plutarch," "Double Elephant" and "Long Double Elephant," and on and on.

4. *The Dictionary of Paper: A Compendium of Terms Commonly Used in the U.S. Pulp, Paper and Allied*

Industries, 4th ed. (New York: American Paper Institute, 1980). The 3rd edition is abundantly available on the Web, and it is the basis of the information for the present volume; see *The Dictionary of Paper: Including Pulp, Paperboard, Paper Properties and Related Papermaking Terms* (New York: American Paper and Pulp Association, 1965). To hint at the complexity of the subject, see "Paper size," Wikipedia, http://en.wikipedia.org/wiki/Paper_size.

RBMS STANDARDS AND GUIDELINES

CHAPTER 2 PRESENTED INFORMATION ABOUT ETHICAL STANDARDS, THE interlibrary loan of rare and unique materials, and borrowing and lending books for exhibition. Chapter 7 presented information on security. For each of those discussions, the RBMS Guidelines were drawn upon. The Rare Books and Manuscripts Section of ACRL has been assiduous in creating guidelines to help librarians to carry out their duties in a responsible, thorough, ethical way. All people working in the rare book world should know these standards and guidelines, and should adhere to their precepts and follow their advice. They have been created by some of the most experienced special collections librarians in the field, and their recommendations are statements of Best Practice in the profession. They have been visited and revisited over the years, with experts in the profession honing their language and perfecting their recommendations.

Booksellers, archivists, librarians, and private collectors should study them because many of these guidelines will have an effect on their own activities. The documents deserve mention because they are key to special collections operations, and they should be familiar to all who work in the field.

The RBMS website[1] gives the following information about these documents:

ACRL/RBMS Guidelines for Interlibrary and Exhibition Loan of Special Collections Materials, approved by ACRL in January 2012. It combines and replaces the separate *ACRL Guidelines for the Interlibrary Loan of Rare and Unique Materials* and *ACRL Guidelines for Borrowing and Lending Special Collections Materials for Exhibition.* (www.ala.org/acrl/standards/special collections)

ACRL/RBMS Guidelines Regarding Security and Theft in Special Collections, approved by ACRL in 2009. It combines and replaces the separate *Guidelines for the Security of Rare Books, Manuscripts, and Other Special Collections* and *Guidelines Regarding Thefts in Libraries.* (www.ala.org/acrl/standards/ security_theft)

ACRL Code of Ethics for Special Collections Librarians; supersedes *ACRL Standards for Ethical Conduct for Rare Book, Manuscript, and Special Collections Libraries and Librarians, with Guidelines for Institutional Practice in Support of the Standards*, 2nd edition, 1994. [Approved Final Revision published in College and Research Libraries News (C&RL News) 54:4, April 1993] (www.rbms.info/standards/code_of _ethics.shtml)

ACRL/SAA Joint Statement on Access to Research Materials in Archives and Special Collections Libraries. [Revised ed., approved July 2009. Former revised ed. published in C&RL News 54:11, Dec. 1993] (www.ala.org/acrl/ standards/jointstatement)

ACRL Guidelines on the Selection of General Collection Materials for Transfer to Special Collections. Third ed., approved July 2008. (www.ala.org/ acrl/standards/selctransfer)

ACRL Guidelines: Competencies for Special Collections Professionals. Approved July 2008. (www.ala.org/acrl/standards/comp4spe collect)

The aim here is not to delve into the details of these documents, but to bring them to the attention of those who can profit from reading them. Full-text versions are available for free from the websites indicated in the quoted list.

NOTE

1. These statements are on the Web at www.rbms .info/standards. These documents are specific to special collections. A more general set of standards is that of ACRL (Association of College and Research Libraries), which can be accessed at www .ala.org/acrl/standards. There are more than thirty ACRL documents at this website.

DEPARTMENT FORMS

THE OPERATIONS OF SPECIAL COLLECTIONS ENTAIL OFFERING MANY KINDS OF services, maintaining rules and regulations about what can and cannot be done in the department and what may or may not be brought into the department, delineating the kinds of fees the unit charges for various services, warning patrons about legal issues, keeping certain kinds of records, preparing for and later dealing with disasters, maintaining standards of operation, showing what the practice is in the institution for the transfer of materials from the general stacks to the special collections department, explaining deaccession policies, and more. The department should have forms that deal with most of these things.

Some of the forms are for internal use only: delineating practices in dealing with theft or mutilation, regulating activities such as shelf-reads or cleaning of the collection, preparing for and dealing with disasters, specifying a telephone tree to guide people on whom to call in emergencies, explaining the department's practice with respect to appraising library materials, and other things. Some of the forms are for the public: sign-in sheets, information sheets about the patrons (patron registration forms), sheets showing fees for services, flyers introducing the department to users and showing what some of the more prominent collections are, photoduplication policies, use-of-camera policies, and many others.

RBMS has published a series of guidelines, and it is acceptable for a rare book department not to create its own in the areas these documents cover. But the department should have in writing a statement that it adheres to the policies promulgated by RBMS in its publications. And the department should have many of the documents listed here *on paper* or clearly delineated on the department's website. Such a formal presentation, in a relatively fixed form, carries more weight than does any policy conveyed orally. For instance, a patron asking a librarian to scan a certain number of pages from a book or a collection of photos might be angry if told that the library allows only up to ten images from any collection or book. But if the patron is given a printed form—or is directed to a "published" website—that explains this limitation, it is clear that this is a formal policy of the library, and it carries the authority of those who wrote and those who approved of the policy.

One key issue, then, is that the librarian must not merely create a policy and implement it. It must be vetted by the administration (possibly also by legal counsel) before it can be put into use. All policies that have a direct impact on patrons should be kept in writing or up to date on the department's website, and the patrons should be shown them upon their first entrance into the department.

So in running a rare book and special collections department, a librarian should have various forms available. To repeat: Many department policies impact the users, and several of these are ultimately for security and to help the staff help the clients. When a patron enters a department, it is good to show that the policies are in place and applicable to all who use the library materials. No patrons should merely be told what the policies are, for they could assume that the regulations are idiosyncratic. A printed (or online) form shows that *all* users are subject to standard, universally applied policies.

The following list is not comprehensive. It cites many kinds of documents that a special collections library may wish to have on hand. Individual departments may have special needs for specific documents not listed here. For instance, a department may have a map showing the location of particular holdings in a reading room or other space accessible to patrons. Or it might have a special guide for the use of a particular collection that has specific strings attached to it by a donor.

There are samples of forms on the Web for many of the following items, but because every institution has its own "problems," its own unique collections, staff, hierarchy, and practices, librarians will need to tailor each form to their own institution's policies and practices.

Some of these forms will need to be filled out by the patrons, and the information may be retained for years, digitally or on paper (or, as in the past, on microfilm). Patron registration information, for instance, may be useful for tracking down lost items years after the patron has used them (though, of course, well-carried-out security measures in the

reading room should prevent such loss in the first place). Also, some of these forms should be revisited regularly (e.g., every five or ten years) to see if they are up to date. As technology changes and as special collections operations and practices evolve, the forms may need to be renewed to reflect new procedures or new laws.

1. **PATRON REGISTRATION FORM.** This document may contain many things, including date (maybe time of sign-in), name, address(es) (home and affiliated institution), phone number(s), e-mail address(es), name of institution of employment, contact points for that institution, intended area(s) of research, intended length of stay, information from a photo ID (some departments make a copy of the ID form and attach it to the registration form), and so forth. This sheet may also contain what is in item 2 below. It may also contain a section allowing the host institution to record each use of the collection. Many institutions now have online registration forms. The longevity of their access and the possibility of the corruption of these records may make the librarian lean toward having paper-based registration forms, either as the primary form of preserving the information or as a backup to the digital one.

2. **INFORMATION SHEET** spelling out the requirements for the use of the department's personnel and materials. (This form could be used to guide patrons *and* staff.) Such information might include handling and use procedures, presence of food or drink in the department, the use of pencils and pens in the reading room, the need for patrons to deposit all personal belongings (including suitcases and briefcases, backpacks, cloth or plastic bags, books and magazines, and the like) into a locker and hang up outer clothes (jackets, coats, shawls, umbrellas), the use of laptop computers and digital cameras, and other policies deemed necessary for the indi-

vidual institution. (The policy on the placement of briefcases and clothes may also apply to casual or part-time employees, or even to the regular staff.) This form should have a statement like, "I have read and will adhere to the requirements of the policies delineated in this document." There should be a line for a signature and date. This may not be a legally binding document, but it drives home the seriousness of the department, and it gives the patron a sense of responsibility to follow the dictates of the document. The document may also contain a statement that prohibits the circulation of materials from the department. It is important to have a written policy that clearly spells out that books do not circulate. A written policy, on paper, that can be handed to anyone requesting this kind of special treatment carries a good deal of authority.

3. **SIGN-IN LOG BOOK** (or Sign-In Cards). Once patrons have registered, they should be required to sign in on each use of the department. Some libraries may not have such a requirement, but this form will generate a record of use of the materials and will record who has been in the department on what days. Sign-in could be digital, too.

4. **INTRODUCTION TO THE DEPARTMENT,** to be available to patrons, giving the names of key personnel, contact points for these people, and the hours the facility is open (along with other information as needed). This is not a standard form that special collections departments generally have on hand. But it is a sign of the department's wish to serve its patrons as well as possible. It is a kind of friendly outreach, telling the patrons that the department wants to help them as much as it can and may offer personal contact if users need it. Some departments may not wish this kind of information to be disseminated. In fact, some departments do not even list their

personnel on the institution's website. As a gesture of goodwill, and to help patrons get their questions answered, this form may be useful.

5. **PHOTOCOPYING/REFORMATTING POLICIES,** including information on lead time; limitations on numbers of items to be copied; fees for the service(s), with an explanation of a sliding scale of costs for academics, students, private researchers, corporate patrons, and so forth; conditions under which no photocopying will be done (fragility, copyright issues, Deed of Gift issues, etc.), with a statement something like, "The ability to copy any item in the collection will be determined by the Department"; expected turnaround time; and so forth. Other fees may be added to the list, including shipping and handling for materials to be sent to remote patrons.

6. **DEED OF GIFT FORMS,** one with and one without ownership of copyright conveyance. It is naturally to the benefit of the institution to be given copyright to donated material (if the donors actually own the rights), but donors generally do not like to grant this. The deed should contain the name(s) of the donor(s), date of gift, a description of the gift (even an itemized list might be in order for a gift of many items, especially if the items are valuable), and a section for listing restrictions or other conditions. It is in the best interest of the recipient institution to limit the number of strings attached to the gift. For instance, such restrictions as long-term inaccessibility to the collection (say, over ten years) should be discouraged. Also to be discouraged are statements like, "This material is available to all researchers except my immediate family" (or vice versa—"available to my immediate family but not to others"). Any string attached that limits access to the material should be carefully considered and strongly discouraged, so the librarian should

discuss with the donor why restrictions are not beneficial to the library or its users and how they discourage research, noting that the primary reason the donor is giving the materials to the library is to encourage their use.[1] Other strings, like how or where the collection is to be housed or what must remain with the collection (especially if the gift comes with things that do not belong in the special collections department) must also be discouraged. (Note: even outright gifts cost the institution money. The recipient should encourage the donor to include in the gift a cash component for cataloging and processing.) Final word: the Deed of Gift must make it clear that the institution becomes the sole owner of the materials to perpetuity. The signatures should be witnessed and, if counsel advises, notarized. Donors should have no recourse to take back anything that is in the gift once the papers are signed and the items are in the possession of the institution.[2]

7. **DEED OF DEPOSIT.** This form should contain the name(s) of the person(s) making the deposit, a clear statement of ownership, a description of the item(s) to be deposited (sometimes with an itemization), restrictions on use, and anything else deemed necessary. Deposits are highly discouraged, but if a librarian is forced to take one, the agreement should contain such information as length of deposit (anything over, say, a year is simply free storage for the owner and should be rejected, if possible); a statement that after a certain agreed-upon time (specified in the form) the item(s) on deposit will become the property of the holding institution; a note detailing the policy if the depositor takes back the material (e.g., a certain amount of advance notice is essential; the depositor will pay for the institution's costs of holding, caring for, and insuring the deposited material, which costs may be determined on the basis of linear feet over a certain amount of

time, for instance; the fee to be set forth and agreed upon at the delivery of the deposited material; the fee to be paid before the materials are released back to their owner[s]); a statement exculpating the institution for any damage or theft that happens to the deposited materials while they are in the institution's facilities; and the like. See more comments under Deed of Gift (item 6).[3]

8. **COPYRIGHT STATEMENT.** The patron is responsible for copyright issues on all materials used from the repository. That is, if a patron wants to publish any of the materials acquired from the library or archive, she must seek out copyright holders herself and get permission when legally required to do so. The form should have a statement something like, "I have read and understand the institution's copyright policies." Getting the patron to sign this form may exculpate the department or library from any misuse of copyrighted materials, and it is a good warning to ignorant or unscrupulous researchers. But, of course, the copyright code itself establishes this principle. Basically, the researcher, not the library, is responsible for securing permissions for commercial use of materials under copyright. This form is a good reminder to the patrons of their responsibilities when it comes to using the works of others.

9. **STATEMENT OF APPRAISAL PRACTICES** (i.e., "The library does not do appraisals"). The department, then, should have on hand the pamphlet *Your Old Books* to help people appraise their own holdings. Copies may be bought inexpensively and handed out to the patrons, or the patrons may be directed to find the text on the Web. The department may also wish to have a list of booksellers available for the patrons to peruse. The ABAA Directory lists booksellers by expertise and geographical location. This form may

also list some common bookselling websites to help patrons do their own appraisals (sites like AbeBooks, BookFinder, AddALL, and many others).

10. **COLLECTION DEVELOPMENT PLAN** for the department.

11. **THEFT GUIDELINES,** to instruct the staff on what to do when a theft is discovered. (See the RBMS Theft Guidelines. These and the two following forms may be created from those on the Web at the RBMS site. See appendix 5.)

12. **GUIDELINES FOR THE TRANSFER OF MATERIALS FROM THE OPEN STACKS TO THE SPECIAL COLLECTIONS DEPARTMENT.** (See the RBMS guidelines on such transfers.)

13. **SECURITY GUIDELINES** (See the RBMS guidelines on security.)

14A. **INTERLIBRARY LOAN GUIDELINES** (for patron use; for exhibition). This could be a long document, spelling out all kinds of things pertaining to the actual handling of the materials, the transfer practices, insurance, physical plant conditions, security measures in place at the borrowing institution, and much more. This should be accompanied by forms 14b and 14c. The RBMS guideline mentioned in appendix 5 may be all the department needs.

14B. **INTERLIBRARY LOAN CONTRACT / LOAN AGREEMENT FORM.**

14C. **EXHIBITIONS POLICY.**

15A. **DEACCESSIONING POLICIES AND PRACTICES.** This can be an extremely complex activity, with many legal twists, and often governed by the institution above the special collections department level. There may even be city or state laws that impact the deac-

cession of materials.[4] Make sure your policy statement is absolutely clear on retention schedules; ownership of materials being considered for deaccession; marking of deaccessioned items; the right of staff or other interested parties (friends, donors, administrators, etc.) to become the owners of deaccessioned materials, or the prohibition of such ownership; public awareness of the deaccessioning policy and of specific items, if necessary; and so forth. And make sure that deaccessioning is permitted in the first place.

15B. **DEACCESSIONING FORM.** This is a paper-based or electronic record of each item removed from the collection.

16. **DISASTER PREPAREDNESS PLAN.** This form should delineate what to do to prepare for a disaster and what to do once a disaster hits. There are many components to this document, including lists of supplies that must be available, a statement of where these supplies are to be located, a regular schedule to look at these materials to make sure that they are in place and that all batteries are still functioning, and much more. The document may prioritize which collections are to be rescued and what to do with them. This plan should contain (or be accompanied by) a telephone tree of people or businesses to contact in case of an emergency (department head, director of the library, police, the institution's own security force, fire officials, lawyers, insurance agents, and other services that might help—freezer companies that can house wet books, for instance). (See item 20 in this list. Also see chapter 12.)

17. **FINDING AIDS FOR THE COLLECTION.** Paper-based or online finding aids are essential as part of public outreach. A finding aid can be a simple checklist, a pamphlet, a booklet, or a published volume. Today the effort at most institutions is to get the finding aids into

digital form and mounted on the Internet. Until such conversion is complete, the paper-based ones should be available to researchers.

18. **OTHER PUBLIC RELATIONS MATERIALS,** including a document or pamphlet on planned giving, donations to the department, and so forth. Beyond item 4 on this list, there may be a brochure introducing the department to visitors, giving names and phone numbers of people, a listing of or even short prose paragraphs on important collections, a history of the department, pictures of highlights from the collection, and anything else that may be glitzy or informative. As with finding aids, these materials are now generally available online, but it might be handy to have a pamphlet about Giving to the Department.

19. **SHELFLISTS WITH NOTES.** Today shelflists are digital. But old ones may be useful to retain because the content of online versions is limited to the data fields that the online system has, while the old paper-based shelflist cards may retain penciled-in information that the online record lacks. The shelflist is not, per se, a "department form," but it is a paper-based "document" that may be useful to librarians or patrons, and it may contain information that does not wind up in the online MARC record.

20. **CONSERVATION PRACTICES / PRESER-VATION POLICIES** (these may be combined into a single form). This document might also contain a list of conservators the department consults or employs. A typical entry in this form may be something like, "For all nineteenth-century leather bindings that need to be rebound, rebacked, or re-covered, conservator X should be consulted." More on this topic may be found in chapter 12. The form spoken of here is not a Treatment Plan; it is a generic document that helps the librarian identify items that are to be conserved, shows what work the items need, and keeps track of their existence. This form, also, may be kept online.

21. **TELEPHONE TREE** showing all people, in prioritized order, to be contacted in case of a disaster or other emergency. (See item 16 in this list.) Although the institution may have its own such tree, a specialized one for the rare book department may be good to have at hand. Also, such a listing may certainly be kept online, but if the disaster involves a power failure, a paper list will be accessible.

22. **CALL SLIPS.** These should be in triplicate. Yes, this is the computer age; but paper call slips are a security tool still in use by special collections departments throughout the country. One copy of the slip goes to the patron and should be kept with the book or other item borrowed (and should be returned with the borrowed material). One copy goes to the pager, who can leave it on the shelf in the open space that held the book. (Special holders are available for this practice.) A third copy may be kept at the circulation desk. One of these should eventually go into a file for future reference. The file may be organized by borrower's name, by call number, by author, or by subject (or in some other way convenient to the department). If the information on these slips is transferred to an online database, it can be searched in all data fields. Many librarians in the past have microfilmed their call slips and discarded the originals. The slips should contain the name and address (and phone number?) of the borrower, the author and title of the book (or information about the identity of the manuscript or other material), the publication information (city, publisher, and date, and maybe also the edition), the call number of the item, the date of use, and whatever other information the library deems necessary.

These slips should be part of the confidential record of the library. If the information is kept in digital form, the database could be searchable more readily than can a well-sequestered paper file.

23. **HYGROTHERMOGRAPH RECORDS** for the collection for at least the previous year. (These may be kept on paper or in digital form.)

24. **LIST OF LOCAL RESEARCHERS** who can help remote patrons or suggestions on how distant researchers can get assistance through local students, history departments, online databases, and so forth.

25. **FREQUENTLY ASKED QUESTIONS** pamphlet (can be online).

26. **OTHER FORMS** that are generated by the collection itself. There may be little pamphlets for individual, well-known, heavily used collections; information about parking at the institution; a listing of local restaurants for patrons; a brochure about local transportation; campus or local maps; and anything else dictated by the individual institution. Of course, this kind of information is easy to mount on the Web, but it might be a cordial gesture to have a paper-based pamphlet for scholars working in the department that they can take with them in their pockets.

NOTES

1. The length of this entry shows how complicated donations can be. See the discussion in chapter 6 in the text.

2. One librarian's experience raises another situation worth mentioning. Two brothers gave a collection of manuscripts to a library, signing a Deed of Gift that delineated no restrictions. About fifteen years later, they approached the library and asked if they could add a restriction: that anyone wanting to use the archive needed to get permission from the brothers. This was, of course, absurd for several reasons, two of which are paramount. First, the institution owns the materials and, because there had never been a restriction for well over a decade, it had no reason to add one now. Second, the brothers, in their request for a modification of the gift, made no provision for a termination of that restriction, many years after the fact. So at what point would that restriction be nullified? The librarian was reluctant to allow any tampering with the original terms of the donation, but because the brothers were friends of the institution and could be important donors someday, she wanted to accommodate them as well as she could. She allowed the request, but in the codicil that was added to the original papers of donation were a few clauses, including that the brothers had to notify the library at least once a year where they were (so a patron could contact the brothers for permission); failing to make this notification of present whereabouts nullified the modification. Another clause in the modification was that at the brothers' deaths, the restriction would be permanently lifted and no permission would thenceforth be needed. Third, this modification could not be passed down to any heirs. The restriction would end at the brothers' deaths or with a year's silence about the present whereabouts of the brothers. Because the brothers were fairly superannuated, the restriction would not be in place for too long. This way the brothers were satisfied, and the library was not forced to restrict access to materials to perpetuity. Some Deed of Gift forms do not have much space (or any at all) for strings to be attached. This could act as a discouragement to the donor to place any restrictions on the gift. Finally, one addition to a Deed of Gift form may be a clause specifying that the library may deaccession anything it wants for any reason. It should not be forced to keep the entire gift, especially if some of the materials given are out of scope or if they duplicate the library's holdings. And the deed may also specify that if the deaccessioned materials are sold, the proceeds must go into future acquisitions for the library. This last is a standard practice.

3. Some obvious things to keep in mind are that the deposited materials are not owned by the library, so it should not expend any resources for their conservation or cataloging, and depositors should be told this in advance; and that the statements about liabilities in case of damage or loss should be spelled out clearly. Deposits are sometimes forced upon departments from above in the hierarchy, despite the librarian's desire to reject them. The

best the librarian can do in such a situation is to minimize the department's efforts and liability on behalf of the collection coming in while maintaining the highest standards of care, security, and access possible under the circumstances. Also, sometimes a department's excellent handling of a long-term deposit will convince the owner of the materials to make the deposit a gift. This does not always happen, but the goodwill generated by the institution may be the deciding factor for the depositor in making the deposit a donation.

4. In some states, all possessions of state-run or -supported institutions are considered state property, and their disposition may be under the state's jurisdiction. The librarian needs to know what the situation is in her state and may be governed by those laws.

CITING SOURCES
AND PLAGIARISM

EARLIER IN THE PRESENT VOLUME ARE STATEMENTS ABOUT HOW IMPORTANT IT is for special collections librarians to publish, to keep them current in the profession and as part of a comprehensive outreach effort. And because of their position—surrounded by research materials of many kinds—librarians are in a perfect position to do research and to let the world know about the materials in their collections. They should be using primary and secondary materials in their writing. Although professionals should know the basics about citing sources, it is amazing to see volume after volume with inadequately cited sources. At best, such practice can be embarrassing and deceptive; at worst, it is plagiarism. This appendix is a brief guide to help librarians and archivists—and anyone else publishing work that relies on and draws from sources—to avoid the pitfalls of improper citation.

In writing in which the author borrows from any sources, the author is absolutely required to cite those sources. Similarly, in visual communication, artists of all kinds must show where borrowed materials come from. Citing sources means showing exactly what words and images come from which sources. This is crucial in scholarly writing because the author or visual artist will be taking from many sources for just about anything she writes (other than an opinion piece or editorial) or for any pictorial presentation.

This idea is worth repeating: If you take anything from a source—anything that is not common knowledge—you must show the reader where it comes from. If you do not, then the material looks as if it is from you. Passing something off as your own that is not your own is a kind of theft, and it may be criminal. In writing it is called *plagiarism*, and it can lead to serious consequences.

Any published text must be the work of the author herself, acknowledging the assistance of others and clearly showing what comes from sources and what is the author's.

Sources must be cited; that is, citations must be given clarifying what is borrowed and from whom. What does not need to be cited is any material that is common knowledge. If you mention that Columbus discovered the New World in

1492; that Babe Ruth hit 714 home runs and was surpassed by Hank Aaron with 755; that the capitol of Iowa is Des Moines; or that Jonas Salk invented the vaccine that conquered polio—all this is common knowledge and need not be cited. But if you use the statement "Always obey your parents when they are present," you must attribute it correctly to Mark Twain.

Direct quotations; indirect quotations; facts and statistics; concepts and arguments; special information about people, places, events, organizations; and so on—anything that the common person does not know "off the top of her head" (please avoid such clichés)—must be cited.

The general rule is this: The reader should know at every point in your writing what is yours and what comes from your sources—and what those sources are. If there is any doubt about what is common knowledge and what needs to be cited, take the cautious route and cite a source.

Look at any article in, say, the *Wall Street Journal* and you will find such phrases as "according to sources close to the defendant," "the CEO's secretary acknowledged that," "a speaker from the office who wishes to remain anonymous claims," "as the Attorney General said," "in a public statement, Governor Smith told reporters," "a report from the Department of the Interior shows," "taped conversations done by the police reveal," and so on. You should always name your source when possible. Even if you cannot name the source, as in some of these examples, you must indicate where the information comes from.

Similarly, in writing any kind of scholarly prose, one must cite sources thoroughly. It is best for the writer to signal to the reader the very point that source material begins to be used. The citation then should be given at the point that the writer stops using the source. This goes for passages or information quoted directly or paraphrased. For instance, "As Hollins points out, 'Politics . . .' (285)." Note that the parenthetical citation of the page number in the Hollins source is part of the sentence, but the parenthesis goes outside the quotation marks and inside the closing period.

If you do not show your sources—that is, if you pass off materials as if they are your own when they are not—you are plagiarizing. To reiterate, plagiarism is presenting other people's words and ideas as if they were your own. It is a form of deception; it is a form of counterfeiting in which trust is undermined.

There are different kinds of plagiarism. One is using another writer's words with perhaps a slight variation here and there—borrowing the full text or only parts of it (like sentences or phrases). Another is the complete rephrasing of another writer's work, rewritten so that there is no exact correspondence of words and sentences from paragraph to paragraph, but with the basic idea of each paragraph presented as your own.

Equivalent warnings apply about the use of images, graphics, or typographical or pictorial materials that originate with anyone other than the writer herself, when these materials are unacknowledged. Artwork or designs that use any part of another artist's or designer's work, or that manipulate another artist's work to create something original but in which the other artist's work is still recognizable, is considered borrowing; such borrowing must be acknowledged. If it is not, the new piece is considered plagiarized.

To reiterate a key suggestion: At the moment you begin to use another writer's ideas or words, mark it by introducing the source: "As Jenkins claims, ..." When you stop using that source, give a footnote number or parenthetical citation. This way the reader will always know what is yours and what is from a source.

INDEX